The Master's Reference gives you instant access to markup syntax and usage details while coding. The accompanying CD has an electronic version of the reference for easy searching.

Mastering™ XHTML
Premium Edition

Ed Tittel

Chelsea Valentine

Lucinda Dykes

Mary Burmeister

SYBEX®

San Francisco • London

Associate Publisher: Dan Brodnitz
Developmental Editor: Bonnie Bills
Editor: Liz Welch
Production Editor: Liz Burke
Technical Editor: Molly Holzschlag
Book Designer: Franz Baumhackl
Graphic Illustrator: Tony Jonick
Electronic Publishing Specialist: Jill Niles, Nila Nichols
Proofreaders: Emily Hsuan, Nancy Riddiough, Dave Nash
Indexer: Ted Laux
CD Coordinator: Christine Detlefs
CD Technician: Kevin Ly
Cover Designer: Design Site
Cover Illustrator: Jack D. Meyers

Library of Congress Card Number: 2001094601

ISBN: 0-7821-2818-1

SYBEX and the SYBEX logo are either registered trademarks or trademarks of SYBEX Inc. in the United States and/or other countries.

The CD interface was created using Macromedia Flash, COPYRIGHT 1994, 1997-1999 Macromedia Inc. For more information on Macromedia and Macromedia Flash, visit http://www.macromedia.com.

Netscape Communications, the Netscape Communications logo, Netscape, and Netscape Navigator are trademarks of Netscape Communications Corporation.

Netscape Communications Corporation has not authorized, sponsored, endorsed, or approved this publication and is not responsible for its content. Netscape and the Netscape Communications Corporate Logos are trademarks and trade names of Netscape Communications Corporation. All other product names and/or logos are trademarks of their respective owners.

Internet screen shot(s) using Microsoft Internet Explorer 5.5 reprinted by permission from Microsoft Corporation.

TRADEMARKS: SYBEX has attempted throughout this book to distinguish proprietary trademarks from descriptive terms by following the capitalization style used by the manufacturer.

The author and publisher have made their best efforts to prepare this book, and the content is based upon final release software whenever possible. Portions of the manuscript may be based upon pre-release versions supplied by software manufacturer(s). The author and the publisher make no representation or warranties of any kind with regard to the completeness or accuracy of the contents herein and accept no liability of any kind including but not limited to performance, merchantability, fitness for any particular purpose, or any losses or damages of any kind caused or alleged to be caused directly or indirectly from this book.

Manufactured in the United States of America

10 9 8 7 6 5 4 3 2 1

Software License Agreement: Terms and Conditions

We'd like to dedicate this book to the victims and families of the terrible tragedies in New York and at the Pentagon, especially to those brave and selfless rescue workers who gave their lives trying to save others.

Software License Agreement: Terms and Conditions

We'd like to dedicate this book to the victims and families of the terrible tragedies in New York and at the Pentagon, especially to those brave and selfless rescue workers who gave their lives trying to save others.

Acknowledgements

Thanks to Cheryl Applewood and Raquel Baker who enlisted our aid on this project and brought us into the fold, so to speak. Special thanks to our author team: Chelsea Valentine, Mary Burmeister, Lucinda Dykes, and Martin DeVore, for their contributions to this book. On the Sybex side, our thanks go to Liz Burke, Liz Welch, Jill Niles, and Nila Nichols for their contributions to this book as well. Finally, we're amazed, pleased, and awed that the inimitable Molly Holzschlag agreed to tech-edit this book. Great job, everybody!

Personally, I'd like to thank the project managers at LANWrights, including Dawn Rader, Mary Burmeister, Kim Lindros, and Karen Annett, for making business at LAN-Wrights possible as we know it today. I'd also like to thank my family for their unwavering affection and support, and my friends for giving me the distractions I needed to keep work and life in perspective. Finally, thanks to Blackie for his single-minded pursuit of the great outdoors, and the many times he lured me away from my desk to enable his perambulations. The 5–7 miles a day we walk not only help keep me fresh, but fit as well.

—Ed Tittel

As always, thanks to Mary for her endless support and dedication to this project. I would also like to thank my co-authors, Ed, Lucinda, and Mary, for their input and guidance. In addition to the team of authors on this project, we have to thank the folks at Sybex. A round of applause goes out to: Liz Burke, Jill Niles, Nila Nichols, Liz Welch, and Molly Holzschlag. Thanks to all of those who helped to keep me sane.

—Chelsea Valentine

With special thanks to Mary Burmeister for her support, humor, patience, and guidance, and just for being such a wonderful person to work with. Thanks to Ed Tittel for giving me the opportunity to write, and to Chelsea Valentine for her knowledge and support. Thanks to all of the LANWrights team for their help and support. Thanks to Steve, for putting up with all my late nights at the computer, and thanks to my parents for teaching me to love books. And above all, thanks to God for everything.

—Lucinda Dykes

Grandma and Grandpa Green, I love you and I'm thankful for the time we recently got to spend with each other. To both Mr. and Mrs. Burmeister's: I love you and thanks for being the best family ever! Thanks to everyone in my life for giving me what's really important in this world: love and friendship. Laura, Teresa, Shailu, Dawn, Deanna, Tara, Tanya, Heather, Angela, Crystal, Dorothy, Nan—each one of you has brought something special to my life and for that, I'm eternally grateful. To my beautiful Goddaughter Morgan: You always bring a smile to my face. And finally, thanks to everyone at LAN-Wrights for being the best. I can't imagine a better group of people to work with.

—Mary Burmeister

Contents at a Glance

Master's Reference

Contents

Introduction

Welcome to *Mastering XHTML, Premium Edition*—your one-stop comprehensive guide to the Extensible Hypertext Markup Language (XHTML)! In this book, you'll find the following elements:

- Comprehensive information about the latest and greatest XHTML specifications, plus what they include and how to use them.

- An exploration of XHTML's profound and interesting relationship with the HTML 4.0 specification.

- Advice and ideas about developing Web pages to accommodate various types and versions of Web browsers.

- Easy-to-follow instructions that help you build XHTML documents one step at a time, or to convert documents from HTML to XHTML.

- Examples of how you can enhance your Web pages with various technologies, including JavaScript and multimedia.

- Design guidelines to help you use XHTML properly and effectively.

- Thorough coverage of XML uses, applications, and structure, along with information about how to integrate XHTML and XML documents.

- Thorough coverage of advanced XHTML topics, such as generating XHTML from a database and creating searchable XHTML.

- Useful information and advice about choosing tools that meet your Web page creation, management, and publishing needs.

- A comprehensive reference on XHTML, style sheets, JavaScript, special characters, browser-safe colors, and the XML specification.

- Sample files and software, located on the companion CD.

XHTML is a reformulation of HTML based on the rules and syntax of XML, and it's the future of the Web. We developed this book so any Web content developer—whether a newbie or a seasoned professional—can learn and use XHTML effectively. For example, if you're new to XHTML, you can start at the beginning and work your way forward as you improve and expand upon your skills. You'll find the step-by-step instructions and examples easy to follow and understand. However, if you're already up to speed on authoring in HTML, you can thumb through later chapters to learn about new topics (including XHTML) and develop new skills, use the Master's Reference to find the information you seek, or jump straight to the sections on XML or converting from HTML to XHTML to see where the future lies. So, if you're involved in any way with creating documents for the Web, you'll find this book an invaluable reference.

What's in This Book?

This book contains seven parts (and a bonus eighth part on the CD), plus the Master's Reference. Here's what to expect:

Part I: Getting Started

In this part, you'll learn about XHTML code, develop your first XHTML page—including all the common page elements and even a few relatively advanced features, such as links, adding images, and working with fancy formatting controls—and learn how to publish your pages for all to see.

Part II: Advancing Your Skills

In this part, you'll move on to some of the more sophisticated and interesting XHTML effects, such as working with tables, frames, and forms. You'll also learn how to convert HTML files into their XHTML equivalents, including some cool tools to help automate this otherwise time-consuming and tedious task.

Part III: Moving Beyond Pure XHTML

In this part, you'll learn how to use Cascading Style Sheets to manage how Web documents appear inside your users' browsers with verve and precision. You'll also learn about incorporating interactivity and flexible controls with JavaScript, and how to include multimedia effects in your Web pages. Armed with this information, you should be able to create XHTML pages with great power and eye appeal!

Part IV: Developing Web Sites

In this part, you'll learn the ins and outs of developing and managing highly functional Web sites that your visitors will want to keep coming back to visit. Here, you'll learn about the XHTML document development process, and you'll find tips and tricks to help you develop specific types of Web sites—including public, personal, and intranet sites—with ease and panache. These chapters show you how to develop and design your pages and sites according to how they'll be used and to meet your target audience's most pressing needs.

Part V: Applying XHTML to Advanced Applications

In this part, you'll learn about some more sophisticated XHTML applications. First, you'll learn how to apply what you've already learned about style sheets and JavaScript to create Dynamic XHTML pages. Next, you'll discover how publishing XHTML directly from a database can ease your workload and help you keep your site entirely up-to-date. Finally, a chapter on creating and managing searchable XHTML gives you the tools you need to let people search your Web site easily and effectively.

Part VI: XHTML: A Bridge to XML

In this part, you'll examine the interesting and powerful relationship between XML and XHTML (the "X" in XHTML stands for XML, after all). First, you'll tackle a review of XML's capabilities and characteristics. Then, you'll find an in-depth discussion of the many and various relationships that it's possible to create between XHTML and other XML applications, with a particular emphasis on how to extend documents beyond XHTML's built-in markup and semantics.

The next two chapters cover the ins and outs of working with the formal definitions of XML markup called Document Type Definitions (DTDs); here, you'll learn how to define and use you own customized markup! Finally, you'll examine the details behind the W3C's efforts to break XHTML into a series of interrelated subsets called modules (which is why this effort is called "modularization") so that certain XHTML documents need only incorporate those components of the markup language that they actually use. (Thus, a cell phone with XHTML support need not incorporate support for tables, frames, or graphics, because they're unlikely to be used on the itty-bitty screen so typical on such a device.)

Part VII: XHTML Development Tools

In this part, you'll survey the ever-changing landscape of Web development tools, including those that work with HTML, XHTML, and XML. You'll learn about some of the capabilities that high-end authoring tools have to offer, as well as explore the value and confidence that validation tools can confer. Next, you'll find out the secrets and importance of validating your XHTML documents.

Part VIII: The XML Family of Applications

This part is on the CD. In this part, you'll get a sense of what the XML fuss is all about, as you look at important ways to use XML-based markup languages to manage and present XML-based documents and data. Starting with an examination of the Extensible Stylesheet Language Transformations (XSLT), you'll learn how to turn XML into HTML or XHTML on the fly for delivery to older Web browsers (or for maximum backward compatibility). After that, you'll get a chance to see what XML's Synchronized Multimedia Integration Language (SMIL) can do to help you coordinate voice, text, and multimedia effects in your Web pages. Next, you learn how to navigate, interrogate, and access the contents of parsed XML documents (including XHTML) using easy programming tools and techniques. Finally, you learn about XML Schemas, another method for defining XML documents that's particularly well suited to capture complex data types and for screening input and output values.

Master's Reference

The Master's Reference includes seven sections:

XHTML Elements and Attributes   A comprehensive list of XHTML elements and attributes, with definitions, explanations, and examples of proper usage.

Cascading Style Sheets Reference   A comprehensive explanation of style sheet markup, with a list of related markup elements and attributes, plus examples of proper usage.

Scripting Reference   A comprehensive list of JavaScript objects, properties, methods, and functions with examples of how to use them.

Working with the W3C Validator   An explanation of how to interpret the sometimes convoluted errors given by the W3C validator.

XHTML Special Characters A collection of pointers to the numerous variants of the ISO-8859 Character sets (also known as ISO-Latin character sets) and to the ISO 10646 Character sets (also known as Unicode).

XHTML Color Codes A list of pointers to color descriptions and equivalent numeric RGB code values.

XHTML 1.0 Specification A copy of the official specification for XHTML 1.0, reproduced with permission from the W3C. This is the "ultimate rulebook" for XHTML markup elements, attributes, and usage.

Conventions in This Book

Throughout this book, we've employed several conventions intended to help you find and use the information it contains more easily.

Text Conventions

The following text conventions will help you easily identify new words, show you how to follow along with the examples, and help you use menu commands.

The first time a new word is used, it appears in *italics* and is followed by a brief definition or example. For example, we explain that *markup* is the formal term used to describe the text that denotes XHTML elements within a document.

Examples of XHTML markup appear in a special font `like this`, and usually appear within a line of copy, or on one or more lines that stand by themselves. If an example requires that you type in new markup for each step, the new markup you enter appears in bold, like this:

```
<p>A line of markup from a previous step.</p>
<p>Another line of markup from a previous step.</p>
<p>New markup to enter in the current step!</p>
```

Finally, instructions for using a menu command appear like this:

1. Choose File ➤ Save As to open the Save As dialog box, and then choose Options.

This sequence means you should go to the File menu, and choose Save As from the drop-down list of entries. The Save As dialog box appears, from which you should choose the Options entry.

Icon Conventions

The following icons indicate helpful tips and warnings. They're flagged to get your attention, and are usually worth reading for that very reason!

Tips include time-saving information to help you make your XHTML authoring easier and faster.

Warnings flag potential trouble spots (or potential sources of trouble, anyway). Ignore them at your own risk!

Exploring Additional Resources

Throughout this book, you'll find plenty of examples to illustrate how to develop markup or that show the results of steps you follow. You'll find many of these examples on the *Mastering XHTML, Premium Edition* Companion CD.

Additionally, on the CD you'll find a wide variety of HTML, XHTML, and XML development tools as well as some multimedia tools, including everything from useful freeware programs to time-limited evaluation versions of high-end commercial software packages. Just put the CD in your computer and use Microsoft Windows Explorer or some similar program to inspect the CD's contents.

Finally, we point you to lots of Web sites—some show you examples of how companies apply XHTML code to their needs, some offer software for you to download, and some are information resources to help you keep up-to-date on XHTML and related topics, tools, and technologies. Remember that Web content changes frequently so you may not find everything exactly as described in this book, or in the location we say it resides. Although we verified everything immediately before this book went to press, we can't guarantee specific content at specific addresses, given the rate and scope of change on the Web.

Contact Us

We're glad you chose *Mastering XHTML, Premium Edition* as your one-stop XHTML resource and reference. Please let us know how it goes—we're always glad to read your comments, ponder your suggestions, and respond to your questions. You can contact us at mxhtml@lanw.com. We look forward to hearing from you!

Part I
Getting Started

In This Part

Getting Acquainted with XHTML, Its Tools, and Its Resources

Chapter 1

The Extensible Hypertext Markup Language (XHTML) is a reformulation of the Hypertext Markup Language (HTML) based on the rules and syntax of the Extensible Markup Language (XML). Despite its reformulation, XHTML remains very much like HTML in that you can use it to create interactive, online pages. You're probably familiar with the most common HTML application, Web pages; XHTML provides the same capabilities. Users can still jump from topic to topic, fill out forms, submit information, and search databases, among other things, rather than slogging through information linearly. However, XHTML is not what you see on screen as a Web page. Instead, XHTML is the behind-the-scenes markup that instructs Web browsers what to display.

In this chapter, we'll introduce you to XHTML—what it looks like, what you use it for, and what tools you need to get started—and give you a foundation for learning to use XHTML throughout the rest of this book. To begin with, we introduce the basic impetus behind HTML and then discuss why markup experts agree that reformulating HTML into XHTML was a good idea. In addition, we cover some special terminology that will help you understand the technical side of the topics we cover throughout this book.

This chapter covers the following topics:

- Understanding XHTML and its related terms and concepts

- Exploring why XHTML is worthwhile and how to use it

- Finding the tools you'll need to get started

- Using other helpful resources

What Are HTML and XHTML?

XHTML is a *markup language*: a system of codes that identify parts and characteristics of documents. As Figure 1.1 shows, XHTML documents are plain-text files. They contain no images, no sounds, no videos, and no animations; however, they can include *pointers*, or links, to these file types, which is how Web pages end up looking as if they contain nontext elements.

```
file-upload[1] - Notepad
File  Edit  Format  Help  Send

<!DOCTYPE html PUBLIC "-//W3C//DTD XHTML 1.0 Transitional//EN"
    "http://www.w3.org/TR/xhtml1/DTD/xhtml1-transitional.dtd">
<html xmlns="http://www.w3.org/1999/xhtml">
<head>
  <title>W3C HTML Validation Service: Upload files</title>
</head>
<body>
  <p>
    <a href="http://www.w3.org/">
    <img align="left" src="http://www.w3.org/Icons/www/w3c_home"
        height="48" border="0" alt="W3C" /></a>
  </p>

  <p align="right" class="navbar">
    <a href="./">Validator home</a> |
    <a href="about.html">About this service</a> |
    <a href="feedback.html">Feedback</a><br clear="all" />
  </p>
  <h1>HTML Validation Service</h1>
  <p>
    This form allows you upload files from your computer to have
    them validated.
  </p>
  <form method="post" enctype="multipart/form-data" action="/check">
    File: <input type="file" name="uploaded_file" size="50" />
    <table cellpadding="0" cellspacing="0">
      <tr>
        <td>
          <input name="ss" type="checkbox" value="" /> Show source input
        </td>
        <td>
          <input name="outline" type="checkbox" value="" /> Show an outline of this
          document<br />
        </td>
      </tr>
      <tr>
        <td>
          <input name="sp" type="checkbox" value="" /> Show parse tree
        </td>
        <td>
          <input name="noatt" type="checkbox" value="" /> exclude
          attributes from the parse tree<br />
        </td>
      </tr>
    </table>
    <input type="submit" value="Validate this document" />
    <input type="reset" value="Reset this form" />
  </form>
</body>
</html>
```

Figure 1.1 *XHTML documents are just text files, containing the code and content you provide.*

As you can see, XHTML documents look nothing like the Web pages you have likely seen before. Instead, XHTML is made up of *elements*, *tags*, and *attributes* (which will all be defined later in the chapter) that work together to identify document parts and tell browsers how to display them. Figure 1.2 shows how the tags and attributes of Figure 1.1 work together to create a Web page.

Figure 1.2 *Browsers interpret the code to determine how to display XHTML documents.*

The roots of *HTML* (which is the predecessor to XHTML) go back to the late 1980s and early 1990s. That's when Tim Berners-Lee first developed HTML to provide a simple way for scientists at CERN (a particle physics laboratory in Geneva, Switzerland) to exchange reports and research results on the Web. HTML is based, in turn, on a formal definition created using a powerful *meta-language*—a language used to create other languages—called the *Standard Generalized Markup Language (SGML)*. SGML is an International Organization for Standardization (ISO) standard tool designed to create markup languages of many kinds.

By 1993, the power and reach of the World Wide Web was becoming well known, and CERN released HTML for unrestricted public use. CERN eventually turned HTML over to an industry group called the World Wide Web Consortium (W3C), which continues to govern HTML and related markup-language specifications. Public release of HTML (and its companion protocol, the *Hypertext Transfer Protocol, or HTTP,* which is what browsers use to request Web pages, and what Web servers use to respond to such requests) launched the Web revolution that has changed the face of computing and the Internet forever.

In the intervening years since the early 1990s when HTML became a public standard, HTML has been the focus of great interest, attention, and use. Today, Web-related traffic dominates the Internet, and Web sites have become a standard part of corporate and organizational information access and delivery. Unfortunately, HTML is a "closed" language, which means that the markup it recognizes is fixed and immutable, except when its underlying SGML-based formal definition is altered. Because of this characteristic, HTML has gone through many versions—from version 1.0 in 1993 to version 4.01 in December 1999—as the language definition sought to keep up with new, but nonstandard, language elements introduced in particular Web browsers such as Microsoft Internet Explorer and Netscape Navigator.

The original definition of HTML provided a mechanism to identify and mark up *content*—specific information judged to be of sufficient importance to deliver online—without worrying too much about how that information looked, or how it was presented and formatted on the user's computer display. But as commercial interest in the Web exploded, graphic designers and typographers involved in Web design found themselves wishing for the kind of presentation and layout controls that they received from software such as PageMaker and QuarkXPress. HTML was never designed as a full-fledged presentation tool, but it was being pulled strongly in that direction, often by browser vendors who sought market share for their software by accommodating the desires of their audience.

Unfortunately, these browser-specific implementations resulted in variations in the HTML language definitions that weren't supported all browsers and in functionality that wasn't part of any official HTML language definition. Web designers found themselves in a pickle—forced either to build Web pages for the lowest common denominator that all browsers could support, or to build Web pages that targeted specific browsers that not all users could necessarily view or appreciate.

*Throughout this book, we use the term **users** to describe the people who view and use the XHTML documents you develop.*

Basically, XHTML was created as a way to clean up this mess. XHTML provides a way to take advantage of a newer, more compact underlying meta-language called XML that is inherently extensible and, therefore, open-ended. More importantly, XHTML helps rationalize and consolidate a Web markup landscape that had become highly fragmented (a result of different and incompatible implementations of HTML). There are many other good reasons for using XHTML instead of HTML, and you'll learn more about them later in this chapter and throughout this book. But first, some coverage of the basic concepts and terminology that make XHTML work!

 As we were completing this book, the W3C advanced the XHTML 1.1 specification to Recommendation status, which means it has become the most current standard for XHTML. We cover the differences between XHTML 1.0 and XHTML 1.1 in Master's Reference Part 8.

Understanding Elements and Tags

Because XHTML uses XML-based terminology, it identifies the markup text that signals the placement of document controls and content containers as *elements*. XHTML elements serve two primary functions. First, they identify logical document parts—that is, major structural components in documents, such as headings (h1, for example), numbered lists (ol, also called ordered lists), and paragraphs (p). Therefore, if you want to include a component in an XHTML document, you type the text and apply the appropriate elements to that text. (We'll show you how in the following sections.) That's pretty much all there is to it.

 *If you're familiar with HTML, you're probably used to hearing the word **tag** to describe HTML markup—for example, a single tag such as <br> and a tag pair such as <title>...</title>. However, in XML, both are called **elements**; an element can be either a single instance of markup **or** a matched pair of markup instances.*

Also, some elements in XHTML documents also refer to other things—that is, elements can include pointers and links to other documents, images, sound files, video files, multimedia applications, animations, applets, and so on. For example, if you want to include an image of your company's product in your XHTML document, rather than pasting an image directly into the document (as you might in a word processing file), you include an element (tag) that identifies the filename for that image, as shown here:

```
<img src="logo.gif" alt="corporate logo" />
```

In this example, the img (image) element points to a logo file (logo.gif) that the browser should display. This illustrates that browsers rely on information within an XHTML document to tell them what to display, as well as how to display it.

In this book, when we refer to an XTHML element in the text, we will omit the opening and closing angle brackets (and other markup, where appropriate) and simply use the element name to refer to an element in general. On the other hand, when we identify a specific tag, we will reproduce it exactly as it should appear in an XHTML document. Thus, we would refer to the element that identifies a document's title as the title element, but we would produce the following snippet of code to specify an actual document title that includes the opening <title> and closing </title> tags (which are the markup items that create the title element):

```
<title>A Title Identifies a Document's Purpose or Primary
Content</title>
```

In the preceding example, the <title> and </title> tags enclose the actual content related to the title element. When the XHTML document appears within a Web browser, the string "A Title Identifies a Document's Purpose or Primary Content" appears in the title bar for the window in which it appears, as shown in Figure 1.3.

Figure 1.3 The title element's content appears in the browser window's title bar.

XHTML tags come in one of two forms:

- A singleton tag, such as <br /> or <img />, is formally called an *empty element* because it includes no actual text content. In XHTML, such tags must end with a space and a slash before the closing right angle bracket. (The space is a little trick that allows older browsers—ones that may not recognize XHTML—to treat such tags as HTML and therefore recognize them. Without the space before those closing characters, older browsers may ignore such tags altogether.)

- A pair of related tags, such as `<title>`...`</title>` or `<head>`...`</head>`, enclose and identify document content. In such cases, the first tag in a pair (for example, `<head>`) is called an *opening tag* because it opens a content container. The second tag in a pair (for example, `</head>`) is called a *closing tag* because it closes the content container opened by the opening tag.

Unlike HTML, which allows great latitude in how markup is included or omitted from documents, XHTML is persnickety about the markup it's willing to recognize. In any XHTML document, all tag text must appear in lowercase; every empty element must end with the closing `/>` string; and every opening tag must be followed by a corresponding closing tag at an appropriate point. Understanding the details of these general rules is important, and they are explained at length in Chapter 2.

Understanding Element Components

As our examples so far should illustrate, XHTML elements, and the tags that represent them in XHTML documents, are reasonably intuitive. Although markup can occasionally be cryptic, you can usually get some idea of an element's function from its name. Let's take a look at the components that go into building tags for XHTML elements.

First, all tags are composed of *element names* that are contained within *angle brackets* (`<` `>`). The angle brackets simply tell browsers that the text between them represents XHTML markup rather than ordinary text content. Some sample tags look like these:

- `<h2>` (for heading level 2)
- `<p>` (for document paragraph)
- `<strong>` (to emphasize a particular section of content strongly)

You'll learn more about these tags and their uses in Chapter 3.

Second, many elements are designed to contain content; they use a pair of tags, where actual content occurs between the opening tag (for example, `<h1>`) and the corresponding closing tag (`</h1>`). Both tags look alike, except the closing tag includes a forward slash (/) to denote the end of the element container. To apply tags to something in your document, place an opening tag before the content that should be associated with the element you wish to use, and place the closing tag after it, as follows:

```
<h1>Information to which the tags apply.</h1>
```

When creating XHTML markup by hand, you can make life easier on yourself by entering both the opening and closing tags at the same time. That way, you won't forget the closing tag. If you do forget a closing tag, most elements will treat all subsequent content after the opening tag as content for the opening element until the browser finds a matching closing tag. On the other hand, if you use an XHTML or HTML editor, most of these tools will create content tags in pairs to absolve you of this responsibility.

You'll also use empty elements, which do not include a closing tag. We'll point these out throughout this book and show you how to use them correctly.

To apply more than one element to a particular piece of content, you nest the tags. *Nesting* means placing one set of tags inside another set. For example, to apply strong emphasis to a word within a paragraph, you nest the strong element within the paragraph (p) element, as follows:

```
<p>The <strong>right</strong> way to use strong emphasis is to
    enclose only those words you wish to emphasize inside a
    strong element</p>
```

Throughout the book, because of the width limits of the printed page, we wrap and indent code lines that are meant to be written all on one line. This doesn't mean you have to; you should type these long lines without a return in your code. (A little later, in the section "Improving XHTML Readability," we'll explain when and why you should type code on multiple lines.)

When you nest elements, the first opening tag must be matched by a corresponding closing tag at the end of the outside block of content, and the second opening tag must be closed with a corresponding closing tag immediately after the internal content block that it relates to. XHTML is quite insistent that you can't use tags out of order; therefore, a block of text like this:

```
<p>The last word gets strong <strong>emphasis.</p></strong>
```

is invalid because it closes the outside p element before closing the nested (or inside) strong element.

Typing Tags Correctly

When typing tags, be particularly careful not to include extra spaces within the tag itself. If you do this, a browser may not recognize the tag and may not display the content associated with the corresponding XHTML element correctly. Sometimes, a browser might display the markup itself because it's unable to distinguish improperly formed markup from normal element content.

For example, a `title` element should look like this:

```
<title>Correctly Formed Title</title>
```

Do *not* include spaces within tags for non-empty elements, as in this erroneous example:

```
< title >Incorrectly Formed Title< /title >
```

This explains the strange appearance of the browser view of this markup shown in Figure 1.4.

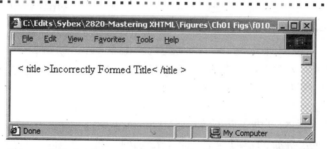

Figure 1.4 *An incorrectly formed* `title` *element's content appears inside the browser window, not in the title bar.*

Of course, the exception to this rule is empty elements, which need a space before the closing `/>`. Type an empty element's tag like this:

```
<img src="picture.jpg" alt="A picture of us" />
```

Improving XHTML Readability

You'll find it easier to read and use tags if you follow a few conventions. In particular, use hard returns between elements to create shorter lines. This does not affect how browsers display an XHTML document; it just makes that document easier for you to read when you're editing its contents.

The following two examples show you how hard returns and indents can improve readability.

```
<!DOCTYPE html PUBLIC "-//W3C//DTD XHTML 1.0 Transitional//EN"
"http://www.w3.org/TR/xhtml1/DTD/xhtml1-transitional.dtd">
<html xmlns="http://www.w3.org/1999/xhtml"><head><title>
Mastering HTML Document Title</title></head><body>Mastering
HTML Document Body</body></html>
```

The preceding code produces exactly the same display as this:

```
<!DOCTYPE html PUBLIC "-//W3C//DTD XHTML 1.0 Transitional//EN"
    "http://www.w3.org/TR/xhtml1/DTD/xhtml1-transitional.dtd">
<html xmlns="http://www.w3.org/1999/xhtml">
    <head>
        <title>Mastering HTML Document Title</title>
    </head>
    <body>
        Mastering HTML Document Body
    </body>
</html>
```

No question which one's easier to read or follow, right?

Those of you who are already familiar with HTML may be wondering why all XHTML element names appear exclusively in lowercase. Perhaps some of you even know that HTML is indifferent to case for tag text. That's not true for XHTML, however: All tag text—except attribute values (covered in the next section) and DOCTYPE declarations—must be lowercase. This is to match how the tags that correspond to XHTML elements are defined formally in the Document Type Definition (DTD). See more about DTDs, the DOCTYPE declarations, and the XHTML rules in Chapter 2.

Understanding XHTML Attributes

Some XHTML elements take modifying values called *attributes*, which provide additional information about such elements, such as:

- What other files should be accessed, such as an image file

- What language is used for an element's content

- Whether an element's content should read right to left or left to right

Attributes are also used to uniquely identify an element instance within a document and to apply some presentation style to an element. Normally, attributes take the form `attribute="value"`; they always follow the tag name within the opening tag of a non-empty element or within an empty element's tag.

Let's assume you want to center a heading 1 in the browser window. You'd start with your heading and tags, like this:

```
<h1>A heading goes here</h1>
```

Next, add the `style` and `type` attributes to the opening tag, like this:

```
<h1 type="text/css" style="align:center">
   A centered heading goes here</h1>
```

All attributes are separated from other attributes and the tag itself by spaces. In XHTML, *all* attributes require quotes. As our example illustrates, you can include multiple attributes in a single tag by placing a space between each attribute–value pair.

Within opening tags, or the tags that correspond to empty elements, attributes can appear in any order after the element name, but the element name must always appear first.

What Can You Do with XHTML?

You're likely most familiar with HTML, or XHTML, because it's used to create Web pages; but either of these markup languages may be put to many other uses:

Developing intranet or extranet sites   XHTML is commonly used to develop intranet Web sites—sites accessed by people within a company or organization from one or more locations—or extranet sites, used by people from a specific group of companies or organizations that routinely share information among themselves.

Developing help files   XHTML can also be used to develop online help files that are accessible on any platform. Online help files allow developers to produce documentation inexpensively.

Developing network applications   XHTML is particularly suitable for creating entire applications, such as training programs, interactive chats, or databases that are available through Web pages.

Developing kiosk applications   XHTML can also be used to create kiosk applications—those stand-alone computers with the neat touch-screen capabilities.

Content delivery for Web-enabled phones, personal digital assistants (PDAs), or handheld computers   In March 2001, a consortium of wireless device manufacturers, including Nokia, Ericsson, Motorola, 3Com, and Handspring, announced that they were adopting XHTML as their standard markup language. This is because XHTML includes special facilities that make it easy to transform and filter XHTML documents for display on wireless devices, as you'll learn in later chapters in this book.

What Tools Do You Need?

For your first XHTML documents, you only need the following basic tools:

- A plain-vanilla text editor, which you will use to create and save your XHTML documents (see the sidebar "HTML Editors" for an explanation as to why we can't currently recommend any XHTML editors)

- An XHTML validator, which you will use to check the syntax and structure of your XHTML documents

- A Web browser, which you will use to view and test your XHTML documents

Text Editors

Although there are dozens of excellent HTML WYSIWYG ("what you see is what you get") editors available, you should learn to code XHTML using a standard text editor. Text editors force you to *hand-code,* meaning that you, not the software, enter tags and attributes. Hand-coding helps you learn XHTML elements, attributes, and structures and lets you see exactly where you've made mistakes. Also, with hand-coding, you can easily include the newest XHTML enhancements into your documents. Some good text editors are Notepad for all Windows versions, vi or pico for Unix, and TeachText or SimpleText for Macintosh.

Learning to hand-code is essential for using the latest-and-greatest XHTML effects—whether it's the current XHTML 1.0 or a future version. Most new XHTML versions are not supported by WYSIWYG editors yet, so you need to hand-code new elements and attributes in your documents anyway, even when using an HTML- or XHTML-savvy tool.

Using a word processing program such as Word, WordPerfect, or even WordPad to create HTML documents often introduces unwanted formatting and control characters, which can cause problems. XHTML requires plain text with no formatting controls, so either make a special effort to save all documents as plain text within such applications, or take our advice and use a text editor instead.

HTML Editors

As we write this chapter, few editors are available that produce native XHTML code, and none that we wanted to include with this book. However, it's possible to use an HTML editor, instead of a simple text editor, to create an initial version of your XHTML documents and then to make use of a special-purpose tool, such as HTML Tidy or HTML-Kit, to transform your HTML into equivalent, properly formatted XHTML. Because this requires a bit more savvy than we assume from our general readership, this material is aimed only at those more experienced readers to whom this kind of approach makes sense.

In general, HTML editors fall into two categories:

- Text- or code-based, which show you the HTML code as you're creating documents
- WYSIWYG, which show the results of code, similar to the way it will appear in a browser, as you're formatting your document

Simple WYSIWYG editors, such as Netscape Composer and Microsoft FrontPage Express, are good for quickly generating HTML documents. These editors only give you a close approximation of page layout, design, and colors, but are good for viewing the general arrangement of features. However, they do not give you, the author, as much control over the final appearance of your document as code-based editors do.

After you've developed a few HTML documents and understand basic HTML principles, you may choose to use both a WYSIWYG editor and a code-based editor. For example, you can get a good start on your document using a WYSIWYG HTML editor and then polish it (or fix it) using a code-based one. For now, though, we recommend that you hand-code XHTML using a standard text editor.

The W3C Validator

One of the primary benefits that XHTML confers to its users is the ability to mechanically—or at least, programmatically—*validate* XHTML documents. In plain terms, this means that after you've created an XHTML document, you can submit it to an online syntax-checking tool for analysis. This tool will tell you whether the document follows the rules for some specific, well-known form of XHTML syntax, or if it finds errors, it will identify them by their location in the document. This means you can check whether your documents follow one or more sets of XHTML syntax rules, and keep working through them until you achieve the XHTML equivalent of Nirvana: a clean bill of health from the validator!

Using this tool is incredibly simple. You need only visit `http://validator.w3.org/file-upload.html`, browse your local hard disk, and upload the file you want validated through its nearly mindless interface. If you're in luck, what you get back looks like what's shown in Figure 1.5. If you're not in luck, you will need to find out how to read and interpret the validator's sometimes cryptic error messages. Because this interpretation is a substantial chore, we've devoted Master's Reference Part 4 to this topic; you may want to read it through before your first encounter with the validator. Of course, if you don't believe us, try using the tool without reading that material—we're convinced you'll want to turn to our reference once you get a look at the validator's output when it finds errors!

Figure 1.5 When the W3C validator finds no errors, its output is both short and very sweet!

Our main point is that you should make validation part of your standard XHTML authoring process. That way, you'll get the best possible guarantee that most browsers will be able to view and display the contents of your XHTML documents.

Web Browsers

If you've ever surfed the Web, you've used a Web browser to view HTML or XHTML documents. The most common browsers are Microsoft Internet Explorer (IE) and Netscape Navigator; however, many other browsers are also available for virtually all computer platforms and online services. We're especially fond of Opera (available free from www.opera.com) and Amaya (available free at www.w3.org/Amaya) because they often support advanced features and functions sooner than the more popular IE and Netscape browsers do.

Exactly how your documents appear, though, varies from browser to browser and from computer to computer. For example, most browsers in use today are *graphical browsers*: they can display elements other than text. A *text-only* browser can display—you guessed it—only text. How your XHTML documents appear in each of these types of browsers differs significantly, as shown in Figures 1.6 and 1.7.

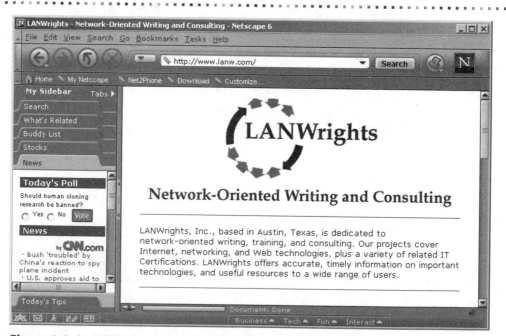

Figure 1.6 *An HTML document displayed in Netscape Navigator*

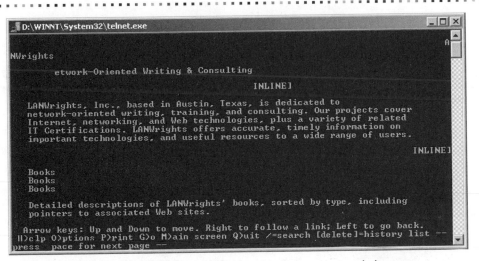

Figure 1.7 *The same HTML document viewed in Lynx, a text-only browser*

Even graphical browsers tend to display things a bit differently. For example, one browser might display a first-level heading as 15-point Times New Roman bold, whereas another might display the same heading as 14-point Arial italic. In both cases, the browser displays the heading bigger and more emphasized than regular text, but the specific text characteristics vary. Figures 1.8 and 1.9 show how two other browsers display the same XHTML document.

Finally, your user's computer settings can also make a big difference in how your HTML or XHTML documents appear. For example, the computer's resolution and specific browser settings can alter a document's appearance.

So, as you're developing and viewing your XHTML documents, remember that what you see may look a bit different to your users. If possible, test your documents in as many different browsers, at as many different resolutions and color settings, on as many different computers as possible. You won't be able to test for all possible variations, but you should be able to get a good idea of what your users might see.

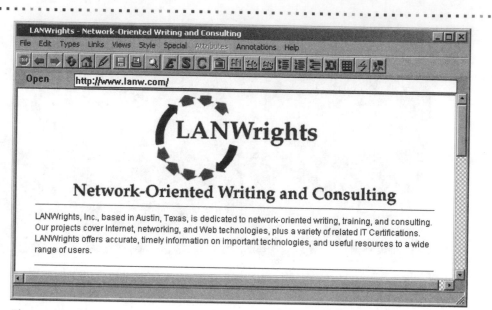

Figure 1.8 *The W3C Amaya browser has its own unique look and feel.*

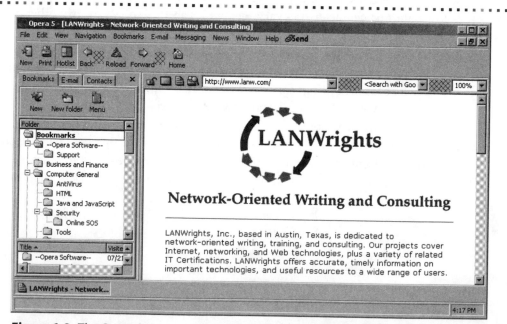

Figure 1.9 *The Opera browser shows the same document with slightly different formatting.*

What Other Resources Can Help?

In addition to this book, you can find information, resources, and specifications on the Web. In particular, the W3C site, as well as several product-specific Web sites, will help you learn, use, and keep up with changes in XHTML.

Visit the W3C

The W3C was created in 1994 at the Massachusetts Institute of Technology (MIT) to oversee the development of Web standards, eventually including the XHTML standard. This consortium defines and publishes XHTML and numerous other Web-related standards, along with information about the elements and attributes that may legally appear within XHTML documents. So, an excellent way to monitor XHTML changes is to visit the W3C site at www.w3.org/MarkUp. There you'll find new releases of XHTML standards and information about HTML standards.

For more information on proposed standards and other developments in Web-related specifications, such as Cascading Style Sheets (CSS) and XML specifications, visit the W3C's home page at www.w3.org.

Can you use new elements and attributes as they become available? For the most part, yes. By the time many popular elements and attributes become part of a standard, they already work with many or most browsers. However, some elements and attributes (including some that were introduced with XHTML 1.0) did not have wide or stable browser support when that specification was released and, to this day, do not have nearly the breadth of support that some other elements and attributes enjoy. We'll point these out throughout this book and show you how they differ from previous versions of HTML.

Monitor Netscape and Microsoft Sites

When HTML was the prevailing Web markup standard, each time Netscape or Microsoft released a new browser version, it would also add new markup *extensions*, which are browser-specific, nonstandard elements and attributes. Some of these extensions were useful, some less so. However, as a whole, any nonstandard elements introduced into HTML caused problems both for Web developers and for users. Fortunately, fewer extensions seem to be introduced now that XHTML has made the scene, but you should still be aware of what's added with each new browser release.

If you're considering using extensions in your XHTML documents, keep in mind that they're not standard and that the W3C validator will not recognize or validate nonstandard markup. Also, extensions that are specific to a particular browser (for example, Netscape) will probably not work in other browsers (such as Internet Explorer or Opera). For this reason, we strongly recommend that you refrain from using extensions and use only standard XHTML elements and attributes. This way, you'll not only be able to validate your documents to make sure they're syntactically correct, but you can also be reasonably sure that all your users can access the information you provide therein.

 In early 2001, about 75 percent of Web surfers use Internet Explorer, about 18 percent use Netscape Navigator, and the remaining 7 percent use a variety of other browsers. Realistically, about 80 to 90 percent of Web users can access most sites that use standard XHTML markup.

You can find Netscape's elements and attributes at

`http://developer.netscape.com/docs/manuals/htmlguid/index.htm`

And you will find Microsoft's elements and attributes at

`http://msdn.microsoft.com/workshop/author/default.asp`

Monitor Other Sites

Although definitive information comes from the W3C, Microsoft, and Netscape, you can check other reliable resources. Here's a list of sites to check regularly.

Organization	URL
Web Design Group	www.htmlhelp.com
Web Developer's Virtual Library	www.wdvl.com
HTML Writer's Guild	www.hwg.org
C|Net's Builder.com	www.builder.com
Zvon	www.zvon.org

Where to Go from Here

This chapter gave you a brief overview of XHTML—what it is, what it's used for, how it relates to its predecessor (HTML), and how and why XHTML came to be. Although you haven't done any XHTML coding yet, you should now possess a good foundation of basic concepts and terminology.

From here, we suggest you proceed to Chapter 2, where you'll learn more details about XHTML document syntax and structure, particularly about the concepts of well-formedness and validity. Because understanding those details is a necessary ingredient for truly understanding and appreciating XHTML (unless you're already familiar with these notions), we strongly urge you to continue on to the next chapter. Otherwise, feel free to skip to Chapter 3, where you will tackle creation of your first XHTML document.

XHTML Structure and Form

Chapter 2

When the World Wide Web Consortium (W3C) made the move from HTML to XHTML, structure and form moved into the spotlight. As Web developers, most of us never *really* paid attention to structure. Some of us knew that DOCTYPE declarations existed, but few of us actually used them. We knew that there were a few required elements, but if we accidentally missed one, no harm, no foul. The time of lazy markup is over!

The usual reaction to this idea is outrage, and if not outrage, a little groaning and moaning. However, we're convinced that after you read this chapter, you'll agree with us. Not only will XHTML's strict rules make it easier for you troubleshoot problems, but they will also make it easier for you to learn the language.

This chapter covers the following topics:

- Recognizing a well-formed document

- Creating a valid document

- Using the three XHTML DTDs

- Understanding DOCTYPE declarations

- Understanding namespaces

A Well-Formed Document

The concept of a "well-formed" document is not new; however, it's central to XHTML and, therefore, is the first item we discuss. As you may know, XHTML is an application of XML. What we mean by "an application of XML" is that it adheres to requirements defined by the XML specification.

XML as a Meta-language

For those of you who don't know about XML yet, XML stands for the Extensible Markup Language, and it's a direct descendant of the Standard Generalized Markup Language (SGML).

SGML has been around since the 1980s, and you can trace the original ideas for it back to the late 1960s. SGML is, like XML, a meta–markup language that defines requirements for creating markup languages. For example, HTML is a markup language that was created following SGML's syntax and document requirements. Whereas the vocabulary (which names all the elements and attributes) is defined by the HTML standard, the syntax rules that HTML adheres to are defined by SGML.

XML is a direct descendant of SGML and was introduced in 1996. XML is a refined version of SGML and is a meta–markup language (a.k.a. meta-language) as well. It would take an entire chapter, if not an entire book, to describe the reason for the evolution from SGML to XML, but we won't do that here. Suffice it to say, XML, as a subset of SGML, retained 90 percent of SGML's power with only 10 percent of its complexity.

One of the primary differences between SGML and XML is that XML's syntax requirements are simpler and therefore stricter. What does this mean for XHTML? Well, whereas HTML is an application of SGML, the vocabulary has not been cast as an application of XML. Hence, the X added to its name. There are many advantages gained, and we will point these out throughout this book. To learn more about XML, visit www.w3.org/XML.

XML defines two types of constraints for documents:

Well-formedness constraints   Every XML document must follow a small handful of XML syntax and document rules. These rules are easy to follow and are a requirement for any XML, and therefore, XHTML document.

Validity constraints   Most validity constraints are optional constraints that deal with associating a DTD. If you include a DTD, the DTD defines rules for your elements and attributes. The document must then adhere to these rules.

All XHTML documents must be *well formed*. This means that all XHTML documents must follow XML's syntax and document rules. There aren't that many of them, and if you're familiar with HTML, you already have a head start. In the following section, we cover each and every well-formedness constraint.

 Throughout this chapter, we refer to "XML" rules and requirements. Because XHTML is an application of XML, it too must follow these rules. We want to be as technically accurate as we can, and technically, the syntax rules are defined by the XML specification.

XML Rules

The rules to which XML documents must adhere make it easier to create tools to parse the documents. These rules also make XML easy to work with. The rules are simple, and some of them will be familiar if you've worked with HTML. We define XML's rules in two categories:

- XML syntax rules are the rules that define basic syntax requirements.
- XML document rules are the rules that govern basic document requirements.

XML Syntax Rules

Many of the syntax rules required for every XHTML document are stricter than those required for HTML documents. For this reason, each rule in this section is accompanied by an HTML example using HTML syntax and an XHTML example following the rules defined by each section. For example:

```
HTML:   <p>This is a paragraph.
XHTML:  <p>This is a paragraph.</p>
```

In the previous example, the XHTML syntax is correct, whereas the HTML example is not considered well-formed XHTML and should not be parsed by a parser. This is not to say that a browser won't parse, interpret, and render the ill-formed markup. In most cases, browsers don't parse XHTML as XHTML, but rather as HTML. This is not expected to remain this way. Eventually, browsers will parse XHTML as XML. However, for the time being, you might want to use a stand-alone parser to check your documents for errors before uploading them to your server. See the section "Parser's Response" later in this chapter for more on parsers.

Close All Elements

All elements must be balanced with an opening and closing tag. This is not the case according to HTML, in which several elements are defined with optional closing tags, such as the p element.

```
HTML:  <p>This is a paragraph.
XHTML: <p>This is a paragraph.</p>
```

The XHTML example defines opening and closing tags that contain character data (its content). The HTML example defines an opening tag that marks the beginning of a paragraph. The only way the processor infers that the paragraph is closed in HTML is if it encounters an opening block-level element, such as another p element. The opening of another block-level element suggests that the previous block-level element is closed. This leaves element relationships a tad open-ended, and to make the distinction clearer, XHTML requires that all elements must be terminated (closed).

Empty Elements Must Be Terminated

If you already know HTML, you're probably wondering what you do with the img and br elements. Both of these elements need to be closed, but because they're empty elements, they follow a different syntax. Empty elements accept attributes but do not contain character data. For example, the following markup defines an element that contains character data (the character data is defined in bold):

```
<p>This is a paragraph.</p>
```

An empty element on the other hand, looks like this:

```
<img src="logo.gif" alt="Corporate Logo" />
```

The img element doesn't contain any character data. Instead, it uses attributes to define its functionality. According to the img element defined in the preceding markup, the source file of the image can be found using "logo.gif" as a relative Uniform Resource Locator (URL), and the alternative text, Corporate Logo, is displayed when a user agent can't interpret images or while the image is loading.

Empty elements must also be terminated, and according to XML syntax rules, you have two options:

- Terminate the tag with a space and a slash, as follows:

```
<img src="logo.gif" alt="Corporate Logo" />
```

- Add a closing tag, as follows:

```
<img src="logo.gif" alt="Corporate Logo"></img>
```

The first option saves space and time, and logically makes a little more sense. You can use either syntax, but we suggest (and most developers use) the first option, rather than the latter.

According to HTML, you didn't need to terminate empty elements. XHTML is a tad different:

```
HTML:  <img src="logo.gif" alt="Corporate Logo">
XHTML: <img src="logo.gif" alt="Corporate Logo" />
```

According to the XML specification, most white space within a tag is not significant. For example: `<img src="logo.gif" alt="Logo"/>` *is the same as* `<img src="logo.gif" alt="Logo" />`*. In the second example, you should notice white space between the closing quotation mark (") and the forward slash (/). However, older browsers have problems interpreting the first example because there is no white space separating these items. If you add a space before the /, you can ensure that most older browsers will interpret the empty element without any problems.*

Quote All Attribute Values

Another XHTML rule is that all attribute values be delimited with quotation marks. HTML allows several attribute values to be defined without quotation marks—although the specification recommends that they always be used.

This rule is easy enough.

```
HTML:  <table align=center>
XHTML: <table align="center">
```

The HTML example does not contain quotation marks, and the XHTML example does.

*In many HTML examples, you're likely to see the attribute value in uppercase (*CENTER*). Most attribute values are not case sensitive. In this book, we generally use lowercase to define attribute values, for readability.*

All Attributes Must Have Values

One of the trickier XML rules is that all attributes must have values. At first glance, this may seem to be an easy rule to grasp, but there's a trick or two you have to master when applying it to XHTML. For most attributes, it's fairly straightforward. For example:

```
<table align="center">
```

In this case, the `align` attribute has to have a value to tell the processor just how to align the table. But what do you do with Booleans that are used as stand-alone attributes? The HTML vocabulary defined a handful of stand-alone attributes that when present, turn the function on, and when absent the function is assumed to be off. For example:

```
<input disabled>
```

In this case, the `disabled` attribute is present and the `input` form control is disabled. If you added other attributes, the element would look something like the following:

```
<input disabled name="pet" value="cat">
```

Because this element is empty, we need to terminate it:

```
<input disabled name="pet" value="cat" />
```

(Note that we added white space before the trailing slash.) Although the preceding attribute syntax is fine according to HTML, it's not well formed according to XHTML, because all attributes must have values. The problem is that these stand-alone attributes do not have any predefined values, and therefore, a value is not really needed. However, according to XML's rules, it must have a value, so a work-around was created: You set the attribute equal to itself:

```
<input disabled="disabled" name="pet" value="cat" />
```

This work-around is perfect because legacy browsers won't have problems with these attributes and the syntax is still well-formed XHTML.

```
HTML:  <dl compact>
XHTML: <dl compact="compact">
```

XML Is Case Sensitive

The rule that XML is case sensitive can also be defined as a validation constraint; however, we define it here because it's a primary concern to proper syntax. XML is case sensitive, which means that however the elements and attributes are named in the associated DTD is how you have to use them.

The XHTML DTDs define elements and attributes in lowercase, so we too have to stick to it. This is a sticky point for many HTML developers who are used to writing their markup in uppercase. Most developers don't want to change, and many of them want to know why they have to. There's no compelling reason that the DTDs defined all elements and attributes in lowercase, but because it was done that way, you have to abide by those rules in your XHTML documents:

```
HTML:   <TABLE>...</TABLE>
XHTML:  <table>...</table>
```

If you choose to not use a DTD, XML still requires that the opening and closing tag match. For example, <P> is not the same as <p>.

Nesting Is Important

The concept of nesting is central to document structure. Nesting defines where an element can occur. For example, the following markup defines a `title` element that is nested with the head element:

```
<head>
    <title>Document title</title>
</head>
```

This may seem straightforward; however, there are cases where people make mistakes. For example, can you spot the mistake in the following markup?

```
<p>You can bold a <b>word</p></b>
```

The problem is that the tags are overlapping; no one element is nested within the other. The golden rule is "what you open first, you close last." To correct this syntax, you would write:

```
<p>You can bold a <b>word</b></p>
```

Notice how the b element is nested completely within the p element.

```
HTML:   <p>You can bold a <b>word</p></b>
XHTML:  <p>You can bold a <b>word</b></p>
```

*When referring to an element that is nested within another element, we call the nested element a **child** of the container element; the container is the **parent** element. Throughout this book we refer to nested elements as "children of a parent element."*

XML Document Rules

If you thought the syntax rules were a snap to understand, you'll be delighted to read this section. There are only a few document rules that govern a well-formed XML document. We also define a few optional rules that we recommend you follow, but they're not necessary.

Required Root Element

All XML documents must have at least one root element. This is a simple rule really. Without at least one root element, there's no content. The root element must contain all other elements on the page. In XHTML, the root element is the html element. You're probably thinking, "Why didn't they change root element from html to xhtml?" XHTML uses the exact same vocabulary as HTML, which makes it easier for parsers, authoring tools, and developers to work with XHTML. That's why! In Chapter 3 we define the html element.

Optional XML Declaration

The XML specification defines an optional XML declaration. The declaration uses the syntax of an XML processing instruction, but it's not one. The XML declaration announces to both developers and processors that the current document adheres to the XML specification. The declaration can accept three attributes: version, encoding, and standalone. The syntax is as follows:

```
<?xml version="1.0" encoding="UTF-8" standalone="no"?>
```

Please note that xml is lowercase and there is no white space separating the < > from the ?.

So far, there's only one version of the XML specification, and because the XML declaration is optional, you could leave it off entirely. After all, every XML document is currently an XML 1 document, so <?xml version="1.0"?> is not really necessary. However, it's unlikely that the XML specification will *never* evolve; XML documents will at some point be declaring themselves with <?xml version="2.0"?>. If you use the XML declaration to begin with, current and future processors will unequivocally know how to handle your document.

A second edition of XML has been released, but it only corrected minor mistakes in the 1.0 specification and did not represent any content-related changes to the standard. Its formal title is XML 1.0 (Second Edition).

If you're creating an XML document, you must include an XML declaration. However, if you're creating XHTML documents, you should use caution when adding the XML declaration. There are a few legacy browsers that have problems interpreting the XML declaration. If you choose to leave it off, your document must be UTF-8 or UTF-16 encoded (UTF-8 is the default encoding type). In this case, you might want to include information about the character set using the `http-equiv="Content-Type"` convention in a `meta` element (see Chapter 3).

Do not include the XML declaration if your users are accessing the Web with non-XML-aware user agents (browsers). Most older versions of browsers (Internet Explorer 5 and earlier and Netscape 4.7 and earlier) are not XML-aware and will have trouble processing the XML declaration.

If you do include the XML declaration, there are two rules you *must* follow:

- It must be the first item in your document.

- It must begin on the first line, and in the first character position (no preceding white space, please).

Optional *DOCTYPE* Declaration

In a few sections, we cover Document Type Definitions (DTDs). DTDs are optional; however, if you use a DTD, you need to reference it within a DOCTYPE declaration. The use of DTDs is optional according to XML. XHTML takes a departure on this rule and requires the use of a DTD.

For a document to be a strictly conforming XHTML document, it must reference (and adhere to) one of the three XHTML DTDs. This rule is defined by the XHTML specification and is not a requirement according to the XML specification. See the section "Referencing the Three Flavors of XHTML."

Comment Tags

In XHTML documents, and throughout this book, you'll see lines enclosed in special characters like these:

```
<!-- This is a comment. -->
```

These are *comments*. The `<!-- -->` markup is used to "hide" something from browsers, which are not supposed to display the comment contents on screen. Its traditional purpose is to include notes about the code—what it does, who wrote it, what changes still need to be made, and so forth. Comment markup is currently used for several other purposes, including carrying script or style sheet information that affects presentation but isn't itself seen by users, as you'll see in later chapters.

Parser's Response

A parser is a program used in conjunction with other applications. A parser prepares your document for other programs and checks for well-formedness to make sure that your document follows all of the syntax requirements. One of the first things a parser does is check that the XML document is well formed. If it's not, it reports an error message and fails to display the document.

This is most definitely not the case with HTML processors. If you break an HTML rule, the processor seems to look the other way and display your document the best it can. With XML, however, you find a stronger reliance on syntax rules and the parsers uphold this idea. If you break one of the well-formedness rules, your document will not render.

The error messages you receive are quite wonderful because most of them (they differ from parser to parser) let you know the line and position where the error occurs, and will even define the mistake. This makes troubleshooting potential problems much easier. Figure 2.1 shows a typical error message presented by Microsoft Internet Explorer.

Figure 2.1 *An error message in Internet Explorer*

A parser's response to XHTML is a little different. Ideally, the parser would verify that the XHTML document is indeed well formed; however, most parsers that are used by browsers produce error messages for XHTML documents. Because most browsers actually view XHTML as HTML, it treats the documents as HTML.

If you want to check your XHTML document for well-formedness, you have to find a non-validating parser other than the ones found in the major browsers. We recommend using the W3C's online validator to check both for well-formedness and validity.

In the future, we expect that browsers will provide better support for XHTML parsers; however, that's up to the browser vendors.

Non-validating Versus Validating Parsers

Essentially, there are two different types of parsers that can parse an XML document: a non-validating parser and a validating parser. A *non-validating parser* only evaluates a document against XML's well-formedness constraints. Issues of validity are not considered. A *validating parser* checks both for well-formedness and validity. For a document to be valid, you have to reference and adhere to a DTD.

The W3C offers an online HTML validating parser that validates both HTML and XHTML documents. You can upload your XHTML document, cut and paste it into a text box, or (if your page is already online) enter the URL. We should warn you that the error messages it presents take some getting used to. For example:

- "Error: Missing DOCTYPE declaration at start of document" means that the document does not reference a DTD, and therefore, the document cannot be validated.

- "Error: Required attribute "ALT" not specified" means that a required attribute (the `alt` attribute, in this case) is missing.

- "Error: End tag for "A" omitted; possible causes include a missing end tag, improper nesting of elements, or use of an element where it is not allowed" means that a closing tag is missing. There are many reasons the validator cannot locate the closing tag:

  - The elements might be incorrectly nested; therefore, the end tag is defined later in the document.

  - The end tag is missing all together.

  - It's an empty element that is not terminated correctly. (In this case, the a element requires a closing tag, so we can rule out this possibility.)

The validator states the exact line and position of the error, so you don't have to blindly search through the entire document trying to locate the mistakes.

You can try out the W3C's validator at `http://validator.w3.org`. Master's Reference Part 4 is a guide to the most common error messages from this validator.

Validity

A document is considered *valid* if it adheres to all the rules defined by an associated DTD. A DTD is a collection of declarations that define element and attribute names and relationships. If you look at the XML specification, you find two common themes:

- It defines syntax and document rules for creating XML documents.

- It defines syntax rules for creating DTDs.

The first function we covered in the previous section, "A Well-Formed Document." In this section, we cover the second function defined: validity. According to the XML standard, adhering to a DTD is optional. In other words, an XML document is not required to be valid.

The XHTML standard, on the other hand, says that not only must an XHTML document be well formed, but it must also be valid. This means that all XHTML documents must adhere to an XHTML DTD.

Outside of it being a requirement, there are many advantages gained by referencing a DTD. The most important of these is troubleshooting. A DTD defines the rules for your markup. For example, the DTD defines element and attribute names, where elements can occur within the document, and where attributes can occur. When creating an XHTML document by hand, you'll undoubtedly make mistakes. If you choose not to use a DTD, you'll have to comb the document with your eyes to find all your mistakes. However, if you use a DTD, you can use a validator to locate them.

DTDs use different syntax than XML, which makes them a little strange to read at first. If you're only working with the XHTML vocabulary, you don't need to know too much about DTDs because they're already created for you. However, in the following section, we provide you with some details on DTDs so you can understand them.

What Is a DTD?

A DTD is a rulebook for your document. DTDs define element and attribute names and relationships and provide the rules that your elements and attributes must abide by. For example, in the XHTML DTD, there's a declaration that requires every document to contain the html element, and requires that the html element contain two child elements: head and body. Therefore, the declaration requires the following:

```
<html>
  <head>...</head>
  <body>...</body>
</html>
```

The previous example is a simplified version of an XHTML document and should only be used to illustrate a point. We intentionally left out some required components. For a complete example of an XHTML document, please visit the end of this chapter.

Simply put, a DTD defines rules for elements and attributes, and these rules can be checked by a validating parser. If a document fails to abide by the DTD's rules, it will produce an error message that tells you where you made mistakes.

The Heart of a DTD

The heart of a DTD consists of declarations. Four types of declarations are defined.

For each declaration example, we've simplified actual XHTML element declarations to make it easier on the eyes. Our examples do not represent the complete declaration for a given element or attribute. Most XHTML DTD declarations use entities, and the syntax can become rather complex. If you're interested in seeing the real thing, feel free to visit www.w3.org/TR/xhtml1/DTD/xhtml1-transitional.dtd.

Element type declarations   define element names and content models. Each content model defines the type of content an element can contain. For example, it could state that an element can only contain data, or that an element can only contain the head and body elements as children—for example,

```
<!ELEMENT html (head, body)>
```

Attribute list declarations   define attribute names and the elements they can modify. Each attribute list declaration also defines default values and datatypes. For example, in XHTML, the img element is required to accept both the alt and src attributes, and the height and width attributes are optional. Here's an example:

```
<!ELEMENT img EMPTY>
<!ATTLIST img src     CDATA   #REQUIRED
              alt     CDATA   #REQUIRED
              height  CDATA   #IMPLIED
              width   CDATA   #IMPLIED   >
```

Entity declarations   define a data item and provide a way to reference that data item. Entities are used to define common data items that will be used throughout the XML document or the DTD itself. Once a data item is declared as an entity, you can reference it using an entity name, saving you time and bytes. You can reference entities from within your document or from within a DTD subset. For example, if you want to create information that you reuse a lot in a DTD subset, such as the group of heading elements, you can create an entity for those values—for example,

```
<!ENTITY % heading "H1|H2|H3|H4|H5|H6">
```

Notation declarations identify objects that are not to be parsed as XML. Because all text in an XML document is parsed by the XML parser (unless otherwise indicated), there must be some way to identify items that are not XML. For example, if you want to include a Graphics Interchange Format (GIF) image, you would need a way to tell the processor to not parse the GIF image as XML. A notation declaration does just that—for example,

```
<!NOTATION gif SYSTEM "image/gif">
```

These are the only four types of declarations that you will find in a DTD. They are not as simple as they may appear. Each declaration type can take on many different forms—although these forms are not necessary for our discussion of DTDs. For more on these declarations, visit the XML specification at www.w3.org/TR/1998/REC-xml-19980210 or Chapters 22 and 23.

Referencing the Three Flavors of XHTML

There are three variations of XHTML: Strict, Transitional, and Frameset. Many developers/writers refer to them as the "three flavors" of XHTML. Each variant is defined by its own DTD. As the document author, you reference which DTD the document supports. When you reference one of the DTDs, you're providing the processor with a list of elements and attributes and with the rules defining their relationships. If your document breaks one of those rules, it's not valid.

The three possible DTDs are as follows:

The Strict DTD Allows for the XHTML elements relating to document structure, leaving out most presentational elements.

The Transitional DTD Allows for most XHTML elements, including presentational elements.

The Frameset DTD Allows for frame markup, and is only used when defining frameset documents.

Before we define each flavor of XHTML, you learn the basic syntax needed to reference each XHTML variant.

DOCTYPE Declarations

As mentioned, DTDs define the rules for a document's elements and attributes. Lucky for us, the XHTML DTDs have already been defined, and all you have to do is learn how to reference them. A *DOCTYPE declaration* is markup that references the DTD that defines the grammar for an XML document. In the following sections, we define DOCYTPE declaration syntax and point out some ways you can use these declarations to improve troubleshooting and validation.

- -

XHTML Opportunities

Because XHTML is an XML application, it's extensible, and therefore you can mix XML vocabularies. For example, you can add Scalable Vector Graphics (SVG) elements to an XHTML document because both are XML vocabularies.

You can also add your own elements and attributes to your XHTML documents. If you use a DTD, you must define all elements and attributes that are used in your document. This means that you would also need to extend your XHTML DTD. To do so requires that you can read and write a DTD. This is covered in Chapters 22 and 23.

- -

Syntax

DOCTYPE declaration syntax is not that complicated. There are a few parts to the declaration, but first you need to understand the delimiters used.

All XML declarations, including DOCTYPE declarations, begin with a less than symbol and an exclamation point (<!). The declaration is closed with just a greater than symbol (>). What we have so far is:

```
<!>
```

Note that this is not a comment tag!

All declarations use a keyword to identify their type. For DOCTYPE declarations, this keyword is DOCTYPE (all uppercase). The keyword must be added directly after the exclamation point. No white space is allowed. If you add the keyword, you have the following:

```
<!DOCTYPE>
```

You're not yet done, because after all, the DOCTYPE declaration must reference the file, and as of yet you've only identified the type of declaration. Four (or three, depending on the type of DOCTYPE declaration) other pieces of information must be added:

Type of document   This is essentially the root element.

```
<!DOCTYPE rootelement>
```

In XHTML, this must be html, in all lowercase, as follows:

```
<!DOCTYPE html>
```

Type of DTD   Identifies whether the document is using a DTD that is not publicly defined (SYSTEM) or one that is and has a public identifier available (PUBLIC).

```
<!DOCTYPE html KEYWORD>
```

For example:

```
<!DOCTYPE html PUBLIC>
```

Public identifier of the DTD   A Uniform Resource Name (URN) that is recognized as a public identifier for the DTD. A public identifier is only used if the keyword PUBLIC is used; when you do include an identifier, the syntax looks like this:

```
<!DOCTYPE rootelement KEYWORD "identifier">
```

For example:

```
<!DOCTYPE html PUBLIC "-//W3C//DTD XHTML 1.0 Strict//EN">
```

URL of the DTD   Defines the location of the external DTD subset (essentially, the DTD). When you've added this component, you get the following:

```
<!DOCTYPE rootelement KEYWORD "identifier" "URL">
```

For example:

```
<!DOCTYPE html PUBLIC "-//W3C//DTD XHTML 1.0 Strict//EN"
    "http://www.w3.org/TR/xhtml1DTD/xhtml1-strict.dtd">
```

As an XHTML developer, if you want to use one of the three XHTML DTDs—and you should—all you have to do is add one of the three DTD declarations. For example, you would include the preceding markup (two lines on our printed page) as the first line of your XHTML document. In the following sections, we define how to include DTD declarations within an internal subset (within the DOCTYPE declaration itself); however, this is not necessary for using the XHTML DTDs. One of the rare reasons you would want to know how to use internal subsets is if you're creating your own declarations.

Internal Versus External

In the previous section, you saw how to reference an external DTD document. However, DTDs can be defined both externally and internally. Although you're not likely to use internal declarations, if you're only using XHTML elements, there's a chance that you will want to extend your markup and add your own elements. If this is the case, you need to know all your options.

DOCTYPE declarations reference DTDs, but just where do those definitions reside? There are several options for referencing definitions; they are as follows:

- Declare all the definitions within the DOCTYPE declaration itself:

  ```
  <!DOCTYPE rootelement [document type definitions]>
  ```

- Declare all definitions in an external document that is referenced using a SYSTEM identifier:

  ```
  <!DOCTYPE rootelement SYSTEM "URL">
  ```

- Declare some definitions in an external document and reference them using a SYSTEM identifier, and also declare some definitions within the DOCTYPE declaration:

  ```
  <!DOCTYPE rootelement SYSTEM "URL"
      [document type definitions]>
  ```

- Reference a PUBLIC DTD:

  ```
  <!DOCTYPE rootelement PUBLIC "identifier" "URL">
  ```

- Reference a PUBLIC DTD, and also define some additional definitions within the DOCTYPE declaration:

  ```
  <!DOCTYPE rootelement PUBLIC "identifier" "URL"
      [document type definitions]>
  ```

In each case, the declarations are either defined internally as an internal subset or externally as an external subset. The DTD is seen as a combination of all internal and external definitions. XHTML only uses an external subset for DTDs; however, if you want to extend the XHTML vocabulary, you might want to add some internal declarations of your own.

To read more on this topic, visit Chapter 22 and 23.

Referencing a System DTD

If you use the SYSTEM keyword, it must be followed by the URL that references the DTD. This URL can be an absolute or relative address, the same as when referencing any document on your server or the Web. For example, if the DTD resides in the same directory as the file that is referencing it, you could use relative addressing:

```
<!DOCTYPE classListing SYSTEM "classlisting.dtd">
```

However, if the DTD resides on another machine, you need to provide an absolute URL to identify it.

```
<!DOCTYPE classListing SYSTEM
    "http://www.lanw.com/DTDs/classlisting.dtd">
```

XHTML DOCTYPE declarations do not use system identifiers; they use public identifiers, as described in the following section.

Referencing a Public DTD

Several common DTDs can also be referenced using a name in addition to a URL. This name is known as the *public identifier* and is a unique string that can be used to reference a DTD. If the processor recognizes the public identifier, it will translate that into the URL of the DTD. If it does not recognize the public identifier, it looks to the URL in the declaration.

For the processor to recognize, and be able to translate, a public identifier, it has be hard-wired into the processor. The idea is that this might all change: there may eventually be public identifier repositories that allow processors to look up a public identifier and download the DTD. However, we'll have to wait for that functionality.

If you do use a public identifier, you have to use the PUBLIC keyword, followed by the public identifier and URL. This is how you reference public XHTML DTDs:

```
<!DOCTYPE html PUBLIC "-//W3C//DTD XHTML 1.0 Strict//EN"
    "http://www.w3.org/TR/xhtml1DTD/xhtml1-strict.dtd">
```

XHTML DTDs

As mentioned, there are three different variations of XHTML. Each has its own DTD. Again, the three variations are: Strict, Transitional, and Frameset. They were also defined in HTML 4, so they may look familiar.

Strict DTD

The Strict DTD is not used often because it doesn't allow the deprecated markup that is sometimes necessary when older browsers are viewing documents.

*Elements and attributes that are defined as **deprecated** are not expected to be included in the next version of the XHTML specification. Most formatting elements and attributes are deprecated in favor of using Cascading Style Sheets.*

The Strict DTD also assumes that you're using style sheets to format your document. This can be a problem because many older browsers don't support style sheets. If you use the Strict DTD, you have to use the following DOCTYPE declaration:

```
<!DOCTYPE html PUBLIC "-//W3C//DTD XHTML 1.0 Strict//EN"
    "http://www.w3.org/TR/xhtml1/DTD/xhtml1-strict.dtd">
```

You can also abbreviate the URL and define the DOCTYPE declaration as the following:

```
<!DOCTYPE html PUBLIC "-//W3C//DTD XHTML 1.0 Strict//EN"
    "DTD/xhtml1-strict.dtd">
```

Some of you may be scratching your head wondering why you could include a relative URL to a page that isn't saved somewhere in your computer. This is a convention allowed by the W3C only for the XHTML DTDs. You cannot make a habit of using relative addresses to point to documents that do not reside on your computer.

Transitional DTD

The XHTML Transitional DTD is based on the HTML 4.0 Transitional DTD (also known as the "loose" DTD) and supports most element and attributes except for frame-related markup. Because this DTD includes support for most deprecated elements and attributes, it's used more than any other XHTML DTD.

If you're creating an XHTML document that will be viewed in older browsers, you'll most likely need to use some of the deprecated presentational elements, such as the font and basefont elements. If you use the Strict DTD, you cannot use these two elements—you'd have to use CSS to define presentational properties.

The syntax is similar to the Strict DOCTYPE declaration; the only difference is the public identifier and URL.

```
<!DOCTYPE html PUBLIC "-//W3C//DTD XHTML 1.0 Transitional//EN"
    "http://www.w3.org/TR/xhtml1/DTD/xhtml1-transitional.dtd">
```

Frameset DTD

The XHTML frameset DTD is based on the HTML 4.0 Frameset DTD and is only used with frameset documents. Frameset documents replace the body element with a frameset element and require the use of frame empty elements. Because a frameset requires specific elements, it gets its very own DTD. (See Chapter 8 for more on creating frames.)

When creating a frameset document, you'll need to use the following DOCTYPE declaration. Notice the public identifier and URL:

```
<!DOCTYPE html PUBLIC "-//W3C//DTD XHTML 1.0 Frameset//EN"
    "http://www.w3.org/TR/xhtml1/DTD/xhtml1-frameset.dtd">
```

XML Namespaces

Although this book is dedicated to XHTML, it's important for you to understand how namespaces work from an XML perspective. XML allows you to create your own elements and attributes. XML also allows developers to combine XML document types. For example, you could embed elements from a document type that you created into an XHTML document. The following would be an example of embedding your own elements into an XHTML document, but there's a possible problem; look at the bolded elements:

```
<!DOCTYPE html PUBLIC "-//W3C//DTD XHTML 1.0 Strict//EN"
    "http://www.w3.org/TR/xhtml1/DTD/xhtml1-strict.dtd">
<html xmlns="http://www.w3.org/1999/xhtml">
    <head>
        <title>Working with Namespaces</title>
    </head>
    <body>
        <h1>Online Class Offerings</h1>
```

```
    <class>
       <title>Introduction to XML</title>
       <instructor>Chelsea Valentine</instructor>
    </class>
    <class>
       <title>TCP/IP for Webmasters</title>
       <instructor>Ed Tittel</instructor>
    </class>
  </body>
</html>
```

The bold lines illustrate the problem of element name conflicts. The first `title` element belongs to the XHTML document type; however, the next two `title` elements belong to our own document type. The problem arises when the processor has to decide what to do with them. How does the processor know which `title` element is which? The answer is XML namespaces.

XML namespaces allow you to use an element from one document type (such as an XML document) and embed it in another document type (such as an XHTML document). Because namespaces uniquely identify a set of elements that belongs to a given document type, they ensure that there are no element name conflicts.

The namespace in the XML recommendation document is seen as a complement to the XML specification and can be found at `www.w3.org/TR/REC-xml-names`. The recommendation document defines a special syntax to identify namespaces. The document defines how a collection of elements can be given unique identifiers; therefore, no matter where an element is used, you can be sure that it belongs to the namespace.

There are two ways to define a namespace:

Default namespace   Defines a namespace using the `xmlns` attribute without a prefix, and all child elements are assumed to belong to the defined namespace. XTHML uses the default namespace construct to define the XHTML namespace.

Local namespace   Defines a namespace using the `xmlns` attribute with a prefix. When the prefix is attached to an element, it's assumed to belong to that namespace.

In both cases, you define a namespace using the `xmlns` attribute. The attribute's value is the name that identifies the namespace. A namespace name can be some Uniform Resource Identifier (URI). A URI can be a URL or a Uniform Resource Name (URN). Most times, you'll find URLs used. This may seem strange, but the namespace is only symbolic and does not point to a document or schema. The value should be unique.

We look at both types in the next two sections.

Default Namespaces

A *default namespace* is considered to apply to the element where it's declared and to all child elements that are not assigned to another namespace. You define the namespace as you would define an attribute: The attribute name is xmlns, and the value is the namespace name.

For example, XHTML uses the default namespace syntax to define the XHTML namespace. The xmlns attribute is defined within the html start tag and is applied to all child elements that do not have a prefix pointing to another namespace. In the following snippet of markup, the XHTML namespace is declared within the html start tag:

```
<html xmlns="http://www.w3.org/1999/xhtml">
  <head>
    <title>Example Transitional XHTML Document</title>
  </head>
  <body>
    <h1>My First XHTML Document</h1>
    <p><font color="#CCCC00" size="+1">After reading this book,
      we will become XHTML gods!</font></p>
  </body>
</html>
```

The namespace name is already defined for us, because it belongs to a public document type. If you visit the URL in the preceding code, you'll find that no content resides there. This is because it's only meant to be a symbolic unique identifier used to resolve possible element name conflicts.

If you created your own XML document, you could create your own namespace name, for example:

```
<classListing
    xmlns="http://www.lanw.com/namespace/onlinetraining/">
    <class>
        <title>Introduction to XML</title>
        <instructor>Chelsea Valentine</instructor>
    </class>
    <class>
        <title>TCP/IP for Webmasters</title>
        <instructor>Ed Tittel</instructor>
    </class>
</classListing>
```

In this case, we've created our own unique namespace that uses our domain name. The `classListing` element and all of its children belong to the `http://www.lanw.com/namespace/onlinetraining` namespace.

Local Namespaces

Local namespaces are similar to default namespaces; however, they add an additional identifier: a prefix. A local namespace can be defined anywhere within the document. In other words, you don't have to declare it within the element that it is to modify (as you do with default namespaces). In this case, you define a namespace and associate a prefix that can later be used to reference the namespace.

Local namespaces are often used when embedding document types within another document. For example, in the previous section "XML Namespaces," we provided an example that uses both XHTML elements and our own class elements. The XHTML elements are uniquely identified by the XHTML default namespace, but what about our class elements? Because we already have a default namespace, we will have to define a local namespace for them. In the following example, we have bolded elements to illustrate this concept:

```
<!DOCTYPE html PUBLIC "-//W3C//DTD XHTML 1.0 Strict//EN"
    "http://www.w3.org/TR/xhtml1/DTD/xhtml1-strict.dtd">
<html xmlns="http://www.w3.org/1999/xhtml"
    xmlns:lanw="http://www.lanw.com/namespace/onlinetraining">
    <head>
        <title>Working with Namespaces</title>
    </head>
    <body>
        <h1>Online Class Offerings</h1>
        <lanw:class>
            <lanw:title>Introduction to XML</lanw:title>
            <lanw:instructor>Chelsea Valentine</lanw:instructor>
        </lanw:class>
        <lanw:class>
            <lanw:title>TCP/IP for Webmasters</lanw:title>
            <lanw:instructor>Ed Tittel</lanw:instructor>
        </lanw:class>
    </body>
</html>
```

In the previous example, a local prefix is defined for the class elements:

```
xmlns:lanw="http://www.lanw.com/namespace/onlinetraining"
```

The `xmlns` attribute is used, but notice the colon and characters that follow (`:lanw`). To define a local namespace, you must define a prefix that can be used as a reference later in the document. The colon separates the `xmlns` attribute name from the prefix. You can create your own prefix for your own document types; however, if you're using someone else's vocabulary, be sure to check and see if they have defined a prefix for you.

After you've defined the local namespace, you can reference it with the prefix. In our example, all elements identified with the prefix (`lanw`) and a colon (`:`) belong to the `http://www.lanw.com/namespace/onlinetraining` namespace. Most local namespaces are defined in the root element and then referenced when needed.

The Required XHTML Namespace

All XHTML elements and attributes belong to the XHTML namespace. Each XHTML element and attribute has its very own name—all of which belong to the same namespace. The XHTML namespace is defined as a default namespace and is a required component of an XHTML document. The `xmlns` is a required attribute of the `html` element, and the `xmlns` value is fixed as `http://www.w3.org/1999/xhtml`. This makes it easy, because there's no mistaking what goes where; you should always define the XHTML namespace like so:

```
<html xmlns="http://www.w3.org/1999/xhtml">
```

Combining Namespaces

In the section "Local Namespaces," our example combined two namespaces. This is becoming a common practice. The future of XHTML is as a document structure language. Gone are the days of using XHTML as a multipurpose language for document structure, presentation, and describing metadata.

The W3C has turned its focus to creating XML applications that have dedicated tasks and that can work together. For example, the following XML applications could be combined:

- XHTML defines document markup.

- MathML (Mathematical Markup Language) defines mathematical expressions.

- SMIL (Synchronized Multimedia Integration Language) defines synchronized multimedia tasks.

- SVG defines a scalable vector graphic language.

For example, you could add mathematical expressions to your XHTML document. The following example is defined by the XHTML specification document (we've added the bold highlighting):

```
<html xmlns="http://www.w3.org/1999/xhtml"
    xml:lang="en" lang="en">
    <head>
        <title>A Math Example</title>
    </head>
    <body>
        <p>The following is MathML markup:</p>
        <math xmlns="http://www.w3.org/1998/Math/MathML">
            <apply>
                <log/>
                <logbase>
                    <cn> 3 </cn>
                </logbase>
                <ci> x </ci>
            </apply>
        </math>
    </body>
</html>
```

There are a few ways to combine these document types. The first way, as demonstrated previously, is to define a default namespace for the root element and then redefine a default namespace for a child element. The nested default namespace is then applied to its current element and all its child elements. For example, all the elements

```
  </head>
  <body>
    <h1>My First Transitional XHTML Document</h1>
    <p><font color="#CCCC00" size="+1">After reading
      this book, we will become XHTML gods!</font></p>
  </body>
</html>
```

LISTING 2.3: A FRAMESET XHTML DOCUMENT

```
<!DOCTYPE html PUBLIC "-//W3C//DTD XHTML 1.0 Frameset//EN"
  "http://www.w3.org/TR/xhtml1/DTD/xhtml1-frameset.dtd">
<html xmlns="http://www.w3.org/1999/xhtml">
  <head>
    <title>Example Frameset XHTML Document</title>
  </head>
  <frameset cols="20%, *">
    <frame src="nav.html" name="navigation" />
    <frame src="index.html" name="content" />
  </frameset>
```

Where to Go from Here

This chapter focused on some basic XHTML concepts that must be understood to take advantage of the language. You learned how to create well-formed XHTML documents, reference DTDs, and declare and combine namespaces. The next step is to start creating your XHTML documents:

- See Chapter 3 to find out how to create your own XHTML documents.

- Check out Chapters 4 through 8 for information on links, images, tables, forms, and frames.

Creating Your First XHTML Document

Chapter 3

If you're ready to create your first XHTML document, you're in the right chapter! Here, we'll help you start a new XHTML document and save it using the appropriate file formats, show you how to add document structure elements (which help browsers identify your XHTML document), and show you how to apply some common formatting elements.

If you're new to XHTML (or rusty at hand-coding), you might want to review the element and attribute information in Chapter 1. Before starting this chapter, you should be familiar with elements and attributes, as well as how to apply them to your content.

Throughout this chapter, we provide lots of code samples and figures to help guide you and to show you what your results should look like. You can substitute your own text and images if you prefer, or you can duplicate the examples in the chapter. The step-by-step instructions will work regardless of the specific content you use. After you work through this chapter, you'll have developed your first XHTML document, complete with text, headings, horizontal rules, and even some character-level formatting.

In this chapter, you'll learn the following markup skills:

- Creating, saving, and viewing XHTML documents

- Including structure elements

- Applying common elements and attributes

- Including fancier formatting

Creating, Saving, and Viewing XHTML Documents

Exactly how you start a new XHTML document depends on which operating system and editor you're using. In general, you'll find that starting a new XHTML document is similar to starting other documents you've created. With Windows or Macintosh, you'll choose File ➔ New from within your editing program. (If you're using Unix, you'll type **vi**, **pico**, or **emacs**, and use the appropriate commands.) You'll make your new document an official XHTML document by saving it as such, which is discussed next.

Before you begin hand-coding XHTML, be aware that you should frequently save and view your work so you can see your progress. By doing so, you can make sure that things appear as you expect them to and catch mistakes within a few new lines of code. For example, we typically add a few new lines of code, save the XHTML document, then view it... then add a few more lines of code, save the document, then view it.... Exactly how often you save and view your documents depends on your preference. Chances are that at the beginning, you'll probably save it frequently.

You create an XHTML document in much same way that you create any plain-text document. Here's the general process:

1. Open your text editor.

2. Start a new document. If you're using Windows or Macintosh, choose File ➔ New. If you're using Unix, type **vi** or **pico** to start the editor.

3. Enter the XHTML code and text you want to include. (You'll have plenty of practice in this chapter.)

We recommend that you practice using XHTML by doing the examples throughout this and other chapters.

4. Save your document. If you're using Windows or Macintosh, choose File ➔ Save or File ➔ Save As.

Guidelines for Saving Files

As you work your way through this chapter, keep these saving and viewing guidelines in mind:

- Name the file with an htm or html extension. Windows 3.x doesn't recognize four-character extensions, so you're limited to htm on that platform.

- If you aren't using a text-only editor such as Notepad or TeachText, verify that the file type is set to Text or ASCII (or HTML, if that's an available menu option). If you use word-processing programs to create XHTML documents (and remember our caveat about this from Chapter 1), save your documents as HTML, Text Only, ASCII, DOS Text, or Text With Line Breaks. The specific options *will* vary depending on the word processor you use.

- Use only letters, numbers, hyphens (-), underscores (_), and periods (.) in your filename. Most browsers also accept spaces in filenames; however, spaces often make creating links difficult, as you will see in Chapter 4.

- Save the document and any other documents and files associated with a particular project all in one folder. You'll find that this makes using links, images, and other advanced technologies easier.

Viewing the XHTML documents that you develop is as simple as opening them from your local hard drive in your browser. If you're working with an open XHTML document in your editor, remember to save your latest changes and then follow these steps in your browser:

1. Choose File ➜ Open, and type the local filename or browse your hard drive until you find the file you want to open. Your particular menu command might be File ➜ Open Page Or File, or Open File, but it's all the same thing.

2. Select the file and click OK to open it in your browser.

Alternative Ways to Open Files

Most browsers provide some clever features that can make developing XHTML files easier.

You can easily see your editing changes in a file by *reloading* it. For example, after you view a document and then save some editing changes, you can reload the document and see the latest changes. You'll probably find that clicking a button is much easier than going back through the File ➜ Open and browse sequence. Generally, you reload documents by clicking a Refresh or Reload button or by choosing a similar option from the View menu.

In addition, you can open a file by selecting it from a list of "bookmarks" or "favorites." *Bookmarking* a file means adding a pointer to the file so you can open the file quickly, just as a bookmark makes it easier to open a book to a specific page. Creating bookmarks, or favorites, is as easy as clicking a menu option (or even just typing a keyboard shortcut) while viewing a page. Whenever you want to go back to that page, simply click the bookmark rather than choosing File ➜ Open and selecting the file. Most browsers have bookmark options; just look for a button or a menu command.

Applying Document Structure Elements

After you create a new document, your first task is to include *document structure elements*, which provide browsers with information about document characteristics. For example, document structure elements identify the version of XHTML used, provide introductory information about the document, and include the title, among other similar things. Most document structure elements, although part of the XHTML document, do not appear in the browser window. Instead, document structure elements work "behind the scenes" and tell the browser which elements to include and how to display them. Although these elements do not directly produce the snazzy results you see in Web pages or help files, they are essential.

Most browsers, including Netscape Navigator and Microsoft Internet Explorer, correctly display documents that do not include document structure elements. However, there's no guarantee that future versions will continue to do so or that your results will be consistent. We strongly suggest that you use the document structure elements because they're required by the XHTML specification.

All XHTML documents should include five document structure elements, nested and ordered as in the following example markup:

```
<!DOCTYPE HTML PUBLIC "-//W3C//DTD XHTML 1.0 Transitional//EN"
    "http://www.w3.org/TR/xhtml1/DTD/xhtml1-transitional.dtd">
<html xmlns="http://www.w3.org/1999/xhtml">
  <head>
    <title>Title That Summarizes the Document's Content</title>
  </head>
  <body>
    Mastering XHTML Document Body
  </body>
</html>
```

You can save time when creating future XHTML documents by saving document structure elements in a master document. That way, you can easily reuse them in other XHTML documents, rather than retyping them time after time. If you use an XHTML authoring program, this markup (or something similar to it) is usually the base of a new document.

The *DOCTYPE* Declaration

The DOCTYPE declaration tells browsers and validation services with which XHTML version the document complies. The XHTML 1 specification requires this nonpaired declaration, and, therefore, you should use it in all your documents. The key part of the DOCTYPE declaration is the *Document Type Definition* (DTD), which tells browsers that the document complies with a particular XHTML version. A DTD specifies the organization that issues the specification (the W3C, in these cases) and the exact version of the specification.

Enter the DOCTYPE declaration at the top of your document, like this:

```
<!DOCTYPE html PUBLIC "-//W3C//DTD XHTML 1.0 Transitional//EN"
    "http://www.w3.org/TR/xhtml1/DTD/xhtml1-transitional.dtd">
```

This example complies with XHTML 1.0 Transitional DTD, which is the most flexible DTD. To use the XHTML 1.0 Strict DTD, you would use this code:

```
<!DOCTYPE html PUBLIC "-//W3C//DTD XHTML 1.0 Strict//EN"
    "http://www.w3.org/TR/xhtml1/DTD/xhtml1-strict.dtd">
```

You can also abbreviate the URL and define the DOCTYPE declaration as the following:

```
<!DOCTYPE html PUBLIC "-//W3C//DTD XHTML 1.0 Strict//EN"
    "DTD/xhtml1-strict.dtd">
```

As new XHTML standards evolve, you can expect this declaration to change to indicate new versions. For example, in a year or so, the DOCTYPE declaration might look like this:

```
<!DOCTYPE xhtml PUBLIC "-//W3C//DTD XHTML 2.0 Transitional//EN"
    "http://www.w3.org/TR/xhtml2/DTD/xhtml2-transitional.dtd">
```

Even after new standards appear, you don't need to revise the DOCTYPE declaration in existing documents. If your document conforms to the XHTML 1 standard, it'll conform to that standard, regardless of more recent XHTML versions.

Which XHTML 1 DTD Should I Use?

The XHTML 1 specification comes in three varieties: Strict, Transitional, and Frameset. The *Strict* version prohibits everything except "pure" XHTML, and you're unlikely to use it unless you're writing XHTML documents that use no formatting elements and are relying on style sheets to make them look good. To indicate that your document complies with the Strict DTD, use the following markup:

```
<!DOCTYPE html PUBLIC "-//W3C//DTD XHTML 1.0 Strict//EN"
   "http://www.w3.org/TR/xhtml1/DTD/xhtml1-strict.dtd">
```

The *Transitional* version is the most flexible for accommodating deprecated but still frequently used elements and attributes, including nearly all formatting elements. To indicate that your document complies with the Transitional DTD, use the following declaration:

```
<!DOCTYPE html PUBLIC "-//W3C//DTD XHTML 1.0 Transitional//EN"
   "http://www.w3.org/TR/xhtml1/DTD/xhtml1-transitional.dtd">
```

The *Frameset DTD* is similar to the Transitional DTD, but also supports the elements needed to use frames. To indicate that your document complies with the Frameset DTD, use the following declaration:

```
<!DOCTYPE html PUBLIC "-//W3C//DTD XHTML 1.0 Frameset//EN"
   "http://www.w3.org/TR/xhtml1/DTD/xhtml1-frameset.dtd">
```

See Chapter 2 for more information on these DTDs.

The *html* Element

The html element identifies the document as either an HTML or XHTML document. To specify that it's an XHTML document, you should also add the XHTML namespace. (See Chapter 2 for more on namespaces.) The html element is necessary for older browsers that do not support the DOCTYPE declaration, and it's required by the specification. It's also helpful to people who read the XHTML markup. To use the html element along with the XHTML namespace, enter it in your document under the DOCTYPE declaration, like this:

```
<!DOCTYPE html PUBLIC "-//W3C//DTD XHTML 1.0 Transitional//EN"
   "http://www.w3.org/TR/xhtml1/DTD/xhtml1-transitional.dtd">
<html xmlns="http://www.w3.org/1999/xhtml">
</html>
```

The *head* Element

Found in every XHTML document, the head element contains information about the document, including its title, scripts used, style definitions, and document descriptions. Not all browsers require this element, but most browsers expect to find any available additional information about the document within the head element. To add the head element, enter it between the html opening and closing tags, like this:

```
<!DOCTYPE html PUBLIC "-//W3C//DTD XHTML 1.0 Transitional//EN"
    "http://www.w3.org/TR/xhtml1/DTD/xhtml1-transitional.dtd">
<html xmlns="http://www.w3.org/1999/xhtml">
    <head>
    </head>
</html>
```

Don't confuse this document head *element, which is a structure element, with* **heading** *elements such as* h1, *which create heading text in a document body. We discuss heading elements later in this chapter in the "Creating Headings" section.*

Additionally, the head element can contain other elements that have information for search engines and indexing programs.

The title Element

The title element, which the XHTML 1 specification requires, contains the document title. The title does not appear within the browser window, although it's usually visible in the browser's title bar, which has limited space. Therefore, make sure your title briefly summarizes your document's content and keep keywords at the beginning of the title. To use the title element, enter it between the opening and closing head elements, like this:

```
<!DOCTYPE html PUBLIC "-//W3C//DTD XHTML 1.0 Transitional//EN"
    "http://www.w3.org/TR/xhtml1/DTD/xhtml1-transitional.dtd">
<html xmlns="http://www.w3.org/1999/xhtml">
    <head>
        <title>
            Title That Summarizes the Document's Content
        </title>
    </head>
</html>
```

Titles should represent the document, even if the document is taken out of context. Some good titles include the following:

- Sample XHTML Code
- Learning to Ride a Bicycle
- Television Viewing for Fun and Profit

Less useful titles, particularly taken out of context, include the following:

- Examples
- Chapter 2
- Continued

The information in the title *element is also used by some search engines and indexing programs.*

Watch out for the default titles produced by WYSIWYG editors. Always be sure to put in your own title.

The meta Element

The meta element is a child of the head element (that is, it can nest within head); it's also an empty element. The meta element is used to embed document meta-information. *Meta-information* contains information about the contents of the document such as keywords, author information, and a description of the document. The primary advantage to including meta elements in your XHTML document is that these elements make it possible for search engine robots and spiders to identify, catalog, and locate the information in your document. Here's an example of some meta elements in an XHTML document:

```
<!DOCTYPE html PUBLIC "-//W3C//DTD XHTML 1.0 Transitional//EN"
    "http://www.w3.org/TR/xhtml1/DTD/xhtml1-transitional.dtd">
<html xmlns="http://www.w3.org/1999/xhtml">
    <head>
        <meta name="author" content="Your name" />
        <meta name="keywords" content="A keyword,a keyword,a
            keyword" />
```

```
<meta name="description" content="This is the Home Page
   of the Web site of Your Name." />
<title>
   Title That Summarizes the Document's Content
</title>
   </head>
</html>
```

When using the meta element, remember to close it with a space and a slash before the final angle bracket (/>) because it's an empty element.

Other Children of the head Element

In addition to the title and meta elements, the head element may also contain the following child elements:

script   Instructs the browser that the enclosed content is part of a scripting language such as Perl, PHP, JavaScript (also called JScript or ECMAScript), or VBScript.

style   Contains internal Cascading Style Sheets (CSS) information.

link   Defines a link. This element functions much like the anchor (a) element (discussed in detail in Chapter 4). The link element is most commonly used to link external CSS style sheets to a document or to link the various frames that make up documents authored under the XHTML Frameset DTD.

isindex   Formerly used to create text controls, the isindex element has been deprecated in favor of the input element.

base   Defines a document's base Uniform Resource Locator (URL) using the href attribute. It must occur as a child of the head element and establishes a base URL for all relative references. This element is often used in conjunction with anchors to enable navigation within a single document. Another popular use of the base element is with a frameset where a frame is named as an attribute of the frame element.

A URL is a type of Uniform Resource Identifier (URI). The value of the href attribute can be any type of URI, such as a Uniform Resource Name (URN).

The *body* Element

The body element encloses all the elements, attributes, and information that you want a user's browser to display. Almost everything else we talk about in this book takes place between the body elements. (Unless you're creating a framed document. See Chapter 8 for more information.) To use the body element, enter it below the closing head element and above the closing html element, like this:

```
<!DOCTYPE html PUBLIC "-//W3C//DTD XHTML 1.0 Transitional//EN"
    "http://www.w3.org/TR/xhtml1/DTD/xhtml1-transitional.dtd">
<html xmlns="http://www.w3.org/1999/xhtml">
    <head>
        <title>
            Title That Summarizes the Document's Content
        </title>
    </head>
    <body>
        All the elements, attributes, and information in the
        document body go here.
    </body>
</html>
```

Throughout this book, we'll provide examples for you that won't include these structural elements. This doesn't mean you shouldn't include them; it just means that we're focusing on the immediate topic.

If you've been following along, save your document, view it in a browser, and compare it with Figure 3.1 to confirm that you're on the right track. The title appears in the title bar, and some text appears in the document window.

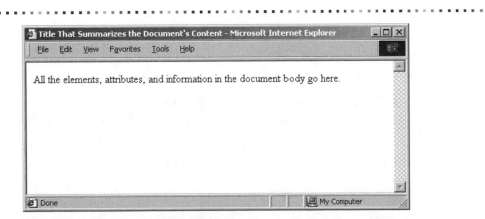

Figure 3.1 *Your first XHTML document, including all structure elements*

Remember that you can also include the XML declaration (`<?xml version="1.0" encoding="UTF-8" standalone="no"?>`), but it's not required by the W3C at this time.

Applying Basic Elements

After you include the structure elements, you're ready to start placing basic content in the document body. The following sections show you how to include headings, paragraphs, lists, and rules (horizontal lines). These elements constitute the basic XHTML document components and, unlike the structure elements, do appear in the browser window. Learning to apply these basic elements and attributes will prepare you to apply practically any XHTML element or attribute.

As you create your content, keep in mind that its exact appearance will vary from browser to browser. As we said in Chapter 1, two browsers will both display a heading bigger and bolder than body text, but the specific font, size, and emphasis will vary. In addition, the user may have specific browser settings on his or her machine that will affect the display of the document.

About Common Attributes

In XHTML, there are several attributes that can be applied to most elements; these are known as the *common* attributes. They include:

id="name"   Assigns a unique name to an element within a document.

style="style"   Allows the author of the document to use CSS style sheets as attribute values or to define the presentation parameters for that specific element. You can use the `style` attribute with all elements except `html`, `head`, `title`, `meta`, `style`, `script`, `param`, `base`, and `basefont`.

class="name"   Assigns a class or a set of classes to an element. This attribute is frequently used with CSS to establish the display properties for a particular subset of elements.

lang="language code"   Declares the language to be applied to the element. For example, `lang="en"` declares that English is the designated language for the element.

dir="ltr|rtl"   Specifies the direction text should be read. This doesn't seem like an important attribute unless you remember that many of the world's languages are not read from left to right. Yes, ltr means "left to right" and rtl means "right to left," so this attribute is most useful in cases where the direction of the text is ambiguous at best and totally confusing at worst.

title="text" Functions in a manner similar to the title element but applies only to a specific element instead of an entire document. Caveat: The attribute's behavior is not defined by the XHTML specification. Instead, the way that behavior is rendered is left up to the browser. This attribute is currently most useful on sites or documents that the author knows will be viewed by users employing Internet Explorer 5.0 or later. The title attribute cannot be used with the following elements: html, head, meta, title, script, param, base, and basefont.

Deprecated Elements Abound

One of the main goals of XHTML is to separate document structure from presentation. This goal alone makes XHTML the antithesis of HTML and its "tag soup" of deprecated elements. *Deprecated elements* are elements that will be phased out of the next version of XHTML.

Although the XHTML 1.0 Transitional DTD permits the use of many of these deprecated elements, it's really better to think toward the future and avoid their use altogether in favor of other elements or other options, such as CSS (which is explained in Chapter 10). Table 3.1 lists the HTML elements that have been deprecated in XHTML 1 but are still used by some authors.

Table 3.1 Deprecated Elements in XHTML 1

DEPRECATED ELEMENT	DESCRIPTION	DEPRECATED IN FAVOR OF
applet	Java applet	The object element
basefont	Base font size	CSS
center	Shorthand for div align="center"	CSS
dir	Directory list	Unordered lists (the ul element)
font	Local change to font	CSS
isindex	Single line prompt	Using input to create text-input controls
menu	Menu list	Unordered lists (the ul element)
s or strike	Strikethrough text	CSS
u	Underlined text	CSS

When we discuss these elements in the following sections, we note that they are deprecated and give alternatives where possible.

Creating Paragraphs

One of the most common elements you'll use is the paragraph element, p, which is appropriate for regular body text. In HTML, you could use just the opening p element to mark your paragraphs. However, in XHTML, the paragraph element should be paired—use the opening element <p> where you want to start a paragraph and the closing element </p> to end the paragraph. It's easier to identify where the element begins and ends if you use both opening and closing tags.

To use the paragraph element, enter the opening and closing tags around the text you want to format as a paragraph, like this:

```
<p>
A whole paragraph goes right here.
</p>
```

 It isn't required to type a tag's content on a separate line; <p>Paragraph goes here.</p> *is also valid. We do this just to make the demonstration code easier to read.*

Figure 3.2 shows a few sample paragraphs.

Sample Text

A whole paragraph goes right here. Just remember, if you use too many paragraphs of plain old text like this, your visitors migh

Another paragraph goes right here. As with the other paragraph, if you use too many paragraphs of plain old text like this, your remember, if you use too many paragraphs of plain old text like this, your visitors might get bored. Just remember, if you use to like this, your visitors might get bored.

Here is another one, just like the other one. As with the other paragraph, if you use too many paragraphs of plain old text like t remember, if you use too many paragraphs of plain old text like this, your visitors might get bored. Just remember, if you use to like this, your visitors might get bored. Just remember, if you use too many paragraphs of plain old text like this, your visitors m

Figure 3.2 *Paragraph text is the most common text in XHTML documents.*

The align attribute can also be used with the paragraph element, but it's deprecated, so we suggest using style sheets to achieve the same effect. The values of align are left, center, right, or justify. To apply this attribute, include it in the opening paragraph element, like this:

```
<p align="center">
Paragraph of information goes here.
</p>
```

You can also apply other paragraph formats instead of the p element to achieve some slightly different paragraph formats, as explained in Table 3.2.

Table 3.2 Other Paragraph-Formatting Elements

ELEMENT	EFFECT
address	Used for address and contact information. Often appears in italics and is sometimes used as a footer.
blockquote	Used for formatting a quotation. Usually appears indented from both sides and with less space between lines than a regular paragraph.
pre	Effective for formatting program code or similar information (short for "preformatted"). Usually appears in a fixed-width font with ample space between words and lines.

Figure 3.3 shows how the address and pre elements appear in Internet Explorer.

Figure 3.3 *Special paragraph-level tags make information stand out.*

Creating Headings

Headings break up large areas of text, announce topics to follow, and arrange information according to a logical hierarchy. XHTML provides six levels of headings; h1 is the largest of the headings, and h6 is the smallest. The paired tags look like this:

```
<h1>...</h1>
<h2>...</h2>
<h3>...</h3>
<h4>...</h4>
<h5>...</h5>
<h6>...</h6>
```

For most documents, limit yourself to two or three heading levels. After three heading levels, many users begin to lose track of your hierarchy. If you find that you're using several heading levels, consider reorganizing your document or dividing it into multiple documents—too many heading levels often indicates a larger organizational problem.

Here's an example of how to use the heading elements:

```
<!DOCTYPE html PUBLIC "-//W3C//DTD XHTML 1.0 Transitional//EN"
    "http://www.w3.org/TR/xhtml1/DTD/xhtml1-transitional.dtd">
<html xmlns="http://www.w3.org/1999/xhtml">
    <head>
        <title>Sample Headings</title>
    </head>
    <body>
        <h1>First Level Heading</h1>
        <h2>Second Level Heading</h2>
        <h3>Third Level Heading</h3>
    </body>
</html>
```

Figure 3.4 shows how Netscape 6 displays a few heading levels.

Figure 3.4 *Heading levels provide users with a hierarchy of information.*

In general, you should use heading elements only for document headings—that is, don't use heading elements for figure captions or to emphasize information within text. Why? First, you don't always know how browsers will display the heading. It might not create the visual effect you intend. Second, some indexing and editing programs use headings to generate tables of contents and other information about your document. These programs won't exclude headings from the table of contents or other information just because you used them as figure captions, for example.

By default, all browsers align headings on the left. However, most browsers support the align attribute, which also lets you right-align, center, and justify headings. To use the align attribute, include it in the heading elements, like this:

```
<h1 align="left">Left-aligned Heading</h1>
<h1 align="center">Centered Heading</h1>
<h1 align="right">Right-aligned Heading</h1>
```

Figure 3.5 shows headings aligned left, center, and right.

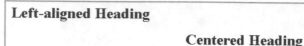

Left-aligned Heading

Centered Heading

Right-aligned Heading

Figure 3.5 *Headings aligned left, center, and right*

XHTML Opportunities

The XHTML 1 specification deprecates (strongly discourages) the use of the `align` attribute. Therefore, although this attribute is still currently supported, if your users will be using current browsers, you should consider using CSS for your formatting needs.

You'll find how-to information about CSS in Chapter 10 and a comprehensive list of CSS options in Master's Reference Part 2.

If you're writing for a wide audience, some of whom might be using older browsers, nest the element that has the `align="center"` attribute inside a `center` element, to ensure that the text actually appears centered. The markup would look similar to this:

```
<center><h1 align="center">Centered Heading</h1></center>
```

Creating Lists

Lists are great ways to provide information in a structured, easy-to-read format. They help your users easily spot information, and they draw attention to important information. A list is a good form for a procedure. Figure 3.6 shows the same content formatted as both a paragraph and a list.

Information in a Paragraph

Providing information in a paragraph is not nearly as effective as putting the same information in a list. By clearly chunking information into a list, you make the information easier to find, easier to read, easier to use, and more attractive.

Information in a List

Providing information in a paragraph is not nearly as effective as putting the same information in a list. By clearly chunking information into a list, you make the information:

- easier to find
- easier to read
- easier to use
- more attractive

Figure 3.6 *Lists are often easier to read than paragraphs.*

Lists come in two varieties: numbered (called *ordered* lists) and bulleted (called *unordered* lists). To create either kind of list, you first specify that you want information to appear as a list, and then you identify each line item in the list. Table 3.3 shows the list and line item elements.

Table 3.3 List and Line Item Elements

Element	Effect
li	Specifies a line item in either ordered or unordered lists.
ol	Specifies that the information appear as an ordered (numbered) list.
ul	Specifies that the information appear as an unordered (bulleted) list.

The following steps show you how to create a bulleted list; use the same steps to create a numbered list but use the ol element instead of the ul element.

1. Start with text you want to format as a list, such as the following:

   ```
   Lions
   Tigers
   Bears
   Oh, My!
   ```

2. Insert the ul elements around the list text.

```
<ul>
Lions
Tigers
Bears
Oh, My!
</ul>
```

3. Put the li opening tag and closing tag around each list item.

```
<ul>
<li>Lions</li>
<li>Tigers</li>
<li>Bears</li>
<li>Oh, My!</li>
</ul>
```

The resulting list, viewed in a browser, looks similar to that shown in Figure 3.7.

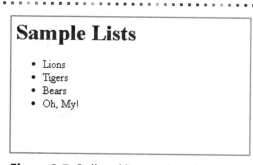

Figure 3.7 *Bulleted lists make information easy to spot on the page and can draw attention to important points.*

To change your list from unordered (bulleted) to ordered (numbered), change the ul element to ol. The resulting numbered list is shown in Figure 3.8.

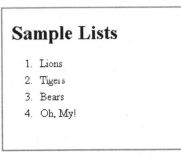

Sample Lists

1. Lions
2. Tigers
3. Bears
4. Oh, My!

Figure 3.8 *Numbered lists provide sequential information.*

Other, less commonly used and deprecated list elements include dir, *to create a directory list, and* menu, *to create a menu list. You use these elements just as you use the* ul *and* ol *elements.*

Setting List Appearance

By default, numbered lists use Arabic numerals, and bulleted lists use small, round bullets. You can change the appearance of these by using the attributes listed in Table 3.4.

Table 3.4 List Attributes

ELEMENT	EFFECT
For numbered lists:	
type="A"	Specifies the number (or letter) with which the list should start: A, a, I, i, or 1 (default).
type="a"	
type="I"	
type="i"	
type="1"	
For bulleted lists:	
type="disc"	Specifies the bullet shape.
type="square"	
type="circle"	

To use any of these attributes, include them in the opening ol or ul tag or in the opening li tag, like this:

```
<ol type="A">
<li>Outlines use sequential lists with letters.</li>
<li>So do some (unpopular) numbering schemes for
    documentation.</li>
</ol>
```

Or like this:

```
<ul type="square">
<li>Use bullets for non-sequential items.</li>
<li>Use numbers for sequential items.</li>
</ul>
```

Or this:

```
<ul>
<li type="circle"> Use bullets for non-sequential items.</li>
<li type="square"> Use different bullets for visual
    interest.</li>
</ul>
```

Figure 3.9 shows how these attributes appear in a browser.

· ·

Sample Lists

1. Lions
2. Tigers
3. Bears
4. Oh, My!

A. Outlines use sequential lists with letters.
B. So do some (unpopular) numbering schemes for documentation.

■ Use bullets for non-sequential items.
■ Use numbers for sequential items.

○ Use bullets for non-sequential items.
■ Use different bullets for visual interest.

Figure 3.9 *You can change the appearance of numbers and bullets using list attributes.*

You can add the compact *attribute in opening* ol *or* ul *elements to tell browsers to display the list as compactly as possible. Generally, this setting will make little difference, because most browsers render lists this way by default. This attribute is deprecated.*

 The type *attribute for unordered lists is currently supported by many (but by no means all) browsers; it is also deprecated.*

More Options for Ordered Lists

Ordered lists have additional attributes that you can use to specify the first number in the list, as well as to create hierarchical information.

First, you can start a numbered list with a value other than 1 (or A, a, I, or i). Simply include the start attribute in the initial ol element, as in <ol start="51"> to start the list at 51. Or you can even change specific numbers within a list by using the value attribute in the li tag, as in <li value="7">.

 Both the start *and* value *attributes are deprecated.*

To use these attributes, include them in the ol element, like this:

```
<ol start="51">
   <li>This is the fifty-first item.</li>
   <li>This is the fifty-second.</li>
   <li type="i" value="7">This item was renumbered to be the
       seventh, using lowercase roman numerals,
       just because we can.</li>
</ol>
```

Figure 3.10 shows how this code appears in a browser.

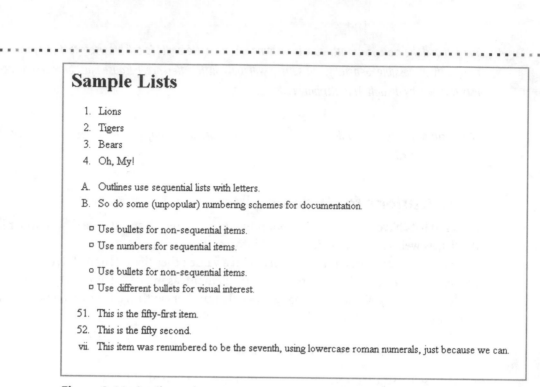

Figure 3.10 *Attributes let you customize ordered lists in several ways.*

Second, you can use nested ordered lists and different type attributes to create outlines. The numbering continues past each lower-level section without the need to manually renumber with a value attribute. Here's an example of what the code looks like:

```
<ol type="I">
   <li>Top Level Item</li>
   <li>Another Top Level Item</li>
   <ol type="A">
      <li>A Second Level Item</li>
      <li>Another Second Level Item</li>
      <ol type="1">
         <li>A Third Level Item</li>
         <li>Another Third Level Item</li>
      </ol>
      <li>Another Second Level Item</li>
   </ol>
   <li>A Top Level Item</li>
</ol>
```

The results are shown in Figure 3.11.

Figure 3.11 *Ordered lists are even flexible enough to format outlines.*

Using Definition Lists

Finally, one special list variant, *definition lists*, can be useful for providing two levels of information. You can think of definition lists as dictionary entries—they have two levels of information: the entry and a definition. You can use these lists to provide glossary-type information, or you can use them to provide two-level lists. Table 3.5 lists the elements and their effects.

Table 3.5 Definition List and Item Elements

ELEMENT	EFFECT
dl	Specifies that the information appear as a definition list.
dt	Child of dl; identifies definition terms.
dd	Child of dl; identifies definitions.

To create a definition list, as shown in Figure 3.12, follow these steps:

1. Enter the dl opening and closing tags to start the definition list.

   <dl>
   </dl>

2. Add the dt opening and closing tags around the definition terms.

   <dl>
   <dt>XHTML</dt>
   <dt>Maestro</dt>
   </dl>

3. Add the dd element to identify individual definitions.

   <dl>
   <dt>XHTML</dt>
   <dd>Extensible Hypertext Markup Language is used to create
       Web pages.</dd>
   <dt>Maestro</dt>
   <dd>An expert in some field. See "Readers of <i>Mastering
       XHTML</i>" for examples.</dd>
   </dl>

 A great way to apply definition lists is in "What's New" lists—a special page that tells people what's new and exciting on your site or at your organization. Try putting the dates in the dt element (maybe with boldface and italics) and the information in the dd element.

Definition List

XHTML
 The Extensible Hypertext Markup Language is used to create Web pages.
Maestro
 An expert in some field. See "Readers of *Mastering XHTML*" for examples.

Figure 3.12 *Definition lists are a formatting option that is useful when presenting dictionary-like information.*

Applying Bold, Italic, and Other Emphases

In addition to creating paragraphs, headings, and lists, you can also apply formatting to individual letters and words. For example, you can make a word appear *italic*, **bold**, underlined, or superscript, as in e^2. You use these character-level formatting elements only within paragraph-level elements—that is, you can't put a p element within a character-level element such as b. You have to close the character-level formatting before you close the paragraph-level formatting.

Correct:

```
<p><b>This is the end of a paragraph that also uses boldface.
    </b></p>
<p>This is the beginning of the following paragraph.</p>
```

Incorrect:

```
<p>This text <b>is boldface.</p>
<p>As is this.</b></p>
```

Although many character-formatting elements are available, you'll probably use b (for **boldface**) and i (for *italic*) most often. Table 3.6 shows a list of the most common character-formatting elements.

Table 3.6 Common Character-Formatting Elements

ELEMENT	EFFECT
b	Applies boldface.
blink	A proprietary Netscape element that makes text blink; usually considered highly unprofessional.
cite	Indicates citations or references.
code	Displays program code; similar to the pre element.
em	Applies emphasis; usually displayed as italics.
i	Applies italics.
s or strike	Apply strikethrough to text; deprecated.
strong	Applies stronger emphasis; usually displayed as bold text.
sub	Formats text as subscript.
sup	Formats text as superscript.
tt	Applies a fixed-width font.
u	Applies underline; deprecated.
var	Displays variables or arguments.

To use these elements, enter them around the individual letters or words you want to emphasize, like this:

```
Making some text <b>bold</b> or <i>italic</i> is a useful
technique, more so than <strike>strikethrough</strike> or
<blink>blinking</blink>.
```

Figure 3.13 shows some sample character formatting. The blinking word doesn't appear in this figure so you can see that it disappears.

Sample Lists

Making some text **bold** or *italic* is a useful technique, more so than ~~strikethrough~~ or

Figure 3.13 *Character formatting helps you emphasize words or letters.*

Spend a few minutes trying out these character-formatting elements to see how they work and how they look in your favorite browser.

XHTML Opportunities

The XHTML 1 specification strongly encourages using CSS for your formatting needs. Although the specification still supports many deprecated individual formatting elements, the use of CSS is the recommended way to include formatting in your XHTML documents. Using CSS, you can apply the following:

- Character-level formatting, such as strikethrough and underline
- Paragraph-level formatting, such as indents and margins
- Other formatting, such as background colors and images

See Chapter 10 and Master's Reference Part 2 for CSS information.

Including Horizontal Rules

Horizontal rules are lines that break up long sections of text, indicate a shift in information, or help improve the overall document design. To use a horizontal rule, which is an empty element, include the hr element where you want the rule to appear, like this:

```
<p>Long passages of text should often be broken into sections
    with headings and, optionally, horizontal rules.</p>
<hr />
<h3>A Heading Also Breaks Up Text</h3>
<p>A new long passage can continue here.</p>
```

By default, horizontal rules appear shaded, span the width of the browser window, and are a few pixels high. You can change a rule's shading, width, height, and alignment by including the appropriate attributes. It should be noted that all horizontal rule attributes have been deprecated in favor of the use of CSS. Table 3.7 shows horizontal rule attributes.

 *Pixels are the little dots on your screen that produce images; **pixel** is an abbreviation for **picture element**. If your display is set to 800×600, you have 800 pixels horizontally and 600 pixels vertically.*

Table 3.7 Attributes of the Horizontal Rule (hr) Element (All Deprecated)

ATTRIBUTE	SPECIFIES
align="…"	Alignment to left, center, or right
noshade="noshade"	That the rule has no shading
size="n"	Rule height measured in pixels
width="n"	Rule width (length) measured in pixels
width="n%"	Rule width (length) measured as a percentage of the document width

To use any of these attributes, include them in the hr element, like this:

```
<hr width="80%" size="8" />
<hr width="50%" />
<hr width="400" align="right" />
<hr noshade="noshade" align="center" width="200" />
```

Figure 3.14 shows some sample horizontal rules with height, width, alignment, and shading attributes added.

Figure 3.14 *Horizontal rules can help separate information, improve page design, and simply add visual interest to the page.*

Specifying Line Breaks

Sometimes you need to break a line in a specific place, but you don't want to start a new paragraph (with the extra spacing). For example, you might not want lines of poetry text to go all the way across the document; instead, you might want to break them into several shorter lines. You can easily break paragraph lines by inserting the empty element br where you want the lines to break, like this:

```
<p>
There was an XHTML writer<br />
Who tried to make paragraphs wider<br />
He found with a shock<br />
All the elements did mock<br />
The attempt to move that text outside-r.<br />
Mercifully Anonymous
</p>
```

Including Fancier Formatting

Now that you have a firm grip on using the basic XHTML formatting options, you can dive into some of the fancier formatting effects. In the following sections, we'll show you how to add colors and specify fonts and sizes. Although most newer browsers support these effects, not all browsers do; your fancier effects might not reach all users. Also, the XHTML 1 specification deprecates many of these effects in favor of CSS. If your users use CSS-capable browsers, you should consider using CSS instead of the deprecated elements and attributes mentioned here.

Adding Colors

One of the easiest ways to jazz up your documents is to add colors to the background or text. You can liven up an otherwise dull Web page with a splash of color or an entire color scheme. For example, add a background color and change the text colors to coordinate with the background. Or highlight a word or two with color and make the words leap off the page. Or, if you're developing a corporate site, adhere to the company's color scheme to ensure a consistent look.

As you'll see in Chapter 14, developing a color scheme is a great way to help unite your pages into a cohesive Web site.

The drawback to setting colors is that you really don't have control over what your users see. Users might set their browsers to display colors they like, or they might be using a text-only browser, which generally displays only black, white, and gray.

You specify colors using hexadecimal numbers, which combine proportions of red, green, and blue—called *RGB numbers*. RGB numbers use six digits, two for each proportion of red, green, and blue. As you're choosing colors, remember that not all RGB numbers display well in browsers; some colors *dither*, meaning that they appear spotty or splotchy. We recommend that you select RGB values that are appropriate for Web-page use, as listed in Table 3.8, which illustrates that each of R, G, and B can each take on the values 00, 33, 66, 99, CC, or FF—giving you 256 possible combinations. Although you'll most likely never go wrong with these "safe" colors, it's most important to use these colors in page backgrounds or in places with large patches of color, where dithering may occur if you don't use these number combinations.

Table 3.8 Recommended RGB Values

R	G	B
00	00	00
33	33	33
66	66	66
99	99	99
CC	CC	CC
FF	FF	FF

To create an RGB number from the values in this table, simply start with a pound sign (#) to indicate the hexadecimal system and then select one option from each column. For example, choose FF from the Red column, 00 from the Green column, and 00 from the Blue column to create the RGB number #FF0000, which has the largest possible red component but no blue and no green; it therefore appears as a pure, bright red. (Note that the color values are not case sensitive.) See Master's Reference Part 6 for pointers to complete lists of the appropriate RGB numbers and corresponding descriptions.

Setting Background Colors

Using a *background color*, which is simply a color that fills the entire browser window, is a great way to add flair to your Web pages. By default, browsers display a white or gray background color, which may be adequate if you're developing pages for an intranet site where flashy elements aren't essential. However, if you're developing a public or personal site, you'll probably want to make your site more interesting and visually appealing. For example, if you're developing a public corporate Web site, you might want to use your company's standard colors—ones that appear on letterhead, logos, or marketing materials. Or you might want to use your favorite color if you're developing a personal site. In either case, using a background color can improve the overall page appearance and help develop a theme among pages.

Check out Chapters 14 and 15 for tips and information about developing coherent Web sites and for specific tips about public, personal, and intranet sites.

As you'll see in the following section, pay careful attention to how text contrasts with the background color. If you specify a dark background color, use a light text color. Conversely, if you specify a light background color, use a dark text color. Contrast is key for ensuring that users can read information on your pages.

To specify a background color for your documents, include the bgcolor attribute in the opening body tag, like this:

```
<body bgcolor="#FFFFFF">...</body>
```

Setting Text Colors

Similar to background colors, text colors can enhance your Web pages. In particular, you can specify the color of the following:

- Body text, which appears throughout the document body
- Unvisited links, which are links not yet followed
- Active links, which are links as they're being selected
- Visited links, which are links previously followed

Changing body text is sometimes essential—for example, if you've added a background color or an image. If you've added a dark background color, the default black body text color won't adequately contrast with the background, making the text difficult or impossible to read. In this case, you'd want to change the text color to one that's lighter so that it contrasts with the background sufficiently.

Changing link colors helps keep your color scheme intact—for unvisited as well as visited links. Set the visited and unvisited links to different colors to help users know which links they've followed and which ones they haven't.

To change body text and link colors, simply add the attributes listed in Table 3.9 to the opening body tag.

Table 3.9 Text and Link Color Attributes (All Deprecated)

Attribute	Sets Color For
text="..."	All text within the document, with a color name or a #RRGGBB value
alink="..."	Active links, which are the links at the time the user clicks them, with a color name or a #RRGGBB value
link="..."	Unvisited links, with a color name or a #RRGGBB value
vlink="..."	Links the user has recently followed (how recently depends on the browser settings), with a color name or a #RRGGBB value

We recommend setting all Web page colors at one time—that way you can see how background, text, and link colors appear as a unit.

To change text and link colors, follow these steps:

1. Within the body element, add the `text` attribute to set the color for text within the document. This example makes the text black.

   ```
   <body text="#000000">
   ```

When setting text colors, using a "safe" color is less important for text than for backgrounds. Dithering is less apparent in small areas, such as text.

2. Add the `link` attribute to set the link color. This example uses blue (#0000FF) for the links.

   ```
   <body text="#000000" link="#0000FF">
   ```

3. Add the `vlink` attribute to set the color for visited links. If you set the `vlink` attribute to the same as the link, links will not change colors even after users follow them. This could be confusing, but also serves to make it look like there is always new material available. This example sets the visited link to a different shade of blue.

   ```
   <body text="#000000" link="#0000FF" vlink="#000099">
   ```

4. Finally, set the `alink`, or active link, color. This is the color of a link while users are clicking it and will not necessarily be visible in Internet Explorer 4, depending on the viewer's settings. This example sets `alink` to red.

   ```
   <body text="#000000" link="#0000FF" vlink="#000099"
       alink="#FF0000">
   ```

Specify fonts and increase font sizes to improve readability with dark backgrounds and light-colored text.

Specifying Fonts and Font Sizes

You can use the `font` element to specify font characteristics for your document, including color, size, and typeface. However, it's worth noting that the `font` element and its attributes have been deprecated in favor of CSS. We suggest you check out the font properties in CSS and use them instead of the font element. Table 3.10 describes the element and attributes you'll use to set font characteristics.

Table 3.10 Font Characteristics (All Deprecated)

ITEM	TYPE	DESCRIPTION
font	Element	Sets font characteristics for text.
color="…"	Attribute of font element	Specifies font color in #RRGGBB numbers or with color names. This color applies only to the text surrounded by the font elements.
face="…"	Attribute of font element	Specifies possible type faces as a list, in order of preference, separated by commas—for example, "Verdana, Arial, Helvetica".
size="n"	Attribute of font element	Specifies font size on a scale of 1 through 7; the default or normal size is 3. You can also specify a *relative* size by using + or − (for example, +2).
basefont	Element	Sets the default characteristics for text that is not formatted using the font element or CSS.

As you're determining which font face to use, keep in mind that the font must be available on your users' computers for them to view the fonts you specify. For example, if you specify Technical and your users do not have it, their computers will substitute a font—possibly one you'd consider unacceptable. As a partial way of overcoming this problem, you can list multiple faces in order of preference; the machine displays the first available. For example, a list of "Comic Sans MS, Technical, Tekton, Times, Arial" will display Comic Sans MS if available, then try Technical, then Tekton, and so forth.

So, which fonts should you choose? Table 3.11 lists fonts that are commonly available on Windows, Mac, and Unix platforms.

Table 3.11 Commonly Available Fonts

WINDOWS	MACINTOSH	UNIX
Arial	Helvetica	Helvetica
Courier New	Courier	Courier
Times New Roman	Times	Times

You might check out Microsoft's selection of downloadable fonts (www.microsoft.com/ typography/free.htm). These fonts are available to users who have specifically downloaded the fonts to their computers, or who are using Internet Explorer 4 or newer, or Windows 98 or newer.

To specify font characteristics, follow these steps. You can set some or all of the characteristics used in this example.

1. Identify the text to format with the `font` element.

   ```
   <font>Look at this!</font>
   ```

2. Select a specific font using the `face` attribute. See Table 3.11 for a list of commonly available fonts.

   ```
   <font face="Verdana, 'Times New Roman', Times">
       Look at this!</font>
   ```

3. Change the font size using the `size` attribute. You set the size of text on a scale from 1 to 7; the default size is 3. Either set the size absolutely, with a number from 1 to 7, or relatively, with + or – the numbers of levels you want to change. Almost all newer browsers, and all XHTML 1–compliant browsers, support `size` to set font size. The only significant downside to setting the font size is that your user might already have increased or decreased the default font size, so your size change might have more of an effect than you expected.

   ```
   <font face="Technical, 'Times New Roman', Times" size="+2">
       Look at this!</font>
   ```

4. Add a `color` attribute to set the color, using a color name or a #RRGGBB value.

   ```
   <font face="Technical, 'Times New Roman', Times" size="+2"
       color="#FF0000">Look at this!</font>
   ```

Figure 3.15 shows the result.

Figure 3.15 *Setting font characteristics can spiff up your pages and help you achieve the visual effect you want.*

Where to Go from Here

Congratulations! You've just learned to apply XHTML code, and you even learned some of the most common elements and attributes. From here, you can jump to just about any chapter in the book. Here are a few suggestions:

- If you've just created your first page during this chapter, check out Chapter 4 to learn how to link XHTML documents.

- If you want to include images in your documents, go to Chapter 5.

- If you want to add some advanced document features, such as tables, forms, and frames, check out Part II.

Linking Your Documents

Chapter 4

inks are the "hyper" part of hypertext—the part that you use to jump from one document to another. Links differentiate XHTML documents from other electronic documents. They connect your XHTML documents to create a unified Web site and connect them to other information on the Internet.

In this chapter, we'll show you how to include various kinds of links in your XHTML documents. Through the examples and instructions, you'll see that links are made up of nothing more than Web addresses and a few XHTML elements, which are easy to include in your Web pages. Specifically, you'll learn to link to pages within your site, to pages at other sites, and to specific places within pages. You'll also learn how to include e-mail links.

This chapter covers the following topics:

- Looking at link anatomy

- Understanding types of URLs

- Constructing link anchors

- Linking to a specific place in a document

- Inserting e-mail links

Link Anatomy

Links, also called anchors, mark text or images as elements that point to other XHTML documents, images, applets, multimedia effects, or specific places within an XHTML document. Links are made up of three parts:

- Opening and closing anchor tags, `<a>`...`</a>`, which mark the text or image as a link.

- An attribute, `href`, which is located within the opening anchor tag, as in `<a href="...">`...`</a>`.

- An address—the value of `href`—that tells browsers the file to link to, identifying a file location on the Web or on your local hard drive. These addresses can be markup-language (such as HTML, XHTML, and XML) documents or elements referenced by documents, such as images, applets, scripts, and other files. The address is always enclosed in quotes—for example, `"address.html"`.

Put these together, and a basic link looks like this:

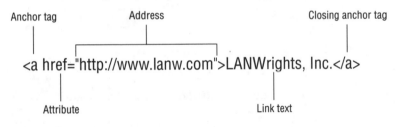

The "link text" part of this example actually appears in the document. Text links usually display as blue and underlined text, but this depends on your user's computer and browser settings and how you specify link formatting.. Image links generally appear in a border. Figure 4.1 shows text and images used as links.

See Chapter 3 for information about setting link colors.

Figure 4.1 *Text links usually appear underlined; image links usually have a border around them.*

All links include opening and closing anchor tags, an attribute, and an address. However, the specific address you use depends on where the documents you link to are located.

Throughout this chapter, **originating document** *refers to the document that is linked* **from** *and contains the anchor element, and* **linked document** *refers to the document that is linked* **to***.*

URL Anatomy

The most common type of address used in hypertext links is a *URL* (usually pronounced yoo-arr-ell; it stands for Uniform Resource Locator), which is an address of a document on the Web or, more accurately, on the Internet. Although a URL can look complex and long, it's generally made up of four basic parts—protocol, hostname, folder name, and filename—each of which has a specific function.

 A URL is one type of Uniform Resource Identifier (URI). The value of the href *attribute can actually be any URI, but because a link to something other than a URL is pretty rare, most people just say URL.*

Protocol

The *protocol* specifies the computer language used to transfer information. Specifically, a protocol tells the browser where the information is located. For example, the information can be located on a Web server, FTP (File Transfer Protocol) server, local hard drive, and so on. The protocol also tells the browser what to expect from the document retrieval process—for example, whether logon is required, what information about the document will be provided by the server, and so on.

The protocol you use in your links depends on where the destination file is. The most common protocol you'll use in links is HTTP, or *Hypertext Transfer Protocol*, which indicates that information is located somewhere on the World Wide Web. Likewise, if you're linking to a document in a specific location on your local computer, you'd use `file:///` as the protocol indicator to specify that a browser should look for the file on its local computer. Or, if you want to link to information located on an FTP server, you'd use `ftp://` as the protocol indicator.

Table 4.1 lists some of the more common protocols you can use in links within your XHTML documents.

Table 4.1 Common Protocols

Protocol Indicator	Use
`http://`	For documents on the Web, including XHTML documents and associated files.
`file:///`	For documents on the local hard drive. The third slash replaces the hostname, so you can simply type the folder and filename.
`ftp://`	For documents on an FTP server.
`gopher://`	For documents on a gopher server.
`telnet://`	To open a telnet connection to a specific host. Good for connecting to library catalogs. However, linking with this protocol indicator is chancy unless you're certain that telnet applications are installed or configured on the user's end.
`wais://`	To connect to a Wide Area Information Server (WAIS) database. This is seldom used because forms and CGI scripts offer a better way to process searches and because few users have WAIS clients installed and properly configured.
`mailto:`	To open a mail message window in which users can send an e-mail message to the specified address. Most browsers support `mailto:`, although it is not a standard or an officially accepted protocol. This indicator does not include `//`.
`news:`	To connect to a newsgroup or a specific article in a group. Such a link is not guaranteed, because you don't know to which newsgroups your users have access. Also, before using the `news:` protocol, consider that articles periodically expire and disappear from the server. This indicator does not include `//`.

Hostname

The *hostname* is the name of the server that holds XHTML documents and related files. Each server has a specific address, and all documents stored on the server share the same hostname. For example, if your Internet service provider's (ISP's) server name is LANW, your hostname might be something like www.lanw.com.

Folder Name

Folder names are the next chunk of information in a URL, indicating the folder in which files are located. You might think of folders as containers for the XHTML documents you create. Just as you might use a manila folder to organize paper documents in your file drawer, you also use folders to contain XHTML and related documents.

*The terms **folder** and **directory** are interchangeable. Folder is more commonly used in the context of current desktop computers; directory is more common for older versions of Windows and for Unix.*

Filename

Filenames are the names of specific documents and consist of two pieces of information:

- A name, which identifies the file to display
- A file extension, which specifies the file type—an XHTML document, an image, a text file, and so on

If you're creating links to other documents and other locations on the Internet, you might use a wide range of filenames. Some will be short and cryptic—`frntmter.htm`, `mynewhmp.htm`—as a result of either the developer using Windows 3.*x* or (far less likely) as a result of the server using Windows 3.*x*. However, you might also see much longer filenames if both the server and the developer use Windows 95 and higher, Macintosh, Unix, or some combination.

We suggest that you don't use spaces in your filenames even though some systems allow them. They can cause problems when you link to the documents.

When you're including links in your XHTML documents, you might not include a filename at all. For example, if you're pointing to a Web site, you may use a URL such as

`http://www.yahoo.com/`

that includes only the protocol and the hostname. The specific filename (and folder name, in this case) is not necessary; users click that link, and the Yahoo! server displays the home page by default because of the specific server settings.

When using URLs in your links, enter them exactly as they're given to you.

Types of URLs

URLs vary depending on the location of the document to which you're linking. For example, a URL will be longer and include more information if the file is on the World Wide Web. A URL will be shorter and include less information if the file is on your local computer or server. Basically, URLs fall into two categories: absolute and relative.

An *absolute URL* contains all the information necessary to identify files on the Internet. A *relative URL* points to files in the same folder or on the same server. In other words, the file linked to is relative to the originating document. Figure 4.2 illustrates absolute and relative URLs.

Figure 4.2 *Relative URLs point only to documents near the originating document, and absolute URLs point to documents on other machines.*

Absolute URLs

You can think of absolute URLs as being similar to official postal service addresses, which include a name, street address, apartment number (if applicable), city, state, and postal code. All this information is necessary for your letter to Aunt Cindy to arrive at her house, and if any piece of information is missing (such as the street address or apartment number), the letter might arrive late, arrive at someone else's house, or not arrive at all.

Likewise, an absolute URL contains the protocol, hostname, folder name, and filename, which are all essential for linking to Web sites. To link to another Web site, you have to provide all these tidbits of information so that the correct server, folder, and document can be found.

Here are some sample absolute URLs:

```
http://www.lanw.com/books/errata/default.htm
http://www.altavista.com
ftp://ftp.w3.org/pub/
```

 Remember, from our discussion in the "Filename" section, that specific filenames are sometimes not necessary because they're set by default on the Web server.

Relative URLs

A relative URL usually contains *only* the folder name and filename, or even just the filename. You can use these partial URLs when you're pointing to a file that's located in the same folder or on the same server as the originating file. In these cases, a browser doesn't need the server name or protocol indicator, because it assumes the files are in a folder or on a server that's relative to the originating document.

Using a relative URL is similar to instructing someone to look "next door" for a piece of information. In this case, next door is relative to where you are; it's accurate and complete only if you originate the request from a place that has a next-door neighbor with the correct information.

You can use relative URLs to refer to documents in relation to the originating document (called a *document-relative URL*) or to the server on which the originating document resides (*called a server-relative URL*). Figure 4.3 illustrates how relative folders and files relate.

Figure 4.3 *You can indicate each of these locations with a relative URL when linking from other nearby documents.*

Document-Relative URLs

You'll often use a document-relative URL when you're developing or testing a set of XHTML documents. As we developed examples for this book, we used document-relative URLs and put all the files in a single folder. In fact, in most cases, we included only the filename. For example, when linking from the index.html document in Figure 4.3, we use these document-relative URLs:

```
services/consulting.html
services/other/tips.html
```

Notice that these URLs include only the folder names and filenames. The protocols and hostnames are not necessary because both these documents are relative to the originating index.html document. However, when linking between these two documents, you have to include the folder names, because these documents are in different folders.

If `consulting.html` and `tips.html` were both in the `services` folder, you could link them by *just* their filenames.

If you're familiar with the Unix and DOS convention of using two periods (`..`) to move up a directory in the hierarchy, you can also use that to link to documents in other folders. For example, to link from `consulting.html` to `names.html`, you could use a link similar to this:

```
<a href="../contacts/names.html">link text</a>
```

The address indicates moving up a level (the `..` part), then into the `contacts` folder, and then to the `names.html` document. Likewise, a link within `tips.html` to the `names.html` file would look like this:

```
<a href="../../contacts/names.html">link text</a>
```

Nested folders that lie deep within the server hierarchy or sets of folders that might be used and moved as a unit can benefit from these links. These relative URLs can link all the documents within the unit, and then you can move the unit to other servers or even to other locations within the specific server hierarchy. All the links among the documents will continue to work.

Server-Relative URLs

A server-relative URL is relative to the *server root*—that is, relative to the hostname part of the URL. Figure 4.4 illustrates how documents and folders relate to servers.

Server-relative URLs have a forward slash (/) at the beginning of the filename, which indicates that you interpret the path of the document from the top of the current server (the server root), rather than from the current document location. For example, from anywhere in our site, we could use a server-relative URL to display our home page with a link to `/index.html`, which would display the `index.html` file right under the top of the server. Some server-relative URLs include:

```
/index.html
/contacts/names.html
```

Likewise, you can link to folders and filenames with a server-relative URL. From the `tips.html` document, you can link to the `names.html` document within the `con-tacts` folder with a link to a URL like the preceding example.

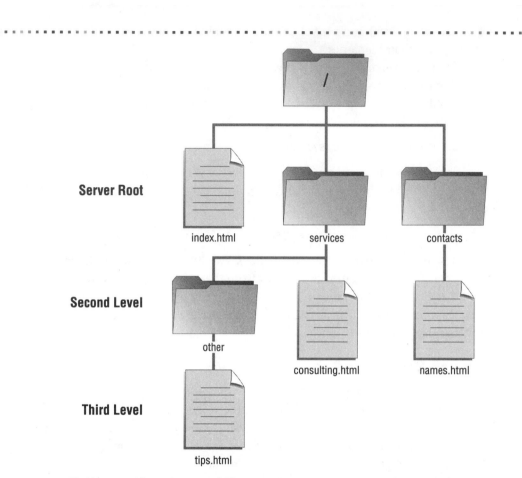

Server Root

Second Level

Third Level

index.html services contacts

other

consulting.html names.html

tips.html

Figure 4.4 *The same set of files as in Figure 4.3, positioned in relation to the server*

Server-relative URLs are useful when you're linking to a specific location on the server (such as contact information) that isn't likely to change and that isn't clearly relative to the current document. For example, you might use a server-relative URL if you're working on a document that does not yet have a specific home on the server but still links to specific pages, such as the home page. If you don't use a server-relative URL, you'd have to code the server name into the URL, and then if you had to change servers or move the documents to a different server, the links would no longer work (in other words, the links would "break").

Use relative URLs whenever possible, because they let you move your documents around without breaking too many links. If you link all your documents with absolute URLs, you'll break all those links each time you move the documents around on a server or move them to a different server.

Setting the Base Location for a Document

A lot of times, you'll develop XHTML documents and put them in one folder, only to later move some of the documents to a different folder. When you move documents to new folders, all the document-relative links will be broken. Rather than changing all the relative URLs, you can use the base empty element with the href attribute in the head element to specify what the relative URLs are relative to.

For example, suppose you want to move a document called www.lanw.com/books/default.htm out of the books folder into the server root. Rather than editing all the links, you can just add the base element within the head element, like this:

```
<head>
    <title>Document Title</title>
    <base href="http://www.lanw.com/books/default.htm" />
</head>
```

Including the base element with the href attribute in the head element resets all relative links in the doument so all relative URLs point correctly to the real locations of the documents. Without base and href, all relative URLs from the default.htm document would point to nonexistent documents.

Constructing Link Anchors

Link anchors are the glue that holds the Web together. Fortunately, they are simple to construct—they require only a single element and careful use of the URL. In this section, we'll look at how to link to documents in the same folder, in different folders, and on different servers.

Linking to Documents in the Same Folder

The basic link connects one document to another file in the same folder. Figure 4.5 shows two documents within the same folder.

DocumentA.html   DocumentB.html

Figure 4.5 DocumentA.html *and* DocumentB.html *both reside in a folder called* FatFolder.

To create a link from DocumentA.html to DocumentB.html, you include the anchor element (a), the href attribute, and a URL that points to the filename of Document B. In this case, the link from the originating document (Document A) might look like this:

```
<a href="DocumentB.html">link text goes here</a>
```

When linking to documents within the same folder, you need to include only the filename. Without additional information, browsers will look in the same folder as the originating document. In this sense, the locations of Document A and Document B are both indicated relative to the folder in which they reside.

Linking to Documents in a Different Folder

Commonly, you'll link two documents that reside in different folders, as Figure 4.6 shows. To create a link from aboutus.html to consulting.html, you include the folder and filename, as in:

```
<a href="services/consulting.html">link text</a>
```

Figure 4.6 aboutus.html *resides in a folder called* ACMEInc; consulting.html *resides in a subfolder called* services.

The folder (services) and filename (consulting.html) are separated by a forward slash (/), which indicates the end of the folder name and the beginning of the filename.

Linking to Documents on the Web

When you link from one document to another document on the Web, the documents likely reside on different servers. Figure 4.7 shows an originating document, acme-info.html, with a link to a document on a different server on the Web. Remember that linking to documents on another server requires an absolute URL so that the correct host, folder, and file can be found. Therefore, to link to the futile.html file in the attempts folder on the www.coyote.org Web site, you need to include an absolute URL, similar to this one:

```
http://www.coyote.org/attempts/futile.html
```

The full link would look like this:

```
<a href="http://www.coyote.org/attempts/futile.html">
    Last Try</a>
```

Figure 4.7 The acmeinfo.html file resides on a server called www.acme.com; futile.html resides on a server called www.coyote.org in the attempts folder.

Linking to a Specific Location in a Document

In addition to linking to a document, you can also link to a specific place within a document. For example, rather than linking to the Web-Based Training document, you can link to a subheading called Class Schedule within that document. By doing so, you can let your users move directly to the information they seek, rather than having them reach a document and scroll to the tidbit of information.

You link to specific places within documents with the help of a *name anchor*, which marks the targeted link location. In this example, you'd put the name anchor at the Class Schedule subheading and then link directly to that anchor from another document. Very cool… and efficient for your users.

Forming Name Anchors

Name anchors are made up of three parts:

- Opening and closing anchor tags, <a>…</a>, which mark the text or the location within a document as a target

- An attribute, name, which identifies the anchor as a name anchor

- A name, enclosed in quotes, which identifies the specific location

Put these together, and a basic name anchor looks like this:

```
<a name="location">Document content goes here</a>
```

The text between the opening and closing anchor tags is visible in your document, but, unlike link anchors, it's not highlighted nor is any other specific visual indicator associated with it. It's simply the place (text) in the document to which you want to link. If you prefer, you can leave the text out and just insert the link, as follows: <a name="location"></a>. You can use the name attribute with the a element with other elements in your document.

Here's a sample process for creating a name anchor:

1. Start with a subheading.

   ```
   <h2>Class Schedule</h2>
   ```

2. Add the anchor element.

   ```
   <h2><a>Class Schedule</a></h2>
   ```

3. Add the name attribute. Use something specific that you'll be able to remember.

```
<h2><a name="schedule">Class Schedule</a></h2>
```

That's all there is to it. You will see nothing different in your document when you view it with your browser, but you have just provided the tools necessary to link directly to a subsection of your document, as described in the following section.

Linking to Name Anchors

After you create a name anchor, you can link to it by using the "pound sign" (#). To continue with our example, the Class Schedule section is in a document that has the filename online.htm, which is in the training folder on the www.lanw.com server.

A link to that document looks like this:

```
<a href="http://www.lanw.com/training/online.htm">Link</a>
```

A link to the Class Schedule section, using an absolute URL, looks like this:

```
<a href="http://www.lanw.com/training/online.htm#schedule">
    Link</a>
```

Notice the #schedule addition in the targeted link, which is what tells the browser to link to that heading. How much information you include in a targeted link and what it looks like depends on where the linked document is located, as shown by the following examples:

Link to the same document:

```
<a href="#schedule">...</a>
```

Link to a different document in the same folder:

```
<a href="online.htm#schedule">...</a>
```

Link to the same server (different folder and document, server-relative URL):

```
<a href="/training/online.htm#schedule">...</a>
```

Link to a different server:

```
<a href="http://www.lanw.com/training/
    online.htm#schedule">...</a>
```

You can't link to name *anchors that don't exist. To ensure that users can link to specific places within your documents, include* name *anchors in places likely to be visited.*

Inserting E-Mail Links

Another handy link you can use is an *e-mail link*, which takes your users from the Web page to an already-addressed blank e-mail message in their e-mail program. By including e-mail links in your Web pages, for example, you can let users easily contact you.

To create an e-mail link, simply add an anchor link with the `mailto:` protocol indicator and the e-mail address. For example, you might include a link to send the authors of this book e-mail with a link like this:

```
<a href="mailto:info@lanw.com">Send Feedback</a>
```

As we mentioned in Table 4.1, the mailto: *protocol is not an XHTML standard, but it's widely used and recognized.*

Pop-Up Opportunity

The HTML 4 specification introduced a feature that allows you to add link descriptions that pop up on the screen when users move their mouse over the link, as shown here:

To add pop-up descriptions, sometimes called tooltips, to your links, simply include the `title` attribute in the a element, like this:

```
<a href="http://www.lanw.com" title="The LANWrights Web Site">
    More Information</a>
```

This feature doesn't work in all browsers; it only works in Internet Explorer 4 and higher and Opera 3 and higher.

Where to Go from Here

In this chapter, you learned about the various flavors of URLs and how to use them to construct links. You also learned how to label locations within your documents with name anchors and link to those locations. Armed with this information, you're now ready to tackle just about any XHTML task.

- In Chapter 5, you'll learn how to include images in your XHTML documents.

- See Chapter 13 for information about publishing XHTML documents on a Web server.

- See Part II, starting with Chapter 6, for information about adding tables, forms, and frames, as well as how to convert your HTML documents to XHTML.

- Visit Part IV for handy tips and advice for developing a coherent Web site, as well as specific techniques for developing public, personal, and intranet sites.

Including Images

XHTML

Chapter 5

Your next step toward becoming an XHTML pro is including images, which can add pizzazz to your Web pages, help provide information, serve as navigational aids, or just add a splash of color. The key to including images is to do so wisely—that is, choose graphics with a purpose, use appropriate file formats, and employ graphics that help you design your pages effectively. By taking the time to use images wisely, you can maximize their effectiveness for your users.

In this chapter, we'll show you how to choose appropriate images, choose file formats, use images for different purposes, and develop image maps (those clickable images with multiple links).

This chapter covers the following topics:

- Selecting appropriate file size, physical size, and image format

- Adding images to XHTML documents

- Specifying image characteristics: height, width, alignment, and borders

- Using images as links

- Creating image maps

- Using images as backgrounds

Developing Images

Although images add life to your Web pages, they can become a liability if they are not developed properly. For example, images can take F-O-R-E-V-E-R to load, becoming an obstacle for your users. Likewise, images can unnecessarily hog page space or disk space, perhaps obscuring important content. So, your goal in using images is to develop them properly by considering three things:

- File size
- Physical dimensions
- File type

Determining File Size

Think of image files as being three-dimensional, having height and width as well as many colors. For example, a 16-color image not only has height and width, which you can see on the screen, but it also has 16 *layers*, one for each color; this is called the *color depth*. An image's basic file size equals width × height × color depth.

With the following techniques, you can reduce file size and, therefore, make your images as efficient as possible:

- Reduce the *number of colors*. This technique is particularly useful for Graphics Interchange Format (GIF) images. You'll find more information on the number of colors in GIFs in the section "Understanding GIFs," later in this chapter.

- Reduce the image's *physical dimensions*. For example, you can reduce an image from 600×400 pixels to 300×200 pixels. The resulting smaller image usually includes the details and clarity of the larger one, yet it occupies significantly less disk space. You'll find guidelines for sizing images in the next section.

- Use a format that *compresses* the file to cram more data into less space. You'll find more details about suitable image formats in the section "Understanding Image Formats," later in this chapter.

Every time you reduce file size, you make it easier for users to download and view your page. But always keep an eye on image quality—if your graphic is too small or too compressed, you might lose the effect of it completely.

Dealing with Physical Dimensions

The physical size (dimensions) of an image is its height and width; this affects not only how the image appears in a browser, but also how quickly it loads. Just how big should images be? Well, that depends. Many sites use itty-bitty images, such as buttons and icons, that effectively add color or dimension to a Web page. Other sites use larger graphics for logos or button bars, which are also effective. There's no "right" size for images; instead, the key is to consider the following:

- The image's purpose
- The overall page design
- Your users' computer settings
- The total file size of the page

Consider Image Purpose

Every time you add an image to a page, you need a good reason for doing so—to illustrate a point, to show a person or a location, to show a product, to outline a process, to make navigation easier and clearer, or simply to add some color and zest to an otherwise hum-drum document. Be sure that every image enhances content, design, or both.

When determining the dimensions of an image, consider its importance. For example, if your users need an image to understand a concept, the image should be larger. On the other hand, an image that merely adds a splash of color should probably be a bit smaller. If you're not sure how important an image is, lean toward smaller. Remember, images are the major contributor to the total file size of a page, and therefore to the loading time of the page, so they can affect how easily a user can access your pages.

Consider Page Design

Images are visually "weighty" objects—that is, they attract attention faster than other page elements. Images that are too large often overwhelm page contents and obscure the message. When determining image size, in particular, consider how the image will appear relative to other page elements. Here are some questions to ask yourself:

- Will the page include multiple graphics?
- Will the page incorporate borders and shading, which are also weightier than text?

- Will the page contain a substantive amount of text or only a few words? Text can make up in volume what it lacks in visual weight. A lot of text balances a graphic more effectively than a small amount of text.

Consider Users' Computer Settings

Your users' computer settings also affect how images appear on screen. An image that's 600×400 pixels will take up almost the entire browser window on Windows computers using the lowest screen resolution of 640×480 pixels (even allowing for most browser interface elements), so that's a good standard for a maximum image size. The most common screen resolution is currently 800×600, and many users use a resolution of 1024×768 or higher; that same 600×400 image will take up much less screen space on their computers. Check your pages at several screen resolutions to make sure that the images and content remain clear at different settings. And, of course, if you can make images smaller, do so to help speed loading time.

To convey content adequately, few images need to be larger than 600×400. Something in the 300×200 pixels range is usually a good size for photographs, and buttons are generally 50×50 pixels or smaller.

Consider Total File Size of the Page

By adding up the size of all files associated with a page, you can calculate the total file size of a page and estimate the download time for that page. We will walk you through an example to show you how to do this. For this example, we will use an example page index.html; the values for this page are shown in Table 5.1.

Table 5.1 File Size Values for index.html

FILENAME	FILE SIZE
index.html	4 KB
header.gif	17 KB
logo.gif	5 KB
navbar.jpg	13 KB
styles.css	1 KB
Total	40 KB

1. Write down the size of all the files associated with a page and add them.

2. Take the total file size in kilobytes (KB) and multiply by 8 to convert to kilobits (Kb; 1 byte = 8 bits).

3. Divide by the modem speed of the user to estimate the actual download time for the page.

In this example, a user using a 28.8 Kbps (kilobits per second) modem would be able to completely download the page `index.html` in about 11 seconds (using the values in Table 5.1, 40 KB × 8 = 320 kilobits; 320 kilobits/28.8 Kbps = 11.1 seconds).

Don't mix up kilobytes (used for file size and abbreviated KB) and kilobits (used for download rate and abbreviated Kb). Many people use just K for both; they refer to 56K modems and also to file sizes such as 56K. But a 56 Kbps modem doesn't download a 56 KB file in one second! (It takes about eight seconds.)

A good rule is to keep the total file size of a page between 30 and 50 KB so download time is reasonable for all users.

Understanding Image Formats

When developing images, you should also consider your format options. Basically, you can use Graphics Interchange Format (GIF), Joint Photographic Experts Group (JPEG), or Portable Network Graphics (PNG) formats, depending on what you want to do.

Understanding GIFs

The most common image format is Graphics Interchange Format (*GIF*), developed by CompuServe for online use. If you check out your image-editing software's Save As options, you might have a choice between two versions of GIF: 87a and 89a. You want to choose version 89a; whether it's called GIF-89a or just GIF, this format includes the following features:

- Transparency
- Animation
- Progressive rendering
- Lossless compression

GIF Supports Transparency

GIF supports *transparency*. This means that you can make any part of a GIF image transparent so that what is underneath the image shows through the transparent areas. In most cases, this will be the background color of the page. For example, in the ASR Outfitters logo image, the corner areas are a different color and set to be transparent. Figure 5.1 shows this image as it appears in Paint Shop Pro, an image-editing program; even if you set the background as transparent, you can still see it. Figure 5.2 shows the same image as it appears in Internet Explorer.

Figure 5.1 *Viewed in an image-editing program, the transparent background is still visible.*

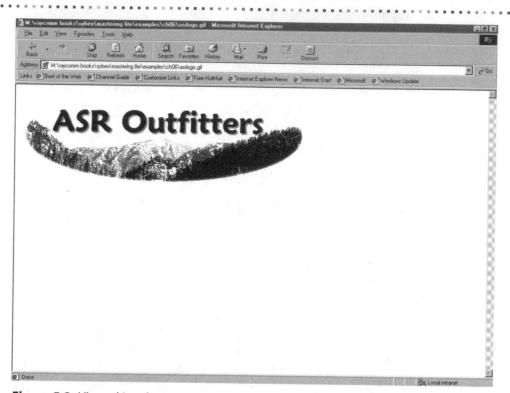

Figure 5.2 *Viewed in a browser, the transparent background is not visible.*

It's often not necessary to use transparency to achieve this effect. If you set the background color of the image to the exact same color as the background color of the page (which is set in the body element—for example, `<body bgcolor="#ffffff">` for a white background—or in an associated style sheet), the image background will blend seamlessly with the page background. This is called *pseudo-transparency* or *fake transparency*.

GIF Supports Animation

Some image-editing programs and specialized image-processing or Web-design programs can combine several GIF images into a single file, which then displays each image or panel in turn. The effect is similar to the effect found in cartoon-flip books—you flip the pages and see the illusion of motion, i.e., animation.

Not all browsers display animated GIFs, although almost all commonly used browsers today support them. Browsers that don't support animated GIFs include text-only browsers and browsers that use text-to-speech software.

Using animated GIFs is a simple way to provide animation without resorting to Java applets or to more sophisticated plug-ins such as Shockwave or Flash. You'll find more information about animated GIFs in Chapter 12.

Animated GIFs are much larger than nonanimated ones, because they contain the equivalent of an additional image for each panel (frame) of animation.

GIF Supports Progressive Rendering

Progressive rendering is also known as *interlacing* and refers to how an image is displayed on the screen while it downloads. A browser displays a noninterlaced image line by line, as it's received over the network or loaded off a disk. The complete image is not visible until it has been completely loaded. A browser displays interlaced images in passes, filling in every eighth line until the entire image is displayed.

The effects of interlacing vary from browser to browser. Some browsers display the downloading image as slowly coming into focus. Other browsers display it like Venetian blinds that are slowly opened until the entire image is displayed. Either way, interlaced images begin to appear on the screen faster than noninterlaced images and allow users who are familiar with the image to get the gist before the whole image appears. Interlaced images also help reassure the user that the image download is occurring.

GIF Supports Lossless Compression

Lossless compression is an efficient way to save files without losing image details. When GIFs are saved, they are compressed to take less space on the disk and less time to download. With lossless compression, the compression algorithm notices broad expanses of single colors, and instead of recording the color for each pixel, it indicates the color and the number of times to repeat the color. The image is not changed; it's simply saved more efficiently.

GIFs can include up to 256 colors. However, if your image does not have this many colors, a smaller file size can be created by limiting the number of colors in the GIF to only as many as you actually need. Therefore, when you save an image as a GIF in an image-editing program, save it with only as many colors as necessary. This will decrease the file size and the download time.

Because GIFs can only include 256 colors, they're not sufficient for true photographic quality. GIF images are best used for line art, icons, and drawings with a limited number of colors. You will probably want to use the JPEG file format for images requiring higher quality.

Understanding JPEGs

JPEG, which is pronounced *jay-peg*, is an acronym formed from Joint Photographic Experts Group (it's sometimes written as JPG because that's the standard file extension). JPEG is the second most popular format for images on the Web. As a whole, JPEG images are less flexible than GIF images, and most significantly, they do not support the variety of rendering options that GIFs support.

The most significant advantage of JPEG is that it supports millions of colors, thereby providing much more realistic photographic reproduction. JPEG images use a *lossy* compression algorithm. Lossy compression discards some details of the image to decrease the file size. JPEG images are best for photographs because the loss of detail is less noticeable with photographs than with line art; in addition, the compression ratio and resulting quality are much better with photographs.

Setting JPEG options in your image-editing program helps control both the eventual file size and the quality. In many programs, you can set the resolution, or number of pixels per inch (ppi), and the level of JPEG compression. If the images are for Web use only—i.e., they won't be used for print publications—a resolution of 100 is more than adequate. Screen resolution is only 72 ppi for Mac monitors and 96 ppi for PC monitors; therefore, using a resolution higher than 100 uselessly increases an image's file size. Depending on the image, the application, and the eventual purpose of the image, you can often increase the compression substantially without losing much detail. If the same image is going to be used both on the Web and in print, save one version as a JPEG for the Web and another version as a higher resolution TIFF for print.

Although JPEG supports progressive rendering, older browsers do not support this feature and will display a broken image icon when you use a JPEG with progressive rendering.

Understanding PNGs

The latest development in Web image file formats is *PNG*, pronounced *ping*, which stands for Portable Network Graphics. This format is only supported by more recent browser versions (Microsoft Internet Explorer 4 or later and Netscape Navigator 4.04 or later). PNG images combine most of the advantages of GIF, including transparency and interlacing, plus the ability to accommodate millions of colors and a tight, lossless compression technique.

Which Image Format Is Right for You?

The image format you choose depends on the features you want to include. Table 5.2 compares the features of the three graphic formats examined.

Table 5.2 Features of GIF, JPEG, and PNG

FEATURES	GIF	JPEG	PNG
Transparency	Yes	No	Yes
Interlacing/progressive rendering	Yes	Yes	Yes
Millions of colors	No	Yes	Yes
Lossless compression	Yes	No	Yes
Good for line art	Yes	No	Yes
Good for photographs	No	Yes	Yes
Accepted on most browsers	Yes	Yes	No

As you can see, GIF and JPEG have complementary advantages and disadvantages. However, as more browsers support PNG, it will probably become the first choice.

XML Opportunities

The W3C's currently finalizing the Scalable Vector Graphics (SVG) 1.0 specification (which is in the Candidate Recommendation phase). SVG is an XML language used to describe two-dimensional graphics. The W3C defines vector graphics as "paths consisting of straight lines and curves." Find out more about SVG at www.w3.org/Graphics/SVG/Overview.htm8 or www.w3.org/TR/2000/CR-SVG-20001102.

Adding Images

In this section, we're going to create some Web pages for ASR Outfitters, a mountaineering and hiking supply company that is a mythical, mini-version of REI, the recreation equipment retailer. In the process, you'll learn how to include images in an XHTML document. Although this may seem like putting the cart before the horse, knowing how to include images makes learning to develop them easier.

Table 5.3 shows the main image element and its attributes, which are used to insert images in Web pages.

Table 5.3 Main Element and Attributes of Images

ITEM	TYPE	SPECIFIES
`img`	Empty element	Marks an image within an XHTML document.
`align="…"`	Attribute of `img`	Image alignment as `top`, `middle`, `bottom`, `left`, or `right`; deprecated.
`alt="…"`	Attribute of `img`	Alternative text to display if an image is not displayed (necessary for accessibility reasons); required.
`border="n"`	Attribute of `img`	The width of a border around an image in pixels; deprecated.
`height="n"`	Attribute of `img`	The final height of an image in pixels.
`src="url"`	Attribute of `img`	An image file and location (URL) to include; required.
`width="n"`	Attribute of `img`	The final width of an image in pixels.

Adding an Image

Adding an image is similar to adding the elements and attributes you've already used. You use the `img` element, which specifies an image, plus the `src` attribute to specify the image filename and location (URL). For example, if you're including an image that's located within the same folder as your document (a relative URL), your code might look like this:

```
<img src="logo.gif" />
```

Or, if you're including an image located on another server, you could include an absolute URL, like this:

```
<img src="http://www.asroutfitters.com/gifs/asrlogo.gif" />
```

The img element is classified as an empty element; it uses a space and a slash (/) before the closing angle bracket.

A URL used in the src attribute is called a *remote reference*. Referencing logos and images remotely has certain advantages and some significant drawbacks. One advantage is that remote references to images ensure that you're always using the current logo. For example, if ASR Outfitters hires a graphic design company to change its corporate image, a franchisee's site that uses remote references to the main site will reflect the changes as soon as the main site changes. Additionally, remote references lighten the load on your server and reduce the number of files you must manage and manipulate.

On the down side, changes that are out of your control can easily break links from your site. If the ASR Outfitters Webmaster decides to move the images from the gifs subdirectory into an images subdirectory, the franchisee's images will no longer work, because the src attribute points to the subdirectory that no longer contains the image files. From the user's perspective, the franchisee simply has a nonfunctional site—the user really doesn't know or care why.

Additionally, network glitches or server problems can also render your images inoperative if you link to them remotely. If the load on your own site is significant and you use remote images, the other site may be swamped with the demand and not even know why. Overall, you're probably better off copying the images to your local folder or at least to a different folder on your server, rather than relying on remote servers.

Be careful about linking to or copying remote images, because those images may be copyrighted material. For example, if Bad Karma Hiking Equipment decided that the ASR Outfitters images were cool and incorporated those cool images in a site design by using them without permission, it would be infringing on ASR Outfitter's copyrighted material. This also applies to background images (covered later in this chapter) and any other document content. So, be careful!

To add images to your document, start with a basic XHTML document that, along with content, includes the following:

- The DOCTYPE declaration
- The html element with the XHTML namespace
- The head element
- The body element

We used the basic document in Listing 5.1 for ASR Outfitters.

LISTING 5.1: THE ASR OUTFITTERS BASIC PAGE

```
<!DOCTYPE html PUBLIC ".//W3C/DTD XHTML 1.0 Transitional//EN"
    "http://www.w3.org/TR/xhtml1/DTD/xhtml1-transitional.dtd">
<html xmlns="http://www.w3.org/1999/xhtml">
    <head>
        <title>ASR Outfitters</title>
    </head>
    <body>
        <h1 align="center">ASR Outfitters</h1>
        <p>We provide mountaineering and hiking equipment
            nationwide via mail order as well as through our
            stores in the Rocky Mountains.</p>
        <hr width="70%" size="8" noshade="noshade" />
        <p>Please select from the following links:</p>
        <ul>
            <li><a href="camping.html">Camping News</a></li>
            <li><a href="catalog.html">Catalog</a></li>
            <li><a href="clubs.html">Clubs</a></li>
            <li><a href="contact.html">Contact Us</a></li>
            <li><a href="weather.html">Check Weather</a></li>
        </ul>
        <hr width="70%" size="8" noshade="noshade" />
        <center>
            <address>ASR Outfitters<br />
                <a href="mailto:info@asroutfitters.com">
                    info@asroutfitters.com</a><br />
                4700 N. Center<br />
                South Logan, UT 87654<br />
                801-555-3422<br />
            </address>
        </center>
    </body>
</html>
```

Attribute–value pairs must be written in full; for example, noshade="noshade" *in Listing 5.1. In HTML, an attribute name could sometimes be specified without an attribute value (e.g., the attribute* checked *for a* form *element). In XHTML, the value must be specified—even in cases such as this where the name and the value are the same.*

To add an image to this basic document, follow these steps:

1. Insert an <img /> tag where you want the image to appear.

    ```
    <h1 align="center">ASR Outfitters</h1>
    <img />
    <p>We provide mountaineering and hiking equipment
        nationwide via mail order as well as through our
        stores in the Rocky Mountains.</p>
    ```

2. Add an src attribute that points to the image filename and location. In this example, the filename is asrlogo.gif, and it's in the same folder as the document; so that's all that's required.

    ```
    <img src="asrlogo.gif" />
    ```

3. In this case, add a line break tag <br /> after the <img /> tag so that the following text starts on the next line (and not in any available space behind or on either side of the image).

    ```
    <img src="asrlogo.gif" /><br />
    ```

4. Because the image duplicates the content of the first-level heading (<h1 align="center">ASR Outfitters</h1>), consider removing the first-level heading.

5. The first-level heading was centered, so add the center element around the logo to center it as well.

    ```
    <center><img src="asrlogo.gif" /><br /></center>
    ```

 The img element supports the align attribute with a value of top, middle, bottom, left, *or* right, *but it does not support horizontal centering. If you want to use horizontal centering, use the* center *element. However, note that the* center *element is deprecated in favor of using style sheets. See the "Aligning the Image" section later in this chapter for more information.*

You can see the resulting image in the ASR Web page shown in Figure 5.3.

Figure 5.3 *An image in the ASR Web page*

Including Alternative Text

Alternative text describes an image you've used in your Web page. You should include alternative text for the following reasons:

- The XHTML 1 specification requires the `alt` attribute for many elements, including `img`. Your documents won't be valid without it, which will mean extra work for you to update them in the future.

- Some of your users may be using text-only browsers.

- Some of your users may be visually impaired and using text-to-speech converters that can't render graphics.

- A user may have turned off images so files will load faster.

- Sometimes browsers don't display images correctly.

- Sometimes images don't display because the links aren't working properly.

- Sometimes browsers display alternative text while images load.

- Search engines may use alternative text as the only source of information on image content.

Alternative text should be clear and concise, and should provide your users with enough information so they can understand the image content without viewing it. Alternative text for a logo can be as simple as the company name and the word *logo*. Even text as brief as "ASR sample photograph" or "ASR content-free image" is helpful to users. If they see only the word *Image* (which they would if you omit the alt attribute), they'll have to load the images to see the content.

To add alternative text to your images, simply add the alt attribute to the img element, like this:

```
<img src="asrlogo.gif" alt="ASR Outfitters Logo" />
```

The resulting alternative text is shown in Figure 5.4.

Figure 5.4 *Alternative text provides information about the image.*

Specifying Height and Width

You can speed up the loading time of images by specifying an image's height and width. As the browser loads the page, it notes the `height` and `width` attributes and leaves that much space for the image. Next, it lays out the remaining text, then it goes back and fills in the image. If you do not include these attributes, the browser has to download enough of the image to get the dimensions before it can lay out the rest of the text, thereby slowing the display of other page elements.

To specify image height and width, add the `height` and `width` attributes in the `img` element, like this:

```
<img src="asrlogo.gif" alt="ASR Outfitters Logo" width="604"
    height="192" />
```

As a rule, use the actual height and width of the image. To get the dimensions, open the image in an image-editing program and use the program's option for finding pixel measurements (usually a properties page, status bar, or Image Size command). You will see something like 604 × 192 × 256, which indicates, in this example, that the `asrlogo.gif` image is 604 pixels wide, 192 pixels high, and 256 colors deep. With this information, you can then add the `width` (604) and `height` (192) attributes to the `img` element.

Reducing these attributes doesn't reduce download times; the same image file still has to load. See the later section "Creating Thumbnails" for a technique to include smaller images that are also less memory intensive.

Aligning the Image

XHTML provides several image alignment options:

- Three vertical options align the image with respect to a line of text.

- Two options align the image to the left or to the right of the window (with corresponding text wrap).

The alignment options within the `img` element override other alignment settings within the XHTML document, such as `<center>...</center>` tags surrounding the `img` element.

By default, images align on the left, with a single line of accompanying text appearing on the same line; however, long text wraps to the following line. To ensure that accompanying text appears beside the image, specify `align="left"` in the `img` element, like this:

```
<img src="asrlogo.gif" alt="ASR Outfitters Logo" width="604"
     height="192" align="left" />
```

The text appears to the right of the left-aligned image, as shown in Figure 5.5.

Figure 5.5 *Specifying left alignment for an image ensures that accompanying text appears to the right of the image.*

Remember that all attribute values must be quoted in XHTML. For example, `align="left"` *is valid code, and* `align=left` *is not valid code.*

You can create attractive effects by combining image alignment and text alignment. For example, setting an image to `align="right"` and then setting the accompanying text to `align="right"` forces the text to be flush against the image with a ragged left margin, as shown in Figure 5.6.

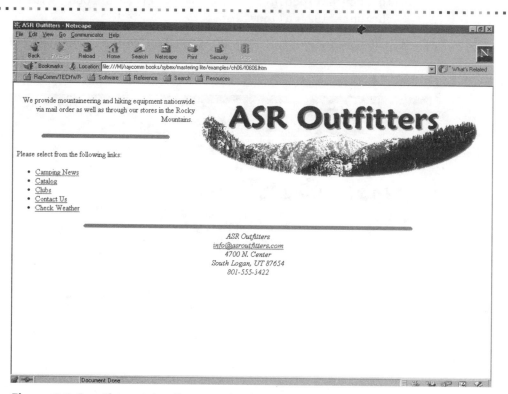

Figure 5.6 *Specifying right alignment for the image and text produces appealing results.*

The remaining alignment options—top, `middle`, and `bottom`—can be used to align the image within the text. For example, using `align="top"` aligns the top of the image with the top of the surrounding text, and the remainder of the image hangs below the text line. Using `align="middle"` places the middle of an image at the baseline of surrounding text. Similarly, using `align="bottom"` places the bottom of an image on the same line as the text, and the remainder of the image extends considerably higher than the surrounding text. The effect of these options is shown in Figure 5.7.

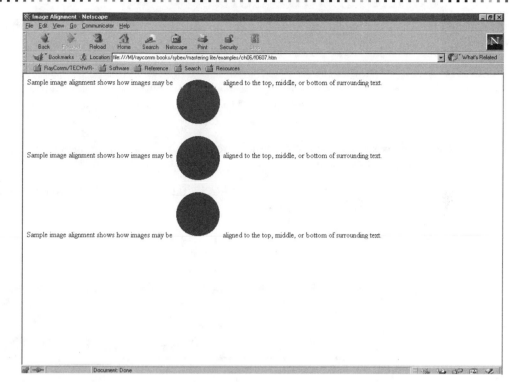

Figure 5.7 *Top, middle, and bottom alignment float the image differently in relationship to the surrounding text.*

XHTML Opportunities

The XHTML specification deprecates presentational markup in favor of style sheets. The `align` attribute and the `center` element are presentational, which means they provide information about the display of a document. Presentational elements and attributes can be used in an XHTML document as long as the document uses the XHTML Transitional DTD. However, if you want to use the XHTML Strict DTD, any alignment must be specified in a style sheet. (See Chapter 2 for further information about XHTML DTDs, Chapter 3 for more about presentational attributes and elements, and Chapter 10 and Master's Reference Part 2 for details on using style sheets to set alignment and other presentational properties.)

Controlling the Border

You control the border around an image with the border attribute. In most browsers, by default, the border is visible only on images that are used as links. To turn the border off for an image, add the border="0" attribute to the img element, resulting in a complete image element:

```
<img src="asrlogo.gif" alt="ASR Outfitters Logo" width="604"
    height="192" border="0" />
```

Likewise, you can increase the border width around an image by increasing the value of the border attribute, like this:

```
<img src="asrlogo.gif" alt="ASR Outfitters Logo" width="604"
    height="192" border="7" />
```

The resulting border looks like the one in Figure 5.8.

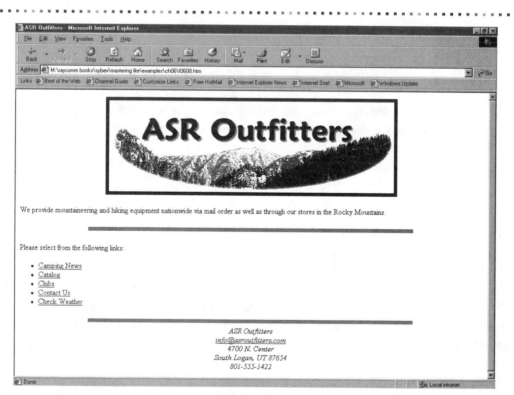

Figure 5.8 *Setting a large border width frames your images.*

Choosing Suitable Colors

When creating your own images—or choosing colors for Web page or table backgrounds—you want to choose colors that look good in most browsers, most of the time. If you're selecting colors for text or for small swatches, choose anything that appeals to you. However, if you're selecting a background color or a color that will appear in broad expanses of your XHTML documents, be careful.

If you choose a color that is not available on a user's system, the browser will dither the color to approximate its appearance. *Dithering* is the technical term for substituting other colors, partially or wholly, to minimize the impact of not having the correct color. Dithering in photographs or small images is rarely noticeable, but dithering in large single-color areas results in blotchy or mottled appearances.

In the past, personal computers only supported 8-bit color, or 256 (2 to the power of 8) colors at a time. Nowadays, the three major operating systems (Macintosh, Unix, and Windows) each use different sets of colors for system functions, and those colors—up to 40—are taken from the available 256, leaving only 216 colors for general use. If you choose one of these 216 colors (also called *Web-safe colors*), you can be certain that the colors will look as good as they can in all browsers on all platforms. These remaining 216 colors are evenly distributed over the color spectrum, giving you a wide range of colors from which to choose.

Today, most personal computers support not only 8-bit color but also 15-bit or 16-bit color (also called *high color*), and many computers support 24-bit color (also called *true color* or *millions of colors*). If your computer is set to display 24-bit color, it can display 16,776,216 colors. However, despite the fact that most users have more than 256 possible colors available, color display is still not completely uniform in different browsers and different platforms.

If you would like to learn more about Web-safe color, including the pros and cons of using the Web-safe color palette, see the article "Death of the Websafe Color Palette?" by David Lehn and Hadley Stern at `http://hotwired.lycos.com/webmonkey/00/37/index2a.html`.

Monitor colors are represented as proportions of their red, green, and blue components, which together form an *RGB value*. In most image-editing programs, you can choose component levels in decimal (base 10) numbers, on a scale of 0–255 for a 256-color system. However, when you're specifying colors within a Web page, the most common format is hexadecimal (base 16) numbers. The "hex" digits are 0123456789ABCDEF, so the hexadecimal version of 0–255 is 00–FF.

If you limit yourself to 256 total colors, you can build a color's RGB value from the numbers in Table 5.4 for each color component. To create a safe (nondithering) color, choose a system (hexadecimal or decimal) and choose one value from each column. For example, a Web-safe "sky blue" color might be 51, 204, 255 for the red, green, and blue components. The corresponding hexadecimal numbers would be 33, CC, FF. (Hex digits aren't case sensitive, so ff is the same as FF.)

Table 5.4 Preferred RGB Values

HEXADECIMAL			DECIMAL		
Red	Green	Blue	Red	Green	Blue
00	00	00	0	0	0
33	33	33	51	51	51
66	66	66	102	102	102
99	99	99	153	153	153
CC	CC	CC	204	204	204
FF	FF	FF	255	255	255

You signal, in your code, that you're using a hexadecimal color value by placing a pound sign (#) before the six digits for the color code; for example, <body bgcolor="#33CCFF">. Decimal color values (which are less common in XHTML) are defined in parentheses: <body bgcolor="rgb(51,204,255)">.

For 16 predefined colors, rather than specify a number for the color value, you can use a keyword. These keywords are listed in Master's Reference Part 6. You'd use them as attribute values in place of the hex code—for example, <body bgcolor="teal">.

As a rule, colors that are close to the 256 colors built from Table 5.4 will also not dither, but there's no hard and fast rule on how "close" is close enough. For example, we tried #000001 and found that it didn't visibly dither on our computers... this time.

Visit Chapter 14 for information about using colors to help create a coherent Web site. Also, you'll find more on browser-safe colors in Master's Reference Part 6.

Using Images as Links

Using images as links offers two distinct advantages to both you and your users. First, images really can be as good as a thousand words. Often, including an image link can replace several words or lines of text, leaving valuable space for other page elements and content.

Second, you can also use *thumbnails*, which are smaller images that link to larger ones. By doing so, you can let users get the gist of an image and choose whether they want to load the larger version. (You'll find details about thumbnails in an upcoming section, "Creating Thumbnails.")

Creating Image Links

To add an image as a link, start by adding the img element. In this example, we are adding a fancy button to the ASR Outfitters page to replace the more prosaic Camping News bulleted list item. The name of the image is camping.gif, and the file it should link to is camping.html.

When you use images as links, alternative text is critical. If clicking the image is the only way users can connect to the other page, the alternative text is their only clue when the image is not displayed (whether because of technical difficulties, because they've turned off images, because they have text-only browsers, or because they use a screen-reading program for the visually impaired).

Here are the steps for adding an image link:

1. Add an img element and an src attribute with the name of the image file as the value to the document.

   ```
   <img src="camping.gif" />
   ```

2. Include alternative text using the alt attribute.

   ```
   <img src="camping.gif" alt="Camping News" />
   ```

3. Add any other attributes you want to include, such as the height, width, and border attributes. If you choose to use border="0" to turn off the border completely, be sure that the image is visually identified as a link. Otherwise, your users might not know it's a link unless they pass their mouse over it and see the pointing-hand cursor.

   ```
   <img src="camping.gif" width="300" height="82" border="0"
       alt="Camping News" />
   ```

4. Add the link anchor opening tag (`<a>`) before and the closing tag (`</a>`) at the end of the image element.

    ```
    <a><img src="camping.gif" width="300" height="82"
        border="0" alt="Camping News" /></a>
    ```

5. Add the `href` attribute to the opening anchor tag (`<a>`) to specify the image filename and location.

    ```
    <a href="camping.html"><img src="camping.gif" width="300"
        height="82" border="0" alt="Camping News" /></a>
    ```

Now you have an image that acts as a link to the `camping.html` file. After adding a couple more images and surrounding them all with the `center` element, the ASR Outfitters page is similar to Figure 5.9.

Figure 5.9 *Image links can make a page much more attractive (and slower to load).*

Creating Thumbnails

As we mentioned earlier, a thumbnail is a smaller version of an image, but it's also a link to the larger version. Thumbnails can also link to multimedia files or to other content that is time-consuming to download or not universally accessible.

For example, ASR Outfitters included a thumbnail of the original photograph that inspired its logo. This thumbnail links to the original photograph, which is a larger image.

To add a thumbnail image, start by having both images—the thumbnail and the larger version—available. Make a thumbnail by starting with the full-size version (scanned from your private collection or from another source—remember the copyright rules). Use your image-editing software to resize or resample the image to a much smaller size—as small as possible while still retaining the gist of the image. Save this second image under a different name and follow these steps:

1. Include the thumbnail image in your document the way you'd include any other image. For example, the code might look like this:

```
<img src="photo-thumbnail.jpg" height="78" width="193"
    align="right" border="1" alt="Thumbnail of original
    photo" />
```

2. Add a link from the thumbnail to the larger image.

```
<a href="photo.jpg"><img src="photo-thumbnail.jpg"
    height="78" width="193" align="right" border="1"
    alt="Thumbnail of original photo" /></a>
```

If you set the border to 0, be sure that the supporting text or other cues in the XHTML document make it clear that the image is, in fact, a link to a larger photograph. Alternatively, do as we did and simply set border="1" to make it clear that an image is a link. Here's the result from the bottom corner of the ASR Outfitters home page:

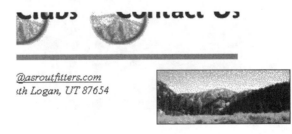

Although you can achieve the same visual effect in your document by using the original image and setting a smaller display size with the `height` and `width` attributes, this technique defeats the purpose of thumbnails. Even if you reset the display size with smaller values for `height` and `width`, the entire full-size image will have to be downloaded to your computer. The trick to effective thumbnails is to reduce both the dimensions and the actual file size to the smallest possible value so the page will load quickly.

Creating Image Maps

An image map, also called a *clickable image*, is a single image that contains multiple links. In your Web travels, you may have used image maps without knowing it. Clicking a portion of an image map takes you to the link connected with that part of the visual presentation. For example, a health-information Web site might present an image map of the human body to a patient, with instructions for the patient to "click where it hurts." Another good use replaces individual images (which browsers could realign depending on the window width) with a single *graphical menu*. Figure 5.10 shows a sample image map from the ASR Outfitter's Web site. Users can click each area for weather conditions—weather at the high peaks and lower elevations—and even the ultraviolet index.

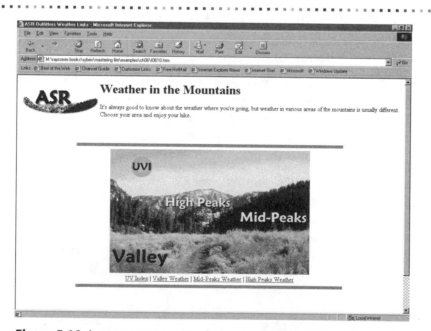

Figure 5.10 *Image maps are single images with multiple links to other information or graphics.*

Understanding Image Map Types

The two types of image maps are *server-side* and *client-side*. The feature distinguishing the two types is where the processing takes place (where a user's mouse-click is translated into a link to another document). The processing can occur either on the server (hence, *server-side image map*) or on the user's computer (hence, *client-side image map*).

Server-Side Image Maps

In a server-side image map, the coordinates of the click are transmitted to the server computer, which determines the instructions that apply to that click. The server sends that information back to the client, which then sends a request for the appropriate document. The server computer does the calculating and tells the client what to do.

The advantages to using server-side image maps are that they have been around longer than client-side maps and they are widely supported. The disadvantages to using server-side image maps include the following:

- Because a server-side image map requires input from the server, it generally responds slower than a client-side image map, depending on network traffic.

- The two-step communication of a server-side image map increases network traffic.

- The server may need supplemental software to process the image map.

- The server administrator may have to specify how the image map is processed.

Client-Side Image Maps

Generally, you'll want to use client-side image maps for several reasons. To start with, they're faster (because there's no need for back and forth communication between client and server to process the map) and more reliable for those browsers that support client-side maps (and most do). For example, if a document with a client-side image map comes from Server A and points to a document on Server B, the client can do the calculations and request the document directly from Server B.

Client-side image maps are more user-friendly than server-side image maps. When a user moves the cursor over an image-map link within a document, the status bar generally displays the URL of the link. Newer browsers, including the latest versions of Netscape Navigator and Internet Explorer, also show information about the link in a small pop-up window. In contrast, when a user places the cursor over a server-side image-map link, the status bar displays only the coordinates of the cursor.

Finally, client-side image maps are better for you, the Web author, because you can use and test them before you put the image map on the server. In contrast, server-side maps do not work until they have been installed on the server, making testing much more difficult.

If your users may be using particularly old browsers, consider using both client-side and server-side image maps. If browsers see a client-side map, they'll use it. If they don't recognize the client-side image map, they'll revert to the server-side map. The only disadvantage to this approach is that you have to do twice as much work.

Making Appropriate Image Maps

Poorly constructed or carelessly selected image maps can be much worse than no image map at all. The inherent disadvantages of images (for example, their download time and their inaccessibility for text-only browsers) apply in spades to image maps. When determining whether an image map is appropriate for your needs, ask the following questions:

Is the image map linking to a stable navigational structure?   If the links will be changing or if the overall site navigation structure isn't completely worked out, it's not time for an image map. Revising image maps is possible, but generally a real hassle. It's often easier to completely redo an image map than to update it.

Is the image final?   If the image hasn't passed all levels of review and isn't polished, you're not ready to make an image map. Changes as trivial as cropping the image slightly or rescaling the image by a few percentage points can completely break your map.

Is the image function appropriate to an image map?   Flashy images on a home page are good candidates for image maps, particularly if the design reflects the corporate image. In many cases, an intricate design must be a single image anyway—browsers cannot always accurately assemble individual images into the arrangement the designer intends—so adding image-map navigation is just using the image more efficiently. However, pages buried within an intranet site or that have a technical and practical focus are less likely to benefit from an image map.

Is the image content appropriate to an image map?   Artificial or gratuitous use of image maps can be a real drawback to otherwise fine Web pages. Is clicking certain spots in an image really the best way for your users to link to the information they need? For example, in a Web site about automobile repair and diagnosis for the layperson, a picture of a car and the instructions to click where the funny sound seems to originate is completely appropriate. In a site directed at experienced mechanics, however, a list of parts (hood, trunk, dashboard, tire) would be much faster and more appropriate.

Does the function or content merit an image map? If both do, that's great. If one does, you can probably proceed with an image map. However, if the links on a page don't need to be flashy and the content is not substantially clarified with an image map, omit the image map entirely. Don't forget that image files add substantially to the download time of a page, so use them wisely.

Can the image map be completely reused? If you are planning to use an image map on several pages (you will use exactly the same image and code), its value increases. In this case, it's more likely to be worth the download time than if it's only being used once.

If you answered no to one or more of these questions, consider using traditional, individual images or navigation aids. For example, if you can easily break the content or image into multiple smaller images with no significant problems, strongly consider doing so. Remember that image maps are time-consuming to develop and may not be available to all your users, so be sure an image map is right for your needs before developing one.

Selecting an Image

When you select a suitable image to use as an image map, follow the same guidelines as you would for choosing other images:

- Be sure that the image supports the content.

- Be sure that the physical size is as small as possible, but large enough to convey the content.

- Be sure that the file size is as small as possible.

- Photos are usually not good choices for image maps. It's hard for the user to know where to click in a photo unless it also includes text that clearly points out the clickable areas.

For example, if you are creating an auto-repair image map for laypersons, use a simple drawing or schematic. At the other extreme is the ASR Outfitters image map, which is primarily a visual attraction with only a tangential function. The image map shown in Figure 5.10, earlier in this chapter, is part of a localized weather page. Users can click an area to get the weather for that region.

Setting Alternate Navigation

Unless you know beyond a doubt that *all* your users have graphical browsers and will choose to view images, you must provide alternate navigation options. Those who don't see the images—for whatever reason—won't be able to link to the information via your image, so provide text-based alternatives. An easy solution is to create a list of links. For example, alternate navigation for the image shown in Figure 5.10, earlier in this chapter, might look like the following code:

```
<br />
<a href="uvi.html">UV Index</a> |
<a href="valley.html">Valley Weather</a> |
<a href="midpeaks.html">Mid-Peaks Weather</a> |
<a href="highpeaks.html">High Peaks Weather</a>
```

In this code, the vertical line or "pipe" character (|) separates the links and creates the menu effect, as shown at the bottom of Figure 5.10.

Creating the alternate navigation before you develop the image map helps remind you of the links to include in the image map.

Creating Client-Side Image Maps

Creating a client-side image map involves three steps:

1. Define the image area.

2. Create the image map.

3. Activate the image map.

Defining Image Areas

All image maps are simply a combination of three shapes:

- Circles

- Rectangles

- Polygons (any shapes other than circles and rectangles)

You can create almost any image by combining these shapes. Figure 5.11 shows the ASR Outfitters image map from within a map-editing program. The UVI link is a circle, the valley temperatures link is a rectangle, and the mid- and high-peak links are polygons.

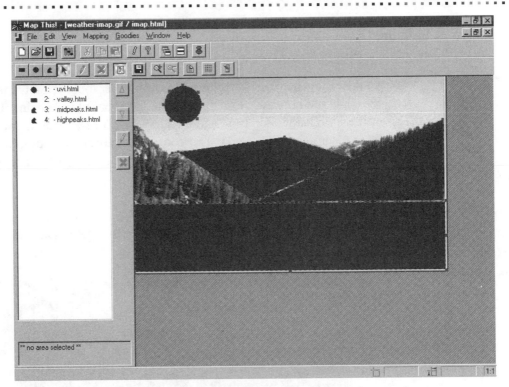

Figure 5.11 *This image map includes a circle, a rectangle, and two polygons.*

You don't have to be precise with most map definitions. You can assume that most users will click somewhere in the middle of the link area; if not, they're likely to try again.

The following three sections show you how to define these three shapes. Before you get started, open an image in an image-editing or -mapping program, such as Paint Shop Pro.

If you'll be developing several image maps, we recommend installing and using image-mapping soft-ware, which is available on the Internet. However, if you're creating simple maps or if you're only doing a few, creating them manually is almost as easy. Most WYSIWYG ("what you see is what you get") editors include image-map tools that are very easy to use.

Defining Circles

To define a circle, follow these steps:

1. Identify the center and the radius. Use the pointer tool to point at the center of the circle and note the coordinates in the status bar of your paint program. For example, in Paint Shop Pro (as shown in Figure 5.12), the pointer tool looks like a magnifying glass, and the *x,y* coordinates are at the bottom of the window. The *x* is the number of pixels from the left edge of the image, and the *y* is the number of pixels from the top.

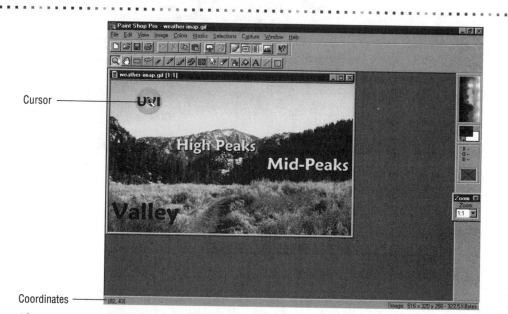

Figure 5.12 *Use your cursor to find the coordinates of various points, such as the center of a circle or corner of a polygon.*

2. Move the cursor horizontally to the edge of the circle, and note the coordinates.

3. Subtract the first *x* coordinate from the second *x* coordinate to get the radius of the circle.

4. Make a note of these coordinates.

Defining Rectangles

To define a rectangle, follow these steps:

1. Identify the upper-left corner and the lower-right corner. Point your mouse at the upper-left corner of the rectangle and record the coordinates; then point at the lower right and record the coordinates.

2. Make a note of these coordinates.

Defining Polygons

To define a polygon, follow these steps:

1. Identify each point on the shape, moving in order around the shape. You can start at any point on the perimeter and proceed clockwise or counterclockwise, as long as you don't skip points. For example, in the ASR Outfitters map, the Mid-Peaks area can be defined with three points—making a right triangle with the long side running between the Mid-Peaks and High Peaks areas. The High Peaks area might include several points across the top of the mountains, or it might be as simple as another triangle.

2. Make a note of these coordinates.

Creating the Image Map

When you create an image map, you include elements and attributes that tell a browser what to do when a user clicks the defined map areas. You can include this information within the XHTML document that contains the image map, or you can include it in a separate document. The first is more common, but if you'll be using the image map (say, as a navigation aid) in several documents, consider storing it in a separate file and referencing it from each of the documents.

You can place the map definition block anywhere within the body of your XHTML document, but it's easier to update and maintain if you place it either immediately after the opening <body> tag or immediately before the closing </body> tag. Table 5.5 explains the most common image-map elements and attributes.

Table 5.5 Main Image-Map Elements and Attributes

ITEM	TYPE	USE
img	Element	Indicates inclusion of an image map.
ismap="ismap"	Attribute of img	Specifies that the image uses a server-side image map.
usemap="…"	Attribute of img	Names the client-side map definition to use.
map	Element	Marks the map definition block within the XHTML document.
id="…"	Attribute of map	Provides an identifier for the map definition block; required attribute.
name="…"	Attribute of map	Provides a name for the map definition block; deprecated.
area	Empty element	Defines an area within the map.
alt="…"	Attribute of area	Provides alternate text (or pop-up text) describing each link; required attribute.
coords="x1,y1,x2,y2…"	Attribute of area	Identifies the shape of an area.
href="url"	Attribute of area	Specifies a link for the area. A click in the area links to this URL.
nohref="nohref"	Attribute of area	Specifies that a click in this area will not link anywhere.
shape="…"	Attribute of area	Identifies the shape of an area as a rectangle (rect), circle (circle), or polygon (poly).

In XHTML, the name attribute for the elements a, applet, form, frame, iframe, img, and map is deprecated. XHTML documents should use the id attribute rather than the name attribute. To ensure maximum compatibility, use both the name and id attributes with identical values; for example, <map name="navmap" id="navmap">.

To include a client-side image map, follow these steps (we'll use the ASR Outfitters page in this example):

1. Within your XHTML document, add opening and closing map tags.

   ```
   <body>
   <map>
   </map>
   </body>
   ```

2. Give the map a clear, descriptive name with name and id attributes. (See the previous warning.) The values used for the name and ID must be exactly the same, and these values may be used only once in the same document. They provide an internal anchor of sorts that you can link to either from the same document or from other documents.

   ```
   <map name="weather_zones" id="weather_zones">
   </map>
   ```

3. Add an area empty element for one of the shapes.

   ```
   <map name="weather_zones" id="weather_zones">
   <area />
   </map>
   ```

4. Add a shape attribute to the area element. In this example, circle represents the UVI area in the ASR example map.

   ```
   <area shape="circle" />
   ```

5. Add the coords attribute with the *x,y* coordinates of the center of the circle and with the radius of the circle.

   ```
   <area shape="circle" coords="82,43,30" />
   ```

6. Add an href attribute pointing to the target file. You can use relative or absolute URLs in client-side image maps, but, as with other links, using relative URLs is a good idea. In this case, the area links to a file called uvi.html in the same folder.

   ```
   <area shape="circle" coords="82,43,30" href="uvi.html" />
   ```

7. Add the `alt` attribute describing the link for use in pop-ups.

```
<area shape="circle" coords="82,43,30" href="uvi.html"
    alt="UV Index" />
```

 As you add areas, some may overlap others. The first area defined overrides overlapping areas.

8. Add additional `area` elements, one at a time. In this example, the next `area` element is for the Valley area, so it is a `rect` (for rectangle). The coordinates for the top left and lower right are required to link to `valley.html`.

```
<area shape="circle" coords="82,43,30" href="uvi.html"
    alt="UV Index" />
<area shape="rect" coords="1,209,516,320"
    href="valley.html" alt="Valley Weather" />
```

9. For the Mid-Peaks area, a triangle will suffice to define the area; so the shape is a `poly` (polygon) with three pairs of coordinates. This links to `midpeaks.html`.

```
<area shape="circle" coords="82,43,30" href="uvi.html"
    alt="UV Index" />
<area shape="rect" coords="1,209,516,320"
    href="valley.html" alt="Valley Weather" />
<area shape="poly" coords="199,207,513,205,514,71"
    href="midpeaks.html" alt="Mid-Peaks Weather" />
```

10. The High Peaks area is easily defined with a figure containing four corners—vaguely diamond-shaped, as in the following example:

```
<area shape="circle" coords="82,43,30" href="uvi.html"
    alt="UV Index" />
<area shape="rect" coords="1,209,516,320"
    href="valley.html" alt="Valley Weather" />
<area shape="poly" coords="199,207,513,205,514,71"
    href="midpeaks.html" alt="Mid-Peaks Weather" />
<area shape="poly"
    coords="63,123,251,98,365,134,198,204"
    href="highpeaks.html" alt="High Peaks Weather" />
```

Refer to Figure 5.11 for a reminder of what this shape looks like.

11. Set the `href` attribute for the remaining areas. You could set the remaining area so that nothing at all will happen when a user clicks there by using the `nohref` attribute. However, you must specify both a name and a value for this attribute, even though both are the same.

```
<area shape="default" nohref="nohref" />
```

That's all there is to it. The final map looks something like the code in Listing 5.2. (We'll come back to this code block when we build server-side maps later in this chapter.)

LISTING 5.2: THE ASR OUTFITTERS IMAGE MAP

```
<map name="weather_zones" id="weather_zones">
<area shape="circle" coords="82,43,30" href="uvi.html"
    alt="UV Index" />
<area shape="rect" coords="1,209,516,320" href="valley.html"
    alt="Valley Weather" />
<area shape="poly" coords="199,207,513,205,514,71"
    href="midpeaks.html" alt="Mid-Peaks Weather" />
<area shape="poly"
    coords="63,123,251,98,365,134,198,204"
    href="highpeaks.html" alt="High Peaks Weather" />
<area shape="default" nohref="nohref" />
</map>
```

Activating the Map

Before you can activate the map, you must place the map image in your document. The `img` element (in a new document from the ASR site), looks like this:

```
<img src="weather-imap.gif" width="516" height="320" border="0"
    alt="Weather Zones in the Mountains" />
```

To connect the image to the map definition created in the previous section, simply add the `usemap` attribute, as in the following example:

```
<img src="weather-imap.gif" width="516" height="320" border="0"
    alt="Weather Zones in the Mountains"
    usemap="#weather_zones" />
```

The usemap *attribute requires a pound sign (#) in the value to indicate that the link goes to a place within a document.*

If you want to link to a map definition in another document, add an absolute URL to the usemap attribute. If you do this, test thoroughly because not all browsers support this feature. The final map is shown in Figure 5.13.

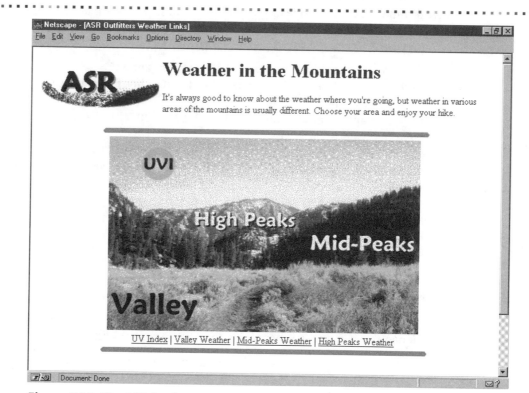

Figure 5.13 *The ASR Outfitters image map*

Creating Server-Side Image Maps

The process for making server-side maps is virtually identical to that of making client-side image maps. The only real differences are in map file format. Each type of server can have a different type of image-map configuration.

However, in practice, only two main server-side map formats exist: NCSA (from the National Center for Supercomputing Applications) and CERN (from the French for what is now the European Organization for Nuclear Research). They function in similar ways, but each requires a slightly different format for map definitions. Each format represents an implementation of server-side image maps from the earliest server software these organizations produced.

Ask your server administrator which image-map format you'll need to use for a server-side image map. Additionally, double-check the URL for the server-side image map.

The only real issue with converting your client-side image map to a server-side image map is that you must know more about (be sure of) the URLs. For example, everything in the ASR example was located initially in one folder. To properly set up a server-side map, we need to determine the full path to the information. Because of limitations in the NCSA image map implementation, the map should be contained in a subdirectory, not in the server root directory. ASR will put the image-map document, the map file, and the associated (linked) files together in the weather subdirectory on www.asroutfitters.com. Therefore, the complete URL to the main file is

```
http://www.asroutfitters.com/weather/asrweather-imap.html
```

You must use server-relative—not document-relative—URLs, or absolute URLs, to ensure that everything works properly. See Chapter 4 for more about URLs.

Creating an NCSA Image Map

In general, the NCSA image-map format is

```
method URL coordinates
```

If we use the same image-map areas from the code back in Listing 5.2, the NCSA server-side map file looks like this:

```
default /weather/asrweather-imap.html
circle  /weather/uvi.html        82,43,30
rect    /weather/valley.html     1,209,516,320
poly    /weather/midpeaks.html   199,207,513,205,514,71
poly    /weather/highpeaks.html  63,123,251,98,365,134,198,204
```

The default item points explicitly back to the file containing the map, so clicks outside active areas will not link to other pages. The remaining lines include the shape, URL, and coordinates, just as the client-side map definition file did, but using a slightly different format.

The NCSA server-side format also supports a point "shape" (in addition to the circle, rectangle, and polygon) with a single pair of coordinates. A click "near" the point takes a user to that URL. If you provide multiple points, the server chooses the closest one to your click. Because other image-map formats do not support the point, we recommend using only the existing shapes.

After you create this map file, save it with a `map` extension. ASR places the map file in the same folder as the rest of the files—that is, in the `weather` folder, just below the server root directory.

Activating NCSA-Style Server-Side Image Maps

Activating the server-side image map makes much more sense if you think of it as making the image a link (with an added level of complexity). Follow these steps:

1. Start with the map in your document (the client-side map, if you choose).

```
<img src="weather-imap.gif" width="516" height="320"
    border="0" alt="Weather Zones in the Mountains"
    usemap="#weather_zones" />
```

2. Add the `ismap` attribute to the `img` element, as shown here:

```
<img src="weather-imap.gif" width="516" height="320"
    border="0" alt="Weather Zones in the Mountains"
    usemap="#weather_zones" ismap="ismap" />
```

3. Add a link around the image.

```
<a>
<img src="weather-imap.gif" width="516" height="320"
    border="0" alt="Weather Zones in the Mountains"
    usemap="#weather_zones" ismap="ismap" />
</a>
```

4. Add the href attribute specified by the network administrator. In all probability, it will look something like this:

```
<a href="http://www.asroutfitters.com/cgi-
    bin/imagemap/weather/weather-imap.map">
<img src="weather-imap.gif" width="516" height="320"
    border="0" alt="Weather Zones in the Mountains"
    usemap="#weather_zones" ismap="ismap" />
</a>
```

If the client recognizes a client-side image map, it disregards the server-side map. If the client does not recognize the client-side map, it uses the server-side map.

When you've finished creating the map, be sure to upload the map file at the same time you upload the rest of your files. That's an easy one to forget.

Implementing CERN-Style Image Maps

CERN-style maps are considerably less common than NCSA-style maps. Again, the same basic information is included, but slightly reshuffled. After converting the original code from Listing 5.2, you end up with the following CERN map file:

```
default /weather/asrweather-imap.html
circle (82,43) 30  /weather/uvi.html
rect   (1,209) (516,320)  /weather/valley.html
poly   (199,207) (513,205) (514,71)  /weather/midpeaks.html
poly   (63,123) (251,98) (365,134) (198,204)
    /weather/highpeaks.html
```

The major differences from NCSA are: the coordinate pairs are enclosed in parentheses; the coordinates go before the URLs; and the rectangle can use any two opposite coordinates, rather than just the top-left and lower-right. The URLs can be either absolute- or server-relative.

Other types of servers exist, and administrators configure their servers differently. Asking up front how to implement a server-side image map will reduce frustration. The bottom line is that client-side image maps are less hassle.

Using Background Images

Most browsers support background images, the patterns or images behind the text in XHTML documents. As a rule, background images are *tiled* throughout the available space, meaning that they are multiple copies of one image placed side by side both horizontally and vertically to fill the screen.

Tiling offers two main advantages. First, you can produce a *seamless background*, meaning that the casual user cannot see where individual images start and stop. Figure 5.14 shows a seamless background.

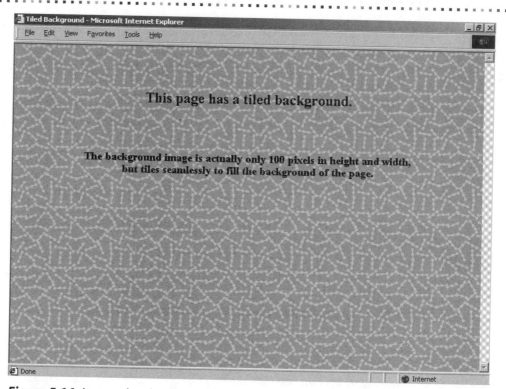

Figure 5.14 *In seamless backgrounds, the tiled images blend together.*

Second, you can develop more visually interesting backgrounds by making background images that are most likely to tile only horizontally or only vertically. For example, an image that is only 10 pixels high and 1280 pixels wide is as wide or wider than most current browser windows. Therefore, the image will most likely repeat vertically but not horizontally. This can produce a vertical band, as shown in Figure 5.15.

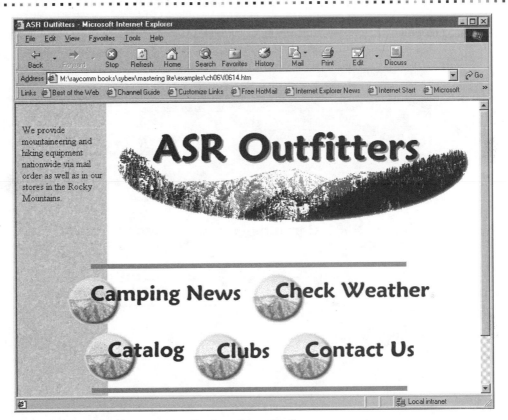

Figure 5.15 *Wide images usually tile only vertically.*

 Many users are currently using at least 17" monitors, and 19" and 21" monitors are becoming more common. Whereas a large monitor does not necessarily mean that the user will open the browser window to any particular size, it's important to remember that, in general, you can't control the size of the user's browser window or the resolution of the user's monitor. Keep this in mind if you're using a large background image, especially if you made the image large to prevent tiling.

Similarly, you can use a tall image to produce a tiled horizontal band, as shown in Figure 5.16. Pay careful attention to the image height. If the image height is less than the window height the user is using, the background will tile. Another good technique is to make the image fade into the background color of the document.

Figure 5.16 *A horizontal band looks like this in a browser.*

Always specify a background color, even if you're using a background image. The color will load faster than the image, so it will be visible while the image is loading. Also, if the image does not load, the background color will still be visible behind the other elements on the page.

To set the background image and color of your page, use the attributes in Table 5.6 in the opening body tag, as shown here:

```
<body background="asrback.jpg" bgcolor="#000000">
```

Table 5.6 Background Attributes of the body Element

ATTRIBUTE	USE
background="…"	Uses a URL to identify the name and location of an image for the background of an XHTML document; deprecated.
bgcolor="…"	Sets a background color for the page; deprecated.

Both of these attributes are deprecated, and style sheets can be used to prevent background images from tiling, or to make them tile only horizontally or vertically. You can also use style sheets to include background images or background color behind individual page elements, rather than behind the entire page. See Chapter 10 for more information on backgrounds.

Where to Go from Here

In this chapter, you learned how to select appropriate images, include them in your XHTML documents, and format them to make them appear as you want. You also learned about two image-map types, client-side and server-side, which give you a useful way to provide multiple links from a single image.

From here, you could move on to one of several chapters, but here are a few suggestions:

- See Chapter 2 for details on well-formed and valid XHTML documents.

- Check out Chapter 3 for more XHTML formatting information.

- See Chapter 6 to see how to include images in tables.

- See Chapter 10 and Master's Reference Part 2 for information about style sheets.

Part II
Advancing Your Skills

In This Part

Developing Tables

XHTML

Chapter 6

This chapter introduces XHTML *tables*, which are grids made up of rows and columns. These rows and columns create individual *cells* that can contain text and images. Tables are an effective design element that allow you to present information visually, yet in a way that is most likely to be presented by the browser in the manner that you intended. The material in this chapter will walk you through the effective use of tables.

This chapter covers the following topics:

- Creating basic tables

- Adding and deleting rows and columns

- Spanning rows and columns

- Adding captions

- Formatting tables

- Using XHTML table features

Using Tables Effectively

Tables serve two functions. First, they help present complex data in a readable format. Traditionally, you use tables when information can more effectively be portrayed visually than described in paragraph form.

Second, you can use tables to incorporate more sophisticated design elements into Web pages. The effect of using tables for page layout is similar to that of using frames (discussed in detail in Chapter 8); however, if you use tables for page layout, users can still bookmark a specific page on your Web site, which they can't do as accurately with frames. In addition, more browsers support tables than frames, so you have little concern about how tables will affect your user's computer or browser settings. Figure 6.1 shows an example of a Web site formatted using tables.

Figure 6.1 Tables help you develop interesting page designs.

If your users are not all using browsers that support XHTML elements (which are the same as HTML 4 elements if you're using the Transitional DTD), using tables for formatting is a good way to go. However, as you'll see in many places throughout this chapter, the HTML 4 and XHTML 1 specifications move away from using this formatting technique in favor of style sheets. Find out how to develop style sheets in Chapter 10, and a complete style sheet reference is in Master's Reference Part 2.

Not all browsers support tables, but most versions of Netscape Navigator, Internet Explorer, and many other browsers do. Furthermore, not all browsers that support tables support all table features. For example, Netscape 6 supports tables, but does not support extended features such as table footers. Table 6.1 lists browsers that support tables and extended table features.

Table 6.1 Browser Support for Standard Tables and HTML 4.01 Tables

BROWSER	STANDARD TABLES	HTML 4.01 TABLES
Netscape Navigator	Yes	Yes (in Netscape 6)
Internet Explorer	Yes	Yes (in IE 4 and later versions)
Lynx	No	No
Opera	Yes	No

Before including tables in an XHTML document, be sure your users use a browser that supports tables. If they don't, the table will not appear properly, if at all.

Table features commonly not supported are noted throughout this chapter.

Creating Basic Tables

Creating tables is a two-step process:

1. Create the table structure—that is, enter the `table` element, specify rows and columns, and specify column headings.

2. Enter the data in table cells.

You may want to sketch a diagram of your table before you begin coding. This will help you make sure you have all the necessary components for your table before you start coding it.

By first creating the table structure and then entering the data, you can avoid errors. Most commonly, Web authors forget the closing </table> tag or omit an entire paired tag. These errors result in an odd-looking table or no table at all. Ensuring that the basic table structure is in place before you start adding text can help you trouble-shoot problems. Table 6.2 describes the basic table elements.

Table elements become complex quickly! Be sure that you open and close tags as needed, that you don't omit elements, and that you properly nest elements. Debugging problems in a table can be tedious and very frustrating.

Table 6.2 Basic Table Elements

ELEMENT	MARKS
table	A table within an XHTML document
tr	A row within a table
td	A cell (table data) within a row
th	A heading cell within a row

Closing tags were optional in HTML 4, but they are required in XHTML. They also help you see where one element ends and another begins.

The following steps show you how to build a table and enter information into it. The sample table in Figure 6.2 represents a product summary on a corporate Web site.

1. Start with a functional XHTML document that contains the appropriate structure elements (the DOCTYPE declaration, html, head, title, and body elements) and any additional information you want to include.

2. Add the table element where you want the table boundaries to appear.

```
<table>
</table>
```

C:\Edits\Sybex\2820-Mastering XHTML\AR\f0602r.htm - Microsoft Internet Explorer

File   Edit   View   Favorites   Tools   Help

Product	Purpose
Binder 1.0	Join multiple objects.
Organizer 2.2	Join multiple objects for easy access and changing.
Splitter 3.2	Divide single object into multiple smaller objects.

Done   My Computer

Figure 6.2 *A basic table includes content, but it does not include formatting or borders—yet.*

For accessibility reasons, you can use a summary *attribute in the* table *element to describe your table's content; its value tells users what the table contains. This is not required by the specification, but it's a good idea to make your Web pages as readable as possible to as many people as you can.*

3. Add a tr element for each row, between the table tags. The sample table includes four tr elements, one for each row.

```
<table>
<tr>
</tr>
<tr>
</tr>
<tr>
</tr>
<tr>
</tr>
</table>
```

4. Add th elements in the first row where you want to include table headings. The sample table includes two th elements. You might include some spaces to set off the table heading (and data) elements so you can easily see which text is associated with each row and cell.

```
<table>
<tr>
    <th></th>
```

```
    <th></th>
</tr>
<tr>
</tr>
<tr>
</tr>
<tr>
</tr>
</table>
```

5. Add td elements to create individual cells in which to include information. The sample table includes six data cells, two in each row.

```
<table>
<tr>
    <th></th>
    <th></th>
</tr>
<tr>
    <td></td>
    <td></td>
</tr>
<tr>
    <td></td>
    <td></td>
</tr>
<tr>
    <td></td>
    <td></td>
</tr>
</table>
```

6. Add the content for each cell. Place table heading information between the opening and closing th tags, and enter data between the opening and closing td tags.

```
<table>
<tr>
    <th>Product</th>
    <th>Purpose</th>
</tr>
<tr>
    <td>Binder 1.0</td>
```

```
        <td>Join multiple objects.</td>
    </tr>
    <tr>
        <td>Organizer 2.2</td>
        <td>Join multiple objects for easy access and
            changing.</td>
    </tr>
    </table>
    <tr>
        <td>Splitter 3.2</td>
        <td>Divide single object into multiple smaller
            objects.</td>
    </tr>
```

This code produces results shown in Figure 6.2. Notice that the content is present, but that the table does not include any formatting or borders.

Adding or Removing Rows and Columns

After you create a table, you can easily add and delete elements as your information changes. The following sections show you how to add and remove rows and columns. The example results in a table that has one more column and one more row than the previous sample.

Adding Rows

To add a row to your table, insert additional tr and td elements where you want the new row to appear. For example, you can add a new row in the middle of a table like this:

```
<table>
<tr>
    <th>Product</th>
    <th>Purpose</th>
</tr>
<tr>
    <td>Binder 1.0</td>
    <td>Join multiple objects.</td>
</tr>
```

```
<tr>
   <td>Organizer 2.2</td>
   <td>Join multiple objects for easy access and changing.</td>
</tr>
<tr>
   <td>Combiner 0.9</td>
   <td>Join multiple objects at the edges.</td>
</tr>
<tr>
   <td>Splitter 3.2</td>
   <td>Divide single object into multiple smaller objects.</td>
</tr>
</table>
```

The table now looks like the one shown in Figure 6.3.

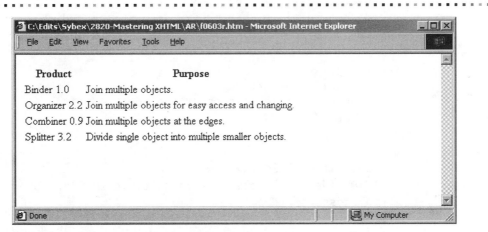

Figure 6.3 *The sample table now has four rows.*

Adding Columns

Adding columns is somewhat more difficult than adding rows because you have to add a cell to each row. However, the general process is the same: You insert the elements where you want the new column to appear, either to the left or to the right of existing columns or somewhere in between.

For example, you can add a new column to the right side of the sample table by adding another th element to the top row and a td element to each of the other rows. The sample code would look like this:

```
<table>
<tr>
    <th>Product</th>
    <th>Purpose</th>
    <th>Industry standard term</th>
</tr>
<tr>
    <td>Binder 1.0</td>
    <td>Join multiple objects.</td>
    <td>Stapler</td>
</tr>
<tr>
    <td>Organizer 2.2</td>
    <td>Join multiple objects for easy access and changing.</td>
    <td>Ring binder</td>
</tr>
<tr>
    <td>Combiner 0.9</td>
    <td>Join multiple objects at the edges.</td>
    <td>Tape</td>
</tr>
<tr>
    <td>Splitter 3.2</td>
    <td>Divide single object into multiple smaller objects.</td>
    <td>Scissors</td>
</tr>
</table>
```

The resulting table looks like that shown in Figure 6.4.

Table Sample

Product	Purpose	Industry standard term
Binder 1.0	Join multiple objects.	Stapler
Organizer 2.2	Join multiple objects for easy access and changing.	Ring binder
Combiner 0.9	Join multiple objects at the edges.	Tape
Splitter 3.2	Divide single object into multiple smaller objects.	Scissors

Figure 6.4 *Adding columns allows you to provide additional information.*

Deleting Rows and Columns

Deleting rows and columns is easier than adding them. However, you have to be careful and make sure you delete all the elements associated with a row or a column:

- When deleting a row, be sure to delete the `tr` opening and closing tags and the `td` elements and other information they surround.

- When deleting a column, be sure to delete the `th` and `td` opening and closing tags (and any other information within them) from each row.

For example, to delete the *bottom row* in the sample table, you delete the elements in strikethrough in the following code:

```
<table>
<tr>
   <th>Product</th>
   <th>Purpose</th>
   <th>Industry standard term</th>
</tr>
<tr>
   <td>Binder 1.0</td>
   <td>Join multiple objects.</td>
   <td>Stapler</td>
</tr>
<tr>
   <td>Organizer 2.2</td>
```

```
      <td>Join multiple objects for easy access and changing.</td>
      <td>Ring binder</td>
   </tr>
   <tr>
      <td>Combiner 0.9</td>
      <td>Join multiple objects at the edges.</td>
      <td>Tape</td>
   </tr>
   <tr>
      <td>Splitter 3.2</td>
      <td>Divide single object into multiple smaller objects.</td>
      <td>Scissors</td>
   </tr>
</table>
```

To delete the *final column* in the sample table, delete the last td element from each table row, like this:

```
<table>
<tr>
   <th>Product</th>
   <th>Purpose</th>
   <th>Industry standard term</th>
</tr>
<tr>
   <td>Binder 1.0</td>
   <td>Join multiple objects.</td>
   <td>Stapler</td>
</tr>
<tr>
   <td>Organizer 2.2</td>
   <td>Join multiple objects for easy access and changing.</td>
   <td>Ring binder</td>
</tr>
<tr>
   <td>Combiner 0.9</td>
   <td>Join multiple objects at the edges.</td>
   <td>Tape</td>
</tr>
<tr>
   <td>Splitter 3.2</td>
   <td>Divide single object into multiple smaller objects.</td>
   <td>Scissors</td>
```

```
</tr>
</table>
```

*If you delete the final cell from each row, your revised table will look just fine. If you delete a random cell from each row, your table will still **look** just fine, but the data will be inaccurate. Be careful to delete the elements and content consistently from each row.*

Spanning Rows and Columns

Spanning refers to stretching a cell over multiple rows or columns. Figure 6.5 shows a sample table in which the cells labeled Merchandise and Descriptive Information span two columns each, indicating that they apply to the multiple columns they span. The Joining Tools cell spans three rows to show which rows apply to that category. To specify column and row spans, use the attributes listed in Table 6.3.

Table Sample

Merchandise		Descriptive Information	
Type	Product	Purpose	Industry standard term
	Binder 1.0	Join multiple objects.	Stapler.
Joining Tools	Organizer 2.2	Join multiple objects for easy access and changing.	Ring binder.
	Combiner 0.9	Join multiple objects at the edges.	Tape.
Dividing Tools	Splitter 3.2	Divide single object into multiple smaller objects.	Scissors.

Figure 6.5 *This sample table features a cell (Joining Tools) that spans three rows.*

Table 6.3 Table Row and Column Span Attributes

ATTRIBUTE	USE
rowspan="n"	Used in th or td elements, rowspan indicates how many rows the cell should span. For example, rowspan="3" spans three rows.
colspan="n"	Used in either the th or td elements, colspan indicates how many columns the cell should cover. For example, colspan="3" spans three columns.

Spanning Rows

You can span rows using either the th or td element, depending on whether you're spanning a table heading or table data. The following example shows you how to span one cell over three rows, as in the Joining Tools cell in Figure 6.5, earlier in this chapter:

1. Add a new column for the tool categories, as shown in Figure 6.5. Place the category text **Type** in the top-left cell with a th element. Place **Joining Tools** in the second cell (with a td element), which will eventually span three rows. Place **Dividing Tools** in the third cell but in the fifth (bottom) row with a td element.

```
<table>
<tr>
    <th>Type</th>
    <th>Product</th>
    <th>Purpose</th>
    <th>Industry standard term</th>
</tr>
<tr>
    <td>Joining Tools</td>
    <td>Binder 1.0</td>
    <td>Join multiple objects.</td>
    <td>Stapler.</td>
</tr>
<tr>
    <td>Organizer 2.2</td>
    <td>Join multiple objects for easy access and
        changing.</td>
    <td>Ring binder.</td>
</tr>
<tr>
    <td>Combiner 0.9</td>
    <td>Join multiple objects at the edges.</td>
    <td>Tape.</td>
</tr>
<tr>
    <td>Dividing Tools</td>
    <td>Splitter 3.2</td>
    <td>Divide single object into multiple smaller
        objects.</td>
```

```
        <td>Scissors.</td>
    </tr>
</table>
```

 Three of the rows now have too many cells. If you display the table in a browser at this stage, you'll see that the cells appear out of alignment.

2. Add the rowspan attribute to the th or td element that affects the cell you want to span. In the sample table, add the rowspan="3" attribute to the Joining Tools td element (which should affect rows 2 through 4), like this:

```
<td rowspan="3">Joining Tools</td>
```

The resulting table now includes a spanned row, which looks like the Joining Tools row shown in Figure 6.5.

Spanning Columns

You can span columns using either the th or td element, depending on whether you're spanning a table heading or a table cell. The following example shows how to add two cells that each span two columns. Start with the code from the previous section, which includes the spanned row:

1. Add a tr element for the new row.

```
<table>
<tr>
</tr>
<tr>
    <th>Type</th>
    <th>Product</th>
    <th>Purpose</th>
    <th>Industry standard term</th>
</tr>
```

2. Add th or td cells that you want to span. In the sample table, add two th cells—one with the word **Merchandise** and one with the phrase **Descriptive Information**.

```
<table>
<tr>
```

```
        <th>Merchandise</th>
        <th>Descriptive Information</th>
    </tr>
    <tr>
        <th>Type</th>
        <th>Product</th>
        <th>Purpose</th>
        <th>Industry standard term</th>
    </tr>
```

3. Add the colspan attribute to the th or td element that affects the cell you
    want to span. In the sample table, add colspan="2" to both the th elements,
    because each cell should span two columns.

```
    <tr>
        <th colspan="2">Merchandise</th>
        <th colspan="2">Descriptive Information</th>
    </tr>
```

The resulting table, complete with a row span and a column span, should now look
like the one in Figure 6.5.

- -

Design Workshop

You can include both the rowspan *and* colspan attributes in one th or td element. For example, a large or complex table might have two heading rows and two columns with descriptive information, such as the following:

The first cell in the table spans two columns (colspan="2") to cover both category columns. It simultaneously
spans two rows (rowspan="2") to cover both heading rows. No content necessarily fits in this area of the table, so
you might use a logo or some sort of graphic to fill the space attractively.

- -

Adding Captions

A caption is explanatory or descriptive text that usually appears above the table. You use captions for two purposes:

- To summarize table contents

- To provide at-a-glance information about table contents

You should position the caption above the table to ensure that your user sees it. If a table is more than one screen tall, a user might not scroll down to read the caption. Also, you should place the caption element right after the opening table tag. Only one caption element is allowed per table.

You can locate the caption in relation to the table visually by adding the align attribute. The caption can be aligned at the top, bottom, left, or right of the table. (Note that the align attribute is deprecated.) To add a caption to the sample table, follow these steps:

1. Add the caption element between the opening and closing table tags. In the sample table, place the caption element below the opening table tag.

   ```
   <table>
   <caption>
   </caption>
   ```

2. Add caption text, like this:

   ```
   <caption>
   Office Product Merchandise and Category Information
   </caption>
   ```

3. Specify whether the caption should appear above or below the table by using the align="top" or align="bottom" attribute, like this:

   ```
   <caption align="top">
   Office Product Merchandise and Category Information
   </caption>
   ```

4. Optionally, add character-level formatting elements to the caption. (See Chapter 3 for a review of character-level formatting.) Without boldface or italics, the caption is often hard to identify in the table.

   ```
   <caption align="top">
   <b>Office Product Merchandise and Category Information</b>
   </caption>
   ```

The resulting caption looks like Figure 6.6.

Table Sample

	Merchandise	Descriptive Information	
Type	Product	Purpose	Industry standard term
	Binder 1.0	Join multiple objects.	Stapler.
Joining Tools	Organizer 2.2	Join multiple objects for easy access and changing.	Ring binder.
	Combiner 0.9	Join multiple objects at the edges.	Tape.
Dividing Tools	Splitter 3.2	Divide single object into multiple smaller objects.	Scissors.

Office Product Merchandise and Category Information

Figure 6.6 *Table captions provide an at-a-glance summary of table contents.*

Formatting Tables

After you set up a table, you can add formatting options that improve its overall appearance. In particular, you can do the following:

- Add borders
- Include background colors and images
- Adjust cell spacing and padding
- Adjust cell alignment
- Specify cell size
- Specify table alignment

XHTML Opportunities

As you'll see in the next several sections in this chapter, you can add a lot of formatting to tables—backgrounds, borders, colors, alignment, and so on. Keep in mind that many of these options are not standard XHTML and that not all browsers support them. Additionally, XHTML 1 strongly encourages you to use style sheets to apply formatting options, because most of these attributes are deprecated.

If you're certain your users use browsers that support HTML 4 table elements, consider using style sheets to format your tables. Style sheets, which are supported by the HTML 4 specification, are the preferred way to apply styles throughout your XHTML documents—tables included! See Chapter 10 and Master's Reference Part 2 to learn to use style sheets.

Adding and Formatting Borders

Borders are the lines that enclose tables and that clearly separate rows, columns, and cells. By default, most browsers display tables without borders; however, tables that have borders are much easier to read and more attractive. For example, the sample tables shown thus far in this chapter have not had borders and have been rather difficult to read—it's hard to tell where one cell stops and the next begins. Without borders, the cells visually run together, and the columns and rows are somewhat obscured, as you can see back in Figure 6.6.

Creating Table Borders

You specify table borders using an attribute and a number, measured in pixels, that tell browsers the width of the border. As shown in Figure 6.7, most browsers display borders as lines with a 3-D effect. Table 6.4 lists the table border attributes.

Table Sample

Office Product Merchandise and Category Information

Merchandise		Descriptive Information	
Type	Product	Purpose	Industry standard term
Joining Tools	Binder 1.0	Join multiple objects.	Stapler.
	Organizer 2.2	Join multiple objects for easy access and changing.	Ring binder.
	Combiner 0.9	Join multiple objects at the edges.	Tape.
Dividing Tools	Splitter 3.2	Divide single object into multiple smaller objects.	Scissors.

Figure 6.7 *A 2-pixel border added around table cells*

Table 6.4 Table Border Attributes

ATTRIBUTE	SPECIFIES
`border="n"`	A table border width, in pixels. The larger the number, the wider the border. `border="0"` removes borders (generally also the default setting).
`bordercolor="…"`	A color for the table border, as `#rrggbb` number or color name. Supported by newer versions of Netscape Navigator and Internet Explorer; however, it's not part of the XHTML specification.

To create a table border and specify its color, follow these steps:

1. Add the `border` attribute to the opening table tag.

   ```
   <table border="2">
   ```

2. Specify the border color using the `bordercolor` attribute and either an RGB number or an accepted color name. Specifying the border color is not essential—the border will be wider because of the `border="2"` attribute, and the color is simply another formatting characteristic that you can add if you choose.

   ```
   <table border="2" bordercolor="#FF0000">
   ```

Figure 6.7 shows the results of using border="2" in the table element.

See Chapter 5 for more information about RGB color values.

Specifying No Table Borders

Although most browsers display tables without borders by default, you can specify no borders to ensure that no borders display. For example, if you're using tables for advanced formatting such as columns, side headings, or juxtaposed text and graphics, you want to ensure that the table appears without borders. Figures 6.2 through 6.6 are all examples of tables that have no visible borders. To specify no table borders, set the border attribute to zero (0), like this:

```
<table border="0">
```

Using Internet Explorer–Specific Border Attributes

Microsoft has implemented two additional elements in Internet Explorer to control border color. In many browsers, the table borders are presented in 3-D—that is, a darker color at the bottom and right edges, with a lighter color at the top and left, as shown in Figure 6.8.

Table Sample

Office Product Merchandise and Category Information			
Merchandise		**Descriptive Information**	
Type	**Product**	**Purpose**	**Industry standard term**
Joining Tools	Binder 1.0	Join multiple objects.	Stapler.
	Organizer 2.2	Join multiple objects for easy access and changing.	Ring binder.
	Combiner 0.9	Join multiple objects at the edges.	Tape.
Dividing Tools	Splitter 3.2	Divide single object into multiple smaller objects.	Scissors.

Figure 6.8 *Internet Explorer allows you to set different colors for the bevel or shadow effect in table borders.*

Internet Explorer recognizes attributes to set the darker and lighter color of the 3-D effect. Table 6.5 lists these attributes.

These attributes are not part of the XHTML specification. They are proprietary Internet Explorer attributes that may not render correctly in other browsers.

Table 6.5 Internet Explorer Table Border Attributes

ATTRIBUTE	SPECIFIES
bordercolorlight="..."	A light border color (in #rrggbb format) for 3-D effect on tables.
bordercolordark="..."	A dark border color (in #rrggbb format) for 3-D effect on tables.

To apply these attributes, insert them in the opening `table` tag, just as you insert standard border attributes, separately or together. These are all well formed:

```
<table bordercolorlight="CCCCCC">...</table>
<table bordercolordark="33FF33">...</table>
<table bordercolorlight="CCCCCC"
    bordercolordark="33FF33">...</table>
```

If you have specific border color needs and you know that your users will be using Internet Explorer, you can further customize border colors by applying the same attributes to individual table cells.

Setting Table Background Options

In addition to specifying border color, you can specify that the table background appear as a particular color or image. Using a background color or image enhances table appearance, makes the table more interesting, provides a place for corporate logos, and helps contrast text and image colors.

Although these background options will still work in Netscape Navigator and Internet Explorer, consider setting table background colors using style sheets because the XHTML specification deprecates table background options.

Setting a Table Background Color

Only the newer versions of Netscape Navigator and Internet Explorer support table background colors. However, you can provide table background colors and images for Netscape Navigator and Internet Explorer users with no adverse effects on those who use other browsers. For example, Figure 6.9 shows a table that uses a background color viewed in Netscape Navigator. If you display this table in an older browser, the background color will be the same as the background color of the browser.

Figure 6.9 *A color background can enhance a table's appearance when viewed in a browser that supports background colors.*

For background colors to be effective, they must adequately contrast with text color(s); otherwise, the text becomes virtually unreadable, as you can see in Figure 6.10.

Figure 6.10 *Consider your page's text colors when choosing table background colors.*

To ensure that your table background color(s) are effective, follow these guidelines:

- Choose a light background color if your text is dark; choose a dark background color if your text is light.

- Choose colors that are aesthetically pleasing and suit the purpose of your document. For example, if your topic is fast-paced, choose bright colors; if your topic is slower-paced, choose paler colors.

- View your XHTML documents in a few different browsers.

- Choose from one of the 216 nondithering colors.

 As we detailed in Chapter 5, nondithering colors appear solid (not splotchy or spotted) in browsers.

The table background color attribute is `bgcolor="#rrggbb"`, and it's used in the opening `table` element. To use a color throughout the background of the table, add `bgcolor` followed by the RGB number or color name, as in the following:

```
<table bgcolor="#CCFFFF">
```

The table background (not including the borders) will be colored, as in Figure 6.11.

Table Sample

Office Product Merchandise and Category Information

Merchandise		Descriptive Information	
Type	Product	Purpose	Industry standard term
Joining Tools	Binder 1.0	Join multiple objects.	Stapler.
	Organizer 2.2	Join multiple objects for easy access and changing.	Ring binder.
	Combiner 0.9	Join multiple objects at the edges.	Tape.
Dividing Tools	Splitter 3.2	Divide single object into multiple smaller objects.	Scissors.

Figure 6.11 *The resulting table background color*

Setting a Table Background Image

Only the newer versions of Netscape Navigator and Internet Explorer support table background images. Other browsers display the browser's default background color instead of the background image.

 To accommodate users with browsers that do not support background images and users who have image options turned off, use background colors even with background images. Users can then view a table enhanced with color, rather than one that uses the browser's default background color.

Table background images are tiled—that is, they are repeated on the screen until the available background space is filled. Not all browsers tile images in the same way. For example, Figures 6.12 and 6.13 show how earlier versions of Netscape Navigator and Internet Explorer display a table that uses a small pair of scissors as the background image.

![HTML Tables - Netscape browser window showing a table titled "Table Sample" with heading "Office Product Merchandise and Category Information" and a scissors background image]

Merchandise		Descriptive Information		
Type	Product	Purpose		Industry standard term
	Binder 1.0	Join multiple objects.		Stapler.
Joining Tools	Organizer 2.2	Join multiple objects for easy access and changing.		Ring binder.
	Combiner 0.9	Join multiple objects at the edges.		Tape.
Dividing Tools	Splitter 3.2	Divide single object into multiple smaller objects.		Scissors.

Figure 6.12 *A table background image viewed in Netscape Navigator*

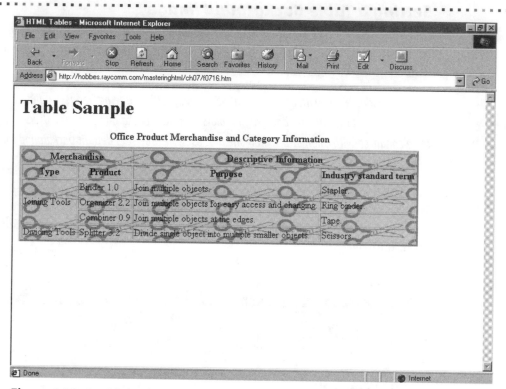

Figure 6.13 *A table background image viewed in Internet Explorer*

Although the image is inappropriately dark and the text is unreadable, the overall effect is quite different in each browser. In Figure 6.12, the tiling restarts at the upper-left corner of *each cell,* and the caption is not considered part of the table for the purpose of background. In Figure 6.13, however, the image is rendered slightly larger and is tiled throughout the table without consideration for individual cells. These differences are not as noticeable in the most recent versions of the browsers (Netscape 6 and Internet Explorer 5.5).

To ensure that the whole image is visible in a table cell (and only once), include the img *element in the table cell, not as a background image.*

Also, as Figures 6.12 and 6.13 show, table background images can easily overpower table content if you use too many shapes, patterns, or colors. The resulting text becomes virtually unreadable.

To ensure that you choose a suitable background image, follow these guidelines:

- Choose small, subtle images that are not essential for conveying information.

- Choose simple background images—ones with few shapes, patterns, or colors.

- Choose background images that enhance the purpose of the document.

- View your XHTML documents in as many browsers as possible.

To indicate a background image in a table, you use the `background` image attribute.

Internet Explorer 3 and newer and Netscape Navigator 4 both support these elements on individual cells as well as for the table as a whole. Add the attribute to the `td` or `th` element, just as you would add it to the `table` element.

Figure 6.14 shows an effective background image. To use a table background image, add `background` followed by the URL, as in the following code:

```
<table background="coolimage.gif">...</table>
```

Table Sample

Office Product Merchandise and Category Information

Merchandise		Descriptive Information	
Type	Product	Purpose	Industry standard term
Joining Tools	Binder 1.0	Join multiple objects.	Stapler.
	Organizer 2.2	Join multiple objects for easy access and changing.	Ring binder.
	Combiner 0.9	Join multiple objects at the edges.	Tape.
Dividing Tools	Splitter 3.2	Divide single object into multiple smaller objects.	Scissors.

Figure 6.14 *An effective table background image enhances the table content.*

Specifying Cell Alignment

Cell alignment refers to the horizontal or vertical alignment of cell contents. Most browsers have the following default cell alignment settings:

- Table *headings* are aligned in the center (horizontally and vertically) in the cell.

- Table *contents* are aligned on the left (horizontally) and center (vertically) in the cell.

Using the attributes described in Table 6.6, you can change the default horizontal and vertical alignment in table cells.

Table 6.6 Table Cell Alignment Attributes

ATTRIBUTE	SPECIFIES
align="…"	Horizontal alignment of cell contents, as left, center, or right.
valign="…"	Vertical alignment of cell contents, as top, middle, bottom, or baseline.

To use these alignment attributes, include them within any tr, td, or th element, as these three examples show:

```
<tr align="right">...</tr>
<td valign="top">...</td>
<th align="center" valign="middle">...</th>
```

You can save some typing by setting the alignment for a row in the tr element, rather than in each individual cell. If you set the alignment in the tr element, you can override it on a cell-by-cell basis in the td or th element.

Specifying Cell Size

Most browsers make cells as large as necessary to hold the contents and wrap text to a new line only after the table is as wide as the browser window and table width settings permit. You can specify cell size to keep the text from wrapping to a new line or to make content easier to read.

Specifying all cell widths decreases perceived download time by allowing some browsers to lay out the table as it arrives, rather than waiting for the whole table to download. The table still takes the same time to download; however, it appears to load faster because it arrives gradually, rather than in one big chunk.

You can specify cell size in two ways:

- As a percentage of the table width
- As a specific size, measured in pixels

Although most browsers support alignment attributes, how they display attributes depends on the table size and other table or cell settings. For example, a cell size that is 50 percent of the table will be wider or narrower, depending on the screen resolution and on the size of the browser window. Likewise, if you set cell width to 100 pixels, it will be exactly that wide in browsers that support cell width tags, regardless of what that does to the overall page layout.

If you can avoid setting specific cell widths in your tables, do so. The more restrictive the table formatting, the less leeway the browser has to reformat the table to fit and the more unpredictable the results.

Use the attributes in Table 6.7 in either the th or td element to control the table width and text wrap.

Table 6.7 Table Width and Text Wrap Attributes

ATTRIBUTE	USE
width="n"	Specifies the width of a cell in either pixels or as a percentage of table width; deprecated.
nowrap="nowrap"	Prohibits text wrapping within the cell, thus requiring all text to appear on one line; deprecated.

The width and nowrap attributes are deprecated in favor of using style sheets. See Chapter 10 for more information on style sheets.

Specifying Cell Width

To specify cell width, simply add the width="n" attribute to the td or th elements. For example, you can specify that a header cell (and, therefore, the cells below it) occupy 15 percent of the table width, like this:

```
<tr>
   <th>Type</th>
   <th>Product</th>
   <th>Purpose</th>
   <th width="15%">Industry standard term</th>
</tr>
```

If you set the `width` in a cell with a `colspan` attribute, similar to the Descriptive Information cell shown in Figure 6.15, the attributes affect individual columns below proportionately.

Table Sample

Office Product Merchandise and Category Information

Merchandise		Descriptive Information	
Type	Product	Purpose	Industry standard term
Joining Tools	Binder 1.0	Join multiple objects.	Stapler.
	Organizer 2.2	Join multiple objects for easy access and changing.	Ring binder.
	Combiner 0.9	Join multiple objects at the edges.	Tape.
Dividing Tools	Splitter 3.2	Divide single object into multiple smaller objects.	Scissors.

Figure 6.15 *The browser determined the sizes of the cells in this table automatically.*

For example, if you add a `width="50%"` to the Descriptive Information cell, the browser attempts to make the columns starting with Purpose and with Industry Standard Term together total approximately 50 percent.

```
<tr>
  <th colspan="2">Merchandise</th>
  <th colspan="2" width="50%">Descriptive Information</th>
</tr>
```

Figure 6.16 shows the resulting table.

Table Sample

Office Product Merchandise and Category Information

Merchandise		Descriptive Information	
Type	Product	Purpose	Industry standard term
Joining Tools	Binder 1.0	Join multiple objects.	Stapler.
	Organizer 2.2	Join multiple objects for easy access and changing.	Ring binder.
	Combiner 0.9	Join multiple objects at the edges.	Tape.
Dividing Tools	Splitter 3.2	Divide single object into multiple smaller objects.	Scissors.

Figure 6.16 *Combine cell size and column span attributes to customize your tables.*

Specifying No Text Wraps

If you reset the width of certain cells, you may want to ensure that the contents do not wrap to multiple lines. Note that nowrap is also a stand-alone attribute and, as such, it must be set equal to itself as indicated in the XHTML specification. Add the nowrap attribute, as in the following example, to encourage the browser not to break the line.

```
<th colspan="2" width="30%" nowrap="nowrap">Descriptive
    Information</th>
```

To set a minimum size for a cell, smaller than which it cannot be displayed, use a transparent GIF image 1 pixel × 1 pixel in size with height and width attributes set to the necessary size.

Adding Cell Spacing and Padding

Cell spacing and padding refer to how much white space appears in a table. In particular, *cell spacing* refers to the spacing between cells, and *cell padding* refers to spacing between cell contents and cell borders.

For many tables, open space around cell contents makes the table much easier to read and more aesthetically pleasing. Table 6.8 describes cell spacing and cell padding attributes.

Table 6.8 Table Cell Spacing and Padding Attributes

ATTRIBUTE	SPECIFIES
cellspacing="n"	Amount of space between cells, in pixels.
cellpadding="n"	Amount of space between cell contents and cell borders, in pixels.

If the table has a border, the cellspacing *attribute enlarges the rule between cells. If there is no border, the space between adjacent cells will simply be somewhat larger.*

To add cell spacing and padding, include the attributes in the table element, like this:

```
<table cellspacing="5" cellpadding="5" border="3">...</table>
```

The resulting table will look like Figure 6.17. As you can see, there is more white space around the text.

Office Product Merchandise and Category Information

Merchandise		Descriptive Information	
Type	Product	Purpose	Industry standard term
Joining Tools	Binder 1.0	Join multiple objects.	Stapler.
	Organizer 2.2	Join multiple objects for easy access and changing.	Ring binder.
	Combiner 0.9	Join multiple objects at the edges.	Tape.
Dividing Tools	Splitter 3.2	Divide single object into multiple smaller objects.	Scissors.

Figure 6.17 *The* cellspacing *and* cellpadding *attributes can increase space between and within table cells.*

Specifying Table Alignment, Width, and Text Wrap

So far in this chapter, most of the elements and attributes have specified the relationship of the table contents to each other or to other table components. However, table width, alignment, and wrap settings specify how the table fits into the XHTML document as a whole.

These settings are important for two reasons:

- Browser and computer settings vary significantly from computer to computer. By using width, alignment, and wrap attributes, you help ensure that your users can easily view your tables.

- By default, text that surrounds tables does not wrap—it stops above the table and starts below the table. The table itself takes up the full browser width. These attributes narrow the space that the table uses and allow the text to wrap around the table.

Table 6.9 describes the table width, alignment, and wrap attributes.

The align *and* clear *attributes are deprecated in favor of using style sheets. See Chapter 10 for more information on using style sheets.*

Table 6.9 Table Width, Alignment, and Wrap Attributes

ATTRIBUTE	USE
width="n"	Specifies table width, in pixels or as a percentage of the window width.
align="…"	Specifies table alignment, as left, center, right, and, for Internet Explorer only, bleedleft, bleedright, and justify; deprecated.
clear="…"	Specifies that new text following the table should appear below the table, when the left, right, all, or no margins are clear (unobstructed by the table); deprecated.

To use any of these attributes, insert them in the opening table tag. The following code uses the width attribute to set the table width to 600 pixels:

```
<table border="3" width="600">...</table>
```

However, as a rule, setting your table width to a percentage of the browser window—not to a fixed number of pixels—results in a more reliable display. For example, if you set the table width to a size wider than users have available, the table could easily run off the edge of the browser window and require them to scroll horizontally.

To restrict the width of the table (for example, to allow text to wrap around it), use percentages, as in the following example:

```
<table border="3" width="70%">...</table>
```

Aligning the table to the left, right, or center is as easy as adding another attribute to the table, as in the following:

```
<table border="3" width="70%" align="right">...</table>
```

When you use these attributes and make the table substantially narrower than the window, you may also have to contend with unwanted text wrapping. For example, the preceding line of code causes text following the table to wind up on the left of the right-aligned table, as in Figure 6.18.

Table Sample

The accompanying table provides basic information about our products. If you have any questions, please contact us and we'll be happy to provide more information.

Office Product Merchandise and Category Information				
Merchandise		Descriptive Information		
Type	Product		Purpose	Industry standard term
Joining Tools	Binder 1.0		Join multiple objects.	Stapler.
	Organizer 2.2		Join multiple objects for easy access and changing.	Ring binder.
	Combiner 0.9		Join multiple objects at the edges.	Tape.
Dividing Tools	Splitter 3.2		Divide single object into multiple smaller objects.	Scissors.

Figure 6.18 *Text wrapping sometimes causes unusual effects.*

Using XHTML Table Features

The table features discussed in this section were introduced with HTML 4 and have carried over into XHTML. These features give you added control over formatting tables. Instead of formatting the table as a whole, you can format specific table parts, such as the table head, body, footer, and column groups. You can also format tables using style sheets, which we recommend.

You can use XHTML table elements to format portions of the table separately—as sections, rather than as individual cells. For example, you can do the following:

- Group similar areas of tables and add borders around the areas.

- Add lines or text formatting to table headings.

- Include a table footer, which is handy if a table has totals at the bottom of the columns.

- Use these additional elements as hooks for style sheets to get into more sophisticated formatting. All style elements can be used with these elements.

See Chapter 10 for more about style sheets.

For example, Figure 6.19 uses XHTML table elements and attributes to create two main columns (Merchandise and Descriptive Information) that group the other columns (Type, Product, Purpose, Industry standard term), and to include two rows of headers.

XHTML table elements work in conjunction with standard table elements—that is, you develop tables using the standard elements, and then you add the XHTML table elements and attributes. The result is that users using the newest browsers can view the XHTML effects and users of other browsers can still view the basic table.

To apply XHTML table elements and attributes, follow these general steps, which are described in detail in the next two sections:

1. Identify table sections.

2. Apply borders and rules to table sections.

Table Sample

Main column groups ⎯
Header ⎯

Office Product Merchandise and Category Information			
Merchandise		Descriptive Information	
Type	Product	Purpose	Industry standard term
Joining Tools	Binder 1.0	Join multiple objects.	Stapler.
	Organizer 2.2	Join multiple objects for easy access and changing.	Ring binder.
	Combiner 0.9	Join multiple objects at the edges.	Tape.
Dividing Tools	Splitter 3.2	Divide single object into multiple smaller objects.	Scissors.

Figure 6.19 *You can use advanced table elements to group table parts.*

Identifying Table Sections

The first step in using XHTML tables is identifying table sections by grouping similar table parts and identifying each part as being part of the table heading, body, footer, or columns. Table 6.10 describes advanced table elements.

Table 6.10 Advanced Table Elements

Element	Use
thead	Labels the header area of a table.
tbody	Labels the body area of table.
tfoot	Labels the footer area of table.
colgroup	Identifies column groups within a table.
col	Identifies columns in a table within a column group. This is an empty element.

Identifying Row Groups

Row groups include parts such as the header, body, and footer—the table parts that contain table rows. To identify row groups, start with the standard table elements and then include the XHTML table elements around them. Take a look at the following code, which nests the standard table elements within the table header element (<thead>...</thead>):

```
<thead>
<tr>
   <th colspan="2">Merchandise</th>
   <th colspan="2">Descriptive Information</th>
</tr>
<tr>
   <th>Type</th>
   <th>Product</th>
   <th>Purpose</th>
   <th>Industry standard term</th>
</tr>
</thead>
```

You can also identify table body parts by using the **tbody** element, like this:

```
<tbody>
<tr>
   <td rowspan="3">Joining Tools</td>
   <td>Binder 1.0</td>
```

```
      <td>Join multiple objects.</td>
      <td>Stapler.</td>
   </tr>
   <tr>
      <td>Organizer 2.2</td>
      <td>Join multiple objects for easy access and changing.</td>
      <td>Ring binder.</td>
   </tr>
   <tr>
      <td>Combiner 0.9</td>
      <td>Join multiple objects at the edges.</td>
      <td>Tape.</td>
   </tr>
   <tr>
      <td>Dividing Tools</td>
      <td>Splitter 3.2</td>
      <td>Divide single object into multiple smaller objects.</td>
      <td>Scissors.</td>
   </tr>
</tbody>
```

Finally, you can identify a table footer by using the tfoot element in the same way. The tfoot element must follow the thead element and *precede* the tbody element.

```
<tfoot>
<tr>
   <td>Tool Combo</td>
   <td>All</td>
   <td>Use for all office needs.</td>
   <td>N/A</td>
</tr>
</tfoot>
```

At this point, the advanced table won't look any different from the standard table. After you've tagged your table with these additional table tags, you can either identify column groups or format the tagged parts with the advanced formatting elements.

Identifying Column Groups

In addition to identifying table headers, body, and footers, you can identify column groups. The colgroup element, which is used in conjunction with the span attribute, is located at the beginning of the table and announces the columns to which it applies. You can also use the width, align, char, charoff, and valign attributes with the colgroup element.

The table shown in Figure 6.7, earlier in this chapter, contains two distinct groups of columns, with two columns in each. Therefore, there will be two colgroup elements with span="2" attributes in each. We also want all these columns to align to the left, as shown in the following example:

```
<caption align="top"><b>Office Product Merchandise and Category
    Information</b></caption>
<colgroup span="2" align="left"></colgroup>
<colgroup span="2" align="left"></colgroup>
<thead>...</thead>
```

Identifying Columns within colgroups

The col empty element allows you to apply formatting to individual columns in a column group (colgroup). For example, in the previous example, we have two colgroups of two columns each all aligned to the left. Let's say we want the first column in the first group to be centered and the second column to be aligned to the left. The markup would look like this:

```
<colgroup>
<col align="center" />
<col align="left" />
</colgroup>
<colgroup span="2" align="left">...</colgroup>
```

XHTML Table Borders

You can use XHTML's formatting capabilities to create custom table borders—called *rules*—which apply to specified sections of the table. Rather than applying borders to an entire table, which is all you can do with standard table capabilities, you can apply borders just to the table heading, body, footer, or specific columns. Table 6.11 describes the advanced table formatting attributes.

Table 6.11 Advanced Table Formatting Attributes

ATTRIBUTE	USE
frame="…"	Specifies the outside edges of the table that will have a border. Possible choices include border (the default), void (no borders), above, below, hsides (top and bottom), lhs (left hand side), rhs (right hand side), vsides (left and right), and box (all sides).
rules="…"	Specifies which internal borders of the table are displayed. none, groups (rules between table groups such as thead, tbody, tfoot, colgroup), rows (rules between table rows), cols (rules between table columns), all.
cols="…"	Specifies the number of columns in the table.

To format the identified table parts, include these attributes in the table element by following these general steps:

1. Add an outside border (the frame) by adding the frame attribute to the table element, like this:

   ```
   <table frame="box">…</table>
   ```

You can still control the border width with the border attribute, covered earlier in this chapter. For example, to set the outside border to 3 pixels wide, the opening table tag would look like this: <table frame="box" border="3">. The border attribute in the table element affects only the width of the outside border, not the width of the internal rules.

2. Add inside borders (called rules) by adding the rules attribute to the table element, like this:

   ```
   <table frame="hsides" rules="none" border="3">…</table>
   ```

The resulting table looks like Figure 6.20, when viewed in Internet Explorer. If you look carefully at Figure 6.20, you'll notice a thin line above the table footer—that's part of the footer formatting, just as the boldface is part of the th formatting.

Table Sample

Office Product Merchandise and Category Information

Merchandise		Descriptive Information	
Type	Product	Purpose	Industry standard term
	Binder 1.0	Join multiple objects.	Stapler.
Joining Tools	Organizer 2.2	Join multiple objects for easy access and changing.	Ring binder.
	Combiner 0.9	Join multiple objects at the edges.	Tape.
Dividing Tools	Splitter 3.2	Divide single object into multiple smaller objects.	Scissors.
Tool Combo	All	Use for all office needs.	N/A

The accompanying table provides basic information about our products. If you have any questions, please contact us and we'll be happy to provide more information.

Figure 6.20 *You use advanced tables to be creative with table design and rules.*

To insert a rule between the groups you defined in the table, add `rules="groups"`. *This is an effective technique, as is* `rules="rows"`.

Additionally, you can specify the number of columns in the table to decrease the perceived download and redraw time. Doing so has no effect on the visual appearance of the table, but still allows the browser to lay out the table more quickly. To use this trick, add the `cols` attribute to the `table` element, like this:

```
<table cols="4">...</table>
```

Because tables are laid out as soon as the whole table is downloaded to the browser (rather than line by line as with regular text), using multiple, smaller tables will improve the perceived download time.

Design Workshop: Creating Newspaper-Style Headings

Here's a handy formatting trick. Use tables to set up a heading with several columns of text below it—like a newspaper:

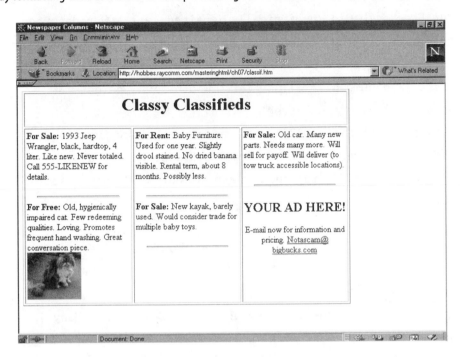

The XHTML that produces this effect follows.

```
<!DOCTYPE html PUBLIC "-//W3C//DTD XHTML 1.0 Transitional//EN"
    "http://www.w3.org/TR/xhtml1/DTD/xhtml1-transitional.dtd">
<html xmlns="http://www.w3.org/1999/xhtml">
<head><title>Newspaper Columns</title></head>
<body bgcolor="FFFFFF" text="000000" link="0000FF"
    vlink="800080" alink="FF0000">
<table cellpadding="3" cellspacing="3" border="1" width="80%">
<tr><td valign="middle" align="center" colspan="3">
    <h1>Classy Classifieds</h1></td></tr>
<tr><td valign="top" width="120"><b>For Sale:</b> 1993 Jeep
```

```
        Wrangler, black, hardtop, 4 liter. Like new. Never
        totaled. Call 555-LIKENEW for details.<br />
<hr width="80%" />
<b>For Free: </b>Old, hygienically impaired cat. Few redeeming
    qualities. Loving. Promotes frequent hand washing. Great
    conversation piece.
<img src="winthumb.gif" align="left" width="100" height="88"
    border="0" alt="Winchester" /></td>
<td valign="top" width="120"><b>For Rent:</b> Baby Furniture.
    Used for one year. Slightly drool stained. No dried
    banana visible. Rental term, about 8 months. Possibly less.
    <br />
<hr width="80%" />
<b>For Sale:</b> New kayak, barely used. Would consider trade
    for multiple baby toys. <br />
<hr width="80%" /></td>
<td valign="top" width="120"><b>For Sale:</b> Old car. Many
    new parts. Needs many more. Will sell for payoff. Will
    deliver (to tow truck accessible locations). <br />
<hr width="80%" />
<center><h2>YOUR AD HERE!</h2>
    E-mail now for information and pricing.
<a href="mailto:Notascam@bigbucks.com">
    Notascam@<br />bigbucks.com</a></center>
</tr></td>
</table>
</body>
</html>
```

Feel free to take this example and adapt it for your own needs. It contains many of the elements and concepts discussed in this chapter.

Where to Go from Here

This chapter showed you how to develop and format standard HTML tables plus tables built with XHTML elements and attributes. If you know how to develop tables, you can effectively present complex data and create interesting page layouts. From here, check out these chapters:

- Check out Chapter 3 for general formatting and design topics.

- See Chapter 10 and Master's Reference Part 2 for complete information about creating and applying style sheets.

- Look at Chapter 5 to see how to include images and use colors wisely.

- See Chapter 8 to see how to create XHTML frames.

- See Master's Reference Part 1 for more table options.

Developing
XHTML Forms

Chapter 7

When you submit credit card information to purchase something online, search the Web with AltaVista or Hot-Bot, participate in a Web-based chat room, or even select a line from a Web-page drop-down menu, you're using a form. Within the scope of plain XHTML—as opposed to extensions such as JavaScript, Java applets, and other embedded programs—forms are the only method of two-way communication between Web browsers and Web sites.

Perhaps because of the name, XHTML developers tend to assume that forms are just for collecting pages of data. In fact, you can use forms to get any kind of information from users without giving them the feeling of "filling out a form." A form is often as simple as a blank entry field and a Submit button.

In this chapter, we'll look at how to develop forms using standard elements and attributes, which virtually all browsers support. We'll develop a form piece by piece, including the following essential tasks in using forms effectively:

- Determining the form content

- Starting a form

- Adding Submit and Reset buttons

- Including check boxes, radio buttons, and other input fields

- Using text areas and select fields

- Processing forms

Determining Form Content

The first step in developing a form is determining which information to include and how to present it, that is, how to break it into manageable pieces. You then need to ensure that users can easily provide the information you want from them, which means that your form needs to be both functional and visually appealing.

Information Issues

When deciding which information to include and how to break it down, consider your purposes for creating the form. You might begin by answering these questions:

- What information do I want? Customer contact information? Only e-mail addresses so I can contact users later? Opinions about the site?

- Why will users access the form? To order something online? To request information? To submit comments or questions about products or services?

- What information can users readily provide? Contact information? Description of their product use? Previous purchases?

- How much time are users willing to spend filling out the form? Would they be willing to describe something in a paragraph or two, or would they just want to select from a list?

After determining what information you want and what information your users are willing to provide, break the information into the smallest chunks possible. For example, if you want users to provide contact information, divide contact information into name, street address, and city/state/postal code. You could even go a step further and collect the city, state, and postal code as separate items so you can sort data according to customers in a particular area, for example. If you don't collect these items separately, you won't be able to sort on them individually.

 Although it's possible to go back and change forms after you implement them, careful planning will save a lot of trouble and work later. For example, if you complete and implement a form and then discover that you forgot to request key information, the initial responses to the form will be less useful or skew the resulting data. Fixing the form takes nearly as much time as doing it carefully at first.

Our sample site, ASR Outfitters, includes a form on its Web site to collect targeted addresses for future product and sale announcements. Although ASR could just as easily (but not as cheaply) use regular mailings by purchasing mailing lists, a Web site form avoids the cost of traditional mailings, collects information from specifically interested users, and keeps the Internet-based company focused on the Web.

Because filling out a Web page form takes some time, ASR created a form, shown in Figure 7.1, that includes only the essentials.

Figure 7.1 *ASR Outfitters' form collects only the basic demographic and marketing information.*

In this case, a little demographic information is needed:

First name   This is necessary to help personalize responses.

Last name   This is also necessary to help personalize responses.

E-mail address   Collecting this information is the main purpose of the form.

Street address, city, state, postal code   These are all necessary for future snail mailings and demographic analysis. Collecting the address, even with no immediate intent to use it, is probably a wise move, because it would be difficult to ask customers for more information later.

Online purchasing habits   ASR wants to learn about the possible acceptance rate for taking orders over the Web.

Areas of interest   ASR wants to find out about the customer's interests to determine areas in which to expand its online offerings.

Referral   The marketing department wants to know how the audience found the Web site.

Other comments   It's always important to give users an opportunity to provide additional information. You may want to limit the space for these comments, so the person who has to read them doesn't have to read a novel's worth of information.

Usability Issues

Usability, as it applies to forms, refers to how easily your users can answer your questions. Most online forms require some user action and usually offer no concrete benefit or reward for the users' efforts. Therefore, if forms are not easy to use, you won't get many (or any) responses. Here are some usability guidelines to consider when creating forms.

Group Similar Categories

When you group similar categories, as shown in Figure 7.1, the form appears less daunting, and users are more likely to fill it out and submit it. ASR can group the information it's soliciting from users into three main categories:

- Contact information
- Purchasing habits and areas of interest
- Referrals and other information

Make the Form Easy

If you've ever completed a long form, you know how tedious it can be. Think of a tax form for an example of how *not* to do it. Although the specifics depend greatly on the information you'll be collecting, the following principles remain constant:

- Whenever possible, provide a list from which users can choose one or more items. Lists are easy to use, and they result in easy-to-process information.

- If you can't provide a list, ask users to fill in only a small amount of text. Again, this takes minimal time, and it provides you with data that is fairly easy to process.

- Only ask users to fill in large areas of text if it's absolutely necessary, because large blocks of text take a lot of time to enter for the user and for you to process. Additionally, many users are likely to ignore a request that requires them to enter a great deal of information.

For more information about how to create lists and areas to fill in, see the section "Creating Forms," later in this chapter.

Provide Incentives

Provide users with incentives to fill out the form and submit it. Offer them something, even if its value is marginal. Studies show that a penny or a stamp included in mailed surveys often significantly improves the response rate. Consider offering a chance in a drawing for a free product, an e-mailed list of tips and tricks, or a discount on services.

ASR Outfitters could have offered anything from a free tote bag, to an e-mailed collection of hiking tips, to a discount on the next purchase, but chose to settle for a small coupon book available on the next visit to the store.

Most drawings and giveaways are legally binding in some way, and you need to be sure of their legal standing.

Design Issues

Perhaps because of the need to address all the technical issues, Web authors often neglect design issues. However, a well-designed form encourages users to give you the information you want.

*For how to incorporate sound Web design on your site, check out **Effective Web Design** by Ann Navarro (Sybex, 2001).*

What constitutes good form design? Good form design is something visually appealing, graphically helpful, and consistent with the remainder of the site. A form at an intranet site that has a white background and minimal graphics and that is managed by conservative supervisors would likely have a simple, vertical design and be none the worse for it. However, a visually interesting or highly graphical Web site calls for a form in keeping with the overall theme.

Although the visual interest of the form should not overwhelm the rest of the page, you'll want to make judicious use of color, alignment, small images, and font characteristics. Here are some guidelines:

- Use headings to announce each new group of information. This helps users move easily through the form.

- Be sure to visually separate groups. This makes the forms easier to use because sections become shorter and easier to wade through. You can use horizontal rules or the `fieldset` element in XHTML to do this.

- Use text emphases to draw the audience to important information. Use emphases sparingly; emphasize only a few words so that they stand out on the page.

- Specify how users should move through the form. Don't make your users scroll horizontally to access information. Consider making a narrow, longer form rather than a wider, shorter form to accommodate users who have lower monitor resolution. If your survey is in multiple columns, make different categories visually obvious.

- Use arrows to help users move through the page in a specified order.

- Be sure that it's clear which check boxes and fields go with the associated descriptive information. For example, if you have a long row of check boxes and labels, it's fairly confusing to figure out whether the check box goes with the text on the right or the text on the left. Use line breaks and spacing to clearly differentiate.

- Specify which fields are optional and which are required. One way to do this is to put optional fields after the required ones. Some browsers and processing programs reject incorrectly filled out or incomplete forms.

- Use a background image. Forms with some texture tend to be less form-ish and friendlier. However, be sure that the image doesn't outweigh the content and that the text adequately contrasts with the image so the text is not difficult to read.

- Make all the text-entry fields the same width and put them on the left if you have a vertical column of name and address information. This allows all the text to align vertically and looks much better. If the text labels go on the left, the fields will not (cannot) align vertically and, therefore, will look more random and less professional.

Check out Master's Reference Part 1 for a comprehensive list of form elements and attributes.

Creating Forms

Forms have two basic parts:

- The part you can see, which a user fills out

- The part you can't see, which specifies how the server should process the information

In this section, we'll show you how to create the part that you can see. We'll show you how to create the other part later in the section "Processing Forms."

Hand-Code Forms or Use a WYSIWYG Editor?

You can create forms using any HTML development tools—alone or in combination. For example, if you plan to develop a lot of forms, you might consider using a WYSIWYG ("what you see is what you get") editor to create the basic form. These editors don't produce consistently good results, but they help ensure that you don't leave out any elements or necessary attributes. You can then manually modify the formatting as necessary. However, if you'll only be doing one or two forms, creating them manually or with the help of a code-based editor is more than adequate and is probably easier than learning how to use a WYSIWYG editor effectively.

Understanding Widgets

Forms consist of several types of widgets, also called *controls*, which are fields you can use to collect data, including:

Submit and Reset buttons   send the form information to the server for processing and return the form to its original settings.

Text fields   are areas for brief text input. Use these for several-word responses, such as names, search terms, or addresses.

Select lists   are sets from which users can choose one or more items. Use them to present a long but finite list of choices—for example, choosing a state or province from a list, or choosing one of 17 options.

Check boxes   allow users to select none, one, or several items from a list. Use them to elicit multiple answers. For example, ASR Outfitters used check boxes to get information about the activities of its customers.

Radio buttons   give users an opportunity to choose only one item—for example, gender, a preference, or anything else that can be only one way.

Text areas   are areas for lengthy text input, as in open-ended comments or free-form responses.

Figure 7.2 shows a sample form that includes these widgets.

Which Widgets Are Best?

When deciding which widget to use, consider the information you want to collect. For example, start by seeing whether you can collect pieces of information using check boxes and radio buttons. These are generally the easiest to use because they specify the options and require only the click of a mouse. Then, look for places you can use select lists, which are also easy to use. Finally, include text areas only if users need to respond in their own words.

In general, radio buttons, check boxes, and select lists are all better choices for accepting input than text areas. If users are selecting choices from a list, you don't need to be concerned with misspellings, inconsistent answers, or free-form answers that don't fit the categories. If you can provide choices and let users choose from among them, do so.

Figure 7.2 *Forms give users different ways of entering information.*

Creating a Form and Adding Submit and Reset Buttons

The first step in creating a form is to insert the form element and add Submit and Reset buttons. Submit and Reset buttons are essential components because they allow users to submit information and, if necessary, clear selections. Although you must add other form fields before the form will do anything worthwhile, the Submit button is the key that makes the form go somewhere.

Forms require two form element attributes (action and method) to specify what happens to the form results and which program on the server will process them. We'll look at these attributes in the section "Processing Forms," later in this chapter.

Table 7.1 lists and describes the basic form button elements. (See Table 7.2 for more attributes to use with the input element.)

Table 7.1 Basic Elements for Form Buttons

ELEMENT	PROVIDES
`<input type="submit" value="..." />`	A Submit button for a form. The `value` attribute produces text on the button.
`<input type="image" name="..." src="url" />`	A graphical Submit button. The `src` attribute indicates the image source file.
`<input type="reset" value="..." />`	A Reset button for a form. The `value` attribute produces text on the button.

In the following example, we'll create a form for the ASR Outfitters site as we show you how to start a form and then add Submit and Reset buttons. The code in Listing 7.1 produces the page shown in Figure 7.3.

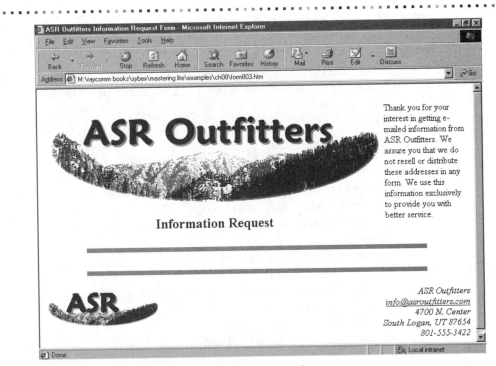

Figure 7.3 The ASR Outfitters form page, sans form

LISTING 7.1: THE ASR OUTFITTERS INFORMATION PAGE, WITHOUT FORM

```
<!DOCTYPE html PUBLIC ".//W3C/DTD XHTML 1.0 Transitional//EN"
  "http://www.w3.org/TR/xhtml1/DTD/xhtml1-transitional.dtd">
<html xmlns="http://www.w3.org/1999/xhtml">
<head>
  <title>ASR Outfitters Information Request Form</title>
</head>
<body background="" bgcolor="#ffffff" text="#000000"
      link="#0000ff" vlink="#800080" alink="#ff0000">
  <table>
    <tr>
      <td valign="top">
        <center>
          <img src="asrlogo.gif" alt="ASR Outfitters Logo"
           width="604" height="192" border="0" /><br />
          <font size="7" face="Times New Roman">
          <h2>Information Request</h2></font>
        </center>
      </td>
      <td>
        <font size="3" face="Times New Roman">
Thank you for your interest in getting e-mailed information
from ASR Outfitters. We assure you that we do not resell or
distribute these addresses in any form. We use this information
exclusively to provide you with better service.</font>
      </td>
    </tr>
  </table>
  <hr width="80%" size="8" noshade="noshade" />
  <hr width="80%" size="8" noshade="noshade" />
  <img src="asrlogosm.gif" align="left" width="200" height="84"
    border="0" alt="ASR Small Logo" />
  <div align="right">
    <address>
      <font face="Times New Roman">
        <br />ASR Outfitters<br />
        <a href="mailto:info@asroutfitters.com">
        info@asroutfitters.com</a><br />
        4700 N. Center<br />
        South Logan, UT 87654<br />
```

```
        801-555-3422<br />
      </font>
    </address>
  </div>
</body>
</html>
```

To add a form to the page, follow these steps:

1. Add the form element where you want the form. We're going to put ours between the horizontal rules.

    ```
    <hr width="80%" size="8" noshade="noshade" />
    <form>
    </form>
    <hr width="80%" size="8" noshade="noshade" />
    ```

 You can avoid problems with your forms by properly nesting your form within other objects in the form. Be careful to place the form outside paragraphs, lists, and other structural elements. For example, you do not want to open a table within the form and close it after the end of the form. Also, be sure to test your forms carefully.

2. Create a Submit button by adding the input empty element, the type="submit" attribute, and the value attribute. Although the Submit button traditionally goes at the bottom of the form (immediately above the closing form tag), it can go anywhere in the form. You can set the text on the face of the Submit button to any text you want—simply substitute your text for the text in the value attribute (just be sure it's still obvious that this button submits something).

    ```
    <form>
    <input type="submit" value="Submit" />
    </form>
    ```

3. Create a Reset button by adding the input empty element, the type="reset" attribute, and the value attribute. Again, although the Reset button traditionally goes at the bottom of the form with the Submit button, immediately above the closing form tag, it can go anywhere in the form. The Reset button can have any text on its face, based on the value attribute. The following example has Start Over on the face.

```
<form>
<input type="submit" value="Submit" />
<input type="reset" value="Start Over" />
</form>
```

Figure 7.4 shows what the buttons look like in a completed form.

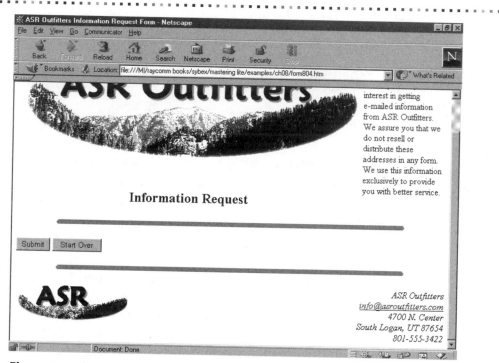

Figure 7.4 *The Submit and Reset (Start Over) buttons are added to the form.*

You cannot control button size directly—the length of the text determines the size of the button.

If the appearance of your form is extremely important to you, consider using a graphical Submit button. However, be sure that your users are using browsers that can handle these buttons. Using images for Submit buttons can cause unexpected or unwanted results in older browsers; for example, they crash old versions of Netscape Navigator. Consider using browser-detection scripts to improve your success with image-based Submit buttons. (See Chapter 5 for information about including images.)

*If you use something other than a submit button (one that says **Submit** on it), be sure it's obvious what it is supposed to be.*

If you want to use an image for your Submit button, substitute the following code for the Submit button (substituting your own image for submitbutton.gif):

```
<input type="image" name="point" src="submitbutton.gif" />
```

The type="image" attribute specifies that an image is used to submit the form when clicked. The name="point" attribute specifies that the *x,y* coordinates where the mouse is located will be returned to the server when the image is clicked. Finally, the src attribute works just as it does with regular images.

Figure 7.5 shows the complete ASR Outfitters form with a graphical Submit button. This button is in the same style as the images from the ASR Outfitters home page, developed in Chapter 5. Using similar images throughout a Web site helps maintain consistency. For more information about creating a coherent Web site, see Chapter 14.

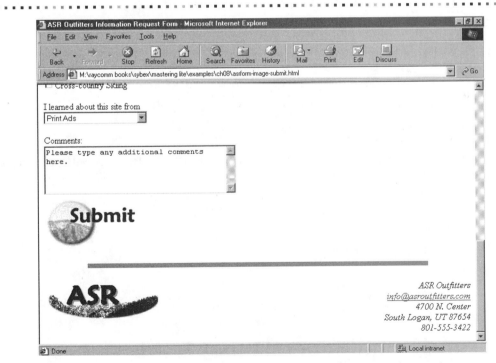

Figure 7.5 *Graphical Submit buttons can make your form more interesting.*

XHTML makes no provision for a Reset button with an image; therefore, if you choose to use an image for your Submit button, dispense with a Reset button. If you don't, you'll have to deal with the potentially poor combination of an image and a standard Reset button.

XHTML Opportunities

If your users are using browsers that comply with HTML 4 and later versions, you can use the `button` element to create a button that you can include instead of or in conjunction with Submit and Reset buttons. Buttons created with the `button` element have no specific action associated with them, as the Submit and Reset buttons do. However, if you're so inclined, you can link the button to JavaScript. Doing so gives you all sorts of functional and flashy possibilities (see Chapter 11).

To provide a Submit button using the `button` element, use code similar to the following:

```
<button type="submit" value="submit" name="submit">
    Click to Submit Form
</button>
```

To provide a graphical Reset button using the `button` element, use code similar to the following:

```
<button type="reset" value="reset" name="reset">
    <img src="gifs/resetbuttonnew.gif" alt="Reset button" />
</button>
```

If you want to use a `button` element to call a script that, for example, verifies a form's contents, you might use something like this:

```
<button type="button" value="verify" name="verify"
    onclick="verify(this.form)">
    Click to Verify Form
</button>
```

Including General Input Fields

You can also develop other types of input fields using various attributes in the `input` element, an empty element that sets an area in a form for user input. Table 7.2 shows the most frequently used attributes of the `input` element. (See Master's Reference Part 1 for a complete listing of attributes you can use with the `input` empty element.)

Table 7.2 Most Common Input Field Attributes

ATTRIBUTE	USE
`accept="…"`	Specifies the acceptable MIME types for file uploads. Wildcards are acceptable, as in `accept="image/*"`.
`maxlength="n"`	Sets the maximum number of characters that can be submitted. Use this attribute with text fields.
`name="…"`	Processes form results.
`selected="selected"`	Indicates the default selection to be presented when the form is initially loaded or reset.
`size="n"`	Sets the visible size for a field. The number *n* equals characters with text input fields and pixels in other fields.
`type="…"`	Sets the type of input field. Possible values are `text`, `password`, `checkbox`, `radio`, `file`, `hidden`, `image`, `submit`, `button`, and `reset`.
`value="…"`	Provides content associated with `name="…"`. Use this attribute with radio buttons and check boxes because they do not accept other input. You can also use this attribute with text fields to provide initial input.

Text Fields

A text field is a blank area within a form and is the place for user-supplied information. As you can see, text fields are commonly used for a name, an e-mail address, and so on:

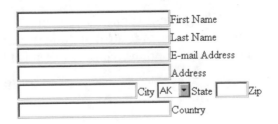

To add a text field to an existing form, follow these steps:

1. Add an `input` element where you want the field.

   ```
   <form>
   <input />
   </form>
   ```

2. Specify the type of input field. In this case, use `type="text"`.

   ```
   <form>
   <input type="text" />
   </form>
   ```

3. Add the `name` attribute to label the content. For example, one of the first fields in the ASR Outfitters form is for the first name of a user; therefore, the field name is `firstname`.

   ```
   <input type="text" name="firstname" />
   ```

The values for name *should be unique within the form. Multiple forms on the same site (or even on the same page) can share values, but if different fields share the same* name *value, the results will be unpredictable.*

4. Specify the size of the field in the form by including the `size` attribute. Although this is optional, you can ensure your user has ample space and can make similar text fields the same size. For example, 30 is a generous size for a name, but still not overwhelmingly large, even on a low-resolution monitor.

   ```
   <input type="text" name="firstname" size="30" />
   ```

5. Add the `maxlength` attribute if you want to limit the number of characters your users can provide (for example, if the field passes into an existing database with length restrictions). Keep in mind that `maxlength` settings should not be less than the `size` attribute; otherwise, your users will be confused when they can't continue typing to the end of the field.

   ```
   <input type="text" name="firstname" size="30"
     maxlength="30" />
   ```

6. Add text outside the `input` field to indicate the information your user should provide. Remember that the name of the field is not visible in the browser; up to this point, you've created a blank area within the form, but you have not labeled that area in any way. You may also want to add a `br` element because the `input` element doesn't insert line breaks.

```
<input type="text" name="firstname" size="30"
    maxlength="30" />First Name<br />
```

Figure 7.6 shows the resulting text field in the context of the form. Use the same process to add other text fields.

Figure 7.6 *Users can enter information in text fields.*

Guidelines for Including Multiple Text Fields

As a rule, forms are much more attractive if the fields are aligned. If they're nearly, but not exactly, aligned, the form looks sloppy, just as a misaligned paper form looks sloppy.

Here are some guidelines to follow when you include multiple text fields in your form:

- Place the fields at the left margin of your page, followed by the descriptive text. If you place the descriptive text (such as "First Name" or "Last Name") to the left of the fields, the fields will not line up vertically. Alternatively, consider putting your form fields and descriptive text in a table so you can ensure that the rows and columns are evenly aligned. Set the text fields to the same size, when appropriate. Of course, you wouldn't set the field for entering an official state abbreviation to 30 characters, but there's no reason that first name, last name, and company name couldn't all be the same length.

- As you add descriptive labels, remember to also add line breaks (`<br />` or `<p>`...`</p>`) in appropriate places. None of the form elements forces a line break, so your form elements will all run together on a single line. In many cases, this is fine, but it can also look a little off.

- Optionally, you can add a `value` attribute to the text input element to "seed" the field with a value or to provide an example of the content you want. For example, you could add `value="First Name Here"` to the input field used for the first name to let your users know what information to type.

  If you're taking a survey, seeding a field is of questionable value. If your users can't figure out what to put in a field, you probably have a design problem. If you include some text, your users are more likely not to complete the field (and submit your sample) or to accidentally leave part of your sample text in the field, thereby corrupting your data.

  The best—possibly only—time to seed a field is if you do not have space on the form for descriptive labels.

Radio Buttons

A *radio button* is a type of input field that allows users to choose one option from a list. Radio buttons are so named because you can choose only one of them, just as you can select only one button (one station) at a time on your car radio. When viewed in a browser, radio buttons are usually small circles, as shown here:

I prefer (choose one only):
- ○ Classic rock
- ○ Soft rock
- ◉ Oldies
- ○ Classical music

In the ASR Outfitters questionnaire, we wanted to find out if users were inclined to make purchases online; the choices range from refusing to purchase to regularly purchasing online. Each choice is mutually exclusive—choosing one excludes the remainder. Radio buttons were our obvious choice.

To add radio buttons to a form, follow these steps:

1. Add any introductory text to lead into the buttons, at the point where the buttons should appear. Also add descriptive text and formatting commands as appropriate. The text of the ASR Outfitters example looks like the following:

   ```
   <p>
   Please choose the most appropriate statement.<br />
      I regularly purchase items online.<br />
      I have on occasion purchased items online.<br />
      I have not purchased anything online, but I would
      consider it.<br />
      I prefer to shop in real stores.<br />
   </p>
   ```

2. Add the input element where the first radio button will go.

   ```
   <input />I regularly purchase items online.<br />
   ```

3. Add the type="radio" attribute.

   ```
   <input type="radio" />I regularly purchase items
      online.<br />
   ```

4. Add the name attribute. The name applies to the collection of buttons, not just to this item (all the radio buttons of a given set repeat the same name attribute value), so be sure the value is generic enough to apply to all items in the set.

   ```
   <input type="radio" name="buying" />I regularly purchase
      items online.<br />
   ```

5. Add the value attribute. In text input areas, the value is what the user types; however, you must supply the value for radio buttons (and check boxes). Choose highly descriptive, preferably single-word values (such as "regular" rather than "yes" or "of course").

   ```
   <input type="radio" name="buying" value="regular" />
      I regularly purchase items online.<br />
   ```

6. If desired, add the attribute checked to one of the items to indicate the default selection. Remember that only one radio button can be selected, so only one button can carry the checked attribute.

```
<input type="radio" name="buying" value="regular"
   checked="checked" />I regularly purchase items
   online.<br />
```

In general, make the most likely choice the default option, both to make a user's job easier and to minimize the impact of their not checking and verifying the entry for that question. Although adding the checked attribute is optional, it ensures that the list records a response.

7. Add the remaining radio buttons.

Use the same name attribute for all radio buttons in a set. Browsers use the name attribute on radio buttons to specify which buttons are related and, therefore, which ones are set and unset as a group. Different sets of radio buttons within a page use different name attributes.

The completed set of radio buttons for the ASR Outfitters form looks like the following:

```
<p>
Please choose the most appropriate statement.<br />
   <input type="radio" name="buying" value="regular" />
      I regularly purchase items online.<br />
   <input type="radio" name="buying" value="sometimes" />
      I have on occasion purchased items online.<br />
   <input type="radio" name="buying" value="might"
      checked="checked" />I have not purchased anything online,
      but I would consider it.<br />
   <input type="radio" name="buying" value="willnot" />
      I prefer to shop in real stores.<br />
</p>
```

When viewed in a browser, the radio buttons look like those in Figure 7.7.

Figure 7.7 *A user can select a radio button to choose an item from a list.*

XHTML Opportunities

XHTML lets you easily group related items using the `fieldset` element. For example, in the ASR Outfitters form, several fields collect personal information, and you could group them within a `fieldset` element, like this:

```
<fieldset>
...various input fields for personal information go here...
</fieldset>
```

Additionally, by adding `legend` elements (aligned to the `top`, `bottom`, `left`, or `right`), you can clearly label content:

```
<fieldset>
<legend align="top">Personal Information</legend>
...various input fields for personal information go here...
</fieldset>
```

Check Boxes

Users can also use *check boxes* to select an item from a list. Each check box works independently from the others; users can select or deselect any combination of check boxes. Using check boxes is appropriate for open questions or questions that have more than one "correct" answer.

In most browsers, check boxes appear as little squares that contain a check mark when selected:

> **I'm willing to listen to (choose all that apply):**
> ☐ Classic rock
> ☐ Soft rock
> ☐ Oldies
> ☐ Classical music

The ASR Outfitters form is designed to find out about activities that interest customers. Any combination of answers from none to all might be possible, so this is a good place to use check boxes.

To add check boxes to your form, follow these steps:

1. Enter the lead-in text and textual cues for each item, as in the following code sample:

    ```
    <p>I'm interested in (choose all that apply):<br />
        Hiking<br />
        Mountain Biking<br />
        Camping<br />
        Rock Climbing<br />
        Off-Road 4WD<br />
        Cross-country Skiing<br />
    </p>
    ```

2. Add an `input` element before the first choice in the list.

    ```
    <input />Hiking<br />
    ```

3. Add the `type="checkbox"` attribute to set the input field as a check box.

    ```
    <input type="checkbox" />Hiking<br />
    ```

4. Add the name attribute to label the item. For check boxes, unlike radio buttons, each item has a separate label. Although the check boxes visually appear as a set, logically the items are completely separate.

```
<input type="checkbox" name="hiking" />Hiking<br />
```

5. Add the value attribute for the item. In the ASR Outfitters form, the value could be yes or no—indicating that hiking is or is not an activity of interest. However, when the form is returned through e-mail, it's useful to have a more descriptive value. If the value here is hiking, the word *hiking* returns for a check mark, and nothing returns for no check mark. The e-mail recipient can decipher this easier than a yes or a no.

```
<input type="checkbox" name="hiking" value="hiking" />
   Hiking<br />
```

6. Add a checked attribute to specify default selections. With check boxes, you can include a checked attribute for multiple items, but be careful not to overdo it. Each checked attribute that you include is an additional possible false positive response to a question.

```
<input type="checkbox" name="hiking" value="hiking"
   checked="checked" />Hiking<br />
```

7. Repeat this process for each of the remaining check boxes, remembering to use different name attributes for each one (unlike radio buttons).

In the ASR Outfitters form, the final code looks like this:

```
<p>I'm interested in (choose all that apply):<br />
   <input type="checkbox" name="hiking" value="hiking" />
      Hiking<br />
   <input type="checkbox" name="mbiking" value="mbiking" />
      Mountain Biking<br />
   <input type="checkbox" name="camping" value="camping" />
      Camping<br />
   <input type="checkbox" name="rock" value="rock" />
      Rock Climbing<br />
   <input type="checkbox" name="4wd" value="4wd" />
      Off-Road 4WD<br />
   <input type="checkbox" name="ccskiing" value="ccskiing" />
      Cross-country Skiing<br />
</p>
```

When viewed in a browser, the check boxes look like those in Figure 7.8.

Figure 7.8 *Users can use check boxes to choose multiple items from a list.*

Password Fields

Password fields are similar to text fields, except the contents of the field are not visible on the screen. Password fields are appropriate whenever the content of the field is confidential—as in passwords, Social Security numbers, or the mother's maiden name. For example, if a site is accessed from a public place and requires confidential information, a user will appreciate your using a password field. Of course, because your users cannot see the text they type, the error rate and problems with the data rise dramatically.

To establish a password field, follow these steps:

1. Add the input field.

   ```
   <input />
   ```

2. Set the type="password" attribute.

    ```
    <input type="password" />
    ```

3. Add the name attribute.

    ```
    <input type="password" name="newpass" />
    ```

4. Specify the visible size and, if appropriate, the maximum size for the input text by using the maxlength attribute.

    ```
    <input type="password" name="newpass" size="10"
        maxlength="10" />
    ```

Viewed in the browser, each typed character appears as an asterisk (*), like this:

 Password

Hidden Fields

Hidden fields are—obviously—not visible to your users. However, they are recognized by the program receiving the input from the form and can provide useful additional information. For example, ASR Outfitters uses the program cgiemail to process its form, which includes a hidden field that essentially says, "When this is form is submitted, show the user the Thanks page." Therefore, when the form is submitted by the user, cgiemail recognizes this hidden field and renders the Thanks page shown in Figure 7.9.

The cgiemail program, which is software for a Unix Web server to return form results with e-mail, is discussed at length in the final section of this chapter, "One Solution: Processing Results with cgiemail."

If you need hidden fields, the program that requires them usually includes specific documentation for the exact values. The cgiemail program that ASR Outfitters uses requires a hidden field such as the following:

```
<input type="hidden" name="success"
    value="http://www.example.com/asr/asrmaildone.html" />
```

The type="hidden" attribute keeps it from being shown, and the name and value attributes provide the information that cgiemail expects.

Hidden fields can go anywhere in your form, but it's usually best to place them at the top, immediately after the opening form tag, so they aren't misplaced or accidentally deleted when you edit the form.

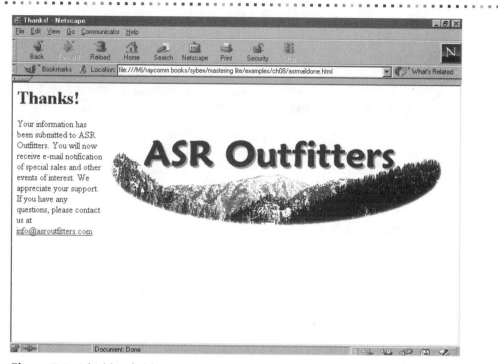

Figure 7.9 *A hidden field can tell the server to send a reference page to the user.*

File Fields

XHTML also supports a special input field, a *file field*, to allow users to upload files. For example, if you want users to submit a picture, a scanned document, a spreadsheet, or a word-processed document, they can use this field to simply upload the files without the hassle of using FTP or e-mailing the file.

This feature must be implemented both in the Web browser and in the Web server, because of the additional processing involved in uploading and manipulating uploaded files. After verifying that the server on which you'll process your form supports file uploads, you can implement this feature by following these steps:

1. Add the appropriate lead-in text to your XHTML document.

   ```
   Please post this photo I took in your gallery!
   ```

2. Add an input field.

   ```
   Please post this photo I took in your gallery!
   <input />
   ```

3. Add the type="file" attribute.

   ```
   Please post this photo I took in your gallery!
   <input type="file" />
   ```

4. Add an appropriate name attribute to label the field.

   ```
   Please post this photo I took in your gallery!
   <input type="file" name="filenew" />
   ```

5. Optionally, specify the field's visible and maximum lengths with the size and maxlength attributes.

   ```
   Please post this photo I took in your gallery!
   <input type="file" name="filenew" size="30"
       maxlength="256" />
   ```

6. Optionally, specify which file types can be uploaded by using the accept attribute. For example, add accept="image/*" to accept any image file.

   ```
   Please post this photo I took in your gallery!
   <input type="file" name="filenew" size="30"
       maxlength="256" accept="image/*" />
   ```

The values for the accept attribute are MIME types. If you accept only a specific type, such as image/gif, you can specify that. If you'll take any image file, but no other files, you could use image/* as ASR Outfitters did. Finally, if you will accept only a few types, you can provide a list of possible types, separated by commas:

```
<input type="file" name="filenew" size="30"
    maxlength="256" accept="image/gif, image/jpeg" />
```

To download a complete list of MIME types, visit `ftp://ftp.isi.edu/in-notes/iana/assignments/media-types/`.

When rendered in most browsers, this code results in a text area plus a button that allows users to browse to a file, as shown in Figure 7.10.

Figure 7.10 *You can use file fields to upload files.*

Including Text Areas

Text areas are places within a form for extensive text input. One of the primary uses for text areas is to solicit comments or free-form feedback from users, as shown here:

The `textarea` element sets an area in a form for lengthy user input. Initial content for the text area goes between its opening and closing tags. Table 7.3 lists and describes the chief attributes used for text areas within XHTML forms.

Table 7.3 Major Attributes of the `textarea` Element

ATTRIBUTE	USE
`cols="n"`	Sets the number of columns (in characters) for the visible field.
`name="..."`	Establishes a label for an input field. The `name` attribute is used for form processing.
`rows="n"`	Sets the number of rows (lines of type) for the visible field.

*Don't confuse text fields with text areas. Text fields are appropriate for shorter input; **text areas** are appropriate for longer input.*

To include a text area in a form, follow these steps:

1. Enter any lead-in text to set up the text area wherever you want it to appear.

    ```
    <p>Comments:</p>
    ```

2. Add the opening and closing `textarea` tags.

    ```
    <p>Comments:</p>
    <textarea></textarea>
    ```

3. Add a name attribute to label the field.

    ```
    <textarea name="comments"></textarea>
    ```

4. Add `rows` and `cols` attributes to set the dimensions of the text area. The `rows` attribute sets the height of the text area in rows, and `cols` sets the width of the text area in characters.

    ```
    <textarea name="comments" rows="5" cols="40"></textarea>
    ```

5. Enter some sample information to let your users know what to type by adding the text between the opening and closing `textarea` tags.

    ```
    <textarea name="comments" cols="40" rows="5">
    Please type any additional comments here.</textarea>
    ```

This `textarea` markup produces a text area field in the XHTML document similar to the one shown in Figure 7.11.

![ASR Outfitters Information Request Form - Netscape browser window showing a form with radio button options under "Please choose the most appropriate statement," checkboxes under "I'm interested in (choose all that apply)," and a Comments text area, with Submit and Start Over buttons.]

Figure 7.11 *A user can type comments in a text area.*

Including Select Fields

Select fields are some of the most flexible fields used in developing forms because you can let users select single and multiple responses. For example, suppose you need users to tell you the state or province in which they live. You could list the regions as a series of radio buttons, but that would take up tons of page space. You could also provide a text field, but users could make a typing mistake or spelling error.

Your best bet is to use a select field, which lets you list, for example, all 50 U.S. states in a minimal amount of space. Users simply select a state from the list without introducing spelling errors or typos.

Select fields, such as the one shown here, can either provide a long (visible) list of items or a highly compact listing, similar to the fonts drop-down list in a word-processing program.

 State

The select element defines an area in a form for a select field. Table 7.4 lists and describes the elements and attributes used to create select fields.

Table 7.4 Important Select Field Elements and Attributes

ITEM	TYPE	USE
select	Element	Sets an area in a form for a select field that can look like a drop-down list or a larger select field.
multiple="multiple"	Attribute of select	Sets the select field to accept more than one selection. Use this attribute along with the size attribute to set to a number as large as the maximum number of likely selections.
name="…"	Attribute of select	Establishes a label for an input field. The name attribute is used for form processing.
size="n"	Attribute of select	Sets the visible size for the select field. The default (1) creates a drop-down list. You can change the default (to 2 or higher) if you want more options to be visible.
option	Element	Marks the items included in the select field. You'll have an option element for each item you include.
selected="selected"	Attribute of option	Lets you specify a default selection, which will appear when the form is loaded or reset.
value="…"	Attribute of option	Provides the content associated with the name attribute.

Use a select field any time you need to list many items or ensure that users don't make spelling or typing errors. To include a select field in a form, follow these steps:

1. Enter the lead-in text for the select field.

   ```
   I learned about this site from:<br />
   ```

2. Add the opening and closing select tags.

   ```
   I learned about this site from:<br />
   <select>
   </select>
   ```

3. Enter a name attribute to label the select field.

```
<select name="referral">
</select>
```

4. Add the choices that your users should see. Because the select field and option element inserts line breaks and other formatting, do not include any line-break elements.

```
I learned about this site from:<br />
<select name="referral">
  Print Ads
  In-Store Visit
  Friend's Recommendation
  Sources on the Internet
  Other
</select>
```

5. Add the opening and closing option tags for each possible selection.

```
<select name="referral">
  <option>Print Ads</option>
  <option>In-Store Visit</option>
  <option>Friend's Recommendation</option>
  <option>Sources on the Internet</option>
  <option>Other</option>
</select>
```

6. Provide a value attribute for each option element. These values are what you will see when the form is submitted, so make them as logical and descriptive as possible.

```
I learned about this site from:<br />
<select name="referral">
  <option value="print">Print Ads</option>
  <option value="visit">In-Store Visit</option>
  <option value="rec">Friend's Recommendation</option>
  <option value="internet">Sources on the Internet</option>
  <option value="other">Other</option>
</select>
```

7. Optionally, let users select multiple items from the list by including the `multiple` attribute in the opening `select` tag.

```
<select name="referral" multiple="multiple">
```

 If you choose to include `multiple`, *your user can select one or all options; you cannot restrict the choices to only, say, two of four items.*

8. Optionally, add the `selected` attribute to the option element to specify a default selection. You can offer more than one default setting if you used the `multiple` attribute.

```
<option value="print" selected="selected">
```

With this, the basic select field is complete. Browsers display this select field as a drop-down list, as in Figure 7.12.

Figure 7.12 Select fields let you provide many choices in a compact format.

Designing Long Select Fields

When developing particularly long select fields—ones that include many items—be sure to make the area as easy to use as possible. Here are some guidelines:

- Be sure that the select field appears within one screen; don't make users scroll to see the entire select field.
- Add a `size` attribute to the opening `select` element to expand the drop-down list to a list box, like this:

```
<select name="referral" multiple="multiple" size="5">
```

The list box can have a vertical scrollbar, if necessary, to provide access to all items, as shown here:

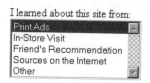

Select boxes are horizontally fixed, meaning that they cannot scroll horizontally.

You can use JavaScript to validate form input. For example, you can ensure that users fill out contact information or credit card numbers you need to process their information or requests. See Chapter 11 for details.

Processing Forms

In general, after a user clicks the Submit button on a form, the information is sent to the Web server and to the program indicated by the `action` attribute in the form. What that program then does with the data is up to you. In this section, we'll look at some, but not nearly all, of your options. The server can

- Send the information to you via e-mail.
- Enter the information into a database.
- Post the information to a newsgroup or a Web page.
- Use the input to search a database.

When you're working out what to do with the data you collect or if you're just checking out what others have done to get some inspiration, your first stop should always be your Web server administrator. In particular, ask which programs are installed to process form input. Depending on what's available, you might be able to take advantage of those capabilities.

Regardless of how you want the information processed, you include specific attributes in the opening form element, as explained in Table 7.5.

Table 7.5 Processing Attributes for the form Element

ATTRIBUTE	USE
action="..."	Indicates the program on the HTTP server that will process the output from the form.
method="..."	Tells the browser how to send the data to the server, with either the post or the get method.

The action and method attributes depend on the server-side program that processes the form.

In general, the documentation that came with your form-processing script or with your Web server will tell you what to use for post and get. For example, ASR Outfitter's Internet service provider (ISP), www.example.com, publishes information on its Web site about how to set up a form to mail the results (using a CGI script called cgiemail, discussed later in this chapter). In this case, the proper opening form element is

```
<form method="post" action="http://www.example.com/cgi-bin/
    cgiemail/~user/user-mail.txt">
```

Remember that we have to break long lines, like this one, in print. You should type this all on one line, because including hard returns in attribute values can lead to unpredictable browser behavior.

Of course, the attributes you use depend on the program processing the information. By changing the attributes, you can also specify a different program. Because this single line of code within an XHTML form determines how the information is processed, you can change what happens to the data without significantly changing the form itself.

Why would you want to change what happens to the data? You'd do so primarily because you discover better ways to manipulate the data. For example, if you want feedback about your company's new product, you want the quickest way to collect the data, which is probably to have it e-mailed to you. Later, you could investigate ways to have the data written directly to an automated database—which isn't as speedy to set up as e-mail, but could save you some work.

Some Web servers have built-in scripts or commands to process form results; others, particularly Unix servers, require additional programs.

In the following sections, we discuss your form-processing options—sending with e-mail, writing to a database, posting to a Web page, and other possibilities. Because your ISP's particular setup can vary significantly, we've provided general information that you can apply to your specific situation—probably with the help of your server administrator. The final section in this chapter gives you a specific example of setting up an e-mail return—an option you're likely to use.

To learn your form-processing options, check with your server administrator or visit your ISP's Web site.

About Using Form Data

Getting a good response rate is the single biggest challenge to survey takers. Using an XHTML form to collect information puts you in a similar role, with the added complication that your users must find your Web site to complete it. After you get the data, you need to use it wisely. Here are some guidelines:

- Tell your users how you're going to use the information. For example, if you ask for users' e-mail addresses, let them know if you plan on sending them e-mail about your product. Better yet, ask them whether they want information sent to them.

- Carefully consider the source, and don't read more into the data than you should. It's quite tempting to assume that the available information is representative of what you might collect from an entire population (customers, users, and so on).

- Take the time to analyze your data carefully, determining what it does and doesn't tell you.

For example, after ASR Outfitters implements its form and receives a few hundred responses, it will have a general idea of how many customers are willing to make purchases online, how many are located in specific areas, how many have certain interests, and even how many use online services. Much of this information was not previously available to ASR, and it is tempting to assume that the data is representative of all ASR customers.

The results of ASR's online survey reflect only the preferences and opinions of that small set of customers who use the Internet, *and* visited the site, *and* took the time to fill out the survey. Even if 95 percent of the people who complete the survey express interest in more rock-climbing gear, that might not reflect the interests of the overall ASR customer base.

Processing Forms via E-Mail

Having the server return form results to you via e-mail isn't always ideal (although it can be depending on your situation); however, it's often useful, nearly always expedient, and cheap. Using e-mail to accept form responses simply sends the information the user submits to you (or someone you designate) in an e-mail message. At that point, you have the information and can enter it (manually) in a database, send a response (manually), or do anything else you want with the data.

If you're collecting open comments from a relatively small number of people, receiving the results via e-mail is a reasonable, long-term solution. That is, it's a reasonable solution if you—or whoever gets the e-mail—can easily address the volume of form responses. E-mail is also a good solution if you do not know what level of response to expect. If the volume turns out to be manageable, continue. If the volume is high, consider other solutions, such as databases.

Database Processing

Writing the information that respondents submit into a database is a good solution to a potentially enormous data management problem. If you're collecting information about current or potential customers or clients, for example, you probably want to quickly call up these lists and send letters or e-mail, or provide demographic information about your customers to potential Web site advertisers. To do that, you'll want to use a database.

Although the specifics of putting form data into a database depend on the server and the software, we can make some generalizations. If you work in a fairly large company that has its own Web server on site, you'll encounter fewer problems with tasks such as putting form results directly into a database or sending automatic responses via e-mail. If you represent a small company and rely on an ISP for Web hosting, you may have more of a challenge.

If your Web server uses the same platform on which you work—for instance, if you use Windows 2000 Professional and your Web server is a Windows NT Web server— feeding the form results directly into a database is manageable. However, if your Web server is, for example, on a Unix platform and you work on a Windows machine, you may face some additional challenges getting the information from a form into a readily usable database.

Posting to a Web Page

Depending on the information you're collecting, you might want to post the responses to a Web page or to a discussion group. For example, if ASR Outfitters sets up a form to collect information about hiking conditions, the natural output might be a Web page.

Other Options

If you find that the options available on your system do not meet your needs, check out Matt's Script Archive at `www.worldwidemart.com/scripts` or Selena Sol's Public Domain CGI Scripts at `www.extropia.com`.

These scripts offer a starting point, for either you or your server administrator, to handle form processing effectively. In particular, the form-processing script from Selena's archive offers everything from database logging to giving audiences the opportunity to verify the accuracy of the data they enter.

Keep in mind, if you choose to install and set up these scripts yourself, that the installation and debugging of a server-side script is considerably more complex and time consuming than installing a new Windows program. Not that it isn't impossible for the novice to do it, and do it successfully, but set aside some time.

If you choose to download and use scripts from the Web, be sure that you get them from a reliable source and that you or your server administrator scan the scripts for possible security holes. Form-processing programs must take some special steps to ensure that malicious users don't use forms to crash the server—or worse. Without your taking precautions, forms can pass commands directly to the server, which will then execute them, with potentially disastrous results.

One Solution: Processing Results with cgiemail

Because you'll likely choose—at least initially—to have form results e-mailed to you, we'll walk you through a form-to-e-mail program. The cgiemail program is produced and distributed for free by MIT, but it's only available for Unix servers. Check out

```
http://web.mit.edu/wwwdev/cgiemail/index.html
```

for the latest news about cgiemail. This program is a good example because many ISPs offer access to it and because it's also commonly found on corporate Internet and intranet servers.

A comparable program for Windows 95/98/NT/2000, MailPost for Windows 32-bit Web, is found at `www.mcenter.com/mailpost`.

Here is the general process for using cgiemail:

1. Start with a complete form—the one developed earlier in this chapter or a different one. Without a functional form, you cannot get the results sent to you via e-mail.

2. Add the `action` and `method` attributes with values you get from your server administrator. (See the "Processing Forms" section, earlier in this chapter, for more information about the `action` and `method` attributes.)

3. Develop a template for the e-mail message to you. This template includes the names of each of your fields and basic e-mail addressing information.

4. Develop a response page that the user sees after completing the form.

Now, let's look at how ASR Outfitters can use cgiemail to implement its form.

1. The Form

You don't need to do anything special to forms to use them with cgiemail. You have the option of requiring some fields to be completed, but that's not essential. For example, because the purpose of the ASR Outfitters form is to collect e-mail addresses, ASR should make the e-mail address required.

The solution? Rename the `name` field from `emailaddr` to `required-emailaddr`. The cgiemail program will then check the form and reject it if that field is not complete. The actual code for that line of the form looks like this:

```
<br /><input type="text" name="required-emailaddr" size="30" />
    E-mail Address
```

Optionally, add `required-` to each field name that must be completed.

2. The action and method Attributes

The server administrator provided ASR Outfitters with the `action` and `method` attributes shown in the following code:

```
<form method="post" action="http://www.example.com/cgi-bin/
    cgiemail/asr/asr-mail.txt">
```

The file referenced in the `action` line is the template for an e-mail message. In this case, the `http://www.example.com/cgi-bin/cgiemail` part of the `action` line points to the program itself, and the following part (`/asr/asr-mail.txt`) is the server-relative path to the file. (With a server-relative path, you can add the name of the server to the front of the path and open the document in a Web browser.)

3. The Template

The plain-text template includes the bare essentials for an e-mail message, fields in square brackets for the form field values, and any line breaks or spacing needed to make it easier to read.

In general, you can be flexible when setting up the template, but you must set up the e-mail headers exactly as shown here. Don't use leading spaces, but do capitalize and use colons as shown. The parts after the colons are fields for the `From` e-mail address, your e-mail address (in both the `To:` line and in the `Errors-To:` line), and any subject field you choose:

```
From: [emailaddr]
To: ASR Webmaster <webmaster@asroutfitters.com>
Subject: Web Form Submission
Errors-To: ASR Webmaster <webmaster@asroutfitters.com>
```

Format the rest of the template as you choose—within the constraints of plain-text files. If you want to include information from the form, put in a field name (the content of a `name` attribute). The resulting e-mail will contain the value of that field (either what a user enters, or the `value` attribute you specify in the case of check boxes and radio buttons).

Be liberal with line breaks, and enter descriptive values as you set up the template. E-mail generated by forms may make sense when you're up to your ears in developing the form, but later it's likely to be so cryptic that you can't understand it.

Following is the complete content of the `asr-mail.txt` file.

```
From: [emailaddr]
To: ASR Webmaster <webmaster@asroutfitters.com>
Subject: Web Form Submission
Errors-To: ASR Webmaster <webmaster@asroutfitters.com>
Results from Information Request Web Form:
[firstname] [lastname]
[emailaddr]
[address]
[city], [state] [zip]
```

```
[country]
Online Purchasing:
[buying]
Interested In:
[hiking]
[mbiking]
[camping]
[rock]
[4wd]
[ccskiing]
Referral:
[referral]
Comments:
[comments]
```

The cgiemail program completes this template with the values from the form, resulting in an e-mail message similar to the following:

```
Return-path: <www@krunk1.example.com>
Envelope-to: asroutfitters@asroutfitters.com
Delivery-date: Sat, 26 May 2001 10:03:55 -0600
Date: Sat, 26 May 2001 10:03:51 -0600 (MDT)
X-Template: /home/users/e/public_html/asr/asr-mail.txt
From: mjones@example.com
To: ASR Webmaster <webmaster@asroutfitters.com>
Subject: Web Form Submission
Errors-To: ASR Webmaster <webmaster@asroutfitters.com>
Results from Information Request Web Form:
Molly Jones
mjones@example.com
402 E 4th
South Logan, UT 84341
USA
Online Purchasing:
might
Interested In:
hiking
camping
rock
Referral:
rec
```

```
Comments:
I'd also like information about outdoor gear.
Thanks!
```

4. Success Page

The only remaining step is to set up a success page—a document that is returned to the user indicating that the form has been received. Although a success page is optional, we recommend that you use one. In the form code, a "success" field is actually a hidden `input` field that looks like this:

```
<input type="hidden" name="success"
  value="http://www.example.com/asr/asrmaildone.html" />
```

A success page can contain any content you choose. If you want, you can point the success page back to your home page or to any other page on your site. On the other hand, many XHTML developers use the success page as a place to thank the user for taking the time to fill out the form, to offer an opportunity to ask questions or make comments, or to confirm what the user submitted.

A nonstandard way of returning forms is to use a `mailto` *URL in the* `action` *line. This hack works with Netscape, and not with all versions at that. A much better solution, unless you can closely control the browsers your users use, is a server-based e-mail program.*

Where to Go from Here

In this chapter, you learned how to determine what information to include in forms and to develop them using a variety of widgets. Additionally, you learned about the different ways to process forms and to get the data back.

What now? Following is a list of chapters that include related topics:

- For more information about WYSIWYG editors, see Chapter 1.

- For more information about using JavaScript to help control forms, see Chapter 11.

- For more information about planning XHTML documents, check out Chapter 13.

Creating Frames

Chapter 8

F rames divide browser windows into several independent sections that each contains a separate XHTML document. Subdividing browser windows can dramatically improve both the appearance and the usability of a site. For example, because frames group information, users can more easily find what they want. Frames can, however, make navigation difficult. For example, if followed links seem to appear randomly in different frames, your users will become confused.

In this chapter, we'll discuss framing principles, create a framed site, and look at navigation issues that arise when you use frames. We'll also discuss floating frames, an Internet Explorer–specific and HTML 4 Frameset specification standard option.

This chapter covers the following topics:

- Understanding frames

- Deciding to use frames

- Creating frames

- Enabling effective navigation

- Creating inline frames

Understanding Frames

Throughout this chapter, we use a few terms you should become familiar with:

Framed pages or framed sites are XHTML documents that use frames.

Frameset specifies the layout for frames, including the locations and characteristics of the frames. The frameset acts as a holder for frame information.

Nonframed pages or nonframed sites are documents that do not use frames.

Nonframed browsers are browsers that do not support frames.

Parent documents are documents that contain frames.

Frames are an HTML 4 standard. Framed sites use a combination of XHTML documents, displayed together in a browser window. Most commonly, frames divide the window into two or more sections, with one larger section containing content and the smaller section(s) containing a logo, navigation links, or both. Figure 8.1 shows a framed site; one section contains content, and the other contains a logo and navigation links.

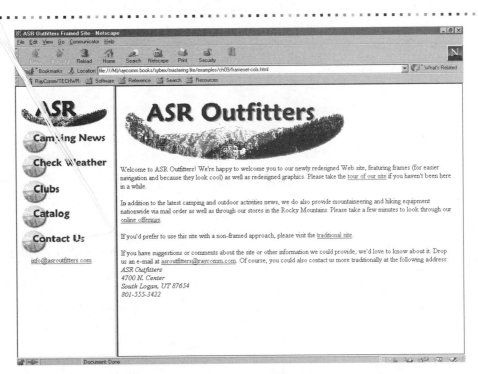

Figure 8.1 *Frames usually contain either the main content or peripheral content such as a navigation menu or a logo.*

The appearance of frames depends on how you design them. For example, the frames in Figure 8.1 are vertical frames, which means that the border between them runs vertically in the window. You can also create horizontal frames, in which the border runs horizontally, as shown in Figure 8.2.

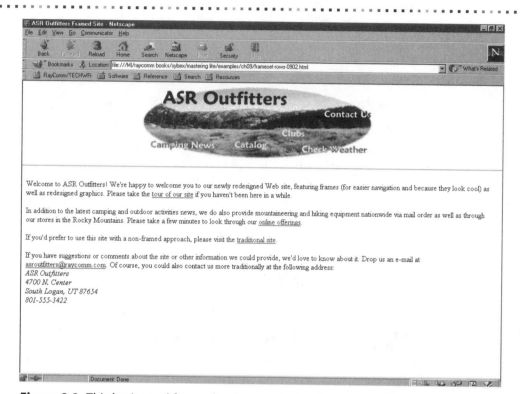

Figure 8.2 *This horizontal frame divides the window into top and bottom sections.*

  Because of the limited space in most browser windows—the result of limited screen resolution—using more than two or three frames is typically not a good choice. Use additional frames only if they're small and unobtrusive.

Deciding to Use Frames

The decision to frame your site will have long-range implications, particularly in terms of development effort. (If you create a complete framed site, you may also need to create a complete nonframed site to accommodate users who have browsers that are not frames compatible.)

When deciding whether to use frames, you should consider both the advantages and the disadvantages of doing so.

Some Advantages of Using Frames

Frames are widely supported by popular browsers, and offer several advantages, both to users and developers, such as:

- Frames are widely used on the Internet and are often perceived as a hallmark of a technically sophisticated site.

- Frames can be implemented so your pages also accommodate older browsers that can't display frames, so if you're willing to take the time and effort, you can effectively serve all users to your site.

- Frames reduce download time. When using frames, users can download only the content pages. The static elements, such as logos and navigation menus, are already downloaded when the user first loads the site.

- Frames can improve site usability. Navigation remains visible as content changes in a separate frame.

- Because frames separate content from navigation elements and structural elements, you can easily and quickly update pages and provide new content. For example, if a framed site uses a top banner and a bottom banner, with scrolling content in the middle, you can replace the content—and only the content— without compromising appearance or navigation.

A Caution About Linking to Outside Sites

Unfortunately, frames have introduced the potential for legal problems. A standard framed site, for example, might use a banner frame at the top, a navigation frame on the left, and a content frame on the right. A user clicks a link in the left frame and views the content in the right frame—the top (banner) and left (navigation) frames remain the same.

This layout works well as long as the links all point to XHTML documents within your site. However, problems occur when the links point to documents outside the site. For example, a company could use this type of frame layout and include a link to a CNN News Web page that, when clicked, loads the CNN page into the right frame. That content is generated by CNN but not labeled as such. This "borrowed" content appears to belong to the company, not to CNN. This could be a huge copyright issue.

When you include links to XHTML documents that are not yours and not created by you, you need to clearly identify the information as belonging to an outside source (and possibly obtain permission to display that information), or, better still, use nonframed pages.

Some Disadvantages of Using Frames

As a result of early implementation problems and site design issues, some drawbacks are associated with using frames. For example, frames have an inconsistent usability record. For the first several months after frames were introduced, the Back button in some browsers returned to the last nonframed page, even if the user had been browsing through multiple pages within a framed site. This inability to move backward through visited pages was frustrating and caused many users to completely reject framed sites. Although this problem is less frequent as more people use newer browsers, you should still accommodate all users by providing a highly visible link, possibly at the top of your site, that will take users to an equivalent, nonframed site. Alternatively, start your users at a nonframed site and then allow them to choose the framed site if they want it.

Frame navigation is a mystery to many, and the mystery is compounded because many framed sites have links that seem to appear randomly in different frames or windows. You need to ensure that your users can easily find what they want.

Frames may take up more space than they are worth. For example, the ASR Outfitters framed site was designed specifically for 800×600 or better resolution and looks good in Figure 8.1, at the proper resolution. However, when the site is viewed at 640×480, as shown in Figure 8.3, appearance degrades drastically. Not only do the graphics appear improperly, but the scrollbars also obscure more of the page.

Figure 8.3 *Lower resolution in browsers can wreak havoc on framed sites.*

Most newer browsers, including the last several versions of Netscape Navigator and Internet Explorer, support frames. Because frame technology—like the rest of XHTML—continues to improve and evolve, both the specification and its implementation could change somewhat.

Creating Frames

Creating frames requires relatively few steps:

1. Create a frameset (or layout) document that determines the location and characteristics of the frames.

   As you may recall from Chapter 3, there are three XHTML DTDs, one of which is used specifically for frameset documents: the Frameset DTD. Therefore, the first line of your frameset document should be as follows:

   ```
   <!DOCTYPE html PUBLIC "-//W3C//DTD XHTML 1.0 Frameset//EN"
        "http://www.w3.org/TR/xhtml1/DTD/xhtml1-frameset.dtd">
   ```

2. Designate the frames and their contents.

3. Format the frames.

4. Make provisions for frames when viewed in nonframed browsers.

Table 8.1 lists and describes the frame elements and attributes used to create frames.

Table 8.1 Frameset Elements and Attributes

ITEM	TYPE	USE
`frameset`	Element	Establishes frames within an XHTML document.
`rows="n1, n2, …"`	Attribute of `frameset`	Sets the size for rows—horizontal frames—in pixels, as a percentage, or as "all remaining space" with `"*"`.
`cols="n1, n2, …"`	Attribute of `frameset`	Sets the size for columns—vertical frames—in pixels, as a percentage, or as "all remaining space" with `"*"`.
`frame`	Empty element	Identifies frame characteristics and initial content.
`src="url"`	Attribute of `frame`	Identifies the source for the frame content, as a standard URI.
`name="…"`	Attribute of `frame`	Labels a frame so it can be targeted or referred to from other frames or windows.
`noframes`	Element	Sets a section of an XHTML document to be visible to nonframed browsers (and invisible to framed browsers).

Determining Frame Size

As with all XHTML, frames render differently on various operating systems and browser combinations, with various display settings. Therefore, as you make decisions about how to frame your site, keep in mind size and scaling of the frames.

Determining Size

The size at which frames display depends on the resolution of your user's monitor and the size at which the browser window is displayed. If a site is designed for a high-resolution monitor, it will be unreadable on a low-resolution monitor even if it has only a couple of frames.

For example, you have two columns. The first is set to a width of 200 pixels for your logo and navigation buttons; the other column fills the remaining space (indicated by an asterisk in the `cols` attribute). At high resolution, you have a potentially attractive page. At 800×600, your logo will take about 25 percent of the window width, and at 1024×768 it will take about 20 percent. Not really a problem. However, at 640×480, your logo will fill 30 percent of the window width, leaving too little space for your content. Figure 8.3, earlier in this chapter, shows a two-frame page viewed at 640×480 resolution.

You can improve this page by setting the columns to 25 percent each, but then the logo column will require horizontal scrolling at lower resolutions.

The only real solution is to think small (or no frames at all), particularly if you do much of your development at a high resolution. Test extensively at lower resolutions, and provide links that users can click to break out of the frames into a full-screen view.

Determining Scaling

Scaling refers to how different screen resolutions and the size of browser windows affect the display of frames. By default, frames are resizable and automatically appear with scrollbars as needed to allow a user to view everything in the frame.

Depending on the layout, however, some frames might be more effective if they cannot be scrolled or resized. In particular, if frames contain only images—either image maps or regular images—set them to a fixed size and disable scrollbars and resizing. Doing so forces frames to accommodate the images and prevents users from resizing them. Your layout is thus preserved.

In general, simpler frames and sizes are better than fancy ones. Just because two frames are good doesn't mean that four frames are twice as good. Besides being ugly, the use of more than two frames leads to frames that are so small that even audiences using a high-resolution monitor must scroll both horizontally and vertically to read the content. Figure 8.4 shows a page with too many frames.

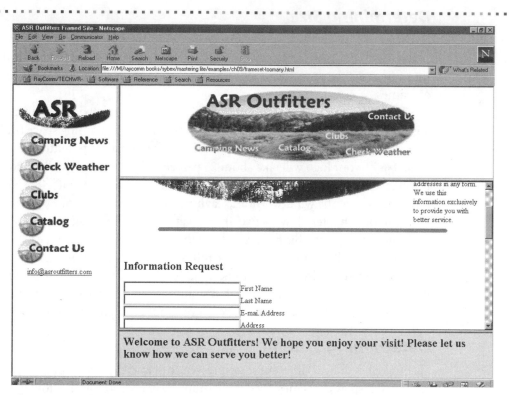

Figure 8.4 *When you use too many frames, your Web pages become busy, confusing, and often difficult to read.*

Creating a Frameset

A frameset is the foundation for individual frames and their content, in which you specify the general frame layout—either vertical (using columns) or horizontal (using rows). The basic frameset document is very similar to a standard XHTML document; however, it uses the Frameset DTD instead of either the Strict or Transitional DTD, and the `frameset` element instead of the body element.

The following example sets up a basic frameset document with two columns. Other examples in this section will develop this sample document further.

Before you start, prepare several XHTML documents with minimal content, but possibly different background colors. This will allow you to easily experiment with and view various frameset combinations.

The source documents in these examples are virtually blank documents, containing different colored backgrounds to make it easier to see different frames.

Follow these steps to start your frameset document:

1. Start with a basic XHTML document, including the DOCTYPE declaration, the html, head, and title elements and meta elements of your choice. Your code should look something like this:

```
<!DOCTYPE html PUBLIC "-//W3C//DTD XHTML 1.0 Frameset//EN"
    "http://www.w3.org/TR/xhtml1/DTD/xhtml1-frameset.dtd">
<html xmlns="http://www.w3.org/1999/xhtml">
<head>
    <title>Frameset Samples</title>
</head>
</html>
```

2. Add the frameset element to establish the frameset:

```
<html xmlns="http://www.w3.org/1999/xhtml">
<head>
    <title>Frameset Samples</title>
</head>
<frameset>
</frameset>
</html>
```

3. Add a cols or rows attribute, depending on whether you want vertical or horizontal frames. We used the cols attribute with values of 50% and * to get two columns, one at 50 percent and one filling the remaining space (the * is a wildcard character):

```
<frameset cols="50%, *">
</frameset>
```

We could also use 50% for the second column in this case, because we know how much space remains, but using the * is a better choice because we can add columns without changing the existing values. If you change the first 50% value here, you don't have to make any other changes. If you specify all values, you must then change all values when you want to add columns.

If you view the document at this point, you won't see anything because you haven't specified any content. That comes when you add frames.

Within a frameset, you can specify either rows or columns, but not both. To divide your browser window into columns and then subdivide each column into rows, you nest `frameset` elements, like this:

```
<frameset cols="200,50%,*">
    <frameset rows="100,*">
    </frameset>
</frameset>
```

Just How Are Frame Sizes Calculated?

When you specify frame sizes within your frameset, the user's browser must accommodate both your specifications and the browser size and resolution. The browser calculates the actual sizes as shown here:

- Browsers apply percentages, which indicate a percentage of the entire browser window, first, if specified in the frameset.
- Browsers apply pixel values, which specify an exact size, second, if specified in the frameset.
- Browsers use wildcard (*) settings to fill the remaining space.

In general, you can use the * to set up proportional columns or rows. For example, the following frameset element has three values after `cols`; therefore, the space is divided into three parts. To allocate those proportionately (evenly), use an * as shown here:

```
<frameset cols="*, *, *">
```

To make the middle frame twice as large as the other two, add a 2 to the *, as in the following:

```
<frameset cols="*, 2*, *">
```

The middle frame fills half the space, and the other two columns fill one-quarter each. If you add a 2 to the third space, the first column fills one-fifth and the remaining two fill two-fifths each, as shown in the following illustration.

```
<frameset cols="*, 2*, 2*">
```

As we mentioned earlier, you can specify frame width in percentages, in pixels, or as a proportion of the remaining space. You can also combine these specifications. For example, a frameset might require one section that is 100 pixels wide, another that is 50 percent of the window, another that fills two parts of the remaining space, and a final section that is one part of the remaining space. That code, including the frame elements (remember that the frame element is an empty element), looks like this:

```
<frameset cols="100, 50%, 2*, *">
    <frame name="first" src="z-maroon.html" />
    <frame name="second" src="z-yellow.html" />
    <frame name="third" src="z-blue.html" />
    <frame name="fourth" src="z-green.html" />
</frameset>
```

This code results in the following frames:

Adding Frames

Adding frames to an existing frameset document is straightforward. You add a `frame` element for each column or row in the frameset document, specify the content for each frame, and then name each frame.

In the following example, we're going to add vertical frames. The process for adding horizontal frames is the same except for the `rows` or `cols` attribute in the `frameset` element.

We'll start with the frameset document that we created in the last section, and then we'll add two frame elements and the content for each frame. The starting document looks like this:

```
<!DOCTYPE html PUBLIC "-//W3C//DTD XHTML 1.0 Frameset//EN"
    "http://www.w3.org/TR/xhtml1/DTD/xhtml1-frameset.dtd">
<html xmlns="http://www.w3.org/1999/xhtml">
<head>
    <title>Frameset Samples</title>
</head>
<frameset cols="50%, *">
</frameset>
</html>
```

Now, follow these steps:

1. Add a `frame` element between the opening and closing `frameset` tags.

   ```
   <frameset cols="50%, *">
       <frame />
   </frameset>
   ```

2. Add the `name` attribute to label the frame. Because browsers fill frames from left to right and top to bottom, this frame name is for the left frame. The second frame name is for the right frame.

   ```
   <frameset cols="50%, *">
       <frame name="first" />
   </frameset>
   ```

3. Add the `src` attribute to specify the XHTML document that will fill the frame. The document filling this frame is `z-yellow.html`.

   ```
   <frameset cols="50%, *">
       <frame name="first" src="z-yellow.html" />
   </frameset>
   ```

The URL you use depends on where the file is located. If you're using a file in the same folder as the frameset document or in an adjacent folder, you can use a relative URL, as we do here. If the file is located elsewhere, you need to adjust the URL accordingly.

4. Add the second `frame` element, with the name `second` and source of `z-blue.html`.

```
<frameset cols="50%, *">
    <frame name="first" src="z-yellow.html" />
    <frame name="second" src="z-blue.html" />
</frameset>
```

This step completes the frameset document. The frames, which include the yellow and blue documents, look like those in Figure 8.5.

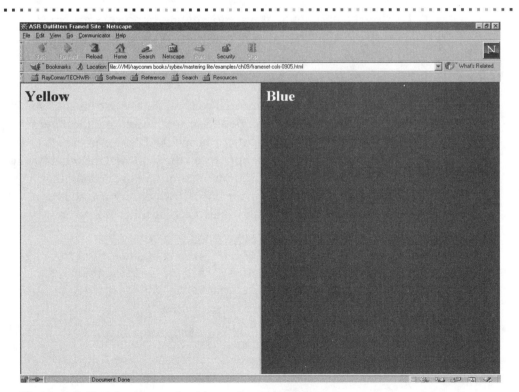

Figure 8.5 *Two frames, each with a separate document*

As you test your documents, you may find that reloading framed documents looks a little random—sometimes the whole document reloads, while at other times only a certain frame reloads. The easiest way to control how browsers reload is to ensure that the item you want to reload is active. To reload a single frame, click inside the frame and then click the Reload (or Refresh) button. To reload the entire frameset, click in the location line or in the address line (depending on the browser you use), and then click the Reload (or Refresh) button.

To add another column, alter your frameset to make space and then add another `frame` element. The current frameset looks like this:

```
<frameset cols="50%, *">...</frameset>
```

The 50% specifies that the first column fill 50 percent of the window. The * specifies that the second column fill the remaining space. To add an additional column, follow these steps:

1. Specify the amount of space for the additional column. For example, if you add a 200-pixel column after the 50% column, the `frameset` element looks like this:

   ```
   <frameset cols="50%, 200, *">...</frameset>
   ```

2. Add another `frame` element. If you add the `frame` element *before* the two existing elements, the new frame appears on the left, and the other two appear in the center and on the right. If you add the `frame` element *after* the two existing elements, the new frame appears on the right, and the other two appear on the left and in the center. The frame columns fill in the order they appear in your code, from left to right in the browser window. If you add the new `frame` element at the beginning, the code looks like this:

   ```
   <frameset cols="50%, 200, *">
       <frame name="third" src="z-maroon.html" />
       <frame name="first" src="z-yellow.html" />
       <frame name="second" src="z-blue.html" />
   </frameset>
   ```

The framed page looks like that shown in Figure 8.6.

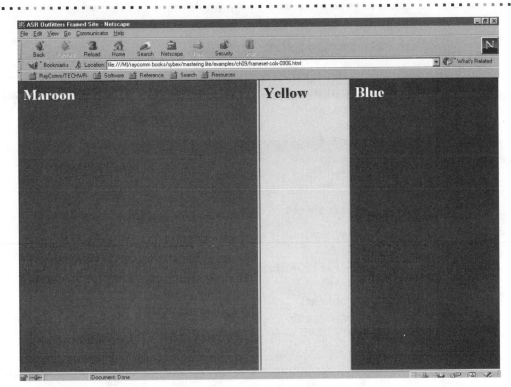

Figure 8.6 *Multiple vertical frames get a little busy.*

You can follow these same steps to add horizontal frames (except you use the rows *attribute).*

Combining Horizontal and Vertical Framesets

Although many of your framing needs probably require only a pair of horizontal or vertical frames, you can easily nest frameset elements to combine vertical and horizontal frames within a single document. Each frame area in a frameset element can contain either a frame element, as in the preceding examples, or another frameset element.

In the next example, we set up a simple frameset with two columns and then divide the columns into two rows each. Follow these steps:

1. Start with a blank XHTML document, similar to the following:

```
<!DOCTYPE html PUBLIC "-//W3C//DTD XHTML 1.0 Frameset//EN"
    "http://www.w3.org/TR/xhtml1/DTD/xhtml1-frameset.dtd">
<html xmlns="http://www.w3.org/1999/xhtml">
<head>
    <title>Frameset Samples</title>
</head>
</html>
```

2. Add the frameset element.

```
<html xmlns="http://www.w3.org/1999/xhtml">
<head>
    <title>Frameset Samples</title>
</head>
<frameset>
</frameset>
</html>
```

3. Create two columns by adding the cols attribute. In this example, one column fills 30 percent of the window, and the other fills the remaining space.

```
<frameset cols="30%, *">
</frameset>
```

4. Add a second frameset tag pair, for two rows, each at 50 percent of the window, as shown in the following code. Within the first frameset tag pair, you could place two frames, two framesets, or one frame and one frameset (as this example shows):

```
<frameset cols="30%, *">
    <frameset rows="50%, 50%">
    </frameset>
</frameset>
```

5. Add the three necessary frame elements so you can view your document. The second frameset requires two frame elements, and the primary frameset element requires only one (because the second frameset is taking one of the two

available columns). Be sure to include both the name and src attributes with the frame elements. Your code should look like the following:

```
<frameset cols="30%, *">
    <frameset rows="50%, 50%">
        <frame name="topleft" src="z-maroon.html" />
        <frame name="lowerleft" src="z-blue.html" />
    </frameset>
    <frame name="right" src="z-white.html" />
</frameset>
```

Your frames should look like those in Figure 8.7.

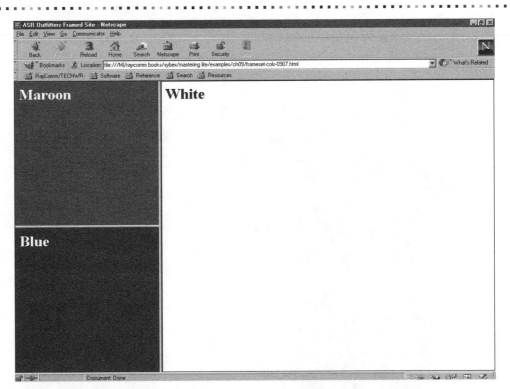

Figure 8.7 *A combination of horizontal and vertical frames is often effective.*

To set a second pair of frames on the right side, replace the final `frame` element with an additional `frameset` element, as well as two `frames` to fill it. The final code looks like this:

```
<frameset cols="30%, *">
   <frameset rows="50%, 50%">
      <frame name="topleft" src="z-maroon.html" />
      <frame name="lowerleft" src="z-blue.html" />
   </frameset>
   <frameset rows="100, *">
      <frame name="topright" src="z-yellow.html" />
      <frame name="lowerright" src="z-white.html" />
   </frameset>
</frameset>
```

When you view the results of this code in a browser, you'll see the frames as shown in Figure 8.8.

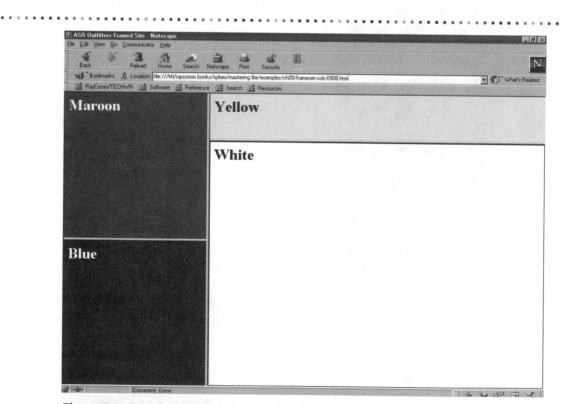

Figure 8.8 *Four frames are easy to create, but visually a little much.*

If your document does not appear in the browser, double-check that you have the correct number of frames and that every frameset *element that you opened has a closing tag. An omitted closing* frameset *tag is usually the villain, particularly if you're nesting multiple framesets.*

Formatting Frames

Formatting a frame primarily involves changing its borders and adjusting its margins. You use the attributes shown in Table 8.2 to do so. According to the XHTML specification, these attributes apply to the frame elements within a frameset. However, the various browsers support the use of these attributes in the frameset element.

Table 8.2 Frame Formatting Attributes

ATTRIBUTE	USE
frameborder="…"	Sets or removes the border around a frame. For uniform results in all browsers, use in conjunction with the border attribute. Possible values are 1 (on) and 0 (off), for IE and the specification. For Netscape, the values can be either 1 or 0, or Yes or No. The default is 1.
border="n"	A proprietary Netscape attribute (that also works in IE 4 and higher) that sets or removes the border around a frame. For uniform results in all browsers, use in conjunction with the frameborder attribute. Possible values are 0 for off, or number of pixels.
noresize="noresize"	Prohibits users from resizing a frame. In the absence of this attribute, users can click and drag the mouse to move the frame borders.
scrolling="…"	Prohibits scrollbars (with a value of no), requires scrollbars (yes), or lets the browser provide scrollbars if required (auto, the default).
marginheight="n"	Sets the number of pixels of the margin above and below the content of the frame.
marginwidth="n"	Sets the number of pixels of the margin to the left and the right of frame content.
bordercolor="…"	Sets the color of the frame border as either a #rrggbb value or a color name.

These options apply to actual frames, not to the content of the frames. Remember that frame content is simply a standard XHTML document and is formatted accordingly.

Removing Borders

By default, all frames have borders. However, you can remove them to give your pages a more streamlined appearance. To remove borders from your frames, follow these steps:

1. Start with a functional frameset document, such as the following.

```
<!DOCTYPE html PUBLIC "-//W3C//DTD XHTML 1.0 Frameset//EN"
    "http://www.w3.org/TR/xhtml1/DTD/xhtml1-frameset.dtd">
<html xmlns="http://www.w3.org/1999/xhtml">
<head>
    <title>Frameset Samples</title>
</head>
<frameset cols="30%, *">
    <frameset rows="50%, 50%">
        <frame name="topleft" src="z-maroon.html" />
        <frame name="lowerleft" src="z-blue.html" />
    </frameset>
    <frameset rows="100, *">
        <frame name="topright" src="z-yellow.html" />
        <frame name="lowerright" src="z-white.html" />
    </frameset>
</frameset>
</html>
```

2. To remove all borders from your frames, add both `border="0"` and `frame-border="0"` to each `frame` element.

```
<frameset cols="30%, *">
    <frameset rows="50%, 50%">
        <frame name="topleft" src="z-maroon.html" border="0"
            frameborder="0" />
        <frame name="lowerleft" src="z-blue.html" border="0"
            frameborder="0" />
```

```
        </frameset>
        <frameset rows="100, *">
            <frame name="topright" src="z-yellow.html"
                border="0" frameborder="0" />
            <frame name="lowerright" src="z-white.html"
                border="0" frameborder="0" />
        </frameset>
    </frameset>
```

These attributes result in the document shown in Figure 8.9.

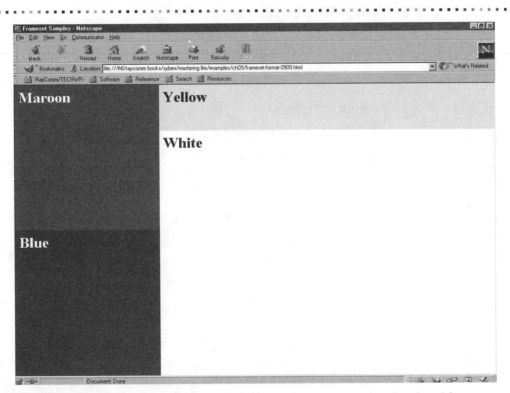

Figure 8.9 *Frames without borders often look more attractive than bordered frames.*

Because of the conflicting elements proposed and supported by Microsoft and Netscape, you must use both the border *and the* frameborder *attributes to turn off borders in all browsers. However, if you're on an intranet and all your users use Netscape browsers exclusively, use only the* border *attribute. If your users use Internet Explorer exclusively, use only the* frameborder *attribute.*

If you remove or set borders in individual frames, remember that the borders that frames share must **both** *be set to 0 to completely remove the border. If one frame is set to no borders and an adjacent frame has borders, you will see borders in the browser.*

Specifying Border Width

Adding borders of a specific size gets a little more complex because of the conflicting attributes supported by the HTML 4 specification, Internet Explorer, and Netscape Navigator. To turn on borders, set frameborder="1" (for Internet Explorer) and border="1" (for Netscape Navigator). To set the border width, increase the value of the border for both browsers.

The HTML 4 (hence the XHTML) specification does not support the border *attribute. In addition, the specification does not support the use of the* frameborder *attribute in the* frameset *element.*

For example, to turn on borders at the default value, use the following:

```
<frameset cols="30%, *" border="1" frameborder="1">
```

To set the borders to a width of 20 pixels (excessively wide, but easy to see if you're following the example), use the following:

```
<frameset cols="30%, *" border="20" frameborder="1">
```

The resulting screen looks like that shown in Figure 8.10.

Internet Explorer supports a framespacing="n" *attribute, which should increase the space between frames (in addition to the border width). However, because of Netscape's lack of support for this attribute and because this attribute is not included in the HTML 4 frames specification, we don't recommend using it.*

Figure 8.10 *A 20-pixel width is excessive, but it makes the change in border width apparent.*

Specifying Border Color

Colored borders can enhance or complement the color schemes of the documents in the frames. However, only the latest versions of Netscape Navigator and Internet Explorer support them, and they're not part of the HTML 4 specification.

To color frame borders, add the `bordercolor` attribute to the `frameset` or (better) `frame` element, as in the following example.

```
<frame name="left" src="navbar.html" border="2" frameborder="2"
    bordercolor="#008000" />
```

When coloring borders, add the color to the individual frames for more consistent results. Although you can often add colors to `frameset` elements, not all browsers consistently support that usage.

Controlling Frames

Depending on your layout, you might want to exercise a little extra control over how frames appear. In particular, you can:

- Prevent users from resizing the frame
- Determine whether scrollbars appear on framed pages
- Set frame margins

Controlling these aspects will help keep your site predictable and thus more usable for your users.

Controlling Frame Size

If you have content of a known size, you might want to establish a fixed size for a frame and choose not to let users resize it. For example, if a frame encloses an image map that is used for site-wide navigation, you would probably size the frame to the image map. If the image map is 390 pixels wide and 90 pixels high, you might set the frame to 400×100 pixels with the following code:

```
<frameset cols="400, *">
    <frameset rows="100, *">...</frameset>
</frameset>
```

You know the exact size of only the first (top-left) frame: It will be 400 pixels wide and 100 pixels high. All other frames on the page will be resized according to the size of the browser window. If the browser window is set to 800×600, the second (variable) column will be about 400 pixels wide. If the browser window is 1024×768, however, the variable column will be about 600 pixels wide.

You can also set a frame to `noresize` to prevent users from resizing it. Although many Web surfers do not know that they can resize frames by simply clicking and dragging the borders, some do and will rearrange the borders to suit themselves. However, if users resize a frameset to avoid scrolling, they might obscure some content without realizing it. To avoid this, simply add the `noresize` attribute to the `frame` element, like this:

```
<frame name="menu" src="imagemap.html" noresize="noresize" />
```

The `noresize` *attribute is set equal to itself. Setting one frame to* `noresize` *also prohibits other adjacent frames from resizing. For example, if the Maroon frame in Figure 8.10 is set to* `noresize`, *users cannot horizontally resize the Yellow frame or vertically resize the Blue frame.*

Controlling Scrollbars

Although scrollbars are essential so users can see all the content in frames, they can be superfluous and visually distracting. Depending on the margin that a browser inserts around an image, scrollbars might appear in some browsers on some platforms and not in others. For example, if the entire image map fits within the frame, little scrolling is necessary, and scrollbars would probably obscure more of the image map than what would be lost through the margins. Therefore, you might set this frame to scrolling="no" to prohibit scrollbars, like this:

```
<frame name="menu" src="imagemap.html" scrolling="no"
    noresize="noresize" />
```

Set scrolling="no" *only if the frame contains an image or an object of a known size. Because browser settings, available fonts, and monitor resolution vary, you cannot predict what text might or might not fit within a frame.*

Conversely, you might also set scrolling="yes" in some cases. For example, if you have a contents page that contains most of the links from your navigation frame, you might set scrolling to yes so the frame always has a scrollbar. If you have shorter documents, the scrollbar will be nonfunctional, but it will appear consistently and make your site look just a wee bit more professional. If you set scrolling to auto (the default), some pages may have a scrollbar and some may not, which can be distracting to a user.

Setting Frame Margins

A frame margin is the space between the edge of the frame and the visible content of the XHTML document. Adjusting the frame margin affects the framed document itself and keeps documents from appearing to touch each other; in other words, adjusting the frame margins gives your documents a little "breathing room."

To set frame margins, add the marginheight (for vertical margins) and marginwidth (for horizontal margins) attributes to the frame element, as shown in the following code:

```
<frame name="topleft" src="z-maroon.html" marginwidth="100"
    marginheight="100" />
```

This code moves the document 100 pixels from the top and left margins, as illustrated in Figure 8.11.

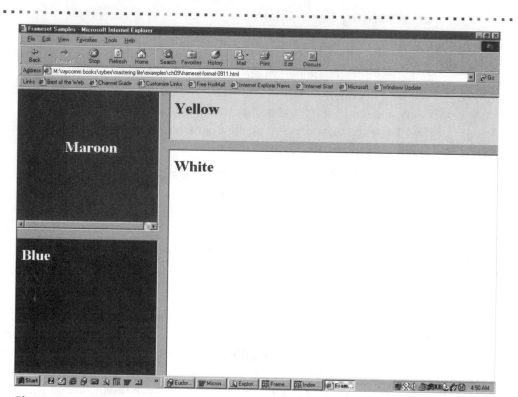

Figure 8.11 *The Maroon document's margins are a little big, but clearly different.*

Accommodating Nonframed Browsers

As mentioned earlier, not all browsers support frames. If a user to your framed site has a nonframed browser, what does he or she see? Nothing. Because that's the last thing you want, you need to accommodate users who are using nonframed browsers. This usually means supplying text that replicates the information in the framed document.

If you're developing a framed intranet site and your company only uses the latest version of a particular browser, you really don't need to worry about this. However, if you're developing a Web site for general use, you need to give careful thought to how you will supply information to users using nonframed browsers. Here are some guidelines.

- Provide some amount of nonframed information. Even if you decide not to accommodate nonframed browsers, display a courtesy message stating (positively) that your site requires the newest graphical browsers and that it's inaccessible with other browsers.

- Use a browser-detection script that automatically redirects nonframed browsers to the nonframed pages. This option requires slightly more work than the preceding guideline; however, it makes the browser do the work, not the user.

- Include alternate text within the noframes section. If you do this carefully, your users may not even know that your site has other content. This option increases your workload substantially. You must maintain two complete documents—the content within the frames and the content within the noframes section.

- Create your home page using frames, but provide a link to the nonframed version. Users thus have the option to use frames, but they aren't forced to do so. This option also doubles your work.

- Develop your home page without frames, and then provide links to the framed version. Again, this is a double-your-work option.

At one time, the Raycomm Web site (real, not hypothetical) used this last solution, as shown in Figure 8.12. The home page looked like a framed site, but was actually a fancy background and a table to separate the navigation features from the content. A link ("Try the High-Tech Site") went to a roughly parallel page that looked the same but used frames.

Tips for Maintaining Framed and Nonframed Documents

One way to lighten your workload is to make extensive use of "server-side includes," so your content and presentation are essentially separate. You include the content in framed pages. In the nonframed pages, you include the content and another document that has navigation links. Check your server documentation for more information about using server-side include capabilities.

Another alternative is to include the navigation links in your document and then use JavaScript to hide the links from framed browsers. This is not an elegant solution, but it works. Almost all browsers that support JavaScript also support frames, and vice versa (unless the user has disabled either frames or JavaScript).

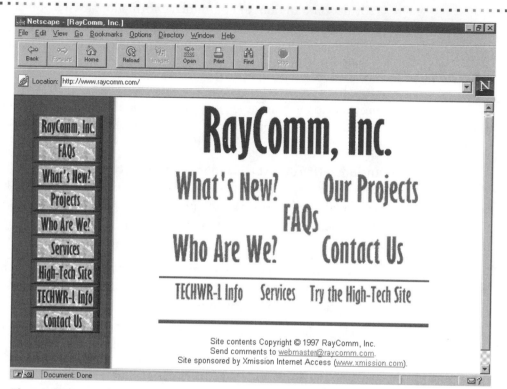

Figure 8.12 *A table can masquerade as a set of framed documents.*

Are Tables or Frames Better for Your Design Needs?

You can use both tables and frames to create interesting page layouts and work around the limitations of XHTML. For example, you can place navigation information beside the text of a document or array two columns of text side by side, using either tables or frames.

So how do you decide which to use? The advantages of tables include the following:

- Tables are more widely recognized by browsers than frames.
- Tables create fewer site navigation difficulties than frames.
- Tables are standard HTML 3.2 and 4.

The advantages of frames include the following:

- Frames are easier to update and maintain because the individual documents are shorter and simpler.

- Framed pages tend to download faster and take up less memory than tables because information doesn't have to be downloaded repeatedly.

- Frames are more flexible for complex layouts. For example, they allow you to have information across the top of a page and scroll other information under that banner.

- Frames offer some useful bells and whistles, such as being able to call up a document in a specific part of the browser window—an effect that can be simulated with tables only at the cost of incredible effort.

- Frames are standard HTML 4.

For more information about tables, see Chapter 6.

Providing Nonframed Content

To accommodate users using nonframed browsers, use the noframes element and include the alternate text. Start with an existing XHTML frameset document such as the following:

```
<!DOCTYPE html PUBLIC "-//W3C//DTD XHTML 1.0 Frameset//EN"
    "http://www.w3.org/TR/xhtml1/DTD/xhtml1-frameset.dtd">
<html xmlns="http://www.w3.org/1999/xhtml">
<head>
    <title>Frameset Samples</title>
</head>
<frameset cols="30%, *" border="0" frameborder="0"
    bordercolor="#008000">
    <frameset rows="50%, 50%">
        <frame name="topleft" src="z-maroon.html" />
        <frame name="lowerleft" src="z-blue.html" />
    </frameset>
    <frameset rows="100, *">
        <frame name="topright" src="z-yellow.html" />
        <frame name="lowerright" src="z-white.html" />
    </frameset>
</frameset>
</html>
```

Now, follow these steps:

1. Add the `noframes` tag pair somewhere in the document between the `frameset` tags. The best choice—for ease of development—is either at the beginning, immediately following the first `frameset` tag, or at the end, just before the closing `frameset` tag.

```
  . . .
          <noframes>
             <body>
             </body>
          </noframes>
       </frameset>
    </html>
```

The body *element is required in the* noframes *element according to the XHTML Frameset DTD. Therefore, if you're going to validate your frameset documents, you should include the* body *element in the* noframes *element.*

2. Add any appropriate content within the `noframes` elements. The approach you take, as mentioned previously, will vary. For an intranet site for a company that has standardized on the latest version of Internet Explorer, you might choose something like the following.

```
<noframes>
  <body>
     <h1 align="center">Intranet Access Problem</h1>
     <p>WAMMI, Inc., has standardized on the newest
version of Internet Explorer. You seem to be using an
older version or a different browser entirely. Please see
your network administrator or check with the Help Desk to
get the proper browser. With the newest browser, you will
be able to access the corporate intranet.</p>
  </body>
</noframes>
```

When viewed in a nonframed browser such as Mosaic, this page looks like Figure 8.13.

Figure 8.13 *The* noframes *content is visible only in browsers that cannot accommodate frames, as shown here.*

Some nonframed browsers support only a limited set of formatting elements. Keep this in mind if you're tempted to get fancy with your nonframes formatting.

Enabling Effective Navigation

Designing with frames and helping your users navigate your site effectively requires moderation and simplicity. The following sections explain the navigation types and show you how to implement navigation.

Choosing Navigation Types

You can design frames so users can navigate in two ways:

- Users can click in one frame and view the resulting document in another frame (as shown in Figure 8.14).

- Users can click in one frame and view the resulting document in that same frame.

Figure 8.14 *Navigation links can lead to a document in the same frame or in another frame.*

When you use the first option, navigation tools remain visible at all times in one frame, and the content appears and changes in another frame. In Figure 8.14, clicking a link on the left changes the content in the frame on the right.

When you use the second option, clicking a link changes the content in the frame that contains the link. For example, in Figure 8.14, clicking a link in the frame on the right changes the content of that frame.

You normally use the second option when content is logically cross-referenced to other documents at the site. However, all frames can contain links, whether they are navigation links or cross-references.

Implementing Navigation

Linking to specific frames requires only one new attribute, target. When used in an anchor (a) element, this attribute directs the content of the link into a different frame.

The frameset document for Figure 8.14 looks like this:

```
<!DOCTYPE html PUBLIC "-//W3C//DTD XHTML 1.0 Frameset//EN"
    "http://www.w3.org/TR/xhtml1/DTD/xhtml1-frameset.dtd">
<html xmlns="http://www.w3.org/1999/xhtml">
<head>
    <title>ASR Outfitters Framed Site</title>
</head>
<frameset cols="230, *">
    <frame name="left" src="lefttoc1.html" />
    <frame name="main" src="content.html" />
    <noframes>
      <body>
        <p>If you can see this, your browser is not capable
            of displaying frames.</p>
      </body>
    </noframes>
</frameset>
</html>
```

The first (left) frame element carries the attribute name="left", and the other frame has the attribute name="main". These attributes allow the frames to be specifically addressed.

The basic code for the left frame is as follows:

```
<!DOCTYPE html PUBLIC "-//W3C//DTD XHTML 1.0 Frameset//EN"
    "http://www.w3.org/TR/xhtml1/DTD/xhtml1-frameset.dtd">
<html xmlns="http://www.w3.org/1999/xhtml">
<head>
    <title>ASR Outfitters</title>
</head>
<body background="" bgcolor="#ffffff" text="#000000"
    link="#0000ff" vlink="#800080" alink="#ff0000">
    <img src="asrlogosm.gif" align="" width="200" height="84"
        border="0" alt="ASR Logo" />
    <ul>
        <li><a href="camping.html">Camping News</a></li>
```

```
      <li><a href="weather.html">Check Weather</a></li>
      <li><a href="clubs.html">Clubs</a></li>
      <li><a href="catalog.html">Catalog</a></li>
      <li><a href="contact.html">Contact Us</a></li>
   </ul>
 </body>
</html>
```

As the document currently stands, clicking a link—say, Camping News—in the left frame displays the new document in the left (same) frame, because frame links, by default, land in the same frame. If you want the linked document to appear in the right frame, follow these steps:

1. Add the target attribute to the a element.

```
      <li><a href="camping.html" target="">Camping News
         </a></li>
```

2. Add the name of the frame to which you want to link. The initial frameset names the frame on the right main, so that's the name you use.

```
      <li><a href="camping.html" target="main">Camping News
         </a></li>
```

Now when you click the Camping News link, the file appears in the right frame, as shown in Figure 8.15.

Of course, in this particular scenario, each link from this document should open in the main frame. To save time and reduce the possibility of error, you can add the target="main" attribute to the base element and force it to affect the entire document.

The base element goes in the document head and sets the rules for the whole document. To set all links from the document in the left frame to open in the main frame, add the element and attribute to the document head as in the following example:

```
<!DOCTYPE html PUBLIC "-//W3C//DTD XHTML 1.0 Frameset//EN"
   "http://www.w3.org/TR/xhtml1/DTD/xhtml1-frameset.dtd">
<html xmlns="http://www.w3.org/1999/xhtml">
<head>
   <title>ASR Outfitters</title>
   <base target="main" />
</head>
```

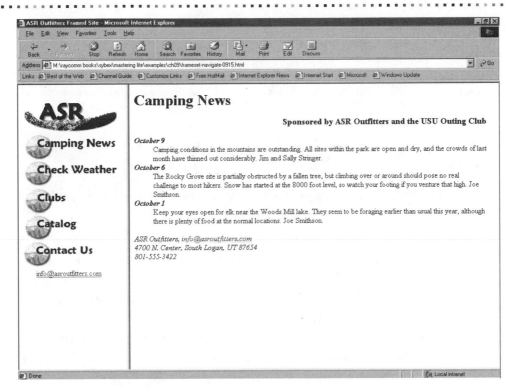

Figure 8.15 The target *attribute controls which frame receives the content of a link. The Camping News link was directed into the "main" frame.*

With the base target defined, you only need the target attributes to link to other locations. The following section discusses some special target locations and names.

Using Image Maps as Navigation Tools in Framed Documents

The target attribute works in all contexts where links occur. For example, you can use an image map in a frame to provide navigation for an entire site. The following code and example show how to include an image map in a framed page:

```
<map name="frame-imagemap">
<area shape="rect" coords="4,4,190,51" href="camping.html"
    alt="Camping" />
<area shape="rect" coords="5,57,191,110" href="weather.html"
```

```
        alt="Weather" />
    <area shape="rect" coords="4,112,191,165" href="clubs.html"
        alt="Clubs" />
    <area shape="rect" coords="3,167,191,220" href="catalog.html"
        alt="Catalog" />
    <area shape="rect" coords="3,222,191,277" href="contact.html"
        alt="Contact" />
    <area shape="default" href="lefttoc1.html" alt="Contents" />
    </map>
```

To force each area, except the last, to open in the main frame, add the `target="main"` attribute to each one, as in the following code:

```
    <map name="frame-imagemap">
    <area shape="rect" coords="4,4,190,51" href="camping.html"
        alt="Camping" target="main" />
    <area shape="rect" coords="5,57,191,110" href="weather.html"
        alt="Weather" target="main" />
    <area shape="rect" coords="4,112,191,165" href="clubs.html"
        alt="Clubs" target="main" />
    <area shape="rect" coords="3,167,191,220" href="catalog.html"
        alt="Catalog" target="main" />
    <area shape="rect" coords="3,222,191,277" href="contact.html"
        alt="Contact" target="main" />
    <area shape="default" href="lefttoc1.html" alt="Contents" />
    </map>
```

Using Special Target Names

In addition to the target names that you define in `frame` elements within the frameset document, you can use other, special target names in all elements that link XHTML documents, such as a, `form`, and `area`. Table 8.3 explains these target names and their functions.

Table 8.3 Special Target Names

Attribute Value	Use
target="..."	Sets the link to open in the frame named between the quotes.
target="_self"	Sets the link to open in the current frame.
target="_blank"	Sets the link to open in a new window.
target="_parent"	Sets the link to open in the parent frameset of the current document. If only one frameset is present, this removes the frameset.
target="_top"	Sets the link to open in the browser window, breaking out of all frames.

By using these special `target` attribute values, in any context, you control where the linked file appears. In general, you can keep the targets predictable and usable by following these guidelines:

- Keep your pages together. If you're linking a closely related page from your site, direct the link into an adjacent frame, not into a separate window, so your site remains visually cohesive.

- Keep your navigation content and regular content in a consistent location. If your navigation links appear in a frame that spans the top of the browser window, the content to which the objects in that frame link should appear in a different frame. Similarly, if a link within your Web content displays related content, use `target="_self"` to ensure that the link appears in the same window, because your users will expect content in that particular frame.

- Link to nonframed pages using `target="_top"` to ensure that your non-framed documents really aren't framed.

- Keep your pages visible. If you link to another site, use `target="_blank"` to open a new browser window for the other site, while keeping your window open and visible. That way, if your user tires of the other site, your site is still easily accessible.

- Don't frame other pages. By setting `target="_blank"` or `target="_top"` for external links, you can ensure that other people's content doesn't appear within your frames. Why? First, if you display content on your site that was created by someone else, that's plagiarism. Second, you don't necessarily want your site associated with content from another site. (See the sidebar "A Caution About Linking to Outside Sites" earlier in this chapter for more information.)

- Don't frame yourself. If your framed site includes an active link to the home page (likely the frameset document for the site), be sure that the link includes `target="_top"`. If you accidentally point the link to your main frameset into a frame within the site, your home page will appear within your home page within your home page and so on. See Figure 8.16 for an example.

Figure 8.16 *Framing your own site, even accidentally, can look odd at best and completely silly at worst.*

A little creativity in `target` *attributes is a good thing, but a lot of creativity will either scare off users or entice them to click every link you have just to see where it goes.*

The Order of *target* Attributes

If `target` attributes appear in more than one place—or don't appear at all—the order of precedence is as follows:

- No `target` attributes means that the link will appear in the same frame.
- `target` attributes in the `base` element apply to all links in the document.
- `target` attributes in a elements override the `base` element.

Creating Inline Frames

Inline frames, often called *floating frames*, appear as part of an XHTML document in much the same way that images appear in an XHTML document. They allow you to insert an XHTML document into an area within another document. In this sense, inline frames blend traditional XHTML documents with framed documents. At the time of writing, only Internet Explorer 3 and higher and Netscape 6 supported inline frames, although they are part of the HTML 4 specification. Figure 8.17 shows a sample inline frame from an ASR Outfitters page.

The basic element you use for your inline frames is the `iframe` element, which identifies a floating frame's characteristics and initial content. Its attributes are listed and explained in Table 8.4.

Table 8.4 Attributes of the `iframe` Element

ATTRIBUTE	DESCRIPTION
`src="url"`	Identifies the source for the frame content as a standard URL.
`name="..."`	Labels the frame so it can be targeted or referred to from other frames or windows.
`frameborder="n"`	Sets or removes borders around the frame.
`scrolling="..."`	Prohibits scrollbars (`no`), requires scrollbars (`yes`), or lets the browser provide scrollbars if required (`auto`, the default).

Table 8.4 continued Attributes of the `iframe` Element

ATTRIBUTE	DESCRIPTION
`marginheight="n"`	Sets the number of pixels in the margin above and below the content of the frame.
`marginwidth="n"`	Sets the number of pixels in the margin to the left and right of the frame.
`height="n"`	Specifies the height of an inline frame in pixels.
`width="n"`	Specifies the width of an inline frame in pixels.
`align="…"`	Specifies the alignment as `left`, `middle`, `right`, `top`, or `bottom`.

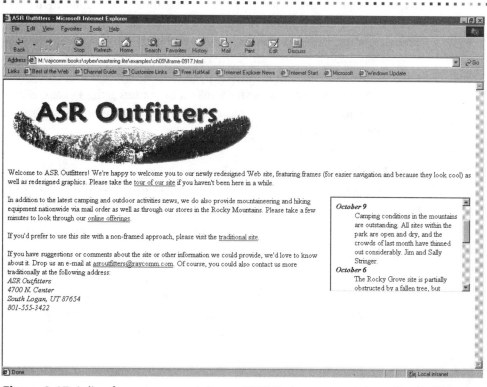

Figure 8.17 Inline frames can contain any XHTML document and can float within another document.

To add an inline frame to your document, start with a functional XHTML document:

```
<!DOCTYPE html PUBLIC "-//W3C//DTD XHTML 1.0 Frameset//EN"
    "http://www.w3.org/TR/xhtml1/DTD/xhtml1-frameset.dtd">
<html xmlns="http://www.w3.org/1999/xhtml">
<head>
    <title>Floating Frame Samples</title>
</head>
<body background="" bgcolor="FFFFFF" text="000000"
    link="0000FF" vlink="800080" alink="FF0000">
    <h1>Floating Frames</h1>
    <p>Documents with floating frames look really cool, but only
        in Internet Explorer.</p>
</body>
</html>
```

Now, follow these steps:

1. Add an iframe tag pair.

    ```
    <body background="" bgcolor="FFFFFF" text="000000"
        link="0000FF" vlink="800080" alink="FF0000">
        <h1>Floating Frames</h1>
        <iframe>
        </iframe>
        <p>Documents with floating frames look really cool, but
            only in Internet Explorer.</p>
    </body>
    ```

2. Add the name attribute to the iframe element. Just as with traditional frames, the name attribute labels the frame so it can be targeted by links.

    ```
    <iframe name="float1">
    </iframe>
    ```

3. Add the src attribute to specify the XHTML document that will fill the frame. Technically, an image could also fill a frame, but that would rather defeat the purpose of a floating frame where an XHTML document can be placed.

    ```
    <iframe src="z-maroon.html" name="float1">
    </iframe>
    ```

4. Include the height and width attributes to specify the dimensions of the floating frame in pixels. These values are analogous to the height and width attributes for an image.

```
<iframe src="z-maroon.html" name="float1" height="200"
    width="300">
</iframe>
```

5. Provide alternate text to accommodate users using browsers other than recent versions of Internet Explorer. This text is similar to the alt text from images, except that you do not use an attribute–value pair here; just enter the alternate text between the iframe tags.

```
<iframe src="z-maroon.html" name="float1" height="200"
    width="300">
    Netscape Navigator users get to see this message.
</iframe>
```

6. Optionally, add an alignment attribute. Generally, you'll use either left or right, but any alignment attribute that you'd use with images will also work with floating frames.

```
<iframe src="z-maroon.html" name="float1" height="200"
    width="300" align="right">
    Netscape Navigator users get to see this message.
</iframe>
```

If you're using Internet Explorer version 3 or later, you'll see something like Figure 8.18.

Because floating frames closely resemble images in the way they are implemented and manipulated within the parent document, you can often treat floating frames in similar ways. For example, you can array them within table cells to force a specific layout scheme. You can also wrap text around the floating frame just as you wrap text around an image, as ASR Outfitters did in Figure 8.17, earlier in this chapter.

Figure 8.18 *Floating frames can be visually interesting and make pages more attractive.*

Navigating in and among floating frames is similar to navigating in regular frames. The name and target attributes serve the same purposes, and you use them the same way whether you're dealing with inline frames or regular frames. For example, use the following code to force a document to appear in a floating frame.

```
<a href="z-blue" target="float1">Click to put the blue document
   in the floating frame.</a>
```

Where to Go from Here

In this chapter, you learned about frames—their uses, advantages, and disadvantages—and about how to include them in your XHTML documents. Keep in mind that not all browsers support frames; so use the guidelines throughout this chapter to determine when and how to include them effectively.

Also in this chapter, you learned how frames relate to other XHTML components. Following is a list of related information you might find useful:

- For information about computer and browser settings, see Chapter 1.

- If you want information about keeping up with standards, also refer to Chapter 1.

- For more information about URLs, see Chapter 4.

- To find out more about images and image maps, see Chapter 5.

- To read more about tables, see Chapter 6.

Converting HTML to XHTML

Chapter 9

T he odds are that you already have a few (or many) HTML documents lying around. It may be that you want to do what we did: Update your entire HTML site to XHTML. That doesn't mean that you have to start over from scratch.

Remember that XHTML uses the exact same elements and attributes as HTML (with the exception of adding the XHTML namespace). This means that you don't have to change your vocabulary much; all you need to do is update your syntax. There are two ways you can do this: by hand or with the help of a tool.

This chapter covers the following topics:

- Converting your HTML documents by hand

- Converting your HTML documents using HTML Tidy

Why Convert Your Documents?

This seems to be the first question that comes out of a Web developer's mouth: "Why should I convert to XHTML?" Because the two languages use the same element set, and they should function the same in a browser, why would you want to take the time to convert them?

To understand why you would want to convert to XHTML, you have to understand where XML is coming from and going to (re-read Chapter 2 if this doesn't make sense). If you still feel the conversion is not worth the time, here are just a few of the reasons you would want to convert your documents to XHTML:

- Because XHTML is an application of XML, an XML processor can process XHTML.

- XHTML can be extended to include other document models (or vocabularies), including Scalable Vector Graphics (SVG), Synchronized Multimedia Integration Language (SMIL), Mathematical Markup Language (MathML), or even your own XML vocabulary.

- XHTML encourages the separation of style from structure.

- XHTML promotes cleaner markup that will be easier for both a processor and human to read.

- Mobile-phone vendors selected XHTML as their markup language of choice.

- XHTML allows traditional HTML content developers and Web designers to continue using what they know, albeit in the framework of a more structured markup environment.

- Although many tool vendors have not yet caught on, most experts think it's just a matter of time before vendors big and small make mechanical validation part of their built-in editing processes.

- Current efforts on XHTML modularization (which breaks markup into categories, and lets each category be used independently of the others in documents) and related forms of XML-based markup—for instance, the outstanding work on XForms that's currently underway—promise to give XHTML documents access to markup and capabilities that HTML does not (and will never) have. Over time, improved functionality will move the market simply because content developers will need the capabilities that other XML applications can deliver.

- More history and experience with XHTML and with the XHTML–XML connection are likely to demonstrate lower costs of ownership, maintenance, and development. If realized, these benefits will move the market inexorably in that direction.

- HTML won't be developed any further by the W3C except as new versions of XHTML; therefore, it's unlikely to be taken any further by browser vendors. (Browser vendors will most likely continue support for HTML, but they just won't develop additional support.)

Converting Documents by Hand

If you're only updating a few documents, and you're dying to get some XHTML practice, you might choose to convert your HTML page to XHTML by hand. To be honest, this will rarely happen. There's no need to, because there's a wonderful free tool (HTML Tidy, discussed in the "Working with Tidy" section) that will do it for you at the click of a button. However, it's important that you understand what the tool is doing, so you can utilize its customizable options.

To understand what the tool is doing, let's take a look at what you would have to do if your tool of choice was your fingers.

Backward Compatibility

XHTML is backward compatible with legacy browsers. Keeping in mind that XHTML uses HTML's vocabulary, the only real obstacle that would prevent XHTML from compatibility with older browsers would be syntactic conventions. Lucky for us, XML syntax is close enough to SGML (and therefore HTML) that the syntactic differences are small.

In Chapter 2, you learned all the rules your XHTML document must follow, most of which were already defined by HTML. A few additions, such as closing all elements and adhering to an empty-element syntax, are new. Whereas older browsers have very few problems processing XHTML documents, you need to abide by a few rules to avoid any problems:

- When using XML's empty-element syntax, include a space before the trailing forward slash (/); for example, `<br />`.

- Most older browsers will render the XML declaration

```
<?xml version="1.0" encoding="UTF-8" standalone="no"?>
```

as content, so it's best to leave it off any XHTML document that will be viewed in older browsers. If you do leave the XML declaration out of your document, the document can only use UTF-8 or UTF-16 character encoding.

- Use external style sheet or script documents, rather than embedding them in the head of your XHTML document. Prior to XHTML, Web developers used HTML comments to hide script and style sheet syntax from older browsers. XHTML uses XML CDATA sections to mark internal scripts and style sheet syntax. Old and new processors are likely to conflict. If you cannot use external scripts or style sheets, be sure that the internal syntax does not contain <, &,]]>, or --.

Currently, no browsers know how to handle XML CDATA sections. However, further support for XML is very likely in the next versions of browsers.

- Do not add line breaks or multiple white-space characters within attribute values. Many XML developers use line breaks to aid document readability, but browsers handle white space inconsistently, and multiple white-space characters can translate into problems when rendering XHTML documents. If you're going to use white space for readability, be sure you include it only between elements.

- Use both the name and id attributes when referring to a fragment identifier that begins with a pound symbol (#value). The name attribute was originally used to refer to named anchors; however, HTML 4 deprecated this attribute and introduced the id attribute to replace it as a way to uniquely identify a given element. For future compatibility, you want to use the id attribute; however, because many current and older browsers don't support this attribute, you use the name attribute as well. For example,

    ```
    <a name="one" id="one">...</a>
    ```

- Again, for forward and backward compatibility, use both the lang and xml:lang attributes to define the language for a given element. The xml:lang attribute takes precedence over the lang attribute.

- Don't use more than one isindex element within the head element. The isindex element is deprecated in favor of the input element.

If you're concerned with creating XHTML documents that support backward compatibility with older browsers, be sure that you use elements that are supported by the older browsers. For example, if you use form markup in your XHTML document, Internet Explorer 2 will not recognize it because it does not support complex forms.

The Rules

As an application of XML, XHTML requires that you follow XML's syntax requirements. These syntax requirements are similar to those followed by HTML and should be easy to get a handle on. In the following sections, we briefly go over the rules one by one.

These rules are defined in detail in Chapter 2. For more information about each specific syntax rule, see Chapter 2.

Terminate all elements. All elements must be balanced with a closing tag, or if considered empty, they should follow XML's empty-element syntax.

Use proper empty-element syntax. Empty elements must also be terminated; however, as the document author, you have two options. You could add a closing end tag to balance the empty element; for example,
</br>. However, because adding a closing tag doesn't seem logical, a shortened syntax was also defined—adding a trailing forward slash to the opening tag; for example, <br />. If you use the empty-element syntax (<br />), you have to add a white-space character before the trailing forward slash, for backward compatibility reasons.

Quote all attribute values. All your attributes' values must be in quotation marks.

Give values for all attributes. HTML allows for a handful of attributes that function as Boolean attributes, which stand alone, without a value. When one of these is present, it turns a function on. When the attribute is omitted, the function is not activated. Because XHTML follows XML's syntax rules, all attributes must have values; for example,

```
<input type="checkbox" checked="checked" />
```

Lowercase element and attribute names because XHTML is case sensitive. The XML specification requires that XML documents obey the rules of an associated DTD, including naming conventions for elements and attributes. If the DTD defines all element and attribute names in lowercase, as developers we have to abide by that rule. Therefore, all XHTML elements and attributes must be lowercased. We also lowercase case-insensitive attribute values to be consistent.

Nest elements correctly. Nesting elements correctly wasn't important to HTML; however, it's a strict requirement for XHTML. Because elements must be balanced with an opening tag and a closing tag, it's necessary to be careful with nesting; it establishes element hierarchy and relationships.

There's an easy way to remember your nesting principles: What you open first, you must close last. Repeat that to yourself over and over and you will never forget how to nest again.

Include a *DOCTYPE* declaration. If you're adhering to one of the XHTML 1 DTDs, you can't use an HTML 4 DTD reference. When you're converting your document from HTML to XHTML, make sure that you're using the correct DOCTYPE declaration. For a listing of the three XHTML DTDs, see Chapter 2.

Add the XHTML namespace. XHTML makes use of XML namespaces to help uniquely identify its collection of elements and attributes. This is especially handy if you plan on mixing (embedding) other XML vocabularies. Namespaces are covered in Chapter 2. Be sure to read more about namespaces if you haven't already. According to the XHTML specification, all XHTML documents must use the default XHTML namespace (xmlns="http://www.w3.org/1999/xhtml"). This namespace is required and must be defined within the html start tag.

Summing It Up

Listing 9.1 is not a well-formed XHTML document, and we're going to make it one.

LISTING 9.1: SLOPPY HTML DOCUMENT

```
<HTML>
<HEAD>
<TITLE>Sloppy HTML</TITLE>
</HEAD>
<BODY>
<H1>Element Rules</H1>
<P><FONT COLOR=RED>Elements provide the structure that holds your
document together.</FONT>
<BR>
<OL COMPACT>
<LI>Close all elements.
```

```
<LI>Empty elements should follow empty-element syntax, and be
sure to add the white space for backward compatibility.
<LI>Convert all stand-alone attributes to attributes with values.
<LI>Add quotation marks to all attribute values.
<LI>Convert all uppercase element and attribute names to
lowercase.
<LI>Use the appropriate DOCTYPE declaration.
<LI>Add the XHTML namespace to the html start tag.
<LI>Make sure you comply with any backward-compatible steps
defined in the section "Backward Compatibility."
</OL>
</BODY>
</HTML>
```

Follow these steps to make the document well formed:

1. Close all elements. Notice that the p element and none of the list item (li) elements have closing tags, so add the closing p and li tags.

    ```
    <P><FONT COLOR=RED>Elements provide the structure that
    holds your document together.</FONT></P>
    <BR>
    <OL COMPACT>
    <LI>Close all elements.</LI>
    <LI>Empty elements should follow empty-element syntax.</LI>
    <LI>Convert all stand-alone attributes to attributes with
    values.</LI>
    <LI>Add quotation marks to all attribute values.</LI>
    <LI>Convert all uppercase element and attribute names to
    lowercase.</LI>
    <LI>Use the appropriate DOCTYPE declaration.</LI>
    <LI>Add the XHTML namespace to the html start tag.</LI>
    <LI>Make sure you comply with any backward-compatible steps
    defined in the section "Backward
    Compatibility."</LI>
    </OL>
    ```

2. Empty elements should follow empty-element syntax, and be sure to add the white space for backward compatibility. The BR element is the only empty element in this document. Change it to <BR />.

3. Convert all stand-alone attributes to attributes with values. Change COMPACT to COMPACT=COMPACT.

4. Add quotation marks to all attribute values.

```
<P><FONT COLOR="RED">Elements provide the structure that
holds your document together.</FONT></P>
<BR>
<OL COMPACT="COMPACT">
```

5. Convert all uppercase element and attribute names (and attribute values) to lowercase.

```
<html>
<head>
<title>Sloppy HTML</title>
</head>
<body>
<h1>Element Rules</h1>
<p><font color="red">Elements provide the structure that
holds your document together.</font></p>
<br />
<ol compact="compact">
<li>Close all elements.</li>
<li>Empty elements should follow empty-element syntax.</li>
<li>Convert all stand-alone attributes to attributes with
values.</li>...
```

6. Use the appropriate DOCTYPE declaration. We're going to use the Transitional DTD:

```
<!DOCTYPE html
  PUBLIC "-//W3C//DTD XHTML 1.0 Transitional//EN"
  "http://www.w3.org/TR/xhtml1/DTD/xhtml1-transitional.dtd">
```

7. Add the XHTML namespace to the html start tag.

```
<html xmlns="http://www.w3.org/1999/xhtml">
```

8. Make sure you comply with any backward-compatible steps defined in the section "Backward Compatibility." Our document doesn't need any adjustments here.

According to the XHTML specification, you should wrap any script or stylesheet syntax with XML CDATA sections to avoid conflicts with < and &, or to avoid the expansion of entities such as & or <. In theory, this would be an additional step in the conversion process. Although this would be ideal, most browsers don't recognize CDATA section syntax. To avoid browser confusion, it's recommended that you use external script and style sheets when possible.

You're resulting code should look like Listing 9.2.

LISTING 9.2: CLEAN XHTML DOCUMENT

```
<!DOCTYPE html PUBLIC "-//W3C//DTD XHTML 1.0 Transitional//EN"
   "http://www.w3.org/TR/xhtml1/DTD/xhtml1-transitional.dtd">
<html xmlns="http://www.w3.org/1999/xhtml">
  <head>
    <title>Sloppy HTML</title>
  </head>
  <body>
    <h1>Element Rules</h1>
    <p><font color="red">Elements provide the structure that
      holds your document together.</font></p>
    <br />
    <ol compact="compact">
      <li>Close all elements.</li>
      <li>Empty elements should follow empty-element syntax, and
        be sure to add the white space for backward
        compatibility.</li>
      <li>Convert all stand-alone attributes to attributes with
        values.</li>
      <li>Add quotation marks to all attribute values.</li>
      <li>Convert all uppercase element and attribute names to
        lowercase.</li>
      <li>Use the appropriate DOCTYPE declaration.</li>
      <li>Add the XHTML namespace to the html start tag.</li>
      <li>Make sure you comply with any backward-compatible
        steps defined in the section "Backward Compatibility."
        </li>
    </ol>
  </body>
</html>
```

In this listing, you'll notice that we indented the markup. We do this to make the markup easier to read.

We don't suggest using the font *element to define presentation. We recommend using Cascading Style Sheets (CSS) to define presentation style rules for your document. If your target audience uses Internet Explorer 5.0 or higher, we recommend you opt for CSS style rules.*

Working with Tidy

HTML Tidy, a tool created by David Raggett, is the answer to any Web developer's prayer. Tidy, which has been around for a while, converts HTML documents into clean XHTML in a matter of seconds. In the beginning, it was designed to clean up HTML markup. Now, Tidy is included as a plug-in with most big-time HTML editors. In addition, Tidy comes in a version you can run from the command prompt and a GUI version (TidyGUI).

You may be wondering just what Tidy can do. Well, it pretty much does everything you need it to do. For example, Tidy corrects the following:

Detects mismatched end tags In most cases, Tidy will locate mismatched end tags and make the appropriate corrections.

Corrects incorrectly nested elements In most cases, Tidy will correct nesting errors.

Locates misplaced elements Tidy will alert the document author if an element is misused—for example, if the td element is nested within a form element.

Lowercases element and attribute names Tidy will correct any uppercase element names and attribute names automatically.

Adds quotation marks to attribute values Tidy will add double or single quotation marks around all attribute values (you can specify which).

This is not the end of what Tidy can do. In fact, you can customize Tidy to do just about anything relating to the conversion process. For example, you can control whether the modified version uses indentation for nested elements, or you can request that Tidy invoke only some, but not all, of the rules. To learn more about HTML Tidy's many, many abilities and options, visit www.w3.org/People/Raggett/Tidy.

The markup shown in Listing 9.3 is the `sloppy.htm` document that we'll convert to clean XHTML. The clean markup that's produced by all methods discussed in the following sections is shown in Listing 9.4.

LISTING 9.3: SLOPPY HTML DOCUMENT

```
<HTML>
<HEAD>
<TITLE>LANWrights Online Training</TITLE>
</HEAD>
<BLOCKQUOTE><B>Note: </B>For a complete bibliography and
publication information, please visit the LANWrights <A
HREF="http://www.lanw.com/books.htm">Book Nook.</BLOCKQUOTE></A>
<H1>LANWrights Web-based Training</H1>
<P>All classes share a similar design approach, including the
following:
<UL COMPACT TYPE=SQUARE>
<LI>A collection of stand-alone lessons equal to about 16 hours
of classroom training
<LI>Online exercises, with built-in feedback on results
<LI>Online discussion group software that allows students to
interact with each other online, and access to a telephone
hotline open during regular business hours
<LI>Automated mastery tests for each lesson, including score
reporting
<LI>Individual student tracking and results reporting available
24/7
<LI>Printable access and how-to instructions for student use
<LI>Printable and/or downloadable versions of all lessons
</UL><P ALIGN=CENTER>If you are interested in hiring us to
provide online training for your company, you can visit our <A
HREF="http://www.lanw.com/training/wbt-brochure.htm">online
brochure</A>, which includes specific information about pricing,
structure, availability, and the instructors.
</BODY>
</HTML>
```

LISTING 9.4: CLEAN XHTML VERSION PRODUCED BY HTML TIDY

```
<!DOCTYPE html PUBLIC "-//W3C//DTD XHTML 1.0 Transitional//EN"
"http://www.w3.org/TR/xhtml1/DTD/xhtml1-transitional.dtd">
<html xmlns="http://www.w3.org/1999/xhtml">
<head>
<meta name="generator" content="HTML Tidy, see www.w3.org" />
<title>Sloppy HTML</title>
</head>
<body>
<blockquote><b>Note:</b> For a complete bibliography and
publication information, please visit the LANWrights <a
href="http://www.lanw.com/books.htm">Book Nook.</a></blockquote>
<h1>LANWrights Web-based Training</h1>
<p>All classes share a similar design approach, including the
following:</p>
<ul compact="compact" type="square">
<li>A collection of stand-alone lessons equal to about 16 hours
of classroom training</li>
<li>Online exercises, with built-in feedback on results</li>
<li>Online discussion group software that allows students to
interact with each other online, and access to a telephone
hotline open during regular business hours</li>
<li>Automated mastery tests for each lesson, including score
reporting</li>
<li>Individual student tracking and results reporting available
24/7</li>
<li>Printable access and how-to instructions for student use</li>
<li>Printable and/or downloadable versions of all lessons</li>
</ul>
<p align="center">If you are interested in hiring us to provide
online training for your company, you can visit our <a
href="http://www.lanw.com/training/wbt-brochure.htm">online
brochure</a>, which includes specific information about pricing,
structure, availability, and the instructors.</p>
</body>
</html>
```

To learn how to work with Tidy, you'll need to read the section appropriate to your computing method:

Working Via	Read This Section
Windows command prompt	"Using Tidy from the Windows Command Prompt"
Windows GUI	"Using TidyGUI" or "Using Tidy in HTML-Kit"
Macintosh	"Using Tidy on the Mac"

Using Tidy from the Windows Command Prompt

If you remember the days of DOS, you may be comfortable using Tidy as a stand-alone tool at the command prompt. Windows users who are uncomfortable working from the MS-DOS prompt should skip forward to the sections "Using TidyGUI" or "Using Tidy in HTML-Kit." Macintosh users need to jump ahead to the "Using Tidy on the Mac" section.

Before we get started with this mini tutorial, download DOS version of HTML Tidy from the Web at `www.w3.org/People/Raggett/tidy`. Click the Downloading Tidy link and select `tidy.exe`. After you've downloaded the executable to your hard drive (maybe save it in a folder called `Tidy` on the C drive), you're ready to begin:

1. To fire up the DOS prompt, select Start → Programs → Command Prompt or MS-DOS Prompt, depending on your version of Windows. (You might need to go to Start → Programs → Accessories → Command Prompt or MS-DOS Prompt.) A window with a black background and text, `C:\Windows`, appears (see Figure 9.1).

Figure 9.1 *Working from the command prompt*

2. Locate the `tidy.exe` file. If you saved it in its own folder, `Tidy`, you can navigate to that folder using the following command:

   ```
   cd ..\Tidy
   ```

   This command says the following:

`cd`	Tells the processor that you're changing folders. You should follow this command with a white-space character.
`..\`	Navigates up one level to the root folder.
`Tidy`	Opens the `Tidy` folder.

   Once you've navigated to the `Tidy` folder, you're ready to use the tool. Tidy allows you to point to an HTML document and use commands to convert the document. To do this, you need an HTML document to work with. We use the document shown in Listing 9.3; we'll assume the document to be converted has a filename of `sloppy.htm`.

   To convert your document to XHTML using Tidy, follow these steps:

1. Type the following command at the Windows command prompt:

   ```
   tidy -asxhtml -m c:\XHTML\sloppy.htm
   ```

The above command breaks down as follows:

`tidy`	Calls the Tidy program.
`-asxhtml`	Tells Tidy to convert the HTML document to XHTML.
`-m`	Tells Tidy to convert the document in its current location, and therefore, modify the original document rather than saving the clean version into a separate file.
`c:\XHTML\sloppy.htm`	Defines the location of the sloppy HTML document that needs to be converted. (Substitute whatever drive, path, and folder your document is in.)

2. After you type this command, press Enter. The `sloppy.htm` document will be replaced with a cleaner XHTML version. The cleaned-up version of our example document is shown in Listing 9.4.

Of course, there might be an instance where you want to preserve the initial HTML document and have Tidy create a new XHTML document. If this is the case, enter the following command line instead of the previous one:

```
tidy -asxhtml c:\XHTML\sloppy.htm > c:\XHTML\output.htm
```

The XHTML document will be saved as a separate document in the XHTML folder. You can name the document whatever you want. In this case, we've named the document `output.htm`.

Using TidyGUI

Many of you might not be inspired by the command prompt. In fact, you may want to run from it. There are also some of you that won't want to download another text editor. If you're interested in using a GUI interface for Tidy, but don't want a full text editor attached, André Blavier created a version that you just might get along with.

This GUI version of Tidy is beyond easy to use. Take a look at the TidyGUI interface shown in Figure 9.2.

![TidyGUI interface screenshot]

Figure 9.2 *The simple TidyGUI interface.*

You simply browse for the file you want to Tidy by clicking the Browse button and then click the Tidy! button. After that, you click the Show Output button and save the Tidied output to a new document to save it as your own. To read more about this version, visit `http://perso.wanadoo.fr/ablavier/TidyGUI/`.

Using Tidy in HTML-Kit

Windows users who don't like to work from the command prompt can also use HTML Tidy in a GUI interface, as a part of HTML-Kit. HTML-Kit is a free text editor that allows you to use predefined templates for HTML documents, and it can do anything a snazzy text editor can do. However, in addition to helping you create HTML documents, it uses HTML Tidy to convert HTML documents to XHTML. There's no extra download needed; all you have to do is download HTML-Kit (from `www.chami.com/html-kit/`) and Tidy comes as a part of the package.

The download size of HTML-Kit is significantly larger than the download size of both `tidy.exe` *and TidyGUI.*

After you've downloaded and installed HTML-Kit, open it to see what its interface looks like. Figure 9.3 shows the main HTML-Kit interface (with a new document open).

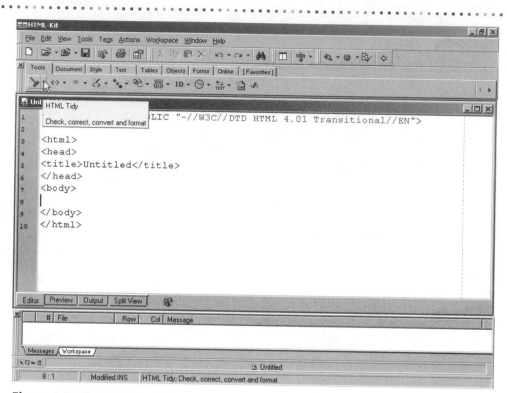

Figure 9.3 *HTML-Kit's interface*

In the top-left corner of the window, you'll see a little broom-like icon (the HTML Tidy icon). To convert all your documents to XHTML, you should customize the conversion options. Select Edit → Preferences and choose the Tidy tab shown in Figure 9.4. For our purposes, make sure the Output says XHTML. After you customize the conversion options, you just click the HTML Tidy icon and your document's converted to XHTML.

Figure 9.4 *The Tidy tab of the HTML-Kit Preferences*

Now, let's convert a document (for example, Listing 9.3) to XHTML using HTML-Kit. Follow these steps:

1. Select File → Open File and find the document.

2. Click the HTML Tidy icon. Alternatively, you could select the down arrow next to the HTML Tidy icon shown in Figure 9.3 and select Convert To XHTML from the drop-down menu. The new output (Listing 9.4) appears on the right side of the screen, and any errors found in the document appear at the bottom of the screen (see Figure 9.5).

Figure 9.5 *Tidy has cleaned up this document, all within HTML-Kit.*

3. If you want to replace the old HTML document with the new XHTML document, right-click in the right window and select Copy Output To Editor from the shortcut menu.

4. Select File ➜ Save, and click the Editor tab at the bottom of the window to continue modifying your document, or just to see the XHTML in all its glory.

Using Tidy on the Mac

Tidy support for the Mac has been around for a while. There are several options for Mac users, all of which are described and available for download at the Tidy for Mac OS site:

```
www.geocities.com/SiliconValley/1057/tidy.html
```

One of the possibilities is comparable to the TidyGUI application for Windows: It's called MacTidy. In fact, TidyGUI was based on MacTidy. However, the most common way to use Tidy with the Mac is to download a plug-in for BBEdit.

BBEdit is one of the premier text editors for Macintosh Web developers and can be found at `www.barebones.com`.

Download the HTML Tidy plug-in from the Tidy for Mac OS page listed earlier. After you've downloaded the StuffIt file that contains the plug-in, copy the BBTidy plug-in to the `BBEdit Plug-ins` folder. After the installation is complete, you can convert your first XHTML document.

To start the conversion process, make sure you have an HTML document (Listing 9.3, for example) open in BBEdit, and then select Tools → Tidy HTML, and BBEdit will begin to work its magic (see Figure 9.6). You will be presented with two documents, one that documents the errors and warning messages and one that provides the output XHTML document (Listing 9.4, for example).

Figure 9.6 *Selecting HTML Tidy from the BBEdit Tools menu*

Where to Go from Here

If you're interested in learning more about XHTML, you should visit the following places in this book:

- Move on to Part III to find out about features beyond XHTML.
- See Part IV for more on how to publish Web sites.

Part III

Moving Beyond Pure XHTML

In This Part

Using Style Sheets

XHTML

Chapter 10

U sing Cascading Style Sheets (CSS) is one of the best ways to format XHTML documents easily and consistently. Style sheets are a major step toward separating presentation from content, allowing the XHTML document to specify structure and content, yet allowing you almost total control over page presentation. The latest CSS recommendation adds even more control, including aural style sheets for screen-reading software, more options for formatting printed documents from the Web, and options for relative and absolute positioning.

Are style sheets here to stay? Yes. In fact, the XHTML specification deprecates formatting elements and attributes (such as the font element and the align attribute) in favor of style sheets.

In this chapter, you'll see how style sheets enhance the effectiveness of XHTML and how you can benefit from using them. You'll learn how to develop style sheets and apply them to your XHTML documents. We include some examples, but you'll want to take a look at Master's Reference Part 2 to get all the specifics.

In this chapter, we'll discuss the advantages and limitations of style sheets to help you decide whether they're right for your needs. And, of course, you'll find out how to implement them. To give you a solid foundation in the use of style sheets, we'll discuss the following topics:

- Understanding style sheets

- Applying style sheets to XHTML documents

- Developing style sheets

- Setting properties: type, box, color, background, lists

- Setting properties: aural, printing, positioning

How Do Style Sheets Work?

As we mentioned in Chapter 2, XHTML is a markup language that you use to identify structural elements in a document. For example, you can specify that one element is a first-level heading, one is a bullet point, one is a block quotation, and so on, by manually inserting formatting elements and attributes. Inserting these elements every place they occur can quickly become a tedious process. With style sheets, however, you specify formatting once, and it's applied throughout the document. If you've used styles in a word processor, you're familiar with this concept.

Style sheets—formally known as the World Wide Web Consortium (W3C) *Cascading Style Sheets* Recommendation—promise to give you layout and format control similar to what you may be accustomed to in programs such as PageMaker or Quark. You can control how page elements look, where they appear, their color and size, the fonts they use, and so on. Now, you—rather than browsers and users—can determine page appearance to a far greater extent than was possible before.

Before you decide to use style sheets, keep in mind that only the newest browsers support most of the features of CSS Level 1 and that the existing support for CSS Level 2 is sketchy. Both Microsoft Internet Explorer 3 (and later) and Netscape Navigator 4 (and later) browsers offer some style sheet support; however, many style sheet features do not work consistently or at all—even in these supporting browsers. Netscape 6 supports almost all features of CSS1, and IE 6 (in beta release at the time this chapter is written) supports all features of CSS1. Both Netscape 6 and IE 6 offer support for many, but not all, features of CSS2.

Browsers, Users, and Style Sheets

Style sheets are available only to users using Internet Explorer 3 (or later), Netscape Navigator 4 (or later), or Opera 3 (or later). Users using earlier versions of these browsers or other browsers may see a plain XHTML document that includes little more than the logical formatting elements, such as headings, paragraphs, tables, and lists.

In addition, because style sheet technology is still relatively new, browsers don't yet provide stable or consistent support. Pages that use style sheets will appear differently in various browsers. However, the latest browsers (IE 6, Netscape 6, and Opera 5) have all made efforts to support Web standards, including CSS1 and some elements of CSS2. Support for Web standards allows Web developers more potential for a consistent appearance of Web pages in different browsers and on different platforms.

Also, your users still have some control over the document appearance, regardless of the formatting you supply in the style sheet. They can disable style sheets or override them with their personal preferences for colors and fonts. CSS2 offers additional support for users, including the capability for users to override designer's style sheets. This is a very important part of making the Web more accessible to users with disabilities, and we can expect more emphasis on users' needs as CSS and the Web develop.

Some Advantages of Using Style Sheets

In addition to giving you more control over how your documents appear to users, style sheets let you manage XHTML documents more easily than if they were filled with for-matting elements. When you place formatting markup in the style sheet, your document is less cluttered.

Style sheets also reduce the time you spend developing and maintaining XHTML documents. Rather than manually formatting paragraphs of text, you simply change the style definition in one place—the style sheet—and the style sheet applies the definition to all occurrences in the XHTML document. No muss, no fuss.

Finally, style sheets give you flexibility from document to document within a Web site. Even if you set up a style sheet that applies to all pages in the site, you can set up individual style sheets to apply to individual XHTML documents. The individual style sheet overrides the global one. In addition, you can further tweak individual style sheets to accommodate special text formatting, such as a document in which certain paragraphs should appear in a different color.

Cascading Style Sheets Level 1

Cascading Style Sheets Level 1 (CSS1) introduced extensive style properties for many features of page layout and text presentation. The CSS1 Recommendation was adopted by the W3C in December 1996 and revised in January 1999. The CSS1 style properties include the following:

- Font properties, including expanded options for setting font size and other font features

- Text properties, including text alignment and decoration

- Box properties, such as margins, padding, borders, and floating elements

- Color and background properties, including background repeat options and background color for elements
- Classification properties, including styles for displaying lists

All of these properties are covered in detail in various sections in this chapter.

 The W3C CSS1 recommendation is available online at www.w3.org/TR/REC-CSS1.

Cascading Style Sheets Level 2

The *CSS2* recommendation was adopted in May 1998. This recommendation builds on the features included in CSS1 and adds new style properties, including the following:

- Media types and properties, including aural style sheets and printed media
- Positioning properties, such as absolute, relative, and fixed positioning
- Downloadable fonts
- Table style properties
- Additional box properties, including new box types
- Visual formatting model, including properties for overflow, clipping, and visibility
- Generated content, used to import content from another Web location
- Text shadows
- System colors
- Cursor styles

The only features of CSS2 that have widespread support as of this writing (and only in newer browsers) are the positioning properties and some of the changes in CSS selectors. (For more on selectors, see "Developing a Style Sheet" later in this chapter.) Aural style sheets, printed media properties, and CSS positioning are discussed in detail later in this chapter.

 The W3C CSS2 recommendation is available online at www.w3.org/TR/REC-CSS2.

Cascading Style Sheets Level 3 and Beyond

Although CSS2 has very limited support in current browsers, CSS3 is currently being developed. Unlike previous versions of CSS, CSS3 is being developed as individual modules. This will make it easier for browsers to support CSS3 on a module-by-module basis, easier for updates in individual modules, and easier for users, Web designers, and Web developers to easily figure out which modules are supported in a particular browser.

CSS3 is still in Working Draft form, but some of the modules currently being developed are

- User-interface enhancements for dynamic and interactive features
- Scalable Vector Graphics (SVG)
- Behavioral extensions (adding the ability to attach dynamic script actions to elements)
- Expanded accessibility features
- International layout properties
- Multicolumn layout

Future additions to CSS will most likely include further accessibility properties, enhanced multimedia support, and expanded dynamic and interactive capabilities.

 For information on all the types of style sheets, including the advanced Extensible Stylesheet Language (XSL), check out the W3C's style site at `www.w3.org/Style`.

Implementing Style Sheets

As you're perusing the rest of this chapter, remember that your XHTML documents and the associated style sheets work as a team. XHTML documents carry the content, and style sheets carry the formatting information. As you'll see, developing style sheets is a two-part process:

1. You associate (or connect) a style sheet with the XHTML document.
2. You develop a style sheet's contents, complete with all the formatting information.

After you become familiar with creating style sheets, you may create the style sheet first and then associate it with an XHTML document. However, for instructing purposes, it makes more sense for us to tell you how to associate the style sheet first.

Associating Style Sheets with XHTML Documents

You can associate style sheets with your XHTML documents in four ways:

- You can embed the style sheet in the document by defining it between the opening and closing head tags.

- You can store the style sheet in a separate document and either link to it or import it.

- You can apply style definitions to specified parts of the document.

- You can use inline style definitions.

Embedding the Style Sheet in the XHTML Document

Embedding the style sheet is the easiest of the four methods of associating it with your XHTML documents. To embed a style sheet, you use the style element, along with style information, between the opening and closing head tags.

Embedding style sheets makes maintaining or updating styles easy because you only have to work with one document—instead of working with a style sheet document and an XHTML document. You simply open the XHTML document and adjust the style sheet code. If you're working with multiple documents or documents that you update frequently, however, you have to adjust the style sheet in every document if you use the internal style sheet; therefore, you probably want to use the external style sheet method instead.

To embed a style sheet in an XHTML document, you'll apply the items shown in Table 10.1, between the opening and closing head tags.

Table 10.1 Style Sheet Code Components

ITEM	TYPE	DESCRIPTION
`style`	Element	Specifies the style sheet area within an XHTML document. Within this section, you can define or import formatting.
`<!--…-->`	Comment markup	Hides style sheet contents from non-style-capable browsers.
`type="text/css"`	Attribute of `style`	Specifies the type of style sheet; required.

To embed a minimal style sheet in an existing document, follow these steps:

1. Start with a functional document header.

```
<!DOCTYPE html PUBLIC "-//W3C//DTD XHTML 1.0 Strict//EN"
    "http://www.w3.org/TR/xhtml1/DTD/xhtml1-strict.dtd">
<html xmlns="http://www.w3.org/1999/xhtml">
<head>
    <title>Embedded Style</title>
</head>
</html>
```

 Use the Strict DTD in a document that contains style sheets, because the Transitional DTD allows formatting elements and the purpose of style sheets is to avoid using them.

2. Add opening and closing `style` tags as well as the `type` attribute.

```
<head>
    <title>Embedded Style</title>
    <style type="text/css">
    </style>
</head>
```

3. Add the comment markup (`<!--…-->`), within the `style` element, to hide the contents from non–style-capable browsers.

```
<head>
    <title>Embedded Style</title>
    <style type="text/css">
```

```
    <!--
    -->
  </style>
</head>
```

Browsers that do not support style sheets ignore the `style` element but display the text that appears between them. Adding comment markup within the `style` tags ensures that the styles will not appear as content in older or less-capable browsers.

4. Add style definitions within the comment markup. In this (minimal) example, we specify that paragraph text is red.

```
<head>
  <title>ASR Outfitters</title>
  <style type="text/css">
    <!--
      p {color: red}
    -->
  </style>
</head>
```

5. Add a body element, a p element, content for the p element, and you're ready to test your embedded style.

```
<!DOCTYPE html PUBLIC "-//W3C/DTD XHTML 1.0 Strict//EN"
    "http://www.w3.org/TR/xhtml1/DTD/xhtml1-strict.dtd">
<html xmlns="http://www.w3.org/1999/xhtml">
<head>
  <title>Embedded Style</title>
  <style type="text/css">
    <!--
      p {color: red}
    -->
  </style>
</head>
<body>
  <p>This paragraph uses an embedded style.</p>
</body>
</html>
```

That's it! To test your embedded style sheet, save this markup, and open the XHTML document in IE or Netscape.

Storing Style Sheets Separately

A separate style sheet (an *external style sheet*) is simply a plain-text file, saved with a .css file extension, that includes style definitions. You should develop an external style sheet any time you're working with several XHTML documents, particularly if they share similar formatting. In this case, you develop a single style sheet and apply it to all the XHTML documents, as shown in Figure 10.1. You can then make formatting changes in all the documents simultaneously by simply changing the external style sheet.

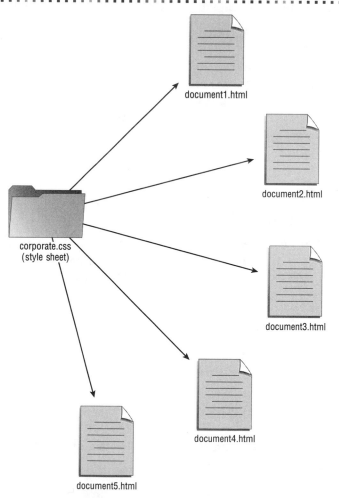

Figure 10.1 *When you develop a separate style sheet, you can easily apply styles to many XHTML documents.*

Even if you're only working with a few XHTML documents, consider developing an external style sheet. You never know how many XHTML documents your site will eventually include.

After you develop the external style sheet document, you associate it with the XHTML document(s) using one of two methods: importing or linking.

Importing a Style Sheet

This method is handy when you're developing multiple style sheets, each with a particular function. For example, as illustrated in Figure 10.2, you can develop a page that applies corporate styles, one that applies styles for your department, and another that specifies particular document formatting. Rather than wading through a 10-page style sheet, you work with multiple smaller ones.

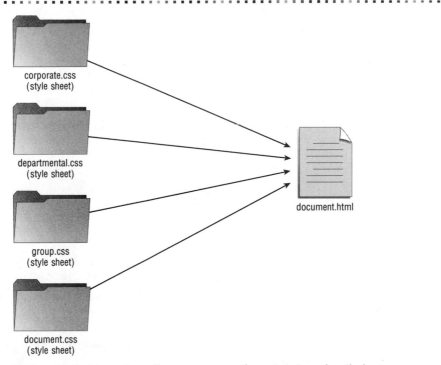

Figure 10.2 *Importing allows you to easily maintain a detailed style sheet.*

Importing style sheets only works well in some browsers. To find out which browsers currently support importing (as well as other CSS properties), check the most current version of the style sheet Reference Guide Master Grid at www.webreview.com/style/css1/charts/mastergrid.shtml.

You import a style sheet by inserting an @import statement within the style element, inside the comment delimiters. The syntax for these imports is @import url(...), with the URL of the imported style sheet inside the parentheses.

To import a style sheet, follow these steps:

1. Start with a complete style block, such as the following code:

```
<!DOCTYPE html PUBLIC "-//W3C/DTD XHTML 1.0 Strict//EN"
    "http://www.w3.org/TR/xhtml1/DTD/xhtml1-strict.dtd">
<html xmlns="http://www.w3.org/1999/xhtml">
<head>
    <title>Imported Style</title>
    <style type="text/css">
       <!--
       -->
    </style>
</head>
```

2. Within a style block or style sheet, add a line similar to the following (substitute the name of your CSS file for red.css):

```
<style type="text/css">
   <!--
       @import url(red.css);
   -->
</style>
```

If you're using @import in addition to other embedded style properties, @import is always the first style declaration listed, followed by any additional @import declarations, and then followed by the additional style declarations.

A complete style block that does nothing but import two style sheets (red.css and blue.css) would look like the following:

```
<style type="text/css">
   <!--
       @import url(red.css);
```

```
        @import url(blue.css);
    -->
</style>
```

 Currently, `@import` *offers no advantages over the link method, which is explained in the following section and is supported in almost all browsers that support style sheets. Therefore, we recommend the link method.*

Linking a Style Sheet

This method has a distinct advantage over the other methods: It gives users a choice of style sheets to use for a specific page. For example, you can link one style sheet to a page for users who will read on screen and link a different style sheet to the same page for users who will print, as shown in Figure 10.3. Theoretically, you could even develop a style sheet (as browsers implement this functionality) optimized for aural presentation.

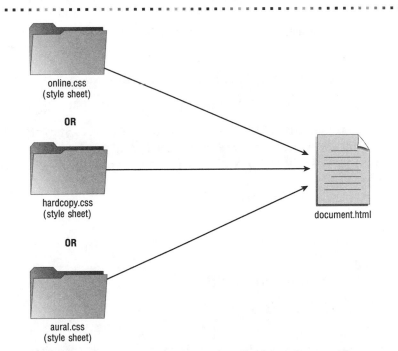

Figure 10.3 *Linking lets you apply style sheets for specific uses.*

Although you can import a style sheet, linking the style sheet is a better long-term choice because future browser versions should offer users more flexibility in handling style sheets, including the option to select from multiple style sheets. Importing offers no choices—it just loads the style sheet. Table 10.2 explains the elements and attributes you use to link style sheets to XHTML documents.

Table 10.2 Elements and Attributes for Linking Style Sheets

ITEM	TYPE	DESCRIPTION
link	Empty element	References a style sheet.
href="url"	Attribute of link	Identifies the style sheet source as a standard URL.
rel="stylesheet"	Attribute of link	Specifies that the referenced file is a style sheet.
title="…"	Attribute of link	Names the style sheet. Unnamed style sheets are always applied; named style sheets are applied by default or provided as options, depending on the rel attribute used.
type="text/css"	Attribute of link	Specifies the type of the style sheet.

To link a style sheet to an XHTML document, follow these steps:

1. Start with a complete XHTML head section, such as the following code:

```
<!DOCTYPE html PUBLIC "-//W3C/DTD XHTML 1.0 Strict//EN"
    "http://www.w3.org/TR/xhtml1/DTD/xhtml1-strict.dtd">
<html xmlns="http://www.w3.org/1999/xhtml">
<head>
    <title>Linked Style</title>
</head>
```

2. Add the link empty element.

```
<head>
    <title>Linked Style</title>
    <link />
</head>
```

3. Specify the rel and type values of stylesheet and text/css, respectively, to link to a standard style sheet.

```
<link rel="stylesheet" type="text/css" />
```

4. Specify the address of the style sheet with the `href` attribute. Specify either a relative URL, as in the sample code, or an absolute URL.

```
<link rel="stylesheet" href="blue.css" type="text/css" />
```

There you go! To link your XHTML document to more than one style sheet, simply include multiple `link` elements, complete with each of the style sheets to which they link. For example, you might link an XHTML document to a generic style sheet that contains basic style definitions and then also link it to a more specific style sheet that contains definitions suitable to a particular style of document—instructions, marketing, and so on. If you link to multiple style sheets, all take effect. However, if you define the same element in multiple sheets, the later links override the previous links.

The XHTML specification indicates that you can also link your XHTML documents to optional style sheets using the `rel="alternate stylesheet"` attribute so that users can choose which styles to use. Theoretically, you can provide optional style sheets that, for instance, let users choose a low-bandwidth style for viewing over a modem connection or a high-bandwidth style with lots of cool images for viewing over a high-speed connection. Or, you can present choices for high-resolution and high-color-depth monitors and provide alternatives for standard monitors at lower color depths. However, at the time of writing, no browsers support optional style sheets.

Applying Style Sheets to Parts of Documents

So far, you've seen how to apply style sheets to entire XHTML documents. You can also apply styles included in a style sheet to specific parts of XHTML documents, as shown in Figure 10.4. This is called applying *style classes*, which you define in your style sheet. For example, suppose you specify in a style sheet that the first line of all paragraphs is indented. You may find that paragraphs after a bulleted list should not be indented because they continue the information from the paragraph before the list. To address this issue, you can manually format the paragraph for this occurrence. However, a better solution is to set up a new paragraph element class within your style definition, called, for example, `continue`. You can use this new paragraph class whenever the first line of a paragraph should not be indented. Table 10.3 describes the elements and attributes you use to apply classes.

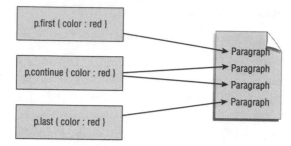

Figure 10.4 *Applying style classes, you can specify how parts of XHTML documents appear.*

Table 10.3 Elements and Attributes for Applying Classes

ITEM	TYPE	DESCRIPTION
div	Element	Holds style attributes and applies them to the XHTML code between the opening and closing tags. Surround paragraphs or other block-level elements with these.
span	Element	Holds style attributes and applies them to the XHTML code between the opening and closing tags. Surround letters, words, and other inline elements with these tags.
class="…"	Attribute of various elements	References a style class to apply to a specified part of an XHTML document.
id="…"	Attribute of various elements	Specifies a unique name associated with a specific style definition. You can use this only once within a style sheet.

You can apply a class to an existing XHTML element, or you can use the div and span elements to specify that the class applies to other elements—such as specific letters or words—not individually specified by an XHTML element.

Applying Classes to an XHTML Element

You apply a class to an existing XHTML element—such as p, h1, ul, and so on—to specify formatting for a group of items. To apply classes within an XHTML document, follow these steps:

1. Start with an existing paragraph within an XHTML document.

   ```
   <p>Many people buy ASR products despite the higher
       cost.</p>
   ```

2. Add the class attribute to the opening p tag, like this:

   ```
   <p class="">Many people buy ASR products despite the higher
       cost.</p>
   ```

3. Add the name of the paragraph class. (You'll see how to define and name classes when you develop the style sheet later in this chapter.)

   ```
   <p class="continue">Many people buy ASR products despite
       the higher cost.</p>
   ```

That's it!

If you have a specific formatting need—a one-time need—you can define a style ID and then apply the id attribute in place of the class attribute in the preceding example. You would end up with something like this:

```
<p id="538fv1">Many people buy ASR products despite the higher
    cost.</p>
```

Applying Classes to Other Document Parts

You can also apply classes to specific parts of an XHTML document that do not have existing elements. For example, suppose you want to make the first few lines in the document body a different color. Because no specific element exists to designate the first few lines, you must specify the paragraph or text to which the style applies.

To apply classes to specific parts of an XHTML document, use the div and span elements, described earlier in Table 10.3. These elements provide a place to apply class formatting when there's no existing formatting.

You use the div element to apply classes to block-level sections of a document—areas where you need the class to apply to more content than just one element. Here are the steps to apply the div class margin, which is defined elsewhere to, say, set the left margin to 40%:

1. Start with a section of an existing XHTML document and text.

```
<p>Many people buy ASR products despite the higher
    cost.</p>
<blockquote>"We sell only the highest quality outdoor
    equipment."</blockquote>
```

2. Add the div tags around the section.

```
<div>
<p>Many people buy ASR products despite the higher
    cost.</p>
<blockquote>"We sell only the highest quality outdoor
    equipment."</blockquote>
</div>
```

3. Add the appropriate class attribute.

```
<div class="margin">
<p>Many people buy ASR products despite the higher
    cost.</p>
<blockquote>"We sell only the highest quality outdoor
    equipment."</blockquote>
</div>
```

The margin class will now apply to both the p and blockquote elements.

Use the span element to apply classes to characters or words—any stretch of content that's *less* than a full, regular element. For example, to apply the firstuse class (that you define elsewhere) to a word, follow these steps:

1. Start with an existing XHTML element—for example, a p element.

```
<p>Many people buy ASR products despite the higher
    cost.</p>
```

2. Add the span opening and closing tags.

```
<p>Many people buy <span>ASR products</span> despite the
    higher cost.</p>
```

3. Add the appropriate `class` attribute.

```
<p>Many people buy <span class="firstuse">ASR
   products</span> despite the higher cost.</p>
```

You might use classes in conjunction with XHTML tables (covered in Chapter 6). Table elements accept `class` *attributes to apply formatting—either to the table sections you specify, to individual cells, rows, and columns, or to the table, cells, rows, or columns as a whole. (See the section "Applying Classes to an XHTML Element" earlier in this chapter.)*

Applying Inline Style Definitions

Applying inline style definitions throughout an XHTML document is similar to adding formatting attributes. For example, just as you can apply an `align` attribute to a paragraph, you can apply a style definition within the p element. Of course, with style sheets you have far more formatting possibilities than with simple XHTML formatting commands.

The technique is simple: add the `style="..."` attribute to any XHTML element. Provide the style definition within quotes (and if there are quoted items within the `style` attribute, put them in single quotes). For that element, then, these values will override any other style definitions that are defined, imported, or linked into the document.

Although you wouldn't use this method to apply styles throughout an XHTML document—it's extremely time-consuming—you could use it for a specific instance in an existing style sheet. For example, your style sheet might specify that paragraphs appear in blue text. You can then apply an inline style to specify that one particular paragraph appears in red text.

To add a style definition to an existing XHTML element, follow these steps:

1. Start with an existing XHTML element—for example, the p element.

```
<p>Many people buy ASR products despite the higher
   cost.</p>
```

2. Add the `style` attribute.

```
<p style="">Many people buy ASR products despite the higher
   cost.</p>
```

3. Add the style definition(s), separated by semicolons. Substitute single quotes for double quotes within the attribute; otherwise, you'll close the attribute prematurely.

```
<p style="color: red; font-family: 'Times New Roman',
     serif"> Many people buy ASR products despite the higher
     cost.</p>
```

Notice that `Times New Roman` *is quoted and* `serif` *is not. This is because* **Times New Roman** *contains white space and, as such, must be quoted. However,* **serif** *does not contain white space; therefore, it does not need to be quoted.*

What Is Cascading?

As you have seen in the preceding sections, there are several ways to specify styles for a document: external style sheets, embedded styles, and inline styles. There may be conflicts between these styles; for example, the external style sheet specifies all text in the document is red, and the embedded style specifies blue text for paragraphs. The browser resolves these conflicting style definitions by applying the precedence rules for style sheets; these rules are called *the cascade*.

The two general cascading rules are:

1. The most specific style rule will be applied—i.e., a style that applies only to paragraphs is more specific than a style that applies to all the document text.

2. If two style rules are equally specific, the style rule that occurs *later* is considered more specific and will be the one applied. If you have two different style definitions for paragraph color, for example,

```
p {color:green}
p {color:blue}
```

the second definition would take precedence; therefore, the paragraph text is displayed in blue.

Style definitions declared in an external style sheet come before style definitions embedded in a document, and these come before inline style declarations. Therefore, the precedence order, from lowest to highest, is:

3. External style sheet

2. Embedded styles (if any, overrides external style sheet)

1. Inline styles (if any, overrides others)

Developing a Style Sheet

In the previous sections, you learned how to associate a style sheet with an XHTML document. Your goal now is to develop the style sheet—that is, to specify the style definitions you want to include. A *style definition* (also called a *style rule)* specifies formatting characteristics.

You can choose from any combination of the eight categories of style properties. We'll cover each of these in its own section later in this chapter.

- Font properties specify character-level (inline) formatting, such as the typeface.

- Text properties specify display characteristics for text, such as alignment or letter spacing.

- Box properties specify characteristics for sections of text, at the paragraph (or block) level.

- Color and background properties specify color, background color, and images at both the inline and block levels.

- Classification properties specify display characteristics of lists and elements (such as p or h1) as inline or block level.

- Aural style sheet properties control the presentation of XHTML documents by sound (CSS2 only).

- Printed style sheet properties add features specifically to control printed output of XHTML documents (CSS2 only).

- Positioning properties add features to precisely control the placement of elements on the display (CSS2 only).

You can easily get carried away with formatting options, but keep things simple. Look through the style sheet information in Master's Reference Part 2 to get an idea of the vast number of options. As you might guess, using even some of these options can quickly get complex.

Before we dive into developing a style sheet, let's take a look at some style sheet code:

Here's what each part does:

The style block includes style elements and comment markup, plus style definitions (or rules).

Selectors are XHTML elements. In this example, the p—as in a paragraph element—is a selector.

Declarations are the properties of the XHTML elements, such as color, background, alignment, and font. In this example color:green and color:red are the declarations. Declarations consist of two parts, a property and a value, separated by a colon. In the second example, color is the property and red is the value. The property/value combination is enclosed within curly brackets or "braces," { }.

Classes specify an additional style definition associated with specific occurrences of an XHTML element. For example, paragraphs tagged with <p class="red"> use this style class.

Each style definition can define the formatting associated with a specific XHTML element, with a specific class, or with a specific id. The formatting associated with XHTML elements appears in the document without any special action on your part (aside from referencing or including the style sheet in your XHTML document). Style definitions for classes or IDs also require that you add the class or id attribute to the appropriate XHTML document section before the formatting can appear in the XHTML document.

To add these elements in an internal style sheet, follow these steps:

1. Be sure the style block is in place, like this.

```
<style type="text/css">
   <!--
   -->
</style>
```

2. Add a selector and braces, as shown here:

```
<style type="text/css">
   <!--
      p { }
   -->
</style>
```

3. Add the declaration between the braces.

```
<style type="text/css">
   <!--
      p { color: aqua }
   -->
</style>
```

Style Sheet Tips

As you're building a style sheet, the process will be easier if you follow these guidelines:

- To include multiple selectors, place them on separate lines, like this:

```
<style type="text/css">

   <!--

      p {color: red}

      h1 {color: blue}

      blockquote {color: green}

   -->

</style>
```

- To provide multiple declarations for a single selector, group the declarations within the braces, separated by semicolons. In addition, you might find the style definitions easier to read if you space them out somewhat, and put only one declaration on a single line. For example, to define p as red text with a yellow background, use the following markup:

```
<style type="text/css">
  <!--
    p { color: red;
        background: yellow; }
  -->
</style>
```

- Start at the highest level—the most general level—within your document, which is probably the body. Format the body as you want most of the document to appear, and then use more specific style rules to override the body settings.

- White space within style definitions and rules is ignored; each of the following lines of code produces the same result:

```
p{color:red}

p {color:red}

p {color: red}

p { color:red}

p { color:red }
```

In addition, become familiar with ways to specify measurements and values, which are discussed in the following two sections.

Specifying Measurements

When specifying locations of elements, you might also want to specify their size. For example, when specifying that the first line of a paragraph is indented, you can also specify the size of the indention. In general, provide measurements in the units shown in Table 10.4. You can also express most measurements as a percentage of the browser window.

Your measurement might look like one of the following lines:

```
p { text-indent: 2px }
p { text-indent: 1em }
```

Table 10.4 Units of Measure in Style Sheets

UNIT	WHAT IT IS	DESCRIPTION
cm	Centimeter	The measurement in centimeters.
em	Em space	In typography, an em is the width of a capital *M* in the typeface being used. In CSS, 1 em is equal to the font size—for example, if the font size is 12 pt, the size of 1 em is equal to 12 points.
ex	X-height	The height of a lowercase letter *x* in the typeface being used.
in	Inch	The measurement in inches.
mm	Millimeter	The measurement in millimeters.
pc	Pica	A typographic measurement that equals 1/6 inch.
pt	Point	A typographic measurement that equals 1/72 inch.
px	Pixel	An individual screen dot.

Relative units such as em are usually preferred to absolute units such as pt when specifying font size, because relative units are scalable by the user. For example, users with visual disabilities may set their browser preferences to "larger" text. If the font size is specified in ems, all of the text will be scaled proportionately; the same text layout relationships exist, just at a larger size.

Specifying Colors in Style Rules

When using style sheets, you can specify colors in the standard XHTML ways (as #rrggbb values or as color names), as well as in two other ways, which use a slightly different approach to specify proportions of red, green, and blue. The following four lines show how to specify red in each method.

Method	Example
Hex Code	p{color: #ff0000}
Color Name	p{color: red}
Decimal	p{color: rgb(255,0,0)}
Percentage	p{color: rgb(100%,0%,0%)}

Although each of these is equally easy to use, we recommend using the #rrggbb option; it's likely to be more familiar, because it matches XHTML color statements.

In the following sections, we'll show you how to develop an embedded style sheet. After you complete an embedded style sheet, you can move it to a separate document and import it or link it.

To follow along with the example, have an XHTML document with the complete structure elements ready, or use Listing 10.1.

LISTING 10.1: AN XHTML DOCUMENT WITH THE COMPLETE STRUCTURE ELEMENTS

```
<!DOCTYPE html PUBLIC "-//W3C/DTD XHTML 1.0 Transitional//EN"
  "http://www.w3.org/TR/xhtml1/DTD/xhtml1-transitional.dtd">
<html xmlns="http://www.w3.org/1999/xhtml">
<head>
  <title>ASR Outfitters</title>
</head>
<body>
  <h1>Welcome to ASR Outfitters!</h1>
  <p>We're happy to welcome you to our newly redesigned Web
site, featuring <b>styles</b> (because they look cool) as well
as redesigned graphics. Please take the <a href="tour.html">
tour of our site</a> if you haven't been here in a while. In
particular, you may appreciate the now automatically updated
camping news, as well as the new weather imagemap. Additionally,
we've been getting some nice kudos from frequent and occasional
visitors.</p>
  <blockquote>Your site always provides timely and useful
  information. Keep up the good work.<br />
  Jim Smith
  </blockquote>
  <hr />
  <h2>What's Here</h2>
  <ul>
    <li><a href="camping.html">Camping News</a> provides the
      latest comments from the trails.</li>
    <li><a href="weather.html">Check Weather</a> offers weather
      updates from a variety of sources.</li>
    <li><a href="clubs.html">Clubs</a> gives local hiking and
```

```
      mountaineering clubs a place to provide information about
      their activities. </li>
    <li><a href="catalog.html">Catalog</a> presents our entire
      inventory, including announcements of the latest sales.
      </li>
    <li><a href="contact.html">Contact Us</a> links to a page
      with a contact form, e-mail addresses, snail mail
      addresses, and phone numbers. If it isn't here, you can't
      find us.</li>
</ul>
<h2>What We Do</h2>
<p>In addition to providing the latest camping and outdoor
activities news, we also provide mountaineering and hiking
equipment nationwide via mail order as well as through our
stores in the Rocky Mountains. Please take a few minutes to
look through our <a href="catalog.html">online offerings</a>.
</p>
<h2>Other Issues</h2>
<ul>
  <li>As you may know, our URL was misprinted in the latest
    <i>Hiking News</i>. Please tell your hiking friends that
    the correct URL is <tt>http://www.asroutfitters.com/</tt>.
    </li>
  <li>To collect a $1000 reward, turn in the name of the
    person who set the fire in the Bear Lake area last
    weekend.
    <ol>
      <li>Call 888-555-1212.</li>
      <li>Leave the name on the recording.</li>
      <li>Provide contact information so we can send you the
        reward.</li>
    </ol>
  </li>
</ul>
<h2>What Would You Like To See?</h2>
<p>If you have suggestions or comments about the site or other
information we could provide, we'd love to know about it. Drop
us an e-mail at <a href="mailto:asroutfitters@example.com">
asroutfitters@example.com</a>. Of course, you could also
contact us more traditionally at the following address:</p>
```

```
<address>ASR Outfitters<br />
   4700 N. Center<br />
   South Logan, UT 87654<br />
   801-555-3422
   </address>
</body>
</html>
```

Without any styles or formatting other than the standard XHTML browser defaults, the document from Listing 10.1 looks something like Figure 10.5.

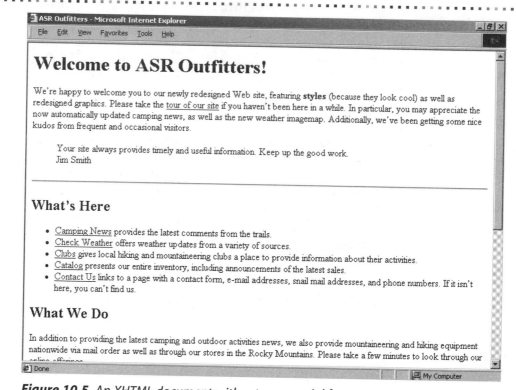

Figure 10.5 *An XHTML document without any special formatting or style sheets*

To add a style block to the document, follow these steps:

1. Add a pair of opening and closing style tags within the document head, as shown in the following code.

```
<!DOCTYPE html PUBLIC
    "-//W3C/DTD XHTML 1.0 Transitional//EN"
  "http://www.w3.org/TR/xhtml1/DTD/xhtml1-transitional.dtd">
<html xmlns="http://www.w3.org/1999/xhtml">
<head>
    <title>ASR Outfitters</title>
    <style type="text/css">
    </style>
</head>
```

2. Add the comment markup (<!-- -->) within the style tags, as shown here:

```
<style type="text/css">
    <!--
    -->
</style>
```

After the style element and comment markup are in place, define the style sheet. You specify style properties, such as fonts, text, boxes, colors, backgrounds and classifications, as discussed in the next section. Think of defining styles as specifying rules for what each element should look like. For example, specify that you want all text blue, all bullets indented, all headings centered, and so on.

Setting Style Sheet Properties

The following sections cover how to set properties for fonts, text, boxes, colors, backgrounds and classifications. The sections do not build on one another; instead, they show you how to set each of the properties separately, based on the sample ASR Outfitters page. Through these examples, you'll see *some* of the style sheet effects you can achieve. For a more complete list of style sheet options, see Master's Reference Part 2.

Setting Font Properties

If the fonts you specify are not available on a user's computer, the browser will display text in a font that is available. To ensure that one of your preferred fonts is used, choose multiple font families and, in addition, always include a generic font family choice. Table 10.5 shows some of the basic font properties and values.

Table 10.5 Font Properties

PROPERTY	POSSIBLE VALUES
font	Any or all of the following `font` properties can be set within this combination font property.
font-family	Font names, such as Times New Roman or Arial, or generic font families, such as `serif`, `sans-serif`, `monospace`, `fantasy`, `cursive`
font-size	`xx-small`, `x-small`, `small`, `medium`, `large`, `x-large`, `xx-large`, or size measurement in length or percentage
font-style	`normal`, `italic`, `oblique`
font-variant	`normal`, `small-caps`
font-weight	`normal`, `bold`, `bolder`, `lighter`, `100`, `200`, `300`, `400`, `500`, `600`, `700`, `800`, `900`

The following example sets a basic font for the whole document—everything between the opening and closing body tags. It sets the basic font for a document to Comic Sans MS, with Technical and Times New Roman as other choices and with a generic serif font as the last choice.

1. Within the style block, add a body selector and braces to hold its properties.

```
<style type="text/css">
  <!--
     body {}
  -->
</style>
```

2. Add the property. To set only the typeface, use `font-family`.

```
<style type="text/css">
  <!--
```

```
        body { font-family }
     -->
   </style>
```

3. Add a colon to separate the property from the value.

```
   <style type="text/css">
     <!--
        body { font-family: }
     -->
   </style>
```

4. Add the value "Comic Sans MS" (the first-choice typeface). (If the font family name contains a space, put the name in quotes. Otherwise, quotes are optional.)

```
   <style type="text/css">
     <!--
        body { font-family: "Comic Sans MS" }
     -->
   </style>
```

5. Add additional values, as you choose, separated by commas. Conclude your list of fonts with either a serif or sans-serif font that's likely to match a font on the user's computer.

```
   <style type="text/css">
     <!--
        body { font-family: "Comic Sans MS", Technical,
               "Times New Roman", serif }
     -->
   </style>
```

Figure 10.6 is the resulting page, complete with the new font for the document body.

Welcome to ASR Outfitters!

We're happy to welcome you to our newly redesigned Web site, featuring **styles** (because they look cool) as well as redesigned graphics. Please take the <u>tour of our site</u> if you haven't been here in a while. In particular, you may appreciate the now automatically updated camping news, as well as the new weather imagemap. Additionally, we've been getting some nice kudos from frequent and occasional visitors.

> Your site always provides timely and useful information. Keep up the good work.
> Jim Smith

What's Here

- <u>Camping News</u> provides the latest comments from the trails.
- <u>Check Weather</u> offers weather updates from a variety of sources.
- <u>Clubs</u> gives local hiking and mountaineering clubs a place to provide information about their activities.
- <u>Catalog</u> presents our entire inventory, including announcements of the latest sales.
- <u>Contact Us</u> links to a page with a contact form, e-mail addresses, snail mail addresses, and phone numbers. If it isn't here, you can't find us.

Figure 10.6 *We've converted our whole page to a new font, without having to insert* font *tags in the document!*

Newer browsers support three additional choices for generic font families. In addition to serif *and* sans-serif, *the three additional generic font families are* cursive, fantasy, *and* monospace.

Setting Link Characteristics

You use three special style classes (also known as *anchor pseudo-classes*) along with font style rules to control the colors of links in your document:

- a:link
- a:active
- a:visited

Use these within your style sheet definition to specify the rules that apply to links, active links, and visited links. For example, to set unvisited links to blue, active links to red, and visited links to magenta, your style block would look like this:

```
<style type="text/css">
  <!--
    a:link { color: blue }
    a:active { color: red }
    a:visited { color: magenta }
  -->
</style>
```

You can also define additional text styles within the document. For example, to set all headings to Arial italic, follow these steps:

1. Add a comma-separated list of all headings to the existing style block, as selectors. The comma-separated list specifies that the style rule applies to each selector individually.

```
<style type="text/css">
  <!--
    body { font-family: "Comic Sans MS", Technical,
                        "Times New Roman", serif }
    h1, h2, h3, h4, h5, h6
  -->
</style>
```

2. Add braces.

```
h1, h2, h3, h4, h5, h6 { }
```

3. Add the `font-family` property, with Arial as the first choice, Helvetica as the second choice, and sans-serif as the third choice.

```
h1, h2, h3, h4, h5, h6 { font-family: Arial,
                         Helvetica,
                         sans-serif }
```

4. After the font family values, add a semicolon and a new line so that you can easily enter (and read) the font style rule.

```
h1, h2, h3, h4, h5, h6 { font-family: Arial,
                         Helvetica,
                         sans-serif;
                       }
```

5. Add the `font-style` property, a colon, and the `italic` value.

```
h1, h2, h3, h4, h5, h6 { font-family: Arial,
                         Helvetica,
                         sans-serif;
                    font-style: italic }
```

6. Continue adding font properties, separated by semicolons, if you want to define other aspects, such as font size or weight. The following lines of code show the headings set to a larger size and weight than usual. You'll see the results in Figure 10.7.

```
<style type="text/css">
  <!--
    body { font-family: "Comic Sans MS", Technical,
                        "Times New Roman", serif }
    h1, h2, h3, h4, h5, h6 { font-family: Arial,
                             Helvetica,
                             sans-serif;
                        font-style: italic;
                        font-size: x-large;
                        font-weight: bolder; }
  -->
</style>
```

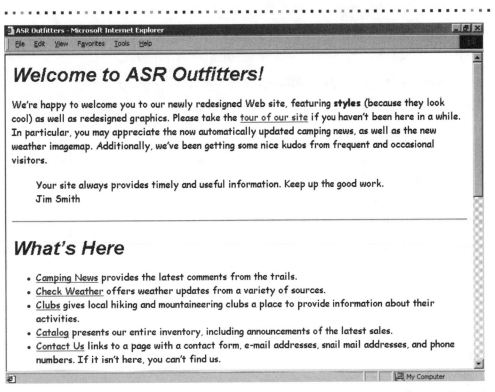

Figure 10.7 *The results of setting the font-family, style, size, and weight for headings*

Combining Font Properties

If you use the special, combination `font` property to set several different font properties at once, the properties must be specified in a certain order or they won't display correctly in a browser.

- The first are `font-style`, `font-weight`, and `font-variant`. They can be in any order, but must come before other font properties. Any of these three properties can be omitted and default values will be used.

- Next is `font-size`, which is required if you use the combination `font` property.

- You can follow `font-size` by a slash (/) and a `line-height` value, which specifies how far apart the lines in a paragraph are:

```
p { font-size: 12pt/14.4pt }
```

Line height can also be set as a separate font property—for example,

```
p { font-size: 12pt; line-height: 14.4pt }
```

(See "Setting Text Properties," the following section in this chapter.)

- Last is `font-family`, which is also required if you use the combination `font` property.

For example, rather than specifying each font property separately, as in the following code sample:

```
<style type="text/css">
   <!--
   body {font-style: italic;
         font-weight: bold;
         font-variant: normal;
         font-size: 1em;
         line-height: 1.2em;
         font-family: "Zapf Renaissance", "Snell Roundhand",
                      cursive}
   -->
</style>
```

The properties could be combined, as follows:

```
<style type="text/css"
   <!--
   body {font: italic bold 1em/1.2em "Zapf Renaissance",
             "Snell Roundhand", cursive}
   -->
</style>
```

Setting Text Properties

Text properties specify the characteristics of *text blocks* (sections of text, not individual characters). Table 10.6 shows some of the most common text properties.

Table 10.6 Text Properties

PROPERTY	POSSIBLE VALUES
`letter-spacing`	Measurement
`line-height`	Number, measurement, or percentage
`text-align`	`left`, `right`, `center`, `justify`
`text-decoration`	`none`, `underline`, `overline`, `line-through`, `blink`
`text-indent`	Measurement or percentage
`text-transform`	`none`, `capitalize`, `uppercase`, `lowercase`
`vertical-align`	`baseline`, `super`, `sub`, `top`, `text-top`, `middle`, `bottom`, `text-bottom`, or a percentage
`word-spacing`	Measurement

You apply these properties to selectors in the same way you apply font-level properties. To indent paragraphs and set up a special, nonindented paragraph class, follow these steps:

1. Within the style block, add a p selector and braces.

```
<style type="text/css">
  <!--
    p { }
  -->
</style>
```

2. Add the `text-indent` property, with a value of 5% to indent all regular paragraphs by 5 percent of the total window width.

```
<style type="text/css">
  <!--
    p { text-indent: 5% }
  -->
</style>
```

3. Add the p.noindent selector (and braces) on a new line within the style block. Using a standard selection, in conjunction with a descriptive term that you make up, you create a new style class within the style sheet.

```
<style type="text/css">
  <!--
    p { text-indent: 5% }
    p.noindent { }
  -->
</style>
```

4. Add the text-indent property, with a value of 0% to specify no indent.

```
<style type="text/css">
  <!--
    p { text-indent: 5% }
    p.noindent { text-indent: 0% }
  -->
</style>
```

5. To specify which text should be formatted without an indent, add a new p element with a class="noindent" attribute, as shown here.

```
<p>We're happy to welcome you to our newly redesigned Web
   site, featuring <b>styles</b> (because they look cool)
   as well as redesigned graphics. Please take the
   <a href="tour.html">tour of our site</a> if you haven't
   been here in a while. In particular, you may appreciate
   the now automatically updated camping news as well as
   the new weather imagemap.</p>
<p class="noindent">Additionally, we've been getting some
   nice kudos from frequent and occasional visitors.</p>
```

Figure 10.8 shows the results. All text tagged with p in the XHTML document is indented by 5 percent of the window width, and special formatting, set up with the class attribute, does not indent.

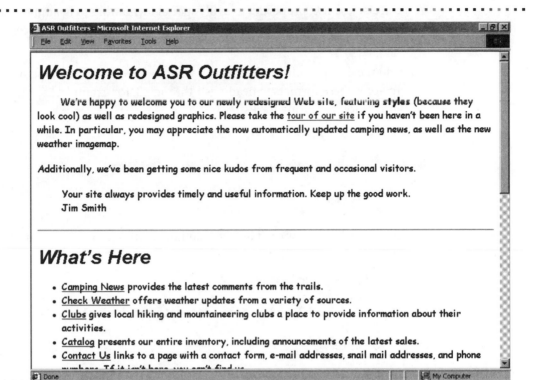

Figure 10.8 *Setting text properties lets you customize your documents—the second paragraph is not indented, while the first one is, because of a style class.*

Specifying Generic Style Classes

You can also specify a class without a selector, as in the following style block:

```
<style type="text/css">
  <!--
    .red { color: #ff0000 }
  -->
</style>
```

You can use a *generic class*, such as red in this example, with any XHTML elements in your document. However, if you specify an element with a class (p . red, for example), you can only use that class with p elements.

You can also use text properties to apply special formatting to headings. To format all headings with a line below them, centered, and with extra spacing between the letters, follow these steps:

1. Add the list of heading selectors you want to format to your basic style sheet. To apply these formats to headings 1 through 3, for example, list h1, h2, h3, with braces following the list.

```
<style type="text/css">
  <!--
    h1, h2, h3 { }
  -->
</style>
```

2. To place a line below each heading, add the text-decoration property with underline as the value:

```
<style type="text/css">
  <!--
    h1, h2, h3 { text-decoration: underline }
  -->
</style>
```

3. Add a semicolon to separate the rules, and add the text-align property with a value of center to center the headings.

```
<style type="text/css">
  <!--
    h1, h2, h3 { text-decoration: underline;
                 text-align: center }
  -->
</style>
```

4. Finally, add another separation semicolon and the letter-spacing property with a value of 5px (5 pixels).

```
<style type="text/css">
  <!--
    h1, h2, h3 { text-decoration: underline;
                 text-align: center;
                 letter-spacing: 5px }
  -->
</style>
```

The sample page looks like Figure 10.9.

Figure 10.9 You can apply text properties to several elements at once—for example, centering all headings.

Specifying Style IDs

You can specify an id for a one-time use—for example, if you're developing a Dynamic XHTML document. Use a # at the beginning of the id selector, as in the following style block:

```
<style type="text/css">
   <!--
      #firstusered { color: red }
   -->
</style>
```

You can use an id, such as firstusered in this example, with any single id attribute in your document. If you specify an element with the id attribute (<p id="firstusered">, for example), you can only use that id once in the document.

Sometimes you may want to set links without underlines. You can use the anchor pseudo-classes and set the text-decoration property to a value of none, as in the following example:

```
<style type="text/css">
  <!--
    a:link, a:visited, a:active {text-decoration: none}
  -->
</style>
```

Just be sure to make it obvious from your page design that these are links!

Setting Box Properties

You use box properties to create box designs—a feature that's not available in standard XHTML. You can box text, such as cautions or contact information, to call attention to it. You can adjust the margins to control how close text is to the border, and you can also remove the border to create floating text. Table 10.7 lists some commonly used box properties.

Table 10.7 Box Properties

PROPERTY	POSSIBLE VALUES
border	Any or all of the following border- attributes
border-color	#rrggbb
border-style	none, dotted, dashed, solid, double, groove, ridge, inset, outset
border-width	Measurement, thick, medium, thin
clear	right, left, none, both
float	right, left, none
height	Measurement or auto
margin	Measurement, or percentage of parent

Table 10.7 continued Box Properties

PROPERTY	POSSIBLE VALUES
margin-bottom	Measurement, or percentage of parent
margin left	Measurement, or percentage of parent
margin-right	Measurement, or percentage of parent
margin-top	Measurement, or percentage of parent
width	Measurement, percentage, or auto

At the time of writing, Internet Explorer and Netscape Navigator support box properties differently—in particular, the relationship between the surrounding text and the box, the size of the box around text, and the interpretation of the width *value are quite inconsistent.*

To create a box, apply these box-level characteristics to existing text in an XHTML document, including paragraphs, block quotes, and headings. The following steps show you how to create a box using an existing block quote. This box will float close to the right margin with a 2-pixel border and will occupy only 50 percent of the window width.

1. Within the style block, add a blockquote selector and braces.

   ```
   <style type="text/css">
     <!--
         blockquote { }
     -->
   </style>
   ```

2. Add a width property, with a value of 50%.

   ```
   <style type="text/css">
     <!--
         blockquote { width: 50% }
     -->
   </style>
   ```

3. Add a semicolon as a separator and the float property with a value of right.

   ```
   <style type="text/css">
     <!--
   ```

```
            blockquote { width: 50%;
                         float: right }
      -->
   </style>
```

4. Add another semicolon as a separator and the border property. In this example, we provide the individual border properties together, rather than as individual entities.

```
<style type="text/css">
  <!--
      blockquote { width: 50%;
                   float: right;
                   border: 2px solid black }
  -->
</style>
```

Figure 10.10 shows the results.

Figure 10.10 *Using boxes is an excellent way to call attention to information.*

The float *property is fully supported in only the latest browsers (Netscape 6, IE 5.5, and Opera 5). Although* float *is partially supported in previous browser editions, results tend to be inconsistent and unpredictable in older browsers.*

Setting Color and Background Properties

To establish color and background properties for the sample document or for any block-level elements, use the properties and values shown in Table 10.8.

Table 10.8 Color and Background Properties

PROPERTY	POSSIBLE VALUES
background	Any or all of the following background- properties
background-color	#rrggbb, transparent
background-image	url(http://example.com) or none
background-repeat	repeat, repeat-x, repeat-y, no-repeat
color	#rrggbb

To include a background color, add the properties to the body element, as shown in the following steps, which add #ffffcc (light yellow) to the background:

1. Within the style block, add a body selector.

    ```
    <style type="text/css">
      <!--
         body
      -->
    </style>
    ```

2. Add braces, the background-color property, and the #ffffcc value, which specifies the light yellow color.

    ```
    <style>
      <!--
         body { background-color: #ffffcc }
      -->
    </style>
    ```

When viewed in a browser, the background will appear lightly colored, just as it would if the `bgcolor` attribute were applied to the body element. Each element within the document inherits the background color from the body. However, you can also specify a separate background color for any inline or block-level element, even if you set a background color for the body element. The more specific style rules override the more general style rules.

You can also add a background image to the body element or other block elements. Remember that block elements are any elements with a line break before and after—for example, body, p, and `h1`.

As shown in the following steps, you can tile the background image either vertically or horizontally:

1. To add a background image to the document body, add the `background-image` property, separated from the previous property with a semicolon.

```
<style type="text/css">
   <!--
      body { background-color: #ffffcc;
              background-image: }
   -->
</style>
```

2. Add the value for the background image as url(pattern.gif). Use any absolute or relative URL in the parentheses.

```
<style type="text/css">
   <!--
      body { background-color: #ffffcc;
              background-image: url(pattern.gif) }
   -->
</style>
```

3. Add `background-repeat: repeat-x` to specify that the background image repeat horizontally (in the direction of the *x* axis). To repeat only vertically, use repeat-y; use no-repeat if you don't want a repeat.

```
<style type="text/css">
   <!--
      body { background-color: #ffffcc;
              background-image: url(pattern.gif);
              background-repeat: repeat-x; }
   -->
</style>
```

Setting Classification Properties

You use classification properties to change specific elements from inline (such as i or b) to block elements with line breaks before and after (such as p and h1), as well as to control the display of lists. Table 10.9 lists some classification properties and their values.

Table 10.9 Classification Properties

PROPERTY	POSSIBLE VALUES
display	inline,block,list-item
list-style-image	url(http://example.com/image.gif)
list-style-type	disc,circle,square,decimal,lower-roman,upper-roman,lower-alpha,upper-alpha,none

To specify that an unordered list uses square bullets, follow these steps:

1. Within the style block, add a ul selector followed immediately by an li selector on the same line. By combining these, the style rule will apply only to an li element within a ul element. If you set a rule for only the li element, it would affect all numbered and bulleted lists in your document, not just those within ul elements.

   ```
   <style type="text/css">
     <!--
        ul li
     -->
   </style>
   ```

2. Add braces.

   ```
   <style type="text/css">
     <!--
        ul li {}
     -->
   </style>
   ```

3. Add a list-style-type property with the value of square.

   ```
   <style type="text/css">
     <!--
   ```

```
        ul li { list-style-type: square }
    -->
</style>
```

You can also set a specific image for use as a bullet by using `list-style-image: url(figure.gif)`, as shown here:

```
<style type="text/css">
  <!--
    ul li { list-style-image: url(figure.gif) }
  -->
</style>
```

 If you specify a list-style-image *property, it's a good idea to also include a* list-style-type *property in case the image is not displayed (i.e., if the browser is unable to download or display the image). The image will be used if available, but if not, the* list-style-type *will be used instead.*

By changing the display property, you can change a list from displaying as a vertical list, as is customary, to an inline list in which each item appears within a line of text. To do so, use the following style rule:

```
<style type="text/css">
  <!--
    ul li { display: inline }
  -->
</style>
```

 Display properties are supported only in the latest browsers: Netscape 6, IE 5.5, and Opera 4 and later.

See Listing 10.2 for an example of an XHTML document with a link to an external style sheet and the code needed to apply these style definitions. Listing 10.3 details the external style sheet code.

LISTING 10.2: AN XHTML DOCUMENT LINKED TO AN EXTERNAL STYLE SHEET

```
<!DOCTYPE html PUBLIC "-//W3C/DTD XHTML 1.0 Transitional//EN"
  "http://www.w3.org/TR/xhtml1/DTD/xhtml1-transitional.dtd">
<html xmlns="http://www.w3.org/1999/xhtml">
<head>
```

```
  <title>ASR Outfitters</title>
  <link rel="stylesheet" type="text/css" href="10_3.css">
</head>
<body>
  <h1>Welcome to ASR Outfitters!</h1>
  <p>We're happy to welcome you to our newly redesigned Web
  site, featuring <span class="emph">styles</span> (because
  they look cool) as well as redesigned graphics. Please take
  the <a href="tour.html">tour of our site</a> if you haven't
  been here in a while. In particular, you may appreciate the
  now automatically updated camping news, as well as the new
  weather imagemap. Additionally, we've been getting some nice
  kudos from frequent and occasional visitors.</p>
    <blockquote>Your site always provides timely and useful
    information. Keep up the good work.<br />
    Jim Smith</blockquote>
  <hr />
  <h2>What's Here</h2>
  <div class="text"><ul>
    <li><a href="camping.html">Camping News</a> provides the
    latest comments from the trails.</li>
    <li><a href="weather.html">Check Weather</a> offers
    weather updates from a variety of sources.</li>
    <li><a href="clubs.html">Clubs</a> gives local hiking and
    mountaineering clubs a place to provide information
    about their activities.</li>
    <li><a href="catalog.html">Catalog</a> presents our entire
    inventory, including announcements of the latest sales.
    </li>
    <li><a href="contact.html">Contact Us</a> links to a page
    with a contact form, e-mail addresses, snail mail
    addresses, and phone numbers. If it isn't here, you
    can't find us.</li>
    </ul></div>
  <h2>What We Do</h2>
  <p>In addition to providing the latest camping and outdoor
  activities news, we also provide mountaineering and hiking
  equipment nationwide via mail order as well as through our
  stores in the Rocky Mountains. Please take a few minutes to
  look through our <a href="catalog.html">online offerings</a>.
```

```
    </p>
    <h2>Other Issues</h2>
    <div class="text"><ul>
      <li>As you may know, our URL was misprinted in the latest
        <span class="ital">Hiking News</span>. Please tell your
        hiking friends that the correct URL is <span
        class="inlineurl">http://www.asroutfitters.com/</span>.
      </li>
      <li>To collect a $1000 reward, turn in the name of the
        person who set the fire in the Bear Lake area last
        weekend.
        <ol>
          <li>Call 888-555-1212.</li>
          <li>Leave the name on the recording.</li>
          <li>Provide contact information so we can send you the
            reward.</li>
        </ol>
      </li>
    </ul></div>
    <h2>What Would You Like To See?</h2>
    <p class="diff">If you have suggestions or comments about the
    site or other information we could provide, we'd love to know
    about it. Drop us an e-mail at <a
    href="mailto:asroutfitters@raycommexample.com">
    asroutfitters@raycommexample.com</a>. Of course, you could
    also contact us more traditionally at the following address:
    </p>
    <div class="text"><address>ASR Outfitters<br />
      4700 N. Center<br />
      South Logan, UT 87654<br />
      801-555-3422
    </address></div>
</body>
</html>
```

LISTING 10.3: AN EXTERNAL STYLE SHEET

```
body
{background-color: #ffffcc;
 margin: 5%;
 font-style: normal;
 font-family: "Comic Sans MS", Verdana, Arial, Helvetica,
```

```
                     sans-serif;
   font-size: 12pt;
   line-height: 16.5pt}


h1, h2
{font-family: "Comic Sans MS", Verdana, Arial, Helvetica,
             sans-serif}


p
{font-style: normal;
   font-family: "Comic Sans MS", Verdana, Arial, Helvetica,
             sans-serif;
   font-size: 12pt;
   line-height: 16.5pt}


blockquote
{color: red;
   font-family: "Comic Sans MS", Verdana, Arial, Helvetica,
             sans-serif;
   font-size: 11pt;
   line-height: 15pt;
   margin-left: 15%;
   width: 300px}


li
{list-style-type: disc;
   font: bold 12pt/16.5pt "Comic Sans MS", Verdana, Arial,
      Helvetica, sans-serif}


li li
{list-style-type: circle}


address
{font-style: normal;
   font-weight: bold;
   font-size: 13pt;
   line-height: 17.5pt}


.emph
{font-weight: bolder}
```

```
.ital
{font-style: italic}

.inlineurl
{font-family: Courier, monospace;
 font-size: 10pt}

.diff
{color: red}

.text
{font-style: normal;
 font-family: "Comic Sans MS", Verdana, Arial, Helvetica,
              sans-serif;
 font-size: 12pt;
 line-height: 16.5pt}
```

Setting Aural Style Sheet Properties

One of the more recent additions to style sheet capabilities is aural properties, which allow you to set properties for documents that will be read aloud by a device. Visually impaired users use these properties; you could use them as supplements to visual presentations or in situations in which reading is not possible—for example, in the car. Aural style sheet properties let you specify that documents be read aloud, specify sound characteristics, and specify other auditory options.

Table 10.10 lists some aural style sheet properties and their values. Visit Master's Reference Part 2 for additional properties and values.

Table 10.10 Aural Style Sheet Properties

Property	Possible Values
pause	Time, percentage
pitch-range	Value
speech-rate	Value, x-slow, slow, medium, fast, x-fast, faster, slower
volume	Value, percentage, silent, x-soft, soft, medium, loud, x-loud

To specify that the document be read aloud with loud volume and fast speech (for efficiency), follow these steps:

1. In a new style block, provide a body selector to make your settings apply to the entire document, followed by braces.

```
<style type="text/css">
  <!--
    body { }
  -->
</style>
```

2. Add a `volume` property with the value of `loud`.

```
<style type="text/css">
  <!--
    body { volume: loud; }
  -->
</style>
```

3. Add a `speech-rate` property with the value of `fast`.

```
<style type="text/css">
  <!--
    body { volume: loud; speech-rate: fast;}
  -->
</style>
```

Aural style sheets are part of the CSS2 specification and are not currently supported by browsers. Check the W3C's Accessibility Features of CSS (`www.w3.org/TR/CSS-access`) for the latest on these features. You can also check Webreview.com's Style Sheet Reference Guide at `www.webreview.com/style/index.shtml`. Note that although the most recent browsers do not support these features, there may be specialized equipment that renders these style rules appropriately.

Setting Printed-Media Properties

Printed-media properties can help you accommodate users who print your documents, rather than read them online. These CSS2 properties let you set values for the page box, which you might think of as the area of your printout. For example, in hardcopy, your page box might be the 8.5"×11" piece of paper; the page box includes the content, margins, and edges. Table 10.11 lists some of the more common printed-media properties and their values. Master's Reference Part 2 provides additional information.

Table 10.11 Printed-Media Style Sheet Properties

PROPERTY	POSSIBLE VALUES
margin	Length, percentage, auto
marks	crop, cross, none
orphans	Value
page-break-after	auto, always, avoid, left, right
page-break-before	auto, always, avoid, left, right
page-break-before	auto, always, avoid, left, right
page-break-inside	auto, always, avoid, left, right
size	Value, auto, portrait, landscape
widows	Value

Like aural style sheets, printed-media properties are part of the CSS2 specification and are not currently supported by browsers.

To specify a page break before all h1 elements in a printed version of your document, follow these steps:

1. In a style block, provide an h1 selector, and braces, to apply your settings to all first-level headings in the entire document.

```
<style type="text/css">
  <!--
    h1 { }
  -->
</style>
```

2. Add a page-break-before property with the value of always.

```
<style>
  <!--
```

```
    h1 { page-break-before: always; }
    -->
</style>
```

See the Web sites listed in the previous section for more on CSS2 features. Although the most recent browsers do not support these features, there may be specialized equipment that renders these style rules appropriately.

Setting Positioning Properties

Using positioning, you can add properties to style rules to control element positioning. For example, you can identify specific locations for elements, as well as specify locations that are relative to other elements. Positioning properties are part of the CSS2 specification, and only the newer browser versions support them. Table 10.12 lists some positioning properties and their values.

Table 10.12 Positioning Properties

PROPERTY	POSSIBLE VALUES
float	left, right, none
overflow	visible, scroll, hidden, auto
position	static, absolute, relative, fixed
top, bottom, left, and right	Length, percentage, auto

Let's look at an example of how positioning properties work. To specify that the .warning classes in the document float to the left with text wrapping around to the right, and that the p.logo class sits at the bottom of the window, follow these steps:

1. In a new style block, provide a .warning selector and braces to hold its properties.

```
<style type="text/css">
  <!--
      .warning { }
  -->
</style>
```

2. Add a `float` property with the value of `left`.

```
<style type="text/css">
  <!--
     .warning { float: left }
  -->
</style>
```

3. Add a `p.logo` selector and braces.

```
<style type="text/css">
  <!--
     .warning { float: left }
     p.logo { }
  -->
</style>
```

4. Add a `position` property and `fixed` value.

```
<style type="text/css">
  <!--
     .warning { float: left }
     p.logo { position: fixed }
  -->
</style>
```

5. Add `bottom` and `right` properties and length of 0 (use any units) for each value.

```
<style type="text/css">
  <!--
     .warning { float: left }
     p.logo { position: fixed; bottom: 0px; right: 0px }
  -->
</style>
```

Positioning properties are a part of the CSS2 specification that is supported by newer browsers. However, relative positioning is supported more fully than absolute positioning at the present.

The Future of Style Sheets in XHTML

It seems likely that *external* style sheets will be the preferred way to use styles with XHTML documents in the future. Embedded and inline styles options are available in XHTML 1.0; however, XHTML 1.1 requires the use of the style sheet module in order to use the `style` element. Using CSS with XML is only possible with external style sheets. External style sheets offer ways to use all of the features of both embedded and inline styles through specifying classes and IDs as well as XHTML element selectors.

In addition, if you're going to venture more into XML, you should check out the Extensible Stylesheet Language (XSL) and XSL Transformations (XSLT). You can find out more at www.`w3.org/Style/XSL`.

Where to Go from Here

In this chapter, you learned how style sheets and XHTML documents relate and how to develop style sheets for your own needs. As you can see, style sheets are certainly more comprehensive than any formatting option previously available.

Next, you might check out some of these chapters:

- See Chapter 3 for more information about standard XHTML elements and formatting options.

- See Chapter 6 to find out more about XHTML tables.

- Check out Chapter 8 to learn about frames.

- Visit Chapter 14 for information about creating a coherent Web site.

Adding JavaScript

XHTML

Chapter 11

Using JavaScript, you can add some pizzazz to your pages, taking them from ho-hum pages to ones that react to user actions, process and check information that users provide, and even deliver information appropriate to each user. With the increasingly sophisticated nature of the Web, you often need these kinds of attractions to hold users' attention and to keep them coming back.

In this chapter, we'll look at what JavaScript is and how to use it, and, with some examples, we'll show you how to include JavaScript in your XHTML documents. We'll start with simple scripts and then build on them. We will concentrate on basic JavaScript capabilities (JavaScript 1.1 and some of 1.2 and 1.3), which is a good compromise between high functionality and broad browser acceptance.

This chapter covers the following topics:

- What is JavaScript?

- Adding JavaScript to your document

- Adding event handlers

- Tracking users using cookies

What Is JavaScript?

JavaScript is a scripting language created by Netscape, which vaguely resembles Sun's Java programming language. Most popular browsers, starting with Netscape Navigator 2 and Internet Explorer 3, support JavaScript. Microsoft's JScript and the international standard ECMAScript are very, very similar to JavaScript and, for our purposes, we just call it all JavaScript.

Microsoft also supports VBScript, a competing scripting approach. We recommend JavaScript (or the Microsoft equivalent JScript) for most purposes because JavaScript is much more widely supported.

You'll find lots of scripts available for public use on the Web. For starters, go to `http://javascript .internet.com.` *You could also search for JavaScript at* `www.yahoo.com` *or visit* `http:// webdeveloper.earthweb.com/pagedev/webjs.`

JavaScript is powerful enough to be truly useful, even though it isn't a full-fledged programming language. What's more, JavaScript is relatively easy and fun to use. JavaScript is simpler and less sophisticated (therefore less complex) than a "real" programming language. Many of the statements—*sentences* for JavaScript—are remarkably natural in their structure and terminology. Table 11.1 shows which browsers support which versions of JavaScript.

Table 11.1 Browser Support for JavaScript

JAVASCRIPT VERSION	NETSCAPE NAVIGATOR	INTERNET EXPLORER
JavaScript 1.0, JScript 1.0	2.0 and higher	3.0 and higher
JavaScript 1.1	3.0 and higher	
JavaScript 1.2, JScript 3.0	4.0 – 4.05	4.0 and higher
JavaScript 1.3	4.06 – 4.75	
JavaScript 1.4, JScript 5.0	5.0*	5.0 and higher
JavaScript 1.5	6.0	

JavaScript 1.4 was part of Netscape Navigator 5, which was not released.

To work with JavaScript, you need to be familiar with the following terms and concepts:

Object   An object is a thing—a check box on a form, the form itself, an image, a document, a link, or even a browser window. Some objects are built into JavaScript and are not necessarily part of your Web page. For example, the Date object provides a wide range of date information. You can think of objects as the "nouns" in the JavaScript language.

Property   A property describes an object. Properties can be anything from the color to the number of items, such as radio buttons, within an object. When users select an item in a form, they change the form's properties. You can think of properties as the "adjectives" in the JavaScript language.

Method   A method is an instruction. The methods available for each object describe what you can do with the object. For example, using a method, you can convert text in an object to all uppercase or all lowercase letters. Every object has a collection of methods, and every method belongs to at least one object. You can think of methods as the "verbs" in the JavaScript language.

Statement   A statement is a JavaScript language "sentence." Statements combine the objects, properties, and methods (nouns, adjectives, and verbs).

Function   A function is a collection of statements that performs actions. Functions contain one or more statements and can therefore be considered the "paragraphs" of the JavaScript language.

Event   An event occurs when something happens on your page, such as the page being loaded, a user submitting a form, or the mouse cursor being moved over an object.

Event handler   An event handler waits for something to happen—such as the mouse moving over a link—and then launches a script based on that event. For example, the onmouseover event handler performs an action when the user moves the mouse pointer over the object. You can think of an event handler as posing questions or directing the action of a story.

Variable   A variable stores data temporarily (usually until the user closes the page or moves to a new page). Each variable is given a name so you can refer to it in your code.

Before we get started, let's take a look at some JavaScript code. Once you can identify the pieces, JavaScript is as easy to read as XHTML code:

```
<!DOCTYPE html PUBLIC ".//W3C/DTD XHTML 1.0 Transitional//EN"
    "http://www.w3.org/TR/xhtml1/DTD/xhtml1-transitional.dtd">
<html xmlns="http://www.w3.org/1999/xhtml">
<head>
    <title>The Basic Page</title>
</head>
<body>
    <h1>Welcome!</h1>
    <a href="http://www.lanw.com/"
        onmouseover="window.status='Check us out!'; return true;"
        onmouseout="window.status=''; return true;">
        Visit our site</a>
</body>
</html>
```

In the preceding code, note the following JavaScript elements:

Object	window is a JavaScript object.
Property	status is a JavaScript property.
Statement	return true is a JavaScript statement.
Event handler	onmouseover and onmouseout are both JavaScript event handlers.

Although we often use extra spaces, indents, and line breaks for readability in our printed code, do not insert any additional spaces or line returns in your JavaScript code. Make sure that each JavaScript statement is on a single line, and allow the text to wrap without a line return. JavaScript sees line returns as JavaScript characters and adds them to your code (which will make the code nonfunctional). It's fine to use line returns at the actual end of a line of code, before you start the next line, but not in the middle of a line of code.

Master's Reference Part 3 includes a comprehensive guide to JavaScript, which you can use to expand on the basics in this chapter.

If you test the previous code in a browser, you'll see the message "Check us out!" appear in the status bar at the bottom of the browser window when you roll the mouse cursor over the "Visit our site" link, and disappear when you roll the mouse cursor off the link.

The JavaScript discussed in this chapter is exclusively client-side JavaScript. This simply means that the user's browser does the work and the server is not involved. Although server-side JavaScript exists, it is outside the scope of this book.

Adding JavaScript to Your Document

You can add JavaScript to your page in three ways:

- Embed the JavaScript in the page.
- Place the JavaScript in the document head.
- Link to JavaScript stored in another file.

The options for placing JavaScript closely resemble the options for placing style sheets, discussed in Chapter 10.

Table 11.2 lists and describes the XHTML elements and attributes you use to add JavaScript to your XHTML documents.

Table 11.2 Elements and Attributes Used to Add JavaScript

ITEM	TYPE	DESCRIPTION
`script`	Element	Identifies the script section in the document.
`language="javascript"`	Attribute of `script`	Specifies the scripting language (and, optionally, version).
`src="url"`	Attribute of `script`	Optionally specifies the location of an external script.
`type="text/javascript"`	Attribute of `script`	Provides the script MIME type; required.
`noscript`	Element	Provides content for non-script-capable browsers.
`<!-- //-->`	Comment markup	Hides the contents of the script from non-script-capable browsers. Note that this differs from comment markup used for style sheets.

Embedding JavaScript

If you're adding a fairly short JavaScript, your best bet is to embed it in the XHTML document in the code that the JavaScript affects. For example, JavaScript that adds the current date to your document is a few lines long, so you can easily embed the script in your XHTML document.

Embedding works like this: When users open your page, their browsers "read" your XHTML source document line by line. If your XHTML code includes JavaScript within the document body, the browser performs the actions as it reads the page. For example, if the body element includes JavaScript, the first task the browser completes is running the script. Or, if you include JavaScript in the first actual text of the document, the browser runs the script as soon as it gets to the text.

Let's embed a JavaScript that prints the current time and date as the page loads. The JavaScript statement—in this case, the whole script—is `document.write(Date())`. Here are the steps:

1. Start with the following XHTML code:

    ```
    <!DOCTYPE html PUBLIC
        "-//W3C/DTD XHTML 1.0 Transitional//EN"
      "http://www.w3.org/TR/xhtml1/DTD/xhtml1-transitional.dtd">
    <html xmlns="http://www.w3.org/1999/xhtml">
    <head>
        <title>The Date Page</title>
    </head>
    <body>
        <h1>Welcome!</h1>
    </body>
    </html>
    ```

2. Add an introductory sentence, like this:

    ```
    <body>
        <h1>Welcome!</h1>
        <p>Today's date is:
        </p>
    </body>
    ```

3. Add `script` tags where you want the script:

```
<p>Today's date is:
   <script>
   </script>
</p>
```

4. Add the `type` attribute to specify the script's MIME type, and the `language` attribute to specify that the scripting language is JavaScript:

```
<p>Today's date is:
   <script type="text/javascript" language="javascript">
   </script>
</p>
```

5. Add comment lines to hide the script from browsers that do not recognize scripting. Include standard XHTML comment markup (`<!--` and `-->`), and preface the closing XHTML comment markup with `//` to hide the comment close from the JavaScript interpreter; if you don't, you'll get an error. The complete comment looks like this:

```
<p>Today's date is:
   <script type="text/javascript" language="javascript">
      <!--
      // -->
   </script>
</p>
```

6. Add the actual JavaScript statement:

```
<script type="text/javascript" language="javascript">
   <!--
      document.write(Date());
   // -->
</script>
```

That's it! The resulting page looks like this:

The Date Page - Microsoft Internet Explorer
File Edit View Favorites Tools Help

Welcome!

Today's date is: Wed May 02 13:50:06 2001

Done   My Computer

Using this method, the initial "Today's date is" text appears in all browsers, regardless of whether they support JavaScript. Browsers that don't support JavaScript display
Today's date is and a blank. To hide the text from browsers that don't support JavaScript,
simply remove the text from the p element and replace the JavaScript statement as
shown in the following code:

```
<script type="text/javascript" language="javascript">
   <!--
      document.write("Today\'s date is: " + Date());
   // -->
</script>
```

This way, users will either see the JavaScript or won't see it, but they won't see a
lead-in with an unfulfilled promise. You get the same effect in JavaScript-capable
browsers and nothing at all in non-JavaScript browsers.

*JavaScript, like all programming languages, has its own punctuation rules, vocabulary, and terminology.
Most of that is beyond the scope of this book, but we'll point out the specifics where we can. In the preceding code, notice that the single quote in* **Today's** *has a backslash in front; that's the "escape character"
that tells JavaScript, "Treat this single quote as a text character, not programming punctuation."*

You're not restricted to a single JavaScript statement, and you can embed several
statements through the page source. The additional statements in the following code
display information about the user's browser in the document:

```
<body>
   <h1>Welcome!</h1>
   <p><script type="text/javascript" language="javascript">
```

```
<!--
    document.write("Today\'s date is: " + Date());
// -->
</script></p>
<p><script type="text/javascript" language="javascript">
    <!--
    document.write("You appear to be using " +
        navigator.appName + " version " +
        navigator.appVersion + ".")
    // -->
</script></p>
</body>
```

In this script, the JavaScript is interpreted line by line as it appears in the XHTML source. In the new statement, the text strings, such as *You appear to be using*, are combined with properties of the `navigator` object—that is, with characteristics of the browser—to display the line shown. See Master's Reference Part 3 for a full run-down of objects, including the `navigator` object, and their properties. The resulting page from this example looks like this:

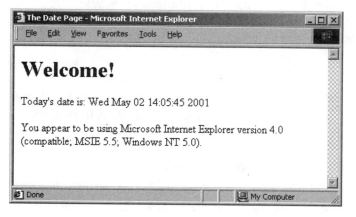

Embedding is a great way to start adding JavaScript to your page. You can use this technique alone or combine it with others.

If you choose to embed the JavaScript, you'll need to provide for older browsers that don't support it. See the section "Providing for Older Browsers" later in this chapter.

Adding a JavaScript Block in the Head

If you repeatedly use JavaScript within documents, consider placing it in the document head element. Collecting individual statements in one place creates a function; creating functions in the head element is convenient and easy to troubleshoot.

In the following examples, we'll show you how to add JavaScript statements to the document head. Here's the code to start with:

```
<!DOCTYPE html PUBLIC "-//W3C/DTD XHTML 1.0 Transitional//EN"
    "http://www.w3.org/TR/xhtml1/DTD/xhtml1-transitional.dtd">
<html xmlns="http://www.w3.org/1999/xhtml">
<head>
    <title>The Date Page</title>
</head>
<body>
    <h1>Welcome!</h1>
    <p>
    </p>
</body>
</html>
```

This XHTML document will include two JavaScript sections. One displays the current date and time, and the other displays the name and version number of the user's browser—the same actions we demonstrated earlier within the body of the document. You include the JavaScript function command in the document head element and then run the function from the document body by calling just its name. Here are the steps:

1. Add the `script` tags to the document head element, like this:

   ```
   <head>
       <title>The Date Page</title>
       <script>
       </script>
   </head>
   ```

2. Add the `type` attribute to specify that the script is a JavaScript, and the `language` attribute to specify that the scripting language is JavaScript:

   ```
   <head>
       <title>The Date Page</title>
       <script type="text/javascript" language="javascript">
       </script>
   </head>
   ```

3. Add comment markup (<!-- //-->) to hide the script from other browsers. Don't forget the slashes.

```
<head>
   <title>The Date Page</title>
   <script type="text/javascript" language="javascript">
      <!--
      // -->
   </script>
</head>
```

Remember, we're putting the script in the document head, so by itself it will not display anything in the browser window. You have to place instructions within the document body to do anything with the script.

4. To make a function out of the JavaScript statement that displays the date, you name the statement and place it in inside "curly brackets" (a.k.a. braces: { }). In this example, the name is printDate. Add the keyword function, the function name (including a set of parentheses), and the braces.

```
<head>
   <title>The Date Page</title>
   <script type="text/javascript" language="javascript">
      <!--
      function printDate() {  }
      // -->
   </script>
</head>
```

 If a function needs parameter values, they're usually inserted in these parentheses. For consistency, even functions without parameters get these parentheses in their names.

5. Add the JavaScript statement within the braces. Use the same code we used within the document body a few pages ago. (Remember, we have to wrap lines to fit them on the printed page; you should type the JavaScript function all on one line.)

```
<head>
   <title>The Date Page</title>
   <script type="text/javascript" language="javascript">
```

```
      <!--
        function printDate() {
          document.write("Today\'s date is: " + Date());}
      // -->
    </script>
  </head>
```

6. To "call" (which means to activate or run) the function from the document body, add another set of script tags within the body tags, as shown here:

```
<body>
  <h1>Welcome!</h1>
  <p>
    <script type="text/javascript" language="javascript">
      <!--
      // -->
    </script>
  </p>
</body>
```

7. Add printDate(), which is the name you gave the function, within the tags.

```
<body>
  <h1>Welcome!</h1>
  <p>
    <script type="text/javascript" language="javascript">
      <!--
          printDate()
      // -->
    </script>
  </p>
</body>
```

Now our code looks like Listing 11.1.

Listing 11.1: Including JavaScript in the head Element

```
<!DOCTYPE html PUBLIC "-//W3C/DTD XHTML 1.0 Transitional//EN"
   "http://www.w3.org/TR/xhtml1/DTD/xhtml1-transitional.dtd">
<html xmlns="http://www.w3.org/1999/xhtml">
<head>
   <title>The Date Page</title>
```

```
<script type="text/javascript" language="javascript">
    <!--
        function printDate() {
            document.write("Today\'s date is: " + Date()); }
    // -->
</script>
</head>
<body>
    <h1>Welcome!</h1>
    <p><script type="text/javascript" language="javascript">
        <!--
            printDate()
        // -->
    </script></p>
</body>
</html>
```

 If you separate the JavaScript into its own section, enclose it within comment markup: `<!--` *and* `//-->`. *Not all browsers can interpret JavaScript, and the comment markup instructs these browsers to ignore the JavaScript section. JavaScript-enabled browsers will see past the comments and recognize the* `script` *element.*

Comments May Not Work in XHTML in the Near Future

The traditional practice of using comments to "hide" scripts from browsers that do not support JavaScript may not work in the near future in XHTML, because XML parsers may silently remove the contents of comments—i.e., your script!

There are two possible solutions to this:

1. Use external scripts (which is recommended). (See the following section "Linking JavaScript.")

2. Wrap the content of the script within a CDATA-marked section, for example:

```
<script>
    <![CDATA[
        ...script content ...
```

```
      ]]>
   </script>
```

At the time this book is being written, no browsers know how to handle XML CDATA sections. However, further support for XML is very likely in the next versions of browsers.

. . . .

Linking JavaScript

If you plan to use script functions in several documents, consider placing them in a separate file and referring to that file from your document. You can build, test, and store working JavaScript code in one location and use it in several Web pages. You can also share this code with others who can link it into their documents.

The linked document is simply a text file that includes all your variable definitions and functions. You can even copy the functions from the headers of your existing XHTML documents if you want. If this document also includes variables and functions that you don't need for the Web page, the browser uses what it needs as the variables and functions are called by the JavaScript code in the XHTML document.

To continue with our date example, you can create a functions.js document that contains the following text:

```
function printDate() { document.write(Date()) }
```

This linked document does not need any special headings or elements—so it doesn't need comment markup or script tags. An external JavaScript file is a text document whose only content is JavaScript code (similar to an external style sheet, which is a text document with only style definitions). It doesn't require any XHTML code, but simply includes the definitions for the variables and functions. You can then link to the script with the following code from the document head element (including all the surrounding tags):

```
<head>
   <title>The Date Page</title>
   <script src="functions.js" type="text/javascript"
      language="javascript">
   </script>
</head>
```

Now, by including this reference to your external script document, you can access any functions included in this external script from any XHTML document you create.

You can include as many functions or variable definitions within your external script document as you like. Alternatively, you can reference multiple external scripts by including additional `script` elements.

Providing for Older Browsers

As you add JavaScript to your pages, you must accommodate older browsers that cannot interpret JavaScript, as well as browsers in which JavaScript is not enabled. If you include JavaScript in the `head` element or if you link the JavaScript from a separate document, you've already provided for older browsers because these don't show up in the document body.

However, if you embed the JavaScript, you must make sure the script doesn't show up. The best way to accommodate older browsers is to make sure that text that is dependent on the JavaScript (such as "Today's date is") is part of the JavaScript statement. You might recall from Listing 11.1 that the embedded code looks like this:

```
<script type="text/javascript" language="javascript">
  <!--
    document.write("Today\'s date is: " + Date());
  // -->
</script>
```

However, if you want to give additional information to script-incapable browsers (rather than just hiding information from them), you can also use the `noscript` element and include alternative text. For example, if you have a form that uses JavaScript to validate input, you might add a statement to the top of the form, within a `noscript` element, that warns users of non-JavaScript browsers that their responses won't be validated and that they should be particularly careful to proofread their responses; for example:

```
<h2>Personal Information Form</h2>
<noscript>
  <p>Please be very careful to proofread your responses.
    If any information is incorrect (particularly your
    e-mail address), we won't be able to contact you.</p>
</noscript>
Please enter your name and address below:<br />
```

In this example, the JavaScript-enabled browser displays only the *Personal Information Form* heading, followed by "Please enter your name and address below:". Other browsers will *also* display the "Please be very careful" text.

For a small amount of JavaScript or for JavaScript that isn't essential to the content of your document, using the noscript element is a convenient way to deal with both situations. If you have more complex JavaScript applications on your page, you'll need to identify users' browsers and automatically direct them to the correct page. In that case, instead of putting content within the noscript tags, a separate page is created for users without JavaScript. To do this, you need a script to perform browser detection, and at least two different versions of the page (one for users with JavaScript enabled and one for users without JavaScript).

See Matt's Script Archive on the Web at www.worldwidemart.com/scripts *for server-side means of identifying browsers and redirecting them appropriately, or visit* www.pageresource.com/jscript/jbrowse.htm *for a client-side version of browser detection using JavaScript.*

Adding Event Handlers

JavaScript relies heavily on event handlers, which react to users' actions by running statements or calling JavaScript functions. Event handlers provide users with additional information by reacting to what is happening or what users are doing on the page—moving their mouse, clicking a button, or selecting options on a form—doing whatever you tell them to do in each instance. For example, with the onmouseover and onmouseout event handlers, you can change the information in your status bar, flash an alert box, or change an illustration.

JavaScript provides a variety of event handlers that can react to users' actions. In this chapter, we discuss only a couple of them, but Master's Reference Part 3 explains all of them.

Using *onmouseover* and *onmouseout* Events

You commonly use an onmouseover event with the anchor element (a) to provide additional information about the link. The onmouseout event, then, generally undoes what the onmouseover event does.

Using these event handlers, you can, among other things, implement timed status bar events, swap images, and alert users. We'll show you how in the next few sections. But first, let's look at how to add the onmouseover and onmouseout event handlers.

 Neither Internet Explorer 3 or earlier nor Netscape Navigator 2 or earlier recognizes the onmouseout *event. If your users use these browsers (which is pretty unlikely anymore), consider using a separate function (described later) to clear the status bar. According to statistics derived from the users of* www.thecounter.com, *only 20 percent of users use a 4.0 or older browser.*

Let's add the onmouseover and onmouseout event handlers to display a new message in the status bar and then remove it. This is handy for displaying information in the status bar that is more descriptive than the URL that the browser automatically displays there. Here are the steps:

1. Start with an XHTML document that includes a link, like this:

```
<!DOCTYPE html PUBLIC
    "-//W3C/DTD XHTML 1.0 Transitional//EN"
  "http://www.w3.org/TR/xhtml1/DTD/xhtml1-transitional.dtd">
<html xmlns="http://www.w3.org/1999/xhtml">
<head>
    <title>Status Bar</title>
</head>
<body>
    <h1>Welcome!</h1>
    <a href="http://www.lanw.com/">
        Visit the LANWrights, Inc. site.</a>
</body>
</html>
```

2. Add the onmouseover event handler to the a element:

```
<a href="http://www.lanw.com/" onmouseover="">
    Visit the LANWrights, Inc. site.</a>
```

3. Add window.status= to the event handler. The window.status property specifies what appears in the status bar.

```
<a href="http://www.lanw.com/"
    onmouseover="window.status=">
    Visit the LANWrights, Inc. site.</a>
```

4. Add the text that will appear in the status bar, enclosed in single quotes (' '). You use single quotes because the window status statement itself is enclosed in double quotes, and you must nest unlike quotes within each other.

    ```
    <a href="http://www.lanw.com/"
       onmouseover="window.status='Check us out!'">
       Visit the LANWrights, Inc. site.</a>
    ```

5. Add a semicolon (to indicate the end of the statement), and add `return true` to the end (just before the closing quotes). This essentially tells the JavaScript interpreter that the action is complete and to do it.

    ```
    <a href="http://www.lanw.com/"
       onmouseover="window.status='Check us out!'; return
       true;">
       Visit the LANWrights, Inc. site.</a>
    ```

If you try this, you'll see that the "Check us out!" statement appears in the browser status bar after you move the cursor over the link. The statement stays in the status bar, which probably isn't what you want.

To restore the status bar after the cursor moves away from the link, add the `onmouseout` event handler, like this:

```
<a href="http://www.lanw.com/"
   onmouseover="window.status='Check us out!'; return true"
   onmouseout="window.status=''; return true;">
   Visit the LANWrights, Inc. site.</a>
```

Using Timed Status Bar Text Events

JavaScript includes a `setTimeout` method that allows you to set up timed events. For example, you can use it in conjunction with the `onmouseover` event handler to display the status bar text for a period of time and then clear it. Although the `setTimeout` method is a bit more complicated than the `onmouseout` event handler, it's more universal. It keeps the status bar text you set from remaining in the status bar, even with older browsers. (There are other JavaScript methods to set timers, but the `setTimeout` method is the only one of these that works in older browsers.)

In general, the function needed to clear the status bar text should do two things:

*   Set the status bar text to a specific text string.

*   Wait for a specified time, and then clear the status bar again.

Because this function is slightly more involved than resetting the status bar onmouseover event, we create the script in the document head, as shown earlier in this chapter. Here's how:

1. In an XHTML document, add the script element and comment lines in the document head:

```
<!DOCTYPE html PUBLIC
   "-//W3C/DTD XHTML 1.0 Transitional//EN"
  "http://www.w3.org/TR/xhtml1/DTD/xhtml1-transitional.dtd">
<html xmlns="http://www.w3.org/1999/xhtml">
<head>
   <title>Status Bar</title>
   <script type="text/javascript" language="javascript">
     <!--
     //-->
   </script>
</head>
<body>
   <h1>Welcome!</h1>
   <a href="http://www.lanw.com/">
     Visit the LANWrights, Inc. site.</a>
</body>
</html>
```

2. Name the function SalesPitch and add the needed braces:

```
<script type="text/javascript" language="javascript">
   <!--
   function SalesPitch() {  }
   //-->
</script>
```

3. Add the window.status statement to set the status bar.

```
<script type="text/javascript" language="javascript">
   <!--
   function SalesPitch() {
      window.status="Check us out!";  }
   //-->
</script>
```

4. Add the new method, setTimeout. Within the parentheses, the first parameter sets the window status to null (' '), and the second specifies to wait 3000 milliseconds (3 seconds).

```
<script type="text/javascript" language="javascript">
   <!--
   function SalesPitch() {
      window.status="Check us out!";
      setTimeout("window.status=''",3000);  }
   //-->
</script>
```

5. Add a return true statement. This serves only to tell the JavaScript interpreter that the function is done and that the interpreter should act on it.

```
<script type="text/javascript" language="javascript">
   <!--
   function SalesPitch() {
      window.status="Check us out!";
      setTimeout("window.status=''",3000);
      return true;  }
   //-->
</script>
```

6. With this SalesPitch script in the document head, now you need to call the script from within the document body to execute the entire function. Add an onmouseover statement to the a element:

```
<a href="http://www.lanw.com/"
   onmouseover="SalesPitch(); return true;">
```

Listing 11.2 shows the complete code.

LISTING 11.2: JavaScript Using a setTimeout Method

```
<!DOCTYPE html PUBLIC "-//W3C/DTD XHTML 1.0 Transitional//EN"
   "http://www.w3.org/TR/xhtml1/DTD/xhtml1-transitional.dtd">
<html xmlns="http://www.w3.org/1999/xhtml">
<head>
   <title>Status Bar</title>
   <script type="text/javascript" language="javascript">
      <!--
```

```
        function SalesPitch() {
            window.status="Check us out!";
            setTimeout("window.status='''",3000);
            return true;   }
        //-->
    </script>
</head>
<body>
    <h1>Welcome!</h1>
    <a href="http://www.lanw.com/"
        onmouseover="SalesPitch(); return true;">
    Visit our site!</a>
</body>
</html>
```

Comments in JavaScript

Add comments (actual notes to yourself, not just comment markup) to your JavaScript to track what the script does. This is useful for future reference and helpful to people with whom you share your JavaScript functions. Comments in JavaScript are preceded by two forward slashes, //. You need to add these slashes at the beginning of each comment line, as in the following code segment:

```
<script type="text/javascript" language="javascript">

    //this function is for a timed event in the status bar

    //set the number of milliseconds

    <!--

        function SalesPitch() {

            window.status="Check us out!";

            setTimeout("window.status='''",3000);

            return true;   }

    //-->

</script>
```

Adding a Little Excitement to the Page Load

Just as events can respond to a user's mouse actions, events can occur when the page loads or unloads. However, anything time consuming (such as playing a sound) or intrusive (such as displaying a welcome alert) can irritate users far more than impressing them with your technical skills.

We suggest that you perform actions with the onload or onunload events only if users will expect it in the context of the page or for other reasons.

See Chapter 12 for more information about adding sounds.

Swapping Images

You can use the onmouseover and onmouseout event handlers to change linked images when the mouse cursor moves over them. These are often called *rollovers*.

This technique works only with Netscape Navigator 3 or later and Internet Explorer 4 or later. Older browsers don't recognize images as objects.

To change an image when the mouse moves over it, you need an anchor element (<a href="url">) and two versions of the image: one is the standard presentation, and the other is the highlighted presentation. When the page initially loads, the standard image is visible. Then, when the mouse moves over the image, the highlighted image replaces the standard image. Finally, when the mouse cursor moves away again, the images change back. Conceptually, the process is the same as changing the status bar text in the preceding example; however, instead of changing the status bar, you swap images.

To set up images to swap, you first need a pair of images that are precisely the same size but visually different.

Next, you need a link using an image in your document. The img element must also have a name attribute so the JavaScript can identify and refer to it. We'll use the following sample document:

```
<!DOCTYPE html PUBLIC "-//W3C/DTD XHTML 1.0 Transitional//EN"
    "http://www.w3.org/TR/xhtml1/DTD/xhtml1-transitional.dtd">
<html xmlns="http://www.w3.org/1999/xhtml">
<head>
    <title>Image Swap</title>
```

```
</head>
<body bgcolor="ffffff" text="000000" link="0000ff"
    vlink="800080" alink="ff0000">
    <center>
        <a href="http://www.example.com/">
            <img src="image1.gif" width="50" height="10" border="0"
                name="catbtn" id="catbtn" alt="catbtn" /></a>
    </center>
</body>
</html>
```

Two images, cleverly titled image1.gif and image2.gif, are available to swap within the img element. To identify the image, you refer to it by name (here, catbtn) and src, which is a property of the catbtn image object. For example, to change the image (but not change it back), you can use a statement such as the following:

```
onmouseover="catbtn.src='image2.gif'; return true;"
```

In the context of the img element set to image1.gif, the onmouseover statement looks like this:

```
<a href="http://www.example.com/"
    onmouseover="catbtn.src='image2.gif'; return true;">
<img src="image1.gif" width="50" height="10" border="0"
    name="catbtn" id="catbtn" alt="catbtn" /></a>
```

Triggering this statement changes the source (src) property of the object named catbtn to image2.gif

Similarly, to change the image back when the cursor moves away, use an onmouseout statement with the opposite image setting, as shown here:

```
<a href="http://www.example.com/"
    onmouseover="catbtn.src='image2.gif'; return true;"
    onmouseout="catbtn.src='image1.gif'; return true;">
<img src="image1.gif" width="50" height="10" border="0"
    name="catbtn" id="catbtn" alt="catbtn" /></a>
```

The complete code for simple image swapping with two images is shown in Listing 11.3. Note that this is just a contrived example. If you enter this code in a text editor, it will only work if you have two images titled image1.gif and image2.gif.

LISTING 11.3: SIMPLE IMAGE SWAPPING WITH TWO IMAGES

```
<!DOCTYPE html PUBLIC "-//W3C/DTD XHTML 1.0 Transitional//EN"
    "http://www.w3.org/TR/xhtml1/DTD/xhtml1-transitional.dtd">
<html xmlns="http://www.w3.org/1999/xhtml">
<head>
    <title>Image Swap</title>
</head>
<body bgcolor="ffffff" text="000000" link="0000ff"
        vlink="800080" alink="ff0000">
    <center>
        <a href="http://www.example.com/"
            onmouseover="catbtn.src='image2.gif'; return true;"
            onmouseout="catbtn.src='image1.gif'; return true;">
        <img src="image1.gif" width="50" height="10" border="0"
            name="catbtn" id="catbtn" alt="catbtn" /></a>
    </center>
</body>
</html>
```

For a series of images, you use a series of if statements in a function to make the changes. Using if statements keeps your XHTML code easier to read and makes it easier to change your script later. You can easily add more statements to reshuffle images in different contexts by adding a function like this in the head section of your XHTML document:

```
function imagereplacer(place) {
    if (place==1) document.catbtn.src="image2.gif";
    if (place==2) document.catbtn.src="image1.gif";  }
```

The if statements check for the value of place and changes the image accordingly. You call this function from the body of your document. Instead of writing the full imagereplacer function in the a element, you put just the function name in the attribute value, with the desired setting for place in the parameter parentheses, as shown here:

```
<a href="http://www.example.com/">
    <img src="image1.gif" width="50" height="10" border="0"
        onmouseover="imagereplacer(1)" alt="catbtn" name="catbtn"
        id="catbtn" onmouseout="imagereplacer(2)" />
</a>
```

If you want to do more—such as change the image *and* change the status bar—you can use a special JavaScript keyword, `switch`, as shown here:

```
function imagereplacer(place) {
    switch (place) {
        case(1): document.catbtn.src="image2.gif";
            window.status="Second Image";
            break;
        case(2): document.catbtn.src="image1.gif";
            window.status="First Image";
            break;  }  }
```

Using this technique, you can list all the options. Similar to the previous `if` statements, the `switch` statement lists each option and the action to take, but with `switch` it's easier to perform multiple or complex actions. In a `switch` statement, each option is a `case`.

In this example, the first line calls the function and includes the number for the variable `place`. You use `place` in the `switch` statement, which has two cases. If `place` is equal to one, use `case(1)`, which sets the source property for the image named `catbtn` (`catbtn.src`) to `image2.gif`.

If you're using objects, methods, properties, or event handlers from early versions of JavaScript, you don't need to add the version to the `language` attribute. However, if you're using expanded capabilities from later versions—as we're going to do with the `switch` statement here—and functions are defined in the document, include the version number within the attribute, for example, `language="javascript1.2"`.

The change from the `if`-statement `imagereplacer` function to the `case`-statement version requires no changes within your XHTML code. When you put JavaScript functions in the document head, you can make changes without editing all the elements in your code.

It's very important to test your JavaScript code in more than one browser. The code in Listing 11.3 works in both Netscape Navigator 3 and later and Internet Explorer 4 and later. However, the code using the `switch` statement works in Internet Explorer 4 and later, but only in Netscape Navigator 6.

Although we often use line breaks for readability in our code, be very careful about inserting any additional line returns in your JavaScript code. Make sure that each JavaScript statement is on a single line, and allow the text to wrap without a line return. JavaScript sees a line return **within** a line of code as a JavaScript character and adds it to your code (which will make the code nonfunctional and cause error messages). It's fine to use line returns at the actual end of a line of code, before you start the next line, but not in the middle of a line of code. JavaScript, in general, ignores extra white space, but be careful about adding extra white space and always test your code when you make any changes.

Using *onclick* and *onchange* Event Handlers

In addition to onmouseover and onmouseout event handlers, you can use onclick and onchange event handlers, which are activated when users click an object or a button or change a form field. Including these event handlers is similar to using the onmouseover and onmouseout event handlers. You can use the onchange or the onclick event handler to set link destinations in forms, among other things.

Alerting Users with *onclick*

A handy use for the onclick event is an alert box, which is a small dialog box that contains a message and an OK button. For example, an alert could be an expanded note about the object, such as "Come to this page for more news on this year's programs!"

At its simplest, you can combine an event handler (to start the process) with an alert, like this:

```
<img src="infolink.jpg" alt="link"
    onclick="alert('Visit LANWrights!'); return true;" />
```

Users see the accompanying dialog box and must click OK to proceed. Alerts can be quite irritating, however, so use them only in conjunction with buttons or other actions so a user can make a conscious choice. For example, you can combine the alert with form validation information and base the alert pop-up on the user's form responses.

Setting Link Destinations in Forms

One of the handiest JavaScript functions is setting link destinations in forms to direct users to information based on their selections in the form. For example, if a form contains a Course Offered selection list, users can select courses that interest them, and you can programmatically set the destination of a jump to meet the needs of the selections. You can also use JavaScript to set destinations so when a user clicks buttons or performs other actions on the page, the script opens new pages—just as traditional links would. This technique can add visual interest to your pages as well as let you interactively produce new pages for your users.

Minimally, to set destinations and activate links, use the onclick event handler, as shown here.

```
<form>
   <input type="radio" name="lesson" value="Lesson 1"
      onclick="self.location='lesson1.htm'" />
   Lesson 1: Getting Started
</form>
```

The self.location='lesson1.htm' entry opens the file lesson1.htm in the same window when a user clicks the radio button. If you want the document to open in a separate window, the process is similar. For example, to open lesson1.htm in another frame, called main, you can use the following:

```
<input type="radio" name="lesson" value="Lesson 1"
   onclick="parent.main.location='lesson1.htm'" />
   Lesson 1: Getting Started
```

The parent.main.location *object name refers to the parent document. In this example, that would be the frameset document; this name then refers to the* main *object (frame) within the frameset, then the* location *property of the frame.*

A single jump can also lead to a variable destination—the document opened depends on the user's selection from a list. Say your document contains catalog information, such as pictures, product descriptions, and prices. A user clicks a category to open the correct page of your catalog. Users might also select activities from a list such as this.

```
<form>
   <select name="Activity"
         onchange="setLink(this.selectedIndex)">
      <option>Hiking</option>
      <option>Camping</option>
      <option selected="selected">Mountain</option>
      <option>Sailing</option>
      <option>Winter</option>
   </select>
</form>
```

The onchange event handler passes information to a function called setLink. The selectedIndex property is the position in the list (starting with zero) of the current selection in the list. So, this.selectedIndex is the numeric value that represents the position in the current list of the value selected.

A relatively simple function setLink, located in the document head, assigns the final URL to the page properties and loads the new URL:

```
<script type="text/javascript" language="javascript">
    <!--
    function setLink(num) {
        if (num = 0) { self.location="hiking.html"   }
        if (num = 1) { self.location="camping.html"   }
        if (num = 2) { self.location="mountain.html" }
        if (num = 3) { self.location="sailing.html"   }
        if (num = 4) { self.location="winter.html"   } }
    //-->
</script>
```

With this type of scripting, it's easier to figure out what's going on, to make changes later, and to accommodate unique, nonsequential names, such as newmountainbikes.html or augustactivities.html.

Using the *onsubmit* Event Handler

One of the most common uses for the onsubmit event handler is to validate form input. You can verify that users fill in required fields, that they make required selections, or that they fill in an appropriate combination of fields. Suppose you provide a form that lets users purchase T-shirts. You can use JavaScript to verify that users include their mailing address, provide a credit card number, and specify a color. If you lack any of this input from users, you won't be able to complete the order.

The following examples, based on the ASR Outfitters general information form, show a couple of approaches to form validation. These examples assume a form with name="survey". If your form is named differently, please adjust accordingly. You can also substitute form[0] for the name of the first form within your page.

You can use the following generic script to loop through your form and check for forgotten or omitted values:

```
<script type="text/javascript" language="javascript">
    <!--
    function checkOut() {
```

```
        for (x = 0; x < document.survey.elements.length; x++) {
            if (document.survey.elements[x].value == "") {
                alert("Sorry, you forgot one of the required
                      fields. Please try again.")
                break;  }  }
        return false;  }
    //-->
  </script>
```

To check your form, use `onsubmit="checkOut(this.form)"` in your form element. The script looks through each of the fields in your form to see whether any are completely empty and, if there's an empty field, an alert flashes with the "Sorry..." text, and then it exits.

If some fields need to be filled and some don't, or if you need to check specific values, you can handle these situations. For example, to ensure that the first name field (called `firstname`) is filled out and not too short (fewer than two characters), add the following `if` statement to the script:

```
if (document.survey.firstname.value.length <= 2) {
    alert("Please enter your full first name.")
    return false;  }
```

The complete script would then look like this:

```
<script type="text/javascript" language="javascript">
  <!--
    function checkOut() {
        for (x = 0; x < document.survey.elements.length; x++) {
            if (document.survey.elements[x].value == "") {
                alert("Sorry, you forgot one of the required
                      fields. Please try again.")
                break;  }  }
        return false;
        if (document.survey.firstname.value.length <= 2) {
            alert("Please enter your full first name.")
            return false;  }  }
    //-->
  </script>
```

You can continue adding other conditions in the same way.

One of the more complex validation problems involves e-mail addresses. Although more complex scripts are available, you'll probably find that a basic check to ensure that the address includes something, an @ sign, and something else will suffice:

```
<script type="text/javascript" language="javascript">
  <!--
  function checkOut() {
    for (x = 0; x < document.survey.elements.length; x++){
        if (document.survey.elements[x].value == "") {
            alert("Sorry, you forgot one of the required
                   fields. Please try again.")
            break;  }  }
    return false;
    if (document.survey.firstname.value.length <= 2){
        alert("Please enter your full first name.")
        return false  }
    if (document.survey.emailaddr.value.indexOf('@') == -1 ) {
        alert("Please correct your email address. It should
               look like you@domain.com")
    return false  }  }
  //-->
</script>
```

This addition verifies that the address contains an @ and that something after the @ exists. If you need more comprehensive validation, check out the scripts at the following Netscape site:

```
http://developer.netscape.com/library/examples/javascript/formval
/overview.html
```

Tracking Users Using Cookies

Cookies are objects you can use to store information about users to your site, and that you can access with JavaScript. You can think of cookies as being high-tech name tags that identify your computer to a server computer. For example, if you visit the Amazon.com Web site and purchase a book there, the Amazon.com server deposits a cookie on your computer. Then, the next time you visit that site, the server looks for the cookie on your computer so it can identify you. The cookie on your computer is then matched to information about you that is stored on the server, such as the information you provided and the books you purchased. In this case, cookies can help make subsequent visits easier because users don't have to re-enter information.

Although the security risk to users is minimal, many people are (understandably) a little sensitive about having information stored about them and read by other computers. For that reason, browsers now offer users a lot of control over how cookies are handled. Early versions of Netscape Navigator simply accepted all cookies. Now, most browsers that recognize cookies have an option to warn users when a cookie is created and give users the option to accept or reject individual cookies.

Newer browsers include options for how to handle cookies. In Netscape Navigator, go to the Edit → Preferences → Advanced for choosing how you want the browser to handle cookies. In Internet Explorer, go to Tools → Internet Options → Security → Custom for cookie options. The default in both browsers is to enable cookies, so you only need to change the options if you want to disable cookies, or if you want to receive a message before allowing a cookie to be placed in your computer.

Either way, the cookie information is not public property; the cookie stores information for you only, and not for public broadcast. It's like having a locker at the gym. Your locker may be in a room with other people's lockers, but only you have the key. Additionally, when the server looks on your computer for the cookie, it can only see and read the cookie it deposited, not other cookies, files, or information.

Cookies are not secret passageways into a user's computer, but rather bookmarks to identify where you and the user were in your adventure together. Creating a cookie is actually a bit of a cooperative venture in that the user answers prompts on the page and you save the information in a cookie.

If you want to track users to your Web site, you can, using two types of cookies:

- Session cookies, which endure only until a user closes the browser
- Persistent cookies, which endure until the expiration date you set

Session Cookies

Suppose you want to keep some information about a user's browsing session, such as the pages browsed or the products purchased. You can do so using *session cookies*. The JavaScript not only records the user's session information, but also sends a message to the user when he or she arrives at and exits your site.

This example shows some of the capabilities and power of cookies. It's also likely to irritate many users. Even if they know that cookies can be set and used, they likely don't want to be reminded of it overtly.

To implement session cookies, first create an empty cookie when the page loads. Start with a functional XHTML document, such as the following:

```
<!DOCTYPE html PUBLIC "-//W3C/DTD XHTML 1.0 Transitional//EN"
    "http://www.w3.org/TR/xhtml1/DTD/xhtml1-transitional.dtd">
<html xmlns="http://www.w3.org/1999/xhtml">
<head>
    <title>ASR Outfitters Cookie Form</title>
</head>
<body>
    Cookie Bearing Document
</body>
</html>
```

Now, follow these steps:

1. Add a function to the document head element that sets the document cookie to the local time and date:

   ```
   <script type="text/javascript" language="javascript">
       <!--
       function homeMadeCookies() {
           var gotHere = new Date();
           document.cookie = gotHere.toLocaleString()  }
       // -->
   </script>
   ```

2. Initialize the cookie from the onload event handler, like this:

   ```
   <body onload="homeMadeCookies()">
   ```

The onload event handler starts the function called homeMadeCookies, which creates and places a value into the variable gotHere. From that information, the next line converts the GMT time to local time and stores that in document.cookie.

By setting up a second function, you can display a message when the user leaves. The fareWell function looks like this:

```
function fareWell() {
    var timedVisit = new Date();
    var tempTime = timedVisit.toLocaleString();
    alert("You got here at: " + document.cookie +
          " and now it's: " + tempTime + ".  " +
          "Thank you for visiting our site.");  }
```

Then, by adding an `onunload` event handler to the body element, you can display the farewell message:

```
<body onload="homeMadeCookies()" onunload="fareWell()">
```

The `fareWell` entry uses an alert to display a brief—cookie-based—message thanking the user, as shown in Figure 11.1.

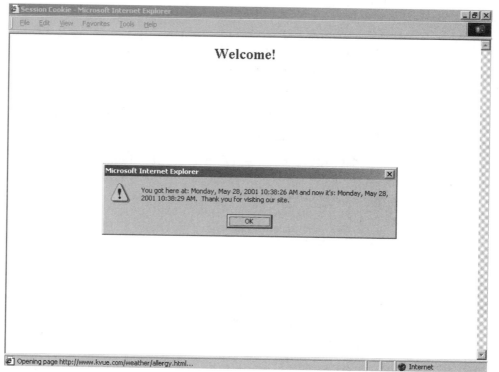

Figure 11.1 *You can use cookies to produce alerts specific to the user's situation.*

Persistent Cookies

You can also store information in cookies for a period of time. You use *persistent cookies* when you want to store information and use it in the future. For example, if a user fills out a form that includes his or her name and other personal information, you'd want to keep that information and use it when the user visits in the future. This is, for example, how the Amazon.com site tracks your visits and seems to know things about you during subsequent visits.

Here are some facts you should know about persistent cookies:

- A browser retains a limited number of cookies. Netscape Navigator retains 300 cookies. Older cookies are discarded to make room for new ones.

- A cookie cannot be larger than 4 KB.

- You can have only 20 cookies per domain. If you're working from a large ISP, you might not be able to set cookies for all users.

These restrictions may not seem limiting at first, but they become so when the demand for feedback increases. Unlike session cookies, persistent cookies need an expiration date. After the cookie expires, a former user is treated as a new user.

Matt's Script Archive includes a section entitled "HTTP Cookie Lib" thatprovides an excellent overview of the subject, pointers to all the importantrelevant resources, and a helpful list of Frequently Asked Questions (a FAQ,in other words). You'll find all this material online at `www.worldwidemart.com/scripts/ faq/cookielib.shtml`*.*

Where to Go from Here

Whew! In this chapter, we introduced you to JavaScript and showed you some of the most basic (and useful!) JavaScript functions. As you can see, JavaScript offers a variety of useful applications and can help you create cutting-edge XHTML documents.

From here, you can wander to several chapters. Here's what we recommend:

- See Chapter 12 to learn about including multimedia in your XHTML documents.

- See Chapter 14 to learn to balance flashy elements with site usability.

- Visit Chapter 16 to learn about publishing your XHTML documents.

- See Master's Reference Part 3 for a comprehensive guide to JavaScript

Including Multimedia

XHTML

Chapter 12

In recent years, Web surfers have seen text-only pages transform into pages that bounce, shimmy, sing, and gyrate. Developers of public sites, in particular, are using flair and excitement in an effort to attract users and to keep them coming back again and again. Flashy elements don't always attract, however. Some users find them such a distraction that they don't continue to browse the site, nor do they return to it. The key is to use glitz wisely and to carefully weigh its benefits and liabilities.

In this chapter, we'll show you how to include special effects—animated Graphics Interchange Format (GIF) files , sounds, videos, Flash animations, Java applets, and ActiveX controls—collectively known as multimedia. (In this book, we define multimedia as anything you can include in a Web page other than basic XHTML code and static images.) We'll look at the pros and cons of various elements and discuss how to include them effectively, if you do choose to include them.

Toward the end of the chapter, we'll show you how to include multimedia as designated by the XHTML 1.0 Recommendation. This chapter covers the following topics:

- Deciding to include multimedia

- Using animated GIFs

- Adding sounds

- Adding video

- Including Java applets

- Adding multimedia using XHTML

Deciding to Include Multimedia

Animated images, sounds, and video can make your pages come alive. Done correctly, multimedia can also give Web pages that "up with technology" look and feel. However, before you run off to gather multimedia elements, take heed: Multimedia poses several challenges, both for users and for the developer.

The principles for including these effects apply to other elements you might discover. For example, if the engineers at your company want to publish their AutoCAD files on your corporate intranet, you can include them in Web pages, following the principles outlined in the "Adding Multimedia Using XHTML 1" section in this chapter.

The Challenges for Users

Multimedia can bring your pages to a virtual halt as users sit and wait (and wait!) for the effects to download. Although some multimedia effects, such as animated GIFs, can be as small as 2 KB, other effects, such as video, can easily grow to 5 MB or more.

In addition, some multimedia effects require plug-ins (which are programs used to view effects that may not come with browsers). In the past, users had to download and install a separate plug-in for each multimedia effect and for each company that provided the effect. However, in newer browsers, support for most multimedia elements is part of the basic browser installation package, including support for streaming audio and video (*streaming media* can be listened to and/or viewed as the download is occurring) and QuickTime video playback, as well as 3-D animation and the *Virtual Reality Markup Language* (VRML). (VRML is one way to provide 3-D simulations on the Web.)

Internet Explorer (versions 3.0 and higher) can download plug-ins automatically if a user needs a feature that's not already installed. Users still have to wait, wait, and wait to view the effect, though. Users using any version of Netscape Navigator, however, may have to click to view the effect and then (in one vividly memorable example):

1. Be informed that they don't have the right plug-in.

2. Be taken to the Netscape Web page to get it.

3. Click to download the plug-in.

4. Fill out a form with personal information (name, address, type of business).

5. Submit the form.

6. Be taken back to the original site (different page).

7. Choose to download the plug-in.

8. Specify where it should be saved.

9. Wait for it to download (much longer than for Internet Explorer).

10. Browse to the downloaded file on the local hard drive.

11. Double-click the installation program to run it.

12. Accept the license agreement.

13. Approve the installation location.

14. Wait for the installation to finish.

15. Exit Netscape Navigator.

16. Restart Netscape Navigator.

17. Browse back to the original site.

18. View the effect (finally).

Eighteen steps and many minutes later, they get to see the multimedia effect, which may not even be worth the time and effort it took.

Luckily, this happens infrequently with the newer versions of Netscape, and the user can always choose not to install a plug-in and not to view a particular multimedia element on a page. Newer versions of Netscape Navigator include many more multimedia features as part of the basic installation.

 Netscape Navigator also includes another useful feature for multimedia. If you go to the Help menu and choose About Plug-ins, you'll find out which plug-ins are currently installed, the version number, and what type of multimedia files they support.

Multimedia Developers

The multimedia developers also offer integrated packages of free software (expanded versions can also be purchased), which support almost all multimedia file formats available on the Web. These software programs include:

- RealPlayer, which supports RealAudio and RealVideo, as well as several other media types available as plug-ins. Currently, there are plug-ins available for RealText, RealPix, WAV, Audio Video Interleave (AVI), Be Here iVideo, RealText 3D, Liquid Music Player, Screenwatch, Learnkey's RealCBT, NetPodium Quickcast, Moving Picture Experts Group (MPEG) Video (Layer 1), GIF, JPEG, MP3 Audio & Playlist (Layer 1), and MIDI formats. Download RealPlayer at:

    `www.real.com`

- QuickTime, which supports more than 200 types of digital media, including MP3, Musical Instrument Digital Interface (MIDI), AVI, AVR, streaming media, and digital video. Download QuickTime at:

    `www.apple.com/quicktime`

- Windows Media Player, which includes seven features in a single application: CD player, audio and video player, media jukebox, media guide, Internet radio, portable device music file transfer, and an audio CD burner. It's available for both PCs and Macintosh computers. Download Windows Media Player at:

    `www.microsoft.com/windows/windowsmedia/EN/default.asp`

The Challenges for Developers

In addition to these resounding indictments of carefree multimedia use in Web pages, it gets worse. For you, the developer, obtaining relevant and useful multimedia objects is often difficult. Your first option is to create the effects yourself, which requires both raw materials (such as photographs, sounds, and video clips) and often special software that you must both purchase and learn to use. In addition, even if you're familiar with the software, developing effective multimedia objects can be time consuming.

You can also browse the Web for multimedia elements, which is a less expensive and less time-consuming option, but you may not find exactly what you want. Although tons of multimedia elements are available on the Web, they're likely to be inappropriate or not in the public domain.

Your goal is to carefully consider the advantages and disadvantages of each multimedia element *before* you include it. Start by asking these questions:

- Does the multimedia element add content that I cannot otherwise provide?

- Does the multimedia element clearly enhance or complement content?

- Do the users have browsers that support these elements?

- Do the users have fast Internet connections?

- Are the users likely to have the appropriate plug-ins or the time, inclination, and technical wherewithal to get and install them?

- Do I have the time and resources to develop or find multimedia elements?

If you answer yes to some or all these questions and you opt to include multimedia, the rest of this chapter is for you.

Throughout this chapter, we point out that you can find multimedia elements on the Web. However, remember that much of what you find is not available for public use. Before you take a file and use it as your own, be sure that it's clearly labeled "for public use." If it's not, you can assume that it's not for you to take and use.

Considering Multimedia Usability

Before you commit to fully multimedia enhanced pages—or even to a single animated GIF on your home page—consider carefully what including multimedia will do to your site's usability. User Interface Engineering (`http://world.std.com/~uieweb/surprise.htm`), presents some alarming findings about the usability of Web pages that incorporate multimedia elements.

In their pilot study, these authors found that "animation did seem to cause delays in the users' performance..." and support that finding with observational research in which Web site visitors sat and waited through several cycles of an animation in order for the page to finish displaying, which of course it never did since the animation continued to cycle.

For the full report based on data from their research, see their book "Web Site Usability: A Designer's Guide" (`http://world.std.com/~uieweb/bookdesc.htm`).

Although some sites were more problematic than others, and other studies show that animations are more effective than static images in advertisements, your site might not benefit from any of these effects.

Developing and Using Animated GIFs

Perhaps the easiest multimedia element to include is an animated GIF, which is a file that, more or less, includes a bunch of images stacked together to give the illusion of movement. Animated GIFs are similar to those little cartoon booklets or "flip books" you had as a kid. When you quickly whirred through the pages, the cartoon seemed to move. Of course, the illusion of movement was nothing more than each drawing being slightly different. Animated GIFs work the same way.

The uses for animated GIFs vary considerably, from flashing commercial messages, to elaborate mini-movies, to small bullets or arrows that appear to grow or move. Animated GIFs are commonly used to help attract users' attention to a specific element.

Developing Animated GIFs

If you're interested in developing your own animated GIFs, we recommend software such as GIF Construction Set for Windows (`www.mindworkshop.com/alchemy/alchemy.html`) or GifBuilder for the Macintosh (`http://homepage.mac.com/piguet/gif.html`). These packages provide the tools to combine individual images into an animated GIF. You can develop individual images with any software that can create GIF images, including Photoshop, ImageReady, Illustrator, and Fireworks. If you want to see what's available on the Web, go to `www.yahoo.com` or `www.altavista.com` and search on **gif animation**. You will find lots of information, software, and software reviews.

Developing an animated GIF often takes more time and effort than you expect. The process can become tedious, especially if you're working with longer animations or animations in which the illusion of smooth motion is needed (rather than simply presenting discrete panes of information, as in ad banners).

The first step is to generate the individual images that will eventually be each panel within the animated GIF. For a basic animated bullet—that appears to move from left to right—you might create a set of images similar to those shown in Figure 12.1.

The easiest way to get smooth animation is to create a single image, select the object that changes or moves, move it into each successive position, and then save the image. In this example, after creating the small ball, we selected the ball, moved it two pixels to the right, saved the image, moved it again, and so forth. The more pixels between images, the jerkier the motion; the fewer pixels between images, the smoother the motion.

After you create the images, use a GIF animation program, such as JASC Animation Shop (Figure 12.2) or any of the graphics programs mentioned earlier, to sequence the images and to set animation properties, such as how often to loop through the animation and how to redraw the images as the animation proceeds.

After you insert each of the frames and preview the image to your satisfaction, simply save it as a GIF file.

Figure 12.1 *Creating a bullet that slides right, in PaintShopPro*

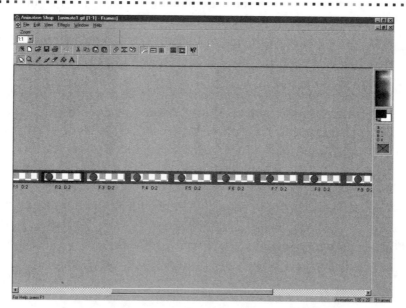

Figure 12.2 *Animating the bullet, in JASC Animation Shop*

Incorporating Animated GIFs into XHTML

Table 12.1 lists and describes the elements and attributes you use to include animated GIFs in your XHTML documents. You can treat animated GIFs just like any other images. (See Chapter 5 for more information on images.)

Table 12.1 Main Elements and Attributes of Animated GIFs

ITEM	TYPE	DESCRIPTION
img	Empty element	Inserts an image in an XHTML document.
src="url"	Attribute of img	Specifies the location of the image file; required.
alt="..."	Attribute of img	Provides alternate text for users who don't view the image; required.

To include an animated GIF in your Web page, follow these steps:

1. Find or create an appropriate animated GIF image.

2. Place the image in your XHTML document, with the regular image elements. Your code could look similar to the following:

```
<img src="animate2.gif" width="99" height="16" border="0"
     alt="animated gif" />
<a href="camping.html">Camping News</a> provides the latest
     comments from the trails.<br />
```

3. Enjoy the experience!

Testing Multimedia

If you're testing your pages either locally or over a direct Internet connection—for example, through your network at the office, connected to the Internet with a dedicated line—take the time to test them with the slowest dial-up connection your users will be using. Check out what happens with 56 Kbps (and possibly slower) modems. What's tolerable with a direct connection can seem interminable over a dial-up connection.

In ideal circumstances, a user with a 56 Kbps modem can download a maximum of 7 KB per second. In real life, that number decreases dramatically, depending on network traffic and a variety of intangibles. If your page contains 2 KB of text, a 4 KB bullet image, a 20 KB photograph, and a 9 KB logo, you're already talking about at least a 5-second download. Add a 60 KB animation or sound file, and you've just bumped that to 15 seconds—best-case scenario. At this point, the user has likely moved on to another site.

However, this is becoming less and less of an issue as more and more users obtain faster Internet connections, such as cable modems and Digital Subscriber Line (DSL) service.

Adding Sounds

Adding audio can produce some fun effects, but if you surf the Web looking for sound, you'll find little of practical use. Generally speaking, Web page sounds come in three varieties:

- Sounds that play when users access the page

- Sounds that play when users click something

- Sounds that are part of a multimedia file such as a Flash animation or a video file

Sounds that play when users access a page are called *background sounds* and can be a short tune or one that plays the entire time a user is at the page. These mooing, beeping, crescendoing background sounds usually do nothing more than entertain (or irritate). Figure 12.3 includes a control box that users can click to play a sound.

Our take on the it-plays-the-whole-time-you're-visiting background sounds is that if we want music to surf by, we'll put a CD in the computer.

Although sounds accessed in this way are primarily for entertainment purposes, they could be of practical use—for example:

- If your car sounds like this *rumble*, you need a new muffler.

- If your car sounds like this *choke*, you might have bad gasoline.

- If your car sounds like this *kaCHUNK* when you shift gears, your transmission is going out.

You get the idea. In lieu of adding the whole control box, however, you could just link directly to an audio file.

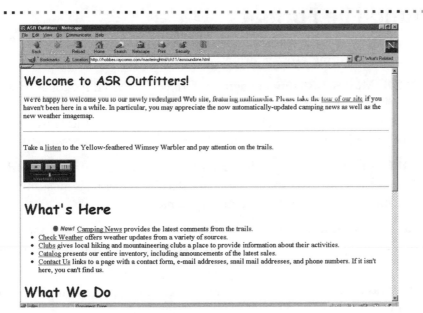

Figure 12.3 *The control box lets users choose whether to play the sound.*

Some Disadvantages of Sounds

Many of the disadvantages associated with using multimedia elements in general are also associated with using sounds:

- Sound files are usually large and load slowly.

- Users need a sound card and speakers to hear sounds.

- Users in a corporate environment might not welcome a loud greeting from their computer.

When choosing to add sound to your page, apply the guidelines we mentioned earlier about using multimedia elements in general. If an audio element does not enhance your message or provide content that is not possible in any other way, you're probably better off not using it.

Sound File Formats

If you do decide to include a sound in your Web page, all you have to do is find a sound file in one of six formats (other formats are available, but are less common):

MIDI (Musical Instrument Digital Interface)   A MIDI file contains synthesized music. If you can find or create one that meets your needs, MIDI is a great choice because the files are small. If you have a MIDI-capable musical instrument (such as an electronic keyboard) and a little skill, you can create your own MIDI files.

AIFF (Audio Interchange File Format)   An AIFF file contains a recorded sound sample, which can be music or a sound effect. This format is most common on Macintosh and usable on most other systems.

AU (or basic AUdio)   An AU file also provides acceptable—but not great—quality sampled sound. These files are accessible on the widest range of browsers and computer systems.

WAV (as in WAVe)   A WAV file provides very good quality sampled sound, but is usable almost exclusively on Windows computers.

RAM or RA (RealMedia)   A RAM or RA file provides high quality streaming sound, but requires the use of RealPlayer software.

MP3   An MP3 file provides outstanding (nearly CD-quality) sound, but it's usable only through browser plug-ins. (The name *MP3* is actually derived from Moving Picture Experts Group, or MPEG, Audio Layer 3.)

If you have a sound card and a microphone, you can record your own sounds. And, of course, you can find thousands if not millions of sounds and samples on the Web.

There are many sources for sound files on the Web. Do a search at www.yahoo.com *for* **audio files***, or use Comparisonics search engine for sound effects on the Web at* www.findsounds.com. *Many of the sound files on the Web are not public domain, which means you can borrow them to experiment with and learn from, but not to publish as your own.*

To include sound files the easiest and most user-friendly way, link to them. For example, as you saw in Figure 12.1 earlier in this chapter, ASR Outfitters added a sound file of a bird call to one of its pages. You add a link to a sound file in the same way that you add a link to an image. The code looks like this:

```
<p>Take a <a href="weirdbrd.aif">listen</a> to the Yellow-
feathered Wimsey Warbler and pay attention on the trails.</p>
```

If you use this option, users can choose whether to hear the sound, which is accessible from most browsers.

If you want to give users additional control over the sound, including volume level, pause, and play, you need to use the object element to add the sound file and to create a viewable sound control box on the page. See "Adding Multimedia Using XHTML 1" later in this chapter for details on using the object element, including a table of supported attributes.

The embed *element is not supported in XHTML 1. The* object *element can be used for sound, video, and text files, although it does not include all the attributes used with the* embed *element.*

Adding Video

You'll find that video—in the right situation—is perhaps the most practical multimedia element. In one quick video clip, you can *show* users a concept or a process, rather than describing it in lengthy paragraphs or steps.

Video files can be huge, however, so you must be sure that a large video file is essential enough to your presentation to ask a user to wait for it to download. Video technology is continuing to develop, and movie clips of reasonable size are increasingly available. Many news and entertainment sites, such as www.cnn.com/videoselect and www.comedycentral.com, offer short movie clips that download quickly.

Newer versions of Internet Explorer support video streaming, MPEG video, and QuickTime movie playback in the basic installation. Netscape Navigator support of video playback and video streaming is more limited, and Netscape requires a plug-in for QuickTime movies.

Video File Formats

You can create your own video files or find them on the Web. Look for files in the following formats:

AVI (Audio Video Interleave)   This format, originally a Windows standard, is now somewhat more widely available. It's a good choice if your users will almost exclusively be using Windows.

Flash   Flash animations are created in Macromedia Flash, which is a vector-based animation program. Because they're vector graphics, Flash files can have a small enough file size to be reasonable to use on many Web sites. For more information on Flash, visit Macromedia's site at www.macromedia.com.

MPEG (Moving Picture Experts Group)   This format is the most widely supported, and viewers are available for most platforms. Because it's highly compressed and usable, MPEG is the best universal choice.

QuickTime   This format, originally a Macintosh standard, is now available for Windows as well. It provides good quality, but users must have the plug-in to view these files in Netscape Navigator. (QuickTime movie playback is a basic feature of later versions of Internet Explorer.)

We recommend linking to video files, rather than directly placing them in a Web page. The code to do this would look similar to this:

```
<p>Take a <a href="weirdbrd.mpg">look at video</a> of the
Yellow-feathered Wimsey Warbler.</p>
```

When video files are linked, users can choose whether to view them.

If you want to add a video file directly on your page, rather than linking to it, you need to use the `object` element to add a video file and to create a viewable movie control box on the page. See "Adding Multimedia Using XHTML 1" later in this chapter.

Including Java Applets

Applets, developed with the Java programming language, are mini-programs with which you can animate objects, scroll text, or add interactive components to your Web pages. Figure 12.4 shows the TicTacToe applet, and Figure 12.5 shows an applet that scrolls a welcome message across the top of a Web page.

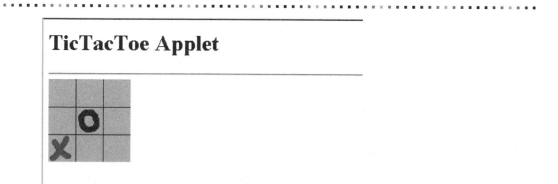

Figure 12.4 *Even a simple applet adds interest and interactivity to a Web page.*

Figure 12.5 *The "Welcome" message scrolling across the top of the page is animated by an applet.*

Java applets have the `.class` filename extension. In the simplest cases, you need only the name of the applet to use it—for example, `TicTacToe.class`. With more complex applets, you must also provide *parameters*. In this section, we'll show you how to send those parameters to the applet, but you'll have to get the exact information to include in the parameter from the documentation that comes with applets.

The software that enables you to program in Java, available at `www.sun.com`, includes tools for developing applets. Unless you're a programmer or have some time on your hands, you'll be better off using prepackaged applets or tools that develop applets on the fly. (Search for **applet** at software archives such as `www.shareware.com`, or visit `http://gamelan.com`, to find these tools.)

Applet files, such as video files, are big and take up to a couple of minutes to download. On the positive side, though, users with most versions of Netscape Navigator or Internet Explorer can use applets without additional software.

Table 12.2 lists and describes the elements and attributes you use to include an applet in your Web pages.

Table 12.2 Applet Elements and Attributes

ITEM	TYPE	DESCRIPTION
`applet`	Element	Embeds a Java applet into an XHTML document. You can include alternate text between `applet` tags. Browsers that support Java ignore all information between the `applet` tags. Deprecated (with all its attributes) in favor of the `object` element (see Table 12.3).
`param`	Empty element	Specifies a parameter passed to an object such as an applet.
`align="…"`	Attribute of `applet`	Specifies the horizontal alignment of the applet displayed as `left`, `right`, or `center`.
`alt="…"`	Attribute of `applet`	Displays a textual description of an applet, if necessary.
`archive="url, url, url…"`	Attribute of `applet`	Specifies a comma-separated list of addresses for archives containing classes and other resources that will be "preloaded." Preloading resources can significantly improve the performance of applets.
`class="…"`	Attribute of `applet`	Assigns a class name or set of class names to an element.
`code="url"`	Attribute of `applet`	Specifies the relative or absolute location of the Java bytecode file.
`codebase="url"`	Attribute of `applet`	Specifies the folder location of all necessary `class` files on the Web server.
`height="n"`	Attribute of `applet`	Specifies the height (in pixels) of the applet object within the document; required.
`hspace="n"`	Attribute of `applet`	Specifies an amount of blank space (in pixels) to the left and right of the applet within the document.
`id="…"`	Attribute of `applet` and `param`	Assigns the applet or parameter an ID so other items in the document can identify it.
`name="…"`	Attribute of `applet` and `param`	Assigns the applet or parameter a name so other items in the document can identify it.

Table 12.2 continued Applet Elements and Attributes

Item	Type	Description
object="…"	Attribute of applet	Names a resource containing a serialized representation of an applet's state; interpreted relative to the applet's codebase.
style="…"	Attribute of applet	Specifies style information.
title="…"	Attribute of applet	Assigns a label to the element.
value="…"	Attribute of param	Specifies the value associated with the parameter passed to the object.
vspace="n"	Attribute of applet	Specifies the amount of vertical space (in pixels) above and below the applet.
width="n"	Attribute of applet	Specifies the width (in pixels) of the applet within the document; required.

XHTML documents should use the id attribute rather than the name attribute. You can use both the name and the id attributes with identical values to ensure maximum compatibility; for example, <param name="gameapplet" id="gameapplet" />.

If you've found an applet to use and want to include it in your Web page, follow these steps. In this example, we'll show you how to add a TicTacToe applet.

1. Start with an XHTML document.

2. Add some introductory text and perhaps a couple of horizontal rules to set off the applet from other page elements.

    ```
    <h1>TicTacToe Game</h1>
    <hr />
    <hr />
    ```

3. Add the applet tags.

    ```
    <h1>TicTacToe Game</h1>
    <hr />
    <applet>
    </applet>
    <hr />
    ```

4. Add the code attribute along with the applet filename (which is case sensitive).

```
<h1>TicTacToe Game</h1>
<hr />
<applet code="TicTacToe.class">
</applet>
<hr />
```

5. Add the width and height attributes to specify the size of the applet.

```
<h1>TicTacToe Game</h1>
<hr />
<applet code="TicTacToe.class" width="120" height="120">
</applet>
<hr />
```

That's it! When we built this code, we only needed one accessory file (TicTactoe.class) to get a page that looked like Figure 12.2.

To add an applet that requires parameters, such as the applet that scrolls the welcome banner, follow these steps:

1. Start with an XHTML document.

2. Add the applet tags.

```
<applet>
</applet>
```

3. Add the applet file.

```
<applet code="Banners.class">
</applet>
```

4. Add the param element that includes the parameter name, ID, and value.

```
<applet code="Banners.class"
<param name="bgColor" id="bgColor" value="White" />
</applet>
```

5. Continue adding parameters as needed by your applet. We recommend adding one at a time to help eliminate coding errors, for example.

```
<applet code="Banners.class" width="400" height="50">
<param name="bgColor" id="bgColor" value="White" />
```

```
<param name="textColor" id="textColor" value="Black" />
<param name="pause" id="pause" value="1" />
<param name="exit" id="exit" value="scrollLeft" />
<param name="align" id="align" value="Center" />
<param name="fps" id="fps" value="20" />
<param name="repeat" id="repeat" value="1" />
<param name="borderWidth" id="borderWidth" value="1" />
<param name="bgExit" id="bgExit" value="None" />
<param name="messages" id="messages" value="Welcome to ASR
    Outfitters!" />
<param name="font" id="font" value="Helvetica" />
<param name="cpf" id="cpf" value="2" />
<param name="enter" id="enter" value="scrollLeft" />
<param name="bgEnter" id="bgEnter" value="None" />
<param name="style" id="style" value="Bold" />
<param name="borderColor" id="borderColor" value="Black" />
<param name="size" id="size" value="36" />
</applet>
```

And that's it! This code displays a scrolling welcome, much like the one shown in Figure 12.3, earlier in this chapter—assuming you have the .class files for the applet. (Ours came from a free tool on the Internet.) Otherwise, use the same process to add an applet you already have.

 The applet element is deprecated in XHTML, and it's recommended that the object element be used instead. Although the applet element can be used if you use a Transitional XHTML DTD, it's likely that future versions of XHTML will not include this element.

Including ActiveX Controls

ActiveX controls are similar to Java applets—they're little programs that provide enhanced functionality to a Web page. For example, ActiveX controls can provide pop-up menus, the ability to view a Word document through a Web page, and almost all the pieces needed for Microsoft's HTML Help. These controls—developed by Microsoft and implemented with Internet Explorer 3—are powerful but Windows-centric. Although you can get a plug-in to view ActiveX controls in Netscape Navigator, you'll find the results are more reliable when you view ActiveX controls with Internet Explorer.

If you want to try out some controls—both free and licensed varieties—check out C|Net's ActiveX site at http://download.cnet.com/downloads/0-10081.html or Gamelan at www.gamelan.com. If you're so inclined, you can create ActiveX controls using popular Windows development packages, such as Visual Basic or Visual C++. You include ActiveX controls in a page just as you include multimedia elements: You use the object element—as discussed in the following section.

Adding Multimedia Using XHTML 1

The future of developing multimedia elements for the Web is clear: instead of using several elements and attributes, you'll simply include the object element and choose from attributes that support this element. In this respect, the XHTML 1.0 Recommendation accommodates any kind of multimedia element. You don't need to specify that you're including a sound, a video, an applet, or whatever; you simply specify that you're including an object. And, you use only the XHTML object element and its attributes, listed in Table 12.3. You no longer need to code separately for both Netscape Navigator and Internet Explorer to use multimedia files on your pages.

Table 12.3 Object Elements and Attributes

ITEM	TYPE	DESCRIPTION
object	Element	Embeds a software object into a document.
align="…"	Attribute of object	Indicates how the object lines up relative to the edges of the browser window and/or other elements within the window. Possible values are left, right, bottom, middle, or top.
archive="url url url…"	Attribute of object	Specifies a space-separated list of addresses for archives containing resources relevant to the object, which may include the resources specified by the classid and data attributes. Preloading archives generally results in reduced load times for objects.
border="n"	Attribute of object	Indicates the width (in pixels) of a border around the object. border="0" indicates no border.
class="…"	Attribute of object	Assigns a class name or set of class names to an object.

Table 12.3 continued Object Elements and Attributes

ITEM	TYPE	DESCRIPTION
codebase="url"	Attribute of object	Specifies the absolute or relative location of the base directory in which the browser will look for data and other implementation files.
codetype="…"	Attribute of object	Specifies the MIME type for the object's code.
class="…"	Attribute of object	Indicates which style class applies to the element.
classid="…"	Attribute of object	Specifies the location of an object resource, such as a Java applet. Use classid="java:appletname.class" for Java applets.
data="url"	Attribute of object	Specifies the absolute or relative location of the object's data.
height="n"	Attribute of object	Specifies the vertical dimension (in pixels) of the object.
hspace="n"	Attribute of object	Specifies the size of the margins (in pixels) to the left and right of the object.
id="…"	Attribute of object	Indicates an identifier to associate with the object.
name="…"	Attribute of object	Specifies the name of the object.
standby="…"	Attribute of object	Specifies a message that the browser displays while the object is loading.
style="…"	Attribute of object	Specifies style information.
title="…"	Attribute of object	Specifies a label assigned to the element.
type="…"	Attribute of object	Indicates the MIME type of the object.
vspace="n"	Attribute of object	Specifies the size of the margin (in pixels) at the top and bottom of the object.
width="n"	Attribute of object	Indicates the horizontal dimension (in pixels) of the object.

Table 12.3 includes the most common attributes of the object *element, but there are many additional attributes for special circumstances. For more information about these additional attributes, see the HTML 4.01 Specification and the XHTML 1.0 Recommendation at* www.w3.org. *Another excellent source of information is the XHTML 1.0 Reference at* www.zvon.org/xxl/xhtmlReference/Output/index.html.

When objects require more information—for example, a Java applet needs specific settings to run—you pass data to the object with the param element. Table 12.4 lists and describes the param elements and attributes.

Table 12.4 Parameter Elements and Attributes

ITEM	TYPE	DESCRIPTION
param	Empty element	Specifies parameters passed to an object. Use the param element within the object or applet element.
ITEM	**TYPE**	**DESCRIPTION**
id="…"	Attribute of param	Assigns the object an ID so other items in the document can identify it.
name="…"	Attribute of param	Indicates the name of the parameter passed to the object; required.
type="…"	Attribute of param	Specifies the MIME type of the data found at the specified URL.
value="…"	Attribute of param	Specifies the value associated with the parameter passed to the object.
valuetype="…"	Attribute of param	Indicates the kind of value passed to the object. Possible values are data, ref, and object.

You can use the object element to include almost any kind of object. Let's start with the Java TicTacToe applet from our previous example.

To add an applet using the object element, follow these steps.

1. Start with a basic XHTML document, like this:

```
<!DOCTYPE html
 PUBLIC "-//W3C//DTD XHTML 1.0 Transitional//EN"
 "http://www.w3.org/TR/xhtml1/DTD/xhtml1-transitional.dtd">
<html xmlns="http://www.w3.org/1999/xhtml">
<head>
    <title>TicTacToe</title>
</head>
<body>
    <h1>TicTacToe Applet </h1>
</body>
</html>
```

2. Add the object tags.

```
<h1>TicTacToe Applet </h1>
<object>
</object>
```

3. Add alternate text between the object tags.

```
<h1>TicTacToe Applet </h1>
<object>
    If your browser supported Java and objects, you could be
    playing TicTacToe right now.
</object>
```

4. Add the classid attribute to indicate the name of the Java class file (program file). You use classid to incorporate programs, such as applets or ActiveX controls.

```
<h1>TicTacToe Applet </h1>
<object classid="java:TicTacToe.class">
    If your browser supported Java and objects, you could be
    playing TicTacToe right now.
</object>
```

5. Add the width and height attributes. A square that is 120×120 pixels should be sufficient.

```
<h1>TicTacToe Applet </h1>
<object classid="java:TicTacToe.class" width="120"
    height="120">
```

```
        If your browser supported Java and objects, you could
        be playing TicTacToe right now.
    </object>
```

6. If you had the `TicTacToe.class` file, and you saved and tested your document, you'd see something similar to the following:

TicTacToe Object

Users using browsers that don't support the `object` element or don't support Java will see something similar to the following:

TicTacToe Object

Unknown Media T)

If your browser supported Java and objects, you could be playing TicTacToe right now.

The process for adding video and sound is similar. The only difference is that you use the `data` attribute instead of the `classid` attribute. Also, you add a `type` attribute to show the MIME type of the object. (You don't need the `type` when you're adding an applet because `java:` precedes the name of the applet, making it clear what kind of object it is.)

To add a sound using the `object` element, follow these steps:

1. Start with an XHTML document.

2. Add the `object` tags.

```
<object>
</object>
```

3. Add the data attribute along with the filename.

```
<object data="weirdbrd.aif">
</object>
```

4. Add the type attribute to specify the type of multimedia.

```
<object data="weirdbrd.aif" type="audio/aiff">
</object>
```

5. Add the height and width attributes to specify the object's size.

```
<object data="weirdbrd.aif" type="audio/aiff" height="50"
    width="100">
</object>
```

There you go! If you had the weirdbrd.aif file, your document would now look like Figure 12.1, shown earlier in this chapter.

Making It Sound Easy

If you're embedding sounds in your pages, consider using a regular link to the sound file rather than using the object element to embed it. The only real advantage to using the object element is a neat little widget in the Web page that users can use to play the sound as if they were using a VCR. However, those neat little widgets aren't the same size in Internet Explorer and Netscape Navigator, so you end up with either a truncated object or one with loads of extra space around it.

We recommend using an icon or a text link to the sound file—it's much easier. Anyway, if the sound takes so long to play that the users have time to click Stop or Pause, the sound file is probably too big.

Where to Go from Here

This chapter showed you some of the more entertaining elements you can include in your XHTML documents. Although multimedia files don't always have practical uses, they do make your pages more interesting and give them the "up with technology" look and feel. You also learned, however, that multimedia effects have a big disadvantage: The files can be enormous, which slows download time considerably.

From here, you can reference several related chapters:

- See Chapter 10 to learn about developing Cascading Style Sheets, which let you add cool formatting to your documents.

- See Chapter 11 to learn how JavaScript can also make your pages shimmy and shake.

- See Chapter 14 to learn how to balance flashy elements (such as multimedia) with usability.

Part IV
Developing Web Sites

In This Part

Understanding the XHTML Document Life Cycle

XHTML

Chapter 13

The life cycle of an XHTML document includes developing, publishing, testing, and maintaining it—whether its ultimate home is on an intranet, on the Internet, in a kiosk, or in a help file. We're going to look at that life cycle step-by-step.

Most of these examples focus on developing Web pages (single documents or whole sites) in a corporate environment. To illustrate parts of the XHTML document life cycle, we'll follow the process for WAMMI, Inc., a mythical auto company. If you're developing XHTML documents for nonprofit organizations, corporate intranets, or departmental sites, you'll still need to go through this same process but probably on a smaller scale without as many steps.

The task of developing XHTML documents often falls (or gets assigned) to those with specific technical skills or to those who have a knack for marketing and sales, but not necessarily to those who have XHTML-related experience. For this reason, we're going to give you a development plan that starts with conception and concludes with maintenance.

We recommend that you start at the beginning and read through the sections in order. Along the way, you'll find advice that will help you make decisions that will improve your site. (Specific information about choosing and using software, coding documents, or applying XHTML effects is in other chapters throughout this book.) If you follow along with the four phases covered in this chapter, and apply the examples and guidelines to your situation, you'll be able to create XHTML documents that are easy for you to maintain and useful to your users. The phases are:

- Developing documents

- Publishing documents

- Testing published documents

- Maintaining documents

Phase 1: Developing Documents

Within the development phase are four subprocesses:

- Planning
- Organizing
- Creating
- Testing

Within these phases are several smaller processes, as shown in Figure 13.1. As you work through this chapter, you may find it helpful to refer to this chart from time to time.

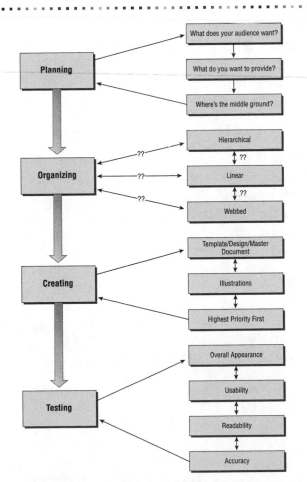

Figure 13.1 *The XHTML document development process*

Planning Documents

XHTML focuses on making tightly structured and standardized information easily available. The resulting XHTML Web and corporate intranet sites are primarily used to provide information to those who need it. In this capacity, XHTML authoring is *user-centered*—in other words, focus on determining what the audience wants and then provide that information.

However, as XHTML and other new Web technologies gain in popularity, Web sites evolve into a marketing tool for millions of companies, organizations, and individuals worldwide. Rather than strictly providing information, the purpose of many Web sites is now to tell users what a company wants them to know, to persuade them to purchase a product or service, and to keep them coming back for more. As a result, XHTML development is simultaneously user-centered and *author-centered*. Now, you not only need to consider what your users want to know, but also what information your organization wants to provide.

Therefore, before you start producing XHTML on the fly, you need to do some planning. In particular, you need to determine what information your users want and what your organization wants to provide. Your goal is to reconcile these "wants" into a single list that accommodates both your users and your organization.

What Do Your Users Want?

When you visit a Web site, you usually have a reason for going there. Although you often stumble onto a site that interests you while browsing, you normally have something specific in mind when you start.

Therefore, as you begin the planning phase, you'll want to think about what users expect to see at your site. A great place to start is with your customers (or co-workers, if you're developing an intranet). For example, they might want general information about you, your company, or your products and services. On the other hand, they might want specific information, such as contact names, troubleshooting advice, safety information, prices, schedules, order forms, and so on.

At WAMMI, a survey revealed that users were interested in knowing what models were available, their cost, and their reliability and safety records. They also wanted to be able to request brochures and locate local dealerships. Their list of wants looked like this:

Available models

Cost

Safety record

Reliability record

Contact information

Request brochure

List of dealerships

What Do You Want to Provide?

Ideally, your Web site will provide all the information that your users want; however, what they want isn't necessarily what you can or want to provide. For example, you might not want to publicize a product's unstable repair history—or at the very least, you might want to downplay it. Or, if you're developing pages for a corporate intranet—say, the R&D department—you don't want to publish *all* the information the department has available. You probably just want to include information about upcoming projects, recent successes and failures, and planned product improvements.

A great way to start figuring out what to include is to take a look at materials you already have on hand. For example, marketing materials often include information about the company, products, and services suitable for use on a Web site. Even if you're developing pages for an intranet, marketing materials often provide a jumping-off place.

If you don't have access to marketing materials (or the marketing guru), ask yourself a few questions:

- What do I want people to know about my organization? What is its mission statement? What are its goals?

- What are my company's products or services? How do they help people? How do people use them?

- How do customers order our products?

- Is repair history or safety information so positive that I want to publicize it?

- Can I include product specifications?

- What product information can I send to people if they request it?

- Can I provide answers to frequently asked questions?

- Do I want to include information about employees? Do their skills and experience play a big part in how well our products are made or sold?

- Can I provide information that is more timely, useful, or effective than other marketing materials, such as brochures or pamphlets, provide?

After you answer these and any other questions that are helpful in your situation, you should be able to develop a list of what you want to provide. WAMMI decided to provide general information about the company, tell potential customers about the various models, show a few snazzy pictures, and brag about the cars' reliability records. WAMMI was unsure about discussing prices because they were higher than those of its competitors. Likewise, WAMMI was unsure whether to publicize safety records, which were only average. The final list looks like this:

Definite

Company information

Car models

Photos

Contact information

Maybe

Prices

Safety records

Reconciling the Want Lists

You may find that users want information that you simply can't provide. For example, they might want to know product release dates or be privy to product previews, which is probably information your company doesn't want to disclose. And, other times, you might want to provide your audience with information that they don't necessarily care about. For example, you might want to tell people that your company received a big award or just reached one million in sales this year—certainly interesting information that's good for marketing, but it's not on your users' priority lists.

As you can see, what WAMMI wanted and what its users wanted didn't necessarily coincide:

Users Want	Company Wants
company information	company information
car selection	car selection
reliability records	
contact information	contact information
	photos
car cost	prices
safety records	safety records
request brochure	
list of dealerships	

Although these two lists have items in common, each list also contains unique items. At the very least, we wanted to include all the items common to both lists. At WAMMI, the reconciled list includes the following:

Company information

Car selection

Safety records

Contact information

Now, what do you do about the items that are unique to each list? We suggest that you consult some of your colleagues, perhaps those in marketing or public relations, and see what they think.

Getting a consensus before you start to build your Web site is always a good rule to follow. The last thing you want after your site goes public is some vice president announcing that you can't publish information that's already flaunted on your Web site.

At WAMMI, we decided to classify the items common to both lists as primary Web-site information and to classify unique items as secondary information.

Planning for Maintenance

Although maintaining your documents after you create them and throughout their existence on your site is a separate phase in the life cycle of documents (see the later section "Developing a Plan"), you also need to include maintenance in the planning phase. This is particularly the case if you answer Yes to any of the following questions:

- Will more than one person be involved in developing the content?

- Will more than one person play an active role in maintaining the site?

- Will your site include more than about 20 XHTML documents?

- Will you frequently add or modify a significant numbers of pages—say, more than 20–25 percent of the total number of documents?

As you can see, you need to plan for both content and site maintenance.

Planning for Content Maintenance

If you'll be depending on others for content, you need to make arrangements at the outset for how you will obtain updates. Will content providers actually develop and update the Web pages, or will they simply send you new information via e-mail? You need to plan accordingly if they're going to merely send you a publication (for example, the annual report) and expect you to figure out what has changed. Planning how you will handle content revisions and updates at the beginning of the project will save you time (and grief) later.

Planning for Site Maintenance

Regardless of whether you or someone else will maintain the site you develop, you need to carefully document the development process and include the following information:

- The site's purpose and goals

- The process through which you determine content

- Who provides content

Documenting the development process will help those who maintain the site (or fill your position when you leave) keep everything up-to-date.

Organizing Your Documents

After you decide what information to include in your site, you need to determine how you will arrange individual XHTML documents. Taking the time to organize the information carefully is often the difference between having frequent users to your site and having none at all. How often do you return to a site that's not well organized? If you can't find what you need easily and quickly, you have no reason to go there, and the same will be true of users to your site.

You can use one or all of these types of organization, depending on your needs:

- Hierarchical
- Linear
- Webbed

Hierarchical Organization

When you organize information in a hierarchical structure, you present a first group of equally important topics, followed by another group of equally important topics, and so on. If you've ever created or used an organizational chart, you're familiar with this technique. The hierarchy starts with top officials, then shows the managers who work for them, the employees who work for those managers, and so on.

A document outline is another example of hierarchical organization. Multiple main points are followed by subpoints, which are followed by more subpoints. In both an organizational chart and a document outline, hierarchical organization allows you to provide multiple levels of structured information.

You can do the same with a Web site. You can provide several main points, and under each point, you can include subpoints. For example, the WAMMI Web site uses hierarchical organization to structure the main pages according to the major topics, as shown in Figure 13.2.

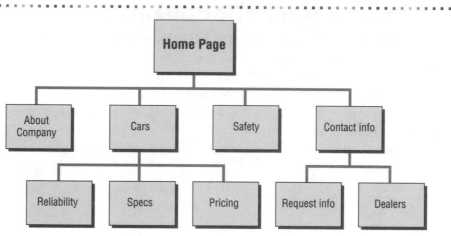

Figure 13.2 *Hierarchical organization accommodates several main topics and subtopics.*

If you choose hierarchical organization, remember to keep it simple. Users to your site will dig through two or three levels of information, but after that, they're likely to give up.

Linear Organization

When you organize information in a linear structure, you impose a particular order on it. Instructions and procedures are examples of this type of organization. If you've ever used a Microsoft Windows–type wizard, you've seen linear organization in action. You start the wizard and then you proceed in order from one screen to the next until you click Finish. You can back up a step or two if necessary, but if you don't complete all the steps, you terminate the procedure.

On a Web site that uses linear organization, a user can move forward and backward within a sequence of pages but cannot jump to other pages. Because this can frustrate users who want to get to other pages, you need to use linear organization only when it's necessary. For example, at our WAMMI site, we used linear organization to walk a user through requesting a brochure, as shown in Figure 13.3.

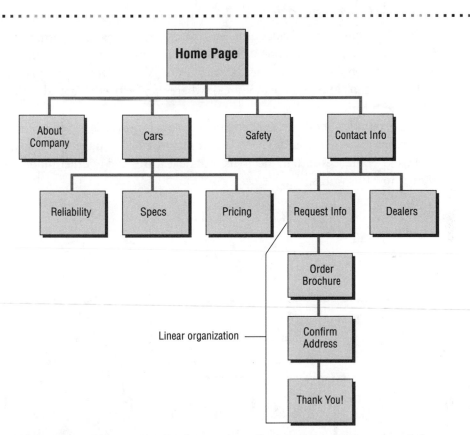

Figure 13.3 *Linear organization works well when you want users to perform actions in a specific order.*

Here are some guidelines to keep in mind when you employ linear organization:

- When your site users are working through linear pages, they can't roam to other pages. Therefore, be sure the linear process is essential to the task at hand.

- Keep the linear sequence as short as possible so users focus on the process and complete it successfully.

Webbed Organization

Webbed organization provides users with multiple, unorganized paths to resources on a site. A user can link from one Web page to many other pages at the same Web site or at another Web site. You often hear stories about Web surfers becoming disoriented or lost—they don't know where they are or where they've been. Webbed organization is often the culprit.

An example of effective webbed organization, however, is an online index that's extensively cross-referenced. The WAMMI site provides an index of the available models and cross-references each model to its specific features and to other models. Figure 13.4 shows how this works.

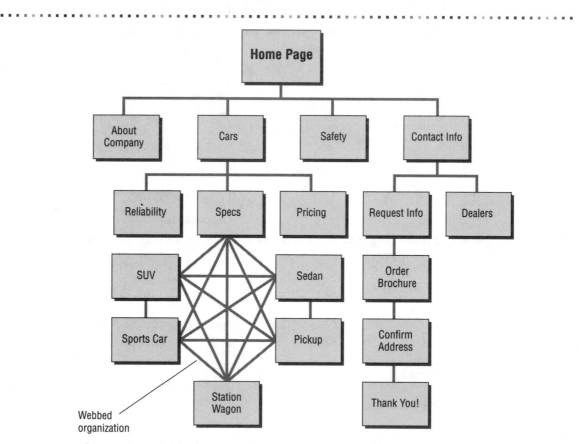

Figure 13.4 *Webbed organization is a good technique to use when you want to cross-reference information.*

Here are some guidelines to keep in mind when you're using webbed organization:

- Provide information on each page that helps users orient themselves. For example, include a running footer or company logo (keep it small) on each page.

- Provide a link to your home page on all pages. If you do so, users can easily return to a familiar page.

Storyboards: An Essential Organizational Tool

Storyboarding is the process of breaking information into discrete chunks and then reassembling it. It's a technique that Web authors borrowed from the film industry, and it's a great way to help you determine the best organizational approach for your site.

Here's one way to do it (and the way the WAMMI site was storyboarded):

1. Write each topic or group of information on a separate note card.

2. Pin the note cards to a wall or spread them out on a table or the floor.

3. Group and rank related information.

4. Continue moving cards around until all the information is organized and ranked to your satisfaction.

5. When you've decided what should link to what, connect those note cards with string.

The resulting groups of information should follow one of the three organization approaches previously discussed or some combination thereof.

Creating Documents

After you've adequately planned your XHTML documents, decided what information to include and how to organize it, you're ready to work on creating your XHTML documents. It's likely that you've already been through many of the specific issues, including choosing software, using elements, adding links and images, and including more advanced effects such as video, sound, frames, JavaScript, and applets. However, just as you need the specifics of markup for those items, you should also take a close look at the overall process to make your XHTML development easier and more efficient.

Create a Master Document

A master XHTML document contains the necessary structure elements, presentation elements rendered via CSS, and the general document format you want to use. When you create a master XHTML document, you establish the look of the site even before you start adding content. Include the elements that you want to appear on every page, such as the following:

- The background
- Repeating images
- The corporate logo
- Icons
- Footer information

If you place these elements in your master document, you need to develop them only once—not every time you start a new document.

After you create a master document, test it (as described shortly in the section "Testing Documents before Publication") to be sure that it appears as you want, that it is usable and readable, and that it is error free. Finding and solving problems early on will save you lots of time in the overall process.

 You can easily use style sheets to create a template for your documents. See Chapter 10 for more on style sheets.

Select Images

Determine which images (graphics) or illustrations are available before you start developing individual pages. Having an idea of what images you can include will help you determine page layout, and you can avoid rearranging pages later.

Create Important Pages First

Web sites, by nature, are always "under construction." You'll find that you will constantly be updating content, adding new pages, and/or removing pages. If you create a few of the most important pages first, test them, and publish them, you can eliminate the tedious task of polishing many pages later. You can then add and modify pages as needed, after you create the initial few.

Testing Documents before Publication

As we mentioned in Chapter 1, the appearance of your pages on your users' screens probably will differ from what you see on your screen, because of browser and operating system differences. Therefore, you need to test your documents on as many computers and browsers as possible. For example, you can check this out if you view a document using Internet Explorer on a computer with a low-resolution display and then look at it using a Netscape browser on a computer with a high-resolution display. By checking documents on various platforms and browsers, you can see how your documents will appear to various users, check readability and usability, and root out any layout or formatting problems. Remember that you want to test for these issues *before* you publish your pages on the Web or an intranet.

Remember that Web pages are similar to the marketing materials your company uses. Just as an editor checks corporate brochures closely for layout, design, organization, and accuracy, carefully check your Web pages or hire an editor to check them.

Getting Ready to Test

Before you start testing, manually "expire" all the links. Most browsers are set by default to remember links that you've visited for about 30 days, and they color those links differently from unvisited links. You can easily see which sites you've visited, which is handy if you'd rather not browse in circles. By expiring links before you test your pages, you can see, for example, that the link colors (for links, active links, and visited links) appear as they should, and you can tell which links you haven't yet followed in your testing process.

Exactly how you expire links varies from browser to browser. The following steps give you the general procedure:

1. Look for a menu option that lets you change browser settings. For example, in the Netscape 6, choose Edit ➤ Preferences. In Internet Explorer 5.5, choose Tools ➤ Internet Options.

2. In the resulting dialog box, look for an option that lets you change document history.

3. Expire the links by clicking the Clear History button.

4. Click OK when you're done.

Testing for Overall Appearance

With your links expired, open your Web pages in your browser, and ask yourself the following questions:

- Is the layout and design aesthetically appealing? Do page elements align as planned?

- Is all the content visible? All text? All images?

- Do all colors appear as they should? Are there any odd patterns or colors?

- Do all pages contain navigation tools?

- Do all frames, applets, and other objects appear as planned?

After you've answered these questions and are satisfied with the results, change the size of your display window and test the overall appearance again. For example, make your display window smaller. You'll find that some elements may not appear on the screen or align as intended. Make any necessary adjustments. Figure 13.5 shows a page that didn't resize well.

Figure 13.5 *Reducing window size can wreck the appearance of your Web page.*

To quickly and easily evaluate different page sizes in Windows, create wallpaper with rectangles at 640×480, 800×600, and 1024×768 pixels. Then, assuming your display is set to at least 1024×768, you can simply resize the browser window to exactly overlap one of the rectangles.

Windows (95, 98, Me, and 2000), Macintosh, and Unix users can all use built-in operating system functions to reset display characteristics. If you use Windows 95, go to www.microsoft.com, download the Microsoft Power Toys, and use the Quick Res Powertoy to change display settings quickly and easily (without rebooting your machine). This utility is built into Windows 98 and higher.

Now, change the color depth (that is, the number of colors being displayed) and see what happens to your pages. View your pages in millions of colors, in 256 colors, and in 16 colors in all your browsers. Check what happens to background and image color when you reduce the color depth. Yes, it's an incredible hassle—but, with some practice, you'll learn how XHTML effects appear at various resolutions, and you can improve your pages accordingly.

Testing for Usability

Usability refers to how easily a user can find and use information. The information may be there, but will users find it, wait for it to download, or go through layers of links to get to it? In testing for usability, consider the following:

- How long do the pages take to download? Remember, you're testing your pages on your local computer; therefore, you can expect the pages to download *much* more slowly when users access them over dial-up Internet connections. Of course, you should also test how the pages load using DSL and cable, if possible.

If your Web pages might be viewed on handheld devices, you'll also want to check your pages there. A better solution is to use XHTML and CSS to create separate, simpler versions of your Web pages for handheld devices.

- Do the benefits of the enhancements outweigh the extra download time? For example, do images or the JavaScript you've added merit the added time required to download?

- How easily can you find navigation tools? Are they readily available, or do you have to scroll to find them? Are they consistent from page to page?

- Do *all* links work—links to information within the site as well as to information outside the site? A variety of tools, both interactive, Web-based tools and downloadable programs, can help you check links automatically. Search on **link validation** at your favorite search service for specifics.

• Are the levels of links appropriate for the information provided? For example, is the information located in a third-level link clearly subordinate to information in the first- and second-level links? Also, if you've provided many link levels, is the information important enough that your users will take the time to wade through the other links?

Pilot Testing Your Documents

When you *pilot test* your documents, you ask real people to look at them and to identify problems and areas for improvement. The two main methods for pilot testing are contextual inquiry and the talking aloud protocol, which are often used in combination.

When you use *contextual inquiry*, you observe users in their own environments. One of the best ways to get started is to simply sit with a notebook and quietly watch your users. Pay attention to everything they do, including which information they refer to, which links they use most, and in what order they visit pages. Make notes about when they refer to your site for information, when they appear to get lost or frustrated, and when they head down the hall to ask someone else. Although this method is time consuming, it can be a real eye-opening experience, particularly if most of your information about your users' needs is based more on conjecture than on observation.

When you use the *talking aloud protocol*, you listen to users describe what they're doing and why they're doing it as they navigate your site. Follow this process:

1. Make a list of five or fewer items that you want each user to find at your Web site.

2. Give the users the list and ask them to find each item.

3. Ask the users to talk out loud throughout the test, saying anything that pops into their heads about the search, the site, or overall tasks.

If possible, record the session. In all likelihood, you'll end up with a transcript that is fairly disjointed but rich in information. For example: "Let's see, I'm supposed to find safety information about this particular car model. Hmmm. No menu items for safety. Maybe it'll be under the Reliability menu. Nope, don't see it. Let's see. Search. No search items. It must be under Reliability. Aha, there it is, hiding under Protection. I saw Protection the first time, but thought that had something to do with undercoating or paint."

Pilot testing your site can identify how people *really* find information at your site and can indicate exactly where you need to make improvements.

Testing for Readability

Readability refers to how easily users can read information—text and images. Because several readability issues—fonts, font sizes, emphases, and colors—contribute to a document's overall appearance, you may have addressed some of them already. However, you need to look at these same issues from a user's point of view.

To test readability, search for a specific piece of information on your site. Observe which information you are drawn to on the page—usually images and headings stand out. Be sure that important information stands out adequately and that you can easily read all text, headings, captions, addresses, and so on.

Reading Online

By nature, reading on a computer screen is more difficult than reading the printed page. Hindrances include the size of the monitor, screen glare, and difficulty in navigating windows. In addition, a computer screen has a much coarser resolution than the printed page (72 to 100 dots per linear inch, as compared with 600 to 2,650 dots for laser-printed or typeset ink on paper). Consequently, users get tired quickly, read more slowly, and frequently skip information when reading on a computer.

As an XHTML author, you can improve readability somewhat with a few design techniques:

- Use headings and subheadings to break up long sections of text and to announce to a reader what information is on the page.
- Use bulleted and numbered lists, which give readers at-a-glance information.
- Use short paragraphs to encourage reading.
- Use text and background colors that adequately contrast.
- Use images to illustrate difficult concepts, rather than describing concepts in words.

Always test readability after changing the size of your display window or decreasing the color depth settings. Often, decreasing the window size or color depth makes pages much more difficult to read. For example, a Web site with a nice menu down the left side, banner on the top, and black text on the right looks great at 1024×768. At lower resolutions, however, the black text can end up over the dark background, as Figure 13.6 shows, and be impossible to read.

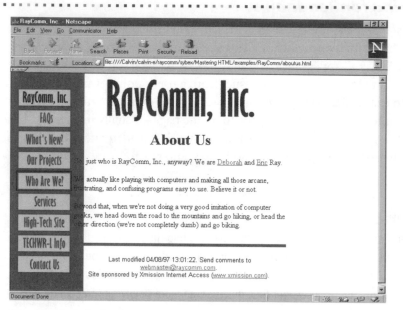

Figure 13.6 *Reducing window size can hinder readability.*

Testing for Accuracy

Finally, be sure the information on your site is accurate. Pay attention to details. In particular, a site littered with typos and glaring grammatical errors has just about zero credibility. Your accuracy checklist also needs to ensure that:

- The content is correct and up-to-date.

- Headings summarize the content that follows.

- References to figures or illustrations are correct.

- The *date last modified* information is current. The date last modified, as the name indicates, tells your users how current the information is and helps them decide whether it's usable.

Can Validation Services Help?

Validation services, accessed either through the Internet or from a program on your local computer, help ensure that you've used standard XHTML. For example, you might check to see that you're using XHTML 1 correctly. Although validation services are not a panacea for solving XHTML coding problems, you can use them to ensure that your code is complete, that it is more or less accurate, and that it is more or less standard. Two online validation services are `http://validator.w3.org` and `www.daimi.au.dk/~olef/validate`. In addition, check out Master's Reference Part 4.

Phase 2: Publishing Documents

Publishing means putting XHTML documents on a Web server and telling people where to look for them. The information in this section applies specifically to publishing your documents on the Internet or an intranet.

The exact process you'll use for publishing documents depends on your situation. Some large organizations have well-defined publishing procedures; in these cases, you might simply fill out an XHTML form and save your files in a specified folder. If your organization doesn't have procedures or if you're publishing on a server you don't own—through, a contractor or Internet service provider (ISP), for example—you need to *upload* your files (which means to copy files from your computer to a server).

Before you can upload your files, you need to obtain the following information from your system administrator or ISP:

- The address of the Web server (for example, `www.lanw.com`).

- The address of the FTP server, if required (`ftp://ftp.lanw.com`, for example). Otherwise, you'll need an address to which to mail the files or the location on the local area network (LAN) where you will place the files.

- A password and any access restrictions.

While you're at it, you should also ask the following:

- What kind of server (Apache, NCSA, WebStar, Netscape, and so on) is it, and on which platform does the server run?

- Can I restrict access to my pages?

- Can I install and run my own scripts?

- What's the default index filename?

- Are access logs maintained? How can I find out how many hits my site gets?

Chapter 16 provides specific information about publishing your documents.

Quick Lookup

The *default index* is the file that automatically appears when you specify the address without a specific filename. For example, if you specify www.lanw.com/books.htm, the server displays the books page. However, if you specify www.lanw.com, the server displays the file default.htm because that's how the server is configured.

On another server, the same address might display the index.htm file or the home.htm file. If you don't identify the index file correctly, your users might be able to view the entire list of files and browse according to their whim—not according to your plan.

Phase 3: Testing Published Documents

Earlier in this chapter, we discussed testing documents on your local computer. Now it's time to test them in the real world, looking for the same issues addressed previously, as well as making sure that all the links work and that the documents all transferred properly to the server. Additionally, at this stage, your goal is not only to look for layout, formatting, and proofreading errors, but also to get an accurate idea of what users will see when they access your pages. In particular, find out how fast pages load, how pages appear at various screen sizes and color depths, and how different browsers display page elements.

When you're testing, you want to do the following:

- Check how fast pages load using several connection types and speeds. Ask a few friends or colleagues to look at your pages and to report problems with layout, links, colors, download time, and so on.

- Check whether the server displays the pages properly. As a rule, everything will look fine, but it's not unheard of to have an incorrectly configured server that displays nothing but XHTML code in the browser.

 If you find that browsers are displaying documents as XHTML code, try changing the file extension to .html *(rather than* .htm*). If that doesn't work, contact the server administrator ASAP.*

- Test your pages using different computers, operating systems, and configurations. Remember to resize your document window and change color depth.

Phase 4: Maintaining Documents

Maintaining XHTML documents is the process of updating and revising existing pages, adding new pages, and deleting outdated pages. Regularly maintaining XHTML documents is essential if you want users to keep returning to your site. Regular maintenance also helps make long-term maintenance less cumbersome.

XHTML documents contain two types of information: static and dynamic. *Static* information remains constant. The company logo, most menus, and even product descriptions are examples of static information. Static information is usually what's included in your style sheet. *Dynamic* information, on the other hand, must be changed or updated regularly. Prices, schedules, specific or timely information, and product lists are examples of dynamic information. Figure 13.7 shows a Web page that includes both types.

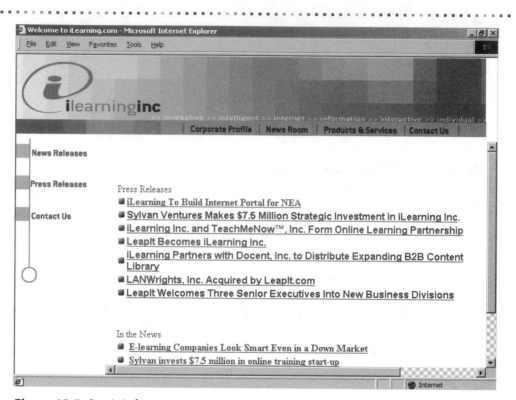

Figure 13.7 *Static information remains constant (here, the logo and menus); dynamic information changes frequently (Press Releases and In the News).*

Developing a Plan

Back in the XHTML document planning stages, you might have taken a few steps to make maintenance easier. In particular, you might have made update arrangements with content providers. Or, you might have developed some sort of documentation to help focus pages as the content changes. If you took either of these steps, you have a head start.

If you didn't plan adequately for maintenance—for example, if you didn't realize how much content you'd have or how difficult it would be to get updated information from your providers—you can still make maintenance a fairly straightforward process. First, devise a maintenance schedule. Set a time every day, every few days, or every few weeks (depending on how frequently the dynamic information changes) to update your documents.

Second, devise a maintenance plan. For example, if you know that you'll only be adding tidbits of information every few weeks, you can probably do that without much problem. If you're likely to receive pages and pages of information to add or if you're likely to make significant changes, however, you'll need to determine how to make the additions and changes most effectively. In these cases, hand-coding the information probably isn't the most effective way; conversion software, which does a lot of the coding for you, might be a better idea. In either case, determine how much you'll be changing and decide how best to handle it.

Keeping Up

As you're adding, deleting, and updating information in your XHTML documents, you'll need to routinely do the following:

- Check for links that don't work or that point to outdated information (which is also known as *link rot*). As you add and remove information from your site, you'll find that some pages suddenly have no links to them, and other existing links don't go anywhere. Manually browse all your links, and take advantage of link-checking programs on the Web. (Look on sites such as www.tucows.com and www.zdnet.com and search for **link checkers**.)

- Balance the latest XHTML specification capabilities with what users' browsers can display. You probably won't want to develop a totally XHTML 1.1–enhanced document if your users' browsers don't support all the version 1.1 effects.

- Ensure that older pages still look good in new versions of browsers. Often, changes in browser software affect how some elements—such as images, tables, and forms—are displayed.

- Check older pages for references to outdated information. For example, you might want to update present-tense references to past presidential elections, sports records, or even products, prices, and schedules.

Where to Go from Here

This chapter provided an overview of the XHTML document life cycle. In particular, it covered planning and organizing issues as well as issues about creating, publishing, publicizing, and maintaining XHTML documents. If you understand these topics, you'll be able to develop XHTML documents and use them for a variety of applications, including Web pages and sites, intranet sites, help files, and kiosks.

From here, you can refer to several chapters, depending on your XHTML proficiency and the specific application you're developing:

- Chapter 14 gives you general tips and advice for developing coherent Web sites.

- Chapter 15 gives you tips and advice for specifically developing public, personal, and intranet sites.

 Check out Steve Krug's book **Don't Make Me Think** *(Que, 2000) for some great tips on how to design an effective and efficient Web site using common sense.*

Implementing a Coherent Web Site

XHTML

Chapter 14

When you or your company prepares materials for written correspondence, you generally choose a paper type and color, emblazon it with a logo, and then send the correspondence in matching envelopes with, perhaps, matching business cards. The result is that you improve the overall appearance of each component and your message (and your company image) appears complete and professional.

Your challenge, as a Web developer, is to do the same for your Web site. In this chapter, we'll show you how to unite individual XHTML documents to develop a coherent, easy-to-use Web site. In particular, we'll discuss how *theme-bearing elements* (items that consistently appear from page to page) and navigation menus can enhance your site and improve its usability. Also, we'll show you how to balance flash with functionality, which is important for making a visually interesting site that's easy to use. This is harder than it looks, but we'll give you numerous examples and illustrations.

This chapter covers the following topics:

- Including theme-bearing elements

- Making your site navigable

- Balancing "flare" with usability

Including Theme-Bearing Elements

Theme-bearing elements are Web page components that help unite multiple pages into a cohesive unit. Your users might not notice that you've included theme-bearing elements, but they will certainly notice if you haven't or if you have used them inconsistently from page to page. In this sense, theme-bearing elements set up users' (usually subconscious) expectations. If your users browse through several pages that contain a logo, they'll begin to expect to see the same logo in the same place on each page. They may not consciously notice that it's there, but they'll certainly notice if it's missing or in a different location—just as you never pay attention to that broken-down car at the house on the corner until it's gone.

Used correctly, theme-bearing elements make your site appear complete and professional, and they also help users know that they are in *your* site as they link from page to page. A user can view only one page at a time, so be sure that each page obviously belongs to the rest of the site and not to a page outside your site.

The following sections describe the theme-bearing elements you can use to unify pages in your site. You may have already included some of them, such as backgrounds and colors, but in addition we'll take a look at how you can use logos, icons, and buttons as theme-bearing elements.

Adding Backgrounds

Using consistent backgrounds—colors or images—is one of the easiest and most effective ways to unify Web pages, just as using the same color and style paper for multipage written correspondence identifies the material as a cohesive package. Using a different background for each Web page can lead to some unwanted results. Users might think they've somehow linked outside your site, or they might pay more attention to the differences in design than to your content.

 Have you ever received business correspondence in which the first page is on heavy, cream-colored, linen-textured letterhead, and the second page is on cheap 20-pound copier paper? Using different backgrounds for Web pages produces a similar effect—users will notice.

Whether you use a solid color or an image depends on the effect you want to achieve. Background colors are less obtrusive and can effectively mark pages as belonging to a specific site. Imagine Figure 14.1 without the textured background and just a plain white or gray background. You could use a solid color to adequately contrast the page elements and unify the other page elements without attracting attention to itself.

The textured background in Figure 14.1, on the other hand, doesn't unify the page elements but instead becomes a visually interesting part of the page. Although the image background isn't overwhelming in itself, it does make reading a little more difficult.

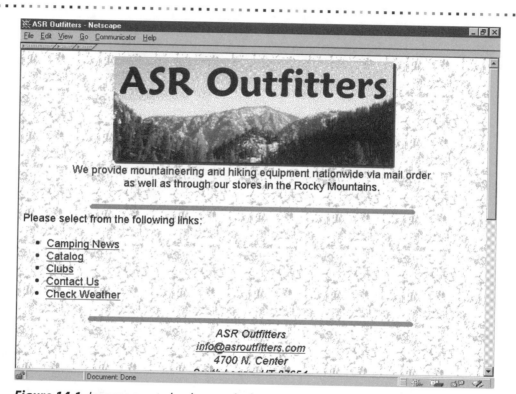

Figure 14.1 *Images create backgrounds that are more visually complex, yet they can complement—not overwhelm—page elements.*

Some Web sites combine colors and images by using a mostly solid color but adding a small repeating graphic, such as the ASR logo shown in Figure 14.2.

In using a small logo—which, in Figure 14.2, appears more like a watermark than an image—the image is less apparent and fades into the background. This is a great way to include a logo without significantly increasing download time or taking up valuable page space.

Figure 14.2 *You can combine colors and images (or text) to create a subtle background.*

Regardless of whether you choose a color or an image background, follow these guidelines:

- Be sure that the background adequately contrasts with the text. Remember that online reading is inherently difficult because of monitor size and quality, resolution, lighting, and screen glare. If you use dark text, use a light background; if you use light text, use a dark background. If you have any doubt about whether the background contrasts adequately, it doesn't.

- Be sure that the background complements—not competes with—other elements such as images. For example, if you include images, be sure that the background doesn't overwhelm them. Often, placing a busy or colorful background under equally busy or colorful images makes online reading more difficult.

- Be sure that the background matches the style and tone of the Web site content. A solid black background makes an impression, but doesn't necessarily soothe and calm the user. It's not a good choice, for example, for the ASR Outfitters pages because it's quite obtrusive.

- Be sure that the foreground text is large and bold enough to be easily read against the background. Use the CSS font properties (or the deprecated font element) to increase the size and, optionally, set a font to help your users easily read text. A slightly increased font size can overcome the visual distractions of a textured or patterned background. (You'll find more information about changing fonts and font sizes in Chapter 3 and more about CSS in Chapter 10.)

- Be sure to choose a nondithering color (one that appears solid and non-splotchy in Web browsers). Because backgrounds span the entire browser window, the colors you choose make a big difference in how the background integrates with the page elements. If, for example, you use a dithering color as a background, the resulting splotches may be more apparent than the page's content. Your best bet is to choose one of the 216 safe colors. To find out more, check out Master's Reference Part 6 or read the excellent, long article at

   `http://hotwired.lycos.com/webmonkey/00/37/index2a.html`

- Be sure you view your Web pages in multiple browsers and with varying color settings—particularly if you use an image background or don't choose from the 216 safe colors. A good background test includes changing your computer settings to 256 colors and then viewing all your pages again. Reducing the computer system's color depth may degrade the quality of the background.

You'll find information about how to include background colors in Chapter 3 and how to add background images in Chapter 5.

Choosing Colors

In most Web sites these days, colors abound—you see them in text, links, images, buttons, icons, and, of course, backgrounds. The key is to use color to enhance your Web pages and identify a theme from page to page.

When developing a color scheme, consider which elements you want to color—text (regular text as well as links, active links, visited links), logos, buttons, bullets, background, and so on. For smaller color areas—text or links—you can choose any color you can imagine. For larger color areas, such as panes or backgrounds, stick to one of the 216 safe colors. The goal is to choose the colors you'll use for each element and use them consistently.

Most Web-development software, from Netscape Composer to Microsoft Front-Page, comes with prepared color schemes. If you're not good with colors, consider using these prematched colors. Because color is the primary visual element in your pages, problematic color choice will be woefully apparent to all users.

The colors you choose should match the site's content. For example, if you're developing a marketing site for a high-tech company, you'll likely choose small areas of bright, fast-paced colors (reds, bright greens, or yellows) that correspond to the site's purpose of catching and holding users' attention. If you're developing an intranet site, you'd likely choose mellow colors, such as beige and blue or dark green, or make the colors match the company colors, because the site's purpose is to inform users, not dazzle them.

If you choose particularly vivid colors, use them in small areas. As the old commercial goes, a little dab will do ya! A small area of red, for example, can attract attention and hold users to the page. A broad expanse of red—such as a background—will likely scare them off or at least discourage them from hanging around.

Including Logos

If you're developing a corporate Web site, consider using a logo on each page. In doing so, you not only help establish a theme, but you also explicitly provide readers with the name of your company or organization throughout the site. You can even make the logo a link to your home page, so regardless of which page users are on, they can jump to the home page via your logo. Logos often include multiple theme-bearing elements: the logo itself, its colors, and the fonts or emphasis of the letters. Take a look at Figure 14.3, which shows a sample logo used on the ASR Outfitters page.

The logo helps set up other page elements. For example, the font appears in other places on the page, the colors are consistent throughout the page, and the image used as the foundation for the logo conveys the appropriate impression.

You may have no control over the logo you use—sometimes you're required to use your company's logo, for example. If you can develop a logo or enhance an existing logo, do so. Logos used online, particularly in Web sites, must carry more information about the company or organization and its style than a logo designed primarily for hard copy. A traditional logo is established by determining paper choice, paper texture, and other elements. Often, an online logo stands nearly alone without the help of other images or background images.

Figure 14.3 *ASR Outfitters Home Page uses a nonscrolling logo as a theme-bearing element.*

Where you place the logo depends on its emphasis. Many sites use a fairly large logo on the home page and a smaller version on subsequent pages. The logo thus appears on all pages, yet more space on subsequent pages is reserved for content.

An effective presentation is to combine small, classy logos with a clever arrangement of frames. For example, as shown in Figure 14.3, a logo can reside in a small frame at the top of a page that does not scroll, remaining visible while users are at the site. Because it does not have to be reloaded, other pages load more quickly.

Incorporating Other Graphical Elements

Other theme-bearing elements include buttons, graphical links, icons, and bullets. These elements, even more than colors and logos, add interest to your pages because they combine color and shape. What's more, these can be (and should be) small; you can include them throughout a page, adding a splash of color with each use. Take another look at Figure 14.3, a Web page that's a good example of how to employ a few graphical elements. Even in this black-and-white figure, the small graphical elements enhance the page.

You can also enhance a page with animated GIF images, which add visual attraction without increasing load time too much. See Chapter 12 for more information about animated GIF images.

Making Your Site Navigable

As mentioned back in Chapter 13, part of what makes a Web site usable is how easily users can access it, browse through it, and find the information they want. Most users access your site through a home page, which is typically a single XHTML document that provides links to the other pages in the site. However, not all your users will drop in using the home page. They can go directly to a page they've viewed before, or they can access your site through a search engine and go straight to a specific page. In either case, you have little control over how users move through your site.

To ensure that your users can link to the information they're looking for and to encourage them to browse your site, you need to make your site easily navigable—that is, make accessing, browsing, and finding information intuitive and inviting. You can do this by using *navigation menus*, which are sets of links that appear from page to page.

Navigation menus come in two varieties:

- Textual, which is a set of text links
- Graphical, which is a set of images (or icons) used as links

Textual Navigation

Textual navigation is simply text that links users to other information in the Web site. As shown in Figure 14.4, a textual navigation menu doesn't offer glitz, but effectively conveys what information resides at the other end of the link.

Textual navigation, though somewhat unglamorous, offers several advantages over graphical navigation. Textual navigation is more descriptive than graphical navigation because, done right, the text clearly tells users about the information in the site. Textual navigation links can be as long as necessary to describe the information at the end of the link; the description is not limited by the size of a button. The smaller (thus faster to download) the button, the less text you can fit on it.

Figure 14.4 *Textual navigation is often the most informative.*

Textual navigation is also more reliable than graphical navigation because the link itself is part of the XHTML document, not a referenced element such as a navigation button.

Finally, text links download much faster than graphical navigation. The links download as part of the page, without the delays associated with images.

If you're considering using textual navigation, follow these guidelines:

- If your textual navigation menu appears as a vertical list, place the most important or most accessed links at the top.

- Make the text informative. Rather than calling links, "More Information," "Contact Information," and "Related Information," add specific summaries. For example, call these links "Product Specs," "Contact Us!," and "Other Sportswear Vendors." Whatever you do, don't use instructions such as "Click Here," which is uninformative and wastes valuable space. Additionally, words such as *Information* rarely do anything but take up space. After all, what would be at the other end of the link besides information?

- Provide the same menu—or at least a similar one—on each page. As your users link from page to page, they become familiar with the setup and location of the menu and actually (unconsciously) begin to expect that it contains certain information in a certain place.

- Customize the menu on each page so the current page is listed, but not as a link. This helps users actually "see" where they are within the site, as well as keeps menu locations consistent.

Graphical Navigation

Graphical navigation is a set of images that link to other information in the site. Most commonly, graphical navigation appears in the form of images with text on them, as shown in Figure 14.5. Graphical navigation can also be images that are pictures (called *icons*) representing what the buttons link to.

Figure 14.5 *These navigation buttons include both text and images.*

Graphical navigation has the distinct advantage of being visually more interesting than textual navigation. For example, because buttons and icons can include colors or patterns and can be almost any shape you can imagine, they are outstanding theme-bearing elements.

As colorful and interesting as graphical navigation might be, it has a few drawbacks. Primarily, it takes longer—sometimes much longer—to download than textual navigation. The download time depends on the file size and your user's connection speed, among other variables that aren't in your control.

Chapter 5 provides information about resizing images and making images quick to download.

Graphical navigation also tends be less informative than textual navigation. For example, if you're using buttons with text on them, you might be limited by the size of the button. The text can be difficult to read, depending on the size of the button and the resolution of the user's computer.

If you want to use graphical navigation, consider these guidelines:

- Be sure that button text is easily readable. Sometimes, when images used to create buttons are made smaller to fit within a navigation menu, the text becomes too small to read or the letters get compacted. Your best bet is to try several button sizes to get a feel for which size is most effective.

- Be sure that the navigation menu integrates well with the other page elements. Images—including graphical navigation—are visually weighty page elements and often make other elements less apparent.

- Plan the navigation menu before you actually create it. Graphical navigation takes longer to develop than textual navigation, and it's much more difficult to change once it's in place. Even if all the pages aren't in place (or fully planned yet), at least create a placeholder for the navigation menu so you don't have to revise the menu as you develop new content.

- Provide the same menu—or as close as possible—on every page. As with textual menus, users link from page to page and expect to see the same menu options in the same location on each page. Also, developing only one menu that you can use from page to page saves you time; you create it once and reuse it on each page.

Rather than creating several navigation buttons, you can create one image that includes several links. This single image with multiple links is called an image map. See Chapter 5 for more information.

Placing Navigation Menus

After you determine which kind of navigation menu to use, decide where to place the menu on your Web pages. Regardless of whether you use textual or graphical navigation, be sure to place menus where users are most likely to use them.

Because navigation menus, particularly graphical ones, often take up a lot of valuable page space, be sure to choose menu location(s) that don't interfere with other page elements. Here are some considerations when choosing a location for navigation menus:

Top of the page   Locating a navigation menu at the top of pages is particularly useful because it's easy to find and access. Users casually surfing your pages can easily link in and out, and those who link to a page in error can easily get out of the page. The big advantage to using the top of the page (from the user's perspective) is that he or she isn't forced to wade through information to access the menu.

Middle of the page   This location is effective in long pages because users can read through some of the information, but are not forced to return to the top or scroll to the bottom just to leave the page. Usually, with mid-page navigation menus, you'll want to use targeted links, as described in Chapter 4.

Bottom of the page   This location works well in a couple of situations. For example, you can put the navigation menu at the bottom when you want users to read the material that precedes it. Keep in mind that users don't want to be forced to read information they're not interested in, but they don't mind browsing through a short page to get to a navigation menu at the bottom. Bottom navigation also works well on pages that already include many elements at the top, such as logos or descriptions; in this case, adding a navigation menu would crowd other important information.

Right and left sides of the page   These locations are becoming more and more common with the use of tables and frames. Although you can put the navigation on the right or left side, it's more commonly found on the left side of the page. For example, you can use a framed layout to place the menu on the left side of the page and the information on the right. A menu at the left creates a two-column page appearance, which can make the page visually interesting and shorten the width of the right column to help readability. In addition, if the navigation menu appears in a separate frame, it can remain on screen at all times, regardless of which pages users link to or how far they scroll down a page. This is very useful for long documents. See Chapters 6 and 8 for more information on tables and frames, respectively.

Multiple locations   For most Web sites, you'll likely use a combination of these locations, which is fine, as long as you use at least one combination consistently. You could, for example, place a main menu at the top of all pages, place a menu of what's on the actual page on the left, and a smaller text version of the main menu at the bottom of the page. Don't use this combination if you're space conscious.

Figure 14.6 shows a Web site that uses a main navigation menu at the top of the page and a secondary navigation menu on the left. In addition, you can scroll the information on the right while the left-side menu remains static.

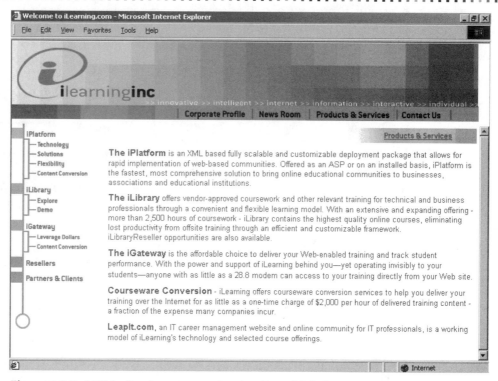

Figure 14.6 *A Web site that uses navigation in multiple locations.*

Balancing Flare with Usability

One of the most important principles of developing a Web site—particularly public and personal sites—is to balance flashy elements (ones that "dazzle" your users) with usability (which makes your site easy to use). If you've spent any time at all surfing the Web, you've probably noticed some really spectacular sites—ones that flash, make sounds, and have moving pictures. In the past, these flashing, beeping, moving sites had one significant drawback: they usually took forever to download. The result was that users ended up waiting for the dazzling stuff, when all they were really looking for was the content. However, as a consequence of increasing computer and Internet access speeds, download times have greatly decreased, generating an explosion of sites that use multimedia technologies such as Flash or Shockwave.

Even with these new developments, flashy elements can still take a while to download. The key is to balance the number and kind of flashy elements you include with usability, which, you may recall from Chapter 12, refers to how easily your users can get to the information throughout your Web site. Yes—absolutely—flashy elements attract users, similar to the way that color and creativity in printed marketing materials help lure in customers and keep them glued to every word. However, if you include too many elements that slow loading time, users will get frustrated, leave your site, and probably won't return. Your goal is to make your site attractive and interesting but not to make users wait too long to access the information they want.

Sites that balance flare and usability include enhancements that download quickly and are quickly available to most of your users. In balancing these, you'll find the following:

- Users spend more time in a balanced site than in one that lacks flare or usability.

- Users return to a balanced site more often than one that's difficult to use.

- Users spend more time in and return to a site that doesn't exclude some users from the effects. For example, you're not likely to get many repeat visits from those using Internet Explorer if you've included only Netscape Navigator–supported effects (or vice versa), or if you continually remind your users that the site was designed expressly for users of other browsers.

*Just because you **can** provide an effect doesn't mean you should. If the effect doesn't help convey information, improve your user's overall experience, or help project your public image, don't include it.*

How do you balance flare and usability? Consider which effects give you the flare, weigh the effects against download time, and consider the availability of the effects in different browsers. We can't tell you exactly how long each takes to download—too many variables exist, such as file size, the type and the speed of the user's Internet connection, and the user's browser capability and computer resources. Table 14.1 summarizes the flashy effects you can add, the impact each can have on download time, and the availability in browsers.

Table 14.1 A Summary of Web-Page Enhancements

ENHANCEMENT	DESCRIPTION	AVAILABILITY
Images	These are the most common enhancements included in Web pages because they add color and flash, yet they're fairly easy to obtain or create. For this reason, they're probably the biggest culprits of waiting, because image files can grow to enormous sizes. However, you can modify images and image files so they take minimal time to download. Chapter 5 shows you how.	All graphical browsers.
Frames	These can slow things down slightly initially, but if used carefully they can speed overall performance considerably because only new information must be downloaded with every new page, leaving logos and other elements in place in adjacent frames.	Available on most versions of Netscape Navigator, Internet Explorer, and Opera.
Java applets	These can slow down pages considerably, particularly for users with older versions of Netscape Navigator. They can add power—both in terms of visual interest and through functional programs embedded in Web pages—but sometimes at a high cost. Java applets are sometimes avoided by the security conscious.	Available on most versions of Internet Explorer, Netscape Navigator, and several other browsers.
JavaScript, also known as JScript or ECMAScript	This slows pages only slightly and can add attractive flash and glitz. However, many JavaScript effects are so overused as to be completely kitschy. Also avoided by the security conscious.	Available on most versions of Internet Explorer, Netscape Navigator, and Opera. Some effects are less widely available.

Table 14.1 continued A Summary of Web-Page Enhancements

ENHANCEMENT	DESCRIPTION	AVAILABILITY
Multimedia	Sounds, video, Macromedia Flash animations, virtual reality worlds, and all the rest of the real flare formerly slowed pages nearly to a standstill. If you're adding important information or if you segregate the flare so only people who really want it will get it, it's okay, but use with consideration toward those with older browser versions or slow Internet connections. See Chapter 12 for more information.	Available on newer browsers either already installed or with the proper plug-ins or controls.
Cascading Style Sheets	These offer great formatting capabilities and lots of flexibility, but aren't universally available. However, browser support for CSS has increased to the point where CSS formatting is preferred for most purposes. Many XHTML formatting elements are deprecated in favor of CSS. See Chapter 10 for more information.	Netscape Navigator 4 and newer, Internet Explorer 3 and newer, and Opera 3 and newer. Specific capabilities vary greatly by browser.

For a list of which browsers support what, check out www.webreview.com/browsers/ index.shtml.

Be aware that some of these effects require users to have plug-ins installed on their computers. A plug-in, discussed in detail in Chapter 12, is an extra program used to view effects within browsers that don't typically support the effect. If you decide to include a Flash or Shockwave animation, for example, users need the appropriate plug-in to view it. If they don't already have the plug-in included in their browser's prepackaged software bundle and want to view the animation, they're forced to download the plug-in off the Internet and install it one time for every browser they use.

Is this a hassle? Yes, without a doubt. Most of your users won't take the time to download and install plug-ins just to view your site, unless the information provided through the plug-in is essential.

However, along with the advent of faster Internet connections, processing speeds, and increased software application bundling, newer versions of browsers may already include many of the major applications that used to require the user to obtain and install a plug-in. According to Macromedia, more than 330 million Flash players are in use, whether packaged with the user's browser or obtained by downloading and installing the plug-in.

Of course, if your information is that important and can be conveyed without the plug-in, include it using a completely hassle-free method, such as text. Also, you can be fairly certain that your users won't open a page in Netscape Navigator and then reopen the same page in Internet Explorer just to view nifty effects.

Where to Go from Here

In this chapter, you learned how using theme-bearing elements and navigation menus can enhance your site's usability, and you learned how balancing flare with usability can make sites inviting for your users. From here, you have several chapters at your fingertips that will add to the topics discussed in this chapter:

- Chapter 5 shows you how to include images in your Web pages and provides more information about choosing colors.

- Chapter 8 discusses the advantages and disadvantages of using frames and shows you how to implement a framed site.

- Chapter 12 provides a discussion of including multimedia in your Web site.

- Chapter 13 provides a thorough discussion about Web site usability. You might also check out that chapter for discussions about providing appropriate information in your Web pages.

- Chapter 15 provides tips and advice for developing specific types of sites— public, personal, or intranet.

Tips for Web Sites: Public, Personal, and Intranet

XHTML

Chapter 15

Throughout this book, we've talked about how to add elements and attributes to create various Web-page effects. In this chapter, we'll go a step further and discuss issues specific to the type of Web site you're developing. Broadly speaking, we can classify sites into three types:

- Public

- Personal

- Intranet

A public site usually focuses on a company or an organization—for example, AltaVista or your local humane society. A personal site is a type of public site, but it focuses on an individual. Both types reside on the Web. However, an intranet is a different type of site altogether; it provides information about a company, but it makes the information available only to that company's employees.

This chapter covers the following topics:

- Developing public sites

- Developing personal sites

- Developing intranet sites

Developing Public Sites

Public sites can address practically any topic and can describe individuals as well as sell or describe products or services. They can also be published on any public Web server in the world. Public sites are those you find on the Internet. Presumably, if you've invested the time and resources to develop a Web site, you have a reason for wanting people to visit it. Although some users may happen upon it, you need to publicize your site to be sure that you reach the audience you intend to reach.

Publicizing Your Site

Your primary option is to publicize by submitting information about your site to directories and indexes. A *directory* is a categorized, hierarchical list. For example, Yahoo! is one of the oldest and best-established directories. It categorizes sites by subject. (Find Yahoo! at www.yahoo.com.)

Indexes (also called *search services*) use computer programs that roam the Internet and record every page they find. The site information, including titles, descriptions, and modification dates, is then fed into a huge database that anyone on the Internet can search. AltaVista (www.altavista.com) is a well-known search service. As time goes by, the distinctions are disappearing—AltaVista licenses a directory for use on the AltaVista site, and Yahoo! licenses search technology for its site.

You can use the publicizing options discussed in the following few sections to publicize your personal site too!

Submitting Documents Yourself

You can easily submit XHTML documents to directories and indexes by accessing their sites and completing online forms. For example, to submit your address to Lycos, follow these steps:

1. Go to the Lycos Web site at www.lycos.com.

2. Choose Add Your Site To Lycos (currently found at the bottom of the page).

3. Enter the URL of your Web site and your e-mail address, and read the other information provided.

4. Click the Add Site To Lycos button to submit your site.

Other services may use slightly different procedures, but the basic process is the same and usually just as easy. Look for a link at the bottom of the directory or index home page—the link is usually labeled "Add Your Site," "Submit Your Site," or "Add A URL." When your site is listed with these services, potential users have a much better chance of finding your site.

Another helpful organization is the Open Directory Project, which maintains a directory compiled by volunteer editors. This directory includes a list of Web addresses and brief descriptions about what you'd find at each site. Visit the Open Directory Project at `http://dmoz.org` and search for **computers** to see how helpful this site is.

Your potential users determine which sites to visit based on these descriptions, so you need to make them informative. Unfortunately, not all services cull descriptions from the same place. For the most part, directories use information that you provide when you submit your site.

Providing Enticing Descriptions in Directories

Most directory services require—or at least request—a brief description about your site as part of the submission process. To draw people to your site, include the description and make it enticing and accurate. Even in the brief space provided by most directory services, you can summarize your site and lure potential users into clicking the link to your site. Here are a few suggestions:

Include key words.   Rather than saying, "Use this site to find tax information," include specific words and phrases, such as, "Find small-business tax tips, tax forms, and tax-filing guidelines."

Start your description with active verbs that describe what users should do with the information.   For example, begin your description with words such as *find, create,* or *develop.*

Include only major categories.   Don't ramble on about obscure or tangential topics.

Announce freebie files.   Many times, potential users are looking for images, sounds, or other information that they can download and use. If you have any freebies for them, let them know!

Announce that you've included updated, cutting-edge, or timely information. Many potential users are looking for the latest information on a topic and will breeze past Web sites that seem to include only old news.

Helping Search Services Find Your Site

Some search services display the first several words of the document body as the site description, regardless of whether the words are headings, paragraphs, or even JavaScript code. For example, visit www.altavista.com and search for **xhtml**. The results list the site addresses and a variety of descriptions.

Note that some nondirectory searches display the part of the page where the search term appears— usually the title, meta *tags (*keywords *or* description*), body, or some combination.*

You'll notice that descriptions vary considerably. Some sound like an introduction; others have nothing but jumbled information. Still others seem to summarize the document content, which is what potential users find most useful.

You can ensure that search services display an enticing description by including a meta element in the head of your XHTML document that specifies the description. Here's the process:

1. Open your XHTML document in a text editor.

2. In the document head (between the head tags), add a meta element, like this:

    ```
    <head>
    <title>ASR Outfitters Home Page</title>
    <meta />
    </head>
    ```

3. Add the name attribute to the element, and give it the value description.

    ```
    <meta name="description" />
    ```

4. Add the content attribute to the element, and fill it with a concise, clear description of your page content. Stick to a line or so, and be sure that the description accurately and effectively portrays your site.

    ```
    <meta name="description" content="ASR Outfitters provides
        hiking and mountaineering equipment through direct
        sales and mail order throughout the continental USA." />
    ```

Remember that we have to break long lines, like this one, in print. You should type this all on one line, because including hard returns in attribute values can lead to unpredictable browser behavior.

5. Save and close your document.

When search engines—such as AltaVista or Lycos—find your page, they display the description found within the meta element along with your site address.

In addition to using the text of your site, you can include keywords to help identify matches for user searches. *Keywords* provide synonyms for common words that might not appear in the actual text of the Web site. In addition, some search sites rank pages higher when the search term is in keywords than when it's just in the body. ASR Outfitters might use keywords such as the following:

affordable	biking	climbing	hiking	tent
backpack	camping	dried food	sleeping bag	

To include keywords, simply add another meta element. Follow these steps:

1. Open the XHTML document.

2. In the document head (between the head tags), add a meta element, as shown here. If you included a description in a meta element, you can place this one above or below it.

```
<head>
<title>ASR Outfitters Home Page</title>
<meta />
</head>
```

3. Add the name attribute to the element, with the value keywords.

```
<meta name="keywords" />
```

4. Add the content attribute to the tag, and fill it with a list of all the likely terms someone might use. Separate the terms with commas, but don't insert spaces after the commas.

```
<meta name="keywords" content="climbing,hiking,biking,
   camping,tent,sleeping bag,backpack,dried food" />
```

For very important terms, it's valuable to list variations of the term—for example, biking,bikes,bicycles.

5. Save and close your document.

Hiding Pages and Folders from Search Engines

If you've created a public site, you probably want robots or spiders to find your site and incorporate your pages into Internet-wide indexes such as AltaVista and Lycos. You might also have specific pages or folders on your server that you want to exclude. For example, many sites have test folders that contain files that need to be on the server for testing purposes, but that are not designed to be accessed by users to the site or by search engines and indexes.

Fortunately, you can keep automated users from accessing specified pages and folders through an agreement called the *Robots Exclusion Standard.* Just put a plain-text document in the root folder of your Web server called robots.txt. In that file, use the following format to specify which robots to exclude and which folders to exclude them from. (All the lines that start with # are comments for you to read—they're disregarded by the robots.)

To keep robots out of your entire site, use a robots.txt file at your server root containing the following.

```
User-Agent: *
# The * specifies all agents or robots
Disallow: /
# The / indicates all documents under the server root.
```

To keep all robots out of the /test folder, for example, use a robots.txt file containing the following:

```
User-Agent: *
# The * specifies all agents or robots
Disallow: /test
# The / indicates that all folders immediately under the server root
# starting with /test should be excluded, including test and tests
```

For more information on search engines, including how they work, search-engine placement tips, and a list of the top search engines and their URLs, go to www.searchenginewatch.com. This site also offers a free e-mail newsletter (as well as an expanded version by paid subscription) that details the latest updates in the frequently changing search engine field.

Using Services to Submit Pages

Dozens of site submission services exist to relieve you of submitting your site manually. Some are free, and others charge a fee. Most free services submit your site to somewhere between 20 and 50 sites, including most of the popular ones, such as AltaVista, Yahoo!, Google, and Lycos. For a fee, they'll submit your site to many more sites—up to several hundred.

Is it worth your time to have your site submitted for free to several dozen sites? You bet it is. Check out www.submitexpress.com for just one example.

Is it worth the cost to have your site submitted for a fee to a few hundred directories and search engines? Possibly, but probably not. First, the 20 to 50 sites to which most services submit include those that your users are likely to use. Second, if your information is so precisely targeted that it wouldn't be adequately listed with the major directory and index services, you can probably market it more effectively through other channels or through specialty search engines and directories that target a specific content area—for example, book printing. You might also consider posting the information to e-mail list servers, newsgroups, or electronic magazines (*e-zines*), where you can target specific markets. Or, you might submit a press release about your site to a newsletter, magazine, or journal that targets specific markets.

 Many search engines and directories now charge a fee for commercial sites. Some offer expedited review of your site for a fee, and others guarantee placement for a fee. If you're launching a new commercial site, it may be worth the fee to get an expedited review of your site by a directory such as Yahoo!. Otherwise, plan on six to eight weeks before your site appears in the search engines and directories.

Other Publicizing Methods

Because of the overwhelming number of new sites that appear on the Internet daily, simply adding your site to existing search engines and directories won't necessarily result in a flood of traffic.

Consider some of the following ways to publicize your new site:

- Include a brief announcement and URL in your e-mail signature.
- Add your URL and e-mail address to business cards and stationery.
- Add your URL to any advertising you do for your business, including yellow-page ads.
- Write an article about your site and submit it to newsletters or journals in your field.
- Send an e-mail message announcing your site to people in your field.
- Include links to other related sites, and ask those sites to provide a link back to your site.

Making Users Want to Browse Your Site

Think of your public Web site as being a retail store. The longer customers browse, the greater the chance that they'll buy something, even if they didn't go into the store intending to purchase anything. You want users to linger in your site for similar reasons. Longer visits likely mean that users will gather more information, notice more products and services, gain a better understanding of your organization, and purchase more merchandise (if you provide that option). Even if your public site serves more as a central clearinghouse for information—mostly providing links to information on the Web—you'll want users to spend time in your site and use the information you provide.

You can use several techniques to help keep users in your site longer. You'll find that you can easily combine these according to the site's purpose.

- Minimize how long users have to wait to download pages, and be sure that your site loads quickly. Pay extra attention to your home page, and make sure that it loads quickly enough that users will stay and visit the rest of the site. Check out Chapter 14 for information about balancing flashy elements with usability.

- Use informative links. Users won't spend much time at your site if you make them guess what information resides at the end of a link. Let them know if a link will take them to a different site. If you use links to graphics or other elements with large file sizes, let the user know in advance by putting the file size next to the link.

- Provide links that go to real information. Users tire easily of linking to pages that say, "This page under construction." At the very least, provide a date they can expect the information to be available—then do it.

- Make the most useful and most-accessed information and links easily accessible. You could force users to scroll through text to get to the information or links, but be careful. Users only tolerate a minimal amount of scrolling, and they're likely to move to another site if they can't reach information quickly.

- Make the navigation obvious and easy for the user to figure out. Never leave users at dead-end pages where they have no option except to leave the pages by using the browser's back button (or by leaving your site).

- Provide services and information to make visiting worthwhile. Offer free samples or added information about whatever you do.

- Provide services that users can use while visiting your site. For example, depending on your products or services, you could include an online mortgage amortization calculator, retirement planning advice, virtual coloring books, or a relocation calculator.

Making Users Yearn to Return

After users complete their business on your Web site, make them want to return to it. Here are some ideas to try:

- Provide new information regularly and often. Users won't return to a site that provides the same information time after time.

- Provide accessible and complete contact information. Many users use the Web as an enormous phone book; rather than looking up your company's phone number, they head to your Web site to find out how to contact you.

- If you provide an e-mail link for contact, make sure to respond quickly to any e-mail you receive from the site. If you're not able to answer right away, see if your ISP or Web hosting service offers auto-responders. These automatically send an e-mail response to let the user know their e-mail was received and will be answered at a later time.

ISP and Web Host: What's the Difference?

Internet service providers (ISPs) are usually the service you use to connect to the Internet. They provide dial-up access to the Internet via modems, and sometimes Digital Subscriber Line (DSL) and Integrated Services Digital Network (ISDN) access. Domain registration and domain hosting are usually available. Some ISPs offer Common Gateway Interface (CGI) bins for you to put your CGI scripts in, but usually do not offer any script templates or support for debugging scripts.

Web hosting services do not provide Internet connections, but instead specialize in domain hosting and other services such as e-commerce, database connections, and Active Server Pages (ASP) services. Web hosts usually offer a variety of script templates for forms, guest books, and discussion forums. Most offer software or templates for e-commerce, and many provide chat services.

- Update existing information, particularly product and service descriptions, to reflect the current availability of your products and services, and make it clear that you've recently updated the information.

- Include summaries of hot-off-the-press information that is related to your Web site.

- Include links to related information. Make your site a central information resource. For instance, we don't search for articles about the latest developments in browser technology; instead, we usually access reliable and current Web sites and link to articles from there.

- Let your users register for e-mail notification of changes to the site. You could collect addresses using a form on your site and send e-mail whenever you make substantive changes, or you could hire a service to automatically notify your registered users of changes.

Maintaining Public Sites

When you're running a public site, you'll probably have a steady stream of users. However, problems crop up when you're updating the site. Your goal is to develop a maintenance plan that eliminates downtime and provides users with uninterrupted service. You want to eliminate even the shortest downtime stints—resulting from uploading files or encountering connectivity problems, for example. If your Web site is occasionally or unpredictably down for maintenance, users will not rely on it as an information resource.

You can avoid these problems if you follow these suggestions:

- Keep backups of your site! Be sure that your ISP, hosting service, and/or server administrator do the same.

- Test the backups and confirm that you can restore the files in a reasonable amount of time. If you house your site at your ISP or hosting service, be sure that you understand under which circumstances it's willing to restore the backup.

- Provide redundant network connections (recommended for larger Web sites) to assure that users can access your site if a network connection goes down.

- Find out what action your ISP or hosting service takes if it has technical difficulties, such as hard disk crashes, system problems, power outages, network disruptions, hackers, and so on. While you—as a content provider—may not have to deal with these issues, you must take responsibility for ensuring that the Web site is adequately covered for all contingencies.

- Use a *test environment* that duplicates your real server as nearly as possible, with the same software, the same physical platform, and the same configuration. Viewing your site in a test environment gives you a good idea of what it will look like when you upload it to the server. See Chapter 16 for more information on test environments.

Using a Tracking Service to Access Site Statistics

Consider using a tracking service as part of the maintenance of your site. There are many free services available, such as the tracker at www.extreme-dm.com/tracking, which includes a counter and multiple site statistics, such as when users visit your site, what browsers they're using, and what keywords they used in the search engines to find your site. The service is free for your home page, or you can purchase an expanded version that tracks every page.

For an expanded and very sophisticated tracking system, check out WebTrends at www.webtrends.com. This software provides a way for you to use your server access logs (these are generally available to you from your ISP or hosting service) to track the users to your site. WebTrends software can create reports about site users, including graphs and tables of information; among the extensive data it provides are these:

- How long do users stay on a page?
- What pages are never accessed?
- What page do they leave the site from?
- What part of the country (or world) are they coming from?

Tracking information can be very useful to you for updating and maintaining your site to best meet the needs of your users.

Putting Ads on Your Site

After developing a public site, consider selling ad space on your pages. You might think about using some margins of your pages to promote related products or to advertise other, complementary sites. If your situation is typical, you probably won't make a fortune (or even a mini fortune). Even high-traffic sites such as Yahoo! don't yield high returns. However, selling ads directly or working with a reciprocal ad exchange service can have some benefits.

If you're sure you want to sell ads and do it all yourself, you'll need to use specialized, and possibly custom, software to track hits. For starters, check into Selena Sol's Public Domain Script Archive (www.extropia.com) and Matt's Script Archive (www.worldwidemart.com/scripts). Both have custom applications to help manage ads and to track hits.

A better option overall is to participate in a link exchange service, such as Link-Trader (www.linktrader.com). This and other link exchanges find homes for your ads while placing ads on your site. After you visit the link exchange site and register, you receive some code to put in your page—that code automatically displays the ad. You then also submit a GIF image for your ad banner. The service counts the number of ads that you show, which is essentially the number of hits to your site. Typically, for every two hits to your site, your ad appears somewhere else once (some services provide an even higher ratio).

 If you represent a company or an organization that's moving toward online sales of products, work with your ISP or Web hosting service to set up secure transactions so credit card transactions from your site are as secure as possible. Check what's available from your ISP or Web host, or go to your favorite search engine and search for **e-commerce** *to get the latest services and software.*

Developing Personal Sites

A personal site is a special type of public Web site that focuses on an individual. Although you can use personal sites to publish general information about yourself, such as your hobbies and interests, you can also use personal sites to market your skills or publish information you've researched or developed—which is what the next few sections show you how to do.

Marketing Your Skills

You can use a personal Web site to market your skills through a Web-based resume, letter of introduction, or personal brochure. Most commonly, you'll market your skills to get a job (or a better job), although you could also use this vehicle to gain contract employment or to let companies know that you exist and are available. With one thoughtfully developed Web site, you can market yourself to millions of people around the world without the hassles or expense of traditional mailings.

A personal Web site represents your skills, experience, and creativity in much the same way that traditional tools do. When you're applying for a job, you generally develop a resume and a letter of application, and you probably pay particular attention to your personal appearance when you go to the interview. You create a package—one that informs a potential employer about your skills, shows your attention to detail and creativity, and projects some information about your personality. Your personal Web site should do the same.

Providing this information on the Web has several advantages over traditional job application materials. For example, your Web-page resume can't get buried on someone's desk, and multiple pages can't get separated or lost in the shuffle. Also, you can provide more details and examples on the Web than you could ever get away with in a traditional resume.

Developing a Web Resume

In developing a Web resume, you have the same options as you do in developing a paper resume—you can focus on experience or education, skills or training, or other aspects that might appeal to a future employer. The approaches break down into essentially two types: functional and skills-based, as shown in Figure 15.1.

Functional Résumé   Skills-Based Résumé

Figure 15.1 *Functional resumes focus on places of employment and educational institutions; skills-based resumes focus on your skills.*

Both types include basically the same sections—contact information, objective, education, employment, activities, and references. They differ only in emphasis, as shown by the summary in Table 15.1. When developing a Web resume, use either of these types or some combination of the two.

Table 15.1 Functional and Skills-Based Resumes

	FUNCTIONAL RESUME	SKILLS-BASED RESUME
Purpose	To provide information about places you worked and/or educational institutions you attended	To provide information about skills you've developed or coursework you've completed
Advantages	Allows you to announce prestigious job titles, company names, university names, and degrees	Allows you to downplay multiple jobs, unfinished degrees, or positions in which you learned a lot without adequate compensation or title
Focus	Places you've worked or education	Skills
Categories	Objective, Education, Employment, Special Skills or Activities, and References	Objective, Skills, Education, Activities, and References

You'll probably combine features of both types of resumes. For example, you may have worked for companies with well-recognized names and held jobs with prestigious titles, but you also want to emphasize your specific skills. In this case, you primarily use a skills-based resume but add an employment history page that lists your previous employers. Or, perhaps you want to show your steady employment history and promotions through each job change. In this case, you want to primarily use a functional resume but include a separate skills page.

Organizing Web resumes is tricky because you must accommodate both a nonlinear read, in which users select topics, and a linear read, in which users start at the top and read sequentially. Many typical Web site users expect your pages to look flashy and provide information quickly. In this case, provide multiple, shorter documents with links between and among them. In doing so, you provide pages that download quickly and display information that's easy to find.

See Chapter 14 for more information about balancing flashy elements with quick loading time.

However, other users may want to print your documents, and you could spend a lot of time printing multiple pages from a site. For this reason, provide the complete resume users can read linearly and print easily.

Essentially, you develop two complete resume packages—one broken into chunks and the other in one document. This way, you accommodate virtually any user (think "potential employer"). These folks can easily view the information or print it, depending on their needs.

To meet both these structural needs, do two things. First, provide each of the resume categories in separate XHTML documents, as shown in Figure 15.2.

Figure 15.2 *Put each resume category in a document of its own.*

Why do this? You might recall from Chapter 1 that online reading produces some difficulties for users. For instance, users face obstacles such as computer resolution, small monitors, and screen glare, all of which make reading online difficult. The result is that users (or more specifically, their eyes) tire quickly, and they tend to gloss over information rather than read it thoroughly. By using multiple, shorter documents, as shown in Figure 15.2, you improve the chances that users take the time to browse. These shorter documents are more inviting because the pages don't appear so difficult to wade through, and very short XHTML documents virtually leap onto the screen, with little wait time. Also, users can choose which information they access and in what order. The result is that users spend more time browsing your site and—essentially— more time considering you as a possible applicant.

Next, provide a link pointing to a single XHTML document that includes the full resume package. You can easily include a link from the home page and let users view a longer single document (as opposed to multiple shorter documents).

Resist the temptation to use the fanciest formatting options in your resume. Your resume should indeed look nice, but keep it quick to download and simply formatted (use standard fonts).

Developing a Web Resume Home Page

Many Web resumes start on a home page, which is the most important page in the site because it's usually the first page that users access. Typically, it states your employment objective and includes links to each category of information, as shown in Figure 15.3.

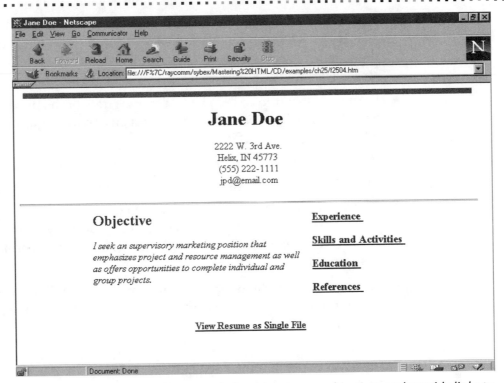

Figure 15.3 *Your resume home page should state your objectives and provide links to other information.*

Don't overlook the *employment objective*, which actually plays a big role in luring users to link to other pages in the resume or deters them from going further. Focus your objective on the skills you can offer a company. For example, rather than saying,

"I seek a position in which I can use my existing skills and learn new ones," state the specific skills you want to use, like this: "I seek a position as Marketing Manager so that I can manage accounts, supervise people, and collaborate on marketing projects." Focus on what you offer the company, rather than on what you want from them.

When developing your resume home page, remember the following guidelines:

- Provide concise information about how, when, and where potential employers can contact you.

- Make browsing inviting—that is, minimize download time, provide links in a useful location, and provide informative link names.

- Be sure your home page portrays the image you want to present. Use colors and layout that express your professionalism and personality and align with those used by your target market. See Chapters 3, 10, and 14 for information about applying formatting effectively.

- Be sure that users can easily link to other pages from the home page. If you provide a list of links, place the most important or most frequently accessed information at the top of it.

- Be sure the information at the end of links is complete. Never provide a link in a resume home page that goes to incomplete or unavailable information.

- Provide a link that goes to a full-length resume in addition to the Web resume that's divided into smaller pieces. That way, users can easily print your resume and have it on hand. (See "Publishing Your Resume in Other Formats" later in this chapter.)

- Include only original information, images, or files. Don't "borrow" materials from other sites and use them as your own. Doing so is illegal, not to mention unethical.

Developing Subsequent Resume Pages

Subsequent pages in the resume should reflect the topics that you announce in the home page. For example, if your home page announces categories such as work history, education, and references, develop a single XHTML document for each category.

When creating these subsequent pages, use the same background, fonts, and color scheme that appear on the home page. This unites pages into a cohesive unit and provides users with visual cues that the pages are part of your site.

See Chapter 14 for information about including theme-bearing elements throughout your Web site.

Here are a few tips to remember when developing subsequent pages:

- Include your contact information on *every* page.

- Provide navigation menus so users can access other main pages in the site easily and quickly.

- Be concise and clear. If you're tempted to go on to a second or third screen, move the less important information to a different page and provide a link to it.

Including a Letter of Introduction

Within your Web resume, you can include a link to a letter of introduction, which provides information that complements—not repeats—your resume. For example, your resume might indicate that you were a team leader on the AlphaDoowhichie project. The letter of introduction can supplement this information by telling users about your specific role in the project, discussing the project's success, or detailing how the company benefited from your performance. Letters of introduction give you the opportunity to highlight your successes and provide the details that aren't always appropriate in resumes.

Here are some guidelines about letters of introduction you might find useful:

- Make the application user-oriented—that is, not only give details about your successes, but also specify how these successes have prepared you to fill the position.

- Limit the letter to three or four paragraphs—long enough to highlight the main points, but not so long that you bore users.

- Provide your contact information.

Publishing Your Resume in Other Formats

Another option is to provide a link from your Web resume (probably from the home page) to your resume saved in other formats. Using Rich Text Format (RTF) and Adobe

Acrobat PDF files, you overcome some difficulties inherent in Web pages—the biggest being that you have no control over how your resume appears in your users' browsers or in printed form.

These files are not actually part of your XHTML document—you link to them just as you link to any other files. Instead of automatically appearing in a user's Web browser as XHTML documents do, the RTF or PDF documents are downloaded to the user's computer and are saved to the hard drive or loaded in an appropriate viewing program (a word processor for RTF files, Acrobat Reader for PDF files). These formats also give you more control over how your document looks when it's printed.

Your easiest and cheapest option is to provide a link to your resume saved as an RTF file. RTF is a fairly standard word-processing format that, in this context, allows your users to view your resume in the word processor of their choice. Most formatting remains intact in RTF documents, and you can create them from the Save As command of most word-processing programs.

A few drawbacks are associated with using an RTF document, however:

- Users must take an extra step to download the file and open it in a word processor.

- Conversion problems can occur in the downloading process.

- Users can easily alter an RTF file.

A better, but more expensive, option is providing a link to a PDF version of your resume. PDF (which is short for *Portable Document Format* and uses the .pdf file extension) is a technology designed to facilitate document sharing and remote printing—keeping all fonts and formatting intact and making it impossible to change the document. Think of it as putting a fax copy of your resume on the Web—users view the document you created, complete with the layout and formatting you specified.

A few drawbacks are also associated with using PDF files. You, the resume provider, have to purchase Adobe Acrobat or have another program available that can create PDF files. PDF files are large, meaning that they take a while to download. Also, users must have an Acrobat reader or download and install one before they can view your resume.

Check out Adobe Acrobat at www.adobe.com *for more information about Acrobat and purchasing information.*

Incorporating Your Web Resume into an Existing Personal Site

If you're developing a Web resume as part of your personal site, consider that the personal site itself becomes part of the resume. In this case, a potential employer might visit your personal pages plus the resume-related pages.

Because of this, we recommend that you take some precautions:

- Make the personal pages as professional as possible.

- Store any potentially offensive documents in a subfolder without links to it. Send the complete URL to this subfolder only to the people you want to be able to see it.

- Use the `robots.txt` file to keep spiders and robots out of your personal stuff, as discussed in "Publicizing Your Site" earlier in this chapter.

- Consider password-protecting your personal pages. Anything from church activities, to hunting, to humor in arguably poor taste could offend some potential employers.

Submitting Your Resume Online

In addition to posting your resume on your own Web site, consider submitting your resume online. A multitude of employment Web sites is now available. These sites offer a variety of services including job listings, career counseling, and often including online services such as tutorials and classes to increase your marketable skills. Most of these sites allow you to post your resume at no charge. Some allow you to post a text document version of your resume, but more often, they have their own forms for you to fill out online with details of your employment history, job skills, training, and education.

Check out several of these sites to see which one is best for the type of work you're looking for. A good place to start is `www.monster.com`, one of the largest online job sites. At this site, you can create up to five different online resumes with cover letters. In addition, an automatic job search service will e-mail you when a job listing matches your criteria. This site currently has 450,000 job postings and includes international listings.

Other well-known employment Web sites are `www.guru.com`, which includes job listings in media, marketing, management, information technology, and multiple types of Web-related employment, and `www.dice.com`, which specializes in job listings and online resumes for information technology jobs. Most employment sites cover both employee positions and contract or freelance work, but there are also sites that specialize in freelance jobs, such as `www.elance.com`. Do a search for **jobs** or **employment** using your favorite search engine to find additional Web sites with job listings and online resume services.

Self-Publishing Information

You might also develop a personal site to *self-publish* information you've researched or developed. For example, you might publish genealogical information, your in-progress soon-to-be-a-hit novel, short stories, class projects, research papers, recommendations, or advice. Whatever the topic, you can self-publish on the Web easily and inexpensively, which is the main reason self-publishing has become so popular.

However, before you self-publish, consider some of the downsides. First, most discerning readers are skeptical about the quality and reliability of self-published information, and your information may be perceived as unworthy. Assure users that the information you provide is reliable, researched, reviewed, or cross-referenced to other sources that support your claims. For example, include a bibliography, a works-cited list, or a list of experts with whom you consulted. Also, consider providing links to other information on the Web that supports your claims.

Second, Web surfers, whether they realize it or not, tend to take self-published information and use it as their own. Most folks don't realize that they're "stealing" your information; self-published information that lacks an official (and highly visible) copyright or statement of ownership appears available for public use. To ensure that your information stays yours, always provide a copyright statement or state that the information is available for reference, but not to be taken and subsumed into other people's work.

Finally, don't publish information that's been published elsewhere—in magazines, journals, newspapers, and so on—without obtaining prior permission. For example, if you're a Dilbert fan and you want to put your 10 favorite Dilbert cartoons on your Web page, remember that someone else holds the copyright to those cartoons. Contact the owners of the Web site and request their permission to use their material. Although most people who publish on the Web (or post information to the Internet on newsgroups or in other forums) don't have lawyers watching for copyright infringements, it's still wrong to take other people's material.

If you're publishing information about people, be sure that they want information published about them.

Has Information Been Taken from Your Site?

If you publish on the Web and you want to find out whether users have taken information and used it as their own, you can. Simply visit AltaVista, HotBot, or another full-text search engine and do the following:

- Search for keywords that appear in your documents.
- Search for unique phrases.

- Search for typing or spelling errors that you find in your pages. For example, a search for **accomodates your needs** will get poor spellers as well as anyone who copied the misspelled text directly.

There's also a great Web site available that searches previously published works for you. It's called Digital Integrity and can be found at www.findsame.com.

When users access self-published research documents, their intent is usually to gather information so they can learn from it or apply it to their own projects. Users might actually read the information from start to finish, or they might print it.

For these reasons, consider presenting the information as one long page, rather than as sections in separate, shorter documents with links between and among them. One long document is easier to read and to print.

Also, because these documents tend to be more than a screen or two, provide multiple navigation menus throughout the document, as shown in Figure 15.4. Place menus at the top and bottom of documents as well as throughout the body.

Figure 15.4 *Placing navigation menus within long documents helps users wade through information.*

Developing Intranet Sites

Intranet sites are enterprise-wide Web sites accessible only by people within an organization. Intranets came about as a result of the need for improved corporate communications. As companies expand geographically, they face the challenges of providing company-wide information quickly and inexpensively—a feat not possible using traditional communication methods such as mailings, memorandums, faxes, or bulletin boards. Using an intranet, however, companies make information immediately accessible to all employees, regardless of their geographic location, and eliminate or significantly reduce the need for other forms of communication.

Although individuals or small groups generally develop and maintain public sites, employees often contribute content for intranets. For example, the information services department might actually run the intranet, but one or more employees in each department within an organization might assume responsibility for providing and updating pages pertaining to that department.

The result can be a hodgepodge of information that doesn't generally fit into a coherent information resource. Your goal as an information coordinator—whether you're the company owner, the head of information services, or the person who also develops and maintains the company's public site—is to ensure that the intranet is a valuable, uniform, usable information resource.

In the following sections, we'll look at how to coordinate content from contributors, suggest some ways that you can put out the word about what's new or updated on your intranet, and introduce intranet discussion groups. The "you" in these sections is the content coordinator for an intranet, and the "users" are employees or members of an organization that uses an intranet.

Determining Intranet Content

Intranets provide substantial, company-specific information that helps employees do their jobs, automates processes, and offers updates or news. If your intranet is part of a corporate environment, a good starting point for content is the human resources department, where you're likely to find company policy manuals, training schedules, safety guidelines, evacuation plans, and much more.

You can also use an intranet to publish product or service descriptions. For example, when you place boilerplate (standardized) information about your products and services on your intranet, users can easily access it and use it in marketing materials, documentation, or whatever.

You might also publish information that's not pertinent to employees' jobs, but that employees would find useful:

- The cafeteria menu

- The company newsletter

- New contract announcements

- Annual budgets

- Company and retirement-fund stock quotes

And if your intranet is connected to the Internet, you can also include links to industry news or to sister-company Web sites.

Your next step is to talk with employees about the information that they provide, distribute, and update to other groups within the company and about the information that they need and might (or might not) get from other departments. Ask about the following:

- Forms

- Reports

- Budgets

- Schedules

- Guidelines

- Procedures

- Policies

- Legacy documents

You can probably obtain some of this information using existing materials such as human resources handbooks, marketing brochures, and company white papers.

Accommodating User Needs

Intranet site users generally have one thing in mind: They're looking for information necessary to do their jobs. They might, for example, use the information to write a report, develop marketing materials, plan their schedules, and so on. For this reason, make absolutely certain that the information you provide is accurate and timely.

Users also expect you to provide accessible information—information they can find consistently from day to day. As a starting point, develop the overall site organization, taking into account all categories of information you will provide. Be sure to leave room for growth—adding new categories and expanding existing categories. For example, in developing a navigation menu, include all the categories of information that you'll eventually need. If you end up including links that don't yet have content, provide a statement about the information coming soon, or better yet, specify a date when you'll provide the information. You can also include contact information for people who can answer questions in the interim.

Finally, users don't usually expect an intranet site to be flashy. After all, they're accessing the site because they need information, not because they expect to be dazzled. Plan a site design that is visually appealing, but don't go overboard with sounds, colors, and other special effects. Consider including your company's logo and using its color scheme, but beyond that, think functional, not fancy.

Helping Others Contribute

As you saw in the previous sections, intranets are not usually the work of one person. Although you may be in charge of developing the site, others will actually provide and update the content. And not all contributors will have the same XHTML proficiency; some will be novices, others will be experts. Striking a balance between consistency and creativity can be challenging. Here are some ideas that may help.

Provide Templates and Examples

If you maintain a consistent look and feel, your intranet will appear more established and polished than it actually is. Relying on information providers to care as much as you do about a consistent appearance is likely too much to hope for, so make it easy for them: Provide templates.

Templates include all the structure elements and other elements that set up the general document format. You can provide templates for departmental home pages, for contact information, for current projects, or for any other pages that are common to several departments. You might also provide references to company-specific graphics and symbols. Using a template complete with these items, contributors can copy and paste the code into their documents and fill in the specific content. Listing 15.1 and Figure 15.5 show a sample template and the resulting document format. Note that you don't see any text formatting in this template because it would be supplied in a separate CSS style sheet.

LISTING 15.1: PROVIDING A TEMPLATE FOR INTRANET CONTENT

```
<!DOCTYPE html PUBLIC "-//W3C/DTD XHTML 1.0 Transitional//EN"
    "http://www.w3.org/TR/xhtml1/DTD/xhtml1-transitional.dtd">
<html xmlns="http://www.w3.org/1999/xhtml">
<head>
    <title>ASR Intranet</title>
    <link rel="stylesheet" href="style.css" type="text/css" />
</head>
<body>
    <div align="center">
    <img src="asrintra.jpg" border="0" alt="ASR intranet logo" />
    </div>
<!--Don't change anything above this line except the title.-->

    <h1 align="center">Put Your Department Name Here</h1>
    <p>Provide content here.</p>
    <p>And here.</p>
    <p>And here.</p>
    <ul>
       <li>List links here.</li>
       <li>And here.</li>
       <li>And here.</li>
    </ul>
<!--Replace department@intranet.asroutfitters.com in the
    following lines with your own e-mail address.-->
    <p>Send all questions to
    <a href="mailto:department@intranet.asroutfitters.com">
       department@intranet.asroutfitters.com</a>.</p>

<!--Please do not change anything below this line. The following
    command applies the document footer with the navigational
    toolbar and related information.-->
<!-- #include virtual="/boilerplate/footer.htm" -->
</body>
</html>
```

If your company has standardized on Netscape Navigator or Internet Explorer 4 or later, consider providing style sheets to contributors. By supplying a style sheet, you help contributors concentrate on content and ensure a more consistent appearance throughout the site. (See Chapter 10 for more information about style sheets.)

Figure 15.5 *The same template viewed in a browser, before being customized for specific departmental use*

Providing Access to Images

An alternative to referencing image files is to store them in a folder that contributors can access. The easiest way is to put them all in a folder immediately off the server root, such as /graphics, and provide copy-and-paste text, like that at the top of the following page.

```
<img src="/graphics/corplogo.gif" alt="ASR Corporate Logo"
    align="left" height="100" width="250" />
```

Moving further into the copy-and-paste realm, you can also include copy-and-paste snippets of code to automatically include document headers and footers by using *server-side includes,* such as:

```
<!--#include virtual="/includes/header.htm"-->
```

You provide the header, including anything that belongs at the top of the document such as the corporate logo, copyright, confidentiality information, and anything else your company requires. The contributor includes the single line in the document, and, when it appears on the Web, all the header information appears in place of the `include` element. Check the Web server documentation for more information about using server-side includes.

Publish Instructions and Guidelines

Publish—on the intranet, of course—instructions and guidelines for providing information on the intranet:

- Documentation for publishing information
- Acceptable versions of XHTML (XHTML 1.0, tables, frames, or whatever)
- Formats for organizing and structuring the information
- Tools (and where to get them)
- Documentation for using tools
- XHTML resources (this book, right?)
- Acceptable enhancements—images, applets, JavaScript, and so on

Also, specify that contributors include their contact information on each page so that content questions will go to them, not you. Make it clear that the "contact the Webmaster" links are only for users having technical difficulties. Contributors need to give users a way to contact them—during and after hours.

Provide Conversion Services

Offer to convert existing documents to intranet pages. Most departments have pages of information that could easily be converted to XHTML.

If you offer this service, you could be overwhelmed with documents to convert. We strongly recommend providing one-time conversion services to help departments get material out on the intranet, but rather than assuming the responsibility for ongoing document conversion, take the time to train the contributors thoroughly so departments can support themselves.

Remind Contributors as Necessary

Most content providers contribute information to the intranet in addition to their regular duties. You can help them manage their sections of the intranet by sending them e-mail reminders. Include information about how frequently users access their information, which information is not accessed, and so on—information that you (or the system administrator) can get from the access logs. If users aren't accessing certain pages, help find out why. Is the information outdated, hard to find, not needed? With this information, you can help weed out information that isn't being used and make room for more.

Automating Processes

If you have programming resources available, consider automating some of the processes discussed in this chapter. For example, you can automatically:

- Generate "What's New" lists.

- Remind content providers of pages that haven't been updated in a specific amount of time.

- Consolidate and summarize access logs, changes to pages, and new sections for reports to management.

- Check incoming documents for compliance with corporate style, the correct version of XHTML, and functional links.

For more information, consult with your system administrator or internal programmers.

Announcing New or Updated Information

Users value new information, so be sure to notify them when the site is updated, and do so consistently. Even if users don't immediately need the information, making them aware that it's available might save them time later. Here are some ways to do so:

- Develop a What's New template that departments can use to feature new or updated information.

- Create New and Updated icons that contributors can include on their pages.

- E-mail employees regularly—say, weekly—and tell them what's new and updated.

- E-mail managers regularly about new and updated information, and request that they pass along the information to their employees.

Setting Up a Discussion Forum

In a real-time discussion forum, users can interact, regardless of time zones or schedules, using the intranet as the communication medium. For example, users can hold informal meetings, chat about projects, or even get live feedback about a document draft—all from their offices at their convenience.

You can choose from several forum options, based on the software you implement. For example, you can use one of the script archives mentioned earlier in this chapter and adapt discussion forums from the scripts. Your ISP or Web hosting service may also offer a discussion-forum package.

If you choose a more advanced software package, such as Ceilidh (pronounced kay-lee, available at www.lilikoi.com), users can post XHTML documents and request that other people edit and comment—right there online. The result is that users can open forums to large groups and get immediate feedback. Other users can monitor discussions for developments or news pertaining to their projects. By conducting meetings online through an intranet, companies move toward a newer, more open approach to communication.

When using scripts and server-side programs, you may need assistance from your system administrator to implement and debug them. Documentation, when available, is included with the scripts or embedded in the code.

Where to Go from Here

Armed with the information in this chapter, you have a running start on developing public, personal, or intranet sites. In fact, you'll likely be one step ahead of the Joneses if you follow the guidelines we provided.

From here, you can follow up with a visit to several chapters:

- See Chapter 13 for more information about the XHTML document development process, which applies to public, personal, and intranet sites.

- See Chapter 14 for tips and advice that apply to all Web sites.

- Check out Chapter 16 if you're interested in more information about servers.

- Visit Chapters 3 and 10 for information about applying formatting wisely.

Publishing Your XHTML Documents

Chapter 16

S o far in this book, you've learned what XHTML documents are, what they look like, and why you'd use them (not to mention much more). And, if you've been doing the examples, you've also created a few documents of your own. To this point, you've been developing and viewing the XHTML documents on your local computer. However, for other people to use and enjoy them, you must *publish* your XHTML documents.

In this chapter, we'll show you options for publishing your documents, and we'll walk you through the publishing process.

This chapter covers the following topics:

- Finding out where you can publish your XHTML documents

- Uploading XHTML documents to a Web server

Places to Publish

When you publish your XHTML documents, all you're doing is putting a copy of the documents on a server so the documents can be available on the Internet. Your XHTML documents are stored on the server and made available to Web site users (or, actually, the computers) that request them. Your users tell the server what to get (by accessing a Web site), and the server displays the requested pages.

In general, you can publish your XHTML documents in three different ways:

- Your Internet service provider (ISP)

- Your corporate IS department

- Your own server

Publishing through Your ISP

One of the most common places to publish XHTML documents is on Web space provided by an Internet service provider (ISP). ISPs usually provide a slew of Internet-related services—including Web space—and help with your Web development needs. You can find out more about ISPs in your area by researching the following resources:

The Web   For a comprehensive list of ISPs, along with contact information and services, visit your favorite search engine and search for **ISP** and your geographic area; for example, search for **ISP TX** if you live in Texas. Also, check out www.isps .com and www.webisplist.com.

Your local paper or yellow pages   Often, you'll find ads for local ISPs in the Technology or Business section of your daily newspaper or in the Internet section of your local yellow pages.

Other people   Ask friends, neighbors, business associates, or folks at your local computer store about the services they use and their experiences. The quality, reliability, and service of both ISPs and Web-hosting services vary, so get all the advice and input you can before you commit.

Look for a guaranteed uptime figure, and always ask what you get if they fail to meet the guarantee. Then, after you find an ISP that appears to suit your needs, start by signing a short contract—say, no longer than six months—until you know that the service is satisfactory.

ISPs often provide a range of services, and you'll need to do some research to find out about them, as well as about start-up and monthly costs. In general, though, most ISPs offer either individual or business accounts.

Finding a Web-Hosting Service

Another option—one that's not quite an ISP, but similar—is a Web-hosting service. A Web-hosting service does not provide dial-up Internet access but simply provides a home from which you can serve your sites.

Generally, you use Web-hosting services in conjunction with an ISP, thus combining the best Web-hosting deal with reliable dial-up access. Although it's possible that a single company could meet all your needs, shopping for these services separately can be useful. For a fairly comprehensive list of Web-hosting services, check out this long but excellent URL:

```
http://dir.yahoo.com/Business_and_Economy/Business_to_Business/
Communications_and_Networking/Internet_and_World_Wide_Web/Network
_Service_Providers/Hosting/Web_Site_Hosting/Directories/
```

Alternatively, follow these steps in Yahoo! to find the Web-hosting information: Go to Home ➜ Business And Economy ➜ Business To Business ➜ Communications And Networking ➜ Internet And World Wide Web ➜ Network Service Providers ➜ Hosting ➜ Web Site Hosting. (Note that the Web changes frequently, so these steps may not be identical by the time you read this book.)

About ISP Individual Accounts

Generally, ISPs provide individual subscribers—as opposed to business subscribers—with access to the Internet, to e-mail, and to a relatively small amount of space on a Web server. Many ISPs also provide other services such as sending you the results of a form via e-mail. Exactly which services you'll need depends on what you want to do with your XHTML pages. For example, if you plan to create and publish simple XHTML documents, you may only need a little bit of Web space. On the other hand, if you plan to create an enormous Web site, one loaded with multimedia and downloadable files, or an e-commerce site, you'll need more space. If you plan to include forms or use server-specific capabilities, you may need some server access or specific programs. Therefore, when choosing an ISP account, figure out what types of XHTML pages you'll be serving, and then find an ISP that can meet your needs.

In addition to finding out what general services an ISP provides, you may also want to ask these questions, depending on your needs:

What kind of server is it, and what platform does the server run on? If you know the server and the platform, you can find the documentation on the Web, which should tell you which scripts you can easily add. For example, if an Apache server is running on a Sun SPARCstation (a likely ISP scenario), you can reasonably request that your server administrator install specific Perl scripts. However, if you're on an intranet with a Windows NT–based Netscape server and you hear of a cool enhancement to the WebStar server on a Macintosh, you can save yourself some embarrassment and just not ask for it.

Can I restrict access to my pages? When testing pages on the server, you don't want the whole world to see them—setting password-restricted access to the whole site helps with this. Additionally, if you have some pages that you want to make available to only a few people (or to everyone except a few people), you need to be able to set passwords and ideally do that with little hassle and without wasting time.

Be careful about publishing pages on the Internet. Even if you don't provide links to a page or publish a page's URL, people may still come across it. Additionally, search engines can also index such pages, making them available.

Can I install and run my own scripts? If you can, you'll have a lot more flexibility and capabilities than you would otherwise. If you're limited to what your ISP has already installed for your use, you're likely to have access to certain limited special capabilities, such as chat rooms, but not the flexibility to go with what you really want.

Do you maintain access logs? How can I find out how many hits my site gets? If you're selling services, promoting your company, or doing anything else that involves a significant number of people seeing your message, you'll need to be sure that accesses are logged, and you'll need to learn how to get to those logs.

Ask your server administrator what kinds of tools are available to view and sort Web server access logs—the "raw" (unprocessed) logs are an ugly mess, but lots of neat programs exist to parse the logs into something useful. Although your server administrator might have some of these programs installed, the access instructions may not be publicized.

Who do I call if the server fails to respond at 2 P.M.? How about 2 A.M.? Does the ISP make backups, or do you need to back up your own site? Under what circumstances will the ISP restore backup files—only if the server crashes or also if you make a mistake and delete your files?

You might also ask these questions if you're thinking about an ISP business account or publishing on a corporate server.

About ISP Business Accounts

If you're running a business and using the Internet (or if you're moving in that direction), consider getting a business account with an ISP. Business accounts, although somewhat more expensive than individual accounts, usually include more Web space, better access to server-side programs, and more comprehensive services, with guaranteed uptime, backups, and more attention to individual needs.

Many ISPs require a business account to have its own *domain name*, which replaces the ISP's name in the URL. For example, instead of our business's URL being:

```
www.example.com/~lanw/index.html
```

(which includes the ISP name and a folder designated for us), it simply reads:

```
www.lanw.com
```

Having your own domain name enhances your professional appearance and can help make your business appear bigger than it really is.

Having your own domain name also offers a few practical advantages. First, you can keep a consistent address even if you move or change ISPs. Users (who may be your customers or potential customers) will always be able to find you because your address remains constant.

Second, you can easily expand your Web site as your needs grow. If you start by having your service provider host your domain (called a *virtual domain*), you can easily expand your capacity or add services, without changing your address or revising your advertising materials.

Virtual Domains

As an information provider, you're not limited to using the server name as the hostname portion of your URL. Instead, you can use a virtual domain, which gives you a hostname of your own, but your files still reside on a host computer. Virtual domains are a very popular way for small companies and organizations to look bigger than they really are.

For example, if you put your files on a server called `example.com`, your Web address might look something like the following:

```
http://www.example.com/~accountname/filename.html
```

In this example, the address includes the protocol indicator, a special folder on the server (indicated by the tilde [~]), an account name, and a filename.

A virtual domain changes the address to eliminate the special folder and account name and replaces these with a new host (domain) name. For example, a Web address using a virtual domain might look like this:

```
http://www.accountname.com/filename.html
```

This example includes the protocol indicator, the domain name (`www.accountname.com`), and the filename (`filename.html`).

The easiest way to get a virtual domain is to ask your ISP to set it up for you. You may pay in the neighborhood of $50 to $100 for setup, plus a $70 fee for registering your domain name for two years with one of the official Internet domain-name registrars. If you do a little homework with your ISP, however, you can set up a virtual domain yourself and save a few dollars. You can find a list of accredited registrars at

```
www.icann.org/registrars/accredited-list.html
```

Finally, using a domain name helps establish your identity. Each domain name is unique and can include the business name itself or other names. For example, our business name is LANWrights, Inc., and our domain name is `www.lanw.com`. We probably could have extended the domain name to `www.lanwrightsinc.com` (or something to that effect) but we went with the shorter version. But beware: If you don't claim your domain name fast, someone else will.

If you have a company name under which you operate, get a domain name immediately, even if you're not likely to use it in the near future. Most of the most popular names are already taken. If you have a small business and aren't incorporated or are just thinking of incorporating, consider getting the domain name first and then incorporating under that name. It seems a little backward, but a domain name must be unique, and competition for good names is stiff. After you obtain your domain name, take care of registering to do business under that name.

Let's look at an example. Suppose your business's name is Laura's Toys and More. You look up www.laurastoysandmore.com and the domain name is already taken. You can try several variations, such as www.laurastoysnmore.com or www.laurastoystore.com, until you find one that is not taken.

At the time of writing, "registrar" companies such as Network Solutions or Inter-Access handle most registration for .com, .org, and .net names. However, you can also access a list of accredited domain registrars at the Internet Corporation for Assigned Names and Numbers (ICANN) site at

```
www.icann.org/registrars/accredited-list.html
```

To register a domain name, follow this process:

1. Go to http://rs.internic.net/whois.html. (InterNIC is the official body that supervises Internet naming; this is their "lookup" page.)

2. Enter your prospective domain name in the query field, and press Enter. If you're lucky, you'll see a No Match message, which means that your domain name is available. If you're less fortunate, you'll see the InterNIC records for whoever owns the name you entered. If you want, you can contact them and see if they want to sell it or give it to you, but you're likely to have more success if you simply look for another name.

3. Either register the name or ask your ISP to do it for you. Most ISPs will register domain names for free if they'll be hosting them, or they charge a reasonable ($100 or less) fee for the service, plus hosting charges. If your ISP attempts to charge significantly more than $100, you might consider either doing it yourself or finding another ISP.

If you really want to do it yourself, all the information and instructions you'll need are available at the InterNIC site, although you'll need to get a little information and cooperation from your ISP to fill out all the forms correctly.

Publishing through a Corporate Server

Another place you might publish your XHTML documents is on a corporate server—at your place of employment, most likely. If you work for a large company or an educational institution or if you work with an organization that handles system administration tasks, you'll probably have little to do when it comes to accessing a Web server. All the necessary pieces—access, administration, and security—are likely to be in place, and you'll simply step in and start using the server. This situation can be either the ideal or the worst possible case, depending on the group that actually runs the Web server.

The level of access and control you have on a corporate server varies from company to company. In the ideal situation, someone else takes care of running the server but lets you do anything you want, within reason. You get help setting up and running server-side programs and can essentially do anything you need to provide information. At the other extreme, you must adhere to a rigid process to submit information to the intranet. You'll submit XHTML documents and then have little control over where they're placed or how they're linked.

In all likelihood, your company will be somewhere in the middle, with an established procedure for accessing the corporate intranet but a substantial amount of freedom to do what you need to do. If not, or if the process of providing content is tightly controlled, you may want to see about running your own server. In any event, you'll need to find out how to contact the server administrators, get emergency contact numbers, find out about the corporate intranet policies, and go from there.

Publishing through Your Own Server

Finally, you might choose to publish your XHTML documents on your own server. If you have the technical savvy and existing infrastructure, running your own server affords you the most flexibility and best range of resources. One good reason to run your own server is that it's a more authentic environment for developing and testing pages. For example, if you have server-relative URLs in links, they'll work properly if you're loading the files from a server, but not if you're loading the same file locally. (See Chapter 4 for more about links and server-relative URLs.)

Particularly in a corporate or educational environment, where a network infrastructure exists, installing and running a server is straightforward. To run a public server, whether at home or at work, you'll need a dedicated network connection—anything from a full-time ISDN line from your ISP to a direct connection will work. If you're just setting up a local server for your own testing purposes, you can even run the server on a stand-alone machine.

If you plan to host your own server, you should follow a couple basic suggestions. We suggest that you have a dedicated Web server with as few applications as possible on it. That will free up the computer for simply hosting the Web pages. You should also have a continuous, high-speed Internet connection.

If you're considering running your own server, here are some issues to consider:

Security Web servers do present a security risk, although not a huge one. Letting other people access files on your computer, through any means, is inherently a little iffy. On an intranet, assuming you don't have highly confidential material on the server machine, you should be fine.

Uptime and access   If you're going to set up and publicize a server, you must ensure that it stays up and available all the time. If you don't have a continuous Internet connection, you shouldn't host your own public Web server.

Time   Running a Web server takes some time. If all you're doing is serving pages, it doesn't take much, but expect a certain investment. If you'll be generating pages from a database or installing and running other add-in programs, it'll take more time, both to keep the server going and to monitor security issues.

Capacity   If your Web server provides only plain XHTML documents and a few graphics to others on an intranet or if it's just for testing purposes, almost any computer will do. If you expect heavy traffic or lots of access, however, be sure that the computer you use can handle the load or can easily be upgraded. If you choose a Windows operating system to host your pages, you'll need about 256 MB of RAM and 8 GB of hard disk space. For a Linux server, you could probably get away with 128 MB of RAM and 4 GB of hard disk space.

Backups   If you're running your own server, you're responsible for backups. If the hard disk on your server suddenly stops working, will you be in a position to restore everything and get it all back up?

Learning More About Running Your Own Server

Installing, configuring, and running a server is beyond the scope of this book; however, if you'd like more information, you can visit the following Web sites:

www.microsoft.com   At this site, you can learn about the latest Microsoft Web server options. At the time of writing, Windows 2000 Server and Windows 2000 Professional ship with Internet Information Services (IIS) 5. Additionally, the Microsoft products also come with FrontPage, which is handy if you use that for Web development.

www.omnicron.ab.ca/httpd/   At this site, a feature-rich server called OmniHTTPd, in both a freeware and a shareware version, is available for Windows 95/98 and NT.

www.apache.org   At this site, you'll find Apache, the most popular Unix-based server software, although it's also available for other platforms, including Windows.

Finally, get the definitive server information at

http://serverwatch.internet.com/webservers.html

The Publishing Process

Before you get started, you'll need the following information:

The address of the HTTP server   For example, www.lanw.com. Depending on your situation, you may need to know the folder name from which your files will be accessed.

The address of the FTP server, if required   For example, ftp://ftp.lanw.com. Depending on how you get your files onto the server, you might have to use the File Transfer Protocol (FTP). Of course, it's also possible, particularly in a corporate or educational environment, that you would simply copy the files to a specific folder on a network drive, and that would be that.

Password and access restrictions   You need a user ID and password to upload files to the server.

Table 16.1 summarizes this information and provides space for you to include your specific information.

Table 16.1 Information You'll Need Before Using FTP

INFORMATION	EXAMPLE	YOUR INFORMATION
FTP server address	ftp.lanw.com	
User ID	jsmith	
Password	JB14mN	Don't write it down!
Folder on server to use	public_xhtml	

Passwords should always be something hard to guess, with a combination of lowercase and uppercase letters, and numbers. You shouldn't write your entire password down near your computer or save it on your computer. Another option is to break your password into two parts: something you know and something you write down.

Armed with this information, you're ready to *upload* your files to the server, which essentially just means to put a copy of your XHTML documents on the server. The process for uploading your documents to a server will be different for most servers and installations. It can be as easy as copying a file to a folder (on a corporate intranet) or as idiosyncratic as completing multiple page online forms and copying files to a folder (on intranets in Dilbert-esque companies—yes, we have examples). It can also be a straightforward process involving an FTP application (the common process on intranets and with ISPs).

The easiest way to upload files to a server is using the publishing tools included in many high-end HTML editing applications. These tools work well if all the files belong in one folder and if you're comfortable letting the programs "adjust" links as the files are uploaded.

*You'll notice that we don't mention **XHTML** publishing tools. It's too early (May 2001) for many applications to fully support XHTML, so you may still have to use HTML tools for a while. Check out the publishing tool that comes with Dreamweaver for a good example:* `www.macromedia.com/software/dreamweaver/`.

However, you'll likely use either an FTP program or your browser to upload your documents, as described next.

Uploading with FTP

FTP is the Internet standard tool for transferring files. Regardless of which FTP program you choose, you'll likely be dealing with the commands outlined in Table 16.2. As you'll see in the following two sections, you can use these commands when uploading with a text-based FTP program or a graphical FTP program.

Table 16.2 FTP Commands for Transferring Files

COMMAND	DESCRIPTION
ftp	Starts an FTP application.
open "…"	Opens an FTP connection to the server name specified.
close	Closes an FTP connection without exiting the FTP application.
quit	Closes an FTP connection and the application.
put	Uploads files to the server computer.
get	Downloads files from the server computer.
ascii	Sets the file type to ASCII, to upload XHTML or other text documents.
binary	Sets the file type to binary, to upload image or class files and other binary documents.
cd	Changes directory on the server. Follow cd with a folder name to change into that folder; follow cd with .. to move up out of the current folder.
pwd	Tells you what folder you're in (stands for *print working directory*).

Uploading Files with a Text-Based FTP Program

Before you get started, you'll need the information specified in Table 16.1, and you'll need your XHTML documents and related files at hand. Follow these steps:

1. At a text prompt (a DOS prompt or the Unix shell), switch to the folder that contains the files you want to upload. For example, if you are at a c: prompt and your files are in the TestWeb subfolder, type **cd testweb**.

2. Type **ftp** to start the FTP application.

3. At the FTP> prompt, type **open** and the address of the FTP server—for example,

   open ftp.lanw.com

4. When prompted, enter your user ID and then your password. Remember that these are case sensitive.

5. Change to the folder where you want to store the files. If you're uploading files to an ISP, your folder name will probably be public_html or www or something similar, such as cd public_html.

6. To upload XHTML documents, set the file type to ASCII. Type **ascii**.

7. Now, upload the documents with the put command. For example, type **put filename.htm**.

   If you have multiple files to upload, you can use the mput command and a wildcard. For example, to upload all files in the folder that have filenames ending with .htm, type **mput *.htm**.

8. To upload binary files (such as graphics), first set the file type to binary. Type **binary**.

9. Now, upload the documents with the put command. For example, type **put filename.htm**.

   If you have multiple files to upload, use the mput command and a wildcard. For example, to upload all files in the folder that have names ending with .gif, type **mput *.gif**.

10. When you're finished, type **quit** to leave the FTP application.

Now, open your Web browser and try to access the files you just uploaded. If you find broken image icons, odds are that you didn't specify binary before you uploaded the files (a common problem). Try again, being careful to specify binary.

If you used a WYSIWYG editor and your links do not work correctly, check out the raw XHTML code to verify that the links were not changed. Netscape Composer and Gold (Composer's predecessor) sometimes arbitrarily change links, causing them not to work.

Uploading Files with Graphical FTP Programs

An arguably easier procedure is available if you have a graphical FTP application (such as WS-FTP for Windows, available from www.ipswitch.com) or Fetch (available from http://fetchsoftworks.com). The specific procedure depends on the software, but generally resembles the following. Before you start, have at hand the same information you gathered for the text-based FTP application.

Use the following procedure to upload files with WS-FTP, a Windows application:

1. Start the application, probably by double-clicking its icon.

2. Choose File → New Site. Enter a name for the site and the host name or IP address.

3. Click Finish.

4. In the main WS-FTP window, fill in the username and password of the site and then click Save to save this info. Check the Save Password checkbox if you want the application to remember your password for you. Leave the other fields blank unless your system administrator gave you that information.

Both user ID and password are case sensitive—if you substitute uppercase for lowercase or vice versa, access will be denied.

3. Click Connect. You'll see a connecting message as your FTP client connects to the FTP server.

4. Select the appropriate local folder on the left side of the window and the appropriate remote folder on the right side of the window. You select folders by double-clicking them or by selecting them and clicking the ChgDir button.

5. When you have the correct folders open on both sides, check the Auto check box to specify how the computers exchange files. Automatic is usually fine. XHTML files transfer as ASCII (because they're plain text), and images transfer as binary (because they're binary, not text, files). If you try automatic and uploaded files don't work properly, set the transfer manually to binary for graphics and to ASCII for XHTML and other text documents.

If you can't open and read the file in Notepad, SimpleText, or vi, it's not a text file. You must transfer all word-processed documents, spreadsheets, and multimedia files as binary.

6. Select the files to transfer, and then click either the arrow (pointing from your local drive to the server drive) or the Copy button.

That's all there is to it. Now, test all your uploaded files.

Uploading with HTTP

Some automatic publishing tools offer the option of uploading via HTTP instead of FTP. However, relatively few ISPs support HTTP uploads because of security considerations.

The primary difference is that with HTTP, you need provide only the Web address at which your files should end up, rather than the FTP server address.

For you, the Web developer, there's no real benefit to either approach as long as the files transfer correctly.

Uploading with Other Tools

In addition to using an FTP program to upload your documents, you can also upload them through your browser or through specialized tools that come with various HTML software. Dreamweaver has an excellent site management tool, illustrated in Figure 16.1. The remote site appears on the left, and the local folders are on the right. This utility works much like an FTP utility and is very convenient. You can develop your pages and upload them to your server, all from the same interface.

If you use a fairly recent version of the Navigator browser, you can upload files by entering **ftp://yourid@yourftpserver.com/** in the Location line. You'll be prompted for your password. The only drawback to this approach is that you must be familiar with the structure of the files on the server. After you browse to the correct folder, choose File ➔ Upload File to select the file to upload (you can upload only one file at a time).

If you upload through your browser, take a second to bookmark that long URL location of your files so you won't have to browse to it again.

Figure 16.1 *The Dreamweaver site management tool*

Where to Go from Here

So, there you have it! You can publish your documents using an ISP, on a corporate network, or on your own server just by transferring a copy of the documents from your computer to a server. By doing so, you make your documents accessible to other people, either at your company or on the Internet.

From here, you have lots of options. Here are a few suggestions:

- Head to Chapter 5 to learn how to include images—and how to do so wisely.

- Visit Chapter 6 to learn how to develop and include tables.

- See Chapter 7 to learn how to include forms (remember, you'll need to get the server to process the form for you!).

- Check out Chapter 8 to learn how to use frames.

- Visit Chapter 15 for more information about public, personal, and intranet sites.

Part V
Applying XHTML to Advanced Applications

In This Part

Bringing Pages to Life with Dynamic XHTML

Chapter 17

When you develop a Web page using dynamic XHTML, your users can view new content without reloading the page, change screen colors with a mouse click, and view animations without installing a plug-in. Dynamic XHTML uses style sheets and scripting (such as JavaScript) in tandem with a browser's Document Object Model (DOM) to produce dynamic effects. Only browsers that support style sheets and scripting can support dynamic XHTML.

In addition, you implement dynamic XHTML one way if you're developing for Microsoft Internet Explorer and another way if you're developing for Netscape Navigator. For example, Internet Explorer users may encounter errors or see nothing at all if they open a page designed for Netscape Navigator. Therefore, taking advantage of the latest and greatest can be disadvantageous if the new feature is not designed for your users' browsers. The recent introduction of standards-compliant versions of browsers, such as Netscape Navigator 6 and Internet Explorer 6 (in preview release at the time of this writing), should make it easier to write dynamic XHTML cross-platform and cross-browser code.

If you're developing for newer browsers and you want to include dynamic effects on your pages, you'll want to know about and use dynamic XHTML. In this chapter, we introduce you to dynamic XHTML, look at some of the advantages and disadvantages associated with using it, and show you how to use it in your documents— for both Netscape Navigator and Internet Explorer. We'll then use dynamic XHTML to develop a practical application: collapsing pages.

This chapter covers the following topics:

- Understanding dynamic XHTML
- The Document Object Model
- Understanding Internet Explorer's implementation
- Understanding Netscape Navigator's implementation
- Using dynamic XHTML and DHTML to create collapsible pages
- Browser detection

What Is Dynamic XHTML?

Dynamic XHTML expands on standard XHTML by giving you the formatting control of style sheets combined with the interactive capabilities of scripting languages such as JavaScript. When you develop pages with dynamic XHTML, users spend far less time accessing information because it's available directly within the browser, rather than needing to be retrieved from the server.

You may see dynamic XHTML referred to as "DXHTML." But because there's no defined DXHTML language, we stick with calling it dynamic XHTML.

Dynamic HTML and dynamic XHTML are not languages; they're simply combinations of technologies.

For example, suppose you have a table of contents page. If you develop it with standard XHTML, users click an item; the browser then requests the document from the server and displays it when it arrives. If you develop the table of contents page with dynamic XHTML, however, the trip to the server is eliminated. Figures 17.1 and 17.2 show this process.

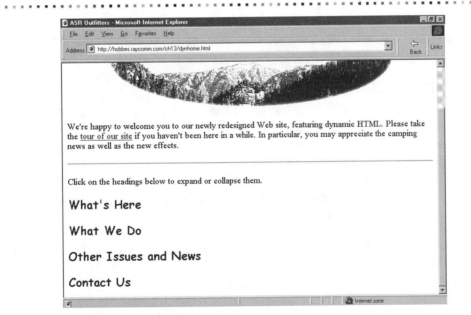

Figure 17.1 *Users can click items in the table of contents.*

Click on the headings below to expand or collapse them.

What's Here

Here's the latest information on the site.

- Camping News provides the latest comments from the trails.
- Check Weather offers weather updates from a variety of sources.
- Clubs gives local hiking and mountaineering clubs a place to provide information about their activities.
- Catalog presents our entire inventory, including announcements of the latest sales.
- Contact Us links to a page with a contact form, e-mail addresses, snail mail addresses, and phone numbers. If it isn't here, you can't find us.

What We Do

Other Issues and News

Contact Us

Figure 17.2 *After selecting an item, the user can view the expanded content.*

We show you how to create collapsible information in the section "Creating a Collapsible Document," later in this chapter.

Before you go sprinting off to add dynamic XHTML capabilities to your documents, you need to be familiar with style sheets and JavaScript. Within dynamic XHTML, style sheets tell browsers what elements should look like, and JavaScript functions change the properties set by style sheets, which is how page elements know to do something—for example, blink, change colors, and so on.

We recommend that you have a firm understanding of style sheets and JavaScript before starting this chapter. For a quick review, flip back to Chapters 10 and 11, respectively.

You might recall from Chapter 11 that you can use JavaScript's onmouseover event handler to change an image when a user moves the mouse over the image. Using the DOM, dynamic XHTML, and event handlers, you can do this with just about any page element. For example, you can change the color of text, increase the text size, or even make the text jump to a new location.

When you implement dynamic XHTML using the W3C's DOM, you use standard elements and attributes. As you'll see in the following section, this approach offers wider support along with better functionality, and it promises more in terms of long-range stability.

For more information on scripting languages in general, including JavaScript, JScript, VBScript, and ECMAScript, see the section "What Is JavaScript?" in Chapter 11.

The Document Object Model

The W3C's DOM is a key (although behind-the-scenes) component of dynamic XHTML. It specifies how individual objects within Web pages (such as images, headings, or other tagged information) should be available to scripts. In browsers that support the DOM, dynamic XHTML will be more flexible, more powerful, and far easier to implement than in other browsers. This is illustrated in this chapter.

Level 0 DOM and the Proprietary DOMs

The DOM is an Application Programming Interface (API) for HTML, XHTML, and XML documents. It provides any scripting or programming language with access to each part of a document (as long as you use the methods and properties of the recommendation). The DOM Level 1 specification became a W3C recommendation in October 1998. You can view the full text of the recommendation at www.w3.org/TR/1998/REC-DOM-Level-1-19981001/.

Understanding the DOM is key to using dynamic XHTML. The DOM is a model of how all the elements on an XHTML page are related to one another and to the document itself. Knowing these relationships allows you to access each of the elements (or groups of elements) and apply dynamic style changes to just that element (or group of elements) using JavaScript or other scripting and programming languages.

The easiest way to understand the DOM is by looking at an XHTML document as a tree structure. The highest level of the tree is the document itself, and all other elements on the page, including the body element, are classified as children of the document.

For example, let's look at a simple piece of code:

```
<html>
<body>
<h1>The document tree</h1>
<p>This is an example of a child element.</p>
<p>This is also a child element.</p>
```

This code can be illustrated as a tree:

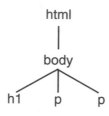

In this simple form of a document tree, html is the parent element. It has one child, body, and the first child element of html (body) also has three children (h1, p, and p).

The Level 0 DOM was developed by Netscape for use in Netscape Navigator 2 with the newly developed scripting language JavaScript. It allowed access only to forms and links. In Netscape 3, access to images was added. Internet Explorer 3 also added implementation of the Level 0 DOM; however, the implementation did not work the same as Netscape's implementation. Even at this point in browser development, cross-browser differences were an issue.

Netscape Navigator 4 and Internet Explorer 4 continued to support the Level 0 DOM, but both also added their own proprietary DOMs. The Netscape proprietary DOM is accessed using document.layers in the JavaScript code, and the Internet Explorer proprietary DOM is accessed using document.all in the JavaScript code. Browser-detection scripts can be used to determine which browser a user is using to access a site, and then his or her browser is directed to the correct version of the page for that browser. More details on browser detection are included at the end of this chapter, as well as a browser-detection script.

The site developer has two choices for scripting:

- Use a browser-detection script and create at least three versions of each page that includes dynamic features—a Netscape Navigator version, an Internet Explorer version, and a version for browsers that don't support style sheets and JavaScript.

- Write a complex script that includes the options for all three of these situations but implements them all from a single document.

Even with different versions of dynamic pages, the features supported by Netscape's DOM and Internet Explorer's DOM are not the same, so similar effects are not always possible in both browsers. We explore some features of each proprietary DOM in more depth in the following section, and then return to the Level 1 DOM and the new Level 6 browsers. According to statistics from www.thecounter.com, about 20 percent of the

Web audience currently uses Netscape 4.*x* or Internet Explorer 4.*x*, so it continues to be important to know how to use both of the proprietary DOMs.

For more details on the history of DOMs and browser development, see Peter-Paul Koch's excellent article, "The Document Object Model: An Introduction, at `www.digital-web.com/features/ feature_2001-5.shtml`.

Level 1 DOM and the Level 6 Browsers

The W3C DOM Level 1 was designed to provide access to every part of an XML document. Because HTML and XHTML documents can also be *parsed* (broken down into component parts) like an XML document, this DOM is also accessible to JavaScript and other scripting and programming languages.

The Level 1 DOM treats each object of the document as a *node*, and the corresponding tree diagram is based on nodes.

If we look at the code sample from the previous section again, we can make a new tree diagram based on nodes:

```
<body>
<h1>The document tree</h1>
<p>This is an example of a child element.</p>
<p>This is also a child element.</p>
```

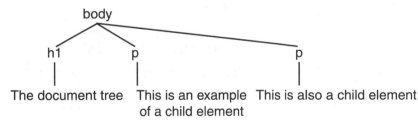

In this diagram, the parts break down as follows:

- body is an element node.
- h1 is an element node (and first child of html).
- The document tree is a text node, which is a child of h1.
- p is an element node (and child of html).

- `This is an example of a child element` is a text node.

- The second p is also an element node (and child of `html`).

- `This is also a child element` is a text node and child of the second p.

You'll use three main node types for scripting in XHTML: element nodes, text nodes, and attribute nodes. For example, if you add an `align` attribute to the second paragraph,

```
<p align="right">This is an example of a child element.</p>
```

`align` is an attribute node, and `right` is a child of this attribute node.

This node structure allows you to access any node individually by giving it an `id` and by using two very useful access methods: `getElementsByTagName` and `getElementById`. Through these methods and `id`, you can apply a style and/or a script to a particular node.

The Level 1 DOM is supported by Netscape 6, Internet Explorer 5, and Opera 4 and 5 (although Opera does not yet support all of the methods and properties of the Level 1 DOM).

Additional DOM Level 1 Information

Peter-Paul Koch's Web site offers several resources for more information on the Level 1 DOM:

- For more information on using the Level 1 DOM, see "Level 1 DOM - Introduction" at `www.xs4all.nl/~ppk/js/dom1.html`.

- For details on browser support and DOM, check out "Browsers" at `www.xs4all.nl/~ppk/js/browsers.html`.

- For a detailed chart of support for DOM properties and methods, see `www.xs4all.nl/~ppk/js/version5.html`.

Although Internet Explorer 5.*x* implements most of the Level 1 DOM, it also supports Internet Explorer's proprietary DOM. On the other hand, Netscape 6 supports the Level 1 DOM but does not offer support for Netscape's proprietary DOM. This means that scripts written for Netscape 4.*x* will not work in Netscape 6. Although you still need to use a browser-detection script for Level 4 browsers (if your audience includes users of these browsers) and separate scripts for Netscape 4.*x* and Netscape 6, the move toward standards compliance in the latest browsers offers the hope that eventually you'll have to create only one version of a Web page for all browsers and all platforms.

Internet Explorer 6 (in preview release at this time) takes a different approach to backward compatibility by making it dependent on the DTD used on your page. If you use an HTML 3.2 DTD, your pages will appear in Internet Explorer 6 as they did in Internet Explorer 4.*x* and 5.*x*. However, if you use the strict form of the HTML 4.0 DTD or XHTML DTD, it will use the Level 1 DOM when executing your scripts.

For more details on creating dynamic pages in Netscape Navigator 6 and Internet Explorer 6, check out the following resources:

- "Scripting for the 6.0 Browsers," by Scott Andrew LePera, at `www.scottandrew.com/index.php/articles/dom_1`.

- "Mozilla Document Object Model Information," by Dave Eisenberg, at `www.alistapart.com/stories/dom/article.html`.

- "IE 6 Switches to Standards," by Jeffrey Veen, at `http://hotwired.lycos.com/webmonkey/01/14/index0a.html?tw=authoring`.

Understanding Internet Explorer's Implementation

Dynamic XHTML in Internet Explorer exposes all page elements to scripting; that is, each page element can be manipulated—recolored, scrolled, jiggled, and so on. If you can specify what the element is, you can format it with style sheets and then change the style sheets using JavaScript. For example, you can identify a heading, specify in the style sheet that the heading is red, and then specify in the JavaScript that the red heading changes to green when a user passes the mouse pointer over the heading.

Internet Explorer 5.x offers implementation of most of the W3C DOM properties and includes backward compatibility for its proprietary DOM (`document.all`); therefore, scripts written for Internet Explorer 4.x will also work in Internet Explorer 5.x. Internet Explorer 5.x offers access to the DOM objects through scripting and also through Component Object Model (COM) interfaces.

If you haven't already done so, you might breeze through Chapters 10 and 11 before starting these examples. In particular, look closely at the `id` attribute description in Chapter 10 and check out the discussion of event handlers and functions in Chapter 11.

Let's take a look at the general process for adding dynamic XHTML capabilities to your XHTML documents using Internet Explorer's implementation:

1. Start with a functional XHTML document. The following code includes the XHTML structural elements and style sheet elements:

```
<!DOCTYPE html PUBLIC "-//W3C/DTD XHTML 1.0
   Transitional//EN"
   "http://www.w3.org/TR/xhtml1/DTD/
   xhtml1-transitional.dtd">
<html xmlns="http://www.w3.org/1999/xhtml">
<head>
  <title>Fix Colors</title>
  <style type="text/css">
<!--
   h1 {color : red}
-->
</style>
</head>
<body bgcolor="#ffffff" text="#000000" link="#0000ff"
   vlink="#800080" alink="#ff0000">
<h1>Need a Break?</h1>

<p>If you'd like to change the color of the heading above
from red to black for better contrast and easier reading,
just click once anywhere in this paragraph.</p>

<p>Click this paragraph to change it back.</p>
</body>
</html>
```

2. Add the id attribute for each instance that will be affected by a dynamic XHTML function. In this example, we'll change the heading color. Remember that id attributes must be unique in each instance.

```
<h1 id="firsthead">Need a Break?</h1>
```

3. Add the JavaScript event handlers. In this example, the event handlers each call a function—swapit() and revert()—to switch the color when a user clicks the text. Because Internet Explorer's dynamic XHTML technology exposes all elements to scripting and style sheets, you can add the event handlers directly to the p elements.

```
<h1 id="firsthead">Need a Break?</h1>
<p onclick="swapit()">
If you'd like to change the color of the heading above
from red to black for better contrast and easier reading,
just click once anywhere in this paragraph.</p>
<p onclick="revert()">
Click this paragraph to change it back.</p>
</body>
</html>
```

4. Add the JavaScript functions, which change the colors on command from the event handlers to the head section of the document (after the closing style element, for example). Each function specifies the color property of the first-head element (identified with the id attribute) and sets it to a specific color.

```
<script type="text/javascript" language="javascript">
<!--
function swapit() {document.all.firsthead.style.color=
    "000000"}
function revert() {document.all.firsthead.style.color=
    "FF0000"}
// -->
</script>
```

See the complete code in Listing 17.1.

LISTING 17.1: DYNAMIC COLOR CHANGES USING DYNAMIC XHTML IN INTERNET EXPLORER 4.x AND 5.x

```
<!DOCTYPE html PUBLIC "-//W3C/DTD XHTML 1.0 Transitional//EN"
    "http://www.w3.org/TR/xhtml1/DTD/xhtml1-transitional.dtd">
<html xmlns="http://www.w3.org/1999/xhtml">
<head>
  <title>Fix Colors</title>
  <style type="text/css">
<!--
   h1 {color :red }
-->
</style>
<script type="text/javascript" language="javascript">
<!--
function swapit() {document.all.firsthead.style.color="000000"}
```

```
function revert() {document.all.firsthead.style.color="ff0000"}
// -->
</script>
</head>
<body bgcolor="#ffffff" text="#000000" link="#0000ff"
    vlink="#800080" alink="#ff0000">
<h1 id="firsthead">Need a Break?</h1>
<p onclick="swapit()">
If you'd like to change the color of the heading above
from red to black for better contrast and easier reading,
just click once anywhere in this paragraph.</p>
<p onclick="revert()">
Click this paragraph to change it back.</p>
</body>
</html>
```

When writing functions, you need to specify exactly which characteristics of which page element (technically, which *object*) the function applies to, and you do this using the full object name (think of it as an address). For example, the address in Step 4 identifies the color property of the firsthead element in the document. The resulting heading in the sample document changes color when a user clicks the paragraphs. Table 17.1 shows you other sample addresses.

Table 17.1: Dynamic XHTML Sample Object and Property Identifiers

THIS SAMPLE ADDRESS	DOES THIS
document.body.style.color	Specifies the color property of the style of the body of the document.
document.all.firsthead.style.top	Specifies the top position property of the style for the specified id name; in this case, firsthead.
document.form(0).style.background	Specifies the background of the first form in the document.

Elements in arrays are numbered starting with 0, as in form(0) in Table 17.1. If your document has three form elements, the form array would include form(0), form(1), and form(2). The numbering is based on when the form element is specified in the document code; the first form is form(0), etc. The length of the array is 3 because there are three form elements.

Understanding Netscape Navigator's Implementation

Rather than using standard XHTML elements and attributes as Internet Explorer does, Netscape's version of DHTML introduced the layer element and special JavaScript style sheets. Because all page elements are not exposed to JavaScript functions, you have to apply the layer element to identify special sections and then apply a script to those sections. This solution does not seamlessly add or hide information.

 The proprietary Netscape elements, layer *and* ilayer, *are not part of the W3C XHTML 1.0 Recommendation. The following example is given to illustrate the difference in DHTML implementation between Netscape Navigator 4.x and Internet Explorer 4.x, but it's not possible to use this as a valid XHTML document. However, Netscape Navigator 6 implements the W3C Level 1 DOM and can be used for dynamic XHTML.*

For example, glance back at Figures 17.1 and 17.2, which show a collapsible table of contents—developed with Internet Explorer's implementation of XHTML. You'll notice that when the topics expand and collapse, they move up and down on the page, depending on how much space the expanded topic needs. However, the same page developed with Netscape's implementation of DHTML leaves space on the page for the expanded topic but doesn't hide that extra space when the topic is collapsed, as shown in Figure 17.3.

If your users use Netscape Navigator 4, you *can* do some useful and interesting things with the Netscape version of DHTML—including moving objects around on the page, using animations, or providing information just when users need it. Netscape's implementation in its 4.*x* browser version did not become widely accepted, simply because it was a move away from, not toward, standards compliance. However, Netscape 6 is standards compliant and implements the W3C Level 1 DOM. Both Netscape 6 and the W3C Level 1 DOM were covered earlier in this chapter.

Table 17.2 lists and describes a few of the Netscape-specific DHTML elements and attributes. See the Master's Reference Part 1 for some other Netscape-specific elements.

Table 17.2 Netscape-Specific Dynamic HTML Elements and Attributes

ITEM	TYPE	DESCRIPTION
layer	Element	Sets up a layer—a section of the document that can be addressed or manipulated.
ilayer	Element	Sets up an inline layer—a section of the document that reserves space for its content and can be addressed or manipulated.

Table 17.2 continued Netscape-Specific Dynamic HTML Elements and Attributes

name	Attribute of `layer` and `ilayer`	Provides an identifying label so the layers can be addressed by style sheets.
visibility	Attribute of `layer` and `ilayer`	Sets the layer to be either visible (`show`) or hidden (`hide`).

Figure 17.3 *A page developed with Netscape's implementation of DHTML doesn't hide the extra space.*

Compared with the rather simple steps that the Internet Explorer implementation of dynamic XHTML requires, the steps that Netscape's implementation requires are more complex. To show you how this works, we'll change the background color of the first document heading we worked with in the previous section. (Netscape's implementation of DHTML won't let you change just the heading color.)

1. Start with a functional HTML document. The following code includes the HTML structural elements and style sheet elements:

```
<!DOCTYPE HTML PUBLIC "-//W3C//DTD HTML 4.0//EN">
<html>
<head>
  <title>Fix Colors</title>
<style type="text/css">
<!--
   h1 {color : red}
-->
</style>
</head>

<body bgcolor="#ffffff" text="#000000" link="#0000ff"
   vlink="#800080" alink="#ff0000">
<h1>Need a Break?</h1>
<p>
If you'd like to change the background color of the heading
above for better contrast and easier reading, just click
here to change color.</p>
<p>
Just click here to change it back.</p>
</body>
</html>
```

2. Add the ilayer tags around the element you'll be changing.

```
<ilayer><h1>Need a Break?</h1></ilayer>
<p>
If you'd like to change the background color of the heading
above for better contrast and easier reading, just click
here to change color.</p>
<p>Just click here to change it back.</p>
</body>
</html>
```

3. Add a name attribute to the ilayer element. We'll call it firsthead.

```
<ilayer name="firsthead"><h1>Need a Break?</h1></ilayer>
<p>
If you'd like to change the background color of the heading
above for better contrast and easier reading, just click
here to change color.</p>
```

```
<p>
Just click here to change it back.</p>
</body>
</html>
```

4. Add event handlers to change the color and change it back. Because the elements are not individually addressable, you have to add a elements.

```
<ilayer name="firsthead"><h1>Need a Break?</h1></ilayer>
<p>If you'd like to change the background color of the
heading above for better contrast and easier reading, just
click <a href="javascript:swapit()">here</a> to change
color.</p>
<p>Just click <a href="javascript:revert()">here</a> to
change it back.</p>
</body>
</html>
```

5. Add the JavaScript functions (which the event handlers you just added refer to) that change the document.layers.firsthead.bgColor attribute (yes, it's case sensitive).

```
<head>
  <title>Fix Colors</title>
 <style type="text/css">
<!--
   h1 {color : red}
-->
</style>
<script type="text/javascript" language="javascript">
<!--
function swapit()
   { document.layers.firsthead.bgColor="yellow" ; }
function revert()
   { document.layers.firsthead.bgColor="white" ; }
// -->
</script>
</head>
```

The complete code is shown in Listing 17.2.

LISTING 17.2: DYNAMIC COLOR CHANGES USING DHTML IN NETSCAPE NAVIGATOR 4.*x*

```
<!DOCTYPE HTML PUBLIC "-//W3C//DTD HTML 4.0//EN">
<html>
<head>
  <title>Fix Colors</title>
<style type="text/css">
<!--
   h1 {color : red}
-->
</style>
<script type="text/javascript" language="javascript">
<!--
function swapit()
   { document.layers.firsthead.bgColor="yellow" ; }
function revert()
   { document.layers.firsthead.bgColor="white" ; }
// -->
</script>
</head>
<body bgcolor="#ffffff" text="#000000" link="#0000ff"
   vlink="#800080" alink="#ff0000">
<ilayer id="firsthead"><h1>Need a Break?</h1></ilayer>
<p>If you'd like to change the background color of the heading
above for better contrast and easier reading, just click
<a href="javascript:swapit()">here</a> to change color.</p>
<p>
Just click <a href="javascript:revert()">here</a> to change
   it back.</p>
</body>
</html>
```

When you try this document in Netscape Navigator 4, you'll see something similar to Figure 17.4.

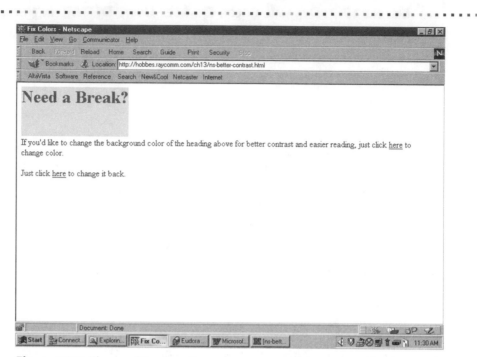

Figure 17.4 *The resulting heading now appears with a colored background.*

Creating a Collapsible Document

A useful dynamic XHTML capability is providing collapsible information, such as the table of contents you saw earlier. We chose this capability not only because it's handy, but also because it illustrates the differences in the Internet Explorer and Netscape Navigator implementations of dynamic XHTML.

Collapsing a Document the Internet Explorer Way

To create a collapsible document, similar to the document shown in Figure 17.1 earlier in this chapter, follow these steps:

1. Start with a basic XHTML document.

```
<!DOCTYPE html PUBLIC "-//W3C/DTD XHTML
   1.0 Transitional//EN"
   "http://www.w3.org/TR/xhtml1/DTD/
   xhtml1-transitional.dtd">
<html xmlns="http://www.w3.org/1999/xhtml">
<head>
<title>ASR Outfitters</title>
<style type="text/css">
<!--
body {font-size : 110%}
h1, h2, h3 {font-family : "Comic Sans MS"}
h1 {font-size : 180% ; font-weight : bold}
-->
</style>
</head>
<body>
<center>
<img src="asrlogo.gif" alt="ASR logo" />
</center>
<p>We're happy to welcome you to our newly redesigned Web
   site, featuring dynamic XHTML. Please take the
   <a href="tour.html">tour of our site</a> if you haven't
   been here in a while. In particular, you may appreciate
   the camping news as well as the new effects. </p>
<hr />
<p>Click on the headings below to expand or collapse
   them.</p>
<h2>What's Here</h2>
<p>Here's the latest information on the site.</p>
<ul>
<li>
<a href="camping.html">Camping News</a> provides the
   latest comments from the trails.</li>
<li><a href="weather.html">Check Weather</a> offers weather
   updates from a variety of sources.</li>
<li><a href="clubs.html">Clubs</a> gives local hiking and
   mountaineering clubs a place to provide information
   about their activities.</li>
<li><a href="catalog.html">Catalog</a> presents our entire
   inventory, including announcements of the latest
```

```
         sales.</li>
     <li><a href="contact.html">Contact Us</a> links to a page
         with a contact form, e-mail addresses, snail mail
         addresses, and phone numbers. If it isn't here, you
         can't find us. </li>
     </ul>
     <h2>What We Do</h2>
     <p>In addition to providing the latest camping and outdoor
         activities news, we do also provide mountaineering and
         hiking equipment nationwide via mail order as well as
         through our stores in the Rocky Mountains. Please take a
         few minutes to look through our <a href="catalog.html">
         online offerings</a>.</p>
     <h2>Other Issues and News</h2>
     <ul>
     <li>As you may know, our URL was misprinted in the latest
         <i>Hiking News</i>. Please tell your hiking friends that
         the correct URL is
         <a href="http://www.asroutfitters.com/">
         http://www.asroutfitters.com/</a>.</li>
     <li>To collect a $1000 reward, turn in the name of the
         person who set the fire in the Bear Lake area last
         weekend.
     <ol>
     <li>Call 888-555-1212. </li>
     <li>Leave the name on the recording. </li>
     <li>Provide contact information so we can send you the
         reward.</li>
     </ol>
     </li>
     </ul>
     <h2>Contact Us</h2>
     <p>If you have suggestions or comments about the site or
         other information we could provide, we'd love to know
         about it. Drop us an e-mail at
         <a href="mailto:asroutfitters@raycomm.com">
         asroutfitters@raycomm.com</a>.
         Of course, you could also contact us more traditionally
         at the following address: </p>
     <address>ASR Outfitters
```

```
<br />
4700 N. Center <br />
South Logan, UT 87654<br />
801-555-3422</address>
</body>
</html>
```

2. Add <div> tags around each of the elements that should individually expand or collapse. Add a unique id attribute to each. You'll use the id attribute to specify the name for later reference from scripts. Also, add a style attribute (display:none) so all elements start out hidden.

```
<h2>What's Here</h2>
<div id="whathere" style="display:none">
<p>Here's the latest information on the site.</p>
<ul>...</ul>
</div>
<h2>What We Do</h2>
<div id="whatwedo" style="display:none">
<p>In addition to providing the latest camping and outdoor
    activities news, we do also provide mountaineering and
    hiking equipment nationwide via mail order as well as
    through our stores in the Rocky Mountains. Please take a
    few minutes to look through our <a href="catalog.html">
    online offerings</a>.</p>
</div>
<h2>Other Issues and News</h2>
<div id="otherstuff" style="display:none">
<ul>...</ul>
</div>
<h2>Contact Us</h2>
<div id="contactus" style="display:none">
<p>If you have suggestions or comments about the site or
    other information we could provide, we'd love to know
    about it. Drop us an e-mail at
    <a href="mailto:asroutfitters@raycomm.com">
    asroutfitters@raycomm.com</a>.
    Of course, you could also contact us more traditionally
    at the following address: </p>
<address>ASR Outfitters<br />
4700 N. Center <br />
```

```
South Logan, UT 87654<br />
801-555-3422</address>
</div>
</body>
</html>
```

3. Add the event handlers that invoke scripts to make the changes.

```
<p>Click on the headings below to expand or collapse
    them.</p>
<h2 onclick="whathere()">What's Here</a></h2>
<div id="whathere" style="display:none">
<p>Here's the latest information on the site.</p>
<ul>…</ul>
</div>
<h2 onclick="whatwedo()">What We Do</h2>
<div id="whatwedo" style="display:none">
<p>In addition to providing the latest camping and outdoor
    activities news, we do also provide mountaineering and
    hiking equipment nationwide via mail order as well as
    through our stores in the Rocky Mountains. Please take a
    few minutes to look through our <a href="catalog.html">
    online offerings</a>.</p>
</div>
<h2 onclick="otherstuff()">Other Issues and News</h2>
<div id="otherstuff"  style="display:none">
<ul>…</ul>
</div>
<h2 onclick="contactus()">Contact Us</h2>
<div id="contactus" style="display:none">
<p>
…
</div>
</body>
</html>
```

4. Add the script at the top that controls all this. The four functions—one for each collapsible element—verify whether the element is hidden (display=="none") and set it to display as a block element (display="block") if it starts out hidden. If it starts out visible, the function sets it to display as hidden. This function allows users to toggle the headings to collapse and expand with each click.

```
<script type="text/javascript" language="javascript">
<!--
function contactus() {
    if (document.all.contactus.style.display=="none")
        (document.all.contactus.style.display="block");
     else
        (document.all.contactus.style.display="none");
    }
function otherstuff() {
    if (document.all.otherstuff.style.display=="none")
        (document.all.otherstuff.style.display="block");
    else
        (document.all.otherstuff.style.display="none");
    }
function whatwedo() {
    if (document.all.whatwedo.style.display=="none")
        (document.all.whatwedo.style.display="block");
    else
        (document.all.whatwedo.style.display="none") ;
    }
function whathere() {
    if (document.all.whathere.style.display=="none")
        (document.all.whathere.style.display="block");
     else
        (document.all.whathere.style.display="none");
    }
// -->
</script>
```

The JavaScript in the previous example uses two similar operators: = and ==. These are easily confused but are actually two different kinds of operators. The first one, =, is the assignment operator, which assigns the value to the right of the = operator to the variable to the left of the = operator. The second one, ==, is a comparison operator, which tests to verify whether the value on the right is the same as the value on the left. If the values are the same, the condition returns as "true", and the next code statement is executed. In the first if statement in this example, if the display value for contactus is equal to "none", the next statement executes and changes the display value to "block".

The complete code for a collapsible document in Internet Explorer 5.5 is shown in Listing 17.3.

LISTING 17.3: COLLAPSIBLE DOCUMENT USING DYNAMIC XHTML IN INTERNET EXPLORER 5.5

```
<!DOCTYPE html PUBLIC "-//W3C/DTD XHTML 1.0 Transitional//EN"
    "http://www.w3.org/TR/xhtml1/DTD/xhtml1-transitional.dtd">
<html xmlns="http://www.w3.org/1999/xhtml">
<head>
<title>ASR Outfitters</title>
<style type="text/css">
<!--
body {font-size : 110% }
h1, h2, h3 {font-family : "Comic Sans MS"}
h1 {font-size : 180% ; font-weight : bold}
-->
</style>
<script type="text/javascript" language="javascript">
<!--
function contactus() {
    if (document.all.contactus.style.display=="none")
        (document.all.contactus.style.display="block");
     else
        (document.all.contactus.style.display="none");
    }
function otherstuff() {
    if (document.all.otherstuff.style.display=="none")
        (document.all.otherstuff.style.display="block");
    else
        (document.all.otherstuff.style.display="none");
    }
function whatwedo() {
    if (document.all.whatwedo.style.display=="none")
        (document.all.whatwedo.style.display="block");
    else
        (document.all.whatwedo.style.display="none") ;
    }
function whathere() {
    if (document.all.whathere.style.display=="none")
        (document.all.whathere.style.display="block");
     else
        (document.all.whathere.style.display="none");
    }
```

```
// -->
</script>
</head>
<body>
<center>
<img src="asrlogo.gif" alt="ASR logo" />
</center>
<p>We're happy to welcome you to our newly redesigned Web
    site, featuring dynamic XHTML. Please take the
    <a href="tour.html">tour of our site</a> if you haven't
    been here in a while. In particular, you may appreciate
    the camping news as well as the new effects. </p>
<hr />
<p>Click on the headings below to expand or collapse them.</p>
<h2 onclick="whathere()">What's Here</h2>
<div id="whathere" style="display:none">
<p>Here's the latest information on the site.</p>
<ul>
<li><a href="camping.html">Camping News</a> provides the latest
    comments from the trails.</li>
<li><a href="weather.html">Check Weather</a> offers weather
    updates from a variety of sources. </li>
<li><a href="clubs.html">Clubs</a> gives local hiking and
    mountaineering clubs a place to provide information about
    their activities.</li>
<li><a href="catalog.html">Catalog</a> presents our entire
    inventory, including announcements of the latest sales.</li>
<li><a href="contact.html">Contact Us</a> links to a page with
    a contact form, e-mail addresses, snail mail addresses, and
    phone numbers. If it isn't here, you can't find us. </li>
</ul>
</div>
<h2 onclick="whatwedo()">What We Do</h2>
<div id="whatwedo" style="display:none">
<p>In addition to providing the latest camping and outdoor
    activities news, we do also provide mountaineering and
    hiking equipment nationwide via mail order as well as
    through our stores in the Rocky Mountains. Please take a
    few minutes to look through our <a href="catalog.html">
    online offerings</a>.</p>
```

```
</div>
<h2 onclick="otherstuff()">Other Issues and News</h2>
<div id="otherstuff"  style="display:none">
<ul>
<li>As you may know, our URL was misprinted in the latest
    <i>Hiking News</i>. Please tell your hiking friends that
    the correct URL is
    <a href="http://www.asroutfitters.com/">
    http://www.asroutfitters.com/</a>.</li>
<li>To collect a $1000 reward, turn in the name of the person
    who set the fire in the Bear Lake area last weekend.
<ol>
<li>Call 888-555-1212. </li>
<li>Leave the name on the recording. </li>
<li>Provide contact information so we can send you the
    reward.</li>
</ol>
</li>
</ul>
</div>
<h2 onclick="contactus()">Contact Us</h2>
<div id="contactus"  style="display:none">
<p>If you have suggestions or comments about the site or other
    information we could provide, we'd love to know about it.
    Drop us an e-mail at
<a href="mailto:asroutfitters@raycomm.com">
    asroutfitters@raycomm.com</a>.
    Of course, you could also contact us more traditionally at
    the following address: </p>
<address>ASR Outfitters<br />
4700 N. Center <br />
South Logan, UT 87654<br />
801-555-3422</address>
</div>
</body>
</html>
```

The resulting collapsible document should look similar to Figure 17.5.

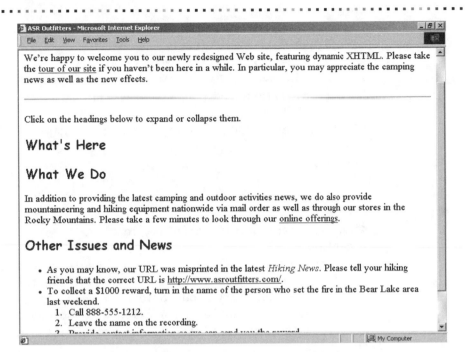

Figure 17.5 Here's Microsoft's version of the collapsible document.

Collapsing a Document the Netscape Navigator Way

To collapse a document the Netscape way, you place menu items together in a line and then include the text below. If you leave the menu items and text lined up, you'll have gross holes in the page, as shown in Figure 17.2 earlier in this chapter.

As noted previously in the section on dynamic color changes using Netscape Navigator 4.x, the `layer` *and* `ilayer` *elements are not part of the XHTML 1.0 Recommendation, and XHTML pages using these elements will not validate. However, it's useful to understand Netscape's proprietary DOM if you'll be creating dynamic pages for Netscape 4.x.*

To do so, follow these steps:

1. Start with a basic HTML document.

```
<html>
<head>
<title>ASR Outfitters</title>
<style type="text/css">
<!--
body {font-size : 110%}
h1, h2, h3 {font-family : "Comic Sans MS"}
h1 {font-size : 180% ;  font-weight : bold}
-->
</style>
</head>
<body>
<center>
<img src="asrlogo.gif" alt="ASR logo" />
</center>
<p>We're happy to welcome you to our newly redesigned Web
   site, featuring dynamic XHTML. Please take the
   <a href="tour.html">tour of our site</a> if you haven't
   been here in a while. In particular, you may appreciate
   the camping news as well as the new effects. </p>
<hr />
<p>Click on the headings below to expand or collapse
   them.</p>
<h2>What's Here</h2>
<p>Here's the latest information on the site.</p>
<ul>
<li>
<a href="camping.html">Camping News</a> provides the
   latest comments from the trails.</li>
<li><a href="weather.html">Check Weather</a> offers weather
   updates from a variety of sources. </li>
<li><a href="clubs.html">Clubs</a> gives local hiking and
   mountaineering clubs a place to provide information
   about their activities. </li>
<li><a href="catalog.html">Catalog</a> presents our entire
   inventory, including announcements of the latest
   sales.</li>
<li><a href="contact.html">Contact Us</a> links to a page
   with a contact form, e-mail addresses, snail mail
   addresses, and phone numbers. If it isn't here, you
   can't find us. </li>
```

```
</ul>
<h2>What We Do</h2>
<p>In addition to providing the latest camping and outdoor
    activities news, we do also provide mountaineering and
    hiking equipment nationwide via mail order as well as
    through our stores in the Rocky Mountains. Please take a
    few minutes to look through our <a href="catalog.html">
    online offerings</a>.</p>
<h2>Other Issues and News</h2>
<ul>
<li>As you may know, our URL was misprinted in the latest
    <i>Hiking News</i>. Please tell your hiking friends that
    the correct URL is
    <a href="http://www.asroutfitters.com/">
    http://www.asroutfitters.com/</a>.</li>
<li>To collect a $1000 reward, turn in the name of the
    person who set the fire in the Bear Lake area last
    weekend.
<ol>
<li>Call 888-555-1212. </li>
<li>Leave the name on the recording. </li>
<li>Provide contact information so we can send you the
    reward.</li>
</ol>
</li>
</ul>
<h2>Contact Us</h2>
<p>If you have suggestions or comments about the site or
    other information we could provide, we'd love to know
    about it. Drop us an e-mail at
<a href="mailto:asroutfitters@raycomm.com">
asroutfitters@raycomm.com</a>.
    Of course, you could also contact us more traditionally
    at the following address: </p>
<address>ASR Outfitters
<br />
4700 N. Center <br />
South Logan, UT 87654<br />
801-555-3422</address>
</body>
</html>
```

2. Add layer tags around each of the sections that will individually appear or disappear. Include in each the `visibility` attribute, set to `hide`. The `name` attributes for each of the layers must be unique—they're how the layers will be referred to from the functions you set up in the next steps. The h2 elements from our original version will not be needed once we add the layer elements in this step and the event handlers in the next step.

```
<layer name="nswhathere" visibility="hide">
<p>Here's the latest information on the site.</p>
<ul>...</ul>
</layer><layer name="nswhatwedo" visibility="hide">
<p>In addition to providing the latest camping and outdoor
   activities news, we do also provide mountaineering and
   hiking equipment nationwide via mail order as well as
   through our stores in the Rocky Mountains. Please take a
   few minutes to look through our <a href="catalog.html">
   online offerings</a>.</p>
</layer>

<layer name="nsotherstuff" visibility="hide">
<ul>...</ul>
</layer>

<layer name="nscontactus" visibility="hide">
<p>If you have suggestions or comments about the site or
   other information we could provide, we'd love to know
   about it. Drop us an e-mail at
<a href="mailto:asroutfitters@raycomm.com">
   asroutfitters@raycomm.com</a>.
   Of course, you could also contact us more traditionally
   at the following address: </p>
<address>ASR Outfitters<br />
4700 N. Center <br />
South Logan, UT 87654<br />
801-555-3422</address>
</layer>
```

3. Add anchor elements (a) with links to JavaScript event handlers to the menu at the top of the page. Each uses an anchor element to call a JavaScript function (which you'll define in the next step).

```
<h2>
<a href="javascript:nswhathere()">What's Here</a> |
<a href="javascript:nswhatwedo()">What We Do</a> |
<a href="javascript:nsotherstuff()">Other Issues and
    News</a> |
<a href="javascript:nscontactus()">Contact Us</a> |
<a href="javascript:clearall()">Collapse All</a> </h2>
```

4. Add the scripts to the top of the page. The clearall() function sets all the layers to hidden. Each other function calls this function to clear the previous text before showing the new text. Otherwise, it would all overlap. The individual functions set the individual sections (named in the individual layer tags) to "show".

```
<script type="text/javascript" language="javascript">
<!--
function clearall() {
    document.layers.nswhathere.visibility="hide";
    document.layers.nscontactus.visibility="hide";
    document.layers.nswhatwedo.visibility="hide";
    document.layers.nsotherstuff.visibility="hide";
}

function nswhathere() {
    clearall();
    document.layers.nswhathere.visibility="show";
}
function nscontactus() {
    clearall();
    document.layers.nscontactus.visibility="show";
}
function nswhatwedo() {
    clearall();
    document.layers.nswhatwedo.visibility="show";
}
function nsotherstuff() {
    clearall();
    document.layers.nsotherstuff.visibility="show";
}
// -->
</script>
</head>
<body>
```

The complete code for this example is shown in Listing 17.4.

LISTING 17.4: COLLAPSIBLE DOCUMENT USING DHTML IN NETSCAPE NAVIGATOR 4.*x*

```html
<html>
<head>
<title>ASR Outfitters</title>
<style type="text/css">
<!--
body {font-size : 110%}
h1, h2, h3 {font-family : "Comic Sans MS"}
h1 {font-size : 180% ;  font-weight : bold}
-->
</style>
<script type="text/javascript" language="javascript">
<!--
function clearall() {
    document.layers.nswhathere.visibility="hide";
    document.layers.nscontactus.visibility="hide";
    document.layers.nswhatwedo.visibility="hide";
    document.layers.nsotherstuff.visibility="hide";
}
function nswhathere() {
     clearall() ;
    document.layers.nswhathere.visibility="show";
}
function nscontactus() {
     clearall() ;
    document.layers.nscontactus.visibility="show";
}
function nswhatwedo() {
     clearall() ;
    document.layers.nswhatwedo.visibility="show";
}
function nsotherstuff() {
     clearall() ;
    document.layers.nsotherstuff.visibility="show";
}
// -->
</script>
```

```
</head>
<body>
<center>
<img src="asrlogo.gif" alt="ASR logo" />
</center>
<p>We're happy to welcome you to our newly redesigned Web
    site, featuring dynamic XHTML. Please take the
    <a href="tour.html">tour of our site</a> if you haven't
    been here in a while. In particular, you may appreciate
    the camping news as well as the new effects. </p>
<hr />
<p>Click on the headings below to expand or collapse them.</p>
<h2>
<a href="javascript:nswhathere()">What's Here</a> |
<a href="javascript:nswhatwedo()">What We Do</a> |
<a href="javascript:nsotherstuff()">Other Issues and News</a> |
<a href="javascript:nscontactus()">Contact Us</a> |
<a href="javascript:clearall()">Collapse All</a> </h2>
<layer name="nswhathere" visibility="hide">
<p>Here's the latest information on the site.</p>
<ul>
<li>
<a href="camping.html">Camping News</a> provides the latest
    comments from the trails.</li>
<li><a href="weather.html">Check Weather</a> offers weather
    updates from a variety of sources. </li>
<li><a href="clubs.html">Clubs</a> gives local hiking and
    mountaineering clubs a place to provide information about
    their activities. </li>
<li><a href="catalog.html">Catalog</a> presents our entire
    inventory, including announcements of the latest sales.</li>
<li><a href="contact.html">Contact Us</a> links to a page with
    a contact form, e-mail addresses, snail mail addresses, and
    phone numbers. If it isn't here, you can't find us. </li>
</ul>
</layer>
<layer name="nswhatwedo" visibility="hide">
<p>In addition to providing the latest camping and outdoor
    activities news, we do also provide mountaineering and
    hiking equipment nationwide via mail order as well as
```

```
    through our stores in the Rocky Mountains. Please take a
    few minutes to look through our <a href="catalog.html">
    online offerings</a>.</p>
</layer>
<layer name="nsotherstuff" visibility="hide">
<ul>
<li>As you may know, our URL was misprinted in the latest
    <i>Hiking News</i>. Please tell your hiking friends that
    the correct URL is
    <a href="http://www.asroutfitters.com/">
    http://www.asroutfitters.com/</a>.</li>
<li>To collect a $1000 reward, turn in the name of the person
    who set the fire in the Bear Lake area last weekend.
<ol>
<li>Call 888-555-1212. </li>
<li>Leave the name on the recording. </li>
<li>Provide contact information so we can send you the
    reward.</li>
</ol>
</li>
</ul>
</layer>
<layer name="nscontactus" visibility="hide">
<p>If you have suggestions or comments about the site or other
    information we could provide, we'd love to know about it.
    Drop us an e-mail at
<a href="mailto:asroutfitters@raycomm.com">
    asroutfitters@raycomm.com</a>.
    Of course, you could also contact us more traditionally at
    the following address: </p>
<address>ASR Outfitters
<br />
4700 N. Center <br />
South Logan, UT 87654<br />
801-555-3422</address>
</layer>
</body>
</html>
```

The resulting document looks like Figure 17.6.

If you try to open this in Netscape 6, it will not work correctly. You must open this markup in Netscape 4.75 or earlier.

Figure 17.6 *Netscape's layers create the collapsible document.*

Implementing Browser Detection

If you plan to include dynamic XHTML capabilities in your XHTML documents, consider implementing a JavaScript to detect which browser your users are using. Remember, if users are not using the browser for which the documents were developed, they'll get error messages.

Browser detection in the past was generally a simple matter of determining whether users were using Netscape Navigator or Internet Explorer using two simple JavaScript methods and properties:

- `navigator.appName` to determine the browser name
- `navigator.appVersion` to determine the browser version

This worked well for both Netscape Navigator and Internet Explorer version 4.*x* or lower, and enabled site developers to redirect users to an appropriate page with the appropriate JavaScript for the version of the browser that they were using and the DOM that the version implemented. With the introduction of newer versions of Internet Explorer (5.5 and 6) and Netscape Navigator 6, other browsers such as Opera, and the multitude of possible operating systems, browser detection became much more complex.

Current browser detection requires use of the userAgent string. The HTTP 1.1 specification uses a header called userAgent. This header identifies the client to the server and includes information about the operating system, the browser name, and the browser version. If you use the following simple script, you can find out the userAgent string returned by your current browser:

```
<script type="text/javascript" language="javascript">
    var agent = navigator.userAgent;
    document.write ("userAgent string: " + agent);
</script>
```

Here are a few examples of the UserAgent string returned by this script:

```
userAgent string: Mozilla/4.75 [en] (Win98; U)
userAgent string: Mozilla/3.0 (compatible; Opera/3.0;
    Windows 95/NT4)
userAgent string: Mozilla/5.0 (Windows; U; Win98; en-US;
    CDonDemand) Gecko/20010131 Netscape6/6.01)
userAgent string:) Mozilla/4.0 (compatible; MSIE 5.5;
    Windows NT5.0)
```

The first string is returned from a computer running Netscape 4.75 on Windows 98 platform, the second from Opera 3.0 on Windows 95, the third from Netscape 6 on Windows 98, and the last from Netscape 4.75 on Windows 2000 (note that the value returned for Windows 2000 is Windows NT5.0). You can see how browser detection has become much more complex!

It's beyond the scope of this chapter to go into the details of pulling out the needed pieces of information from the userAgent string, but for more information on how browser detection works, see the Browser Detection tutorial by Richard Blaylock at http://hotwired.lycos.com/webmonkey/99/02/index2a.html?tw=authoring.

An excellent JavaScript called "The Ultimate JavaScript Client Sniffer: Version 3.02" is available from www.mozilla.org/docs/webdeveloper/sniffer/browser_type .html. This script is provided in Listing 17.5, and copyright permission is given from Netscape for reuse and distribution of this script. This script covers every currently known combination of browser, operating system, and platform, and also includes WebTV and AOL. This script is updated as needed, so as future browser versions become available, check the previous URL for an updated script. It's a long script, but it offers the most comprehensive browser detection currently available, and can be modified to suit your browser detection needs.

This script goes in the head section of your XHTML document, but you must also use another JavaScript in the body section of your document so the browser knows what action to take for the various combinations. Most commonly, you'll want to redirect your users to a particular version of your XHTML page for that browser and browser version. Therefore, an additional script using location.replace has been added to Listing 17.5 that redirects the user to a page specifically designed for Netscape 4.*x*, Internet Explorer, Netscape 6.*x*, or a standard page for all other combinations. You can expand this script to include all the possibilities you want, such as an Internet Explorer 4.0 page, an Internet Explorer 5.5 page, and so on.

 You can link to an external JavaScript the same way you can link to an external style sheet. This browser-detection script is very comprehensive, but also quite long. You can save the script itself as a text file with a .js extension to indicate that it's JavaScript; for example, save it as browserdetect.js. *Then, in the head section of the XHTML document, use the* link *element to link to the script:* <link rel= "script" type="text/javascript" href="browserdetect.js"/>. *For more information, see "Linking JavaScript" in Chapter 11.*

LISTING 17.5: THE ULTIMATE JAVASCRIPT CLIENT SNIFFER WITH PAGE REDIRECTS

```
<!DOCTYPE html PUBLIC "-//W3C/DTD XHTML 1.0 Transitional//EN"
    "http://www.w3.org/TR/xhtml1/DTD/xhtml1-transitional.dtd">
<html xmlns="http://www.w3.org/1999/xhtml">
<head>
<title>Browser Version</title>
<script language="javascript" type="text/javascript">
//<!--
// Ultimate client-side JavaScript client sniff. Version 3.02
// (C) Netscape Communications 1999.  Permission granted to
// reuse and distribute.
// Revised 17 May 99 to add is_nav5up and is_ie5up (see below).
// Revised 20 Dec 00 to add is_gecko and change is_nav5up to
// is_nav6up also added support for IE5.5 Opera4&5 HotJava3
// AOLTV
// Revised 22 Feb 01 to correct Javascript Detection for IE
```

```
// 5.x,
// Opera 4, correct Opera 5 detection add support for winME
// and
// win2k synch with browser-type-oo.js
// Revised 26 Mar 01 to correct Opera detection

// Everything you always wanted to know about your JavaScript
// client but were afraid to ask. Creates "is_" variables
// indicating:
// (1) browser vendor:
//     is_nav, is_ie, is_opera, is_hotjava, is_webtv,
// is_TVNavigator, is_AOLTV
// (2) browser version number:
//     is_major (integer indicating major version number:
// 2, 3, 4 ...)
// is_minor (float   indicating full  version number: 2.02,
// 3.01, 4.04 ...)
// (3) browser vendor AND major version number
// is_nav2, is_nav3, is_nav4, is_nav4up, is_nav6, is_nav6up,
// is_gecko, is_ie3, is_ie4, is_ie4up, is_ie5, is_ie5up,
// is_ie5_5, is_ie5_5up, is_hotjava3, is_hotjava3up, is_opera2,
// is_opera3, is_opera4, is_opera5, is_opera5up, is_aol3,
// is_aol4, is_aol5, is_aol6
// (4) JavaScript version number:
// is_js (float indicating full JavaScript version number:
// 1, 1.1, 1.2 ...)
// (5) OS platform and version:
// is_win, is_win16, is_win32, is_win31, is_win95, is_winnt,
// is_win98, is_winme, is_win2k
// is_os2
// is_mac, is_mac68k, is_macppc
// is_unix
// is_sun, is_sun4, is_sun5, is_suni86
// is_irix, is_irix5, is_irix6
// is_hpux, is_hpux9, is_hpux10
// is_aix, is_aix1, is_aix2, is_aix3, is_aix4
// is_linux, is_sco, is_unixware, is_mpras, is_reliant
// is_dec, is_sinix, is_freebsd, is_bsd
// is_vms
//
```

```
// See http://www.it97.de/JavaScript/JS_tutorial/bstat/
// navobj.html and
// http://www.it97.de/JavaScript/JS_tutorial/bstat/
// Browseraol.html
// for detailed lists of userAgent strings.
//
// Note: you don't want your Nav4 or IE4 code to "turn off" or
// stop working when new versions of browsers are released, so
// in conditional code forks, use is_ie5up ("IE 5.0 or
// greater")
// is_opera5up ("Opera 5.0 or greater") instead of is_ie5 or
// is_opera5
// to check version in code which you want to work on future
// versions.

    // convert all characters to lowercase to simplify testing
    var agt=navigator.userAgent.toLowerCase();

    // *** BROWSER VERSION ***
    // Note: On IE5, these return 4, so use is_ie5up to
    // detect IE5.
    var is_major = parseInt(navigator.appVersion);
    var is_minor = parseFloat(navigator.appVersion);

    // Note: Opera and WebTV spoof Navigator. We do strict
    // client detection.
    // If you want to allow spoofing, take out the tests
    // for opera and webtv.
    var is_nav  = ((agt.indexOf('mozilla')!=-1) &&
(agt.indexOf('spoofer')==-1)
                && (agt.indexOf('compatible') == -1) &&
                    (agt.indexOf('opera')==-1)
                && (agt.indexOf('webtv')==-1) &&
                    (agt.indexOf('hotjava')==-1));
    var is_nav2 = (is_nav && (is_major == 2));
    var is_nav3 = (is_nav && (is_major == 3));
    var is_nav4 = (is_nav && (is_major == 4));
    var is_nav4up = (is_nav && (is_major >= 4));
    var is_navonly = (is_nav && ((agt.indexOf(";nav")
      != -1) ||
```

```
     (agt.indexOf("; nav") != -1)) );
var is_nav6 = (is_nav && (is_major == 5));
var is_nav6up = (is_nav && (is_major >= 5));
var is_gecko = (agt.indexOf('gecko') != -1);


var is_ie     = ((agt.indexOf("msie") != -1) &&
(agt.indexOf("opera") == -1));
var is_ie3    = (is_ie && (is_major < 4));
var is_ie4    = (is_ie && (is_major == 4) &&
(agt.indexOf("msie 5")==-1) );
var is_ie4up  = (is_ie && (is_major >= 4));
var is_ie5    = (is_ie && (is_major == 4) &&
(agt.indexOf("msie 5.0")!=-1) );
var is_ie5_5  = (is_ie && (is_major == 4) &&
(agt.indexOf("msie 5.5") !=-1));
var is_ie5up  = (is_ie && !is_ie3 && !is_ie4);
var is_ie5_5up =(is_ie && !is_ie3 && !is_ie4 && !is_ie5);

// KNOWN BUG: On AOL4, returns false if IE3 is embedded
// browser
// or if this is the first browser window opened.  Thus the
// variables is_aol, is_aol3, and is_aol4 aren't 100%
// reliable.
var is_aol    = (agt.indexOf("aol") != -1);
var is_aol3   = (is_aol && is_ie3);
var is_aol4   = (is_aol && is_ie4);
var is_aol5   = (agt.indexOf("aol 5") != -1);
var is_aol6   = (agt.indexOf("aol 6") != -1);

var is_opera = (agt.indexOf("opera") != -1);
var is_opera2 = (agt.indexOf("opera 2") != -1 ||
agt.indexOf("opera/2") != -1);
var is_opera3 = (agt.indexOf("opera 3") != -1 ||
agt.indexOf("opera/3") != -1);
var is_opera4 = (agt.indexOf("opera 4") != -1 ||
agt.indexOf("opera/4") != -1);
var is_opera5 = (agt.indexOf("opera 5") != -1 ||
agt.indexOf("opera/5") != -1);
var is_opera5up = (is_opera && !is_opera2 && !is_opera3
&& !is_opera4);
```

```
var is_webtv = (agt.indexOf("webtv") != -1);

var is_TVNavigator = ((agt.indexOf("navio") != -1) ||
(agt.indexOf("navio_aoltv") != -1));
var is_AOLTV = is_TVNavigator;

var is_hotjava = (agt.indexOf("hotjava") != -1);
var is_hotjava3 = (is_hotjava && (is_major == 3));
var is_hotjava3up = (is_hotjava && (is_major >= 3));

// *** JAVASCRIPT VERSION CHECK ***
var is_js;
if (is_nav2 || is_ie3) is_js = 1.0;
else if (is_nav3) is_js = 1.1;
else if (is_opera5up) is_js = 1.3;
else if (is_opera) is_js = 1.1;
else if ((is_nav4 && (is_minor <= 4.05)) || is_ie4) is_js
= 1.2;
else if ((is_nav4 && (is_minor > 4.05)) || is_ie5) is_js
= 1.3;
else if (is_hotjava3up) is_js = 1.4;
else if (is_nav6 || is_gecko) is_js = 1.5;
// NOTE: In the future, update this code when newer
// versions of JS are released. For now, we try to
// provide some upward compatibility so that future
// versions of Nav and IE will show they are at least*
// JS 1.x capable. Always check for JS version
// compatibility with > or >=.
else if (is_nav6up) is_js = 1.5;
// NOTE: ie5up on mac is 1.4
else if (is_ie5up) is_js = 1.3

// HACK: no idea for other browsers; always check for JS
// version with > or >=
else is_js = 0.0;

// *** PLATFORM ***
var is_win   = ( (agt.indexOf("win")!=-1) ||
(agt.indexOf("16bit")!=-1) );
// NOTE: On Opera 3.0, the userAgent string includes
```

```
// "Windows 95/NT4" on all
//          Win32, so you can't distinguish between Win95
// and WinNT.
var is_win95 = ((agt.indexOf("win95")!=-1) ||
(agt.indexOf("windows 95")!=-1));

// is this a 16 bit compiled version?
var is_win16 = ((agt.indexOf("win16")!=-1) ||
            (agt.indexOf("16bit")!=-1) ||
            (agt.indexOf("windows 3.1")!=-1) ||
            (agt.indexOf("windows 16-bit")!=-1) );

var is_win31 = ((agt.indexOf("windows 3.1")!=-1) ||
            (agt.indexOf("win16")!=-1) ||
            (agt.indexOf("windows 16-bit")!=-1));

var is_winme = ((agt.indexOf("win 9x 4.90")!=-1));
var is_win2k = ((agt.indexOf("windows nt 5.0")!=-1));

// NOTE: Reliable detection of Win98 may not be possible.
// It appears that: - On Nav 4.x and before you'll get
// plain
// "Windows" in userAgent.
// - On Mercury client, the 32-bit version will return
// "Win98", but the 16-bit version running on Win98 will
// still return "Win95".
var is_win98 = ((agt.indexOf("win98")!=-1) ||
                (agt.indexOf("windows 98")!=-1));
var is_winnt = ((agt.indexOf("winnt")!=-1) ||
                (agt.indexOf("windows nt")!=-1));
var is_win32 = (is_win95 || is_winnt || is_win98 ||
                ((is_major >= 4) &&
                (navigator.platform == "Win32")) ||
                (agt.indexOf("win32")!=-1) ||
                (agt.indexOf("32bit")!=-1));

var is_os2   = ((agt.indexOf("os/2")!=-1) ||
            (navigator.appVersion.indexOf("OS/2")!=-1) ||
            (agt.indexOf("ibm-webexplorer")!=-1));

var is_mac   = (agt.indexOf("mac")!=-1);
```

```
        // hack ie5 js version for mac
        if (is_mac && is_ie5up) is_js = 1.4;
        var is_mac68k = (is_mac && ((agt.indexOf("68k")!=-1) ||
                                    (agt.indexOf("68000")!=-1)));
        var is_macppc = (is_mac && ((agt.indexOf("ppc")!=-1) ||
                                    (agt.indexOf("powerpc")!=-1)));

        var is_sun   = (agt.indexOf("sunos")!=-1);
        var is_sun4  = (agt.indexOf("sunos 4")!=-1);
        var is_sun5  = (agt.indexOf("sunos 5")!=-1);
        var is_suni86= (is_sun && (agt.indexOf("i86")!=-1));
        var is_irix  = (agt.indexOf("irix") !=-1);    // SGI
        var is_irix5 = (agt.indexOf("irix 5") !=-1);
        var is_irix6 = ((agt.indexOf("irix 6") !=-1) ||
(agt.indexOf("irix6") !=-1));
        var is_hpux  = (agt.indexOf("hp-ux")!=-1);
        var is_hpux9 = (is_hpux && (agt.indexOf("09.")!=-1));
        var is_hpux10= (is_hpux && (agt.indexOf("10.")!=-1));
        var is_aix   = (agt.indexOf("aix") !=-1);      // IBM
        var is_aix1  = (agt.indexOf("aix 1") !=-1);
        var is_aix2  = (agt.indexOf("aix 2") !=-1);
        var is_aix3  = (agt.indexOf("aix 3") !=-1);
        var is_aix4  = (agt.indexOf("aix 4") !=-1);
        var is_linux = (agt.indexOf("inux")!=-1);
        var is_sco   = (agt.indexOf("sco")!=-1) ||
                       (agt.indexOf("unix_sv")!=-1);
        var is_unixware = (agt.indexOf("unix_system_v")!=-1);
        var is_mpras    = (agt.indexOf("ncr")!=-1);
        var is_reliant  = (agt.indexOf("reliantunix")!=-1);
        var is_dec   = ((agt.indexOf("dec")!=-1) ||
                       (agt.indexOf("osf1")!=-1) ||
            (agt.indexOf("dec_alpha")!=-1) ||
            (agt.indexOf("alphaserver")!=-1) ||
            (agt.indexOf("ultrix")!=-1) ||
            (agt.indexOf("alphastation")!=-1));
        var is_sinix = (agt.indexOf("sinix")!=-1);
        var is_freebsd = (agt.indexOf("freebsd")!=-1);
        var is_bsd = (agt.indexOf("bsd")!=-1);
        var is_unix  = ((agt.indexOf("x11")!=-1) || is_sun ||
                   is_irix || is_hpux ||
                   is_sco ||is_unixware || is_mpras ||
```

```
                    is_reliant ||
            is_dec || is_sinix || is_aix || is_linux ||
                is_bsd
            || is_freebsd);

    var is_vms   = ((agt.indexOf("vax")!=-1) ||
          (agt.indexOf("openvms")!=-1));

if (is_gecko)
  {
  location.replace("Netscape6.htm");
  }
  else if (is_nav4)
  {
  location.replace("Netscape4.htm");
  }
  else if (is_ie5up)
  {
  location.replace("MSIEPage.htm");
  }
  else
  {
  location.replace("StandardPage.htm");
  }
//--> end hide JavaScript
</script>
</head>
<body>
<noscript>
   <h2>This website requires a browser supporting
   scripting</h2>
</noscript>

</body>
</html>
```

Where to Go from Here

As you learned in this chapter, dynamic XHTML offers lots of potential for making your pages leap off the screen. Although this chapter covered only the basics, you can combine any style sheet characteristic with a JavaScript function to make your pages flash, change, and move.

If you feel confident using style sheets and JavaScript, we recommend that you experiment with combining these two aspects. You'll find a complete style sheet reference and JavaScript reference in the Master's Reference (Master's Reference 2 and 3, respectively). Or, if you're not quite up to speed with these two topics, we recommend visiting the following chapters:

- See Chapter 10 for information about developing and applying style sheets.

- See Chapter 11 to learn how to use JavaScript in your XHTML documents.

Generating XHTML from a Database

XHTML

Chapter 18

A *database* is simply a collection of information arranged so you can easily access and use it. A phone directory, a catalog, and a mailing list are examples of databases you've probably used.

In a way, the Web is a database—the world's largest. It's a collection of information that anyone connected to the Internet can access and use. The Yahoo! site (at www.yahoo.com), which is a collection of information about Web sites, including descriptions and URLs, is another database within the larger World Wide Web database.

As an XHTML guru (you are one if you've made it to this chapter), you might need to move information from a database into a format that you can publish in an XHTML document. In this chapter, we'll show you how to convert database information into XHTML documents, look at a range of database tools, and step you through a general process for generating XHTML from a database.

This chapter covers the following topics:

- Enhancing your Web site with databases

- Determining your database needs

- Choosing database software

- Generating XHTML pages from databases

- Maintaining database documents

Why Generate XHTML from a Database?

Although it sounds complicated (it's not too bad, actually), generating XHTML from a database saves a tremendous amount of time. For example, suppose you work for a company that manufactures nuts and bolts. Management decides to make the enormous product catalog—which includes thousands of items—available on the corporate Web site. You could spend weeks doing the data entry, or you could spend almost as much time moving pages from the catalog into and out of your favorite XHTML tools.

Your best bet is to develop the online catalog by pulling information directly from a database. Even developing a new database specifically for online information is a better choice than entering information into an XHTML document from scratch. Why? A computerized database is a dynamic entity, which means that you can constantly add, change, and remove information. If you use database software to create the online catalog, updating your XHTML documents is almost automatic—and a snap. The alternative is to find and manually edit each and every affected Web page every time some itty-bitty scrap of information changes.

When you generate XHTML from a database, you can also provide online information in any number of segments. For example, you can list products by size, weight, color, or whatever, and you can fairly easily change how you present information once you have a database in place.

Generating XHTML from a database is a good solution for the company that manufactures nuts and bolts; however, a database is not an ideal solution in all cases, particularly if the cost of setting up and maintaining the database outweighs the benefits. For example, if your company manufactures only one or two products, you might just as easily—perhaps more easily—develop an online catalog by simply creating a few XHTML documents.

Exploring Your Options

How you generate XHTML from a database depends on your specific needs and resources, which vary according to the size of your company and the size of the database. We're going to look briefly at the options for a very large company and for a small company. However, most situations fall somewhere in between—the basic principles apply in any situation.

Tools for Database Publishing

You'll need two sets of tools to use a database to generate content for XHTML documents:

Database   A database is where the content for your XHTML pages is stored. Databases save content in tables, which are similar to spreadsheets. Each table has rows and columns, which create individual fields. A field has properties, such as what kind of data it can contain, how many characters the data can contain, and whether the field must contain data or can be empty.

Database management systems (DBMS) can use large and complex programs and servers, such as Oracle, Sybase, Informix, or Microsoft SQL Server. For smaller sites, a less complex combination—for example, Microsoft Personal Web Server (PWS)—and a desktop database program—such as Microsoft Access, FileMaker Pro, or Paradox—may be all that's needed.

Application   These applications are referred to as *middleware*. They are designed to do two things with databases:

- They request data from the database using a server-side scripting language. The script contains the necessary information to make a connection to a database.

- They take the results of the database *query* (a request for information from a database) to a template so the results can be displayed on a Web page.

ColdFusion, UltraDev, or PHP can be used as your application, or you can use any application that can create Active Server Pages (ASP) or JavaServer Pages (JSP) pages. These software options will be discussed later in this chapter in the section "Choosing Software."

The Large Company Scenario

If you work for a large organization that has company-wide database solutions in place, you're probably using Oracle, Sybase, or Informix software. You probably also have programming resources at your disposal or have access to high-end (and fairly expensive) software, such as ColdFusion, that can automatically generate XHTML documents from your database.

If you have programming resources and can create a custom database solution, that's your most sophisticated and flexible option. Your goal, regardless of resources, is to develop a database that's suitable for Web publication, and you need an expedient solution to push the data onto the Web. Most of the solutions discussed in this chapter will work for you.

Structured Query Language (SQL)

If you're a fairly motivated or savvy Web developer, or know someone who is, generating XHTML directly from a relational database management system (RDBMS), such as Oracle, Sybase, or Informix, using Structured Query Language (SQL) is a great technical solution for creating database-driven Web sites, and it can be a workable and flexible solution on most platforms and most servers at a reasonable cost. Check out any of these tutorials for more information on SQL:

- Simple SQL: Getting Started with SQL http://wdvl.internet.com/Authoring/DB/SQL/Start/

- Introduction to Structured Query Language http://w3.one.net/~jhoffman/sqltut.htm

- Interactive/Online SQL Tutorial with SQL Interpreter and live practice database http://sqlcourse.com/

The Small Company Scenario

In this situation, you generate XHTML from a database using moderately priced and easily accessible tools that also give you a broad range of capabilities. We assume that you have access to Windows (95/98/NT/2000, or XP), have access to the data (either from a high-end database or from a desktop database), and need to get the information onto the Internet (or an intranet).

You can generate XHTML pages from a database using Microsoft Personal Web Server (included with Windows 95/98 or can be downloaded free from Microsoft's site at http://msdn.microsoft.com/library/default.asp?URL=/library/officedev/office97/settinguppersonalwebserver.htm), Microsoft Peer Web Services (included with Windows NT 4), or Internet Information Services 5.0 (included with Windows 2000 Professional) and Microsoft Access. This will be covered in more detail in the section "Generating XHTML Pages from Databases" later in this chapter. This is an easy and inexpensive solution for a small database and Web site, but will not work well for a busy site with a large database. If you're working on the Macintosh platform, Personal Web Server and ASP will not work for you; in this case, consider PHP (an open-source scripting language—find more information at www.php.net).

Deciding to Use a Database

If you don't have a database in place yet—and, therefore, don't know whether generating information from a database will best meet your needs—here are some questions to ask yourself:

- Do you have a variety and/or large quantity of information?

- Does the data change frequently or require regular updates or maintenance?

- Do you realistically have the technical and financial resources to create a database?

If you answered yes to the first or second question, you probably have some need for a database. If you also answered no to the third, reassess your needs before you jump into it—this isn't a one-day project.

Our fictitious company, ASR Outfitters, decided to use a database for part of its site because of the variety of its products and ever-changing availability. Rather than editing every product page every time prices, products, or availability changes, ASR Outfitters developers want to update the master database and then quickly and easily make that information available through the Web.

As you consider a database, keep in mind that it could contain data in the traditional sense (as the examples in this chapter show) or it could contain text or other content. Most of the high-traffic sites on the Internet store articles in databases and serve XHTML pages directly from the databases to ease site maintenance.

Deciding Which Information Should Go on the Web

At some point in this process, you'll need to decide which information within your database you should publish on the Web. You may want to publish all the information, but if you don't, here are some other considerations:

- Which information will users find most useful? ASR Outfitters wants users to see all the available product information, so the company publishes it all.

- Which information won't users need? Aside from internal documentation, pricing, and marketing information (which is all kept in different databases), ASR decided that publishing nearly all product information was appropriate.

- Which information do you not want provided to the public? Because its product database is separate from confidential information, ASR did not have to contend with this problem. Management chose not to make cryptic acronyms and abbreviations available. This was not for security purposes, but was an effort to reduce users' confusion.

You don't have to answer these questions now, but keep them in mind as you're working through the remaining sections in this chapter.

Choosing Software

You need to select software that matches your budget, platform, and database size. Although we can't tell you exactly what you need (there are simply too many variables), we can tell you what your options are.

Database application programs (middleware) operate on the server side to link the Web server to the database content. These programs do not create databases—you can use a desktop database program such as Access, FileMaker Pro, or Paradox to do that— but they do help you create XHTML pages that can dynamically connect to a database and access its contents by using a server-side scripting language.

There are several choices for the scripting language:

- ColdFusion Markup Language (CFML)
- Server-side JavaScript or JScript *
- Perl
- Visual Basic Script (VBScript)

* *Both JavaScript and JScript have both client-side and server-side scripting features.*

For a review of server-side scripting languages, see "Server-Side Scripting Shootout" at `http://hotwired.lycos.com/webmonkey/99/46/index1a.html?tw=programming`.

The following list contains some of your database application software choices:

ColdFusion   ColdFusion Markup Language is a tag-based language, like XHTML; however, the set of tags is executed on the server side (unlike XHTML, which is executed on the client side). ColdFusion also has a powerful server, which, among many other features, offers integration with databases and remote database administration, including database connections. The ColdFusion server can be used on many operating systems, including Windows, Solaris, HP-UX, and Linux.

Macromedia and Allaire merged in March 2001, but at the time of this writing, the Allaire Web site is still the main resource for information on ColdFusion.

For more information on ColdFusion, visit Allaire's Web site at `www.allaire.com`, or check out the ColdFusion tutorial at `http://hotwired.lycos.com/webmonkey/programming/coldfusion/tutorials/tutorial2.html`.

ASP   ASP is a Microsoft technology that can be used to create dynamic pages that are a combination of XHTML, scripting, and ActiveX components. These pages can be used to access databases, among other things. ASP pages can be created using any text editor, and some software programs such as Microsoft FrontPage can create ASP pages. Any scripting language can be used in an ASP, but VBScript is the most common.

For more information on ASP, see the "Introduction to Active Server Pages" tutorial at `http://hotwired.lycos.com/webmonkey/98/39/index2a.html`.

ASP now exists in forms that can be used on non-Windows platforms, such as Sun Chili!Soft ASP. For more details, visit the Web site at `www.chilisoft.com`.

UltraDev

UltraDev is a Web application development program that allows you to create database-driven Web sites using one of three models: ColdFusion, ASP, or JSP. ColdFusion is tag based, and both ASP and JSP are script based. Any of these three can be used to create XHTML pages that are a mix of XHTML and either scripts or CFML.

For more information on UltraDev, visit Macromedia's Web site at `www.macromedia.com`. Macromedia and Allaire merged in March 2001, but currently both UltraDev and ColdFusion are available as separate products, or as a combined UltraDev/ColdFusion Studio.

The next version of ASP is ASP.NET. It's a completely new version of ASP, and it's part of Microsoft's .NET platform for XML Web services. The .NET platform is a direct way for applications to interact with one another on the Web. ASP.NET is written in C# (pronounced C sharp). ASP.NET uses programming languages to write Web applications. The applications are compiled on the server and then served to the browser as HTML. ASP.NET is currently in Beta 2 release. For more information on ASP.NET, see `www.asp.net`. *For more information on the .NET platform, see* `www.microsoft.com/net/whatis.asp`.

JSP   JSP is similar to ASP, but it's a Sun technology based on the Java programming language. JSP can be used to create pages that include XHTML and scripting in Java, and can also be written in XML using Extensible Stylesheet Language Transformations (XSLT). JSP is available on all major Web platforms. Although similar to ASPs, JSPs do require some Java knowledge.

For more information on JSP, see the "Intro to JSP" tutorial at `http://hotwired.lycos.com/webmonkey/01/22/index3a.html?tw=programming`, or the Sun online JSP course at `http://developer.java.sun.com/developer/onlineTraining/JSPIntro/`.

PHP/MySQL   PHP is another server-side scripting language that can be used to create dynamic database XHTML pages. It's usually used in combination with MySQL, a free, open-source database management system. PHP/MySQL is cross-platform and can be used on Windows, Macintosh, and Unix. PHP also supports XML.

For more information on PHP/MySQL, check out the introductory PHP tutorial at `www.php.net/tut.php`, the introduction to MySQL at `www.mysql.com/doc/W/h/What-is.html`, and the PHP/MySQL tutorial at `http://hotwired.lycos.com/webmonkey/programming/php/tutorials/tutorial4.html`.

Each of these applications can save XHTML documents and exchange data through a server, thereby making them reasonable candidates for almost any database you'd want to create. You'll find that these software packages are flexible and easy to use to provide your database information as XHTML.

ASR Outfitters chose to use Microsoft Access as its desktop database program simply because the company uses Microsoft Office products; the consistent interface was a driving force. The company then chose ColdFusion as its database application software because it's easy to use and because developers could quickly get up to speed with it.

Generating XHTML Pages from Databases

If you decide to generate an XHTML page from a database, you'll find that the process is complicated, but certainly doable. You have to provide a way for the server (where your Web pages are published) to communicate with the database software.

The software, covered in the previous section, that allows this communication resides on the same computer system as the Web server, and it links the Web server to the data sources.

Exactly how you generate XHTML from a database depends on the software you choose; however, the general process is as follows:

1. Set up the data source. If you already have the data in a database—anything from Access to Oracle—this part is done.

2. Set up the intermediary software (ColdFusion, in our case) to communicate with the database and with the Web server. The intermediary software usually connects directly to the database (the information) itself and not to the data via the program used to create the data.

3. Set up query and change forms to get information out of and put information into XHTML documents.

4. Edit the documents to fit into the overall site appearance.

ASR used the ColdFusion Web Application Wizard to select information to display, to select fields to search on, and to select additional data to present on request. The result was a simple XHTML form in which users can enter search terms. Developing the form—linked to the data—is as simple as choosing options from menus, as shown here.

Furthermore, in addition to the plain-text boxes and the drop-down lists shown in Figure 18.1, users can add check boxes and radio buttons to their search form interface.

Figure 18.1 *A simple and easily generated ColdFusion search form*

The XHTML markup for this search form has a .cfm extension. You'll find it easy to edit manually or with any XHTML editing application, but you'll need to edit it to create well-formed and valid XHTML.

Using Predefined Searches

One technique that can save time for you and your users is a *predefined search*. Instead of users typing the search terms or even selecting terms from a list, they can simply click a link to automatically search in ways you define.

The easiest way to establish these searches is to go to the search form and run the query. Then, copy and paste the URL from the location line in the browser into the XHTML editing program. For example, at the hypothetical ASR site, a detailed view of information about skis is at http://www.example.com/ASROutfitters/Detail .CFM?Products__ProductID=6.

Adding this URL to the a element (to create a link):

```
<a href="http://www.example.com/ASROutfitters/
    Detail.CFM?Products__ProductID=6" >Ski Information,
    Detailed</a>
```

makes it much easier for your users to find information.

Using Microsoft Personal Web Server and ASP

You can create a database in Microsoft Access (or other desktop database programs such as FileMaker Pro or Paradox) and serve XHTML pages with ASP technology using Microsoft Personal Web Server running on your own computer. This is a good way to test database concepts and get an idea of what's involved in creating data-driven Web pages. Note that we chose to use Personal Web Server in this example because it's available at no charge to anyone using a PC, and it's easy to set up.

The details of setting up a database connection and writing a script to access a database are beyond the scope of this book. However, in this section, we go through the process of setting up Personal Web Server and serving a sample XHTML page on your computer. Many resources for learning how to use databases are available, and we discuss some of these at the end of this section.

Here's how to use Personal Web Server to serve a sample XHTML page on your computer:

1. Check whether the appropriate server is already installed on your computer. Go to Start ➤ Find ➤ Files Or Folders and search by the server name: Personal Web Server (on Windows 95/98), Peer Web Services (on Windows NT), or Internet Information Services 5.0 (Windows 2000/XP).

   Table 18.1 shows where you can find the setup files for the various operating systems.

Table 18.1 Where to Find Setup Files

Operating System	Location
Windows 95	Download the Windows NT 4 Option Pack*
Windows 98	Windows 98 installation CD
Windows 2000/XP	Windows 2000/XP installation CD
Windows NT	Download the Windows NT 4 Option Pack*

*You can download the Windows NT Option pack from `http://msdn.microsoft.com/library/default.asp?URL=/library/officedev/office97/settinguppersonalwebserver.htm`.

2. Follow the setup instructions and install your server. Check the Main page in the Personal Web Manager window—you can access Personal Web Manager by double-clicking the PWS icon in the Taskbar. Find the address of your home directory. Write it down so you can access it later. This is the folder where your server gets the pages. The default address is usually something similar to `C:\Inetpub\www.root`.

3. Go to Control Panel and double-click the Network icon, and then click the Identification tab. Check the name listed in the Computer Name box. Write down this name because you need it to access your server.

4. Test your server in a browser. For the address, type **http://Computer Name/** where **Computer Name** is the name of your computer. For example, one of our computers is named Frank. To test the server, we type the address `http://Frank/` in the browser. You can also test directly from the Personal Web Manager Main window. Just click the link after "Your home page is available at."

Make sure you get something other than an error message when you do this so you know your installation is functioning. If you do get an error message, you may need to uninstall and reinstall the server.

5. Now that Personal Web Server (or the equivalent for your operating system) is installed and running, you have the ability to serve XHTML/ASP Web pages from your computer. Next, you'll create a page called `default.asp` to test your server. Start with an XHTML header:

```
<!DOCTYPE html PUBLIC "-//W3C/DTD XHTML 1.0
    Transitional//EN"
"http://www.w3.org/TR/xhtml1/DTD/xhtml1-transitional.dtd">
<html xmlns="http://www.w3.org/1999/xhtml">
<head>
<title>Example</title>
```

6. Add markup to specify that you're using VBScript as the scripting language for your ASP between the head tags. (You don't have to use VBScript as the scripting language, but it's the usual choice for ASP.) Enclose this within a `script` element and a CDATA section.

```
<head>
    <title>Example</title>
    <script language="vbscript" type="text/vbscript">
    <!--<![CDATA[
    <% language= VBScript %>
    //]]> -->
    </script>
</head>
```

 Note that we used a CDATA section to enclose the VBScript. Although, as we mentioned in Chapter 11, no current browsers know how to handle XML CDATA sections, we have provided a workaround here, i.e., enclosing the CDATA section within two groups of comments: an XHTML comment (<!--...-->) and a scripting comment (//).

7. Add markup for the body of the page, including one line of VBScript that tells the browser to write to the page.

```
<body bgcolor="teal">
    <p>
    <% response.write ("Someday I will have database results
```

```
    to display here.") %>
</p>
</body>
</html>
```

8. Save this page as default.asp. Put it in the home directory for your server, and then go to a browser and type **http://Computer Name/** (where **Computer Name** is the name of your computer).

    default.asp is now the home page for your server, and should be the page that displays.

Lising 18.1 shows the complete code.

LISTING 18.1: XHTML AND ASP

```
<!DOCTYPE html PUBLIC "-//W3C/DTD XHTML 1.0 Transitional//EN"
    "http://www.w3.org/TR/xhtml1/DTD/xhtml1-transitional.dtd">
<html xmlns="http://www.w3.org/1999/xhtml">
<head>
<title>Example</title>
<script language="vbscript" type="text/vbscript">
<!--<![CDATA[
<% language= VBScript  %>
//]]> -->
</script>
</head>
<body bgcolor="teal">
    <p>
    <% response.write ("Someday soon I will have database
    results to display here!") %>
    </p>
</body>
</html>
```

If you would like to go further with ASPs and Personal Web Server, see Jay Greenspan's tutorial "Your First Database." He provides sample Access databases and sample ASPs in this excellent introduction to using databases on the Web: http://hotwired.lycos.com/webmonkey/backend/ databases/tutorials/tutorial3.html?tw=eg20010201.

For more information about using databases to update Web site content, see Jeffrey Veen's tutorial "Object-Oriented Publishing" at `http://hotwired.lycos.com/webmonkey/01/21/index2a.html`.

Maintaining Pages Generated from a Database

After you generate XHTML from a database, you need to keep the pages current. Just because they're automatically generated does not mean that they require no maintenance. Unlike maintaining regular XHTML documents, maintaining database-generated documents involves both the data and the presentation.

First, you update the data or information in the database using the software in which you developed the database. When a browser requests the page from the Web server, the server-side script (which is part of the XHTML page) accesses the database for the information. Setting up a connection to the database to retrieve the database information is part of the server-side script. After you've updated your data, this new information is then displayed on the Web page in accordance with the presentational structure you've specified in the XHTML.

You can change the XHTML in order to change the presentation as often as you feel is necessary just as you would maintain any of the XHTML pages on your Web site. When your changes are made, you can upload the new XHTML pages to the Web server so that the changes can take effect.

You can also change the code in the server-side script in your pages to access different information from the database.

Where to Go from Here

In this chapter, we showed you how generating XHTML from a database can be useful, which tools you have at your disposal, which kinds of databases you can create, and—finally—how to generate XHTML from a database. Knowing how to integrate databases into your Web site can save hundreds of hours of writing XHTML pages and can add a whole new world of functionality to your site. Whether you're at a big company or organization, a small one, or somewhere in between, generating XHTML from a database offers you a powerful tool for giving users easy-to-use information.

Where to now?

- Chapter 7 covers XHTML forms.

- Chapter 16 gives you more information about Web servers.

- Chapter 19 shows you how to make your entire site searchable.

Making Your Web Site Searchable

XHTML

Chapter 19

When you make your Web site searchable, you give users much more flexibility: They can jump immediately to the information they've come to get without necessarily following your predefined path. In this chapter, we're going to look at the techniques and tools you can use to add a search capability to your site.

First, we'll discuss the pros and cons of making your site searchable (doing so is not for every site), and then we'll talk about which search tools, known as search engines, are available and how to use them. Although some of this information gets into advanced concepts, your comfort level will be fine if you've read Chapter 16, which talks about understanding and using Web servers, and if you have a good grasp of the issues involved in XHTML coding.

This chapter covers the following topics:

- Choosing how to let users navigate your site

- Exploring the possibilities of site-wide search engines

- Examining search engine products

- Implementing a fully functional search engine on your site

Letting Users Search Your Site

One of the most important decisions that you, as a Web developer, must make is how to present navigation choices to your users. Some sites are carefully mapped to guide users through every step from point A to point B. Other sites use common navigation shortcuts, such as headers and footers or frames, to allow users to jump to specific points. Still other sites use database searches, and, of course, some sites combine any or all of these methods.

In addition to these methods, you have a more general tool for helping users find their way around your site: a search engine. A *search engine* is a tool that users can use to find words or phrases within any or all of your Web pages.

 If you've spent any time on the Internet, you've already used a search engine. For example, you may have tried AltaVista (www.altavista.com), Excite (www.excite.com), Google (www.google.com), or Yahoo! (www.yahoo.com), which provides expedient ways to search the Internet. All you do is enter a search query; the search engine plugs and churns for a second or two and then provides a list of results containing documents that should match your query.

Of course, as with everything, there are benefits and liabilities to adding a search engine to your site. Let's look at the benefits first.

The Benefits of Adding a Search Engine

Search engines help users quickly determine whether your site has the information they want and helps them retrieve it. If users can enter the word *hiking* and instantly receive a listing of every single page on the ASR Outfitters site that contains that word, they can retrieve the information they need with much greater speed than by clicking through page after page of menus.

Search engines also help users navigate from one part of the site to another, which can frequently be difficult. Users often have to find their way back to the home page of the site and then start over. With search engines, they can search for what they want and immediately receive a link to it.

In addition, search engines help users view the sections of your site in a unified manner. At many sites, sections do not have a lot in common. Even though the information in all the sections may be useful, moving from one to another can be difficult, and a user may not know that another section exists. A search engine helps users obtain this information.

The Liabilities of a Search Engine

As useful as a search engine is, there are some good reasons for *not* making your site searchable. For starters, adding a search engine can eat up significant resources (time and money). Before you make your site searchable, be absolutely sure that you have the resources to maintain it. In addition, once your site is searchable, you have to keep it current. A search engine that returns outdated information or dead links is a sure way to drive users from your site.

Privacy may also be a concern if your site contains sensitive documents. When dealing with search engines, there's no such thing as "security by obscurity." Be sure that you index only those pages that you want to be searchable, or don't add a search engine to your site. See the sidebar "A Word about Indexing" for information about how this works.

Another concern is site coherency. If your site has a clear, predefined path that you want users to traverse, adding a search engine may defeat the purpose of the predefined path. In your planning process, consider the type of site you're building and whether a search engine fits with the scheme.

- -

A Word about Indexing

The terms *index, indexing,* and *indexer* appear often in this chapter, and their use in this electronic context is similar to their traditional use. In the index at the back of this book, important words appear in alphabetic order along with the number of the page(s) on which they're located. The purpose of an index is to help readers quickly locate a topic of interest.

The purpose of a computer index is very similar. All, or most, of the words in a group of files are listed along with their locations. If you want a specific word or concept, you can simply look it up in the index.

Once the index exists, special programs called *search front ends* allow users to search the index for relevant documents. The programs that create the index are called *indexers* and include applications such as Glimpse (`http://glimpse .cs.arizona.edu/`), Wide Area Information Server (WAIS), Netscape's Catalog Server, and Microsoft's Index Server.

- -

Using Low-Tech Alternatives

If you think a search engine may not be the best solution for your Web site but you would still like to add some searching functionality, you might consider some of the following alternatives. These approaches don't involve the overhead or resource drain associated with adding and maintaining a search engine.

Most of the best sites on the Internet use a combination of the approaches we describe in this chapter. As you can see, you can improve site navigation without resorting to a search engine.

Taking the Guided Tour Approach

The guided tour approach is basically a series of XHTML pages with, at the extreme, only one link on each page: the link to the next page. This is probably the simplest and the least-flexible solution. Most sites that use this approach also provide links to the previous page and to the home page. However, it all amounts to the same thing—the user travels a set path and is not encouraged to deviate from that path.

Whether this approach will work for you depends on the type of site you're creating. This approach works well, for example, in the context of an online book, which might include links only to the next page, to the previous page, and to the table of contents.

Taking the "Everything Is a Link" Approach

On a site that uses the "everything is a link" approach, each page links to all other relevant pages on or off the site for any word that users might associate with such a link. You'll recognize these sites because many or most of the words in the site link to something. Here's how it works. If you have the text

```
The quick brown fox jumps over the lazy dog.
```

you might have the following links:

- *The* links to a dictionary definition of the word *the*.
- *quick* links to a page listing the relative velocities of land animals.
- *brown* links to a page discussing pigmentation in mammal fur.
- *fox* links to a page describing the animal.

And so on. You get the point.

This can be a problem because too many underlined words are very difficult to read. In addition, it might be difficult for the user to select the correct word to which he or she wants to link because the linked words are so close together.

Using Hierarchical Menus

Shortly before the advent of the Web, another method of information distribution became popular: gopher. *Gopher* is a predominantly text-based series of menus, similar to the one shown in Figure 19.1, that consists of links to either files or other menus, which may be on the same server or another.

Although the Web stole gopher's glory, gopher sites still exist and you can view them with any major Web browser. Many of the first Web sites looked just like gopher sites. Of course, the documents were more attractive because HTML could do what plain text never could, but the interface was still a series of hierarchical menus leading to a file.

If you want simplicity and ease of use, consider using hierarchical menus—built with XHTML, however—on your site. Users are familiar with menu structures and know how to use them. But let's face it: Menus are boring when compared with the many visually appealing approaches.

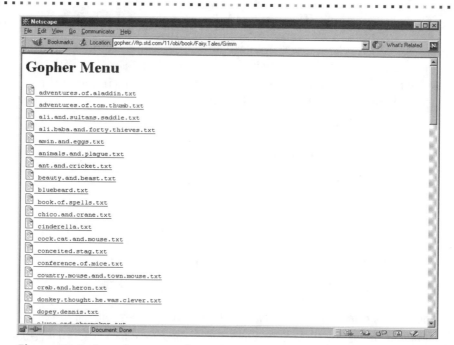

Figure 19.1 A gopher menu site

Using a Back-of-the-Book Index

For many people seeking information in books, the traditional back-of-the-book index is an invaluable tool. You can create a similar tool for your Web site users by either manually (and somewhat laboriously) or automatically providing a site index. Although site indexes can require tedious maintenance, they do have the potential for helping your users find and use information on your site quickly and easily.

Figure 19.2 shows an index produced by HTML Indexer, a tool that helps you automatically generate a site index. You can find out more about this tool at www .html-indexer.com.

Figure 19.2 *HTML Indexer is a handy tool for generating a site index.*

Using JavaScript

Perhaps one of the most useful JavaScript applications is one that allows users to search your site. It's fairly simple to run and does not require a full-blown search engine. Similar to the site index, a JavaScript search application can require a lot of maintenance, but it helps users find information quickly. You'll find JavaScript that you can copy, paste, and add to your site at `http://javascript.internet.com`.

Adding a Site Map

Even if you've lived in the same neighborhood your entire life, you probably need a map to get around the rest of the city. And when you visit a city for the first time, you most definitely need a map to find your way around. The same is true when you visit Web sites. After you've visited a site several times, you usually know where to find what you want, but on your first visit (especially if you arrive via a link), you may have no idea where you've landed or what else is on the site.

One solution to this problem is a *site map*, which is a page that includes a structural overview of the site. It could take the form of a traditional map, a tree structure, or simply a list of pages and their locations. From site maps, users can gauge the breadth and depth of the site, determine where they are within the site, and figure out how to go to another section.

The simplest site map is a directory listing of all the files at the site. This solution is not necessarily ideal (or fascinating), but it can be effective. On the other hand, a site map can be completely graphical, giving users an instant, visual sense of what the site contains. You can create an animated, interactive site map using Java or similar technology.

Many commercial Web servers (such as SuiteSpot from Netscape, `http://home` `.netscape.com/suitespot/v3.5/index.html`) come with tools that allow you to easily generate graphical site maps. In addition, NetObjects Fusion (`www.netobjects.com`), Microsoft FrontPage (`www.microsoft.com/frontpage`), Macromedia Dreamweaver (`www.macromedia.com/software/dreamweaver/`), and Adobe GoLive (`www.adobe.com/` `products/golive/main.html`) include site-mapping programs. These programs do not generate XHTML site map pages for the public, but instead generate site maps for your use. With these, you can add and modify pages and move them around the hierarchy of your site, among many other things.

Enabling Users to Search within Your Site

If you've examined all the options and have decided that adding a search engine to your site is worth the effort, the next step is to decide how to enable users to search within your site. Before you index your first page, answer the following two questions (which are discussed in detail in the following sections):

- How much of your site will be indexed?

- Who can access your search engine?

How Much of Your Site Will Be Indexed?

If you're absolutely confident that you want everyone to be able to hunt down every word on your site, the answer to this question is easy: Index the entire site. However, for most people, there are gray areas, and this question requires a great deal of thought. The following are some sections of your site that probably should not be indexed:

- Pages that exist only to help you maintain the site

- Any password-protected pages

 You want password-protected information hidden from the public. Therefore, you can index those pages on a separate search engine that is accessible only from the password-protected area. Also, you don't want to annoy users by allowing them to link to a blocked area that they're then forbidden to access.

Before you put your search engine online, go through each page on your site (or each section if you have a large site) and decide whether you want to allow it on the search engine. If other people have a stake in the content of your site, be sure to have their consent before making their pages available via the search engine. Do not assume that a page should be on a search engine just because it's publicly available.

Who Can Access Your Search Engine?

As with the first question, if you want your site available to all users, this answer is easy: everybody. However, you may want to restrict access to the search engine to a selected group of people or keep a selected group of people out.

The easiest way to do this is to place the Common Gateway Interface (CGI) program within a password-protected area of your site. With most search engines, you can create separate indexes for different parts of your site. This allows you to restrict access on a section-by-section basis.

As we mentioned earlier, be sure that it's not possible to retrieve a reference to a password-protected page from a publicly available area of your Web site.

After you choose the parts of your site to index and decide who will have access to the index, make a list of all the directories that you will index. Almost all search engines index by directory. If you have a directory in which you want some files to be indexed but not other files, you'll probably have to split the directory into two directories—only one of which will be searchable. After you have a list of all the directories and files on your server, select the directories you want to index.

If your Web server is on a Unix machine, run the command `ls -lR` *from the root of your Web site to produce a list of all files within the site (not counting pages in user directories). From a Windows machine, use* `dir /s` *at a DOS prompt. On a Macintosh machine, use the system utilities to view a directory tree.*

Finding and Implementing Search Engines

Choosing the right search engine depends on your equipment and resources. The search engine choices for a Unix server are different from those for a Windows or Macintosh system. However, one commonality is the need for power. In general, search engines are resource intensive. Large amounts of hard disk space (often in the tens-of-gigabytes range) are needed to store the site index, and fast CPUs with lots of RAM are needed to run the front end for the searches. As in most cases, trade-offs are possible, and you can run a functional search engine with modest hardware. Still, if you want the performance of, for example, AltaVista (in which a large portion of the entire Web is indexed but searches can still seem instantaneous), you have to pay for AltaVista-level hardware, which is expensive.

Unix Solutions

If you're running a Unix-based Web server, you have a wide range of choices. Unlike the Windows world, few Unix solutions depend on a specific Web server. Some of these products are based on a scripting language such as Perl, in which case you need the language interpreter on your Web server machine. Still other products are distributed in source-code-only form. In such cases, you need a C compiler (and for some products, a C++ compiler) on your Web server machine.

If special software is needed, we've noted the requirement in the following descriptions.

Here is a list of the most popular Unix search solutions:

Simple Search   Simple Search is a Perl script, offered by Matt's Script Archive, that implements a search according to your XHTML documents' `title` element. It's fairly straightforward to implement, and it's a great solution for small or low-traffic sites. Find Simple Search at `www.worldwidemart.com/scripts/`.

Glimpse   The University of Arizona created Glimpse as a kinder, gentler text-searching mechanism. Glimpse includes a text indexer and searching program with a myriad of simple, easy-to-use options for creating powerful searches. Additionally, an offshoot project called Webglimpse makes an entire site searchable. Find Glimpse at `http://glimpse.cs.arizona.edu/`.

ht://Dig   San Diego State University created ht://Dig to index its (then small) campus Web site. Designed for small sites and intranets, ht://Dig is fast and easy to use. It's not limited to a single server and can index pages from several related Web servers. It includes many features not found in larger search engines, such as *fuzzy searching* (searching for words using phonetic sounds or synonyms). You need a C compiler and a C++ compiler to implement this search engine on your site. You can find this search engine at `www.htdig.org`.

WAIS   In many ways, Wide Area Information Server (WAIS) is the grandfather of the current crop of search engines such as SWISH (see below), Glimpse, and the like. The official WAIS is a commercial product that has passed through several owners in the past few years, and is currently not available. However, there are a couple of freely available offshoots, such as freeWAIS and freeWAIS-sf. All versions of WAIS are robust and include many types of searches and even different ways of searching. Depending on the version you're using, creating a search interface can range from moderately tricky to downright impossible. You can find freeWAIS at `www.ensta.fr/internet/unix/wais/freewais.html`, and freeWAIS-sf is available at `http://ls6-www.informatik.uni-dortmund.de/ir/projects/freeWAIS-sf/`.

SWISH   SWISH is a combination indexing/searching solution that you can also use as a searching-only front end to the WAIS indexer. SWISH was developed by Kevin Hughes of EIT as a WAIS-like indexing program and has many of the features of that system. SWISH has the advantage of small index files (generally about 1 to 5 percent of the total files you are indexing) and fast response time. You can find the latest version of SWISH, SWISH-E, at `http://sunsite.berkeley.edu/SWISH-E/`. A C++ version, SWISH++, is available at `http://homepage.mac.com/pauljlucas/software/swish/` and can be run not only on Unix but also on Windows 95/98/NT.

Windows Solutions

In the world of Microsoft Windows, the type of search engine you use for your Web site depends largely on the Web server you're running. Few third-party search engine front ends, and fewer still Web indexers, are available for Windows. Luckily, almost all the major commercial Web servers for Windows come with tools that allow you to index your site and make it searchable.

If you install Perl on the machine running your Web server, you can also use the Perl-based Unix solutions previously mentioned, such as Simple Search.

The most common utility for Microsoft is Index Server, which is a search application included with Windows NT Server 4 as part of Internet Information Server (IIS). It can search and index ASCII text files, HTML files, and files created by the Microsoft Office and BackOffice suites of products. It can also search for document properties and HTML tags. It requires that IIS or Peer Web Server run continuously. However, once you've set it up, all index updates, optimization, and even crash recovery are automatic.

Cross-Platform Solutions: Atomz Search

Atomz Search is a hosted Web site search engine service. No special software is required to use Atomz Search because the application is hosted on the Atomz Search server. Three different types of services are currently available:

Atomz Express Search   Free for sites with fewer than 500 pages, it indexes page title, keyword `meta` tags, description `meta` tags, and page content. Templates are provided, but the design layout can be changed to match the rest of your site. An Atomz Search logo appears on the search results page, but no additional banners or ads are required to use this free service.

Atomz Prime Search   Atomz Prime offers advanced features, such as search reports showing what words or phrases users are using to search your site. You can set up daily site re-indexing if the content changes that frequently, or request re-indexing on demand when site content changes. Price is based on the number of pages in the site.

Atomz Enterprise Search   More advanced features are available in Atomz Enterprise, including incremental indexing, parallel indexing, e-commerce support, and intranet support.

Find out more information on Atomz Search at `www.atomz.com`.

Recommendations for Searching Solutions

After you've investigated all the search engine options, you must select what is best for your site. In doing so, you'll want to consider the following:

- The size of your site
- The number of users
- Your technical support resources

Moderately Sized Unix Sites

Perhaps the most common type of Web site found throughout the Internet is medium sized and powered by a Unix-based (usually a free Unix such as Linux or FreeBSD) server running the Apache Web server. Because of the power and affordability of free Unix derivatives, as well as the decreasing costs of a permanent Internet connection, almost anyone can set up a Web server. Sometimes it seems as if almost everyone has.

Creating a search engine for a site like this usually involves some programming, but the results can be effective. A free indexing system such as Glimpse is usually a good choice in this situation. You can then use either Webglimpse or SWISH as a search front end, but, in most cases, if you have the programming help available, the best bet is to create your own search front end that allows customized searches. We'll discuss a simple example of this shortly.

Windows Sites

The next largest (and fastest-growing) segment of the Web server population consists of corporate sites that use Windows NT Server, and possibly even Windows 2000 Server. Most of these sites run Netscape SuiteSpot or the Microsoft Internet Information Server (called Internet Information Services in Windows 2000 and XP).

Creating a search engine for either of these servers is a simple matter of using the indexing tools that come with the server. Netscape Catalog Server and Microsoft Index Server are almost identical in form and function: Both allow you to easily select the areas of your site that you want to index and then automatically update the index. Both provide front ends and allow most common searches. With either, you can create a custom front end, but neither makes it easy, and it's usually more trouble than it's worth.

Sample Search: A Medium-Sized, Unix Solution

H-Net, Humanites OnLine (www.h-net.msu.edu), is a prototypical example of the medium-sized, Unix system that forms the bulk of the Web. Its main search page (at http://www2.h-net.msu.edu/search) includes many options. You can search

- Discussion logs
- Book reviews
- Web pages
- Job guides
- Academic announcements

Users can search one or more of the site's sections or the entire site. In addition, many pages include search forms that allow searches automatically restricted to the current section. The searching capabilities of the site are driven by a Glimpse index and a custom front end (written in Perl) that is loosely based on WWWWais by Kevin Hughes of EIT.

Leveraging the Work of Internet Search Engines

In addition to the methods we've discussed so far, there's another way to allow users to search your site. It's completely free and requires no modification to your existing setup. This technique involves "piggybacking" off existing search engines, such as AltaVista, Lycos, WebCrawler, Yahoo!, and so on.

These super search engines index as much of the Web as they can, which can be a *lot*. (At the time of this writing, AltaVista's index includes 250 million individual Web pages from more than a million servers.) If your site has been indexed by one of these search engines, anyone on the Internet can find your site through the search engine. The trick is to cull your site from the thousands of other sites that could be returned for a particular search query. There are some interesting ways to do this:

- Be sure your site contains lots of links to other resources.
- Use the title and meta elements in your documents properly.

- Use the keywords that you put in the `meta` element in the body of your document frequently.

- Include the `alt` attribute in your images.

Other utilities are available that can help you achieve a higher ranking in search engines. See the excellent article at `www.selfpromotion.com/improve.t` for more information on some of these tools.

Registering with Search Engines

With the number of search engines out there, it would take you forever and a day to register your site with every existing search engine. Luckily, there are services available that will do the dirty work for you. These services sometimes cost money, but if your site is a large portion of your revenue, it's worth your time, effort, and money to use them. Here are a couple services that we know about:

- CyberRegister.com at `www.123-cyber-register.com`

- Linkosaurus at `http://sffa.com/linkosaurus.html`

You can also register your site yourself. Check out the following sites on how to do this effectively:

- `www.selfpromotion.com`

- `www.searchengineguide.com`

- `www.searchengineshowdown.com`

In addition, you can just visit the search engines of your choice and look for a link that says something like "Add your site to blah" or "Submit a site." Ironically enough, you can just go to your favorite search engine and type **search engine** to see a plethora of search engine sites. We suggest you start with the following sites:

- AltaVista at `www.altavista.com`

- Ask Jeeves at `www.ask.com`

- Excite at `www.excite.com`

- Google at `www.google.com`

- HotBot at `www.hotbot.com`

- GO.com at www.go.com

- LookSmart at www.looksmart.com

- Lycos at www.lycos.com

- Microsoft at http://.search.msn.com

- NBCi at www.nbci.com

- Netscape at www.netscape.com

- WebCrawler at www.webcrawler.com

- Yahoo! at www.yahoo.com

After your site is registered, it will be retrieved by relevant searches without much additional work on your part if you followed the guidelines listed earlier (referring to page titles, keywords, links, and alt attributes for images).

AltaVista's Special Search Function

If AltaVista has indexed enough of your pages, you can use a special search function to create a custom search engine for your site at no cost. To get a preferential list of pages from your site, use the following in your search term:

```
host:www.myhost.com
```

If you want only pages from, say, the Sybex site returned, include **+host:www.sybex.com** in your search term (notice the + symbol).

By including +host:www.myhost.com in your query, you're guaranteed to be searching only your site (assuming your site is named www.myhost.com, that is). Because AltaVista uses simple HTML forms to interface with its search engine, it's possible to replicate an AltaVista search form on any or all of your XHTML pages. You can thus add a search capability to any of your pages. A simple form to allow an AltaVista search might look like this:

```
<form method="post" action="http://altavista.com/cgi-
    bin/query">
<input type="hidden" name="pg" value="q" />
Search the Web:<br />
<input name="q" size="55" maxlength="200" /><br />
<input type="submit" value="Submit" />
</form>
```

You can also choose between searching the Web and searching Usenet newsgroups, and you can display the results in one of three forms of varying detail.

 Use your favorite Web browser to view the source code of the AltaVista home page (`www.altavista` `.digital.com`*) to get some more ideas.*

To restrict the search to your specific site, filter the query through a CGI program that adds `+host:www.myserver.com` to the query and then forwards it to AltaVista for the results. The form on the Web page would be almost identical, except for a couple of small changes:

```
<form method="post"
    action="http://www.myserver.com/~me/av.cgi">
<input type="hidden" name="addon1"
    value="+host:www.myserver.com" />
Search the Web:<br />
<input name="q" size="55" maxlength="200" /><br />
<input type="submit" value="Submit" />
</form>
```

The form no longer refers to the AltaVista CGI program (`www.altavista.com/` `cgi-bin/query`), but rather to a custom-made CGI program on your server. This CGI program simply adds the extra information to the query and sends it to AltaVista for processing. You can do this in just a few lines of Perl:

```
#!/usr/bin/perl -w ## Your Perl Goes Here

use CGI; ## Require the CGI.pm module
$output = new CGI; ## Get all of the CGI information

$query = $output->param('q');

$i = 1;
while ($addon = $output->param("addon$i") ) {
    $q .= " $addon";
    $i++;
}

print "Location:
    http://www.altavista.com/cgi-bin/query?pg=q&q=$q\n\n";
```

This script will run without any modification on your Web server, provided Perl is installed. In addition, this script uses the CGI.pm Perl module, which provides easy-to-use CGI-related functions. This module is not a standard part of Perl but can be downloaded from the Comprehensive Perl Archive Network (CPAN) at www.perl.com/CPAN/.

Even though it's only ten lines, the previous script is actually somewhat more complicated than it needs to be. That's because AltaVista added a little extra feature that makes your site searches even more powerful.

In addition to the host:www.myhost.com feature, AltaVista provides another search enhancement. If you add url:mypage.html to an AltaVista search, pages that contain mypage.html in the URL will be given precedence in the result. As shown previously, +url:mypage.html returns only those pages that contain mypage.html.

This is useful for two reasons. First, suppose that your site is not the only site on your server, and instead of a base URL such as www.myhost.com, your base URL is more like www.myisp.com/~me. Adding +host:www.myisp.com restricts the search to www.myisp.com, but that may return more hits than just your specific site. However, adding +url:~me along with +host:www.myisp.com guarantees that only pages from your specific branch of the server will return from the search.

Second, you can use this feature to limit the search to a specific page or section of pages within your site. Suppose you want to restrict your search to the archives directory. Along with the +host:www.myisp.com, add +url:~me/archives; only pages from the archives directory of your specific site will be found.

With this script in place, you can use the following XHTML form to search any part of your Web site:

```
<form method="post" action="http://www.myisp.com/~me/av.cgi">
<input type="hidden" name="addon1"
    value="+host:www.myisp.com" />
<input type="hidden" name="addon2" value="+url:~me/archives">
Search the Web: /><br />
<input name="q" size="55" maxlength="200" /><br />
<input type="submit" value="Submit" />
</form>
```

You can add as many hidden fields with addon1, addon2, addon3, and so on as you like, and the script aligns them and sends them with the user's query to AltaVista.

You may have noticed that this script does not display any HTML of its own. It simply forwards the request to AltaVista. This means that the page will not be in the same style as the rest of your site, but rather it will be an AltaVista search results page.

AltaVista currently forbids the modification of its search results pages in any way, unless you have a special deal with Compaq Computer Corporation. Sending your users to the standard AltaVista search page is the price you have to pay for using a maintenance-free, cost-free solution for Web searching.

AltaVista at Michigan State University (http://altavista.msu.edu), right across the street from H-Net, is the Computer Center that houses MSU's AltaVista machine. Except for the green and white logo at the top of the page, this site could easily be mistaken for AltaVista's main page. It provides a complete AltaVista style search of every major server on campus (including H-Net's). MSU's AltaVista is powered by the AltaVista Intranet Search Private Extension running on an Alpha with Digital Unix.

Where to Go from Here

In this chapter, we explored the world of interactive search engines. We looked at the various styles of site navigation and the benefits of each. We examined many of the most popular searching and indexing tools and discussed how to index your site and provide a searchable interface. Adding a search engine to your site provides a valuable service to your users.

Where to now?

- Chapter 7 explains the XHTML forms that present your database to others.

- In Chapter 8, find out how to use frames to provide navigation shortcuts to your users.

- See Chapter 18 to find out how to use databases to provide other types of searches at your site.

Part VI
A Bridge to XML

An Overview of XML

XHTML

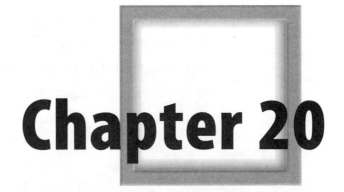

Chapter 20

Web technologies have already provided much more useful and valuable tools than anyone could have envisioned only a few years ago. Along with the changes in Web site use and purpose have come many technological advances in Web-based information delivery. For example, Microsoft and Netscape have repeatedly extended HTML, adding features that provide flashy, useful effects that help you work around the limitations of basic, standard HTML. (Not all these features became part of the W3C recommendations, however.) The W3C has expanded the HTML standard on several occasions, each time adding a slew of features (some from the browser vendors and some not) that let you better control document appearance as well as make documents more accessible and usable.

However, these advances focus primarily on formatting Web sites. What's absent is an emphasis on technology that makes online information easy to present, maintain, and reuse. Even though you can create visually appealing Web sites, you're limited to using simple document structures (this is a heading; this is a paragraph). You must employ complex and convoluted systems to automate information delivery, and maintaining documents is an exercise in tedium. That is, until now.

The *Extensible Markup Language (XML)* offers unique capabilities and flexibility. In particular, it bridges the gap between the two main markup languages, Standard Generalized Markup Language (SGML) and HTML, making the development of online information easier, more accessible, and more affordable. In this chapter, we'll introduce you to XML and show you how it handles specific needs that neither SGML nor HTML addresses directly.

This chapter covers the following topics:

- Understanding the purposes of markup languages
- Exploring the advantages and disadvantages of SGML
- Exploring the advantages and disadvantages of HTML
- Understanding how XML bridges the gap between SGML and HTML

Why Another Markup Language?

With HTML, SGML, and other markup languages already available, you might be wondering why we need yet another such language. XML meets a specific need and compensates for certain limitations inherent in both SGML and HTML. We can most easily understand XML in the context of these other languages and their well-defined roles. So, before we dive into XML specifics in the "Understanding XML Markup" section, let's look at how these markup languages—SGML, HTML, XHTML, and XML—all relate to one another.

Understanding SGML Basics

SGML stands for Standard Generalized Markup Language and is based on work that Charles Goldfarb, Ed Mosher, and Ray Lorie undertook in the 1970s to create a platform-independent way of representing documents and their contents. This effort was so successful, in fact, that by 1986, SGML became enshrined as ISO standard 8879.

SGML is the original and the most powerful of the three markup languages we cover here. In fact, SGML lays a strong foundation for creating complex, large, or highly structured document sets. Using SGML, you can set up document rules that let you identify any structural part of a document, such as titles and subtitles, authors and editors, paragraphs and definitions, dates and times, and any other part you can imagine.

SGML is a *meta-language* used to describe and define other markup languages. The SGML rules that define these other markup languages are contained within a *Document Type Definition (DTD)*, which outlines what the language can and cannot do. Think of a DTD as defining a specific subset of SGML that contains only the SGML capabilities necessary to meet specific needs. For example, an SGML DTD originally defined HTML's capabilities; essentially, it included only those aspects of SGML needed for very simple Web information delivery. Therefore, HTML includes only the pieces necessary for its purpose and becomes markedly easier to use than SGML, but it also becomes more limited in its flexibility and effectiveness.

A meta-language can define other, more specific markup languages.

The key to understanding DTDs is realizing that they're completely customizable, meaning that you can specify which elements and attributes may be contained in documents and what rules they must follow. For example, the HTML DTD specifies that you can include a maximum of six levels of headings (h1 through h6) and that you can include any heading at any point in a document—above or below paragraphs, images, other headings, addresses, or any other page element.

The result of this flexibility is that SGML DTDs can meet practically any need. In fact, many large and small organizations worldwide use SGML, including Lockheed-Martin, Boeing, the U.S. Department of Defense, the Association of American Publishers, Hewlett-Packard, Kodak, the publications office of the European Community, Oxford University Press, the International Organization for Standardization (ISO), and even the publishers of this book, Sybex Inc., to name just a few. Although these organizations have very different document needs, their custom DTDs give them the specific capabilities needed to manage, use, and reuse hundreds of thousands of pages (or screens) of information.

SGML DTDs can require that you comply with the rules precisely as specified—that is, if the DTD says that a Chapter SubTitle follows a Chapter Title, you must include both the title and subtitle and include them in the order specified. If you don't follow the DTD exactly, you likely won't be able to view the documents because most SGML tools will refuse to display or use documents that don't validate successfully against a specific DTD. In this sense, the DTD ensures that documents always conform to an organization's standards; however, this strict compliance also makes developing documents tedious and time-consuming—even when using custom software that helps tailor the information to the DTD.

The Advantages of SGML

First, because the SGML standard is accepted by the International Organization for Standardization (ISO 8879:1986), it lets you easily transfer and reuse information, with the confidence that the document format is mainstream and widely accepted. This helps both today—with the hodgepodge of available document formats—and in the future, for reusing documents, no matter how old those documents become. For example, you could create an SGML document set now and almost certainly be able to change, add to, or otherwise modify the documents 10 years from now.

Why is this significant? Well, imagine creating a document 10 years ago using a word processing program, and then consider the problems you might have trying to edit, add to, or modify that document using today's word processing software—that is, if you can even open the document file. SGML documents are not linked to specific software, companies, or versions; if you can create an SGML document today, you should always be able to use or modify that document in the future.

Second, using SGML, you can custom-build SGML applications to meet your organization's needs. Rather than making do with an existing structure for a manual, you can tailor the SGML application to meet the specific needs of your organization. For example, if you create a series of manuals that must each have an introduction but have no need for glossaries, you can develop a DTD that requires introductions but makes no provision for glossaries.

Third, SGML's capabilities are limitless; therefore, SGML is ideal for extremely large or complex document sets, up to and including the documentation for a Boeing 777. If you developed 777 documentation using any other tool, you could easily suffer through many software versions, be limited by software restrictions, or be bound to the specific brand of software you choose. With SGML, you could create this documentation over a period of years, revise entire sections as information changed, and readily reuse information from other documentation sets, independent of tools or other limitations.

The Disadvantages of SGML

Although SGML offers limitless capabilities and flexibility, it does have a few drawbacks. First, with SGML, you must have a complete DTD *before* you can start creating documents or content. Planning first and creating later is usually a good idea, but you might not always have the time or resources to complete a DTD beforehand. Also, although you can (technically) change a DTD's organization and structure after you create it, you would also need to change all the existing documents to comply with the revised DTD.

Second, SGML is very expensive to implement and use. The SGML specifications alone total 500 pages, and the software required to implement SGML can easily cost hundreds of thousands of dollars in equipment, software, and training. For this reason, your entire organization would have to commit to using SGML as its document-development tool to justify the investment.

Third, SGML's complexity makes constructing generalized parser software to support it quite costly. The SGML specification accommodates unlimited numbers and combinations of elements and attributes, plus different DTDs for different documents, which requires a more flexible and complex browser. Therefore, you're not likely to find many free or very inexpensive SGML browsers (such as Netscape Navigator or Microsoft Internet Explorer with SGML) on the Internet—at least not any time soon.

For more information about SGML, check out Robin Cover's comprehensive site at www.oasis-open .org/cover/sgml-xml.html. *Note the increasing emphasis on XML coverage. You'll have to search individual topic categories for SGML-specific entries.*

Why HTML Was Built

HTML was developed as a specific SGML DTD that offered a relatively limited—but manageable—portion of SGML's most basic text-handling capabilities. HTML was developed at *CERN* (now the European Organization for Nuclear Research) as a simple and concise way for physicists to exchange information and publish papers over the fledgling Internet. SGML was just too big and complicated to address this relatively simple need, so the folks at CERN (mostly Tim Berners-Lee) developed a new markup language—HTML's first version—that included only a small set of SGML capabilities.

Although intentionally limited in its capabilities, HTML has become the most widely used markup language because it's easy to use and straightforward. HTML includes basic formatting and document-structuring capabilities, such as the ability to identify headings, boldface, and italic, and to link to other documents, making it an ideal tool for publishing simple documents.

However, as the Web has grown, HTML has changed to meet some of the increased demands on it. For example, people wanted better, more accurate page layout and design, and they wanted a less tedious way to maintain existing documents. As a result, today's HTML ventures way beyond its original capabilities and intent and includes much more functionality and capability in version 4.01 than was available in earlier versions. XHTML was created to circumvent these problems. See Chapter 1 for a reminder of why XHTML was developed and how it changes HTML.

The Advantages of HTML and XHTML

One of HTML's key features is that it's easy to learn and use, making it an ideal tool for not-so-techie people. As you've learned throughout this book, HTML and XHTML include a simple code structure, consisting of relatively few element and attribute names, angle brackets (<>), and a slash (/). Therefore, you can easily learn to apply elements and not be bogged down with complex code or overwhelming element choices.

Because these two markup languages are so simple, Web browsers—such as Netscape Navigator and Microsoft Internet Explorer—can adequately present virtually any HTML or XHTML document you might create (with the exception of documents designed expressly to take advantage of browser-specific capabilities). This makes exchanging, presenting, and sharing information with HTML and XHTML easy and reliable for many purposes.

Finally, Web browsers do not require strict compliance with a DTD—that is, you can use elements for things other than their intended purposes and still be able to view your documents in a browser. For example, whereas excluding a subtitle in an SGML document might cause a parser to completely reject a document, HTML browsers casually skip over unrecognized components, adapt to missing elements, and nonetheless present documents fairly accurately.

The Disadvantages of HTML and XHTML

Although HTML's simplicity lets you easily learn and use its markup, it also limits you in providing context for words on the page. For example, if we publish a chapter of this book on the Web, all the text and headings would look fine—and anyone reading the document online could certainly get as much out of the chapter as they would on paper. However, the chapter would lack several structural components, such as a chapter subtitle, notes, or sidebars, because HTML and XHTML Frameset and Transitional do not provide elements that correspond to these document parts.

Because HTML and the XHTML Frameset and Transitional DTDs don't provide elements for every possible document part, we could not accurately provide contexts for all page elements. Therefore, we have to use the elements that are available to represent the document parts that we need. For example, we would likely use a heading element (h1) for the subtitle, use an italic element (i) for notes, and use a table element (table) to insert sidebars, but neither users nor computers could automatically differentiate these parts from other headings, italicized words, or tables. Listing 20.1 shows how we might use heading 1, italic, and table elements to format subtitle, note, and sidebar elements using XHTML Transitional.

LISTING 20.1: USING ELEMENTS IN AN XHTML TRANSITIONAL DOCUMENT TO REPRESENT DOCUMENT PARTS

```
<!DOCTYPE html PUBLIC "-//W3C//DTD XHTML 1.0 Transitional//EN"
    "http://www.w3.org/TR/xhtml1/DTD/xhtml1-transitional.dtd">
<html xmlns="http://www.w3.org/1999/xhtml">
<head>
  <title>HTML Formatting Example</title>
</head>
<body bgcolor="#FFFFFF" text="#000000" link="#0000FF"
    vlink="#FF0000" alink="#80080">
<basefont face="Arial, Helvetica" size="4" />
<h1 align="center">Headings Foreshadow Information</h1>
<p><font size="-1">The first paragraph under a heading usually
    presents the key points about the topic and offers a brief
    sample of the information to follow.</font></p>
```

```
<table border="0">
<tr>
<td valign="top">
   <p>Following paragraphs further clarify the information
      and provide more detail. Some information is quoted from
      <cite>The Bible</cite>, whereas other text might be
      <em>emphasized</em> for other reasons.</p>
   <p><strong>Warnings</strong> might be strongly emphasized,
      as well.</p>
</td>
</tr>
</table>
<table border="1" bgcolor="#E0E0E">
<tr>
<td>
   <h3>Sidebars Offer Extras</h3>
   Sidebars offer additional information on specific topics
   that aren't necessarily central to the issues discussed in
   the main flow.
</td>
</tr>
</table>

<p><font size="-1">
   The information above is in two different tables and
   includes a number of elements that describe the appearance
   but not the logical structure of the document.</font></p>
</body>
</html>
```

Figure 20.1 shows how this code appears in a browser; you'll notice that multiple document elements share similar formatting.

A related drawback is that XHTML Transitional requires no definite document structure because the XHTML Transitional DTD is very flexible (as is the way most browsers interpret HTML documents). For example, suppose you're developing an XHTML document featuring your company's MongoMug product. You can choose to include a descriptive document title (using the title element), as in:

```
<title>MongoMug, the Choice of Serious Cocoa Drinkers</title>
```

Figure 20.1 *You can use XHTML Transitional elements to help format information, but the formatting does not describe the content.*

Although the XHTML DTD requires the `title` element and you cannot validate an XHTML document without including this element, you still don't have to include it! Browsers will still display the document even if you omit the title, or most other parts for that matter. Likewise, you might choose to use a heading level 6 (using the `h6` element) to provide your contact information, rather than using the heading element for its intended purpose—a heading.

```
<h6>All MongoMug pages are the property of BigGlug, Inc.
    Contact us at MongoMug@BigGlugInc.com.</h6>
```

Revisit Chapter 3 for more information about the XHTML `title` *element.*

Although misusing these elements may help you format a document the way you want it to appear, doing so also introduces all kinds of potential problems. For example, if you wanted to generate a table of contents from the headings, the table would include all elements you define as headings at any level, including the heading level 6 that is attached to your contact information. Also, rather than a document title appearing at the top of browser windows, the title area would be blank. Listing 20.2 shows an XHTML document that lacks a `title` element (which would normally follow the opening `head` element) and misuses the h6 element. Figure 20.2 shows how it appears in a browser (and it does render despite its inability to be validated in its current form).

LISTING 20.2: XHTML DOCUMENT THAT LACKS A title ELEMENT

```
<!DOCTYPE html PUBLIC "-//W3C//DTD XHTML 1.0 Transitional//EN"
    "http://www.w3.org/TR/xhtml1/DTD/xhtml1-transitional.dtd">
<html xmlns="http://www.w3.org/1999/xhtml">
<head>
</head>

<body bgcolor="#FFFFFF" text="#000000" link="#0000FF"
vlink="#FF0000" alink="#80080">
<basefont face="Arial, Helvetica" size="4" />

<h1 align="center">MongoMug, the Choice of Serious
Cocoa Drinkers</h1>

<p><font size="-1">Once you've gulped from MongoMug, you'll
never sip again.</font></p>

<h6>All MongoMug pages are the property of BigGlug, Inc.
Contact us at MongoMug@BigGlugInc.com.</h6>

</body>
</html>
```

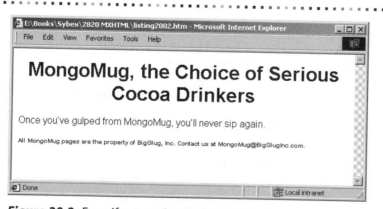

Figure 20.2 *Even if you omit certain XHTML elements or use an element incorrectly, browsers will usually display the document as you intended.*

Understanding XML Markup

XML is a meta-language derived from SGML. It offers you virtually all the power of SGML and nearly all the simplicity of HTML. This is particularly true for XHTML, which is nothing more than a reformulation of HTML according to XML's rules and syntax requirements. XHTML is XML that uses HTML 4.01 as its vocabulary. You can control virtually any document structure and meet any organizational need—and you can do so without dealing with an overwhelmingly complex language; without waiting for a committee to review, approve, and publish the new standards; and without dealing with expensive development and parsing tools.

Why are these features important? Let's look at an example: Suppose you must develop a Frequently Asked Questions (FAQ) document for maintaining houseplants. The FAQ would likely include those questions (and answers, obviously) that come up over and over again, as well as some basic information about the document, such as who maintains it and when it was last modified.

If you were to develop this FAQ page using HTML or XHTML, you'd be bound to the relevant DTD, which provides only limited predefined structure elements. For example, you'd likely end up using heading elements (such as h1 or h3) to list questions, use a paragraph element (p) or blockquote element (blockquote) to provide answers, and perhaps use an italic (i) element for the basic document information, such as the author and date. Take a look at Listing 20.3 and Figure 20.3 (which shows the resulting document viewed in a browser).

LISTING 20.3: A DOCUMENT THAT USES LIMITED STRUCTURE ELEMENTS

```
<!DOCTYPE html PUBLIC "-//W3C//DTD XHTML 1.0 Transitional//EN"
    "http://www.w3.org/TR/xhtml1/DTD/xhtml1-transitional.dtd">
<html xmlns="http://www.w3.org/1999/xhtml">
<head>
<title>House Plant FAQ</title>
</head>

<body bgcolor="#FFFFFF" text="#000000" link="#0000FF"
    vlink="#FF0000" alink="#80080">

<h1 align="center">Plant Care FAQ</h1>
<h3 align="center"><i><b>Motto:</b> All the plant questions
    you've lost sleep over, and then some.</i></h3>
<p align="center"><i>Maintained by Digit Brown</i><br />
```

```
<i>Last revised May 29, 2001</i></p>

<h2>Problems with Dying Plants</h2>
<ul>
   <li><h3>Why are my plants limp and yellow?</h3>
   <blockquote>Because you water them too much!</blockquote>
   </li>
   <li><h3>Why are my plants crispy and brown?</h3>
   <blockquote>Because you don't water them enough!
   </blockquote></li>
   <li><h3>Why don't my plants have a neat pattern like
   they should?</h3>
   <blockquote>Because we're not talking about tie-dying
   plants! </blockquote></li>
</ul>

</body>
</html>
```

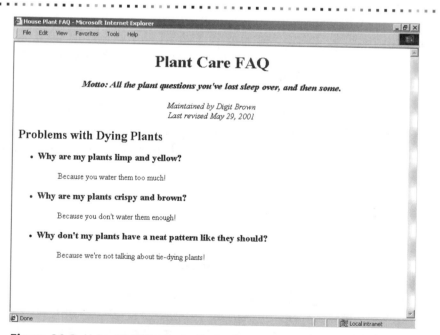

Figure 20.3 *Using XHTML, you're limited to the elements that the XHTML Transitional DTD provides. Often, you end up using elements for purposes other than their intended uses.*

As Figure 20.3 shows, these XHTML elements only specify (to some extent) what each element will look like when viewed in a browser—that is, the questions will appear bigger and bolder than the answers, and the document information will appear in italics. They provide little context as to each element's purpose or the document structure.

If you used XML to create this FAQ, you could develop your own markup elements that not only specify what each element is, but also establish document structure. For example, your XML DTD could include a `question` element for questions, an `answer` element for answers, a `maintainer` element to list who maintains the page, and a `date` element to specify when the page was updated, as shown in Listing 20.4.

LISTING 20.4: THE FAQ WITH XML MARKUP

```
<?xml version="1.0"?>
<!DOCTYPE faq SYSTEM "figure6.dtd">
<faq>
<title>House Plant FAQ</title>
<motto>Motto: All the plant questions you've lost sleep over,
    and then some. </motto>
<maintainer>
    <who>Maintained by Digit Brown</who>
    <date>April 1, 1999</date>
</maintainer>

<category>
    <topic>Problems with Dying Plants</topic>
    <question>Why are my plants limp and yellow?</question>
    <answer>Because you water them too much!</answer>
    <question>Why are my plants crispy and brown?</question>
    <answer>Because you don't water them enough!</answer>
    <question>Why don't my plants have a neat pattern like
      they should?</question>
    <answer>Because we're not talking about tie-dying
      plants!</answer>
</category>
</faq>
```

These elements are much more logical for this purpose than the ones that XHTML Transitional provides, and they establish a specific document structure, as Figure 20.4 shows. XML documents can look like regular documents—this particular application formats the document as a "tree" so you can more easily see the structure.

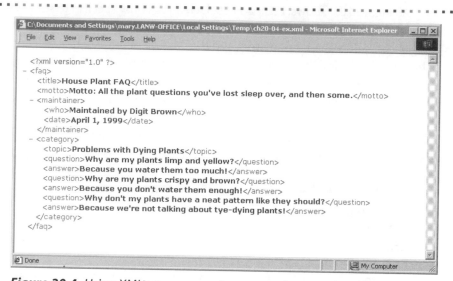

```
<?xml version="1.0" ?>
- <faq>
    <title>House Plant FAQ</title>
    <motto>Motto: All the plant questions you've lost sleep over, and then some.</motto>
  - <maintainer>
      <who>Maintained by Digit Brown</who>
      <date>April 1, 1999</date>
    </maintainer>
  - <category>
      <topic>Problems with Dying Plants</topic>
      <question>Why are my plants limp and yellow?</question>
      <answer>Because you water them too much!</answer>
      <question>Why are my plants crispy and brown?</question>
      <answer>Because you don't water them enough!</answer>
      <question>Why don't my plants have a neat pattern like they should?</question>
      <answer>Because we're not talking about tye-dying plants!</answer>
    </category>
  </faq>
```

Figure 20.4 *Using XML, you can create custom elements that not only meet your specific document needs, but also help define document structure.*

In addition to creating custom elements, you could specify document rules to ensure that you or whoever uses the DTD to create future FAQ documents completes the FAQ documents correctly. For example, you could specify that all questions must have answers, that all FAQ documents must have at least one Q&A set, and so on. You do not have to specify such rules, but you certainly have the capability to do so.

Or you could create interesting FAQ presentations. A user could view a list of FAQs, click a FAQ, and then see the answer pop up on screen—something you cannot do with HTML or unmodified XHTML. True, you could create the same general effect with dynamic XHTML (as described in Chapter 17), but to do so, you'd have to add scripts and specialized code to every FAQ and maintain them all. With XML, you could make this happen automatically in all your documents.

Dynamic XHTML expands on standard XHTML by giving you precise formatting control and interactive capabilities, such as those provided by JavaScript. Take a look at Chapter 17 for more information.

If you're thinking that all this is a lot of work for a lonely FAQ page, you're right. But look at the bigger picture—that is, you might be developing a FAQ format that you will use for hundreds of documents or that other people could use to create compatible documents. In such cases, XML would be invaluable.

The Advantages of XML

The example in the previous section showed you a single comparison between HTML and XML, and in particular, it showed how XML can overcome HTML's limitations in a practical application. Let's take a broad look at XML's advantages, which apply to any XML application.

XML Provides Context for Words

XML gives you the capability to provide context for words on the page. For example, in traditional HTML documents, the word *author* would have the same context (or lack thereof) no matter where it occurred in the document. That is, a casual mention in a paragraph of text (the author of the book was…), in a title (*Author, Author: The Story of Playwrights*), or in data about the publication itself (…author: Neil Simon) would simply be a word that appears in the document. Listing 20.5 shows how you might code the word *author* in a Web page as text, a title, or as the name of the person who wrote something. Notice that there's no specific context information in the markup itself that identifies Neil Simon as the author of the book under discussion. Figure 20.5 shows the resulting Web page.

LISTING 20.5: THE WORD *AUTHOR* IN A WEB PAGE AS TEXT, A TITLE, OR AS THE NAME OF THE PERSON WHO WROTE SOMETHING

```
<!DOCTYPE html PUBLIC "-//W3C//DTD XHTML 1.0 Transitional//EN"
    "http://www.w3.org/TR/xhtml1/DTD/xhtml1-transitional.dtd">
<html xmlns="http://www.w3.org/1999/xhtml">
<head>
<title>Author Section: Authoring a play can be hard
    work</title>
</head>

<body bgcolor="FFFFFF">
<h1 align="center">Author Section: Authoring a play can
    be hard work</h1>
<p>Many a would-be author (or playwright) has yearned for
the time that an audience will sing out "author, author" in
admiration for the hard work; however, as you might read in
the (actually not ever written) book by Neil Simon,
<i>Author, Author: The Story of Playwrights</i>,
this rarely comes to pass.
</p>
```

```
Title: <cite>Author, Author: The Story of
    Playwrights</cite><br />
Author: Neil Simon<br />
Published: Not really<br />
</body>
</html>
```

Again, notice that in the preceding code and in Figure 20.5 that the XHTML elements don't help identify the contexts for the different uses for the word *author*.

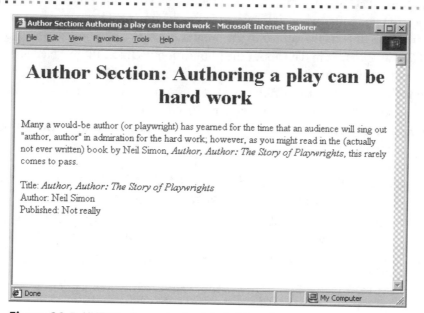

Figure 20.5 *XHTML elements don't help identify context for document parts—that is, author, in any part of this example, is really just a word.*

XML, on the other hand, lets you identify the context for each element by letting you specify how each is used. You could develop customized elements, such as the ones shown in bold in the following code, including the author element, which clearly identifies Neil Simon as the author of the hypothetical book under review. Thus, the markup itself provides lots of context information and clearly labels what's what.

```
<?xml version="1.0"?>
<!DOCTYPE review SYSTEM "review.dtd">
<review>
```

```
<heading>Author Section: Authoring a play can be hard work
    </heading>
<blurb>Many a would-be author (or playwright) has yearned
    for the time that an audience will sing out <quote>author,
    author</quote> in admiration for the hard work; however,
    as you might read in the (actually not ever written) book
    by Neil Simon, <booktitle>Author, Author: The Story of
    Playwrights</booktitle>, this rarely comes to pass.</blurb>

<citation>
    <title>Author, Author: The Story of Playwrights</title>
    <author>Neil Simon</author>
    <pub>Not really</pub>
</citation>

</review>
```

Using XML, you could also add attributes to provide additional information about any of the elements. For example, the following code shows how you might add pubdate, publisher, and isbn attributes to the title element and a gender attribute to the author element. Adding these attributes further adds context to words, as the following code shows:

```
<title pubdate="010199" publisher="Back Yard Press, Inc."
    isbn="1234123412">Author, Author: The Story of
    Playwrights</title>
<author gender="Male">Neil Simon</author>
```

XML Specifies Document Structure

In addition to specifying context for words, XML lets you specify document structure—XML's second advantage. For example, a document might use italic for emphasis, for headings, and for the titles of publications. However, specifying that a word should be italicized does not indicate the role that the word plays in the document; it's simply a formatting tweak. If you indicate that a string of words is a publication title and the following string of words is the author, you add structure to the document. Using XML, you can develop your own elements that help identify the document structure, as in this example with a publication element enclosing title, author, and summary information about the publication:

```
<publicationrecord>
```

```
<title>Author, Author: The Story of Playwrights</title>
<author>Neil Simon</author>
<summary>Book provides a good range of readable
    information.</summary>
</publicationrecord>
```

XML Allows Effective Search Capabilities

Because XML provides context and structure, it lets users effectively search for information within your documents. Rather than simply searching for the word *author*, users can search for that word in a particular segment of the document, such as documents with *author* in a document title, or search only for that word in the body of a document. This control would clearly surpass the whole-text searches (available, for example, through AltaVista and Excite) necessary to find information on the Internet today.

For more information about AltaVista's Internet Search Service, visit www.altavista.com. *For more information about Excite, visit* www.excite.com.

XML Is Flexible

XML documents do not absolutely require a DTD (you just can't validate the documents without one or something else equivalent to one), giving you more flexibility during the development process. For example, when you're developing a document, you can produce XML code and change it as necessary, without the hassles and process of changing a DTD every time you change your mind. After you've developed a structure and set of rules that suit your needs, you can then codify those rules by implementing a DTD that spells out the structure and organization you want. This flexibility makes XML ideal for trying out structured documents with minimal effort and time investment.

XML Is Accessible

Average people using average tools can use and access XML documents, so you can reach a wide audience. Already, a wide variety of software programs (Java applets, primarily) let you provide XML data directly in conventional Web pages. For example, you could provide information about your favorite books and authors (stored in XML format) directly in your (HTML-based) Web page, without recoding or converting your HTML documents. In doing so, you can keep structured XML information and still provide easy access to the information for all potential users.

The Disadvantages of XML

XML is a relatively new technology, and consequently, there's no plethora of tools available to develop and implement XML documents. The potential for widespread acceptance and popularity is certainly there—the number and quality of tools available improves daily—but you currently do not have the breadth of options that you get with other technologies, such as HTML.

For these reasons, you'll also need to take extra steps to ensure that people can view your XML documents. For example, when JavaScript became available, not all browsers supported it. HTML developers had to make decisions about disregarding the technology until it was more commonly available, developing an alternate non-JavaScript site so all possible users could access and view the pages, or living with the knowledge that some sites would be inaccessible to a portion of users.

The same idea applies to XML: You must take extra steps to ensure that users can view your pages because not all users will be able to directly access XML documents. Even when the newest generation of Web browsers adds XML capabilities, you still must take extra steps until a significant portion of your users begin using the newer browsers. These extra steps include providing CSS to add formatting information to XML documents, if users are permitted to access them directly, or providing XSLT style sheets to turn XML documents into HTML to make sure they'll work properly with the vast majority of Web browsers available today.

Where to Go from Here

In this chapter, we've explored XML in terms of how it differs from SGML and HTML and how it meets needs that neither SGML nor HTML addresses. SGML and HTML sit at opposite ends of the spectrum—SGML being a highly powerful tool and HTML being a less capable, but more accessible tool—where XML combines the best features of each of the other two markup languages.

Armed with this information, you're ready to get started with XML:

- Move on to Chapter 21 to learn about XML's special relationship with XHTML, and how that relationship can be expanded using namespaces.

- Visit Chapters 22 and 23 to find out how to create your own XML DTDs.

- Visit Chapter 24 to learn about XHTML modularization, a great technique that lets you pick only the parts of XHTML that your Web pages will actually use (designed for PDAs and Web-enabled cell phones, where memory and screen space are at an absolute premium).

Extending XHTML
Using Namespaces

Chapter 21

As you know, XHTML is an application of XML. Several benefits, such as simplicity and interoperability, can be gained by following XML's syntax requirements. In this chapter, we focus on the benefits of XML's extensibility.

Since XML was introduced, a number of optional modules have been developed that provide element sets for specific tasks. For example, the Extensible Stylesheet Language (XSL) is a formatting vocabulary that defines presentation for XML documents. The XML Linking Language (XLink) defines a standard mechanism for adding hyperlinks to XML documents. The Mathematical Markup Language (MathML) provides document authors with a language for conveying mathematical expressions. If we wanted to stick with one language for the Web, we would have to extend the element set indefinitely. Instead, the XML community has separated specific tasks into workable modules.

To work with all of these different XML vocabularies, you must learn how to combine them within the same document. XML namespaces were created to resolve possible naming conflicts between combined vocabularies (such as the XHTML `title` element and the `title` element for a book-listing vocabulary). An XML namespace provides a formal mechanism for uniquely identifying a vocabulary. If you want to combine different XML vocabularies, you need to be familiar with XML namespaces.

This chapter covers the following topics:

- Extending XHTML markup
- Declaring namespaces
- Working with default namespaces
- Defining a namespace prefix
- Combining XML vocabularies

Benefits of Extending XHTML

The W3C is promoting extensibility as the primary goal of the future of the Web. At the heart of extensibility is a collection of XML technologies. By separating functionality, Web developers will gain the advantages of flexibility. Combining XML vocabularies such as XLink and Scalable Vector Graphics (SVG) with XHTML will allow developers to take advantage of modularizing tasks.

The *X* in XML means the vocabulary is extensible and that the author working with the markup can create his or her own elements and attributes. Therefore, as with XML, XHTML can be extended.

In a nutshell, the benefits to extending XHTML are:

- You can take advantage of emerging XML technologies, such as MathML, SVG, and XForms.

- You can embed your own XML vocabulary within an XHTML document.

- You can better organize the XML vocabularies you use.

- You have a more extensive toolset for problem solving.

In this chapter, we focus on XML namespaces because they are at the heart of extending XHTML.

Working with Namespaces

As you already know, XML allows you to create your own elements and attributes. Because extensibility is at the heart of XHTML, it's important for you to understand how to use namespaces to help you combine different XML vocabularies. You can embed XHTML elements with MathML or your own XML vocabulary. Listing 21.1 is an example of embedding your own elements into an XHTML document.

LISTING 21.1: EMBEDDING ELEMENTS INTO AN XHTML DOCUMENT

```
<html xmlns="http://www.w3.org/1999/xhtml">
   <head>
      <title>Working with Namespaces</title>
   </head>
   <body>
      <h1>Online Class Offerings</h1>
      <online-classes>
```

```
          <class>
              <title>Introduction to XML</title>
              <instructor>Chelsea Valentine</instructor>
          </class>
          <class>
              <title>TCP/IP for Webmasters</title>
              <instructor>Ed Tittel</instructor>
          </class>
          </online-classes>
      </body>
  </html>
```

In Listing 21.1, there's a naming conflict we have to help the processor resolve. The first instance of the `title` element belongs to XHTML; however, the remaining instances of the `title` element belong to our own online-classes vocabulary. The problem arises when the processor has to decide what to do with them. How does the processor know which `title` element is which? The answer is XML namespaces.

Your first reaction may be to expect DTDs to resolve any naming conflicts; however, DTDs are not prepared to handle namespaces. DTDs have been around since the days of SGML. If a given document is to conform to a DTD, there must be one (and only one) element type declaration for each element type. Therefore, the XHTML `title` and the online-class `title` element would have to be defined using the same content model. Even if this was possible, element type declarations don't provide information that could resolve the naming conflict. For this, we have to use namespaces.

A namespace allows you to attach a unique identifier for each collection of elements. For example, we could attach the XHTML namespace to the XHTML elements, and our very own online-class namespace to our own vocabulary. Then, the processor would know that the XHTML `title` element is different from the online-class `title` element.

 The namespace in the XML recommendation document is seen as a complement to the XML specification and can be found at www.w3.org/TR/REC-xml-names. *The recommendation document defines a special syntax to identify namespaces. The document defines how a collection of elements can be given unique identifiers; therefore, no matter where the element is used, you can be sure that it belongs to the namespace.*

But just how do you use XML namespaces? We will cover that topic in the following sections.

Declaring Namespaces

To declare a namespace, you must use a unique Uniform Resource Identifier (URI). The URI is the value of the `xmlns` namespace. A URI can be a Uniform Resource Locator (URL) or a Uniform Resource Name (URN). URLs are used most often. For example, `xmlns="http://www.lanw.com/namespaces/onlinetraining/"` is a namespace that we created to uniquely identify our online-training vocabulary. However, the URI is only a symbolic reference; therefore, there's no document or schema at the URI defined. Think of a namespace as a symbolic last name. For an example, visit the XHTML namespace found at `http://www.w3.org/1999/xhtml`.

You can define a namespace in one of two ways:

Default namespace   Defines a namespace using the `xmlns` attribute without a prefix, and all child elements are assumed to belong to the defined namespace. XHTML uses the default namespace construct to define the XHTML namespace.

Local namespace   Defines a namespace using the `xmlns` attribute with a prefix. When the prefix is attached to an element, it's assumed to belong to that namespace.

In both cases, you define a namespace using the `xmlns` attribute. The attribute's value is the namespace name that identifies the namespace. As mentioned, a namespace name can be some URI. We look at both types of namespaces in the following two sections.

Default Namespace

A default namespace applies to the element where it's declared, and to all child elements that do not have a namespace prefix assigned to another namespace. There's specific syntax for defining XML default namespaces. It looks much like defining an attribute, where the attribute name is `xmlns` and the value is the namespace URI.

For example, XHTML uses the default namespace syntax to define the XHTML namespace. The `xmlns` attribute is defined within the `html` start tag and therefore applies to all child elements that do not fall within the scope of another namespace:

```
<html xmlns="http://www.w3.org/1999/xhtml" xml:lang="en"
  lang="en">
  <head>
    <title>Example Transitional XHTML Document</title>
  </head>
  <body>
    <h1>My First XHTML Document</h1>
```

```
    <p>Extending XHTML allows developers to take advantage
        of the new and improved Web!</p>
    </body>
</html>
```

You'll notice that we don't use a DOCTYPE declaration in this markup. See the "Validation" section later in this chapter for an explanation.

The namespace URI is already defined for us, because it belongs to a public vocabulary. However, for vocabularies that you define yourself, such as our online-class vocabulary, you have to create your own namespace URI. For example:

```
<classListing
    xmlns="http://www.lanw.com/namespace/onlinetraining/">
<class>
    <title>Introduction to XML</title>
    <instructor>Chelsea Valentine</instructor>
</class>
<class>
    <title>TCP/IP for Webmasters</title>
    <instructor>Ed Tittel</instructor>
</class>
</classListing>
```

In this case, we've created our own unique namespace that uses our domain name. The classListing element and all of its children belong to the http://www.lanw.com/ namespace/onlinetraining namespace. If you visit that URL, you wouldn't find a document there because the URL is, as mentioned, only a symbolic unique identifier used to resolve possible element name conflicts.

Local Namespaces

Local namespaces are similar to default namespaces; however, they add an additional identifier: *a prefix.* A local namespace can be defined anywhere within the document. In other words, you don't have to declare it within the element that it is to modify (as you do with default namespaces). In this case, you define a namespace and associate a prefix that can later be used to reference the namespace.

Local namespaces are often used when embedding document types within another document. For example, in the previous section, we provided an example that uses both XHTML elements and our own online-training elements. The XHTML elements are uniquely identified by the XHTML default namespace. But what about our online-training elements? Because we already have a default namespace, we will have to define a local namespace for them. The following example demonstrates this concept. The local namespace is bolded:

```
<html xmlns="http://www.w3.org/1999/xhtml"
    xmlns:lanw="http://www.lanw.com/namespace/onlinetraining"
    xml:lang="en" lang="en">
    <head>
      <title>Working with Namespaces</title>
    </head>
<body>
    <h1>Online Class Offerings</h1>
    <lanw:class>
      <lanw:title>Introduction to XML</lanw:title>
      <lanw:instructor>Chelsea Valentine</lanw:instructor>
    </lanw:class>
    <lanw:class>
      <lanw:title>TCP/IP for Webmasters</lanw:title>
      <lanw:instructor>Ed Tittel</lanw:instructor>
    </lanw:class>
</body>
</html>
```

The `xmlns` attribute is used along with the colon and the prefix (`:lanw`). To define a local namespace, you must define a prefix that can be used as a reference later in the document. The colon separates the `xmlns` attribute name from the prefix (`lanw`). You can create your own prefix for your own document types; however, if you're using someone else's vocabulary, be sure to see whether they have a predefined prefix.

After you've defined the local namespace, you can reference it with the prefix. Notice in our example that all elements with the prefix (`lanw`) followed by a colon (`:`) belong to the `http://www.lanw.com/namespace/onlinetraining` namespace. Most local namespaces are defined in the root element and then referenced when needed.

Combining Namespaces

In the section, "Local Namespaces," our example combined two namespaces. This is becoming common practice. The future of XHTML is as a document structure language. Gone are the days of using XHTML as a multipurpose language for document structure, presentation, and metadata description.

The W3C has turned its focus to creating XML applications that have dedicated tasks and that can work together. For example, the following XML applications could be combined:

- XHTML to define document markup

- MathML to define mathematical expressions

- Synchronized Multimedia Integration Language (SMIL) to define synchronized multimedia tasks

- SVG to define a scalable vector graphics language

For example, you can add mathematical expressions to your XHTML document, as shown in the following example from the XHTML specification document:

```
<html xmlns="http://www.w3.org/1999/xhtml"
    xml:lang="en" lang="en">
    <head>
      <title>A Math Example</title>
    </head>
    <body>
      <p>The following is MathML markup:</p>
      <math xmlns="http://www.w3.org/1998/Math/MathML">
       <apply>
         <log/>
         <logbase>
           <cn> 3 </cn>
         </logbase>
         <ci> x </ci>
       </apply>
      </math>
    </body>
</html>
```

There are a few ways to combine these document types. The first way, as demonstrated previously, is to define a default namespace for the root element, and then redefine a default namespace for a child element. The nested default namespace is then applied to its current element and all its child elements. For example, all the elements that are children of the math element belong to the MathML namespace, as shown in this example:

```
<html xmlns="http://www.w3.org/1999/xhtml"
    xml:lang="en" lang="en">
```

```
<head>
  <title>A Math Example</title>
</head>
<body>
  <p>The following is MathML markup:</p>
  <math xmlns="http://www.w3.org/1998/Math/MathML">
    <apply> <log/>
      <logbase>
        <cn> 3 </cn>
      </logbase>
      <ci> x </ci>
    </apply>
  </math>
</body>
</html>
```

The second way to combine namespaces is to define a default namespace and a local namespace in the root element. In this case, all elements that do not have a prefix belong to the default namespace, and all the elements that have a prefix belong to the associated local namespace. You can find an example of this in the "Local Namespaces" section earlier.

Finally, you can define only local namespaces and add prefixes to all the elements within the document. This is the least commonly used approach; however, there are times when you might want to use only local namespaces.

Common Namespaces

Several namespaces have already been defined for common languages. As you begin to extend XHTML, you will be forced to use some of these common namespaces. Here's a rather extensive list of namespaces:

- Chemical Markup Language (CML)
  `http://www.xml-cml.org`

- Extensible Stylesheet Language (XSL) Working Draft 16-December-1998
  `http://www.w3.org/TR/WD-xsl`

- Extensible Stylesheet Language (XSL) Version 1.0
  `http://www.w3.org/1999/XSL/Format`

- Mathematical Markup Language (MathML)
  `http://www.w3.org/1998/Math/MathML`

- Resource Description Framework (RDF) Model and Syntax Specification
  `http://www.w3.org/1999/02/22-rdf-syntax-ns#`

- Resource Description Framework (RDF) Schema Specification 1.0
  `http://www.w3.org/2000/01/rdf-schema#`

- Scalable Vector Graphics (SVG) 1.0
  `http://www.w3.org/2000/svg`

- Simple Object Access Protocol (SOAP) 1.1 - Encoding
  `http://schemas.xmlsoap.org/soap/encoding/`

- Simple Object Access Protocol (SOAP) 1.1 - Envelope
  `http://schemas.xmlsoap.org/soap/envelope/`

- Synchronized Multimedia Integration Language (SMIL) 1.0 Specification
  `http://www.w3.org/TR/REC-smil`

- Synchronized Multimedia Integration Language (SMIL) 2.0 Specification
  `http://www.w3.org/TR/REC-smil/2000/SMIL20/LC/`

- The Schematron Assertion Language 1.5
  `http://www.ascc.net/xml/schematron`

- XHTML 1.0: The Extensible Hypertext Markup Language
  `http://www.w3.org/1999/xhtml`

- XInclude
  `http://www.w3.org/1999/XML/xinclude`

- XML Linking Language (XLink) Version 1.0
  `http://www.w3.org/1999/xlink`

- XML Schema Part 1: Structures
  `http://www.w3.org/1999/XMLSchema`

- XML Schema Part 2: Datatypes
  `http://www.w3.org/1999/XMLSchema-datatypes`

- XSL Transformations (XSLT) Version 1.0
  `http://www.w3.org/1999/XSL/Transform`

- XSL Transformations (XSLT) Specification Version 1.0 (Working Draft)
  `http://www.w3.org/TR/WD-xsl`

If you visit any of these namespace URIs, you would not find much because the namespace is only a symbolic identifier. With that said, some languages, but not all, use the namespace location to provide additional information about the standard. It also helps if you use an XML-capable browser to display some of these pages.

Combining XML Vocabularies with XHTML

To demonstrate how you might combine XML vocabularies, we chose two of the most widely implemented XML vocabularies. In the following sections, we look at MathML and SVG, as well as an example using our own XML vocabulary.

MathML

Before we dive into how you might use MathML within an XHTML document, let's take a look at what MathML is. The MathML standard defines presentation elements *and* content elements. The presentation elements define how an expression should be displayed, whereas the content elements define the content of the expression.

MathML has been around for a while now—it's one of the longest-living XML applications. For this reason, several browsers, plug-ins, and Java applets are already available that allow users to view MathML data (such as Amaya, at `www.w3.org/Amaya/`). MathML is almost always embedded into another document type, such as XHTML. This makes sense because, after all, who would want to view a page of strictly mathematical expressions?

The following are some common MathML elements from the W3C specification:

- `math` is the single top-level math element that contains all other MathML markup within the XHTML page.

- `mi` indicates that its content should be displayed as an identifier. Single-character identifiers (such as x or h) are commonly displayed in italics. Multicharacter identifiers (such as sin and log) are commonly displayed in an upright font.

- `mn` specifies that its content should be rendered as a number, which is commonly displayed in an upright font.

- `mo` specifies that its contents should be displayed as an operator. There's no specific presentation format defined for operators. The presentation varies.

- `mrow` may contain any number of child elements. Its content is displayed aligned along the baseline in a horizontal row. In addition, `mrow` is commonly used to group terms into a single unit.

- `mfrac` may contain only two children. The first child is positioned as the numerator of a fraction, and the second is the denominator. It's commonly used for binomial coefficients; to do so, you must set the `linethickness` attribute to 0.

- `msqrt` may contain any number of children and displays them under a radical sign.

- `mroot` is similar to the `msqrt` element, except that it requires a second child, which is displayed above the radical in the location of the `n` in an `nth` root.

- `mfenced` is similar to the `mrow` element, except that it displays enclosed in parentheses. Using attributes, you can set the beginning and ending delimiter characters, as well as internal separator characters such as commas.

- `mstyle` is similar to the `mrow` element except that it handles attributes differently. The `mrow` element has almost no attributes of its own, and the `mstyle` elements can be used to set any MathML attribute.

The focus of this section is on how to embed MathML within an XHTML document, not necessarily on how to use MathML. Therefore, we focus on the MathML namespace and embedding MathML in an XHTML document.

Both languages are XML vocabularies and can therefore be combined using namespaces.

MathML Namespace

Embedding MathML within other XML vocabularies, such as XHTML, requires that you keep track of namespaces. The MathML namespace is:

```
http://www.w3.org/1998/Math/MathML
```

When you decide to embed MathML within another XML vocabulary, you have to identify all MathML markup as belonging to the scope of the MathML namespace. You do this by using a default namespace or using a namespace prefix, as described earlier.

The root MathML element is the `math` element; therefore, you use the `xmlns` attribute with the MathML namespace in it as shown here:

```
<math xmlns="http://www.w3.org/1998/Math/MathML">
<mrow>...</mrow>
</math>
```

When defined as a default namespace, the namespace is defined for the element to which it is attached, as well as any child elements.

If you choose to use a namespace prefix, the xmlns attribute is used with a prefix. The prefix can then be used to associate elements and attributes within the document with the defined namespace. For example:

```
<html xmlns:m="http://www.w3.org/1998/Math/MathML">

...

<m:math>
   <m:mrow>
     ...
   </m:mrow>
</m:math>

...

</html>
```

You can use these two namespace declaration methods interchangeably. For example, you might declare a default XHTML namespace, while adding a document-wide namespace prefix for any MathML elements. You could accomplish the same thing by defining a default XHTML namespace and then adding a default MathML namespace to the outermost math element, thereby localizing the default MathML namespace.

Working with MathML namespaces

It's common for MathML processors to use explicit namespace prefixes to attach rendering behaviors to an element. This is a common practice and is used for XSLT processors as well. On the other hand, several MathML authoring tools do not recognize namespaces and therefore lack the ability to use namespace prefixes.

If this is the case, it's likely that you'll want to use a combination of default and prefixed namespaces. For example:

```
<body xmlns:m="http://www.w3.org/1998/Math/MathML">

...

<m:math xmlns="http://www.w3.org/1998/Math/MathML">

<mrow>...<mrow>

</m:math>

...

</body>
```

Embedding MathML in XHTML

Listing 21.2 is an example of an XHTML document containing MathML expressions.

LISTING 21.2: AN XHTML DOCUMENT WITH MATHML EXPRESSIONS

```
<!DOCTYPE html PUBLIC "-//W3C//DTD XHTML 1.0 Transitional//EN"
    "http://www.w3.org/TR/xhtml1/DTD/xhtml1-transitional.dtd">
<html xmlns="http://www.w3.org/1999/xhtml"
       xmlns:m="http://www.w3.org/1998/Math/MathML">
<head>
<title>Quadratic Equations</title>
</head>
<body>
<h1>Quadratic Equations</h1>
<p>Any quadratic equation may be reduced to the form:</p>
<m:math>
<m:apply><m:equals/>
   <m:apply><m:plus/>
     <m:apply><m:plus/>
      <m:apply><m:times/>
        <m:ci>a</m:ci>
        <m:apply><m:power/>
          <m:ci>x</m:ci>
          <m:cn>2</m:cn>
        </m:apply>
      </m:apply>
      <m:apply><m:times/>
        <m:ci>b</m:ci>
   <m:ci>x</m:ci>
      </m:apply>
     </m:apply>
     <m:ci>c</m:ci>
   </m:apply>
   <m:cn>0</m:cn>
</m:apply>
</m:math>

<p>In that case,</p>

<m:math>
<m:apply><m:equals/>
```

```
          <m:ci>x</m:ci>
            <m:apply><m:quotient/>
             <m:apply><m:plus/>
               <m:apply><m:minus/>
           <m:ci>b</m:ci>
               </m:apply>
               <m:apply><m:root/>
           <m:apply><m:minus>
                   <m:apply><m:power/>
                     <m:ci>b</m:ci>
                     <m:cn>2</m:ci>
                   </m:apply>
                   <m:apply><m:times/>
                     <m:cn>4</m:cn>
                     <m:ci>a</m:ci>
                     <m:ci>c</m:ci>
             </m:apply>
                 </m:apply>
                 <m:cn>2</m:cn>
               </m:apply>
             </m:apply>
             <m:apply><m:times/>
               <m:cn>2</m:cn>
               <m:ci>a</m:ci>
             </m:apply>
             </m:apply>
 </m:apply>
 </m:math>

<p>If <var>a</var>, <var>b</var>, and <var>c</var> are real,
   then:</p>
<ul>
   <li>If <var>b<sup>2</sup> - 4ac</var> is positive,
      the roots are real and unequal;</li>
   <li>If <var>b<sup>2</sup> - 4ac</var> is zero, the
      roots are real and equal;</li>
   <li>If <var>b<sup>2</sup> - 4ac</var> is negative,
      the roots are real and unequal.</li>
</ul>
<p>Definition taken from <cite>CRC Mathematical Tables</cite>,
   26th Edition, CRC Press, Boca Raton, FL, 1981.</p>
```

```
<p>Note: the actual formula uses a "plus or minus" operator in
    the numerator of the quotient shown. MathML does not provide
    that operator, so we show only the "plus" case in this
    example for brevity.
</p>
</body>
</html>
```

SVG

In case you're not familiar with SVG, let's take a moment to explain what it is. As defined by the W3C, SVG is a language for describing two-dimensional graphics in XML. Three types of graphical objects can be defined by SVG: vector graphic shapes, images, and text. SVG objects use the Document Object Model (DOM) to allow them to be both dynamic and interactive. Therefore, you can use event handlers such as `onmouseover` and `onclick` to attach behaviors to SVG objects. Many of the element and attribute names should be obvious. For example, the `circle` element is used to define a circle, and the `rect` element is used to define a rectangle. Attributes such as the familiar XHTML `style` attribute allow you to use Cascading Style Sheet (CSS) properties, such as `fill`, `stroke`, and `stroke-width`, to control appearance.

Working with SVG is not that different from working with MathML. Because this is a book on XHTML, we focus on embedding other XML vocabularies within an XHTML document. However, it's important for you to understand that you can use namespaces to embed other XML vocabularies within SVG or MathML documents too.

Many of the same rules that we defined in the MathML section apply when you're working with SVG. For example, you'll want to use a namespace prefix when declaring elements because it's best to use only one default namespace to help ensure uniqueness. Because XHTML is the parent vocabulary, it will be defined using a default namespace. For stylistic reasons, we declare the SVG prefixed namespace within the `html` root element. For our documents, we like to define all namespaces at the top of the document. With all namespaces defined at the same level, it's easier to maintain them.

The SVG namespace is

```
http://www.w3.org/2000/svg
```

You'll most likely define the SVG namespace using the `svg` prefix. Listing 21.3 is a sample XHTML document with embedded SVG elements.

LISTING 21.3: A SAMPLE XHTML DOCUMENT WITH EMBEDDED SVG ELEMENTS

```
<html xmlns="http://www.w3.org/1999/xhtml"
   xmlns:svg="http://www.w3.org/2000/svg">
   <head>
     <title>Shapes</title>
   </head>
   <body>
     <p>Rectangle</p>
   <svg:svg id="body" width="21cm" height="13.5cm"
     viewBox="0 0 210 135">
     <svg:rect x="15" y="25" width="150" height="70"
       style="fill:blue; stroke:red; stroke-width:2" />
   </svg:svg>

   <p>Circle</p>
   <svg:svg width="20cm" height="10cm">
     <svg:circle style="stroke:#33CCCC; stroke-width:.2cm;
       stroke-opacity:1; fill:#000000; fill-opacity:0" cx="10cm"
       cy="5cm" r="3cm" />
   </svg:svg>
   </body>
</html>
```

Listing 21.3 uses the XHTML namespace as its default namespace; therefore, we don't need to use element prefixes. It also declares an additional namespace for some SVG. These elements are prefixed using the XML namespaces notation. The svg prefix indicates the namespace in use by the svg, rect, and circle elements. If you add other elements and attributes that fall within the scope of other namespaces, you must prefix them to prevent any ambiguity.

 To learn more about SVG, visit the W3C's Web site dedicated to the topic at www.w3.org/ Graphics/SVG/.

Your Own Vocabulary

More often than not, you'll want to mix XHTML elements with a grab bag of your own elements. When this is the case, you'll use a combination of default and prefix namespaces. For example:

```
<html xmlns="http://www.w3.org/1999/xhtml"
   xmlns:pdt="http://www.lanw.com/namespaces/products">
  <head>
    <title>Products</title>
  </head>
  <body>
    <pdt:product name="fertilizer" price="5.00" />
    <pdt:product name="Aloe Vera" price="15.00" />
    <pdt:product name="Orchid" price="25.00" />
    <pdt:product name="Sand" price="3.00" />
    <pdt:product name="Cactus" price="15.00" />
  </body>
</html>
```

As with the SVG and MathML examples, the rules stay the same. XHTML uses the default namespace, and our vocabulary uses a prefixed namespace.

 In the previous example, the product information would not be rendered in the browser window because the data is defined using attribute values. If you want to create a document that displays the data, you want to define the data using elements (or you could use XSLT to convert the document structure). If you choose to use elements, you'll need to use CSS style rules to define presentation information for the data. Remember that your own elements do not carry presentation information—all they do is describe the content.

Validation

One notable drawback to using DTDs is that they are not namespace aware—which means that they do not recognize namespace prefixes. To an XML validating processor, a namespace prefix (m:math) is just part of the element name. Therefore, the element type declaration for that element must define the qualified name as m:math. This is impractical if you're using multiple namespaces.

Namespace prefixes create problems for the DTD validation of documents that contain other XML vocabularies. DTD validation requires knowing the literal (possibly prefixed) element names used in the document. However, the namespaces in the XML recommendation allow the prefix to be changed at arbitrary points in the document, because namespace prefixes may be declared on any element.

There are a few ways around this problem; however, none of them is elegant. First, you can add the namespace prefix to the qualified name defined with the element type declaration; for example:

```
<!ELEMENT book:book (book:title, book:author)>
   <!ATTLIST book:book
             book:isbn CDATA #IMPLIED
             xmlns:book CDATA #FIXED "http://www.nspc.com/">
<!ELEMENT book:title (#PCDATA)>
<!ELEMENT book:author (#PCDATA)>
```

Although this syntax is legal, understand that the qualified names in the DTD have no special meaning. For example, book:title is just book:title. The processor does not recognize title as the element name to which the prefix book is mapped.

If you want to avoid namespace prefixes altogether, you can opt to use default namespaces. If you choose this method, remember that the xmlns attribute must be declared within the DTD. It's common practice to define the value as fixed; for example:

```
<!ELEMENT book (title, author)>
   <!ATTLIST book
             isbn CDATA #IMPLIED
             xmlns CDATA #FIXED "http://www.nspc.com/">
<!ELEMENT title (#PCDATA)>
<!ELEMENT author (#PCDATA)>
```

It's important to remember that no matter whether you choose to use XML namespaces or not, the same rules apply for validity. You must include declarations for elements and attributes. Those declarations define qualified names. Although those qualified names may contain namespace prefixes, the process just views them as names with no special meaning. See the following section for validation tips and tricks.

Suggestions and Tips

In the ideal Web, you could follow our document examples, implement solutions, and walk away knowing all is well. Oftentimes, however, various processing agents are not in alignment with the W3C recommendations. XML-related technologies are evolving at a fast pace, and it's unrealistic to expect software products to keep up. In addition, many of the standards being defined by the W3C are still in flux. Even though we're in what you might call a transitional period, it's important to keep the following tips in mind:

- Do not create your own MathML namespace prefix. Use m: as a conventional prefix for the MathML namespace.

- When using namespace prefixes, pick one and use it consistently within a document.

- Declare the MathML namespace on all math elements.

- Avoid using DTDs and namespaces unless you're aware of the implications.

- Always declare all xmlns attributes in the DTD.

- Be sure to use the same qualified names in the DTD as used in the body of the document.

- Define only one prefix per XML namespace.

- Be careful to not use the same prefix for more than one XML namespace.

- Try not to use more than one default XML namespace. This will ensure uniqueness.

Where to Go from Here

In this chapter, we focused on extending XHTML using namespaces. If you want to extend XHTML, you need to read more about modularization techniques. Understanding namespace behavior is important, but the next step is to learn how to incorporate DTDs into the picture:

- See Chapter 24 to learn more about the modularization of XHTML.

- See any chapter found in Part VII covering many of the common XML vocabularies, such as XSL, XSLT, and SMIL.

Getting Started with DTDs

Chapter 22

A Document Type Definition (DTD) serves two purposes: To specify which elements and attributes you can use to develop markup language documents and to specify the document structure and rules you must adhere to while developing markup language documents.

You might think of DTDs as grammar rules of markup languages. For example, the English language includes parts of speech such as nouns, verbs, adjectives, and prepositions, and each of these parts appears in a particular order, depending on the kind of sentence and the amount of detail within the sentence. Likewise, a DTD specifies which elements you can include in markup language documents (such as HTML, XHTML, and XML), much the same way that the rules of English grammar specify all the possible parts of speech you can use. Also, a DTD specifies the order in which the elements should appear and specifies the details that each element can, may, or cannot include, similar to the way that the rules for English grammar specify how to build sentences.

As you've learned in the last few chapters, creating a DTD is often a big part of developing XML applications; therefore, you need to take the time to plan, organize, and develop DTDs thoroughly. In this chapter, we'll introduce you to DTD fundamentals, including the basic rules that govern how DTDs can be assembled and how they connect to XML documents. With this information, you'll not only gain a better understanding of DTDs, but you'll also gain the foundation necessary to read and write them—you'll start applying this information in the next chapter.

This chapter covers the following topics:

- Understanding DTD rules and concepts
- Viewing the pieces and parts of a DTD
- Connecting DTDs to XML documents

Understanding DTD Rules and Concepts

Your first task in developing DTDs is to understand a few rules and concepts. Taking the grammar analogy one step further, think of DTD rules as the spelling rules (such as, *i* before *e* except after *c*) and structure basics (such as, put a period, question mark, or exclamation point at the end of a sentence). These are the unexciting parts of developing DTDs, but they do provide the essential background you need. In the following few sections, we introduce you to these rules and concepts and show you how to apply them. Listing 22.1 illustrates a simple XML DTD.

In this chapter, we use the term processing application *generically to refer to a stand-alone parser or a specialized application or browser that includes the parser and other processing components. There are two types of parsers: validating and non-validating parsers. The validating parser parses a document according to the rules in the DTD and then passes the resulting information to the processor. A non-validating parser, the type found in most Web browsers, only checks the document (including any DTD subset) for well-formedness. If you're familiar with the XHTML DTD, many of the concepts discussed in this chapter should be easy to understand. See Chapter 2 to learn more about XHTML DTDs.*

LISTING 22.1: AN XML DTD

```
<!NOTATION gif SYSTEM "image/gif">
<!NOTATION jpeg SYSTEM "image/jpeg">
<!NOTATION png SYSTEM "image/png">
<!ENTITY mxhtml SYSTEM "graphics/mxhtml.gif" NDATA gif>
<!ENTITY jdgexj SYSTEM "graphics/jdgexj.gif" NDATA gif>
<!ENTITY jdgsj SYSTEM "graphics/jdgsj.gif" NDATA gif>
<!ELEMENT publications (book+)>
<!ATTLIST publications xmlns CDATA #FIXED
    "http://www.lanw.com/namespaces/pubs">
<!ELEMENT book (title, authors, pubDate, publisher, size,
   cover?, topics, errata?, description, website?)>
<!ATTLIST book
         isbn CDATA #REQUIRED
         edition CDATA #REQUIRED
         cat NMTOKENS #REQUIRED
         id ID #IMPLIED
   >
```

```
<!ELEMENT authors (author+)>
<!ATTLIST size pp CDATA #REQUIRED>
<!ELEMENT size EMPTY>
<!ELEMENT cover EMPTY>
<!ATTLIST cover img ENTITY #REQUIRED>
<!ELEMENT topics (topic+)>
<!ELEMENT errata EMPTY>
<!ATTLIST errata code CDATA #REQUIRED>
<!ELEMENT title (#PCDATA)>
<!ELEMENT pubDate EMPTY>
<!ATTLIST pubDate year CDATA #REQUIRED>
<!ELEMENT publisher (#PCDATA)>
<!ELEMENT description (#PCDATA)>
<!ELEMENT website (#PCDATA)>
<!ELEMENT author (#PCDATA)>
<!ELEMENT topic (#PCDATA)>
```

Characters and Names

When you're developing an XML document, you can use virtually any characters from any language in the world. You're limited only by what the processing application can interpret, and XML processing applications are very accommodating; by default, they support most characters available in most languages. So, for example, you can create XML documents with any combination of Western and Asian characters, rather than being restricted to the characters you can type on your computer keyboard.

For more information about characters in DTDs, see Chapter 23.

When developing DTDs for XML documents, you must specify anything you want to include in the XML document by name. And you're required to use *legal names*, which are a grouping of characters that begin with a letter and include letters, numbers, hyphens, underscores, colons, or periods, as in `title`, `heading.2`, or `doc:info`.

Names carry two restrictions:

- They can only contain four punctuation symbols—hyphens (-), underscores (_), colons (:), and periods (.). Any other punctuation characters are not acceptable in XML and will be rejected by the parser.

- They cannot begin with the character string "xml," "XML," or any other capitalization variation. All "xml" variations are reserved for future use by XML standards.

Valid sample names include card, s2c, or card-shark, which start with a letter and include only the allowed characters and symbols.

 Although it's perfectly legal to use a colon within an attribute or element name, it should be avoided. Colons are reserved for use with namespaces, and any namespace-aware processor will mistake the element or attribute name as a namespace prefix.

DTD Declarations

Although Chapter 23 covers how to create DTD declarations, this chapter expects you to understand basic declaration syntax. All DTD declarations follow the same basic structure:

```
<!KEYWORD …>
```

The delimiters are the same for all declarations (<! >), and a keyword is always used to define the type of declaration. All keywords must be in uppercase. The two most common types of declarations are element type and attribute list declarations. The basic syntax for both declaration types are:

```
<!ELEMENT elementname contentmodel>
```

```
<!ATTLIST elementname attributename datatype defaultoption>
```

For example, you could define a book element with an isbn attribute:

```
<!ELEMENT book (#PCDATA)>
```

```
<!ATTLIST book isbn CDATA #REQUIRED>
```

You'll learn more about creating DTD declarations in Chapter 23.

Logic in a DTD

Logic refers to the characters and symbols you use to construct a DTD. As you develop a DTD, you must have some way of connecting elements and of specifying the rules by which they can or must be applied.

Think of it this way. If you're making a sandwich, you have all sorts of pieces, such as bread, cheese, meat, lettuce, and perhaps mustard and/or mayonnaise. Also, you probably have a specific way of putting the pieces together, such as building it from the bottom up or putting goodies on both slices of bread and then putting the two slices together—goodies on the inside, of course. When describing how you build the sandwich, you need some way to specify what the pieces are, how they relate, and how they should be added. Without some sort of logical method in place (even if unstated), you could have all sorts of problems when building a sandwich, such as omitting the bottom piece of bread or adding the mustard to the outside of the bread.

Likewise, in developing an XML document DTD, you need some way to specify which elements can or must be included, how the elements relate, and how the elements should (or must) be put together in the XML document. DTDs use a system called *Extended Backus-Naur Format*, which gives you a method for specifying elements in XML documents, indicating how they relate and how they should be put together. Table 22.1 lists the Extended Backus-Naur operators and describes the function of each.

Table 22.1 Extended Backus-Naur Format Options

USE THIS...	TO DO THIS...	EXAMPLE
( )	Encloses a sequence or group of choices	`(bread, meat, cheese)`
,	Separates items in a list of required elements that must appear in order	`(bread, filling, bread)`
|	Separates items in a list of choices	`(wheat | white | rye)`
?	Shows that elements can occur zero or one time, but no more than once	`(bread, filling, mustard?, bread)`
*	Shows that elements can occur zero or more times	`(bread, filling, mustard?, pickles*, bread)`
+	Shows that elements occur one or more times	`(bread, meat+, bread)`

So, back to the sandwich example, you might specify

`(bread, filling, bread)`

indicating that bread, filling, and bread are each required, one time, and must occur in that order. You could also specify different bread choices, as in

`((white | rye | wheat), filling, (white | rye | wheat))`

which would give people the option to use white, rye, or wheat on either side of the sandwich. Additionally, you might specify that filling could occur multiple times, but at least once, like this:

`((white | rye | wheat), filling+, (white | rye | wheat))`

You might also specify that mustard can optionally be present, but no more than once, and it must go between the first bread and the filling:

```
((white | rye | wheat), mustard?, filling+,
   (white | rye | wheat))
```

Finally, you might add the option of having none, one, or many pickles:

```
((white | rye | wheat), mustard?, filling+, pickles*,
   (white | rye | wheat))
```

As you can see, using the Backus-Naur format involves nothing more than using a few symbols and putting the information in a specific order. You'll apply this system as you develop DTDs.

Data Types

When you write DTDs, you create elements for items such as headings, text, numbered lists, and links (among other elements) that will be parsed (processed) as part of the XML document. These parsed elements are called *parsed data* and will make up the vast majority of your XML documents.

In a DTD, you specify that you want elements to be parsed; you do so using the *parsed character data* (#PCDATA) content model, which will be processed by the XML parser as it looks for other elements or other variables that need to be changed or manipulated. For example, a section of an XML document that could contain other elements—such as a chapter that could contain paragraphs or notes—would be parsed to find the tags that indicate those embedded paragraphs or notes.

In some instances, however, you might not want all the data to be parsed and interpreted. Suppose you're creating an XML document that gives instructions for creating XML. How would you show XML markup within the instruction document? That is, if you say, Step 1: Type in <coolness>Awesome idea</coolness>, how do you indicate that you want the markup displayed as is and not parsed and interpreted by the processing application? In this case, you could not use parsed data to show the XML markup; it would be parsed and interpreted just like the rest of the document contents (and the parser would likely generate error messages because it didn't expect to see a <coolness> element). This is where *unparsed* data becomes handy. It lets you include XML markup (among other things) within a document that will appear exactly as you enter it—essential, in this case, for displaying the markup you want users to type.

You could also use character entities to display otherwise prohibited characters, such as <, >, or &. See Chapter 23 for more information.

Whereas you specify parsed data in a DTD, you specify unparsed data in the XML document itself using *character data* (CDATA). Character data goes through a parser without being processed and, instead, gets passed directly to the processing application. In the XML document, then, you would include character data markup like this:

```
<![CDATA[Type in <coolness>Awesome idea</coolness>)]]>
```

Everything between <![CDATA[and]]> is not parsed and is passed directly to the processing application.

Character data also occurs in DTDs, not just in XML documents. We'll talk more about this in Chapter 23.

Comments in a DTD

Comments are simply notes that you can include in a DTD that will not be processed along with the other DTD content. Think of a comment as a little yellow sticky note that you include in a DTD (or XML document). You can use comments to include reminders about the purpose for an element, make notes to other people developing or using a DTD, or include special instructions for revisions.

You can use comments in the XML documents as well—they are identical (<!-- comment here -->) in structure and purpose.

Your only restriction in using comments is that you must place them between tags (not inside them), and you must use only character data, not markup tags. The following markup shows how you might include a comment within a DTD:

```
<!ELEMENT faq (title, motto, maintainer, category)>
<!ELEMENT category (topic,(question, answer)+)>
<!-- Included date on maintainer element because of possibility
    of different maintainers at different times -->
<!ELEMENT maintainer (who, date)>
```

Include/Ignore

When you're writing DTDs, you may want to either include or exclude parts of the DTD for processing. For example, after you've developed a fairly solid DTD, you might want to experiment with restructuring some of it to better meet your needs. You could create a set of new DTDs, copy and paste parts of the old DTD into them, and then change your XML documents to point to each different DTD to try them out. A better option, however, would be to use INCLUDE and IGNORE options. In using these, you can take an existing DTD and specify that only parts of it (such as experimental sections or working sections) should be read and used by the parser.

Let's look at an example. Suppose you've developed a FAQ DTD and want to begin adding new elements to it so the DTD supports extra information about questions, problem reporting, and resolutions. You can add to or tweak the DTD to include declarations for both purposes using the IGNORE and INCLUDE options. In the following example, a multipurpose DTD uses IGNORE and INCLUDE options to specify which parts the parser should parse or ignore:

```
<![IGNORE[
<!ELEMENT faq (title, motto, maintainer, category)>
<!ELEMENT category (topic,(question, answer)+)>
]]>
<![INCLUDE[
<!ELEMENT faq (title, motto, maintainer+, category)>
<!ELEMENT category (topic,(question, questioner, (answer,
    supporttech)+)+)>
]]>
```

Everything between the <![IGNORE[and]]> is ignored by the parser (the old part of the DTD that works and that you don't want to toss away until all the bugs are worked out), and everything between the <![INCLUDE[and]]> (the new stuff that should expand the DTD to address these new issues) is processed by the parser. Don't worry—we'll talk about the specific elements and how to define them in Chapter 23.

Understanding How DTDs Connect to XML Documents

Finally, before you start developing a DTD, you should be aware of how DTDs and XML documents are connected. Remember that each provides a parser with different information—the XML document provides content, and the DTD provides structure and rules for the XML document. For a processing application to read and display the XML document correctly, you need to tell it where to find the DTD so it knows which rules to apply.

You have three choices:

- You can embed the DTD within the XML document. In this case, the DTD is part of the XML document.

- You can reference a separate DTD. In this case, the DTD is a separate file.

- You can do both—embed declarations and reference an external file.

Embedding the DTD

When you embed DTD declarations in the XML document, you include the DTD information within the XML document itself. Specifically, you include the complete DTD, known as the *internal subset*, within the <!DOCTYPE> declaration, which you must include to create a valid XML document. The following markup shows a DTD embedded in the <!DOCTYPE> declaration:

```
<?xml version="1.0"?>
<!DOCTYPE faq [
<!ELEMENT faq ANY>
]>
<faq>
Some content might go here, as defined in the internal subset.
</faq>
```

The advantage to embedding the DTD is that you only have to deal with a single document, rather than separate ones. You might find an embedded DTD useful, particularly if you're debugging a new DTD and editing both an XML document and the DTD while you're experimenting. Additionally, if you're creating a relatively short DTD or one that you'll use for smaller documents, this would be a good option.

There are two drawbacks to embedding the DTD. In particular, your document could potentially become packed with markup, which makes the document more difficult to read. Rather than viewing only XML document content or DTD information, as you would with separate documents, you'll be forced to wade through the DTD information every time you want to view or modify the XML content. Also, the data in the XML document would be less readily reused and repurposed if it's physically tied to a DTD.

For these reasons, if you plan to create a complex DTD or one that you'll use repeatedly or for large documents (as you'll likely be doing), we recommend that you create a separate DTD and reference it in the <!DOCTYPE> declaration, as discussed in the following section.

Referencing the DTD

Your best choice for connecting the DTD to the XML document is to reference it within the XML document—that is, create a separate DTD document and point to it from the XML document. Referencing external DTD declarations, also known as the *external subset*, is similar to embedding it in that you use the <!DOCTYPE> declaration. The difference, as shown in the following markup, is that you include only the reference and provide no additional information about how your document should be structured:

```
<?xml version="1.0"?>
<!DOCTYPE faq SYSTEM "faq.dtd">
<faq>
```

The advantage to referencing a separate DTD is that it's ideal for long or complex DTDs. You can more easily access and modify DTD markup if it's in a separate file than you can if it's embedded in the XML document.

Additionally, having a separate DTD makes reusing the DTD for other XML documents much easier. Rather than having to copy and paste DTD information, as you would if it's embedded, you can simply reference the DTD from multiple XML documents. You create the DTD one time and reference it as many times as you need.

The disadvantage to referencing a separate DTD is that you have to deal with two documents. For many uses, this may not be a problem; however, for small, simple DTDs, experimental DTDs, or ones under development, embedding the DTD might be a better option.

Combining External and Internal DTDs

External DTD subsets are good for defining a common vocabulary for a collection of XML documents. On the other hand, internal DTD subsets are beneficial for defining customized grammar rules for a specific document. More times than not, you'll find yourself wanting to take advantage of both of these approaches. The XML specification allows document authors to combine both internal and external subsets as a complete collection of declarations for a given document.

The syntax for combining internal and external subsets is as follows:

```
<?xml version="1.0"?>
<!DOCTYPE faq SYSTEM "faq.dtd" [
  <!ENTITY copy "Copyright 2001">
 ]>
<faq>
```

In the previous example, the XML document references the external DTD subset (faq.dtd), while including an internal ENTITY declaration. Although it's not recommended that you create conflicting declarations, if this does occur, the declaration that is read first by the processing application (the internal subset declarations) takes precedence.

Where to Go from Here

In this chapter, we introduced you to basic DTD rules and concepts and showed you how DTDs connect to XML documents. You may be thinking that these nitpicky rules, concepts, and markup are a lot to remember—and you're right. Keep in mind, though, that applying them (as you'll do starting in Chapter 23) is much easier than keeping them straight in your mind. With the information you learned in this chapter, you're ready to learn about the DTD development process and then move on to developing your first DTD.

- See Chapter 23 to develop your first DTD.

- See Chapter 30 for information on XML Schemas, which may someday replace DTDs.

Creating a DTD

Chapter 23

n Chapter 22, you examined the basic rules and concepts you apply when developing DTDs. In this chapter, we'll examine the basic DTD development process and DTD components that you'll need to become familiar with before you develop your first DTD.

As we'll show you, developing DTDs is basically a two-phase process:

1. You provide processing information, which tells parsers or specialized applications how to process the XML document. This step is the short and simple one—not many decisions to make here.

2. You fill in DTD content, which tells parsers or specialized applications the structure and rules it should apply.

In learning about these two phases, keep in mind that you'll complete the second one iteratively. Particularly when filling in DTD content, you'll undoubtedly add to, delete from, or otherwise modify the DTD so it meets your specific needs. These two phases, however, are the basic aspects—one short and fixed, one longer and iterative—in building DTDs.

This chapter covers the following topics:

- Specifying the processing instructions

- Filling in DTD content

- Putting it all together

Specifying Processing Instructions

Your first task in developing a DTD is to include some basics about how processing applications (parsers or other programs such as editors or browsers) should process DTD information. This information, called *processing instructions*, gives processing applications details about the XML document and helps ensure that they process the XML document correctly.

Although you don't have to include processing instructions (and whether you do depends completely on what your processing application requires), you should, at a minimum, include the *XML declaration*. In doing so, you state that the processing application adheres to the rules of a specific XML version, such as XML version 1.0 (currently) or version 3.4 (hypothetically) or whatever. Just like the HTML specification, the XML specification might change a bit with new versions, so you need to tell processing applications with which version the XML document complies.

Although XML declarations use the same syntax as processing instructions, and even perform similar functions to other processing instructions, they're not technically processing instructions. The XML declaration is its very own unique piece of markup that defines version and encoding information about an XML document. This distinction may seem trivial, but it's important to understand.

As shown in the following brief excerpt from a DTD, the XML declaration is the first element in the DTD:

```
<?xml version="1.0"?>
<!ELEMENT faq (title, motto, maintainer, category)>
<!ELEMENT category (topic,(question, answer)+)>
<!ELEMENT maintainer (who, date)>
<!ELEMENT question (#PCDATA)>
<!ELEMENT answer (#PCDATA)>
<!ELEMENT motto (#PCDATA)>
<!ELEMENT title (#PCDATA)>
<!ELEMENT topic (#PCDATA)>
<!ELEMENT who (#PCDATA)>
<!ELEMENT date (#PCDATA)>
```

In this example, the XML declaration includes only information about the XML version—in this case, version 1.0—which is sufficient for telling processing applications to which XML version to adhere.

You can, however, also include two other bits of information in the XML declaration. First, you can specify that the DTD stands on its own and that it does not reference or link to other DTDs. To do this, simply add the standalone attribute, as shown in the following markup:

```
<?xml version="1.0" standalone="yes"?>
```

Or you can specify that the DTD does not stand on its own—that is, it references (includes) other DTDs. In this case, you add a no value to the standalone attribute, like this:

```
<?xml version="1.0" standalone="no"?>
```

You'll find more information about referencing other DTDs later in this chapter in the "Parameter Entities" section.

Second, you can specify an encoding for the DTD and XML document. *Encodings* specify character sets used, such as a Western character set, a Cyrillic character set, or various Asian character sets. By specifying that the processing application should expect a particular encoding, you help eliminate ambiguity in how it processes the information.

The default encoding is UTF-8, which includes all common ASCII characters in addition to most characters in common Western languages. The following markup adds the encoding attribute:

```
<?xml version="1.0" standalone="no" encoding="UTF-8"?>
```

You'll find more information about encodings in the "More about Encodings" sidebar at the end of this section.

In addition to including the XML declaration, you can add other processing declarations that meet your specific needs. Keep in mind that these instructions are just bits of information you provide so the processing application knows how to parse and process your XML documents. To use other declarations, you'll either add them according to instructions provided with the processing application, or if you're writing a processing application, you can specify the instructions. Your only limitation in writing your own instructions is that you do *not* start them with <?xml, <?XML, or any variation in capitalization because this chunk of markup is reserved for future XML uses.

So, for example, if you want to create custom processing instructions for an application that counts the number of times a page is viewed, you might include markup that looks like

```
<?CustomProcessingApp increment PageViews?>
```

and `CustomProcessingApp` would presumably know what to do with the instructions. You begin the markup with an opening angle bracket (<) and question mark (?), and you end with a question mark (?) and a closing angle bracket (>). The information, or instructions, to be processed appears between these, but exactly what you fill in between the <? and the ?> depends on what your processing application requires. The documentation should tell you.

That's all there is to specifying processing instructions. At a minimum, you include the XML declaration, which specifies the XML version, whether the DTD stands alone, and encodings. Other declarations are optional.

More about Encodings

XML supports *Unimarkup*, which is an international standard for character encodings. By requiring Unimarkup support for all XML applications, XML developers ensure that XML documents are internationally portable—unlike many other document formats. This means that you can include virtually any characters used in any language in the world in your XML documents by simply specifying the correct encoding.

All XML processors must be able to recognize and read UTF-8 encodings (which include ASCII characters and Western language characters) and UTF-16 encodings (which include UTF-8 encodings plus *most* other possible characters available internationally). If you're using either of these encodings, you don't have to include an encoding declaration—although it'd be a good idea to clearly specify which encoding you use anyway.

If you plan to use other encodings, you *must* specify them in the DTD.

Filling in DTD Content

After including processing instructions, your next step is to fill in DTD content, which consists of four general types of declarations:

- Element
- Attribute
- Entity
- Notation

As you're beginning to understand what each of these declarations does, keep in mind that you use these declarations to specify the rules and structure you must follow when developing an XML document. Each declaration directly corresponds to what you can or cannot include in an XML document. We'll show you markup samples throughout the following sections, but you might also refer to the "Putting It All Together" section to see how these declarations fit into a DTD.

Element Type Declarations

Element type declarations are perhaps the most common declarations you'll use because they let you identify specific and common parts of XML documents (called elements, logically). For example, using element type declarations, you can specify that an XML document contain items such as headings, citations, addresses, paragraphs, figure captions, and lists. Each of these refers to a different part of an XML document, and, therefore, each requires a separate element type declaration in the DTD. As a start, your element type declarations might look similar to the following bits of markup:

```
<!ELEMENT heading …>
<!ELEMENT citation …>
<!ELEMENT address …>
<!ELEMENT paragraph …>
<!ELEMENT caption …>
<!ELEMENT list …>
```

Keep in mind that elements identify content, not presentation. In other words, a list *element might indicate an enumeration of items; however, it does not necessarily mean that the items would appear aligned vertically with bullet characters in front of each item. You need to use style sheets to achieve that.*

In addition to specifying various elements that can occur within an XML document, you use element type declarations to identify what can be included within the element—that is, which elements will nest in the first element. In particular, you can specify the following:

- Only specified elements can be included.

- Only data, such as words, numbers, or characters, can be included.

- Both specified elements and data can be included.

- Any element or data can be included.

- No elements or data can be included (the element is empty).

Quick Lookup

In Chapter 22, we used the term *elements* generically to describe parts of an XML document—as in the elements that make up an XML document. In this chapter, we again use the term *element*, but in this more precise use, it refers to the *element* as used in an XML document, as in <!ELEMENT...>. An *element type declaration*, then, resides in the DTD.

Specifying That Elements Can Be Included

Within element type declarations, you'll commonly want to specify that other elements can be included. For example, the XHTML DTD specifies that an XHTML document must include an html element; it then further specifies that a head element *and* a body element be included with it. In doing so, it specifies that a particular element can be included within an existing element. The final markup looks like this:

```
<!ELEMENT html (head, body)>
```

For a reminder about the meanings and uses of parentheses and commas, refer to Chapter 22.

Notice that each of these element type declarations begins with an opening angle bracket (<), includes !ELEMENT, identifies the name of the particular element being defined, and closes with a closing angle bracket (>). You'll use this format for all element type declarations.

This element type declaration, which declares an element and specifies what can be included in it, would allow you to create the following markup in an XHTML document:

```
<html>
   <head>...</head>
   <body>...</body>
</html>
```

As defined by the html element declaration, the html element includes the head element, *followed* by the body element.

Specifying That Data Can Be Included

You can also specify that data can be included within an element. Data can include things such as words, numbers, or individual characters—practically any text that's not an element. All you have to do is include (#PCDATA) in the element type declaration, like this:

```
<!ELEMENT code (#PCDATA)>
```

For a reminder about PCDATA, see Chapter 22.

In this example, (#PCDATA) tells processing applications that any data can be included within the code element and that the data in the code element will be parsed. In using #PCDATA, you create what's called a *mixed content model*, which basically means that the element can contain mixed content, including normal characters and numbers, as well as entities, other elements (although the preceding example doesn't allow elements), numbers, or characters.

Find out more about entities in the "Entity Declarations" section later in this chapter.

In the following XML document markup, the data defined by (#PCDATA) appears as text included between opening and closing tags:

```
<code>info@example.com</code>
```

Specifying That Both Elements and Data Can Be Included

In other cases, you might want to specify that both elements and data can be included. For example, you might want to have a preferred element within an address element to show which address the owner prefers to use. In this case, you'd structure the markup like this:

```
<!ELEMENT p (#PCDATA | b | em | i)*>
```

This is another example of a mixed content model, in which the element can be accompanied by data and a specific element. Notice the order in which the information appears. Like other element type declarations, it begins with <!ELEMENT, continues with the element name and an expression that closes with *, and concludes with >. Any time you mix data and elements, you must specify #PCDATA first, and then specify the element or elements and include the * to show that it can occur or recur any number of times.

An expression is a combination of logical operators and other objects that define what may or may not occur in parts of an XML document.

The resulting XML document markup might look like the following sample:

```
<p>The paragraph element may contain both text, <b>bold</b>,
    <em>emphasis</em>, and <i>italic</i> elements.</p>
```

Specifying That Anything Can Be Included

Occasionally, you might want to specify that anything—data, elements, or characters—can be included. In doing so, you perhaps make it simpler to know what can and cannot be included with an element; however, you also make the resulting XML document less structured, which can make using and reusing the information more difficult. How? Well, if many elements can have any content, you could have as little structure or logic as you'd have in a merely well-formed, but not valid, document. You could not require that document developers adhere to any particular standard, which could lead to inconsistent document content and structure.

If, however, it's not important to guarantee consistency, use ANY in the element type declaration, as follows:

```
<!ELEMENT p ANY>
```

Specifying That Nothing Can Be Included

Finally, you may want to specify that nothing can be included with an element—that the element is empty. If, for example, you provide specific information within attributes for an element but plan to have no information enclosed between the element's opening and closing tags, you would ensure that the element itself does not contain any information by defining it as empty.

To specify that nothing can be included with an element, use EMPTY in the element type declaration, like this:

```
<!ELEMENT meta EMPTY>
```

The resulting XML document markup might look like this:

```
<meta attributes="optional" />
```

or this:

```
<meta attributes="optional"></meta>
```

Several empty elements are defined for XHTML, such as img, br, hr, meta, input, area, base, col, frame, link, *and* param.

Attribute List Declarations

In XML documents, you often use elements in conjunction with attributes that provide additional information about the element. Logically, because you use an element type declaration to set the rules for the elements, you use an *attribute list declaration* to specify rules for using an attribute.

If you're thinking that you can already specify additional information about elements using elements nested within an element, you're right. In this sense, you're specifying additional information about elements, much the same way that attribute list declarations do. However, the difference is somewhat arbitrary—you could feasibly use nested elements to function as attributes or use attributes to function as nested elements. In deciding which declaration to use, consider the type of information you're specifying. Typically, you'll want to use element type declarations to include information that XML document users will view, and you'll want to use attribute list declarations for behind-the-scenes information that's only relevant to you, other developers, or perhaps processing applications.

For example, suppose you're developing a bibliography. Using element type declarations, you would likely declare a book element that requires a title element and specify that additional information be included as elements, such as authors and publication dates:

```
<!ELEMENT book (title | author | pubdate)>
```

The resulting markup in an XML document would look like this:

```
<book>
<title>Mastering XML</title>
<author>Ray and Ray</author>
<pubdate>1998</pubdate>
</book>
```

This additional information would be useful to potential XML document users; therefore, it makes sense to make it available as individual elements within the XML document.

In some XML applications, however, you'll want to specify information that's not necessarily useful to users. For example, you might want to provide information about the shelving category or potential audience. This information is useful for two reasons: It helps provide information that's valuable when developing and reusing XML documents, and it gives processing applications the context and targets that are necessary to sort or search for information. Because these reasons focus more on what's useful to you, as the developer, and a processing application—not a potential XML document user—you should consider including this information using attribute list declarations.

 As a general rule, use element type declarations *to provide additional information that's useful to XML document users. Use* attribute list declarations *to provide additional information that's useful to you or a processing application.*

You use attribute list declarations to do the following:

- Define the set of attributes for a given element type.

- Establish constraints for attributes.

- Provide default values for attributes.

- Provide information about whether the attribute is required and, if not, how the processing application should react if a declared attribute is absent.

Like element type declarations, attribute list declarations consist of specific information and are structured in a particular way. For example, the XHTML img element can accept a number of attributes. For simplicity sake, however, we pretend it can only accept one attribute, src:

```
<!ELEMENT img EMPTY>
```

To specify additional information about the img element, such as the kind of information that can go in it, you could develop an attribute list declaration:

```
<!ATTLIST img src CDATA #REQUIRED>
```

Notice that the attribute list declaration does the following:

- Begins with an opening angle bracket (<)

- Includes !ATTLIST, which specifies the declaration as an attribute list declaration

- Specifies the element name, img, that corresponds with the name of the element

- Specifies the attribute name, src

- Specifies the data type, CDATA

- Specifies an attribute setting, #REQUIRED

- Closes with an angle bracket (>)

No matter what information the attribute includes, you'll always follow this basic convention for forming attribute list declarations. Most of the information within the attribute list declaration will be fairly consistent from declaration to declaration; however, you'll always need to determine two essential components: name-value pairs and attribute settings.

Specifying Attribute Name-Value Pairs

Name-value pairs include the attribute name, which describes the attribute, and a value, which specifies parameters for the attribute. In developing a name-value pair, first determine the attribute name; you simply choose one that describes the attribute.

Determining the type of value, however, is a bit more complex because you can add three types of values. Your first option is to use *string values*, which include characters and/or numbers (such as 285, "One Fine Day," or "Pennsylvania6500"). These examples identify a specific attribute value—that is, the value associates with the attribute name. You could also develop a less specific string value that contains simply data, as follows:

```
<!ATTLIST img alt CDATA #REQUIRED>
```

In this example, the CDATA data type indicates that the attribute could contain any string for the value of the img attribute. So, for example, the corresponding attribute in the XML document might look like this:

```
<img alt="alternative text"/>
```

In most cases, however, you'll want to allow for any old string. As here, the value of the alt attribute is up to the document author. However, if there are only a few options for an attribute value, it might be more useful to precisely specify the acceptable values in the DTD.

Your second option is to use *enumerated values*, which specify the possible values (such as yes or no, or 1, 0, or unknown). You use enumerated values when you know the possible values for any given attribute. The following markup indicates that the border attribute for the img element could be either 1 or 0:

```
<!ATTLIST img border (1|0) "1">
```

This markup would require that either 1 or 0—and nothing else—be used as the value for the border attribute. (The final "1" sets the default value, as covered in the "Specifying Attribute Settings" section later in this chapter.)

Your third option is to use *tokenized values*, which refer to specific information within the DTD or XML document (such as the unique ID of an element in the document). These values are somewhat more complicated to develop—basically because you have even more options to choose from—but they can come in handy. In particular, you can use one of several tokenized attribute values, as listed in Table 23.1.

You'll recognize CDATA *from discussions in Chapter 21 and 22.*

Table 23.1 Tokenized Attribute Values

TOKENIZED VALUE	FUNCTION	EXAMPLE
CDATA	Textual data—the broadest and most general possibility.	`<!ATTLIST img alt CDATA #IMPLIED)>`
ID	Provides a unique ID within a document. (Works similarly to ID in XHTML style sheets.)	`<!ATTLIST img id ID) #IMPLIED>`
IDREF, IDREFS	References an ID from the same document. It must be present and accurate for the parser to accept it.	`<!ATTLIST td headers IDREFS #IMPLIED>`
ENTITY, ENTITIES	References external, binary entity or entities, such as an image. Entity jpeg must be declared in the DTD for this example to work.	`<!ATTLIST img photo jpeg ENTITY #IMPLIED)>`
NMTOKEN, NMTOKENS	Provides for attribute values as a name or names that must be proper XML names, not simply unparsed data like the CDATA example. Provides more specific information than CDATA.	`<!ATTLIST contact photoformat NMTOKEN #IMPLIED >`
NOTATION	Refers to the name of a declared notation. In this example, the value provided in the XML document must correspond to a notation declared in the DTD. The NOTATION (enumerated) option would generally be better.	`<!ATTLIST contact photoformat NOTATION (viewer | editor) #IMPLIED >`
Enumerated	Provides a list of specific options, in this case, the value can only be ismap.	`<!ATTLIST img ismap (ismap) #IMPLIED >`
NOTATION (enumerated)	Itemizes the names of a declared notation. In this example, the value provided in the XML document must correspond to the viewer and editor notations declared in the DTD.	`<!ATTLIST contact photoformat NOTATION (viewer | editor) #IMPLIED >`

For the examples in Table 23.1, we used XHTML attribute list declarations. However, the XHTML DTD does not use each data type, and therefore, we had to create a few of our own.

Specifying Attribute Settings

In addition to specifying name-value pairs, you need to specify *attribute settings*, which specify characteristics of the name-value pairs—whether the attribute and value must be present (#REQUIRED), whether they're implied when not specifically included (#IMPLIED), whether they must always contain a specific value (#FIXED), or whether default values (rather than specific settings) are provided.

Your first setting choice is required (#REQUIRED), which means that the element requires the attribute. In this case, the attribute must be included with the element; otherwise, parsers will reject the document because the document doesn't follow the rules specified in the DTD. You add #REQUIRED to an attribute list declaration like this:

```
<!ATTLIST img src CDATA #REQUIRED>
```

Your next choice is implied (#IMPLIED), which means that the element does not require that an attribute be specified but that the default attribute value (null) be sent to the processing application if nothing else is specified. The following attribute list declaration specifies that the width attribute for the img element is optional:

```
<!ATTLIST img width CDATA #IMPLIED>
```

Another choice is fixed (#FIXED), followed by the value the attribute must take, which means that the attribute must contain the default attribute setting or it will be rejected by the parser. In the following example, the xmlns attribute must have the value http://www.w3.org/1999/xhtml:

```
<!ATTLIST html xmlns CDATA #FIXED
    "http://www.w3.org/1999/xhtml">
```

You might notice that value has the XHTML namespace. Because the XHTML specification requires the XHTML namespace to be defined as a part of the html element, the XHTML DTD defines that value as fixed.

Finally, rather than using these specific settings, you can simply provide a default value, if appropriate, by placing the value at the end of the attribute list declaration. Using a default value is handy for making sure information is provided to the processing application. The following markup shows that the attribute value can be either 1 or 0 and that the default value is 1:

```
<!ATTLIST img border (1|0) "1">
```

Handling White Space

When writing DTDs, you can indicate how processing applications should handle white space. *White space* refers to spaces, carriage returns, line feeds, and tabs included in XML documents. In all cases, parsers must pass white space in XML documents to the processing application, but processing applications will likely ignore insignificant white space and present only the significant white space used. For example, in the following XML document fragment, the processing application would ignore the white space around elements because it's used only to make the XML markup easier to read:

```
<body>
<h1>House Plant FAQ</h1>
<p>Motto: All the plant questions you've lost sleep over,
    and then some. </p>
<div class="footer">
    <p>Maintained by Digit Brown</p>
    <p>April 1, 1999</p>
</div>
</body>
```

You include white space in XML documents primarily to make the (often-crowded) document easier to read.

In some instances, however, you might want to include white space in an XML document that should be retained and presented by a processing application. For example, if you're writing poetry or providing examples of computer programming languages, all spaces are likely significant. To indicate that the spaces matter, you simply add an extra instruction to the DTD—in particular, a special attribute, xml:space, for each element that you want the processing application to retain white space for in the processed document. In your DTD, you could include xml:space in the following attribute list declaration:

```
<!ATTLIST someelement xml:space  'preserve'>
```

In this example, the value default would signal that applications' default white-space processing modes are acceptable for this element. The value preserve would signal that applications preserve all the white space. The default value for the xml:space attribute is set to be preserve.

Entity Declarations

Entity declarations let you substitute information in a DTD, which is handy for easily reusing information in an XML document or even within the DTD itself. For example, if your company name is long and complex, you might want to use an entity declaration to allow people to use a shorter, substitute name in its place. By declaring an entity for a complex and hard-to-type name, anyone developing a document can use the short entity and rely on the XML parser to put in the long name.

You can use three kinds of entity declarations—general entities, parameter entities, and character entities—each of which gives you specific capabilities.

General Entities

General entities are substitutions that are made in the XML documents (as opposed to substitutions within the DTD). You define them in the DTD, but the changes and effects show up in the XML documents after processing.

Suppose your company is takeover-prone and you want a simpler way of replacing the old company name with a new company name. Rather than doing a search-and-replace through all your documents, you could more easily use general entities. All you have to do is use a general entity declaration in the DTD and then include the entity in the XML document. In doing so, every time the company name changes, you would only have to change the entity declaration in the DTD, and the parser would apply the new information in all the documents for you. No muss, no fuss.

For example, you might include an entity declaration in the DTD like this:

```
<!ENTITY companyname "John Smith and Sons">
```

In an effort to keep our examples readable, throughout this section we do not use examples from the XHTML DTD. The XHTML DTD makes ample use of entities; however, they do not serve well as introductory examples. If you would like to see the XHTML entities in action, visit www.w3.org/TR/xhtml1/ DTD/xhtml1-transitional.dtd.

Then, your XML markup in a document associated with this DTD would look like

```
<P>Just remember, &companyname; has your best interests at
heart, and we'll always be here for you, whenever you need
us.</P>
```

The resulting parsed document would look like this:

```
Just remember, John Smith and Sons has your best interests
at heart, and we'll always be here for you, whenever you
need us.
```

What's particularly handy about general entities is that you can make changes to the DTD and easily apply them. For example, if your company name changes a week or so later, you could simply change the companyname entity in the DTD to specify the new name. Then all documents referencing the DTD would automatically be updated. The new parsed document might look like this:

```
Just remember, MegaCorporation has your best interests at
heart, and we'll always be here for you, whenever you need us.
```

In general, creating an entity is as easy as entering

```
<!ENTITY name "expansion">
```

In this example, *name* specifies the entity name (you make this up), and *expansion* specifies the replacement text that the parser should substitute whenever it encounters the entity. An entity name can include letters, numbers, dashes (-), underscores (_), periods (.), and colons (:), and it must begin with a letter or underscore.

Here, you're using a general entity in one DTD to substitute information in one or more XML documents—any documents that use that particular DTD. This is called an *internal entity* because it's completely contained within the DTD. You can also use what's called an *external entity* to reference an entity contained in a different file. For example, taking the company name change example one step further, suppose your company uses multiple DTDs, rather than just one. To change the company name throughout all XML documents, you'd need to replace the general entity in all the DTDs that include the company name. In this case, rather than making one quick change, you'd again be forced to change information in multiple documents. Instead, you could create a separate document—an external entity—that would contain the information to be changed and reference that document from every other document. Taking this approach, you could make the change one time in a single document and have that change affect many different XML documents. The following markup declares a companyname entity with the content of the companyinfo.txt file:

```
<!ENTITY companyname SYSTEM "companyinfo.txt">
```

External entities are either *system entities* or *public entities*; system entities are currently the most common and useful. Using system entities, you could reference information on the Internet or reference a graphics file, such as your company logo. To continue with the takeover-prone company example, in addition to substituting the company name, you may also want to substitute a company logo in your document.

Therefore, if you wanted to include a reference to a .jpg format logo in the DTD, you could include something similar to the following:

```
<!ENTITY companylogo SYSTEM "johnsmithsonslogo.jpg" NDATA jpg>
```

In this example, the SYSTEM entity refers to a JPEG image, which is *non-text data* located outside the DTD. Non-text data can include such items as images or other binary files. You identify the non-text data using a *Uniform Resource Indicator (URI)*, which in this particular case is simply a graphic's filename, `johnsmithsonslogo.jpg`.

A URI is similar to a URL: It identifies a particular resource on the Internet. As a matter of fact, a URL is a type of URI.

If you're referencing non-text data, as we are here, you must also include a non-data reference (NDATA) and specify the type of data, in this case, `jpg`, so the processing applications know what kind of information to expect. If you're referencing text data, such as words or numbers or company names, you would not include the NDATA reference.

A Word about Public Entities and Identifiers

In addition to system entities and identifiers, as discussed here, you can use *public entities* and *identifiers*, which are commonly used by SGML applications. Confusingly, because anything on the Internet tends to be freely accessible and information in corporate networks tends to be restricted, "public entities" and "public identifiers" are the least public or accessible of anything you'll use in your XML journey.

You use public entities when you want to refer to standardized and publicly available data, such as a markup language standard. For example, an XHTML DOCTYPE declaration references a public identifier:

```
<!DOCTYPE HTML PUBLIC
    "-//W3C//DTD XHTML 1.0 Transitional//EN">
```

In this, the declaration (`"-//W3C//DTD XHTML 1.0 Transitional//EN"`) provides several bits of information: the organization that publishes the standard (W3C), what type of document it is (a DTD), what standard it references (XHTML 1.0), and which language it's written in (English).

You won't use public identifiers very often, unless you're coming from an SGML background and plan to continue to use the existing SGML tools for development.

Parameter Entities

You use parameter entities to build and reuse DTDs more effectively. Parameter entities follow the same general principle outlined for general entities—they let you make automatic substitutions so you can more easily reuse information. Rather than making a substitution in the resulting XML document, however, the substitution occurs in the DTD.

Again, with parameter entities, you have both internal and external entities. You use an internal entity to expand information within a DTD. For example, you might use an internal parameter entity like this:

```
<!ENTITY % name definition>
```

Notice that this markup begins with a percent sign (%), followed by the entity name (name), and then the expansion text or definition of the entity (definition). The entity name must begin with a letter or an underscore (_), but you can use letters, numbers, dashes (-), underscores (_), periods (.), and/or colons (:) in the rest of the name.

If you have a set of elements in your current DTD that all have a common set of attributes (for example, ModifiedDate and ModifiedBy), you could define those attributes one time at the top of the DTD, as shown here:

```
<!ENTITY % commonAttributes
"ModifiedDate CDATA #REQUIRED
ModifiedBy CDATA #REQUIRED">
```

Then for each element that requires those two attributes, you can simply include the parameter entity commonAttributes, rather than the complete text. For instance, in this example:

```
<!ELEMENT report (#PCDATA | content )*>
<!ATTLIST report %commonAttributes;>
<!ELEMENT evaluation (#PCDATA | content )*>
<!ATTLIST evaluation %commonAttributes;>
```

a parser would expand the entity references to look like this:

```
<!ELEMENT report (#PCDATA | content )*>
<!ATTLIST report
ModifiedDate CDATA #REQUIRED
ModifiedBy CDATA #REQUIRED>
<!ELEMENT evaluation (#PCDATA | content )*>
<!ATTLIST evaluation
ModifiedDate CDATA #REQUIRED
ModifiedBy CDATA #REQUIRED>
```

You use an external parameter entity to reference standard parts of a DTD that are to be included in other DTDs. To return to the company name example, you could create a DTD that contains authoritative information about the company name and include an external parameter entity that specifies the company name. In doing so, you could change the company name one time in the master DTD and automatically make the change throughout the other DTDs.

So, in the master DTD, called `companyinfo.dtd`, you might have a `companyname` entity declaration, like this:

```
<!ENTITY companyname "John Smith and Sons">
```

and all other DTDs would reference the master DTD, like this:

```
<!ENTITY % companyinfo SYSTEM
    "http://www.company.com/companyinfo.dtd">
```

In this case, you could include the `companyinfo.dtd` file in all DTDs that referenced it and apply all entities (and everything else) defined in the DTD to all documents referencing it.

Finally, you can also use parameter entities to shorten DTDs and make them easier to use. For example, rather than creating a lengthy DTD that includes a set of commonly used character entities, elements to establish basic document structure for a memo, and additional elements to provide a structured status report within the memo, you might create three smaller, modular DTDs: one with common character entities, one with memo elements, and one with status report elements. Then, you can use parameter entities to include the three DTDs by reference. In doing so, you can reference the memo DTD for any or all memos you use, just as you can reference the character entities DTD for all documents that require those characters.

Character Entities

You use character entities to add special characters and symbols to DTDs that you could not otherwise include. For example, suppose you need to include an opening angle bracket (<) in your DTD. In a non-markup language document, you could simply use the angle bracket key on your keyboard. However, because angle brackets are part of XML markup (for example, `<element>`), you cannot simply use the angle bracket key on your keyboard and have the symbol remain part of the document. Processing applications would treat the angle bracket as part of the behind-the-scenes markup, which gets processed. So, to include an opening angle bracket and have it remain as part of the DTD, you must substitute the characters `&lt;`, which translate to an opening angle bracket. XML comes with five built-in entities, as shown in Table 23.2.

You can include these five character entities in any XML document without having to specify that you've used them.

To include these, you simply include the markup directly in the XML document, like this:

```
<p>Few people have B&amp;W televisions any more.</p>
```

to yield

```
Few people have B&W televisions any more.
```

The & entity tells parsers to replace the entity with the ampersand symbol (&).

Table 23.2 Built-in XML Character Entities

CHARACTER ENTITY	RESULTING SYMBOL
&amp;	&
&lt;	<
&gt;	>
&apos;	'
&quote;	"

You're not limited to these five built-in character entities. You can use literally thousands of character entities derived from practically any language known internationally. You'll find a list of references to special characters in Master's Reference 5, which will meet most of your needs, or you can refer to specific resources for the language from which the characters are derived.

If you choose to use a character entity that's not built into XML, you must specify the entity in the DTD. For example, if you want to include a musical sharp symbol (#) in an XML document, you include markup like this in the DTD:

```
<!ENTITY sharp  "&#x266F;">
```

The resulting XML document markup would look something like this:

```
<tip>Musicians must always remember the significance of
    the &sharp; symbol.</tip>
```

And, the parsed document would look something like this:

```
Musicians must always remember the significance of
    the # symbol.
```

Character references that begin with &#x are a hexadecimal representation of the character number in the ISO/IEC 10646 standard. Character references that begin with &# are a decimal representation of the character number.

Notation Declarations

You use notation declarations to help processing applications determine how to process non-XML references or information. For example, suppose you want to reference a document published in the Portable Network Graphics (PNG) image format. Because PNG is not an XML format, processing applications are not required to know what to do with the reference (although they might) and, therefore, may not be able to use the referenced image. In this case, you could use a notation entity to provide a suggestion about how the PNG file might be processed:

```
<!NOTATION png SYSTEM "graphview.exe">
```

Notice that this declaration includes !NOTATION, a name (png), and an external reference (graphview.exe). This markup suggests, but does not require, that processing applications use a graphics viewer (graphview.exe) to process the PNG file. Also, because the reference is platform specific, the suggestion does not provide useful information for Macintosh or Unix users—that's okay, though, because the external reference is only a suggestion for processing and does not require that the processing application actually use it.

Putting It All Together

In this chapter, we've given you lots of information—mostly bits and pieces of information you need to keep track of as you're developing DTDs. We expect that you'll probably refer to this chapter several times, at least until you get some practice developing DTDs. To see how all these tidbits fit together, take a look at the following:

- Listing 23.1 shows a sample DTD.
- Listing 23.2 shows the XML document.
- Listing 23.3 shows the style sheet.
- Figure 23.1 shows how all these pieces come together in the parsed document.

Listings 23.1–23.3 can be found on the companion CD that comes with this book. We also recommend that you take a peek at the XHTML Transitional DTD found at www.w3.org/TR/xhtml1/DTD/ xhtml1-transitional.dtd.

LISTING 23.1: A SAMPLE DTD

```
<!-- This is a comment in a DTD -->
<!ENTITY sponsor "John Smith and Associates, Inc.">
<!ENTITY % qa "(question, answer)+">

<!ELEMENT faq (title, motto, maintainer, category)>
<!ELEMENT category (topic,%qa;)>
<!ATTLIST category reviewed CDATA #FIXED "Jane Smith">

<!ELEMENT maintainer (who, date)>
<!ELEMENT question (#PCDATA)>
<!ELEMENT answer (#PCDATA)>
<!ELEMENT name (#PCDATA)>
<!ELEMENT motto (#PCDATA)>
<!ELEMENT title (#PCDATA)>
<!ELEMENT topic (#PCDATA)>
<!ATTLIST topic term (adv|elem) "adv">
<!ATTLIST topic revised (yes|no) "yes"
    import CDATA "low" >
<!ELEMENT who (#PCDATA)>
<!ELEMENT date (#PCDATA)>
```

LISTING 23.2: POSSIBLE RESULTING XML MARKUP THAT COMPLIES WITH THE DTD IN LISTING 23.1

```
<?xml version="1.0"?>
<?xml-stylesheet type="text/css" href="faq.css"?>
<!DOCTYPE faq SYSTEM "faq.dtd">
<faq>
<title>House Plant FAQ</title>
<motto>Motto: All the plant questions you've lost sleep over,
    and then some. </motto>
<maintainer>
    <who>Maintained by Digit Brown</who>
    <date>April 1, 1999</date>
</maintainer>

<category>
<topic revised="yes" term="adv">Problems with Dying Plants
    </topic>
```

```
<question>Why are my plants limp and yellow?</question>
<answer>Because you water them too much! </answer>
<question>Why are my plants crispy and brown?</question>
<answer>Because you don't water them enough! </answer>
<question>Why don't my plants have a neat pattern like
they should?</question>
<answer>Because we're not talking about tie-dying
plants! </answer>
</category>
</faq>
```

LISTING 23.3: ADD A STYLE SHEET TO ADD FORMATTING TO THE XML DOCUMENT

```
faq         {font-family : Arial}
motto       {display : block ;
             font-style : normal ;
             font-weight : normal ;
             font-size 14pt ;
             margin : 1em 1em 1em 1em ;
             font-family : "Comic Sans MS" ;
             float : right ;
             border : 1px black solid ;
             width : 50% ;
             padding : 8px
             }
maintainer {display : block ;
             font-style : normal ;
             font-weight : normal ;
             margin : 1em 1em 1em 1em ;
             font-family : Technical
             }
email       {margin : 1em ; font-style : italic ;}
qacombo     {display : block ;
             margin-top : 1em}
topic       {display : block ;
             font-style : italic ;
             font-weight : bold ;
             font-size : 18pt ;
             margin-top : 2em}
question    {display : block ;
```

```
                   font-style : italic ;
                   font-weight : bold ;
                   margin-top : 1em
                   }
     answer        {display : block ;
                    font-style : normal ;
                    font-weight : normal ;
                    margin-left : 2em}
     title         {display : block ;
                    font-size : 24pt ;
                    font-weight : bold ;
                    border-top : solid 2px red ;
                    font-family : "Comic Sans MS"}
```

Figure 23.1 *The DTD, XML document, and style sheet all come together in this parsed document.*

Where to Go from Here

In this chapter, we've examined the basic DTD development process, which gives you the foundation necessary to build DTDs. In particular, DTDs include two major components: processing information, which tells parsers or specialized applications how to process the XML document, and the rest of the DTD content, which specifies the elements and attributes that can be used in XML documents.

From here, you're ready to take these pieces and begin developing your own DTDs and XML documents. You'll likely refer to this chapter frequently as you're developing these.

- Look back to Chapter 2 to refresh your memory on the XHTML DTDs.

- Refer to Chapter 22 for information about developing an XML document and connecting it to a DTD.

- Revisit Chapter 10 for a refresher on style sheets.

XHTML 1.1 and XHTML Modularization

Chapter 24

On May 31, 2001, the W3C released a recommended specification titled "XHTML 1.1 - Module Based XHTML." (Note that when a W3C specification attains recommended status, it's become an official standard for all intents and purposes.) As the name for this specification indicates, this particular formulation for XHTML 1.1 follows "The Modularization of XHTML" specification closely, which itself attained recommended status on April 10, 2001 (www.w3.org/TR/2001/REC-xhtml-modularization-20010410).

To make a long and potentially tedious story as painless as possible, we decided to use this chapter to not only cover the ins and outs of XHTML Modularization, but also to cover the XHTML 1.1 requirements. Because those requirements depend almost entirely on XHTML Modularization, this combination makes sense in the overall context of this book.

This chapter covers the following topics:

- Understanding XHTML Modularization and XHTML 1.1

- Exploring the XHTML abstract modules

- Using DTDs for XHTML abstract modules

- Using schemas for XHTML abstract modules

- Mixing and matching XHTML abstract modules

Understanding XHTML Modularization

Basically, *modularization* breaks up the entire collection of markup defined in XHTML 1.0 (and, by direct extension, HTML 4.0) into a collection of independent markup subsets called abstract modules. Each abstract module is meant to address some specific set of data or functions—the specification states that each abstract module "...defines one kind of data that is semantically different from all others." The idea is to define individual sets of markup that may be mixed and matched to create tailored document types without requiring document designers to understand their underlying schemas or Document Type Definitions (DTDs) fully and completely.

The most important reason for modularizing XHTML is to support applications or platforms where displays may not support, or document data may not need, all the markup defined in the entire monolithic XHTML 1.0 DTDs (whether it be the Strict, Transitional, or Frameset version).

A popular example used to justify modularization is a Web-enabled personal digital assistant (PDA) or cell phone, where frames, tables, and graphics support may be overkill and may not display properly. Likewise, with all kinds of non-desktop devices adding Internet access (LG Electronics already offers an Internet-ready refrigerator and microwave oven, with other Internet-ready appliances under development) more uses for this technology are inevitable, if still not completely understood or familiar.

In a nutshell, XHTML Modularization lets document designers create document types that omit unwanted or unusable markup. It also creates flexible target document descriptions for documents created on the fly from XML data, for delivery to non-desktop devices. In turn, selecting a subset of XHTML abstract modules supports smaller, simpler parsers, smaller files, faster downloads, and so on—highly desirable for any kind of embedded or compact systems like the ones we've described. In fact, a cellular telephone manufacturers' consortium announced on March 21, 2001, that it will adopt XHTML for future wireless Internet applications for these very reasons.

Encapsulating XHTML Abstract Modules

In XHTML lingo, an *abstract XHTML module* is a subset of elements, attributes, and related content models, associated with a particular kind of markup or function within a typical XHTML document. In the abstract sense, an XHTML module is nothing more than a strict subset of some full-blown XHTML 1.0 DTD (or equivalent schema), taken as a stand-alone definition, ready for incorporation into some XHTML document or into some more general DTD or schema.

In practice, each module implementation consists of a set of element types, a set of attribute list declarations, and a set of content model declarations. This also explains how individual modules can be combined as needed to meet specific document requirements. Better yet, the modularization framework makes it possible to integrate multiple DTDs to create a new document type that can be validated using XML validation techniques. This makes the X in XHTML—which stands for *extensible*—more attainable using XHTML Modularization. (By extension, this applies to XHTML 1.1, as you'll learn in the following section.)

Table 24.1 provides a brief description of the abstract modules currently defined for XHTML; these will be more fully described later in this chapter.

Table 24.1 XHTML Abstract Modules

MODULE NAME	DESCRIPTION
CORE MODULES	All four core modules are needed for minimal modular XHTML
Structure	XHTML structure elements (body, head, etc.)
Text	Basic text container elements
Hypertext	Basic hyperlinking (a element)
List	List-oriented elements
FORMS MODULES	
Basic Forms	Minimal set of forms markup
Forms	Complete set of forms markup
TABLE MODULES	
Basic Tables	Minimal set of table markup
Tables	Complete set of table markup
TEXT EXTENSION MODULES	
Presentation	Supports simple presentation markup
Edit	Supports del and ins elements
Bi-directional Text	Permits text to run right-to-left or left-to-right
OTHER STANDARD MODULES	
Image	Provides basic image embedding
Client-Side Image Map	Handles client-side image maps
Server-Side Image Map	Handles server-side image map formats

Table 24.1 continued XHTML Abstract Modules

MODULE NAME	DESCRIPTION
Object	Supports general inclusion of external objects
Frames	Supports (X)HTML frames
Target	Supports destination targets for selections
Iframe	Supports use of inline frames
Intrinsic Events	Supports intrinsic XHTML events (`onblur`, `onfocus`, `onload`, `onunload`, and `onchange`)
Metainformation	Supports `meta` element
Scripting	Enables/disables support for executable scripts
Style Sheet	Enables declaration of internal style sheets
Style Attribute	Enables use of the `style` attribute
Link	For defining links to external resources
Base	Provides context for relative URLs
DEPRECATED MODULES	
Applet	Supports the deprecated `applet` element
Name Identification	Supports the deprecated `name` attribute
Legacy	Supports other deprecated elements and attributes from HTML 4.0

Meet the XHTML 1.1 Specification

Here's some great news: XHTML 1.1 is nearly exactly equivalent to the version of XHTML 1.0 defined by the Strict XHTML DTD. This is the very same DTD invoked by the following DOCTYPE declaration:

```
<!DOCTYPE html PUBLIC "-//W3C//DTD XHTML 1.0 Strict//EN"
    "DTD/xhtml1-strict.dtd">
```

Because Appendix A of the XHTML 1.1 Specification describes the differences between XHTML 1.1 and XHTML 1.0 Strict, we quote the relevant sections document here, but add our own emphasis in bold:

> XHTML 1.1 represents a departure from both HTML 4 and XHTML 1.0. Most significant is the **removal of features that were deprecated**. In general, the strategy is to define **a**

markup language that is rich in structural functionality, but that relies upon style sheets for presentation.

The differences can be summarized as follows:

- *On every element, the **lang** attribute has been removed in favor of the **xml:lang** attribute (as defined in [XHTMLMOD]).*

- *On the **a** and **map** elements, the **name** attribute has been removed in favor of the **id** attribute (as defined in [XHTMLMOD]).*

- *The "ruby" collection of elements has been added (as defined in [RUBY]).*

For more information about the various items previously quoted or mentioned, please visit:

- XHTML 1.1 Appendix A: `www.w3.org/TR/xhtml11/changes.html#a_changes`

- XHTMLMOD: `www.w3.org/TR/2001/REC-xhtml-modularization-20010410`

- Ruby: `www.w3.org/TR/2001/REC-ruby-20010531/`

When approaching the contents of this book, if you want to stick strictly to XHTML 1.1, rather than the looser, more HTML-like XHTML 1.0 (using the Transitional or Frameset DTDs, that is), please consider the following observations and provisos:

- The XHTML 1.0 Strict DTD omits numerous elements found in earlier implementations of HTML. Many of these omitted elements are used to control document appearance, including `basefont` for establishing a base document font, `font` for managing font selections explicitly, `center` for centering text, plus several text appearance and list style elements. Going forward, the W3C makes style sheets the only proper way to handle such things in XHTML 1.1. (Please note that deprecated modules can make this markup available if absolutely necessary.)

- Deprecated elements and attributes disappear from XHTML 1.1 entirely. This means that many existing HTML or XHTML 1.0 documents must be "cleaned up" to validate to the XHTML 1.1 DTDs. Other elements in this category—some style-related ones are mentioned in the previous list element—include the `applet` element (replace with the `object` element) and the `isindex` element (replace with the `input` element). We provide a complete list of deprecated elements and attributes in Chapter 3, and also indicate which elements and attributes are deprecated in Master's Reference 1.

- XHTML 1.1 adheres to XHTML Modularization rules and naming conventions. Later in this chapter, we'll discuss what these rules are and how they work.

- Ruby annotations permit short runs of text to appear alongside base text in an XHTML 1.1 document. Such annotations are used in many East Asian languages to supply pronunciation guides and ancillary notes. Ruby is defined in the form of an XHTML module for easy inclusion or omission. (Those creating documents in English or other European languages are less likely to use Ruby than those creating documents in East Asian languages, in any case.) For completeness, we also cover this module in this chapter, even though it's not part of the XHTML Modularization effort but rather belongs to the XHTML 1.1 specification. For examples of this markup at work, see the examples section of the Ruby Annotation specification at www.w3.org/TR/2001/REC-ruby-20010531/.

- Replacing the lang attribute with the xml:lang attribute, and the name attribute with the id attribute for a and map elements, makes XHTML syntax entirely consistent with XML going forward. Consider this a kind of practical simplification introduced in XHTML 1.1 to make XHTML more consistent with other forms of XML.

The removal of deprecated elements and attributes plus mandatory use of modularization are clearly the most significant changes here. Implementing these changes means that considerable effort, and in some cases, real redesign work, will be needed to convert XHTML 1.0 or HTML documents to XHTML 1.1. HTML-Tidy can help with this task, but until it's updated properly (no word yet on when this might happen) manual effort will also be involved. Only you can decide if converting documents to XHTML 1.1 is something you should embrace, avoid, or postpone.

On the other hand, careful examination of Table 24.1 (and the related expanded sections on XHTML abstract modules that follow) shows that although the strict definition of XHTML 1.1 forbids the use of deprecated and presentation markup, abstract modules to support such markup have been defined and are available. In practice, this means you can start migrating to XHTML 1.1 and abstract XHTML modules without having to completely revise your code base. Nevertheless, we think planning for such a revision (and a possible redesign) is a good idea, because it's possible that the W3C may elect to make this deprecated markup obsolete in a future XHTML specification.

In plain English, markup that is deprecated in XHTML 1.1 may no longer be legal or usable in subsequent revisions of XHTML. Please plan accordingly!

XHTML Modules: Abstract and Otherwise

In addition to the various specific abstract modules represented in Table 24.1, XHTML modules include various named attribute collections. To invoke an XHTML module within a document, however, you must include a definition of or a pointer to a real (not an abstract) module therein. Today, the W3C has defined DTDs that correspond to the XHTML abstract modules, and work is under way to build schema-based equivalents (more on that later in this chapter). For completeness, we include the complete URL for each XHTML module in the section that covers the elements and attributes that any module contains. Later on, as we present examples, we'll show how to use that information in a custom DTD to invoke the predefined module's DTD.

Because the Core XHTML modules must be included in any XHTML document definition to meet basic core markup requirements, it's not surprising that related core attribute sets are likewise required. These various attribute collections will be covered first in our detailed discussions of the various XHTML modules, and will be followed by the XHTML modules in their order of appearance in Table 24.1. Except for the Ruby module, which we cover last and is defined in the XHTML 1.1 Specification at `www.w3 .org/TR/xhtml11/`), all other predefined XHTML modules are documented at `www.w3.org/TR/2001/REC-xhtml-modularization-20010410`.

Modularization Rules and Naming Conventions

Because XHTML 1.1 essentially rests on the work done in the XHTML Modularization Specification, it should come as no surprise that XHTML 1.1 also follows basic XHTML Modularization rules and naming conventions. These may be briefly and succinctly stated as follows:

- All module names must be unique, so no conflicts are possible. A corollary to this rule is that you cannot define a module with the same name as an existing module, unless you intend to replace the existing module with the new one.

- Where any two modules contain definitions for the same markup elements or attributes, only one of those two modules may be referenced in a related DTD. (Note that this does not apply when one module extends another module's definition, as in adding a new attribute or default. Rather, it explains why we have basic and regular forms and table modules, and why you can use only the basic or regular module of each kind in a DTD.)

- Where attributes and elements have been renamed or replaced (for example, the lang attribute) to conform to XML syntax requirements and conventions, XHTML 1.1 conforms strictly to those requirements and conventions. (See Appendix A of the XHTML 1.1 Specification at www.w3.org/TR/2001/REC-xhtml11-20010531/changes.html#a_changes for more details.)

Attribute Collections

Although abstract modules require specialized attributes, they are normally defined within the context of the module's DTD. However, modular XHTML incorporates a collection of four named sets of attributes that are sometimes called common attributes. Two of these named sets—the *Core* and *I18N* (an abbreviation for "Internationalization") attributes—apply to many XHTML modules. The other two named sets—the *Events* and *Style* attributes—are defined only when related XHTML modules are invoked as part of an XHTML document's governing description. To be more specific, Events attributes are defined only when the Intrinsic Events module is invoked, and Style attributes are defined only when the Style Attribute module is invoked.

Table 24.2 describes all four of these attribute collections and their associated attribute names and data types. Note that this information is from the W3C site.

Table 24.2 XHTML Attribute Collections

COLLECTION NAME	ATTRIBUTES CONTAINED (DATA TYPE)
Core	class (NMTOKENS), id (ID), title (CDATA)
I18N	xml:lang (NMTOKEN)
Events	onclick, ondblclick, onmouseup, onmouseover, onmousemove, onmouseout, onkeypress, onkeydown, onkeyup (all event attributes of type Script)
Style	style (CDATA)
Common	Core + Events + I18N + Style

Note that for convenience, another named collection of attributes—namely *Common*—represents the combination of all four of the previously named attribute collections.

Core XHTML Modules

All four of the core modules—*Structure*, *Text*, *Hypertext*, and *List*—must be present in any document that conforms to minimal requirements for valid XHTML markup. Each of these core modules is covered in more detail in the following sections.

XHTML Structure Module

The XHTML Structure module defines major document structure elements in XHTML. These elements thus define the basis for the content model instantiated in any XHTML document. Table 24.3 enumerates the relevant elements, attributes, and models.

Table 24.3 XHTML Structure Module

ELEMENT	ATTRIBUTES	MINIMAL CONTENT MODEL
body	Common	(Heading|Block|List)
head	I18N, profile (URI)	title
html	I18N, version (CDATA), xmlns (URI="http://www.w3.org/1999/xhtml")	head, body
title	I18N	PCDATA

For definitions of the Heading and Block content sets, see the text following Table 24.4; for the List content set, see Table 24.6. For further details on the Structure module, see

```
www.w3.org/TR/2001/REC-xhtml-modularization-20010410/
    dtd_module_defs.html#a_module_Structure
```

The module's DTD uses the following identifiers:

```
PUBLIC "-//W3C//ELEMENTS XHTML Document Structure 1.0//EN"
SYSTEM "http://www.w3.org/TR/xhtml-modularization/DTD/
    xhtml-struct-1.mod"
```

Although we insert white space for readability here, each identifier should appear on one line with no spaces in the URL.

XHTML Text Module

This module defines all basic XHTML text container elements, attributes, and related content models. This information appears in Table 24.4; be sure to read the explanation that follows to fully understand the named content sets used.

Table 24.4 XHTML Text Module

ELEMENT	ATTRIBUTES	MINIMAL CONTENT MODEL
abbr	Common	(PCDATA|Inline)*
acronym	Common	(PCDATA|Inline)*
address	Common	(PCDATA|Inline)*
blockquote	Common, cite (URI)	(PCDATA|Heading|Block|List)*
br	Core	EMPTY
cite	Common	(PCDATA|Inline)*
code	Common	(PCDATA|Inline)*
dfn	Common	(PCDATA|Inline)*
div	Common	(PCDATA|Flow)*
em	Common	(PCDATA|Inline)*
h1 - h6	Common	(PCDATA|Inline)*
kbd	Common	(PCDATA|Inline)*
p	Common	(PCDATA|Inline)*
pre	Commmon, xml:space="preserve"	(PCDATA|Inline)*
q	Common, cite (URI)	(PCDATA|Inline)*
samp	Common	(PCDATA|Inline)*
span	Common	(PCDATA|Inline)*
strong	Common	(PCDATA|Inline)*
var	Common	(PCDATA|Inline)*

The minimal content models for these elements introduce some content sets that must also be further defined:

- Heading: h1 | h2 | h3 | h4 | h5 | h6
- Block: address | blockquote | div | p | pre

- Inline: abbr | acronym | br | cite | code | dfn | em | kbd | q | samp | span |strong | var

- Flow: Heading | Block | Inline

You can easily distinguish content set names from element names because elements are all lowercase and content set names start with an initial capital (Heading, Block, Inline, and Flow). Strings in ALL CAPS are standard DTD data types (PCDATA and EMPTY, in the preceding table; other entries elsewhere include NMTOKENS, CDATA, ID, URI, URL, and so on).

For further details on the Text module, see

```
www.w3.org/TR/2001/REC-xhtml-modularization-20010410/
    dtd_module_defs.html#a_module_Text
```

The module's DTD uses the following identifiers:

```
PUBLIC "-//W3C//ELEMENTS XHTML Text 1.0//EN"
SYSTEM "http://www.w3.org/TR/xhtml-modularization/DTD/
    xhtml-text-1.mod"
```

XHTML Hypertext Module

The Hypertext module provides the a element used to define standard hyperlinks to other resources in an XHTML document. Table 24.5 defines the related attributes and content model.

Table 24.5 XHTML Hypertext Module

ELEMENT	ATTRIBUTES	MINIMAL CONTENT MODEL
a	Common, accesskey (Character), charset (Charset), href (URI), hreflang (LanguageCode), rel (LinkTypes), tabindex (Number), type (ContentType)	(PCDATA|Inline - a)*

For definitions of the data types mentioned in Table 24.5, please consult the XHTML Modularization Specification at

```
www.w3.org/TR/2001/REC-xhtml-modularization-20010410/
    abstract_modules.html#s_hypertextmodule
```

where each type name is a hyperlink to its definition. For further details on the Hypertext module itself, please see

```
www.w3.org/TR/2001/REC-xhtml-modularization-20010410/
    dtd_module_defs.html#a_module_Hypertext
```

The module's DTD uses the following identifiers:

```
PUBLIC "-//W3C//ELEMENTS XHTML Hypertext 1.0//EN"
SYSTEM "http://www.w3.org/TR/xhtml-modularization/DTD/
    xhtml-hypertext-1.mod"
```

XHTML List Module

The List module incorporates list-related XHTML elements to support basic list structures in even the most minimal XHTML documents. (Some designers disagree with this module's inclusion in the Core; however, because it adds only six elements, we don't view it as a major gaffe—if in fact it does represent an unnecessary inclusion, as some have argued.) Table 24.6 defines the elements, attributes, and content models associated with basic XHTML list structures.

Table 24.6 XHTML List Module

ELEMENT	ATTRIBUTES	MINIMAL CONTENT MODEL
dl	Common	(dt|dd)+
dt	Common	(PCDATA|Inline)*
dd	Common	(PCDATA|Flow)*
ol	Common	li+
ul	Common	li+
li	Common	(PCDATA|Flow)*

The module also defines a named content set, List, with an associated minimal content model of (dl | ol | ul)+. For further details on the List module, see

```
www.w3.org/TR/2001/REC-xhtml-modularization-20010410/
    dtd_module_defs.html#a_module_List
```

The module's DTD uses the following identifiers:

```
PUBLIC "-//W3C//ELEMENTS XHTML Lists 1.0//EN"
SYSTEM "http://www.w3.org/TR/xhtml-modularization/DTD/
    xhtml-list-1.mod"
```

XHTML Forms Modules

XHTML Modularization recognizes two forms modules: a *Basic Forms* module for bare-bones forms, and a *Forms* module for full-blown forms. These are described in the following sections.

XHTML Basic Forms Module

As its name is meant to suggest, the Basic Forms module supplies a minimal set of forms-related elements, attributes, and content models. These are described in Table 24.7.

Table 24.7 XHTML Basic Forms Module

ELEMENT	ATTRIBUTES	MINIMAL CONTENT MODEL
form	Common, action* (URI), method ("get"*|"post"), enctype (ContentType)	(Heading|List|Block-form)+
input	Common, accesskey (Character), checked ("checked"), maxlength (Number), name (CDATA), size (Number), src (URI), tabindex (Number), type ("text"*| "password"| "checkbox"| "radio"|"submit"|"reset"| "hidden"), value (CDATA)	EMPTY
label	Common, accesskey (Character), for (IDREF)	(PCDATA|Inline - label)*
select	Common, multiple ("multiple"), name (CDATA), size (Number), tabindex (Number)	option+
option	Common, selected ("selected"), value (CDATA)	PCDATA
textarea	Common, accesskey (Character), cols* (Number), name (CDATA), rows* (Number), tabindex (Number)	PCDATA

For further details on the Basic Forms module, see

www.w3.org/TR/2001/REC-xhtml-modularization-20010410/
    dtd_module_defs.html#a_module_Basic_Forms

The module's DTD uses the following identifiers:

PUBLIC "-//W3C//ELEMENTS XHTML Basic Forms 1.0//EN"
SYSTEM "http://www.w3.org/TR/xhtml-modularization/DTD/
    xhtml-basic-form-1.mod"

XHTML Forms Module

The Forms module supports all the forms-related markup found in HTML 4, including the elements, attributes, and content models included in Table 24.8.

Table 24.8 XHTML Forms Module

ELEMENT	ATTRIBUTES	MINIMAL CONTENT MODEL
form	Common, accept (ContentTypes), accept-charset (Charsets), action* (URI), method ("get"*|"post"), enctype (ContentType)	(Heading|List| Block-form | fieldset)+
input	Common, accept (ContentTypes), accesskey (Character), alt (Text), checked ("checked"), disabled ("disabled"), maxlength (Number), name (CDATA), readonly ("readonly"), size (Number), src (URI), tabindex (Number), type ("text"*|"password"|"checkbox"| "button"|"radio"| "submit"| "reset"|"file"|"hidden"|"image"), value (CDATA)	EMPTY
select	Common, disabled ("disabled"), multiple ("multiple"), name (CDATA), size (Number), tabindex (Number)	(optgroup|option)+
option	Common, disabled ("disabled"), label (Text), selected ("selected"), value (CDATA)	PCDATA

Table 24.8 continued   XHTML Forms Module

ELEMENT	ATTRIBUTES	MINIMAL CONTENT MODEL
textarea	Common, accesskey (Character), cols* (Number), disabled ("disabled"), name (CDATA), readonly ("readonly"), rows* (Number), tabindex (Number)	PCDATA
button	Common, accesskey (Character), disabled ("disabled"), name (CDATA), tabindex (Number), type ("button"|"submit"*|"reset"), value (CDATA)	(PCDATA|Heading| List|Block-Form| Inline-Formctrl)*
fieldset	Common	(PCDATA|legend| Flow)*
label	Common, accesskey (Character), for (IDREF)	(PCDATA|Inline-label)*
legend	Common, accesskey (Character)	(PCDATA|Inline)+
optgroup	Common, disabled ("disabled"), label* (Text)	option+

The Forms module also mentions two named content sets—Form and Formctrl. These may be further described as follows:

- Form: form | fieldset
- Formctrl: input | select | textarea | label | button

When the Forms module is invoked, it adds the Form content set to the Block content set, and the Formctrl content set to the Inline content set as those are defined in the Text module.

The Forms module is a superset of the Basic Forms module. Both modules may not appear together in any single document type; use only one or the other, as necessary.

For further details on the Forms module, see

www.w3.org/TR/2001/REC-xhtml-modularization-20010410/
   dtd_module_defs.html#a_module_Forms

The module's DTD uses the following identifiers:

```
PUBLIC "-//W3C//ELEMENTS XHTML Forms 1.0//EN"
SYSTEM "http://www.w3.org/TR/xhtml-modularization/DTD/
    xhtml-form-1.mod"
```

XHTML Tables Modules

There are two XHTML Tables modules: Basic Tables and Tables. These two modules are explained in the following sections.

XHTML Basic Tables Module

The XHTML Basic Tables module provides access to a minimal set of table-related markup so that XHTML documents can accommodate simple tables when this module is invoked. The relevant markup, attributes, and content models appear in Table 24.9.

Table 24.9 XHTML Basic Tables Module

ELEMENT	ATTRIBUTES	MINIMAL CONTENT MODEL
caption	Common	(PCDATA|Inline)*
table	Common, summary (Text)	caption?,tr+
td	Common, abbr (Text), align ("left"|"center"|"right"), axis (CDATA), colspan (number), headers (IDREFS), rowspan (Number), scope ("row"|"col"), valign ("top"|"middle"|"bottom")	(PCDATA| Flow - table)*
th	Common, abbr (Text), align ("left"|"center"|"right"), axis (CDATA), colspan (number), headers (IDREFS), rowspan (Number), scope ("row"|"col"), valign ("top"|"middle"|"bottom")	(PCDATA| Flow - table)*
tr	Common, align ("left"|"center"|"right"), valign ("top"|"middle"|"bottom")	(td|th)+

When the Basic Tables module is invoked in an XHTML document, it adds the `table` element to the Block content set defined in the Text module.

For further details on the Basic Tables module, see

```
www.w3.org/TR/2001/REC-xhtml-modularization-20010410/
    dtd_module_defs.html#a_module_Basic_Tables
```

The module's DTD uses the following identifiers:

```
PUBLIC "-//W3C//ELEMENTS XHTML Basic Tables 1.0//EN"
SYSTEM "http://www.w3.org/TR/xhtml-modularization/DTD/
    xhtml-basic-table-1.mod"
```

XHTML Tables Module

As the Basic Tables module provides minimal XHTML table markup, the XHTML Tables module provides complete XHTML table markup. The elements, attributes, and content models involved are documented in Table 24.10.

Table 24.10 XHTML Tables Module

ELEMENT	ATTRIBUTES	MINIMAL CONTENT MODEL
caption	Common	(PCDATA|Inline)*
table	Common, border (Pixels), cellpadding (Length), cellspacing (Length), frame ("void"|"above"|"below"| "hsides"|"lhs"|"rhs"|"vsides"|"box"| "border"), rules ("none"|"groups"| "rows"|"cols"|"all"), summary (Text), width (Length)	caption?, (col*| colgroup*), ((thead?, tfoot?, tbody+)|(tr+))
td	Common, abbr (Text), align ("left"| "center"|"right"|"justify"| "char"), axis (CDATA), char (Character), charoff (Length), colspan (number), headers (IDREFS), rowspan (Number), scope ("row"|"col"|"rowgroup"| "colgroup"), valign ("top"|"middle"| "bottom")	(PCDATA|Flow - table)*

Table 24.10 continued XHTML Tables Module

ELEMENT	ATTRIBUTES	MINIMAL CONTENT MODEL
th	Common, abbr (Text), align ("left"| "center"|"right"), axis (CDATA), colspan (number), headers (IDREFS), rowspan (Number), scope ("row"| "col"), valign ("top"|"middle"| "bottom"|"baseline")	(PCDATA|Flow - table)*
tr	Common, align ("left"|"center"| "right""justify"|"char"), char (Character), charoff (Length), span (Number), valign ("top"|"middle"| "bottom"|"baseline")	(td|th)+
col	Common, align ("left"|"center"| "right""justify"|"char"), char (Character), charoff (Length), span (Number), valign ("top"|"middle"| "bottom"|"baseline"), width (MultiLength)	EMPTY
colgroup	Common, align ("left"|"center"| "right""justify"|"char"), char (Character), charoff (Length), span (Number), valign ("top"|"middle"| "bottom"|"baseline"), width (MultiLength)	col*
tbody	Common, align ("left"|"center"| "right""justify"|"char"), char (Character), charoff (Length), valign ("top"|"middle"| "bottom"|"baseline")	tr+
thead	Common, align ("left"|"center"| "right""justify"|"char"), char (Character), charoff (Length), valign ("top"|"middle"| "bottom"|"baseline")	tr+
tfoot	Common, align ("left"|"center"| "right""justify"|"char"), char (Character), charoff (Length), valign ("top"|"middle"| "bottom"|"baseline")	tr+

When this module is invoked, it adds the `table` element to the Block content set defined in the Text module. For further details on the Tables module, see

```
www.w3.org/TR/2001/REC-xhtml-modularization-20010410/
    dtd_module_defs.html#a_module_Tables
```

The module's DTD uses the following identifiers:

```
PUBLIC "-//W3C//ELEMENTS XHTML Tables 1.0//EN"
SYSTEM "http://www.w3.org/TR/xhtml-modularization/DTD/
    xhtml-table-1.mod"
```

The Tables module is a superset of the Basic Tables module. Both modules may not appear together in any single document type; use only one or the other, as necessary.

XHTML Basic Defines Bare-bones XHTML

Let's assume that you wanted to declare the barest minimum collection of markup elements and related modules (where applicable) necessary to define a workable XHTML implementation. Perhaps it's because you want to send content to a cell phone, PDA, embedded system of some kind, or some other network-attached device with minimal display characteristics and a very small screen.

If you created a customized module declaration that included only the following markup:

- Basic text elements (including headings, paragraphs, and lists)—these are the h1 - h6 heading elements, the p element, and all the elements in the List module mentioned earlier in this chapter

- Hyperlinks and links to related documents (in other words, the Hypertext module)

- Basic forms (the module of the same name)

- Basic tables (the module of the same name)

- Images (the Image module, or `img` element, mentioned later in this chapter)

- Meta information (the `meta` element, covered in the Metainformation module later in this chapter)

and added the Common Attributes module to this mix, you'd define a minimalist collection of XHTML markup that even a cell phone could learn to live with. In fact, the

W3C has done this for you: it's called XHTML Basic, and you can visit its equally short and minimal specification at `www.w3.org/TR/xhtml-basic/`.

Two closing remarks about this brief tour-de-force of XHTML Modularization:

- It does indeed define the bare usable markup minimum for XHTML and as such is eminently well suited to modest or minimal devices with small, character-only displays.

- It shows the power of the principles of modularization at work, which makes Appendix B of its specification—particularly the discussion and examples of the XHTML Basic Driver DTD—eminently worth reading and using to inspire any XHTML module customization you might wish to undertake.

Text Extension Modules

The Text Extension modules encompass a grab bag of text markup capabilities, including some limited presentation markup in the Presentation module, editing-related markup to mark insertions and deletions in the Edit module, and the Bi-directional Text module, which permits text to be displayed right-to-left instead of the more typical left-to-right. These modules are covered in the following sections.

XHTML Presentation Module

The Presentation module provides some basic presentation elements, attributes, and content models for managing limited text presentation markup. Here again, markup purists find this questionable because style sheets can handle all the functions that this markup provides, but we believe the W3C's decision to include this very basic markup was sound, because handheld and embedded devices will have far less need of style sheets because of what this module contains. The various elements, attributes, and content models for the Presentation module appear in Table 24.11.

Table 24.11 XHTML Presentation Module

ELEMENT	ATTRIBUTES	MINIMAL CONTENT MODEL
b	Common	(PCDATA|Inline)*
big	Common	(PCDATA|Inline)*
hr	Common	EMPTY
i	Common	(PCDATA|Inline)*

Table 24.11 continued XHTML Presentation Module

ELEMENT	ATTRIBUTES	MINIMAL CONTENT MODEL
small	Common	(PDDATA|Inline)*
sub	Common	(PCDATA|Inline)*
sup	Common	(PCDATA|Inline)*
tt	Common	(PCDATA|Inline)*

When this module is invoked, it adds the hr element to the Block content set defined in the Text module; likewise, it adds the other elements—b, big, i, small, sub, sup, and tt—to the Inline content set defined in the Text module. For further details on the Presentation module, see

```
www.w3.org/TR/2001/REC-xhtml-modularization-20010410/
    dtd_module_defs.html#a_module_Presentation
```

The module's DTD uses the following identifiers:

```
PUBLIC "-//W3C//ELEMENTS XHTML Presentation 1.0//EN"
SYSTEM "http://www.w3.org/TR/xhtml-modularization/DTD/
    xhtml-pres-1.mod"
```

XHTML Edit Module

The Edit module supports markup used to flag insertions and deletions in documents, which makes it easier to denote additions and removals therein. Table 24.12 describes the relevant elements, attributes, and content models.

Table 24.12 XHTML Edit Module

ELEMENT	ATTRIBUTES	MINIMAL CONTENT MODEL
del	Common, cite (URL), datetime (Datetime)	(PCDATA|Flow)*
ins	Common, cite (URL), datetime (Datetime)	(PCDATA|Flow)*

When this module is invoked, it adds the del and ins elements to the Inline content set defined in the Text module. For further details on the Edit module, see

```
www.w3.org/TR/2001/REC-xhtml-modularization-20010410/
    dtd_module_defs.html#a_module_Edit
```

The module's DTD uses the following identifiers:

```
PUBLIC "-//W3C//ELEMENTS XHTML Editing Markup 1.0//EN"
SYSTEM "http://www.w3.org/TR/xhtml-modularization/DTD/
    xhtml-edit-1.mod"
```

XHTML Bi-directional Text Module

The Bi-directional Text module supports an element that governs the direction in which its content should be read. The relevant element, its attributes, and its content model are described in Table 24.13.

Table 24.13 XHTML Bi-directional Text Module

ELEMENT	ATTRIBUTES	MINIMAL CONTENT MODEL
bdo	Core, dir*("ltr"|"rtl")	(PCDATA|Inline)*

When this module is invoked, it adds the bdo element to the Inline content set defined in the Text module. For further details on the Bi-directional Text module, see

```
www.w3.org/TR/2001/REC-xhtml-modularization-20010410/
    dtd_module_defs.html#a_module_Bi-directional_Text
```

The module's DTD uses the following identifiers:

```
PUBLIC "-//W3C//ELEMENTS XHTML BDO Element 1.0//EN"
SYSTEM "http://www.w3.org/TR/xhtml-modularization/DTD/
    xhtml-bdo-1.mod"
```

Other Standard XHTML Modules

The remaining 14 standard XHTML modules aren't grouped in the specification (even though several, such as those related to frames markup, could have been). Thus, we simply present them here in their order of occurrence in Table 24.1.

XHTML Image Module

The Image module supports an element that permits images to be embedded in XHTML documents. The relevant element, its attributes, and its content model are described in Table 24.14.

Table 24.14 XHTML Image Module

ELEMENT	ATTRIBUTES	MINIMAL CONTENT MODEL
img	Common, alt* (Text), height (Length), longdesc (URI), src* (URI), width (Length)	EMPTY

When this module is invoked, it adds the img element to the Inline content set defined in the Text module. For further details on the Image module, see

```
www.w3.org/TR/2001/REC-xhtml-modularization-20010410/
    dtd_module_defs.html#a_module_Image
```

The module's DTD uses the following identifiers:

```
PUBLIC "-//W3C//ELEMENTS XHTML Images 1.0//EN"
SYSTEM "http://www.w3.org/TR/xhtml-modularization/DTD/
    xhtml-image-1.mod"
```

XHTML Client-Side Image Map Module

The Client-Side Image Map module supports elements to enable use of client-side image maps. Because this requires an image to map to, the Image module must also be included in a document that uses this module, or some other reasonable alternative that supports the img element must be included. The relevant elements, their attributes, and their content models (where applicable) are described in Table 24.15.

When this module is invoked, it adds the map and area elements to the Inline content set defined in the Text module. For further details on the Client-Side Image Map module, see

```
www.w3.org/TR/2001/REC-xhtml-modularization-20010410/
    dtd_module_defs.html#a_module_Client-Side_Image_Map
```

The module's DTD uses the following identifiers:

```
PUBLIC "-//W3C//ELEMENTS XHTML Client-side Image Maps 1.0//EN"
SYSTEM "http://www.w3.org/TR/xhtml-modularization/DTD/
    xhtml-csismap-1.mod"
```

Table 24.15 XHTML Client-Side Image Map Module

ELEMENT	ATTRIBUTES	MINIMAL CONTENT MODEL
a&	coords(CDATA), shape("rect"|"circle"|"poly"|"default")	No change
area	Common, accesskey (Character), alt* (Text), coords (CDATA), href (URI), nohref ("nohref"), shape("rect"* | "circle"|"poly"|"default"), tabindex (Number)	EMPTY
img&	usemap (IDREF)	No change
input&	usemap (IDREF)	No change; applies only when a Forms module is included
map	I18N, Events, class (NMTOKEN), id* (ID), title (CDATA)	((Heading|Block)|area)+
object&	usemap (IDREF)	Applies only when an Object module is included

The notation img& *that appears in the Element column in Table 24.15 indicates that this module adds attributes to elements defined elsewhere. Thus, a corresponding "No change" entry in the content model means that the original content model is unchanged; when other modules must be included in a document for an element change to occur, it will be so noted, as with the* object *element in that table.*

XHTML Server-Side Image Map Module

The Server-Side Image Map module supports use of server-side image maps, which means a mechanism to select coordinates on a client-side image, and to transmit those selections to the server's image map–handling facility. The relevant elements, their attributes, and content models are described in Table 24.16.

Table 24.16 XHTML Server-Side Image Map Module

ELEMENT	ATTRIBUTES	MINIMAL CONTENT MODEL
img&	ismap ("ismap")	No change
input&	ismap ("ismap")	No change; applies only when a Forms module is included

When this module is invoked, it adds no elements to the XHTML Core (it only defines additional attributes), but for this module to be used, the Image module (or some equivalent that defines the img element) must also be included. For further details on the Server-Side Image Map module, see

```
www.w3.org/TR/2001/REC-xhtml-modularization-20010410/
    dtd_module_defs.html#a_module_Server-side_Image_Map
```

The module's DTD uses the following identifiers:

```
PUBLIC "-//W3C//ELEMENTS XHTML Server-side Image Maps 1.0//EN"
SYSTEM "http://www.w3.org/TR/xhtml-modularization/DTD/
    xhtml-ssismap-1.mod"
```

XHTML Object Module

The Object module supports an element that permits objects, such as applets, scripts, or other executables, to be embedded in XHTML documents. The relevant element, its attributes, and its content model are described in Table 24.17.

Table 24.17 XHTML Object Module

ELEMENT	ATTRIBUTES	MINIMAL CONTENT MODEL
object	Common, archive (URIs), classid (URI), codebase (URI), codetype (ContentType), data (URI), declare ("declare"), height (Length), name (CDATA), standby (Text), tabindex (Number), type (ContentType), width (Length)	(PCDATA|Flow|Param)*
param	id (ID), name* (CDATA), type (ContentType), value (CDATA), valuetype ("data"* | "ref" | "object")	EMPTY

When this module is invoked, it adds the object element to the Inline content set defined in the Text module. For further details on the Object module, see

```
www.w3.org/TR/2001/REC-xhtml-modularization-20010410/
    dtd_module_defs.html#a_module_Object
```

The module's DTD uses the following identifiers:

```
PUBLIC "-//W3C//ELEMENTS XHTML Embedded Object 1.0//EN"
SYSTEM "http://www.w3.org/TR/xhtml-modularization/DTD/
    xhtml-object-1.mod"
```

XHTML Frames Module

The Frames module supports elements associated with framed document structures, and thereby permits frames to be used with XHTML documents. Table 24.18 describes the relevant elements, their attributes, and content models.

Table 24.18 XHTML Frames Module

ELEMENT	ATTRIBUTES	MINIMAL CONTENT MODEL
frameset	Core, cols (MultiLength), rows (MultiLength)	(frameset|frame)+, noframes?
frame	CCore, frameborder ("1"|"0"), longdesc (URI), marginheight (Pixels), marginwidth (Pixels), noresize ("noresize"), scrolling ("yes"|"no"|"auto"*), src (URI)	EMPTY
noframes	Common	body

When this module is invoked, it changes the minimal content model for the html element to (head, frameset). For further details on the Frames module, see

```
www.w3.org/TR/2001/REC-xhtml-modularization-20010410/
    dtd_module_defs.html#a_module_Frames
```

The module's DTD uses the following identifiers:

```
PUBLIC "-//W3C//ELEMENTS XHTML Frames 1.0//EN"
SYSTEM "http://www.w3.org/TR/xhtml-modularization/DTD/
    xhtml-frames-1.mod"
```

XHTML Target Module

The Target module supports the use of the target attribute in various XHTML elements so you can specify a frame target when you're defining a potential hypertext link or related context information. The relevant elements, the target attributes, and their content models are described in Table 24.19.

Table 24.19 XHTML Target

Element	Attributes	Minimal Content Model
a&	target (CDATA)	No change
area&	target (CDATA)	Applies when the Client-Side Image Map module is included
base&	target (CDATA)	Applies when the Legacy module is included
link&	target (CDATA)	Applies when the Link module is included
form&	target (CDATA)	Applies when a Forms module is included

When this module is invoked, it simply adds the `target` attribute to the various elements specified in the previous table. (When these go beyond the XHTML core, the applicable modules are mentioned in Table 24.19.) For further details on the Target module, see

```
www.w3.org/TR/2001/REC-xhtml-modularization-20010410/
    dtd_module_defs.html#a_module_Target
```

The module's DTD uses the following identifiers:

```
PUBLIC "-//W3C//ELEMENTS XHTML Target 1.0//EN"
SYSTEM "http://www.w3.org/TR/xhtml-modularization/DTD/
    xhtml-target-1.mod"
```

XHTML Iframe Module

The Iframe module contains the `iframe` element, which is designed to support use of inline frames in XHTML documents. The relevant element, its attributes, and its content model are described in Table 24.20.

Table 24.20 XHTML Iframe Module

Element	Attributes	Minimal Content Model
inframe	core, frameborder ("1"|"0"), height (Length), longdesc (URI), margin-height (Pixels), marginwidth (Pixels), scrolling ("yes"|"no"| "auto"*), src (URI), width (Length)	(PCDATA|Flow)*

When this module is invoked, it adds the iframe element to the Inline content set defined in the Text module. For further details on the Iframe module, see

```
www.w3.org/TR/2001/REC-xhtml-modularization-20010410/
    dtd_module_defs.html#a_module_Iframe
```

The mod   sule's DTD uses the following identifiers:

```
PUBLIC "-//W3C//ELEMENTS XHTML Inline Frame Element 1.0//EN"
SYSTEM "http://www.w3.org/TR/xhtml-modularization/DTD/
    xhtml-iframe-1.mod"
```

XHTML Intrinsic Events Module

The Intrinsic Events module defines attributes associated with handling events that occur when users perform specific actions. Note also that attributes covered in Table 24.21 are added to the indicated element only when the modules in which those elements are initially defined are also included in the XHTML document's DTD invocation. This set of attributes corresponds to the Events attribute set mentioned in the "Attribute Collection" section earlier in this chapter. The relevant elements and attributes are described in Table 24.21.

Table 24.21 XHTML Intrinsic Events Module

ELEMENT	ATTRIBUTES	NOTES
a&	onblur (Script), onfocus (script)	No change
area&	onblur (Script), onfocus (script)	Applies when the Client-Side Image Map module is included
frameset&	onload (Script), onunload (Script)	Applies when the Frames module is included
form&	onreset (Script), onsubmit (Script)	Applies when a Forms module is included
body&	onload(script), onunload (Script)	No change
label&	onblur (Script), onfocus (script)	Applies when a Forms module is included
input&	onblur (Script), onchange (Script), onfocus (Script), onselect (Script)	Applies when a Forms module is included
select&	onblur (Script), onchange (Script), onfocus (Script)	Applies when a Forms module is included

Table 24.21 continued XHTML Intrinsic Events Module

ELEMENT	ATTRIBUTES	NOTES
textarea&	Conblur (Script), onchange (Script), onfocus (Script), onselect (Script)	Applies when a Forms module is included
button&	onblur (Script), onfocus (Script)	Applies when a Forms module is included

For further details on the Intrinsic Events module, see

```
www.w3.org/TR/2001/REC-xhtml-modularization-20010410/
    dtd_module_defs.html#a_module_Intrinsic_Events
```

The module's DTD uses the following identifiers:

```
PUBLIC "-//W3C//ELEMENTS XHTML Intrinsic Events 1.0//EN"
SYSTEM "http://www.w3.org/TR/xhtml-modularization/DTD/
    xhtml-events-1.mod"
```

XHTML Metainformation Module

The Metainformation module supports an element used to describe document contents, audience, and other attributes within the head element in an XHTML document. The relevant element, its attributes, and its content model are described in Table 24.22.

Table 24.22 XHTML Metainformation Module

ELEMENT	ATTRIBUTES	MINIMAL CONTENT MODEL
meta	I18N, content* (CDATA), http-equiv (NMTOKEN), name (NMTOKEN), scheme (CDATA)	EMPTY

When this module is invoked, it adds the meta element to the content model for the head element defined in the Structure module. For further details on the Metainformation module, see

```
www.w3.org/TR/2001/REC-xhtml-modularization-20010410/
    dtd_module_defs.html#a_module_Metainformation
```

The module's DTD uses the following identifiers:

```
PUBLIC "-//W3C//ELEMENTS XHTML Metainformation 1.0//EN"
SYSTEM "http://www.w3.org/TR/xhtml-modularization/DTD/
    xhtml-meta-1.mod"
```

XHTML Scripting Module

The Scripting module supports the invocation of executable scripts for user agents that can handle them, and provides information to user agents that cannot, in XHTML documents. The relevant elements, attributes, and content models are described in Table 24.23.

Table 24.23 XHTML Scripting Module

ELEMENT	ATTRIBUTES	MINIMAL CONTENT MODEL
noscript	Common	(Heading|List|Block)+
script	charset (Charset), defer ("defer"), src (URI), type* (ContentType), xml:space="preserve"	PCDATA

When this module is invoked, it adds the script and noscript elements to the Block and Inline content sets defined in the Text module. The script element is also added to the head element's content model as defined in the Structure module. For further details on the Scripting module, see

```
www.w3.org/TR/2001/REC-xhtml-modularization-20010410/
    dtd_module_defs.html#a_module_Scripting
```

The module's DTD uses the following identifiers:

```
PUBLIC "-//W3C//ELEMENTS XHTML Scripting 1.0//EN"
SYSTEM "http://www.w3.org/TR/xhtml-modularization/DTD/
    xhtml-image-1.mod"
```

XHTML Style Sheet Module

The Style Sheet module supports an element that supports use of internal style sheets in XHTML documents. The relevant element, its attributes, and its content model are described in Table 24.24.

Table 24.24 XHTML Style Sheet Module

ELEMENT	ATTRIBUTES	MINIMAL CONTENT MODEL
style	CI18N, media (MediaDesc), title (Text), type* (ContentType), xml:space="preserve"	PCDATA

When this module is invoked, it adds the style element to the content model for the head element defined in the Structure module. For further details on the Style Sheet module, see

```
www.w3.org/TR/2001/REC-xhtml-modularization-20010410/
    dtd_module_defs.html#a_module_Style_Sheet
```

The module's DTD uses the following identifiers:

```
PUBLIC "-//W3C//ELEMENTS XHTML Style Sheets 1.0//EN"
SYSTEM "http://www.w3.org/TR/xhtml-modularization/DTD/
    xhtml-style-1.mod"
```

XHTML Style Attribute Module

The Style Attribute module adds support for the style attribute to the Core attributes set, and must be defined before the Core attributes so as to be included when the Core attributes are invoked. Use this module if you want to add inline styles within an XHTML document body.

When this module is invoked, it adds the style attribute to the vast majority of XHTML core elements. For further details on the Style Attribute module, see

```
www.w3.org/TR/2001/REC-xhtml-modularization-20010410/
    dtd_module_defs.html#a_module_Style_Attribute
```

The module's DTD uses the following identifiers:

```
PUBLIC "-//W3C//ELEMENTS XHTML Inline Style 1.0//EN"
SYSTEM "http://www.w3.org/TR/xhtml-modularization/DTD/
    xhtml-inlstyle-1.mod"
```

XHTML Link Module

The Link module supports an element that supports links to external resources. The relevant element and its attributes are described in Table 24.25.

Table 24.25 XHTML Link Module

ELEMENT	ATTRIBUTES	MINIMAL CONTENT MODEL
link	Common, charset (Charset), href (URI), hreflang (LanguageCode), media (MediaDesc), rel (LinkTypes), rev (LinkTypes), type (ContentType)	EMPTY

When this module is invoked, it adds the link element to the content model for the head element defined in the Structure module. For further details on the Link module, see

```
www.w3.org/TR/2001/REC-xhtml-modularization-20010410/
    dtd_module_defs.html#a_module_Link
```

The module's DTD uses the following identifiers:

```
PUBLIC "-//W3C//ELEMENTS XHTML Link Element 1.0//EN"
SYSTEM "http://www.w3.org/TR/xhtml-modularization/DTD/
    xhtml-link-1.mod"
```

XHTML Base Module

The Base module supports an element that supplies a base URI against which relative URIs in XHTML documents can be resolved. The relevant element and its attributes are described in Table 24.26.

Table 24.26 XHTML Base Module

ELEMENT	ATTRIBUTES	MINIMAL CONTENT MODEL
base	href* (URI)	EMPTY

When this module is invoked, it adds the base element to the content model for the head element defined in the Structure module. For further details on the Base module, see

```
www.w3.org/TR/2001/REC-xhtml-modularization-20010410/
    dtd_module_defs.html#a_module_Base
```

The module's DTD uses the following identifiers:

```
PUBLIC "-//W3C//ELEMENTS XHTML Base Element 1.0//EN"
SYSTEM "http://www.w3.org/TR/xhtml-modularization/DTD/
    xhtml-base-1.mod"
```

This concludes our discussion of standard XHTML modules. Next, we present three additional modules that we categorize as Deprecated (which is entirely valid, but is not used to characterize them in the XHTML Modularization Specification), after which we conclude the modules section of this chapter with a discussion of the Ruby module introduced in XHTML 1.1.

Deprecated XHTML Modules

Primarily for backward compatibility reasons, the XHTML Modularization Specification includes three additional modules that provide support for markup that would otherwise be unusable in the XHTML environment. This added support could be a significant boon to site designers, developers, and maintainers with Web sites that include older versions of HTML markup (HTML 4 or earlier) because it allows immediate migration to modularized XHTML—and, by extension, to XHTML 1.1—without requiring outright removal and replacement of all deprecated markup elements and attributes.

XHTML Applet Module

The Applet module supports the now-deprecated applet and param elements, which originally supported invocation of executable images embedded in HTML (particularly Java applets, hence the name for one of the elements involved). These elements have been superseded by the object element in HTML 4 and newer versions, but are supported for backward compatibility. The relevant elements, their attributes, and content models are described in Table 24.27.

When this module is invoked, it adds the applet and param elements to the Inline content set defined in the Text module. For further details on the Applet module, see

```
www.w3.org/TR/2001/REC-xhtml-modularization-20010410/
    dtd_module_defs.html#a_module_Applet
```

The module's DTD uses the following identifiers:

```
PUBLIC "-//W3C//ELEMENTS XHTML Java Applets 1.0//EN"
SYSTEM "http://www.w3.org/TR/xhtml-modularization/DTD/
    xhtml-applet-1.mod"
```

Table 24.27 XHTML Applet Module

ELEMENT	ATTRIBUTES	MINIMAL CONTENT MODEL
applet	Core, alt* (Text), archive (CDATA), code (CDATA), codebase (URI), height* (Length), object (CDATA), width* (Length)	(PCDATA|Flow|param)*
param	id (ID), name* (CDATA), type (ContentType), value (CDATA), valuetype ("data"*|"ref"|"object")	EMPTY

XHTML Name Identification Module

The Name Identification module adds the name attribute to numerous XHTML elements. The name attribute was used (historically) to identify specific elements in HTML documents. Modern usage, in keeping with the Document Object Model (DOM) and document parse trees, dictates that the id attribute (part of the XHTML Core) should be used instead. Here again, support is provided for backward compatibility, and the relevant elements, the name attribute, and relevant annotations appear in Table 24.28.

Table 24.28 XHTML Name Identification Module

ELEMENT	ATTRIBUTES	NOTES
a&	name (CDATA)	Part of Core
applet&	name (CDATA)	Applies when the Applet module is included
form&	name (CDATA)	Applies when a Forms module is included
frame&	name (CDATA)	Applies when the Frames module is included
iframe&	name (CDATA)	Applies when the Iframe module is included
img&	name (CDATA)	Applies when the Image module is included
map&	name (CDATA)	Applies when the Client-Side Image module is included

When this module is invoked, it adds the name attribute to various modules, as described in the Notes column in Table 24.28. For further details on the Name Identification module, see

```
www.w3.org/TR/2001/REC-xhtml-modularization-20010410/
    dtd_module_defs.html#a_module_Name_Identification
```

The module's DTD uses the following identifiers:

```
PUBLIC "-//W3C//ELEMENTS XHTML Name Identifier 1.0//EN"
SYSTEM "http://www.w3.org/TR/xhtml-modularization/DTD/
    xhtml-nameident-1.mod"
```

XHTML Legacy Module

The Legacy module supports a grab bag of deprecated HTML elements that are included solely to provide backward compatibility for XHTML implementations. The relevant elements, their attributes, and content models are described in Table 24.29; various legacy attributes, plus related elements and notes, are described in Table 24.30.

Table 24.29 XHTML Legacy Module Elements

ELEMENT	ATTRIBUTES	MINIMAL CONTENT MODEL
basefont	color (Color), face (CDATA), id (ID), size (CDATA)	EMPTY
center	Common	(PCDATA|Flow)*
dir	Common, compact ("compact")	(li)+
font	Core, I18N, color (Color), face (CDATA), size (CDATA)	(PCDATA|Inline)*
isindex	Core, I18N, prompt (Text)	EMPTY
menu	Common, compact ("compact")	(li)+
s	Common	(PCDATA|Inline)*
strike	Common	(PCDATA|Inline)*
u	Common	(PCDATA|Inline)*

Table 24.30 XHTML Legacy Module Attributes

ELEMENT	ATTRIBUTES	NOTES
body&	alink (Color), background (URI), bgcolor (Color), link (Color), text (Color), vlink (Color)	Belongs to Core
br&	clear ("left"|"all"|"right"|"none"*)	Belongs to Core
caption&	align ("top"|"bottom"|"left"|"right")	Belongs to Core
div&	align ("left"|"center"|"right"|"justify")	Belongs to Core
dl&	compact ("compact"), type (CDATA)	Belongs to Core
h1-h6&	align ("left"|"center"|"right"|"justify")	Belongs to Core
hr&	align ("left"|"center"|"right"|"justify"), noshade ("noshade"), size (Pixels), width (Length)	Belongs to Core
img&	align ("left"|"center"|"right"|"justify"), border (Pixels), hspace (Pixels), vspace (Pixels)	Belongs to Core
input&	align ("top"|"middle"|"bottom"|"left"|"right")	Applies when a Forms module is included
legend&	align ("left"|"center"|"right"|"justify")	Applies when a Forms module is included
li&	type (CDATA), value (Number)	Belongs to Core
ol&	compact ("compact"), start (Number), type (CDATA)	Belongs to Core
p&	align ("left"|"center"|"right"|"justify")	Belongs to Core
pre&	width (Number)	Belongs to Core
script	language (CDATA)	Applies when the Scripting module is included
table&	align ("left"|"center"|"right"), bgcolor (Color)	Applies when the Table module is included
tr&	bgcolor (Color)	Applies when the Table module is included

Table 24.30 continued XHTML Legacy Module Attributes

ELEMENT	ATTRIBUTES	NOTES
th&	bgcolor (Color), height (Pixels), nowrap ("nowrap"), width (Length)	Applies when the Table module is included
td&	bgcolor (Color), height (Length), nowrap ("nowrap"), width (Length)	Applies when the Table module is included
ul&	compact ("compact"), type (CDATA)	Belongs to Core

When this module is invoked, it adds the various elements and attributes listed in Tables 24.29 and 24.30 to various modules. For further details on the Legacy module, see

```
www.w3.org/TR/2001/REC-xhtml-modularization-20010410/
    dtd_module_defs.html#a_module_Legacy
```

The module's DTD uses the following identifiers:

```
PUBLIC "-//W3C//ELEMENTS XHTML Legacy Markup 1.0//EN"
SYSTEM "http://www.w3.org/TR/xhtml-modularization/DTD/
    xhtml-legacy-1.mod"
```

This concludes our coverage of all modules covered in the XHTML Modularization Specification. In the following section, we provide similar coverage of the Ruby module added to the XHTML 1.1 specification. (It, too, can be included in an XHTML 1.1 document using the same techniques we'll describe later in this chapter.)

The XHTML 1.1 Ruby Annotation Module

The Ruby Annotation module supports short runs of text that occur alongside the base text, most commonly used in East Asian documents to provide pronunciation details and other short annotations. The text involved is called "ruby text"—hence, the name of the module—and often provides a character-by-character or ideogram-by-ideogram translation from one Asian language to another. Thus, base text may be in Mandarin with ruby text in Hanggul, for instance, where for each Mandarin ideogram, a corresponding Hanggul ideogram is positioned immediately above it. The relevant Ruby markup elements, their attributes, and their content models are described in Table 24.31.

Table 24.31 XHTML 1.1 Ruby Module

Element	Attributes	Minimal Content Model
ruby	Common	`(rb, (rt|(rp,rt,rp)))`
rbc	Common	`rbⅰ`
rtc	Common	`rt+`
rb	Common	`(PCDATA|Inline-ruby)*`
rt	Common, rbspan (CDATA)	`(PCDATA|Inline-ruby)*`
rp	Common	`PCDATA*`

When this module is invoked, it adds the elements from Table 24.31 to the Inline content set defined in the Text module. For further details on the Ruby module, including some nicely formatted examples of what this baby can do, please visit:

`www.w3.org/TR/2001/REC-ruby-20010531/#module`

The module's DTD uses the following identifiers:

```
PUBLIC "-//W3C//ELEMENTS XHTML Ruby 1.0//EN"
SYSTEM "http://www.w3.org/TR/ruby/xhtml-ruby-1.mod"
```

Using XHTML Modules

When it comes to using modularized XHTML—be it to invoke and use the predefined modules covered earlier in this chapter or to invoke and use other publicly available or entirely custom-built modules—the technique is so simple that it's entirely anticlimactic. In a nutshell, you must create an internal DTD section in your XHTML documents, or make reference to an external DTD in your XHTML documents, that invokes the XHTML (or other) modules that you want to use.

It's important to observe, however, that the order of placement when invoking such modules is quite significant. Therefore, if you use modules that modify other modules (for example, the Style Attribute module or the Legacy module), you *must* invoke those modules before invoking the modules they modify. This is the only way that the parsing process that internalizes the document definition can satisfy the references that those modifying modules make to the modules that they modify. In simpler terms, this means the extra modifications that modules outside the Core set make must occur before the Core modules—or other modified modules—can be invoked.

In practice, this means if the section on a module mentions that it alters or adds to a content set, you must invoke that module prior to invoking the module within which the altered content set is initially defined. This means it's smart to invoke the Core modules last, and other modules first, when custom-building a modularized XHTML DTD. We annotate the XHTML Basic DTD later in this section to provide a basic working example, with relevant explanations.

That said, the basic syntax for invoking an XHTML module is quite simple, and takes the following general form:

```
<!ENTITY % module-name.mod
     PUBLIC "-//W3C//ELEMENTS XHTML module-name 1.0//EN"
            "xhtml-mod-abbrev-1.mod" >
%module-name.mod;
```

Here, the module-name term is our notation for the string that appears in the PUBLIC string in our documentation of the various modules earlier in this chapter, and the mod-abbrev term is our notation for the related string that appears in the SYSTEM string in that same documentation. Thus, the equivalent Standard Generalized Markup Language (SGML) for the Text module (a member of the XHTML Core modules) is as follows (to demonstrate the substitutions involved):

```
<!ENTITY % xhtml-text.mod
     PUBLIC "-//W3C//ELEMENTS XHTML Text 1.0//EN"
            "xhtml-text-1.mod" >
%xhtml-text.mod;
```

Thus, the term text replaces both module-name and mod-abbrev in the real DTD invocation of that module. Because these terms sometimes differ for other XHTML modules, we used two terms in our description of the general form of this invocation. Please do not assume you can always use the same string to replace both substitution terms.

Because using XHTML modules to create custom or special-purpose DTDs essentially limits your DTD writing efforts to nothing more than a carefully crafted series of invocations of other, publicly available XHTML module DTDs, it should come as no surprise that the W3C has come to call such DTDs *Driver DTDs*. We think this is because they simply invoke other necessary DTDs in the right order, and drastically limit the amount of original or custom SGML declarations and code otherwise. This makes them look a lot like old-fashioned Unix or Linux driver files, which often consist of nothing more than a bunch of invocations themselves. By looking for Driver DTDs in the XHTML 1.1 Specification, the XHTML Basic Specification, and so forth, you can find plenty of lengthy examples of this new abbreviated method of DTD composition to learn from. That's why we discuss the XHTML Basic DTD in this chapter as well.

At this time, some of the currently available XHTML validation tools cannot yet validate documents based on modularized XHTML. See the sidebar "Validating Modularized XHTML" to help you cope with this problem, should it happen to you.

Validating Modularized XHTML

As mentioned in the previous warning, some of the currently available XHTML validation tools cannot yet validate documents based on modularized XHTML. We hope this will change by the time you read this book. If not, you can use a "trick" to get through validation by invoking the XHTML 1.0 DTD of your choice in documents as you validate them, then replacing your DTD invocation with a modularized equivalent for the production versions of your XHTML documents.

As long as you steer clear of Ruby Annotation and other external XHTML modules in your documents in the short term, this technique works fine. This is because the XHTML 1.0 Strict DTD is exactly equivalent to the non-deprecated XHTML modules (and the other XHTML 1.0 DTDs also work, as long as you invoke the necessary deprecated or additional standard modules to support legacy or frame-handling needs).

Looking at a more involved real-world example should help to cement your understanding of the process of constructing a modularized XHTML DTD. XHTML Basic is a subset of XHTML that became a W3C Recommendation in December 2000. It was designed to create the absolute minimum set of XHTML elements and attributes for use on handheld devices, cell phones, PDAs, and other systems with limited display capabilities. XHTML Basic defines a proper subset of the XHTML 1.0 DTD that includes the following modules:

- Text module
- Hypertext module
- List module
- Image module
- Tables module (basic only)
- Forms module (basic only)
- Link module
- Metainformation module
- Base Element module
- Param Element module
- Embedded Object module

Note that we reproduce the basic DTD from the W3C's Web site in Listing 24.1, except that where we remove tangential or extraneous information, or where we annotate the DTD, the SGML comments appear in italics below (and are not part of the original document itself). To see the document in its original form, please visit `www.w3.org/ TR/xhtml-basic/#a_dtd`.

LISTING 24.1: THE BASIC DTD FROM THE W3C SITE

```
<!-- XHTML Basic 1.0 DTD -->
<!-- file: xhtml-basic10.dtd -->
<!-- XHTML Basic 1.0 DTD
     This is XHTML Basic, a proper subset of XHTML.

The Extensible HyperText Markup Language (XHTML)
Copyright 1998-2000 World Wide Web Consortium
(Massachusetts Institute of Technology, Institut National de
Recherche en Informatique et en Automatique, Keio University).
All Rights Reserved.

Permission to use, copy, modify and distribute the XHTML Basic
DTD and its accompanying documentation for any purpose and
without fee is hereby granted in perpetuity, provided that
the above copyright notice and this paragraph appear in all
copies. The copyright holders make no representation about the
suitability of the DTD for any purpose. It is provided "as is"
without expressed or implied warranty.
```

SNIP: Editorial attribution and revision history deleted here

```
-->
<!-- This is the driver file for version 1.0 of the XHTML
     Basic DTD.

This DTD is identified by the PUBLIC and SYSTEM identifiers:
     PUBLIC: "-//W3C//DTD XHTML Basic 1.0//EN"
     SYSTEM: "http://www.w3.org/TR/xhtml-basic/xhtml-basic10.dtd"
-->

<!ENTITY % XHTML.version  "-//W3C//DTD XHTML Basic 1.0//EN" >
<!-- Use this URI to identify the default namespace:
          "http://www.w3.org/1999/xhtml"
```

```
    See the Qualified Names module for information on the use of
    namespace prefixes in the DTD.
-->


<!ENTITY % NS.prefixed "IGNORE" >
<!ENTITY % XHTML.prefix  "" >


<!-- Reserved for use with the XLink namespace:
-->
<!ENTITY % XLINK.xmlns "" >
<!ENTITY % XLINK.xmlns.attrib "" >


<!-- For example, if you are using XHTML Basic 1.0 directly,
     use the FPI in the DOCTYPE declaration, with the xmlns
     attribute on the document element to identify the default
     namespace:
       <?xml version="1.0"?>
       <!DOCTYPE html PUBLIC "-//W3C//DTD XHTML Basic 1.0//EN"
          "http://www.w3.org/TR/xhtml-basic/xhtml-basic10.dtd">
    <html xmlns="http://www.w3.org/1999/xhtml" xml:lang="en" >
Unless you're invoking other modules outside the XHTML modules,
or modifying those modules, this is exactly what you must do!
    ...
    </html>
-->


<!-- SNIP: Extraneous content related to document profiles and
     the Bi-directional Text module removed here -->


<!-- :::::::::::::::::::::::::::::::::::::::::::::::::::::::::: -->

<!ENTITY % xhtml-events.module   "IGNORE" >
<!ENTITY % xhtml-bdo.module      "%XHTML.bidi;" >

<!ENTITY % xhtml-model.mod
    PUBLIC "-//W3C//ENTITIES XHTML Basic 1.0
      Document Model 1.0//EN"
      "xhtml-basic10-model-1.mod" >
<!-- This invokes changes to the XHTML content model introduced
     in the XHTML Basic implementation. The related DTD is fully
     documented at
```

```
                http://www.w3.org/TR/xhtml-basic/#a_customization -->

<!ENTITY % xhtml-framework.mod
    PUBLIC "-//W3C//ENTITIES XHTML Modular Framework 1.0//EN"
      "xhtml-framework-1.mod" >
%xhtml-framework.mod;
<!-- This invokes the basic XHTML Modularization Framework that
     allows the monolithic XHTML 1.0 DTD to be broken into
     modules -->

<!ENTITY % pre.content
      "( #PCDATA
       | %InlStruct.class;
       %InlPhras.class;
       %Anchor.class;
       %Inline.extra; )*"
>
<!-- This defines changes to preformatted content element in
     the Text module, which is why it must appear before the
     Text module is invoked in the next set of DTD definitions.
  -->

<!ENTITY % xhtml-text.mod
    PUBLIC "-//W3C//ELEMENTS XHTML Text 1.0//EN"
          "xhtml-text-1.mod" >
%xhtml-text.mod;

<!ENTITY % xhtml-hypertext.mod
    PUBLIC "-//W3C//ELEMENTS XHTML Hypertext 1.0//EN"
          "xhtml-hypertext-1.mod" >
%xhtml-hypertext.mod;

<!ENTITY % xhtml-list.mod
      PUBLIC "-//W3C//ELEMENTS XHTML Lists 1.0//EN"
            "xhtml-list-1.mod" >
%xhtml-list.mod;
<!-- This concludes the invocation of the XHTML Core modules
     that are unaltered by other invoked modules. Please note
     that the Structure module is invoked last herein because
     it's altered by some of the other modules that precede it.
  -->
```

```
<!-- :::::::::::::::::::::::::::::::::::::::::::::::::::::::: -->

<!-- Image Module  ..................................... -->
<!ENTITY % xhtml-image.module "INCLUDE" >
<![%xhtml-image.module;[
<!ENTITY % xhtml-image.mod
    PUBLIC "-//W3C//ELEMENTS XHTML Images 1.0//EN"
           "xhtml-image-1.mod" >
%xhtml-image.mod;]]>
<!-- Notice that the syntax is more convoluted for the non-Core
    modules. Basically, it's necessary to create an internal
    image module entity, xhtml-image.module, to correspond to the
    external image module DTD before invoking that external
    module itself. The same approach applies to the Tables,
    Forms, Link, Metainformation, Base Element (Base), Param
    Element (Param), and Embedded Object (Object) modules that
    follow. -->

<!-- Tables Module .................................... -->
<!ENTITY % xhtml-table.module "INCLUDE" >
<![%xhtml-table.module;[
<!ENTITY % xhtml-table.mod
    PUBLIC "-//W3C//ELEMENTS XHTML Basic Tables 1.0//EN"
           "xhtml-basic-table-1.mod" >
%xhtml-table.mod;]]>

<!-- Forms Module  ...................................... -->
<!ENTITY % xhtml-form.module "INCLUDE" >
<![%xhtml-form.module;[
<!ENTITY % xhtml-form.mod
    PUBLIC "-//W3C//ELEMENTS XHTML Basic Forms 1.0//EN"
           "xhtml-basic-form-1.mod" >
%xhtml-form.mod;]]>

<!-- Link Element Module  ............................... -->
<!ENTITY % xhtml-link.module "INCLUDE" >
<![%xhtml-link.module;[
<!ENTITY % xhtml-link.mod
    PUBLIC "-//W3C//ELEMENTS XHTML Link Element 1.0//EN"
           "xhtml-link-1.mod" >
```

```
%xhtml-link.mod;]]>

<!-- Document Metainformation Module  ..................... -->
<!ENTITY % xhtml-meta.module "INCLUDE" >
<![%xhtml-meta.module;[
<!ENTITY % xhtml-meta.mod
    PUBLIC "-//W3C//ELEMENTS XHTML Metainformation 1.0//EN"
           "xhtml-meta-1.mod" >
%xhtml-meta.mod;]]>

<!-- Base Element Module  ................................ -->
<!ENTITY % xhtml-base.module "INCLUDE" >
<![%xhtml-base.module;[
<!ENTITY % xhtml-base.mod
    PUBLIC "-//W3C//ELEMENTS XHTML Base Element 1.0//EN"
           "xhtml-base-1.mod" >
%xhtml-base.mod;]]>

<!-- Param Element Module  ............................... -->
<!ENTITY % xhtml-param.module "INCLUDE" >
<![%xhtml-param.module;[
<!ENTITY % xhtml-param.mod
    PUBLIC "-//W3C//ELEMENTS XHTML Param Element 1.0//EN"
           "xhtml-param-1.mod" >
%xhtml-param.mod;]]>

<!-- Embedded Object Module  ............................ -->
<!ENTITY % xhtml-object.module "INCLUDE" >
<![%xhtml-object.module;[
<!ENTITY % xhtml-object.mod
    PUBLIC "-//W3C//ELEMENTS XHTML Embedded Object 1.0//EN"
           "xhtml-object-1.mod" >
%xhtml-object.mod;]]>

<!ENTITY % xhtml-struct.mod
    PUBLIC "-//W3C//ELEMENTS XHTML Document Structure 1.0//EN"
           "xhtml-struct-1.mod" >
%xhtml-struct.mod;

<!-- end of XHTML Basic 1.0 DTD  ........................ -->
```

Modular XHTML and Schemas

Currently, the only way to build additional XHTML modules and to invoke such modules when constructing document definitions for related XHTML documents is to use DTDs. A *working draft*—or a formal statement of work in progress in a W3C working group that is still building a specification—titled "Modularization of XHTML in XML Schema" is available at www.w3.org/TR/2001/WD-xhtml-m12n-schema-20010322/. This document shows the state of the XML Schema equivalents to the existing DTDs that describe the various XHTML modules as of March 22, 2001. To find the latest version of this work, be sure to visit the HTML home page at www.w3.org/MarkUp/ and check the "News" and "Recommendations" sections to learn the latest status of this effort.

Many XML and XHTML experts believe that building and using XHTML modules will become easier when XML Schema-based descriptions of such modules become possible (when developing new modules or customizing existing ones) or available (when using predefined modules like the ones documented earlier in this chapter). Although this is a subject of some controversy that pits the "pro-SGML" or "pro-DTD" factions against the "pro-Schema" factions in the XML community, we believe most content developers will use whichever approach works best for them.

In the meantime, those interested in XML Schema-based implementations of XHTML modules will find section 3 of the working draft of "Modularization of XHTML in XML Schema" of great interest, because it documents proposed versions of XML Schemas for XHTML content models, infrastructure, and the individual modules themselves in detail. However, because the XML Schema definition only recently attained recommended status (May 5, 2001), we expect this draft to go through some minor changes and adjustments before it, too, attains recommended status. That's why we're unable to cover this information in depth in this book. Suffice it to say, in closing, that XML Schema-based modules should become available soon, perhaps even by the time you read this book. Please check www.w3.org/MarkUp to ascertain this important effort's current status as you read this material.

Where to Go from Here

In this chapter, we explored XHTML modules and modularization. We explored what motivates use of this technology for subsetting a monolithic definition of XHTML, and learned that XHTML Modularization produces more compact documents that are easier to parse and process, especially on handheld devices, cell phones, or embedded systems with Internet and Web access. We examined the contents and capabilities of the existing modules defined in the XHTML Modularization Specification and the Ruby module added to this collection in the XHTML 1.1 Specification. You should not only be ready to make use of this technology if your needs suggest or dictate its use, but should also be able to use the examples presented in this chapter to create and validate modular XHTML documents.

Where to now?

- Chapters 22 and 23 explore and explain the uses, syntax, and semantics of DTDs, should you wish to dig more deeply into the DTDs that describe XHTML modules, or the DTDs that pull them together (such as the XHTML Basic DTD presented earlier in this chapter).

- Chapter 30 explains XML Schemas, should you wish to investigate and learn more about XML Schema-based XHTML modules.

Part VII

XHTML Development Tools

In This Part

Choosing XHTML
Development Tools

Chapter 25

Because XHTML is still relatively new as markup languages go, the only fully powerful development software choices you have are HTML and XML software. You can use a combination of the two to achieve clean XHTML markup, or you can use HTML software and a utility such as HTML Tidy to convert your markup to clean XHTML.

Choosing the development tools that are right for you can be a daunting task. You'll find tons of software out there—both for developing documents and for developing and editing images.

In this chapter, we'll examine the options and take a look at some specific tools (HTML and XML). We'll discuss what each one has to offer, point out any drawbacks, and recommend some tools. We can't tell you which tool to choose, but we can provide you with information that will help you determine which tools are best for your needs.

This chapter covers the following topics:

- Selecting development tools

- Comparing text editors and WYSIWYG editors

- Discovering XML development tools

- Getting to know some image-editing software

Choosing an Editing Tool

In general, there's no "right" kind of tool for developing HTML documents. It depends on you—your needs, preferences, and budget. In the following sections, we'll examine the three categories of development tools:

- Text editors

- WYSIWYG editors

- High-end WYSIWYG editors

Text Editors

You use a text editor when you want to manually enter XHTML elements and attributes. If you've been following the sample markup in this book and entering elements and attributes, you've been using a text editor.

Although hand-coding XHTML is somewhat time-consuming and requires careful proofreading, doing so gives you much more flexibility and control over the documents you create. For example, when the XHTML specification became available, developers using text editors could immediately incorporate the latest XHTML rules and changes. However, developers using WYSIWYG editors could not immediately make their documents XHTML–compliant; they're still waiting for the software to catch up with the latest specification.

Text editors come in two varieties:

- Plain text

- Enhanced

Plain-text editors, such as Notepad (Windows), Simple Text (Macintosh), and vi (Unix), offer nothing more than text-editing capabilities. Figure 25.1 shows a basic XHTML document in Notepad.

Enhanced editors, such as HomeSite and HTML-Kit (shown in Figure 25.2), give you editing capabilities and automated commands that let you add markup with a click of the mouse.

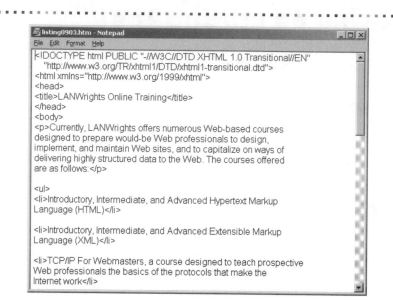

Figure 25.1 *Plain-text editors, such as Notepad, give you a screen in which to create an XHTML document.*

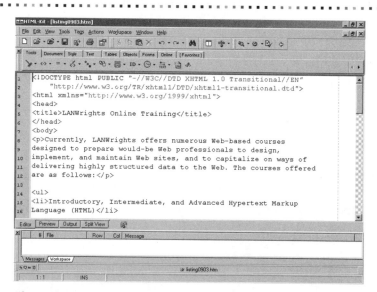

Figure 25.2 *Some editors, such as HTML-Kit, provide space for you to enter code, as well as buttons and menu options that add code for you.*

HTML-Kit also offers a preview mode that mimics WYSIWYG (shown in Figure 25.3) as well as integration with HTML Tidy. The difference between these and true WYSIWYG editors is that you cannot make any editing changes in the preview mode.

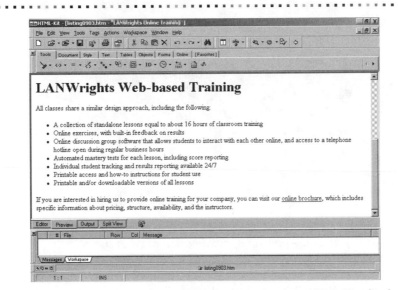

Figure 25.3 *Some enhanced text editors, such as HTML-Kit, display previews of the results.*

Whether you use a plain-text editor or an enhanced editor depends on your specific needs. If you want some help entering elements and attributes, use an enhanced editor. If you don't mind doing all the typing yourself or if you simply prefer a smaller, faster editor, you'll probably choose a plain-text editor.

WYSIWYG Editors

A WYSIWYG (What You See Is What You Get) editor lets you see roughly how the XHTML document will look in a browser as you're creating it. Rather than entering elements and attributes and then viewing the results in a browser, you can preview documents as you create them. Most WYSIWYG editors display only the actual text, not the XHTML markup (unless you choose to view the markup). Figure 25.4 shows how this works in Dreamweaver. For more information on Dreamweaver 4, visit www.macromedia.com/software/dreamweaver/.

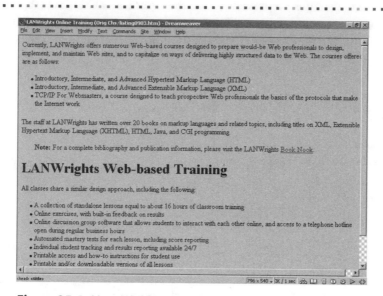

Figure 25.4 *Most WYSIWYG editors, such as Dreamweaver, don't display markup by default—only an approximation of what the page will look like in a browser.*

Other HTML WYSIWYG editors include:

- NetObjects Fusion MX www.netobjects.com/products/html/nfmx.html
- Adobe GoLive 5 www.adobe.com/products/golive/main.html
- Microsoft FrontPage www.microsoft.com/frontpage/

Although these editors can be rather expensive, they give you great control over formatting and can help you develop really spiffy Web pages.

High-end WYSIWYG editors treat page elements as objects, meaning that you can click and drag elements around on the page and place them where you want. In doing so, you can create interesting layouts that should look fairly consistent from browser to browser.

Most WYSIWYG editors also provide site-management services, which help you see how pages in the site connect and relate. For example, take a look at Figure 25.5, which shows Microsoft FrontPage. Each time you create a page, FrontPage automatically adds the page to the overall structure. All you have to do is name the page and add content to it.

Many WYSIWYG editors also include templates. For example, using the FrontPage Wizard, you can choose from several templates (called *themes* in FrontPage lingo), dozens of page options, and various color and background options. Similarly, in NetObjects

Fusion, most templates include a banner, link buttons, bullets, and other formatting options. Templates come in a range of styles, from fun, as shown in Figure 25.6, to the more practical. And, if you want, you can pick and choose elements from the templates or start from scratch and create your own.

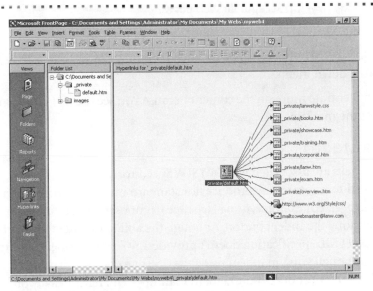

Figure 25.5 *WYSIWYG editors, such as FrontPage, help you manage your site.*

Figure 25.6 *FrontPage templates provide formatting for all kinds of page elements.*

Advantages

WYSIWYG editors offer you a middle ground between ease of use and the ability to do exactly what you want with your Web pages. With a WYSIWYG editor, you can do the following:

- Quickly develop acceptable Web pages.

- Create XHTML documents about as fast as you can type.

- Add XHTML effects just by clicking a button or by choosing an option from a drop-down menu.

- Concentrate more on the content because you see the text and formatting, and not the markup.

Disadvantages

Some drawbacks are associated with WYSIWYG editors, however. The biggest is that WYSIWYG editors commonly produce nonstandard markup to provide the effects most users expect. For example, using Netscape Composer you can indent page elements simply by clicking the Indent button. Although the ability to indent elements might be handy, the XHTML specification doesn't provide any sort of element or attribute for indention (although you can indent using the CSS1 `text-indent` property). So, in this example, Composer produces nonstandard markup—and relies heavily on luck to work in most browsers.

Another drawback is that the WYSIWYG aspect is somewhat misleading. As we've mentioned throughout this book, the exact results of XHTML markup can vary significantly from browser to browser and from computer to computer. If you compare the WYSIWYG preview in any of these editors with the results in an actual browser, you might find that the display is somewhat different.

 Check out Chapters 9 and 26 to find out how to validate XHTML markup and avoid the nonstandard markup that WYSIWYG editors sometimes produce.

A third drawback is that you can't use WYSIWYG editors to add the latest and greatest XHTML effects. For example, you couldn't use a WYSIWYG editor to add style sheets shortly after the release of the HTML 4 specification. The software companies had to develop the application after the latest specification or draft becomes available. For the time being, the best option is to use HTML Tidy (in one of its many forms) to clean up your XHTML and make sure it's valid and well formed. Chapter 9 of this book is devoted to converting HTML to XHTML and has an entire section on the various forms of HTML Tidy.

Discovering XML Development Tools

Some serious XHTML developers skip (X)HTML editors altogether and go straight for XML editors. Although XML editors do not recognize XHTML elements and attributes, they support DTDs, namespaces, and other XML-related features. If you choose to use an XML editor, we recommend that you create some basic XHTML templates to save you a little time.

You should be able to provide the editor with the appropriate DTD so you can use the XHTML elements and attributes. There's a chance, though, you may not be able to, so using these editors may be the equivalent of working with a text editor. However, if you use these tools, you can be sure that your XHTML documents comply with the XML and the associated DTD, and therefore, XHTML rules, so your documents will definitely be well formed and valid.

XML Spy

XML Spy by Altova is more than just an XML editor. Using XML Spy, you can edit, create, and use existing DTDs; edit, view, and output XSL; edit XML Schemas, and more. If all of these terms seem too complicated, visit Chapters 20 and 21 and think about using an HTML editor to create your XHTML documents.

XML Spy allows you to assign an existing DTD or schema to your documents. Therefore, using one of the XHTML DTDs with this tool is a definite possibility. Find out more about XML Spy at www.xmlspy.com.

XML Pro

XML Pro v2.0 by Vervet Logic isn't as versatile as XML Spy—it's simply an XML editor. You can't convert documents or create DTDs using XML Pro, but you can find out whether DTDs are valid. In addition, you need to have some in-depth knowledge of XML to be able to comfortably use XML Pro. If you're feeling brave, you can find out more information about XML Pro at www.vervet.com.

 For information on a slew of XML tools, check out XMLSoftware at www.xmlsoftware.com. You'll find references to XML browsers, editors, parsers, conversion tools, and more on this site.

Choosing an Image-Editing Tool

Just as there's no "right" tool to generate HTML, there's also no one image-editing tool that will meet every need for every person. Which one you choose is up to you, your needs, and your budget. Here are some of the more popular image-editing tools:

Paint Shop Pro   Offers a wide range of capabilities, it's easy to use, and it's affordable. In fact, we used Paint Shop Pro to create the images used in the sample Web sites throughout this book. For more information, visit `www.jasc.com`.

Photoshop   Is a more expensive tool, but you can literally do anything with it. Take a look at any book or magazine cover—most were probably created with Photoshop. Unless you have very sophisticated image-editing needs or are already experienced with high-end image editing, this product might offer much more than you need. However, it's *the* tool if you're looking for power. For more information, check out `www.adobe.com/products/photoshop/main.html`.

Image Composer   Offers a new paradigm. Rather than working with bitmapped images, you can move and manipulate parts of images—just as you can use drawing capabilities in Microsoft Word or PowerPoint. If you're already familiar or proficient with Photoshop or similar products, you might find the paradigm shift a little challenging, but if you're starting from scratch, this is likely to be both easy and fun to learn. Image Composer comes with the stand-alone version of FrontPage 2000 and is shipped with FrontPage 98. If you use Office 2000 Premium, you're offered Microsoft PhotoDraw 2000 instead. Find more information about Image Composer at `www.microsoft.com/frontpage/imagecomposer/imagecomposer1.htm`.

Where to Go from Here

So, those are your basic choices, folks! In this chapter, you saw the advantages and disadvantages of using text editors, WYSIWYG editors, and XML tools. You also got an idea of the image-editing tools you can use. Exactly which tools you choose depends on your specific needs.

From here:

- Visit Chapter 5 to learn how to include images in your XHTML documents.
- Take a look at Chapter 9 to learn more about converting your HTML documents to XHTML.
- See Chapters 14 and 15 to learn how to develop coherent public, personal, and intranet sites.
- Go to Chapter 26 to learn about validation services.

Validating XHTML Documents

Chapter 26

If you recall, the distinction between well-formed and valid XML—and by extension, XHTML—is that well-formed markup need only follow the general rules of syntax for XML, whereas valid markup must adhere specifically to the markup element and attribute definitions, plus content models, defined in one or more specific DTDs or XML Schemas. In this chapter, we make the case for validation as something desirable, and we cover the ins and outs of working with various validators available for local or remote use.

We begin the chapter with definitions for the terms *valid* and *validation*. A valid document is one that is formally tested against the syntax and content rules expressed in a DTD or XML Schema and found to contain no syntax errors or content rule violations. Validation is the process whereby such a formal test of syntax and content rules is performed.

This chapter covers the following topics:

- Understanding validation

- Using a validator

- Working with various validators

- Downloading validation tools

Why Validate Your Documents?

The question that heads this section of the chapter is especially poignant for longtime HTML designers and developers who are used to incredibly forgiving browsers that make an effort to display just about any kind of markup, even when it's not well formed. Given such a loose rendering environment for one's markup, it's not unheard of for professionals to ask in no uncertain terms, "Why bother with validation?"

The answers to this question are both interesting and unsatisfying, given the current state of browser software. To a degree, buying into validation also requires buying into the whole notion of XML in general, and XHTML in particular. The primary impetus in creating XHTML from HTML was to bring the power and expressiveness of XML to bear on a hitherto frozen, nonextensible set of markup. In exchange for extensibility—and the ability to incorporate other XML applications within an XHTML environment that goes along with it—designers and developers must be willing to give up the loosey-goosey, unstructured, and often irregular syntax and semantics that old-fashioned HTML allows (and appears to encourage, by virtue of the forgiving way that modern Web browsers parse and present HTML and XHTML documents).

Ultimately, only you can decide if validation is a worthwhile exercise for your documents; however, we urge you to consider the pros and cons we present in this section. We want to candidly confess that we believe strongly in the virtues of validation and hope to sway you in that direction as you read through the pluses and minuses related to validation that we present. Our hope is that we'll remain objective, but perhaps the best retort to the question "Why validate?" is another question: "If you have to ask, why even bother with XHTML?"

First the validation pros:

- At a bare minimum, successful validation provides a guarantee that a document is syntactically correct and meets all constraints created by content models.

- Even better, when XML Schemas are used for validation, data type and constraint checking (to make sure that attribute values fall within specific ranges or belong to specific sets of values, for instance) also become possible. This permits considerable quality assurance checks to become part and parcel of the validation process.

- With more and more markup being generated programmatically—such as from Active Server Pages (ASP), JavaServer Pages (JSP), PHP, database management systems, ColdFusion, and so forth—validation helps ensure that mechanically generated code is sound and error-free.

- Conformance to certain DTDs or XML Schemas is essential to ensure that specific modularizations for XHTML are used; therefore, when documents must work on personal digital assistants (PDAs), cell phones, or embedded systems, validation ensures that only legal markup is used.

- Next-generation software tools—including Web browsers—are expected to demand definitions for governing DTDs or XML Schemas to drive document parsing. As is already the case with some XML (and SGML) tools, such software may refuse to parse (and therefore, to display) documents that do not include DTD or XML Schema references and that do not validate against such references. Because this approach greatly simplifies (and therefore shrinks) the client software used to read and display XML and XHTML documents, it's expected to become an outright requirement for those same PDAs, cell phones, and embedded systems we mentioned in the preceding list item.

- The bottom line is that valid HTML ideally works in virtually all Web browsers, whereas invalid HTML works in some but not in others. Because what works best for the broadest range of users is eminently desirable, what better argument for validation could we propose?

And now for the validation cons:

- Careful coding and development may be required to create documents that will validate, if you build them by hand. Alternatively, if you use a development tool that requires a DTD or an XML Schema from which to work, it's impossible to create invalid documents!

- Extra work and effort is required both to submit XML or XHTML documents for validation and to keep working with them until they validate successfully.

- Validators don't always track new developments, specifications, or related DTDs and XML Schemas exactly. (As we write this chapter, in fact, to validate an XHTML 1.1 document certain workarounds are necessary—these include validating to the XHTML 1.0 Strict DTD instead of an XHTML 1.1 modularized DTD—and hand-checks are required to make sure no markup outside the restricted subset occurs in any XHTML document that uses only a subset of legal XHTML 1.0 markup.)

On the whole, we think the pros beat the cons hands down, but you can make your own decision on the subject. (Hint: if you decide against validation, you don't need to read any further in this chapter!)

The Validation Process

Although the details vary, here's a step-by-step breakdown of what's involved in performing validation of XHTML documents after the fact:

1. Grab the XHTML document you want to validate or some other relevant document—we also cover a couple of Cascading Style Sheets (CSS) validators in this chapter—you'd like to check for correctness and completeness.

2. Present that document to a validator (such as those we discuss throughout much of this chapter).

3. Read the validator's output, and respond to any error messages or warnings you might find by correcting the code.

4. Repeat the previous two steps until the validator produces no error messages—only warnings that you do not feel compelled to heed (usually, this requires changing your document to avoid certain markup elements, particularly deprecated elements).

It's quite interesting to loop around the final three steps in this four-step process, repairing or rewriting your markup in response to the validator's output. For us, this process usually consists of recognizing some typical errors that are very often caught during the validation process, such as:

Ampersands in URLs Many URLs contain ampersands; however, because the ampersand is a reserved character for XHTML, it's necessary to replace ampersands in URLs with the character entity (&) so the validator does not flag this as an error. In fact, older browsers might also be unable to parse such URLs, so this is a good idea in any case.

Invalid content model usage When one markup element is nested within another, such nesting must be explicitly (or implicitly) part of the content model for the outermost element. The best way to be sure what's legal is to check the relevant XHTML DTD or to look in Master's Reference Part 1 of this book.

Illegal element sequences When we explained the rules for XML syntax, we mentioned that well-formedness requires that elements be properly nested. Thus, the sequence `<strong><cite>Gulliver's Travels</strong></cite>` is invalid, because the innermost element must be closed before the outermost element is closed; in this case `<strong><cite>Gulliver's Travels</cite> </strong>` is well formed (and might therefore also be valid).

Invalid FPI   The name of the string that appears in quotes after the PUBLIC keyword in a DOCTYPE processing instruction is called a formal public identifier (FPI). The FPI is case sensitive; therefore, it's essential to match the formal declaration for any FPI exactly, or "-//W3C/DTD XHTML 1.0 Strict//EN" as an example. For precise FPI syntax, please visit "Choosing a DOCTYPE" at www.htmlhelp.com/tools/validator/doctype.html.

With a little practice, you'll become quite comfortable with your validator of choice (we usually start with HTML-Kit, and then go to the W3C validator for a final pass, but you can use whichever tools work best for you). In the following sections, in fact, we present some of the better choices for such tools that are readily available online.

The W3C Validator

The paragon of HTML and XHTML validators (although not always the most current kernel in the crop) is the W3C's validator, available online at http://validator.w3.org/. As an official outgrowth of the W3C's Web site, this tool offers excellent validation capabilities for a variety of DTDs that include virtually all known HTML DTDs and XHTML DTDs through XHTML 1.0 (with 1.1 support expected virtually any day now). For a complete list of DTDs supported, visit http://validator.w3.org/sgml-lib/catalog.

You can use the W3C's validator in one of two ways:

- By supplying a URI for an Internet-accessible Web document through the primary validator at http://validator.w3.org/. You simply type or paste this information into the Address text box at the midpoint of this page, as shown in Figure 26.1.

- By using the file-upload version of the service, you can browse a local hard disk and then send the file to be validated directly to a Common Gateway Interface (CGI) version of the validator code. For this version, visit http://validator.w3.org/file-upload.html, and use the Browse button to enter the desired file specification in the File text box. Then, click the Validate This Document button to trigger the upload for subsequent analysis. This is depicted in Figure 26.2.

Figure 26.1 *The primary interface for the W3C validator checks Internet-accessible documents.*

Figure 26.2 *The file-upload interface for the W3C validator lets you select and upload single files.*

Either way, the validator returns a Web page that summarizes the status of your Web document, including error messages and/or warnings as appropriate. Using this tool follows the general approach to validation outlined earlier in this chapter—namely, present the document to the validator, read the output, respond to errors or inappropriate warnings, and repeat until such items no longer appear in the validator's output.

For more information on working with this excellent tool, please consult Master's Reference Part 4. This reference covers most of the other things you'll need to know to become comfortable and familiar with the W3C validator.

If you're interested in validation, and in keeping up with the latest and greatest validation tools and techniques, we recommend that you sign up for the www-validator mailing list at `http://lists.w3.org/Archives/Public/www-validator/`. *You can also troll the list archives from this Web page. Past postings and current traffic are excellent sources of information about HTML, XHTML, related DTDs and schemas, and validation tools or techniques of all kinds.*

The developer of the W3C validator, Liam Quin, also offers a Windows-compatible, downloadable version of the same tool, called "A Real Validator," at `http://arealvalidator.com/`. *A 30-day evaluation copy is available for free; registration of this excellent tool costs a mere US$30.00.*

The W3C Online CSS Validator

Because modern XHTML design virtually demands the use of style sheets to manage document presentation as rendered in a Web browser (or other display software), inclusion of inline or external style sheets in such documents is becoming commonplace. Just as you use an HTML or XHTML validator to check syntax and content models for markup against specific DTDs, you can use a CSS validator to check inline or external style sheets against their governing specifications. The W3C CSS Validation Service page appears at `http://jigsaw.w3.org/css-validator/`, as shown in Figure 26.3.

In fact, the W3C CSS validator supports four ways to validate CSS instructions, whether they appear as inline text in XHTML or HTML documents, or in the form of stand-alone style sheets (ASCII text files that normally end with a `.css` extension):

- You can download the CSS validator to your local machine and perform validation there. Windows and a range of Unix systems are supported.

- You can validate a stand-alone CSS style sheet by URI—that is, by providing an Internet-accessible URL where the validator can access the document. An example of such access appears in Figure 26.4.

- You can validate an inline CSS style sheet by cutting the content of the <style>...</style> element and pasting it into a text area for analysis.

- You can validate a stand-alone CSS style sheet by uploading the file in which it resides for analysis, in much the same way you uploaded HTML or XHTML documents to the W3C validator in the preceding section.

Figure 26.3 *The W3C CSS validator provides four ways to validate CSS instructions.*

Figure 26.4 *The W3C CSS Validation Service's URI-based interface lets you specify an Internet-accessible style sheet for analysis.*

Working with this tool will help you improve your understanding of style-sheet structures and syntax, because you'll learn as you interpret and act on its sometimes-arcane error and warning messages. As we started getting familiar with this tool, we found it extremely helpful to keep a good CSS reference handy to help us figure out exactly what the validator was trying to tell us. Some good references include either of Eric A. Meyer's excellent CSS books from O'Reilly & Associates: *Cascading Style Sheets: The Definitive Guide*, ISBN 1565926226, or *CSS Pocket Reference*, ISBN 0596001207, as well as a couple of Web sites he's worked on, such as www.meyerweb.com and http://style.webreview.com.

STG's Online XML Validator

Brown University in Providence, RI, is home to the Scholarly Technology Group (STG). This organization offers a general-purpose XML validation tool at www.stg.brown.edu/service/xmlvalid/. This tool is capable of handling XHTML documents, provided you edit such documents to use XML processing instructions rather than the more typical HTML processing instructions normally associated with XHTML. The beauty of this tool is that it's useful for documents that include references to other XML namespaces, DTDs, or Schemas above and beyond those associated strictly with XHTML. If you're working with such hybrids, you'll find this tool an invaluable item in your validation toolbox, because it can handle just about anything you throw at it.

Although part of the interface to the STG XML Validation Form appears in Figure 26.5, the tool is capable of handling various kinds of input, including:

- File downloads, as shown in Figure 26.5, where a Browse button supports identification of the file to be uploaded and analyzed.

- URI access, where an Internet-accessible document may be identified for subsequent analysis.

- Text box entry, where XML code can be pasted into a text area for delivery to the validator for subsequent analysis.

Figure 26.5 *The STG XML Validation Form handles file uploads, URIs, and a paste buffer.*

This tool is both easily accessible and quite convenient, particularly if you work in an environment where both XML and XHTML are broadly used (as many organizations are starting to do).

The WDG Validator

Under the oversight of Liam Quin, one of the developers of the W3C validator, the Web Design Group (WDG) has operated the HTML Help Web site for several years. An invaluable source for tools and information of all kinds, this site offers its own WDG validator at `www.htmlhelp.com/tools/validator/`. This tool appears to keep up with new and changed specifications much more quickly than its more official counterpart. In fact, the WDG validator supported the XHTML 1.1 specification less than a month after its elevation to recommended status.

As with so many of the other tools of its ilk, the WDG validator supports URI-based validation of Internet-accessible files, upload and validation of local files from your current computer, and a text area into which you can paste markup for upload and subsequent analysis. Unlike many other such tools, however, this one also supports batch mode operation, where you can throw multiple URLs at it in a single file (one URL per line of text only) and it will happily chunk through as many of them as you'd care to line up in a row. The basic interface to the service, with its various options, appears in Figure 26.6.

Figure 26.6 *The WDG Validator offers extra features, plus great documentation and support.*

What we like best about the WDG validator is its infrastructure—that is, there's lots of documentation, additional information, and even access to source code for those alpha geeks interested in looking under the hood. Consequently, you'll find more information about common validation errors, tips on using the validator itself, rationales for validation, and so forth, than you'll find at other sites. Because it helps to soften the blow of learning to use a complex tool, this validator is strongly recommended for those whose background in SGML, HTML, and markup terminology may not be as strong as they might like. This is particularly true for those who try the W3C validator and find themselves intimidated by its many and sometimes unintelligible error messages. In general, we find this validator's error messages a bit friendlier and therefore easier to understand.

WDG's CSSCheck

Simply as a friendlier alternative to the W3C's CSS validator, the WDG's CSSCheck is worth investigating. However, be warned that although this validator generally does a good job with CSS2 properties and selectors, it's not yet fully updated to support CSS2. For more information, or to try this tool, please visit `www.htmlhelp.com/tools/ csscheck/`. If you work with CSS and find the output from the W3C's tool intimidating, you might find that this one makes it a bit easier for you to understand what it's trying to tell you!

Page Valet

As we write this chapter, Page Valet is the only other XHTML validator already equipped to handle XHTML 1.1. Page Valet is actually part of a suite of Web site–management tools called Site Valet (from a company named WebThing) that's available on a subscription basis. Although Page Valet is based on the W3C validator, it also does a good job of softening its error-reporting and warning messages, and it provides a generally friendlier validation tool than its official counterpart. You can access Page Valet at `http://valet .webthing.com/page/`. If properly invoked, Page Valet can also use an accessibility-enhanced DTD developed by the Web Design Group (mentioned previously in this chapter) to check XHTML and HTML documents for potential accessibility or backward compatibility problems with older Web browsers. For those interested in maximally accessible Web pages, this is a valuable added bonus! For more information about this DTD, please visit `www.htmlhelp.org/design/dtd/`.

CAST's Bobby

In British English a bobby is a (helpful and friendly) police officer; in the parlance of CAST (the Center for Applied Special Technology) Bobby is a friendly validation tool that looks for accessibility and usability violations that might keep those with disabilities from accessing or understanding content in a Web site. Section 508 of the U.S. Federal Rehabilitation Act requires that federal Web sites be accessible to people with disabilities, and Bobby is an important tool that can help organizations and agencies down the road meet this Act's requirements. Also, because many federal contractors are also required to comply with this legislation, we see an "accessibility revolution" heading straight for the Web. Here again, Bobby can be a tremendous help. Please visit www.cast.org/bobby for all kinds of information about accessibility and to access the Bobby service to check your HTML and XHTML documents for compliance with the Web accessibility initiative.

The National Cancer Institute has a great site on Section 508 information and initiatives at www.niehs .nih.gov/websmith/508/home.htm. *For the W3C's take on accessibility issues, please visit the Web Accessibility Initiative home page at* www.w3.org/WAI/.

Where to Go from Here

In this chapter, we explored the validation process for XML and XHTML documents. We covered the pros and cons regarding validation, and tried hard to make the case that validation is a good idea. Next, we examined the validation process in general, and took a look at a half-dozen available validation tools of several kinds. Now, not only should you be ready to make use of validation in working with XML and XHTML documents, but you should also be reasonably familiar with some interesting choices of tools and techniques to put the validation process to work.

Where to now?

- Chapter 9 includes a discussion of a great authoring tool called HTML-Kit.

- Chapters 22 and 23 explore and explain the uses, syntax, and semantics of DTDs, should you wish to dig more deeply into the DTDs that describe monolithic or modularized XHTML documents.

- Chapter 30 explains XML Schemas, should you wish to investigate and learn more about XML Schema-based XHTML modules and markup.

- Master's Reference Part 4 provides a description about working with the W3C validator (probably the most popular such tool in use today), and is worth reading if you'd like to try out this tool on your XHTML documents.

Master's
Reference

In This Section

XHTML Elements and Attributes

XHTML

Master's Reference
Part 1

XHTML Elements and Attributes

This section is a comprehensive reference guide to all XHTML elements, including standard elements and some introduced by Netscape Navigator and Microsoft Internet Explorer. For each element, we provide sample code and indicate:

Standard/Usage:	The version of XHTML or HTML in which the element was introduced
Widely Supported:	Whether browsers widely support the element
Empty:	Whether the element is an empty element

For each element, we also list the available attributes; then, for each attribute, we again describe its use with values, provide the HTML version and browser-support information, and show some sample code.

If an element or attribute says it was introduced in HTML 2, 3.2, or 4 and doesn't say that it's deprecated, you can safely use that item in XHTML as well.

If elements and attributes appear in the HTML 4, HTML 3.2, or HTML 2 specifications, the version number appears next to Standard/Usage. For browser-specific elements and attributes, Standard/Usage tells you which browsers or browser versions support them.

You can safely use all HTML 2 elements and attributes—they provide basic functionality, but few layout or design-oriented features.

HTML 3.2 remained backward compatible with HTML 2 but provided many new elements. Included in HTML 3.2 was support for tables, client-side image maps, embedded applets, and many new attributes that help control alignment of objects within documents. You can assume that all common browsers support all HTML 3.2 elements and attributes.

HTML 4 remained backward compatible with other versions of HTML and expanded the capabilities to better address multiple languages and browser technologies, such as speech or Braille. Additionally, most formatting elements and attributes were deprecated in HTML 4 in favor of style sheets, which provide better formatting capabilities.

Because XHTML is a reformulation of HTML 4 as XML, the elements and attributes used are the same. Therefore, if an element or attribute can be used with HTML 4 or earlier, it can be used with XHTML. However, it's suggested that you use style sheets instead of the deprecated elements or attributes.

The current XHTML specification provides three subtypes: XHTML Transitional, XHTML Strict, and XHTML Frameset. The XHTML Transitional DTD accepts the elements and attributes that are deprecated for use in HTML 4 and XHTML 1. For general-purpose Web authoring, this continues to be the best choice. The XHTML Frameset DTD supports frames.

The XHTML Strict DTD focuses on document structure elements, and leaves out all deprecated elements (shown in Table MR1.1) and attributes. This DTD is good if you're authoring for either or both Netscape Navigator 4 and higher or Internet Explorer 4 and higher. We strongly emphasize using clean XHTML markup and style sheets. See Chapter 2 for details on the different specifications and when to use them.

If you want to comply with the XHTML 1.1 specification (released May 31, 2001), you need to stay away from the deprecated elements shown in Table MR1.1. See Master's Reference Part 8 for more on the XHTML 1.1 specification.

Table MR1.1 Deprecated Elements in XHTML 1.0

DEPRECATED ELEMENT	DESCRIPTION	NOTES
applet	Java applet	Deprecated in favor of the object element
basefont	Base font size	Deprecated in favor of CSS
center	Shorthand for div align="center"	Deprecated in favor of CSS
dir	Directory list	Deprecated in favor of unordered lists
font	Local change to font	Deprecated in favor of CSS
isindex	Single line prompt	Deprecated in favor of using input to create text-input controls
menu	Menu list	Deprecated in favor of unordered lists
s	Strikethrough text	Deprecated in favor of CSS
strike	Strikethrough text	Deprecated in favor of CSS
u	Underlined text	Deprecated in favor of CSS

To see a table that shows which attributes are deprecated in which elements in HTML 4.01, visit www.w3.org/TR/html4/index/attributes.html *and check out the Depr column.*

Elements labeled as deprecated throughout this section are acceptable to the XHTML Transitional and Frameset DTDs, but not to the Strict DTD. Elements labeled with earlier versions of HTML but not as deprecated are acceptable for all HTML DTDs, including XHTML Strict. Elements in the XHTML Frameset DTD are labeled as HTML 4 (Frames).

Specifying that an element or attribute is Widely Supported means that approximately 75 to 80 percent of browsers in common use accommodate the element. All recent versions of both Internet Explorer (5.5 and higher) and Netscape Navigator (6 and higher) recognize Widely Supported elements and attributes.

We indicate common variables as follows:

Variable	What You Substitute
n	A number (such as a size)
url	Some form of address (as in a hyperlink)
#rrggbb	A color value (in hex format) *or* a standard color name
...	Some other value, such as a title or a name

Where values are given as a comma-separated list, the values are variable. Where values are given as a pipe-separated list, they're fixed values and you shouzzld choose one.

Common Attributes

A couple attributes apply to almost all elements. These are called *common attributes,* and they are as follows.

lang="..."

Specifies the language used within the section. This attribute is used most often within documents to override site-wide language specifications. Use standard codes for languages, such as DE for German, FR for French, IT for Italian, and HE for Hebrew. See ISO International Standard 639 at

```
http://www.oasis-open.org/cover/iso639a.html
```

for more information about language codes.

Although these codes aren't case sensitive as XHTML attribute values, the ISO requires them to be uppercase in other contexts, such as SGML, so it's better to use capital letters.

Standard/Usage:	HTML 4	Widely Supported:	No

Sample:
```
<p>The following quote is in German. <q lang="DE">Guten tag!</q></p>
```

dir="ltr|rtl"

Specifies the direction (left to right or right to left) for the text used within the section. This attribute is used most often within documents to override site-wide language direction specifications.

Standard/Usage:	HTML 4	Widely Supported:	No

Sample:
```
<p>The following quote is in Hebrew; therefore, it's written right to left, not left
   to right. <q lang="HE" dir="rtl">Hebrew text goes here and is presented right to left,
   not left to right.</q></p>
```

Event Handlers

Each of the following event handlers helps link user actions to scripts. See Master's Reference Part 2, on scripting, for a fuller explanation of their uses, and see Chapter 11 for JavaScript instructions.

onload="..."

Occurs when the browser finishes loading a window or all frames within a frameset. This handler works with body and frameset elements.

onunload="..."

Occurs when the browser removes a document from a window or frame. This handler works with body and frameset elements.

onclick="..."

Occurs when a user clicks the mouse over an element. This handler works with most elements.

ondblclick="..."

Occurs when a user double-clicks the mouse over an element. This handler works with most elements.

onmousedown="..."

Occurs when a user presses the mouse button over an element. This handler works with most elements.

onmouseup="..."

Occurs when a user releases the mouse button over an element. This handler works with most elements.

onmouseover="..."

Occurs when a user moves the mouse over an element. This handler works with most elements.

onmousemove="..."

Occurs when a user moves the mouse while still over an element. This handler works with most elements.

onmouseout="..."

Occurs when a user moves the mouse away from an element. This handler works with most elements.

onfocus="..."

Occurs when a user moves the focus to an element, either with the mouse or the Tab key. This handler works with label, input, select, textarea, and button.

onblur="..."

Occurs when a user moves focus away from an element, either with the mouse or the Tab key. This handler works with label, input, select, textarea, and button.

onkeypress="..."

Occurs when a user presses and releases a key over an element. This handler works with most elements.

onkeydown="..."

Occurs when a user presses a key over an element. This handler works with most elements.

onkeyup="..."

Occurs when a user releases a key over an element. This handler works with most elements.

onsubmit="..."

Occurs when a user submits a form. This handler works only with the form element.

onreset="..."

Occurs when a user resets a form. This handler works only with the form element.

onselect="..."

Occurs when a user selects text in a text field. This handler works with the input and textarea elements.

onchange="..."

Occurs when a user modifies a field and moves the input focus to a different control. This handler works with the input, select, and textarea elements.

XHTML Elements and Attributes

!

<!-- -->

Inserts comments into a document. Browsers do not display comments, although comments are visible in the document source.

Standard/Usage:	HTML 2	**Widely Supported:**	Yes	**Empty:**	No

Sample:

```
<!-- This paragraph was modified on 8-15-01 -->
<p>XML is the latest and greatest in markup languages.</p>
```

<!DOCTYPE>

Appears at the beginning of the document and indicates the version of the document.

Standard/Usage:	HTML 2	**Widely Supported:**	Yes

Samples:

The XHTML Strict standard:

```
<!DOCTYPE html PUBLIC "-//W3C//DTD XHTML 1.0 Strict//EN"
    "http://www.w3.org/TR/xhtml1/DTD/xhtml1-strict.dtd">
```

The XHTML Transitional standard:

```
<!DOCTYPE html PUBLIC "-//W3C//DTD XHTML 1.0 Transitional//EN"
    "http://www.w3.org/TR/xhtml1/DTD/xhtml1-transitional.dtd">
```

The XHTML Frameset standard:

```
<!DOCTYPE html PUBLIC "-//W3C//DTD XHTML 1.0 Frameset//EN"
    "http://www.w3.org/TR/xhtml1/DTD/xhtml1-frameset.dtd">
```

 DOCTYPE *is not an element; therefore, it's not written with a closing tag or a trailing* /. *It's a document type declaration and should be written as it presented in this section.*

a

a

Also called the *anchor* element; identifies a link or a location within a document. You commonly use this element to create a hyperlink, using the href attribute. You can also use the a element to identify sections within a document, using the name attribute.

Standard/Usage:	HTML 2	**Widely Supported:**	Yes	**Empty:**	No

Sample:

```
<a href="http://www.lanw.com/">Visit LANWrights, Inc.</a>
```

accesskey="..."

Assigns a keyboard key to the element.

Standard/Usage: HTML 4   **Widely Supported:**   No

Sample:

```
<a href="help.html" accesskey="h">Help</a>
```

charset="..."

Specifies character encoding of the data designated by the link. Use the name of a character set defined in RFC2045. The default value for this attribute, appropriate for all Western languages, is ISO-8859-1.

Standard/Usage: HTML 4   **Widely Supported:**   No

Sample:

```
<a href="help.html" charset="ISO-8859-1">Help</a>
```

class="..."

Indicates the style class to apply to the a element. Note that you must define the class in a style sheet.

Standard/Usage: HTML 4   **Widely Supported:**   No

Sample:

```
<a href="next.html" class="casual">Next</a>
```

coords="x1,y1,x2,y2,..."

Identifies the coordinates that define a clickable area in a client-side image map. Measures coordinates, in pixels, from the top-left corner of the image.

Standard/Usage: HTML 4   **Widely Supported:**   No

Sample:

```
<a shape="rect" coords="20,8,46,30" href="food.html">Food</a>
```

href="url"

Specifies the relative or absolute location of a file to which you want to provide a hyperlink.

Standard/Usage: HTML 2   **Widely Supported:**   Yes

Sample:

```
<a href="details.html">More Info</a>
```

hreflang="..."

Specifies the language used in the document linked to. Use standard codes for languages, such as DE for German, FR for French, IT for Italian, and HE for Hebrew. See ISO International Standard 639 at

www.oasis-open.org/cover/iso639a.html

for more information about language codes.

Standard/Usage: HTML 4   **Widely Supported:**   No

Sample:

```
<a href="german.html" hreflang="DE">Read this in German!</a>
```

id="..."

Assigns a unique ID selector to an instance of the a element. When you then assign a style to that ID selector, it affects only that one instance of the a element.

Standard/Usage: HTML 4   **Widely Supported:** No

Sample:

```
<a href="next.html" id="123">Next</a>
```

name="..."

Marks a location within the current document with a name. The browser can then quickly move to specific information within a document. You can link to existing named locations in a document by using a partial URL, consisting of just a pound sign (#) and the name (from within that document), or by using a more complete URL with a pound sign and a name at the end (from other documents or sites). This attribute is deprecated; use the id attribute instead of or together with name.

Standard/Usage: HTML 2; deprecated   **Widely Supported:** Yes

Sample:

```
<a href="#ingredients">Ingredients</a>
...
<a name="ingredients" id="ingredients"><h1>Ingredients</h1></a>
```

rel="..."

Specifies relationship hyperlinks.

Standard/Usage: HTML 3.2   **Widely Supported:** No

Sample:

```
<a rel="next" href="otherdoc.html">Other Doc</a>
```

rev="..."

Specifies reverse relationship hyperlinks.

Standard/Usage: HTML 3.2   **Widely Supported:** No

Sample:

```
<a rev="Prev" href="http://www.lanw.com/default.htm">Link</a>
```

shape="rect|circle|poly"

Specifies the type of shape used to represent the clickable area.

Value	Shape Indicated
rect	Rectangle
circle	Circle
poly	Polygon bounded by three or more sides

Standard/Usage: HTML 4   **Widely Supported:** No

Sample:

```
<a shape="rect" coords="20,8,46,30" href="food.html">...</a>
```

style="..."

Specifies style sheet commands that apply to the contents of the a element.

Standard/Usage:	HTML 4	**Widely Supported:**	No

Sample:
```
<a style="background: red" href="page2.html">Page 2</a>
```

tabindex="n"

Indicates where the element appears in the tabbing order of the document.

Standard/Usage:	HTML 4	**Widely Supported:**	No

Sample:
```
<a href="food.html" tabindex="4">Food</a>
```

target="..."

Indicates the name of a specific frame into which you load the linked document. You establish frame names within the frame element. The value of this attribute can be any word.

Standard/Usage:	HTML 4 (Frames)	**Widely Supported:**	Yes

Sample:
```
<a href="/frames/frame2.html" target="pages">Go to Page 2</a>
```

title="..."

Specifies text assigned to the element that you can use for context-sensitive help within the document. Browsers may use this to show tooltips over the hyperlink.

Standard/Usage:	HTML 4	**Widely Supported:**	Yes

Sample:
```
<a href="page2.html" title="Go to the next page">Next page</a>
```

type="..."

Indicates the MIME type of the linked file or object. For example, specify text/html, image/jpeg, application/java, text/css, or text/javascript. For the full list of types, see

```
ftp://ftp.isi.edu/in-notes/iana/assignments/media-types/
```

Standard/Usage:	HTML 4	**Widely Supported:**	No

Sample:
```
<a href="shocknew.dcr" type="application/x-director">Choose Shockwave</a>
```

Other Attributes

The a element also accepts the lang, dir, onclick, ondblclick, onmousedown, onmouseup, onmouseover, onmousemove, onmouseout, onkeypress, onkeydown, and onkeyup attributes.

abbr

Indicates an abbreviation in a document.

Standard/Usage:	HTML 4	**Widely Supported:**	No	**Empty:**	No

Sample:
```
<p><abbr>ABBR</abbr> is an abbreviation for abbreviation.</p>
```

class="..."

Indicates which style class applies to the abbr element.

Standard/Usage:	HTML 4	Widely Supported:	No

Sample:

```
<p><abbr class="casual">ABBR</abbr> is short for abbreviation.</p>
```

id="..."

Assigns a unique ID selector to an instance of the abbr element. When you then assign a style to that ID selector, it affects only that one instance of the abbr element.

Standard/Usage:	HTML 4	Widely Supported:	No

Sample:

```
<p><abbr id="123">ABBR</abbr> is short for abbreviation.</p>
```

style="..."

Specifies style sheet commands that apply to the definition.

Standard/Usage:	HTML 4	Widely Supported:	No

Sample:

```
<p><abbr style="background: blue; color: white">abbr</abbr> is short for abbreviation.</p>
```

title="..."

Specifies text assigned to the element. For the abbr element, use this to provide the expansion of the term. You can also use this attribute for context-sensitive help within the document. Browsers may use this to show tooltips over the text.

Standard/Usage:	HTML 4	Widely Supported:	No

Sample:

```
<p><abbr title="Abbreviation">ABBR</abbr> is short for abbreviation.</p>
```

Other Attributes

The abbr element also accepts the lang, dir, onclick, ondblclick, onmousedown, onmouseup, onmouseover, onmousemove, onmouseout, onkeypress, onkeydown, and onkeyup attributes.

acronym

Indicates an acronym in a document.

Standard/Usage:	HTML 4	Widely Supported:	No	Empty:	No

Sample:

```
<p><acronym>HTTP</acronym> stands for Hypertext Transfer Protocol</p>
```

class="..."

Indicates which style class applies to the acronym element.

Standard/Usage:	HTML 4	Widely Supported:	No

Sample:

```
<p><acronym class="casual">HTTP</acronym> stands for Hypertext Transfer Protocol</p>
```

id="..."

Assigns a unique ID selector to an instance of the acronym element. When you then assign a style to that ID selector, it affects only that one instance of the acronym element.

Standard/Usage: HTML 4 **Widely Supported:** No

Sample:
```
<p><acronym id="123">HTTP</acronym> stands for Hypertext Transfer Protocol</p>
```

style="..."

Specifies style sheet commands that apply to the definition.

Standard/Usage: HTML 4 **Widely Supported:** No

Sample:
```
<p><acronym style="background: blue; color: white">ESP</acronym> stands for
  extra-sensory perception.</p>
```

title="..."

Specifies text assigned to the element. For the acronym element, use this to provide the expansion of the term. You can also use this attribute for context-sensitive help within the document. Browsers may use this to show tooltips over the text.

Standard/Usage: HTML 4 **Widely Supported:** No

Sample:
```
<p><acronym title="Hypertext Transfer Protocol">HTTP</acronym>stands for Hypertext
  Transfer Protocol</p>
```

Other Attributes

The acronym element also accepts the lang, dir, onclick, ondblclick, onmousedown, onmouseup, onmouseover, onmousemove, onmouseout, onkeypress, onkeydown, and onkeyup attributes.

address

Used to provide contact information in a document. This element is sometimes used to contain footer information. The enclosed text is rendered in italics.

Standard/Usage: HTML 2 **Widely Supported:** Yes **Empty:** No

Sample:
```
<address>LANWrights, Inc.<br />
  <a href="mailto:webmaster@lanw.com">Webmaster</a><br />
</address>
```

class="..."

Indicates the style class to apply to the address element.

Standard/Usage: HTML 4 **Widely Supported:** No

Sample:
```
<address class="casual">Author info</address>
```

id="..."

Assigns a unique ID selector to an instance of the address element. When you then assign a style to that ID selector, it affects only that one instance of the address element.

Standard/Usage:	HTML 4	Widely Supported:	No

Sample:

```
<address id="123">Author info</address>
```

style="..."

Specifies style sheet commands that apply to the contents of the address element.

Standard/Usage:	HTML 4	Widely Supported:	Yes

Sample:

```
<address style="background: red">Author info</address>
```

title="..."

Specifies text assigned to the element. You can use this attribute for context-sensitive help within the document. Browsers may use this to show tooltips over the address text.

Standard/Usage:	HTML 4	Widely Supported:	No

Sample:

```
<address title="My Address">Author info</address>
```

Other Attributes

The address element also accepts the lang, dir, onclick, ondblclick, onmousedown, onmouseup, onmouseover, onmousemove, onmouseout, onkeypress, onkeydown, and onkeyup attributes.

applet

Embeds a Java applet object into an XHTML document. Typically, items that appear inside the applet element allow browsers that do not support Java applets to view alternative text. Browsers that do support Java ignore all information between the applet tags. This element is deprecated in HTML 4 in favor of the object element.

Standard/Usage:	HTML 3.2; deprecated	Widely Supported:	Yes	Empty:	No

Sample:

```
<applet code="game.class">It appears your browser does not support Java. You're missing
    out on a whole world of neat things!</applet>
```

align="left|center|right"

Specifies the relative horizontal alignment of the Java applet displayed. For example, a value of center tells the browser to place the applet evenly spaced between the left and right edges of the browser window. This attribute is deprecated in HTML 4 in favor of style sheets.

Standard/Usage:	HTML 3.2; deprecated	Widely Supported:	No

Sample:

```
<applet align="center" code="hangman.class">You lose. Would you like to play again?
    Hit the RELOAD button.<br /></applet>
```

alt="..."

Displays a textual description of a Java applet, if necessary.

Standard/Usage: HTML 3.2   **Widely Supported:** No

Sample:

```
<applet code="hangman.class" alt="A Game of hangman">We could have had a relaxing game of
    hangman if your browser supported Java applets.</applet>
```

archive="url, url"

Used to provide a comma-separated list of URIs of classes and other resources to be preloaded to improve applet performance.

Standard/Usage: HTML 4   **Widely Supported:** Yes

Sample:

```
<applet code="hangman.class" archive="hgman.htm, hgman2.htm">Hangman</applet>
```

code="url"

Specifies the relative or absolute location of the Java bytecode file on the server.

Standard/Usage: HTML 3.2   **Widely Supported:** No

Sample:

```
<applet code="hangman.class">Hangman</applet>
```

codebase="url"

Specifies the directory where you can find all necessary Java class files on a Web server. If you set this attribute, you don't need to use explicit URLs in other references to the class files. For example, you would not need an absolute reference in the code attribute.

Standard/Usage: HIML 3.2   **Widely Supported:** No

Sample:

```
<applet codebase="http://www.lanw.com/" code="hangman.class">If your browser supported
    inline Java applets, you'd be looking at a hangman game right now.</applet>
```

height="n"

Specifies the height (in pixels) of the Java applet object within the document.

Standard/Usage: HTML 3.2   **Widely Supported:** No

Sample:

```
<applet height="200" code="hangman.class">Because your browser does not support inline
    Java applets, we won't be playing Hangman today.</applet>
```

hspace="n"

Specifies an amount of blank space (in pixels) to the left and right of the Java applet within the document.

Standard/Usage: HTML 3.2   **Widely Supported:** No

Sample:

```
<applet hspace="10" code="hangman.class">Sorry. Because your browser does not support
    embedded Java applets, you'll have to play Hangman the old way.</applet>
```

name="..."

Assigns the applet instance a name so other elements can identify it within the document. This attribute is deprecated; use the id attribute instead of or together with name.

    Standard/Usage: HTML 3.2; deprecated   **Widely Supported:** No

    Sample:

```
<applet code="hangman.class" name="Hangman" id="Hangman"></applet>
```

object="url"

Specifies the relative or absolute location of the locally saved Java program.

    Standard/Usage: HTML 4   **Widely Supported:** No

    Sample:

```
<applet object="http://www.lanw.com/hangman.class">Whoops! Your browser does not support
    serialized Java applets. You may want to install a newer Web browser.</applet>
```

title="..."

Specifies text assigned to the element. You can use this attribute for context-sensitive help within the document. Browsers may use this to show tooltips over the embedded applet.

    Standard/Usage: HTML 4   **Widely Supported:** No

    Sample:

```
<applet code="/java/thing.class" title="Thing">Thing</applet>
```

vspace="n"

Specifies the amount of vertical space (in pixels) above and below the Java applet.

    Standard/Usage: HTML 3.2   **Widely Supported:** No

    Sample:

```
<applet vspace="10" code="/hangman.class">If you had a Java-capable browser, you could
    be playing hangman!</applet>
```

width="n"

Specifies the width (in pixels) of a Java applet within a document.

    Standard/Usage: HTML 3.2   **Widely Supported:** No

    Sample:

```
<applet width="350" code="hangman.class">Hangman can be a lot of fun, but it's more fun
    if your browser supports Java. Sorry.</applet>
```

Other Attributes

The applet element also accepts the lang, dir, onclick, ondblclick, onmousedown, onmouseup, onmouseover, onmousemove, onmouseout, onkeypress, onkeydown, and onkeyup attributes.

area

Defines an area within a client-side image map definition (see the map element). It indicates an area where audiences can choose to link to another document.

    Standard/Usage: HTML 3.2   **Widely Supported:** Yes   **Empty:** Yes

    Sample:

```
<area shape="rect" coords="20,8,46,30" href="food.html" />
```

alt="..."

Provides a textual description for users who have text-only browsers.

Standard/Usage: HTML 4; required   **Widely Supported:**   Yes

Sample:
```
<area alt="This blue rectangle links to blue.html" href="blue.html" />
```

accesskey="..."

Associates a keyboard key sequence with the area.

Standard/Usage: HTML 4   **Widely Supported:**   No

Sample:
```
<area accesskey="b" />
```

class="..."

Indicates the style class you want to apply to the area element.

Standard/Usage: HTML 4   **Widely Supported:**   No

Sample:
```
<area class="casual" shape="rect" coords="20,8,46,30" href="food.html" />
```

coords="x1,y1,x2,y2..."

Identifies the coordinates within an image map that define the image map area. Measure coordinates, in pixels, from the top-left corner of the image.

Standard/Usage: HTML 3.2   **Widely Supported:**   Yes

Sample:
```
<area shape="rect" coords="20,8,46,30" href="food.html" />
```

href="url"

Identifies the location of the document you want to load when the indicated image map area is selected.

Standard/Usage: HTML 3.2   **Widely Supported:**   Yes

Sample:
```
<area shape="rect" coords="20,8,46,30" href="food.html" />
```

id="..."

Assigns a unique ID selector to an instance of the area element. When you then assign a style to that ID selector, it affects this instance of the area element.

Standard/Usage: HTML 4   **Widely Supported:**   No

Sample:
```
<area id="123" />
```

nohref="nohref"

Defines an image map area that does not link to another document.

Standard/Usage: HTML 3.2   **Widely Supported:**   Yes

Sample:
```
<area shape="rect" coords="20,8,46,30" nohref="nohref" />
```

shape="default|rect|circle|poly"

Specifies the type of shape used to represent the image map area.

Value	Shape Indicated
rect	Rectangle
circle	Circle
poly	Polygon bounded by three or more sides
default	Any area not otherwise defined

Standard/Usage: HTML 3.2   Widely Supported: Yes

Sample:

```
<area shape="rect" coords="20,8,46,30" href="food.html" />
```

style="..."

Specifies style sheet commands that apply to the image map area.

Standard/Usage: HTML 4   Widely Supported: No

Sample:

```
<area shape="rect" coords="20,8,46,30" href="food.html" style="background: red" />
```

tabindex="n"

Indicates where the image map area appears in the tabbing order of the document.

Standard/Usage: HTML 4   Widely Supported: Yes

Sample:

```
<area shape="rect" coords="20,8,46,30" href="food.html" tabindex="4" />
```

target="..."

Identifies the named frame in which the linked document should load. For example, when users select an area within an image map, the linked document may load in the same frame (the default if target is omitted) or in a different frame, specified by the value of target.

Standard/Usage: HTML 4 (Frames)   Widely Supported: Yes

Sample:

```
<area shape="rect" coords="20,8,46,30" href="food.html" target="leftframe" />
```

title="..."

Specifies text assigned to the element. You can use this attribute for context-sensitive help within the document. Browsers may use this to show tooltips over the image map area.

Standard/Usage: HTML 4   Widely Supported: No

Sample:

```
<area shape="rect" coords="20,8,46,30" href="food.html" title="food" id="food"/>
```

Other Attributes

The area element also accepts the lang, dir, onclick, ondblclick, onmousedown, onmouseup, onmouseover, onmousemove, onmouseout, onkeypress, onkeydown, and onkeyup attributes.

b

b

Indicates text that should appear in boldface.

| Standard/Usage: | HTMI 2 | Widely Supported: | Yes | Empty: | No |

Sample:
```
The afternoon was <b>so</b> hot!
```

class="..."

Indicates which style class applies to the b element.

| Standard/Usage: | HTML 4 | Widely Supported: | No |

Sample:
```
<b class="casual">Boom!</b>
```

id="..."

Assigns a unique ID selector to an instance of the b element. When you assign a style to that ID selector, it affects only that one instance of the b element.

| Standard/Usage: | HTML 4 | Widely Supported: | No |

Sample:
```
I work for <b id="123">Widgets Inc.</b>
```

style="..."

Specifies style sheet commands that apply to the contents of the b tags.

| Standard/Usage: | HTML 4 | Widely Supported: | No |

Sample:
```
<b style="background: red">text with red background</b>
```

title="..."

Specifies text assigned to the element. You can use this attribute for context-sensitive help within the document. Browsers may use this to show tooltips over the boldface

| Standard/Usage: | HTML 4 | Widely Supported: | No |

Sample:
```
<b title="Species">Dog Species</b>
```

Other Attributes

The b element also accepts the lang, dir, onclick, ondblclick, onmousedown, onmouseup, onmouseover, onmousemove, onmouseout, onkeypress, onkeydown, and onkeyup attributes.

base

Identifies the location where all relative URLs in your document originate.

| Standard/Usage: | HTML 2 | Widely Supported: | Yes | Empty: | Yes |

Sample:
```
<base href="http://www.lanw.com/info/" />
```

href="url"

Indicates the relative or absolute location of the base document.

> Standard/Usage: HTML 2; required **Widely Supported:** Yes
> Sample:

```
<base href="http://www.lanw.com/" />
```

target="..."

Identifies the named frame in which you load a document (see the href attribute).

> Standard/Usage: HTML 4 (Frames) **Widely Supported:** Yes
> Sample:

```
<base href="http://www.lanw.com/frames/" target="main" />
```

basefont

Provides a font setting for normal text within a document. Font settings (see the font element) within the document are relative to settings specified with this element. Use this element in the document header (between the head tags). The basefont element is deprecated in HTML 4 in favor of style sheets.

> Standard/Usage: HTML 3.2; deprecated **Widely Supported:** Yes **Empty:** Yes
> Sample:

```
<basefont size="5" />
```

color="#rrggbb" or "..."

Sets the font color of normal text within a document. Color names may substitute for the explicit RGB hexadecimal values. This attribute is deprecated in HTML 4 in favor of style sheets.

> Standard/Usage: HTML 3.2; deprecated **Widely Supported:** Yes
> Sample:

```
<basefont size="2" color="#ff00cc" />
```

face="..., ..."

Specifies the font face of normal text within a document. You can set this attribute to a comma-separated list of font names. The browser selects the first name matching a font available. This attribute is deprecated in HTML 4 in favor of style sheets.

> Standard/Usage: HTML 3.2; deprecated **Widely Supported:** Yes
> Sample:

```
<basefont face="Verdana, Helvetica, Arial" />
```

id="..."

Assigns a unique ID selector to an instance of the basefont element. When you then assign a style to that ID selector, it affects only that one instance of the basefont element.

> Standard/Usage: HTML 4 **Widely Supported:** No
> Sample:

```
<basefont size="+2" id="d3e" />
```

size="n"

Specifies the font size of normal text within a document. Valid values are integer numbers in the range 1 and 7, with 3 being the default setting. This attribute is deprecated in HTML 4 in favor of style sheets.

Standard/Usage: HTML 3.2; deprecated   **Widely Supported:** Yes

Sample:
```
<basefont size="5" />
```

Other Attributes

The basefont element also accepts the lang and dir attributes.

bdo

Indicates text that should appear with the direction (left to right or right to left) specified, overriding other language-specific settings. The bdo element accepts the lang and dir attributes.

Standard/Usage: HTML 4   **Widely Supported:** No   **Empty:**   No

Sample:
```
<p lang="HE" dir="rtl">This Hebrew text contains a number, <bdo="ltr">29381</bdo>,
    that must appear left to right.</p>
```

bgsound

Embeds a background sound file within documents. Use in the document head of documents intended for users who use Internet Explorer.

Standard/Usage: Internet Explorer 2   **Widely Supported:** No   **Empty:**   Yes

Sample:
```
<bgsound src="scream.wav" />
```

loop="n|infinite"

Specifies the number of times a background sound file repeats. The value infinite is the default.

Standard/Usage: Internet Explorer 2   **Widely Supported:** No

Sample:
```
<bgsound src="bugle.wav" loop="2" />
```

src="url"

Indicates the absolute or relative location of the sound file.

Standard/Usage: Internet Explorer 2   **Widely Supported:** No

Sample:
```
<bgsound src="wah.wav" />
```

big

Indicates that text displays in a larger font. Although this element is not deprecated, it's a presentational element and its use is discouraged in favor of style sheets.

Standard/Usage: HTML 3.2   **Widely Supported:** Yes   **Empty:**   No

Sample:
```
<big>Lunch</big>
<p>Lunch will be served at 2 P.M.</p>
```

class="..."

Indicates which style class applies to the big element.

Standard/Usage: HTML 4   **Widely Supported:** No

Sample:

```
<big class="casual">Instructions</big>
```

id="..."

Assigns a unique ID selector to an instance of the big element. When you then assign a style to that ID selector, it affects only that one instance of the big element.

Standard/Usage: HTML 4   **Widely Supported:** No

Sample:

```
<big id="123">REMINDER:</big>
Eat five servings of fruits and vegetables every day!
```

style="..."

Specifies style sheet commands that apply to the contents of the big tags.

Standard/Usage: HTML 4   **Widely Supported:** No

Sample:

```
<big style="background: red">This text is red and big</big>
```

title="..."

Specifies text assigned to the element. You can use this attribute for context-sensitive help within the document. Browsers may use this to show tooltips over the text inside the big tags.

Standard/Usage: HTML 4   **Widely Supported:** No

Sample:

```
<big title="Bigger">This text is bigger</big>
```

Other Attributes

The big element also accepts the lang, dir, onclick, ondblclick, onmousedown, onmouseup, onmouseover, onmousemove, onmouseout, onkeypress, onkeydown, and onkeyup attributes.

blink

A Netscape-specific element that makes text blink on and off. Style sheets offer the same functionality in a more widely recognized syntax (the text-decoration property with a value of blink).

Standard/Usage: Netscape Navigator 1   **Widely Supported:** No   **Empty:** No

Sample:

```
<p><blink>NEW INFO</blink>: We moved!</p>
```

class="..."

Indicates which style class applies to the blink element.

Standard/Usage: HTML 4   **Widely Supported:** No

Sample:

```
<blink class="casual">NEW INFORMATION</blink>
```

id="..."

Assigns a unique ID selector to an instance of the blink element. When you then assign a style to that ID selector, it affects only that one instance of the blink element.

Standard/Usage: HTML 4 **Widely Supported:** No

Sample:
```
<blink id="123">12 Hour Sale!</blink>
```

style="..."

Specifies style sheet commands that apply to the contents of the blink elements.

Standard/Usage: HTML 4 **Widely Supported:** No

Sample:
```
<blink style="background: red">This text is blinking and has a red background if you're using
Netscape Navigator.</blink>
```

blockquote

Useful for quoting a direct source within a document (a block quotation).

Standard/Usage: HTML 2 **Widely Supported:** Yes **Empty:** No

Sample:
```
In So Long and Thanks for All the Fish, Douglas Adams wrote:
<blockquote>Man had always assumed that he was more intelligent than dolphins because he had
achieved so much... the wheel, New York, wars, and so on, whilst all the dolphins had ever
done was muck about in the water having a good time. But conversely the dolphins believed
themselves to be more intelligent than man for precisely the same reasons.</blockquote>
```

cite="..."

Specifies a reference URL for the quotation.

Standard/Usage: HTML 4 **Widely Supported:** No

Sample:
```
<blockquote cite="http://www.clementmoore.com/">Twas the night...</blockquote>
```

class="..."

Indicates which style class applies to the blockquote element.

Standard/Usage: HTML 4 **Widely Supported:** No

Sample:
```
<blockquote class="holiday">Twas the night before Christmas...</blockquote>
```

id="..."

Assigns a unique ID selector to an instance of the blockquote element. When you then assign a style to that ID selector, it affects only that one instance of the blockquote element.

Standard/Usage: HTML 4 **Widely Supported:** No

Sample:
```
In So Long and Thanks for All the Fish, Douglas Adams wrote:
<blockquote id="DAq1">Man had always assumed that he was more intelligent than dolphins
because he had achieved so much...</blockquote>
```

style="..."

Specifies style sheet commands that apply to the contents of the blockquote tags.

Standard/Usage: HTML 4   **Widely Supported:**   No

Sample:

```
<blockquote style="background: red">This quote is red.</blockquote>
```

title="..."

Specifies text assigned to the element. You can use this attribute for context-sensitive help within the document. Browsers may use this to show tooltips over the quoted text.

Standard/Usage: HTML 4   **Widely Supported:**   No

Sample:

```
<blockquote title="Quotation">Quoted text goes here.</blockquote>
```

Other Attributes

The blockquote element also accepts the lang, dir, onclick, ondblclick, onmousedown, onmouseup, onmouseover, onmousemove, onmouseout, onkeypress, onkeydown, and onkeyup attributes.

body

Acts as a container for the body of the document. It's a child of the html element and appears after the head element. In previous versions of HTML, the body element was used to set various color settings and background characteristics of the document; however, in HTML 4 and XHTML, those formatting attributes are deprecated in favor of style sheets.

Standard/Usage: HTML 2; required   **Widely Supported:**   Yes   **Empty:**   No

Sample:

```
<html xmlns="http://www.w3.org/1999/xhtml">
    <head> … </head>
    <body>
        <h1>hello!</h1>
    </body>
</html>
```

alink="#rrggbb" or "..."

Indicates the color of hyperlink text while the text is selected. Color names can substitute for the RGB hexadecimal values. This attribute is deprecated in HTML 4 in favor of style sheets.

Standard/Usage: HTML 3.2; deprecated   **Widely Supported:**   Yes

Sample:

```
<body bgcolor="#000abc" text="#000000" link="#ffffff" vlink="#999999" alink="#ff0000">
    The rest of your XHTML document
</body>
```

background="url"

Specifies the relative or absolute location of an image file that tiles across the document's background. This attribute is deprecated in HTML 4 in favor of style sheets.

Standard/Usage: HTML 3.2; deprecated   **Widely Supported:**   Yes

Sample:

```
<body background="images/slimey.gif">The rest of your XHTML document</body>
```

bgcolor="#rrggbb" or "..."

Indicates the color of a document's background. Color names can substitute for the RGB hexadecimal values. This attribute is deprecated in HTML 4 in favor of style sheets.

Standard/Usage: HTML 3.2; deprecated **Widely Supported:** Yes

Sample:
```
<body bgcolor="#000abc" text="#000000" link-"#ffffff" vlink="#999999" alink="#ff0000">
   The rest of your XHTML document
</body>
```

bgproperties="fixed"

Specifies the behavior of the background image (see the background attribute.) The only current value for this attribute is fixed, which indicates that the background image remains in place as you scroll the document, creating a watermark effect.

Standard/Usage: Internet Explorer 1 **Widely Supported:** No

Sample:
```
<body background="waves.jpg" bgproperties="fixed">The rest of your XHTML document</body>
```

class="..."

Indicates which style class applies to the body element.

Standard/Usage: HTML 4 **Widely Supported:** No

Sample:
```
<body class="casual">The rest of your XHTML document</body>
```

id="..."

Assigns a unique ID selector to an instance of the body element. When you then assign a style to that ID selector, it affects only that one instance of the body element.

Standard/Usage: HTML 4 **Widely Supported:** No

Sample:
```
<body id="123">The rest of your XHTML document</body>
```

leftmargin="n"

Specifies the width (in pixels) of a margin of white space along the left edge of the entire document.

Standard/Usage: Internet Explorer 2 **Widely Supported:** No

Sample:
```
<body leftmargin="30">The rest of your XHTML document</body>
```

link="#rrggbb" or "..."

Indicates the color of hyperlink text within the document for documents not already visited by the browser. Color names can substitute for the RGB hexadecimal values. This attribute is deprecated in HTML 4 in favor of style sheets.

Standard/Usage: HTML 3.2; deprecated **Widely Supported:** Yes

Sample:
```
<body bgcolor="#000abc" text="#000000" link="#ffffff" vlink="#999999" alink="#ff0000">
   The rest of your XHTML document
</body>
```

scroll="yes|no"

Indicates whether scrolling is possible within the document body.

    Standard/Usage: Internet Explorer 4   **Widely Supported:** No

    Sample:

```
<body bgcolor="silver" scroll="no">The rest of your XHTML document</body>
```

style="..."

Specifies style sheet commands that apply to the document body.

    Standard/Usage: HTML 4   **Widely Supported:** No

    Sample:

```
<body style="background: red">The rest of your XHTML document</body>
```

text="#rrggbb" or "..."

Indicates the color of normal text within the document. Color names can substitute for the RGB hexadecimal values. This attribute is deprecated in HTML 4 in favor of style sheets.

    Standard/Usage: HTML 3.2; deprecated   **Widely Supported:** Yes

    Sample:

```
<body bgcolor="#000abc" text="#000000" link="#ffffff" vlink="#999999" alink="#ff0000">
   The rest of your XHTML document
</body>
```

title="..."

Specifies text assigned to the element. You can use this attribute for context-sensitive help within the document. Browsers may use this to show tooltips.

    Standard/Usage: HTML 4   **Widely Supported:** No

    Sample:

```
<body title="Document body">The rest of your XHTML document</body>
```

topmargin="n"

Specifies the size (in pixels) of a margin of white space along the top edge of the entire document.

    Standard/Usage: Internet Explorer 2   **Widely Supported:** No

    Sample:

```
<body topmargin="10">The rest of your XHTML document</body>
```

vlink="#rrggbb" or "..."

Indicates the color of hyperlink text within the document for documents already visited by the browser. Color names can substitute for the RGB hexadecimal values. This attribute is deprecated in HTML 4 in favor of style sheets.

    Standard/Usage: HTML 3.2; deprecated   **Widely Supported:** Yes

    Sample:

```
<body bgcolor="#000abc" text="#000000" link="#ffffff" vlink="#999999" alink="#ff0000">
   The rest of your XHTML document</body>
```

Other Attributes

The body element also accepts the `lang`, `dir`, `onload`, `onunload`, `onclick`, `ondblclick`, `onmousedown`, `onmouseup`, `onmouseover`, `onmousemove`, `onmouseout`, `onkeypress`, `onkeydown`, and `onkeyup` attributes.

br

Breaks a line of continuous text and prevents text alignment around images.

Standard/Usage: HTML 2   **Widely Supported:** Yes   **Empty:** Yes

Sample:
```
I live at: <p>123 Nowhere Ave.<br />New York, NY 12345</p>
```

class="..."

Indicates which style class applies to the element.

Standard/Usage: HTML 4   **Widely Supported:** No

Sample:
```
<br class="casual" />
```

clear="all|left|right|none"

Discontinues alignment of text to inline graphic images. The sample demonstrates how you can force the text to appear after the image and not alongside it.

Standard/Usage: HTML 3.2; deprecated   **Widely Supported:** Yes

Sample:
```
<img src="portrait.jpg" align="right" /><br clear="all" />
<p>The above photo was taken when I was in Florida.</p>
```

id="..."

Assigns a unique ID selector to an instance of the br element. When you then assign a style to that ID selector, it affects only that one instance of the br element.

Standard/Usage: HTML 4   **Widely Supported:** No

Sample:
```
<br id="123" />
```

style="..."

Specifies style sheet commands that apply to the br element.

Standard/Usage: HTML 4   **Widely Supported:** No

Sample:
```
<br style="background: red" />
```

title="..."

Specifies text assigned to the element. You can use this attribute for context-sensitive help within the document. Browsers may use this to show tooltips.

Standard/Usage: HTML 4   **Widely Supported:** No

Sample:
```
<br clear="all" title="stop image wrap" />
```

button

Sets up a button to submit or reset a form as well as to activate a script. Use the img element between the opening and closing button elements to specify a graphical button.

Standard/Usage: HTML 4   **Widely Supported:** No   **Empty:** No

Sample:
```
<button type="button" value="Run Program" onClick(doit)>
   <img src="button.gif" alt="Button" /></button>
```

accesskey="..."

Associates a keyboard key sequence with the button.

| Standard/Usage: | HTML 4 | Widely Supported: | Yes |

Sample:
```
<button accesskey="B">Click Me! </button>
```

class="..."

Indicates which style class applies to the button element.

| Standard/Usage: | HTML 4 | Widely Supported: | No |

Sample:
```
<button class="casual" type="submit" value="Submit">
   <img src="submit.gif" alt="submit" /></button>
```

disabled="disabled"

Denies access to the input method.

| Standard/Usage: | HTML 4 | Widely Supported: | No |

Sample:
```
<button type="submit" disabled="disabled"><img src="button.gif" alt="button" /></button>
```

id="..."

Assigns a unique ID selector to an instance of the input element. When you then assign a style to that ID selector, it affects only that one instance of the input element.

| Standard/Usage: | HTML 4 | Widely Supported: | No |

Sample:
```
<button id="123" type="submit" value="Submit">
   <img src="button.gif" alt="Button" /></button>
```

name="..."

Gives a name to the value you pass to the form processor.

| Standard/Usage: | HTML 4 | Widely Supported: | Yes |

Sample:
```
<button type="button" name="runprog" value="Click to Run">
   <img src="button.gif" alt="Button" /></button>
```

style="..."

Specifies style sheet commands that apply to the element.

| Standard/Usage: | HTML 4 | Widely Supported: | No |

Sample:
```
<button style="background: red" type="button" name="runprog" value="Click to Run">
   <img src="button.gif" alt="Button" /></button>
```

tabindex="n"

Specifies where the input method appears in the tab order. For example, `tabindex="3"` places the cursor at the button element after the user presses the Tab key three times.

Standard/Usage: HTML 4 **Widely Supported:** No

Sample:
```
<button type="button" name="runprog" value="Click to run" tabindex-"5">
   <img src="button.gif" alt="Button" /></button>
```

title="..."

Specifies text assigned to the element. You can use this attribute for context-sensitive help within the document. Browsers may use this to show tooltips over the input method.

Standard/Usage: HTML 4 **Widely Supported:** No

Sample:
```
<button type="submit" name="cc" value="visa" title="VisaCard">
   <img src="visacard.gif" alt="Visa Card button" /></button>
```

type="submit|button|reset"

Indicates the kind of button to create. `submit` produces a button that, when selected, submits all the name-value pairs to the form processor. `reset` sets all the input methods to empty or default settings. `button` creates a button with no specific behavior that can interact with scripts.

Standard/Usage: HTML 4 **Widely Supported:** Yes

Sample:
```
<button type="button" value="Send Data" onClick(verify())>Send Data
   <img src="button.gif" alt="Button" /></button>
```

value="..."

Sets the default value for the button face.

Standard/Usage: HTML 4 **Widely Supported:** No

Sample:
```
<button type="button" name="id" value="Press Me">
   <img src="button.gif" alt="Button" /></button>
```

Other Attributes

The button element also accepts the `lang`, `dir`, `onfocus`, `onblur`, `onclick`, `ondblclick`, `onmousedown`, `onmouseup`, `onmouseover`, `onmousemove`, `onmouseout`, `onkeypress`, `onkeydown`, and `onkeyup` attributes.

C

caption

Used inside a `table` element to specify a description for the table.

Standard/Usage: HTML 3.2 **Widely Supported:** Yes **Empty:** No

Sample:

```
<table>
   <caption valign="top" align="center">Test Grades For Cooking 101</caption>
   <tr><th>Student</th>   <th>Grade</th> </tr>
   <tr><td>B. Smith</td> <td>88</td>    </tr>
   <tr><td>J. Doe</td>    <td>45</td>    </tr>
</table>
```

align="top|bottom|left|right"

Indicates whether the caption appears at the top or bottom, left or right of the table. The values left and right were added in HTML 4, but this attribute is deprecated in HTML 4 in favor of style sheets.

Standard/Usage: HTML 3.2; deprecated   **Widely Supported:**   Yes

Sample:

```
<caption align="top">Seattle Staff Directory</caption>
```

class="..."

Indicates which style class applies to the caption element.

Standard/Usage: HTML 4   **Widely Supported:**   No

Sample:

```
<caption class="chemical">Hydrogen vs. Oxygen</caption>
```

id="..."

Assigns a unique ID selector to an instance of the caption element. When you then assign a style to that ID selector, it affects only that one instance of the caption element.

Standard/Usage: HTML 4   **Widely Supported:**   No

Sample:

```
<table>
   <caption id="123">Great Painters</caption>…
</table>
```

style="..."

Specifies style sheet commands that apply to the contents of the caption element.

Standard/Usage: HTML 4   **Widely Supported:**   No

Sample:

```
<caption style="background: red">This title caption will have a red background.</caption>
```

title="..."

Specifies text assigned to the element. You can use this attribute for context-sensitive help within the document. Browsers may use this to show tooltips over the caption.

Standard/Usage: HTML 4   **Widely Supported:**   Yes

Sample:

```
<caption title="Table caption">Great Painters</caption>
```

Other Attributes

The caption element also accepts the lang, dir, onclick, ondblclick, onmousedown, onmouseup, onmouseover, onmousemove, onmouseout, onkeypress, onkeydown, and onkeyup attributes.

XHTML Elements and Attributes

center

Positions text an equal distance between the left and right edges of the document. This element, now officially replaced by the `<div align="center">`, was included in HTML 3.2 only because of its widespread use.

Standard/Usage:	HTML 3.2; deprecated	**Widely Supported:**	Yes	**Empty:**	No

Sample:

```
<center><blink><h1>ONE-DAY SALE!</h1></blink></center>
```

cite

Provides an in-text citation of a proper title such as the title of a book. Most browsers display the text inside the `cite` tags in italics.

Standard/Usage:	HTML 2	**Widely Supported:**	Yes	**Empty:**	No

Sample:

```
<p>I've read <cite>The Hitchhiker's Guide to the Galaxy</cite> by Douglas Adams.</p>
```

class="..."

Indicates which style class applies to the `cite` element.

Standard/Usage:	HTML 4	**Widely Supported:**	No

Sample:

```
This came from Homer's <cite class="classic">Odyssey</cite>.
```

id="..."

Assigns a unique ID selector to an instance of the `cite` element. When you then assign a style to that ID selector, it affects only that one instance of the `cite` element.

Standard/Usage:	HTML 4	**Widely Supported:**	No

Sample:

```
I read about this in <cite id="123">World Weekly News</cite>.
```

style="..."

Specifies style sheet commands that apply to the contents of the `cite` tags.

Standard/Usage:	HTML 4	**Widely Supported:**	No

Sample:

```
<cite style="background: red">…</cite>
```

title="..."

Specifies text assigned to the element. You can use this attribute for context-sensitive help within the document. Browsers may use this to show tooltips over the cited text.

Standard/Usage:	HTML 4	**Widely Supported:**	No

Sample:

```
<cite title="citation">FDA Vegetable Pamphlet</cite>
```

Other Attributes

The `cite` element also accepts the `lang`, `dir`, `onclick`, `ondblclick`, `onmousedown`, `onmouseup`, `onmouseover`, `onmousemove`, `onmouseout`, `onkeypress`, `onkeydown`, and `onkeyup` attributes.

code

Embeds excerpts of program source code into your document text. This is useful if you want to show program source code within a paragraph of normal text. For showing formatted segments of source code longer than one line, use the pre element.

| **Standard/Usage:** | HTML 2 | **Widely Supported:** | Yes | **Empty:** | No |

Sample:

```
To see the variable's value, use the <code>printf("%0.2f\n", cost);</code> function call.
```

class="..."

Indicates which style class applies to the code element.

| **Standard/Usage:** | HTML 4 | **Widely Supported:** | No |

Sample:

```
The <code class="casual">html</code> element is required.
```

id="..."

Assigns a unique ID selector to an instance of the code element. When you then assign a style to that ID selector, it affects only that one instance of the code element.

| **Standard/Usage:** | HTML 4 | **Widely Supported:** | No |

Sample:

```
<code id="123">while(x) x--;</code>
```

style="..."

Specifies style sheet commands that apply to the contents of the code tags.

| **Standard/Usage:** | HTML 4 | **Widely Supported:** | No |

Sample:

```
<code style="background: red">while(x) x--;</code>
```

title="..."

Specifies text assigned to the element. You can use this attribute for context-sensitive help within the document. Browsers may use this to show tooltips over the code text.

| **Standard/Usage:** | HTML 4 | **Widely Supported:** | No |

Sample:

```
<code title="c code">exit(1);</code>
```

Other Attributes

The code element also accepts the lang, dir, onclick, ondblclick, onmousedown, onmouseup, onmouseover, onmousemove, onmouseout, onkeypress, onkeydown, and onkeyup attributes.

col

Specifies properties for table columns.

| **Standard/Usage:** | HTML 4 | **Widely Supported:** | No | **Empty:** | Yes |

Sample:

```
<table>
  <colgroup>
    <col align="right" />
    <col align="center" />
  </colgroup>
  <tr>
    <td>This cell is aligned right.</td>
    <td>This cell is centered.</td>
  </tr>
</table>
```

align="left|right|center|justify|char"

Specifies how text within the table columns will line up with the edges of the table cells, or if the value is char, on a specific character (the decimal point by default).

Standard/Usage: HTML 4   **Widely Supported:**   No

Sample:

```
<col align="center" />
```

char="..."

Specifies the character on which cell contents will align, if align="char". If you omit the char attribute, the default value is the decimal point in the specified language.

Standard/Usage: HTML 4   **Widely Supported:**   No

Sample:

```
<col align="char" char="," />
```

charoff="n"

Specifies the number of characters from the left at which the alignment character appears.

Standard/Usage: HTML 4   **Widely Supported:**   No

Sample:

```
<col align="char" char="," charoff="7" />
```

id="..."

Assigns a unique ID selector to an instance of the col element. When you assign a style to that ID selector, it affects only that one instance of the col element.

Standard/Usage: HTML 4   **Widely Supported:**   No

Sample:

```
<col id="123" />
```

span="n"

Indicates the number of columns in the group.

Standard/Usage: HTML 4   **Widely Supported:**   No

Sample:

```
<colgroup><col align="right" span="2" /></colgroup>
```

style="..."

Specifies style sheet commands that apply to the columns.

Standard/Usage:	HTML 4	**Widely Supported:**	No

Sample:
```
<col style="background: black" />
```

title="..."

Specifies text assigned to the element. You can use this attribute for context-sensitive help within the document. Browsers may use this to show tooltips over the table column.

Standard/Usage:	HTML 4	**Widely Supported:**	No

Sample:
```
<col title="Table column" />
```

width="n"

Specifies the horizontal dimension of a column (in pixels or as a percentage). Special values of "0*" force the column to the minimum required width, and "2*" requires that the column receive proportionately twice as much space as it otherwise would.

Standard/Usage:	HTML 4	**Widely Supported:**	No

Sample:
```
<col width="100" />
```

valign="top|bottom|middle|baseline"

Vertically position the contents of the table column.

Value	Effect
top	Positions the contents flush with the top of the column
bottom	Positions the contents flush with the bottom of the column
middle	Centers the contents between the top and bottom of the column
baseline	Aligns the contents with the baseline of the current text font

Standard/Usage:	HTML 4	**Widely Supported:**	No

Sample:
```
<col valign="top" />
```

Other Attributes

The col element also accepts the lang, dir, onclick, ondblclick, onmousedown, onmouseup, onmouseover, onmousemove, onmouseout, onkeypress, onkeydown, and onkeyup attributes.

colgroup

Specifies characteristics for a group of table columns.

Standard/Usage:	HTML 4	**Widely Supported:**	No	**Empty:**	No

Sample:

```
<table>
   <colgroup valign="top">
      <col align="right" />
      <col align="center" />
   </colgroup>
   <tr>
      <td>This cell is aligned top and right.</td>
      <td>This cell is aligned top and centered.</td>
   </tr>
</table>
```

align="left|right|center|justify|char"

Specifies how text within the table columns lines up with the edges of the table cells, or if the value is char, on a specific character (the decimal point by default).

Standard/Usage:	HTML 4	Widely Supported:	No

Sample:

```
<colgroup align="center">…</colgroup>
```

char="..."

Specifies the character on which cell contents align, if align="char". If you omit the char attribute, the default value is the decimal point in the specified language.

Standard/Usage:	HTML 4	Widely Supported:	No

Sample:

```
<colgroup align="char" char=",">…</colgroup>
```

charoff="n"

Specifies the number of characters from the left at which the alignment character appears.

Standard/Usage:	HTML 4	Widely Supported:	No

Sample:

```
<colgroup align="char" char="," charoff="7">…</colgroup>
```

id="..."

Assigns a unique ID selector to an instance of the element. When you then assign a style to that ID selector, it affects only that one instance of the element.

Standard/Usage:	HTML 4	Widely Supported:	No

Sample:

```
<colgroup id="123">…</colgroup>
```

span="n"

Indicates how many consecutive columns exist in the column group and to which columns the specified attributes apply.

Standard/Usage:	HTML 4	Widely Supported:	No

Sample:

```
<colgroup span="2" align="left">…</colgroup>
```

style="..."

Specifies style sheet commands that apply to the contents of the colgroup tags.

Standard/Usage: HTML 4   **Widely Supported:**   No
Sample:

```
<colgroup style="color: red">…</colgroup>
```

title="..."

Specifies text assigned to the element. You can use this attribute for context-sensitive help within the document. Browsers may use this to show tooltips over the column group.

Standard/Usage: HTML 4   **Widely Supported:**   No
Sample:

```
<colgroup title="column group">…</colgroup>
```

width="n"

Specifies the horizontal dimension of columns within the column group (in pixels or as a percentage).

Standard/Usage: HTML 4   **Widely Supported:**   No
Sample:

```
<colgroup width="100"><col align="right" />…</colgroup>
```

valign="top|bottom|middle|baseline"

Vertically positions the contents of the table column.

Value	Effect
top	Positions the contents flush with the top of the column group
bottom	Positions the contents flush with the bottom of the column group
middle	Centers the contents between the top and bottom of the column group
baseline	Aligns the contents with the baseline of the current text font

Standard/Usage: HTML 4   **Widely Supported:**   No
Sample:

```
<colgroup valign="top">…</colgroup>
```

Other Attributes

The colgroup element also accepts the lang, dir, onclick, ondblclick, onmousedown, onmouseup, onmouseover, onmousemove, onmouseout, onkeypress, onkeydown, and onkeyup attributes.

d

dd

Contains a definition in a definition list (dl). Use this element inside the dl element. The dd element can contain block-level elements.

Standard/Usage: HTML 2   **Widely Supported:**   Yes   **Empty:**   No
Sample:

```
<dl>
   <dt>Butter</dt>
   <dd>Butter is a dairy product.</dd>
</dl>
```

class="..."

Indicates which style class applies to the dd element.

Standard/Usage:	HTML 4	**Widely Supported**:	No

Sample:

```
<dl>
    <dt>IITML</dt>
    <dd class="casual">Hypertext Markup Language</dd>
</dl>
```

id="..."

Assigns a unique ID selector to an instance of the dd element. When you then assign a style to that ID selector, it affects only that one instance of the dd element.

Standard/Usage:	HTML 4	**Widely Supported**:	No

Sample:

```
<dl>
    <dt>RS-232C</dt>
    <dd id="123">A standard for serial communication between computers.</dd>
</dl>
```

style="..."

Specifies style sheet commands that apply to the definition.

Standard/Usage:	HTML 4	**Widely Supported**:	No

Sample:

```
<dd style="background: blue; color: white">...</dd>
```

title="..."

Specifies text assigned to the element. You can use this attribute for context-sensitive help within the document. Browsers may use this to show tooltips over the definition.

Standard/Usage:	HTML 4	**Widely Supported**:	No

Sample:

```
<dd title="Definition">...</dd>
```

Other Attributes

The dd element also accepts the lang, dir, onclick, ondblclick, onmousedown, onmouseup, onmouseover, onmousemove, onmouseout, onkeypress, onkeydown, and onkeyup attributes.

del

Indicates text marked for deletion in the document. May be either block-level or inline, as necessary.

Standard/Usage:	HTML 4	**Widely Supported**:	No	**Empty**:	No

Sample:

```
<p>HTTP stands for Hypertext Transfer <del>Transport</del>Protocol</p>
```

cite="url"

Indicates the address of the reference (a definitive source, for example) for the deletion.

Standard/Usage:	HTML 4	Widely Supported:	No

Sample:
```
<del cite="http://www.w3.org/">HTML 3.0 was used for 10 years.</del>
```

class="..."

Indicates which style class applies to the del element.

Standard/Usage:	HTML 4	Widely Supported:	No

Sample:
```
<del class="casual">POP stands for Post Office Protocol.</del>
```

datetime="..."

Indicates the date and time in precisely this format: YYYY-MM-DDThh:mm:ssTZD. For example, 2001-07-14T08:30:00-07:00 indicates July 14, 2001, at 8:30 A.M., in U.S. Mountain Time (7 hours from Greenwich time). This time could also be presented as 2001-07-14T08:30:00Z.

Standard/Usage:	HTML 4	Widely Supported:	No

Sample:
```
<del datetime="2001-07-14T08:30:00Z">POP stands for Post Office Protocol.</del>
```

id="..."

Assigns a unique ID selector to an instance of the element. When you then assign a style to that ID selector, it affects only that one instance of the del element.

Standard/Usage:	HTML 4	Widely Supported:	No

Sample:
```
<del id="123">WWW stands for World Wide Web.</del>
```

style="..."

Specifies style sheet commands that apply to the deleted text.

Standard/Usage:	HTML 4	Widely Supported:	No

Sample:
```
<del style="background: blue; color: white">ESP stands for extra-sensory perception.</del>
```

title="..."

Specifies text assigned to the element. You can use this attribute for context-sensitive help within the document. Browsers may use this to show tooltips over the text.

Standard/Usage:	HTML 4	Widely Supported:	No

Sample:
```
<del title="Definition">More deleted text.</del>
```

Other Attributes

The del element also accepts the lang, dir, onclick, ondblclick, onmousedown, onmouseup, onmouseover, onmousemove, onmouseout, onkeypress, onkeydown, and onkeyup attributes.

dfn

Indicates the definition of a term in the document.

| Standard/Usage: | HTML 3.2 | Widely Supported: | No | Empty: | No |

Sample:
```
<dfn>HTTP stands for Hypertext Transfer Protocol.</dfn>
```

class="..."

Indicates which style class applies to the dfn element.

| Standard/Usage: | HTML 4 | Widely Supported: | No |

Sample:
```
<dfn class="computer">POP stands for Post Office Protocol.</dfn>
```

id="..."

Assigns a unique ID selector to an instance of the dfn element. When you then assign a style to that ID selector, it affects only that one instance of the dfn element.

| Standard/Usage: | HTML 4 | Widely Supported: | No |

Sample:
```
<dfn id="123">WWW stands for World Wide Web.</dfn>
```

style="..."

Specifies style sheet commands that apply to the definition.

| Standard/Usage: | HTML 4 | Widely Supported: | No |

Sample:
```
<dfn style="background: blue; color: white">ESP stands for extra-sensory perception.</dfn>
```

title="..."

Specifies text assigned to the element. You can use this attribute for context-sensitive help within the document. Browsers may use this to show tooltips over the definition text.

| Standard/Usage: | HTML 4 | Widely Supported: | No |

Sample:
```
<dfn title="Definition">...</dfn>
```

Other Attributes

The dfn element also accepts the lang, dir, onclick, ondblclick, onmousedown, onmouseup, onmouseover, onmouse-move, onmouseout, onkeypress, onkeydown, and onkeyup attributes.

dir

Contains a directory list. Use the li element to indicate list items within the list. Use ul rather than this deprecated element.

| Standard/Usage: | HTML 2; deprecated | Widely Supported: | Yes | Empty: | No |

Sample:
```
Choose a music genre:
<dir>
   <li><a href="rock/">Rock</a></li>
   <li><a href="country/">Country</a></li>
   <li><a href="newage/">New Age</a></li>
</dir>
```

class="..."

Indicates which style class applies to the dir element.

Standard/Usage:	HTML 4	**Widely Supported:**	No

Sample:
```
<dir class="food">
    <li>Apples</li>
    <li>Kiwis</li>
    <li>Mangos</li>
    <li>Oranges</li>
</dir>
```

compact="compact"

Causes the list to appear in a compact format. This attribute probably will not affect the appearance of the list because most browsers do not present lists in more than one format. It's deprecated in HTML 4.

Standard/Usage:	HTML 2; deprecated	**Widely Supported:**	No

Sample:
```
<dir compact="compact">...</dir>
```

id="..."

Assigns a unique ID selector to an instance of the dir element. When you then assign a style to that ID selector, it affects only that one instance of the dir element.

Standard/Usage:	HTML 4	**Widely Supported:**	No

Sample:
```
<dir id="123">
    <li>Thingie 1</li>
    <li>Thingie 2</li>
</dir>
```

style="..."

Specifies style sheet commands that apply to the dir element.

Standard/Usage:	HTML 4	**Widely Supported:**	No

Sample:
```
<dir style="background: blue; color: white">
    <li>Thingie 1</li>
    <li>Thingie 2</li>
</dir>
```

title="..."

Specifies text assigned to the element. You can use this attribute for context-sensitive help within the document. Browsers may use this to show tooltips over the directory list.

Standard/Usage:	HTML 4	**Widely Supported:**	No

Sample:
```
<dir title="Directory List">...</dir>
```

Other Attributes

The dir element also accepts the lang, dir, onclick, ondblclick, onmousedown, onmouseup, onmouseover, onmouse-move, onmouseout, onkeypress, onkeydown, and onkeyup attributes.

div

Indicates logical divisions within a document. You can use this element to apply alignment, line-wrapping, and particularly style sheet attributes to a section of your document. `<div align="center">` is the official replacement for the center element—although it's also deprecated in favor of using style sheets.

| Standard/Usage: | HTML 3.2; deprecated | Widely Supported: | No | Empty: | No |

Sample:
```
<div align="center" style="background: blue">All About Formic Acid</div>
```

align="left|center|right|justify"

Specifies whether the content of the section aligns with the left or right margins (left, right), if it's evenly spaced between them (center), or if it stretches between the left and right margins (justify). This attribute is deprecated in HTML 4 in favor of style sheets.

| Standard/Usage: | HTML 3.2; deprecated | Widely Supported: | No |

Sample:
```
<div align="right">Look over here!</div>
<div align="left">Now, look over here!</div>
```

class="..."

Indicates which style class applies to the div element.

| Standard/Usage: | HTML 4 | Widely Supported: | No |

Sample:
```
<div class="casual">…</div>
```

id="..."

Assigns a unique ID selector to an instance of the div element. When you then assign a style to that ID selector, it affects only that one instance of the div element.

| Standard/Usage: | HTML 4 | Widely Supported: | No |

Sample:
```
<div id="123">…</div>
```

nowrap="nowrap"

Disables line-wrapping for the section.

| Standard/Usage: | Internet Explorer 4 | Widely Supported: | No |

Sample:
```
<div align="left" nowrap="nowrap">The contents of this section will not automatically
   wrap as you size the window.</div>
```

style="..."

Specifies style sheet commands that apply to the contents of the div tags.

| Standard/Usage: | HTML 4 | Widely Supported: | No |

Sample:
```
<div style="background: red">…</div>
```

title="..."

Specifies text assigned to the element. You can use this attribute for context-sensitive help within the document. Browsers may use this to show tooltips over the contents of the div tags.

Standard/Usage:	HTML 4	**Widely Supported:**	No

Sample:
```
<div title="Title" class="casual">...</div>
```

Other Attributes

The div element also accepts the lang, dir, onclick, ondblclick, onmousedown, onmouseup, onmouseover, onmousemove, onmouseout, onkeypress, onkeydown, and onkeyup attributes.

dl

Contains the dt and dd elements that form the term and definition portions of a definition list.

Standard/Usage:	HTML 2	**Widely Supported:**	Yes	**Empty:**	No

Sample:
```
<dl>
   <dt>Hygeine</dt>
   <dd>Being clean.</dd>
</dl>
```

class="..."

Indicates which style class applies to the dl element.

Standard/Usage:	HTML 4	**Widely Supported:**	No

Sample:
```
<dl class="computer">
   <dt>RAM</dt>
   <dd>Random Access Memory</dd>
</dl>
```

compact="compact"

Causes the definition list to appear in a compact format. This attribute probably will not affect the appearance of the list because most browsers do not present lists in more than one format. It's deprecated in HTML 4.

Standard/Usage:	HTML 2; deprecated	**Widely Supported:**	No

Sample:
```
<dl compact="compact">...</dl>
```

id="..."

Assigns a unique ID selector to an instance of the dd element. When you then assign a style to that ID selector, it affects only that one instance of the dd element.

Standard/Usage:	HTML 4	**Widely Supported:**	No

Sample:
```
<dl id="123">
   <dt>food</dt>
   <dd>We will be eating three meals/day.</dd>
</dl>
```

style="..."

Specifies style sheet commands that apply to contents of the dl tags.

Standard/Usage: HTML 4   **Widely Supported:** No

Sample:

```
<dl style="background: red">…</dl>
```

title="..."

Specifies text assigned to the element. You can use this attribute for context-sensitive help within the document. Browsers may use this to show tooltips over the definition list.

Standard/Usage: HTML 4   **Widely Supported:** No

Sample:

```
<dl title="Definition List">…</dl>
```

Other Attributes

The dl element also accepts the lang, dir, onclick, ondblclick, onmousedown, onmouseup, onmouseover, onmousemove, onmouseout, onkeypress, onkeydown, and onkeyup attributes.

dt

Contains the terms inside a definition list. Place the dt element inside dl tags.

Standard/Usage: HTML 2   **Widely Supported:** Yes   **Empty:** No

Sample:

```
<dl>
   <dt>Hygeine</dt>
   <dd>Being clean.</dd>
</dl>
```

class="..."

Indicates which style class applies to the dt element.

Standard/Usage: HTML 4   **Widely Supported:** No

Sample:

```
<dl>
   <dt class="casual">CUL8R</dt>
   <dd>See You Later</dd>
</dl>
```

id="..."

Assigns a unique ID selector to an instance of the dt element. When you then assign a style to that ID selector, it affects only that one instance of the dt element.

Standard/Usage: HTML 4   **Widely Supported:** No

Sample:

```
<dl>
   <dt id="123">Caffeine</dt>
   <dd>What most people need to start their days</dd>
</dl>
```

style="..."

Specifies style sheet commands that apply to the contents of the dt tags.

| Standard/Usage: | HTML 4 | Widely Supported: | No |

Sample:

```
<dt style="background: red">...</dt>
```

title="..."

Specifies text assigned to the element. You can use this attribute for context-sensitive help within the document. Browsers may use this to show tooltips over the definition term.

| Standard/Usage: | HTML 4 | Widely Supported: | No |

Sample:

```
<dt title="Term">XHTML</dt>
<dd>HTML reformulated as an XML application</dd>
```

Other Attributes

The dt element also accepts the lang, dir, onclick, ondblclick, onmousedown, onmouseup, onmouseover, onmousemove, onmouseout, onkeypress, onkeydown, and onkeyup attributes.

e

em

Makes the text stand out. Browsers usually render the enclosed text in italics or boldface.

| Standard/Usage: | HTML 2 | Widely Supported: | Yes | Empty: | No |

Sample:

```
It's <em>very</em> important to read the instructions before beginning.
```

class="..."

Indicates which style class applies to the em element.

| Standard/Usage: | HTML 4 | Widely Supported: | No |

Sample:

```
Did you say my house was on <em class="urgent">FIRE?!</em>
```

id="..."

Assigns a unique ID selector to an instance of the em element. When you then assign a style to that ID selector, it affects only that one instance of the em element.

| Standard/Usage: | HTML 4 | Widely Supported: | No |

Sample:

```
I have complained <em id="123">ten</em> times about the leaking faucet.
```

style="..."

Specifies style sheet commands that apply to the contents of the em tags.

| Standard/Usage: | HTML 4 | Widely Supported: | No |

Sample:

```
You want this <em style="background: red">when</em>?
```

title="..."

Specifies text assigned to the element. You can use this attribute for context-sensitive help within the document. Browsers may use this to show tooltips over the emphasized text.

Standard/Usage: HTML 4   **Widely Supported:** No

Sample:
```
<em title="Emphasis">...</em>
```

Other Attributes

The em element also accepts the lang, dir, onclick, ondblclick, onmousedown, onmouseup, onmouseover, onmousemove, onmouseout, onkeypress, onkeydown, and onkeyup attributes.

embed

Places an embedded object into a document. Examples of embedded objects include MIDI files and digital video files. Because the embed element is not part of the HTML standard, we suggest you use the object element instead. If the browser does not have built-in support for an object, users will need a plug-in to use the object within the document. This element was introduced in Netscape Navigator, but it's also supported by Internet Explorer.

Standard/Usage: Netscape Navigator 1, Internet Explorer 3   **Widely Supported:** No   **Empty:** Yes

Sample:
```
<embed src="fur_elise.midi" />
```

accesskey="..."

Specifies a keyboard key sequence that binds to the embedded object.

Standard/Usage: Internet Explorer 4   **Widely Supported:** No

Sample:
```
<embed src="st.ocx" accesskey="e" />
```

align="left|right|center|texttop|top|absbottom|absmiddle|baseline|bottom"

Indicates how an embedded object is positioned relative to the document borders and surrounding contents.

Value	Effect
left	Floats the embedded object between the edges of the window, on the left side
right	Floats the embedded object between the edges of the window, on the right side
center	Floats the embedded object between the edges of the window, evenly between left and right
texttop	Aligns the top of the embedded object with the top of the current text
top	Aligns the top of the embedded object with the top of the current text
absmiddle	Aligns the middle of the embedded object with the middle of the current text
absbottom	Aligns the bottom of the embedded object with the bottom of the current text
baseline	Aligns the bottom of the embedded object with the baseline of the surrounding text
bottom	Aligns the bottom of the embedded object with the baseline of the surrounding text

Standard/Usage: Internet Explorer 4   **Widely Supported:** No

Sample:
```
<embed src="song.mid" align="center" />
```

height="n"

Specifies the vertical dimension of the embedded object.

| Standard/Usage: | Netscape Navigator 1.1, Internet Explorer 3; required | Widely Supported: | No |

Sample:

```
<embed src="rocket.avi" width="50" height="40" />
```

src="url"

Indicates the relative or absolute location of the file containing the object you want to embed.

| Standard/Usage: | Netscape Navigator 1.1, Internet Explorer 3; required | Widely Supported: | No |

Sample:

```
<embed src="beethoven_9.midi" />
```

title="..."

Specifies text assigned to the element. You can use this attribute for context-sensitive help within the document. Browsers may use this to show tooltips over the embedded object.

| Standard/Usage: | Internet Explorer 4 | Widely Supported: | No |

Sample:

```
<embed src="explode.avi" title="movie" />
```

width="n"

Indicates the horizontal dimension of the embedded object.

| Standard/Usage: | Netscape Navigator 1.1, Internet Explorer 3; required | Widely Supported: | No |

Sample:

```
<embed src="cartoon.avi" width="50" />
```

Other Attributes

The embed element also accepts the lang, dir, onclick, ondblclick, onmousedown, onmouseup, onmouseover, onmousemove, onmouseout, onkeypress, onkeydown, and onkeyup attributes.

f

fieldset

Groups related form elements.

| Standard/Usage: | HTML 4 | Widely Supported: | No | Empty: | No |

Sample:

```
<form>
   <fieldset>
      ...Logically related field elements...
   </fieldset>...
</form>
```

class="..."

Indicates which style class applies to the fieldset element.

Standard/Usage: HTML 4   **Widely Supported:** No

Sample:
```
<fieldset class="casual">...</fieldset>
```

id="..."

Assigns a unique ID selector to an instance of the fieldset element. When you then assign a style to that ID selector, it affects only that one instance of the fieldset element.

Standard/Usage: HTML 4   **Widely Supported:** No

Sample:
```
<fieldset id="123">...</fieldset>
```

style="..."

Specifies style sheet commands that apply to the contents of the fieldset tags.

Standard/Usage: HTML 4   **Widely Supported:** No

Sample:
```
<fieldset style="background: red">...</fieldset>
```

title="..."

Specifies text assigned to the element. You can use this attribute for context-sensitive help within the document. Browsers may use this to show tooltips over the font text.

Standard/Usage: HTML 4   **Widely Supported:** No

Sample:
```
<fieldset title="Personal data fields">...</fieldset>
```

Other Attributes

The fieldset element also accepts the lang, dir, onclick, ondblclick, onmousedown, onmouseup, onmouseover, onmousemove, onmouseout, onkeypress, onkeydown, and onkeyup attributes.

font

Alters or sets font characteristics of the font the browser uses to display text. This element is deprecated in HTML 4 in favor of style sheets.

Standard/Usage: HTML 3.2; deprecated   **Widely Supported:** Yes   **Empty:** No

Sample:
```
That cat was really <font size="+3">BIG!</font>.
```

color="#rrggbb" or "..."

Indicates the color the browser uses to display text. Color names can substitute for the RGB hexadecimal values. This attribute is deprecated in HTML 4 in favor of style sheets.

Standard/Usage: HTML 3.2; deprecated   **Widely Supported:** Yes

Sample:
```
<font color="#ff0000"><h2>Win A Trip!</h2></font>
<font color="lightblue"><p>That's right! A trip to Hawaii can be yours if you scratch off
    the right number!</font>
```

face="…, …"

Specifies a comma-separated list of font names the browser uses to render text. If the browser does not have access to the first named font, it tries the second, then the third, and so forth. This attribute is deprecated in favor of style sheets.

Standard/Usage:	HTML 4; deprecated	**Widely Supported:**	Yes

Sample:

```
<font size="+1" face="AvantGarde, Helvetica, Lucida Sans, Arial">This text will appear
  in AvantGarde if it's available.</font>
```

size="n"

Specifies the size of the text affected by the font element. You can specify the size relative to the base font size (see the basefont element), which is normally 3. You can also specify the size as a digit in the range 1 through 7. This attribute is deprecated in HTML 4 in favor of style sheets.

Standard/Usage:	HTML 3.2; deprecated	**Widely Supported:**	Yes

Sample:

```
<basefont size="4" />
<font size="+2">This is a font of size 6.</font>
<font size="1">This is a font of size 1.</font>
```

form

Sets up a container for a form element. Within the form element, you can place form input elements such as fieldset, input, select, and textarea.

Standard/Usage:	HTML 2	**Widely Supported:**	Yes
Empty:	No		

Sample:

```
<form method="post" action="/cgi-bin/search.pl">
  Search: <input type=text name="name" size="20" /><br />
  <input type="submit" value="Start Search" />
  <input type="reset" />
</form>
```

accept-charset="…"

Specifies the character encodings for input data that the server processing the form must accept. The value is a list of character sets as defined in RFC2045, separated by commas.

Standard/Usage:	HTML 4	**Widely Supported:**	No

Sample:

```
<form method="post" accept-charset="ISO-8859-1" action="/stat-collector.cgi">…</form>
```

accept="…"

Specifies a list of MIME types, separated by commas, that the server processing the form will handle correctly.

Standard/Usage:	HTML 4	**Widely Supported:**	No

Sample:

```
<form method="post" accept="image/gif, image/jpeg" action="/image-collector.cgi">…</form>
```

action="url"

Specifies the explicit or relative location of the form-processing CGI application.

Standard/Usage: HTML 2; required   **Widely Supported:** Yes

Sample:

```
<form method="post" action="/stat-collector.cgi">…</form>
```

class="..."

Indicates which style class applies to the form.

Standard/Usage: HTML 4   **Widely Supported:** No

Sample:

```
<form method="post" class="casual" action="/stat-collector.cgi">…</form>
```

enctype="..."

Specifies the MIME type used to submit (post) the form to the server. The default value is "application/x-www-form-urlencoded". Use the value "multipart/form-data" when the returned document includes files.

Standard/Usage: HTML 4   **Widely Supported:** No

Sample:

```
<form method="post" enctype="application/x-www-form-urlencoded"
    action="/stat-collector.cgi">…</form>
```

id="..."

Assigns a unique ID selector to an instance of the form element. When you then assign a style to that ID selector, it affects only that one instance of the form element.

Standard/Usage: HTML 4   **Widely Supported:** No

Sample:

```
<form action="/cgi-bin/ttt.pl" method="get" id="123">…</form>
```

method="post|get"

Changes how form data is transmitted to the form processor. When you use get, the form data is given to the form processor in the form of an environment variable (query_string). When you use post, the form data is given to the form processor as the standard input to the program.

Standard/Usage: HTML 2   **Widely Supported:** Yes

Sample:

```
<form method="post" action="/cgi-bin/www-search">
    Enter search keywords: <input type="text" name="query" size="20" />
    <input type="submit" value="search" />
</form>
```

name="..."

Assigns the form a name accessible by bookmark, script, and applet resources. This attribute is deprecated; use the id attribute instead of or together with name.

Standard/Usage: HTML 4; deprecated   **Widely Supported:** No

Sample:

```
<form method="post" action="/cgi-bin/ff.pl" name="ff" id="ff">…</form>
```

style="..."

Specifies style sheet commands that apply to the contents of the form tags.

Standard/Usage:	HTML 4	**Widely Supported:**	No

Sample:

```
<form style="background: red">...</form>
```

target="..."

Identifies in which previously named frame the output from the form processor should appear.

Standard/Usage:	HTML 4 (Frames)	**Widely Supported:**	Yes

Sample:

```
<form target="output" method="get" action="/cgi-bin/thingie.sh">...</form>
```

title="..."

Specifies text assigned to the element. You can use this attribute for context-sensitive help within the document. Browsers may use this to show tooltips over the fill-out form.

Standard/Usage:	HTML 4	**Widely Supported:**	No

Sample:

```
<form method="post" action="/cgi-bin/ff.pl" title="Fill-out form">...</form>
```

Other Attributes

The form element also accepts the lang, dir, onsubmit, onreset, onclick, ondblclick, onmousedown, onmouseup, onmouseover, onmousemove, onmouseout, onkeypress, onkeydown, and onkeyup attributes.

frame

Defines a frame within a frame set (see the frameset element). The frame element specifies the source file and visual characteristics of a frame.

Standard/Usage:	HTML 4 (Frames)	**Widely Supported:**	Yes	**Empty:**	Yes

Sample:

```
<frameset rows="*,70">
    <frame src="frames/body.html" name="body" />
    <frame src="frames/buttons.html" name="buttons" scrolling="no" noresize="noresize" />
</frameset>
```

bordercolor="#rrggbb" or "..."

Specifies the color of the border around the frame. Use the color's hexadecimal RGB values or the color name.

Standard/Usage:	Internet Explorer 4, Netscape Navigator 3	**Widely Supported:**	Yes

Sample:

```
<frame src="hits.html" bordercolor="red" />
```

class="..."

Indicates which style class applies to the frame.

Standard/Usage:	HTML 4	**Widely Supported:**	No

Sample:

```
<frame src="hits.html" class="casual" />
```

frameborder="1|0"

Indicates whether the frame's border is visible. A value of 1 (default) indicates that the border is visible; 0 indicates that it's invisible. Note that Netscape Navigator lists the values as Yes and No.

Standard/Usage: HTML 4 (Frames)   **Widely Supported:** Yes

Sample:
```
<frame src="weather.html" frameborder="0" />
```

id="..."

Assigns a unique ID selector to an instance of the frame element. When you then assign a style to that ID selector, it affects only that one instance of the frame element.

Standard/Usage: HTML 4   **Widely Supported:** No

Sample:
```
<frame src="weather.html" id="123" />
```

longdesc="url"

Specifies the URL of a long description of the frame.

Standard/Usage: HTML 4 (Frames)   **Widely Supported:** Yes

Sample:
```
<frame src="cats.html" longdesc="whycatsrcool.htm" />
```

marginheight="n"

Specifies the vertical dimension (in pixels) of the top and bottom margins in a frame.

Standard/Usage: HTML 4 (Frames)   **Widely Supported:** Yes

Sample:
```
<frame src="cats.html" marginheight="10" />
```

marginwidth="n"

Specifies the horizontal dimension (in pixels) of the left and right margins in a frame.

Standard/Usage: HTML 4 (Frames)   **Widely Supported:** Yes

Sample:
```
<frame src="dogs.html" marginwidth="10" />
```

name="..."

Gives the frame you're defining a name. You can use this name later to load new documents into the frame (see the target attribute) and within scripts to control attributes of the frame. Reserved names with special meaning include _blank, _parent, _self, and _top. This attribute is deprecated; use the id attribute instead of or together with name.

Standard/Usage: HTML 4 (Frames); deprecated   **Widely Supported:** Yes

Sample:
```
<frame src="/cgi-bin/weather.cgi" name="weather" id="weather" />
```

noresize="noresize"

Makes a frame's dimensions unchangeable. Otherwise, if a frame's borders are visible, users can resize the frame by selecting a border and moving it with the mouse.

Standard/Usage: HTML 4 (Frames)   **Widely Supported:** Yes

Sample:
```
<frame src="bottom.html" name="bottom" id="bottom" noresize="noresize" scrolling="no" />
```

scrolling="yes|no|auto"

Indicates whether a scroll bar is present within a frame when text dimensions exceed the dimensions of the frame. Set scrolling="no" when using a frame to display only an image.

> **Standard/Usage:** HTML 4 (Frames)   **Widely Supported:** Yes
>
> **Sample:**

```
<frame name="titleimg" id="titleimg" src="title.gif" scrolling="no" />
```

src="url"

Specifies the relative or absolute location of a document that you want to load within the defined frame.

> **Standard/Usage:** HTML 4 (Frames)   **Widely Supported:** Yes
>
> **Sample:**

```
<frame name="main" id="main" src="intro.html" />
```

style="..."

Specifies style sheet commands that apply to the frame.

> **Standard/Usage:** HTML 4   **Widely Supported:** No
>
> **Sample:**

```
<frame name="main" id="main" src="intro.html" style="background: red" />
```

title="..."

Specifies text assigned to the element. You can use this attribute for context-sensitive help within the document. Browsers may use this to show tooltips over the fill-out form.

> **Standard/Usage:** HTML 4   **Widely Supported:** No
>
> **Sample:**

```
<frame name="main" id="main" src="intro.html" title="Main Frame" />
```

frameset

Contains frame definitions and specifies frame spacing, dimensions, and attributes. Place frame and noframes elements inside frameset tags.

> **Standard/Usage:** HTML 4 (Frames)   **Widely Supported:** Yes   **Empty:** No
>
> **Sample:**

```
<frameset cols="*,70">
   <frame src="frames/body.html" name="body" id="body" />
   <frame src="frames/side.html" name="side" id="side" />
</frameset>
```

border="n"

Specifies the thickness of borders (in pixels) around frames defined within the frameset. You can also control border thickness with the frame element.

> **Standard/Usage:** Netscape Navigator 3, Internet Explorer 4   **Widely Supported:** No
>
> **Sample:**

```
<frameset cols="*,150" border="5">
   <frame src="left.html" name="main" id="main" />
   <frame src="side.html" name="side" id="side" />
</frameset>
```

bordercolor="#rrggbb" or "..."

Sets the color of the frame borders. Color names can substitute for the hexadecimal RGB color values.

Standard/Usage: Netscape Navigator 3, Internet Explorer 4	**Widely Supported:** Yes

Sample:

```
<frameset bordercolor="red" rows="100,*">
  <frame src="top.html" name="title" id="title" />
  <frame src="story.html" name="story" id="story" />
</frameset>
```

class="..."

Indicates which style class applies to the frameset.

Standard/Usage: HTML 4	**Widely Supported:** No

Sample:

```
<frameset bordercolor="red" class="casual">
  <frame src="top.html" name="title" id="title" />
  <frame src="story.html" name="story" id="story" />
</frameset>
```

cols="..."

Specifies the number and dimensions of the vertical frames within the current frameset.

Set cols to a comma-separated list of numbers or percentages to indicate the width of each frame. Use the asterisk (*) to represent a variable width. A frame of variable width fills the space left over after the browser formats space for the other frames (<frameset cols="100,400,*">).

Setting cols with percentage values controls the ratio of frame horizontal space relative to the amount of space available within the browser (<frameset cols="10%,*">).

You cannot use cols and rows in the same element.

Standard/Usage: HTML 4 (Frames)	**Widely Supported:** Yes

Sample:

```
<frameset cols="*,100,*">
  <frame src="left.html" name="left" id="left" />
  <frame src="middle.html" name="middle" id="middle" />
  <frameset rows="2">
    <frame src="top.html" name="top" id="top" />
    <frame src="bottom.html" name="bottom" id="bottom" />
  </frameset>
</frameset>
```

framespacing="n"

Specifies the space (in pixels) between frames within the browser window.

Standard/Usage: Internet Explorer 3	**Widely Supported:** No

Sample:

```
<frameset rows="*,100" framespacing="10">
  <frame src="top.html" name="top" id="top" />
  <frame src="middle.html" name="middle" id="middle" />
</frameset>
```

id="..."

Assigns a unique ID selector to an instance of the frameset element. When you then assign a style to that ID selector, it affects only that one instance of the frameset element.

Standard/Usage: HTML 4   **Widely Supported:**   No

Sample:
```
<frameset rows="*,100" framespacing="10" id="123" >
   <frame src="top.html" name="top" id="top" />
   <frame src="middle.html" name="middle" id="middle" />
</frameset>
```

rows="..."

Specifies the number and dimensions of the horizontal frames within the current frameset.

Set rows to a comma-separated list of numbers or percentages to indicate the height of each frame. Use the asterisk (*) to represent a variable height. A frame of variable height fills the space remaining after the browser formats space for the other frames (<frameset rows="100,400,*">).

Setting rows to a comma-separated list of percentages allows you to control the ratio of frame vertical space relative to the space available within the browser (<frameset rows="10%,*">).

You cannot use rows and cols in the same element.

Standard/Usage: HTML 4 (Frames)   **Widely Supported:**   Yes

Sample:
```
<frameset rows="*,100,*">
   <frame src="top.html" name="top" id="top" />
   <frame src="middle.html" name="middle" id="middle" />
   <frameset cols="2">
      <frame src="bottom1.html" name="left" id="left" />
      <frame src="bottom2.html" name="right" id="right" />
   </frameset>
</frameset>
```

style="..."

Specifies style sheet commands that apply to the contents of the frameset element.

Standard/Usage: HTML 4   **Widely Supported:**   No

Sample:
```
<frameset rows="100,*" style="background: red">
   <frame src="top.html" name="title" id="title" />
   <frame src="story.html" name="story" id="story" />
</frameset>
```

title="..."

Specifies text assigned to the element. You can use this attribute for context-sensitive help within the document. Browsers may use this to show tooltips over the fill-out form.

Standard/Usage: HTML 4   **Widely Supported:**   No

Sample:
```
<frameset rows="100,*" title="Stories">
   <frame src="top.html" name="title" id="title" />
   <frame src="story.html" name="story" id="story" />
</frameset>
```

Other Attributes

The frameset element also accepts the onload and onunload attributes.

h

h*n*

Specifies headings in a document. Headings are numbered 1–6, with h1 representing the heading for the main heading in the document and h3 representing a nested subtopic. Generally, text inside heading elements appears in boldface and may be larger than normal document text.

Standard/Usage: HTML 2   **Widely Supported:**   Yes   **Empty:**   No

Sample:
```
<h1>Caring For Your Canary</h1>
<p>This document explains how you should take care of a canary.</p>
<h2>Feeding</h2>
<h2>Caging</h2>
```

align="left|center|right"

Positions the heading in the left, right, or center of a document. This attribute is deprecated in HTML 4 in favor of style sheets.

Standard/Usage: HTML 3.2; deprecated   **Widely Supported:**   Yes

Sample:
```
<h3 align="center">History Of The Platypus</h3>
```

class="..."

Indicates which style class applies to the h*n* element.

Standard/Usage: HTML 4   **Widely Supported:**   No

Sample:
```
<h1 class="casual" align="left">River Tours</h1>
```

id="..."

Assigns a unique ID selector to an instance of the h*n* element. When you then assign a style to that ID selector, it affects only that one instance of the h*n* element.

Standard/Usage: HTML 4   **Widely Supported:**   No

Sample:
```
<h2 id="123">Paper Products</h2>
```

style="..."

Specifies style sheet commands that apply to the heading.

Standard/Usage: HTML 4   **Widely Supported:**   No

Sample:
```
<h1 style="background: red">Heading 1</h1>
```

title="…"

Specifies text assigned to the element. You can use this attribute for context-sensitive help within the document. Browsers may use this to show tooltips over the heading.

Standard/Usage:	HTML 4	Widely Supported:	No

Sample:

```
<h1 title="Headline">Meals On Wheels Gets New Truck</h1>
```

Other Attributes

The hn elements also accept the lang, dir, onclick, ondblclick, onmousedown, onmouseup, onmouseover, onmousemove, onmouseout, onkeypress, onkeydown, and onkeyup attributes.

head

Contains document head information. The following elements can be used within the document head: link, meta, title, script, base, and style.

Standard/Usage:	HTML 2; required	Widely Supported:	Yes	Empty:	No

Sample:

```
<html>
   <head>
      <title>Making a Peanut-Butter and Jelly Sandwich</title>
      <link rel="parent" href="sandwiches.html" />
   </head>
…</html>
```

profile="url"

Specifies the address of data profiles. You can use this attribute to specify the location of, for example, meta element information.

Standard/Usage:	HTML 4	Widely Supported:	No

Sample:

```
<head profile="http://www.lanw.com/books.htm">…</head>
```

Other Attributes

The head element also accepts the lang and dir attributes.

hr

Draws horizontal lines (rules) in your document. This is useful for visually separating document sections.

Standard/Usage:	HTML 2	Widely Supported:	Yes	Empty:	Yes

Sample:

```
<h2>Birthday Colors</h2>
<hr align="left" width="60%" />
<p>Birthdays are usually joyous celebrations so we recommend bright colors.</p>
```

align="left|center|right"

Positions the line flush left, flush right, or in the center of the document. These settings are irrelevant unless you use the width attribute to make the line shorter than the width of the document. This attribute is deprecated in HTML 4 in favor of style sheets.

> **Standard/Usage:**   HTML 3.2; deprecated   **Widely Supported:**   Yes
>
> **Sample:**

```
<h2 align="left">Shopping List</h2>
<hr width="40%" align="left" />
<ul type="square">
   <li>eggs</li> <li>butter</li> <li>bread</li> <li>milk</li>
</ul>
```

class="..."

Indicates which style class applies to the hr element.

> **Standard/Usage:**   HTML 4   **Widely Supported:**   No
>
> **Sample:**

```
<hr class="casual" width="50%" />
```

color="#rrggbb" or "..."

Specifies the color of the line. A color name can be substituted for the hexadecimal RGB values. Only supported by Internet Explorer; style sheets provide equivalent functionality for a wider variety of browsers.

> **Standard/Usage:**   Internet Explorer 3   **Widely Supported:**   No
>
> **Sample:**

```
<hr color="#09334c" />
```

id="..."

Assigns a unique ID selector to an instance of the hr element. When you then assign a style to that ID selector, it affects only that one instance of the hr element.

> **Standard/Usage:**   HTML 4   **Widely Supported:**   No
>
> **Sample:**

```
<hr id="123" />
```

noshade="noshade"

Specifies that the browser should not shade the line.

> **Standard/Usage:**   HTML 3.2   **Widely Supported:**   Yes
>
> **Sample:**

```
<hr noshade="noshade" align="center" width="50%" />
<img src="bobby.jpg" align="center" border="0" alt="bobby" />
<br clear="all" />
<hr noshade="noshade" align="center" width="50%" />
```

size="n"

Specifies the thickness of the line (in pixels). This attribute is deprecated in HTML 4 in favor of style sheets.

> **Standard/Usage:**   HTML 3.2; deprecated   **Widely Supported:**   Yes
>
> **Sample:**

```
<hr size="10" />
```

style="..."

Specifies style sheet commands that apply to the horizontal rule.

Standard/Usage: HTML 4   Widely Supported: No

Sample:
```
<hr width="50%" style="color: red" />
```

width="n"

Specifies the length of the line. You can specify the value with an absolute number of pixels or as a percentage to indicate how much of the total width available is used. This attribute is deprecated in HTML 4 in favor of style sheets.

Standard/Usage: HTML 3.2; deprecated   Widely Supported: Yes

Sample:
```
<h2 align="center">The End!</h2>
<hr width="85%" />
```

title="..."

Specifies text assigned to the element. You can use this attribute for context-sensitive help within the document. Browsers may use this to show tooltips over the horizontal rule.

Standard/Usage: HTML 4   Widely Supported: No

Sample:
```
<hr title="A line" />
```

Other Attributes

The hr element also accepts the onclick, ondblclick, onmousedown, onmouseup, onmouseover, onmousemove, onmouseout, onkeypress, onkeydown, and onkeyup attributes.

html

Contains the entire document. Place the opening html tag at the top and the closing html tag at the bottom of all your HTML files. (The only code outside of the html tag should be the required DOCTYPE declaration and the optional XML declaration.) The html element is required. Don't forget the XHTML namespace for XHTML documents.

Standard/Usage: HTML 2; required   Widely Supported: Yes   Empty: No

Sample:
```
<?xml version="1.0" encoding="UTF-8" standalone="no"?>
<!DOCTYPE html PUBLIC "-//W3C//DTD XHTML 1.0 Transitional//EN"
    "http://www.w3.org/TR/xhtml1/DTD/xhtml1-transitional.dtd">
<html xmlns="http://www.w3.org/1999/xhtml">
    <head><title>Test Page</title></head>
    <body><h1>Is this working?</h1></body>
</html>
```

version="..."

Specifies the version of HTML used. This attribute is deprecated in XHTML because it contains the same information as the DOCTYPE declaration.

Standard/Usage: HTML 4; deprecated   Widely Supported: No

Sample:
```
<html version="-//W3C//DTD HTML 4.0 Transitional//EN">This is an HTML 4.0 document.
    Not valid XHTML...</html>
```

xmlns="..."

Specifies the XHTML namespace. There's only one possible value for XHTML at this time: xmlns="http://www.w3.org/1999/xhtml".

Standard/Usage:	XHTML 1; required	**Widely Supported:**	No

Sample:

```
<html xmlns="http://www.w3.org/1999/xhtml">...</html>
```

Other Attributes

The html element also accepts the lang and dir attributes.

i

i

Italicizes text.

Standard/Usage:	HTML 2	**Widely Supported:**	Yes	**Empty:**	No

Sample:

```
Mary told me to read <i>Mostly Harmless</i>.
```

class="..."

Indicates which style class applies to the i element.

Standard/Usage:	HTML 4	**Widely Supported:**	No

Sample:

```
This mouse is <i class="casual">enhanced</i>.
```

id="..."

Assigns a unique ID selector to an instance of the i element. When you then assign a style to that ID selector, it affects only that one instance of the i element.

Standard/Usage:	HTML 4	**Widely Supported:**	No

Sample:

```
He called it a <i id="123">doohickie</i>!
```

style="..."

Specifies style sheet commands that apply to italicized text.

Standard/Usage:	HTML 4	**Widely Supported:**	No

Sample:

```
<i style="color: green">green, italicized text</i>
```

title="..."

Specifies text assigned to the element. You can use this attribute for context-sensitive help within the document. Browsers may use this to show tooltips over the italicized text.

Standard/Usage:	HTML 4	**Widely Supported:**	No

Sample:

```
<i title="italicized">italicized text</i>
```

Other Attributes

The i element also accepts the `lang`, `dir`, `onclick`, `ondblclick`, `onmousedown`, `onmouseup`, `onmouseover`, `onmouse-move`, `onmouseout`, `onkeypress`, `onkeydown`, and `onkeyup` attributes.

iframe

Creates floating frames within a document. Floating frames differ from normal frames because they can be manipulated independently within another HTML document.

Standard/Usage:	HTML 4 (Frames)	Widely Supported:	No	Empty:	No

Sample:
```
<iframe name="new_win" id="new_win" src="http://www.lanw.com">…</iframe>
```

align="left|center|right"

Specifies how the floating frame lines up with respect to the left and right sides of the browser window. This attribute is deprecated in favor of style sheets.

Standard/Usage:	HTML 4; deprecated	Widely Supported:	No

Sample:
```
<iframe align="left" src="goats.html" name="g1" id="g1">…</iframe>
```

frameborder="1|0"

Indicates whether the floating frame has visible borders. A value of 1 (default) indicates that the border is visible, and a value of 0 indicates that it is not visible.

Standard/Usage:	HTML 4 (Frames)	Widely Supported:	No

Sample:
```
<iframe src="main.html" name="main" id="main" frameborder="0">…</iframe>
```

height="n"

Specifies the vertical dimension (in pixels) of the floating frame.

Standard/Usage:	HTML 4 (Frames)	Widely Supported:	No

Sample:
```
<iframe src="joe.html" name="Joe" id="Joe" width="500" height="200">…</iframe>
```

hspace="n"

Indicates the size (in pixels) of left and right margins within the floating frame.

Standard/Usage:	Internet Explorer 4	Widely Supported:	No

Sample:
```
<iframe src="joe.html" name="Joe" id="Joe" hspace="10" vspace="10">…</iframe>
```

id="…"

Assigns a unique ID selector to an instance of the `iframe` element. When you then assign a style to that ID selector, it affects only that one instance of the `iframe` element.

Standard/Usage:	HTML 4 (Frames)	Widely Supported:	No

Sample:
```
<iframe src="joe.html" name="Joe" id="Joe">…</iframe>
```

marginheight="n"

Specifies the size of the top and bottom margins (in pixels) within the floating frame.

Standard/Usage: HTML 4 (Frames)   **Widely Supported:**   No

Sample:

```
<iframe src="top.html" name="topbar" id="topbar" marginheight="50">...</iframe>
```

marginwidth="n"

Specifies the size of the left and right margins (in pixels) within the floating frame.

Standard/Usage: HTML 4 (Frames)   **Widely Supported:**   No

Sample:

```
<iframe src="body.html" name="body" id="body" marginwidth="50">...</iframe>
```

name="..."

Assigns the frame a unique name. You can use this name within other frames to load new documents in the frame and to manipulate the attributes of the frame. This attribute is deprecated; use the id attribute instead of or together with name.

Standard/Usage: HTML 4 (Frames); deprecated   **Widely Supported:** No

Sample:

```
<iframe src="jane.html" name="Jane" id="Jane" width="500" height="200">...</iframe>
```

scrolling="yes|no|auto"

Indicates whether the floating frame has scroll bars. The default is auto.

Standard/Usage: HTML 4 (Frames)   **Widely Supported:**   No

Sample:

```
<iframe src="top.html" scrolling="auto">...</iframe>
```

src="url"

Specifies the relative or absolute location of the document file to load in the floating frame.

Standard/Usage: HTML 4 (Frames)   **Widely Supported:**   No

Sample:

```
<iframe name="pics" id="pics" src="pics.htm">...</iframe>
```

style="..."

Specifies style sheet commands that apply to the floating frame.

Standard/Usage: HTML 4 (Frames)   **Widely Supported:**   No

Sample:

```
<iframe src="dots.html" name="dots" id="dots" style="background: red">...</iframe>
```

width="n"

Specifies the horizontal dimension (in pixels) of the floating frame.

Standard/Usage: HTML 4 (Frames)   **Widely Supported:**   No

Sample:

```
<iframe src="joe.html" name="Joe" id="Joe" width="500" height="200">...</iframe>
```

vspace="n"

Indicates the size (in pixels) of top and bottom margins within the floating frame.

Standard/Usage: Internet Explorer 4   **Widely Supported:**   No

Sample:

```
<iframe src="joe.html" name="Joe" id="Joe" hspace="10" vspace="10">…</iframe>
```

Other Attributes

The iframe element also accepts the lang, dir, onclick, ondblclick, onmousedown, onmouseup, onmouseover, onmousemove, onmouseout, onkeypress, onkeydown, and onkeyup attributes.

img

Places an inline image in a document. You can use the attributes ismap and usemap with the img element to implement image maps.

Standard/Usage: HTML 2   **Widely Supported:**   Yes   **Empty:**   Yes

Sample:

```
<img src="images/left_arrow.gif" alt="&lt;-" />
```

align="left|right|top|middle|bottom"

Specifies the appearance of text that is near an inline graphic image. For example, if you use right, the image appears flush to the right edge of the document, and the text appears to its left. Using left produces the opposite effect.

HTML 2 mentions only attribute values of top, middle, and bottom. top aligns the top of the first line of text after the img element to the top of the image. bottom (the default) aligns the bottom of the image to the baseline of the text. middle aligns the baseline of the first line of text with the middle of the image.

HTML 3.2 added left and right to the list of attribute values.

You can use the br element to control specific points where text stops wrapping around an image and continues below the instance of the image.

The align attribute is deprecated in HTML 4 in favor of style sheets.

Standard/Usage: HTML 2; deprecated   **Widely Supported:**   Yes

Sample:

```
<img src="red_icon.gif" align="left" />
It's about time for volunteers to pitch in.<br clear="all" />
```

alt="..."

Provides a textual description of images, which is useful for users who have text-only browsers. Some browsers may also display the alt text as a floating message when the user places the mouse pointer over the image.

Standard/Usage: HTML 2; required   **Widely Supported:**   Yes

Sample:

```
<img src="smiley.gif" alt=":-)" />
```

border="n"

Specifies the width (in pixels) of a border around an image. The default value is usually 0 (no border). The border color is the color of normal text within your document. This attribute is deprecated in favor of style sheets.

Standard/Usage: HTML 3.2; deprecated   **Widely Supported:**   Yes

Sample:

```
<img src="portrait.jpg" border="2" />
```

class="..."

Indicates which style class applies to the image.

Standard/Usage:	HTML 4	Widely Supported:	No

Sample:
```
<img class="casual" src="dots.gif" />
```

controls="control"

If the image is a video file, indicates the playback controls that appear below the image.

Standard/Usage:	Internet Explorer 2	Widely Supported:	No

Sample:
```
<img dynsrc="foo.avi" controls="controls" />
```

dynsrc="url"

Specifies the relative or absolute location of a dynamic image (VRML, video file, and so on).

Standard/Usage:	Internet Explorer 2	Widely Supported:	No

Sample:
```
<img dynsrc="foo.avi" />
```

height="n"

Specifies the vertical dimension of the image (in pixels). If you don't use this attribute, the image appears in its default height. Use this attribute, along with the width attribute, to fit an image within a space. You can fit a large image into a smaller space, and you can spread a smaller image. Some Web designers use the width and height attributes to spread a single pixel image over a large space to produce the effect of a larger solid-color image.

Standard/Usage:	HTML 3.2	Widely Supported:	Yes

Sample:
```
<img src="images/smiley.jpg" width="50" height="50" />
```

hspace="n"

Establishes a margin of white space (in pixels) to the left and right of a graphic image. (See the vspace attribute for how to control the top and bottom margins around an image.) This attribute is deprecated in favor of style sheets.

Standard/Usage:	HTML 3.2; deprecated	Widely Supported:	Yes

Sample:
```
<img src="pics/pinetree.jpg" hspace="20" vspace="15" />
```

id="..."

Assigns a unique ID selector to an instance of the img element. When you then assign a style to that ID selector, it affects only that one instance of the img element.

Standard/Usage:	HTML 4	Widely Supported:	No

Sample:
```
<img src="grapes.jpg" id="123" />
```

ismap="ismap"

Indicates that the graphic image functions as a clickable image map. The ismap attribute instructs the browser to send the pixel coordinates to the server image map CGI application when a user selects the image with the mouse pointer. When HTML 2 established the ismap attribute, image maps were implemented in a server-side fashion only. Now, client-side image maps are more popular (see the usemap attribute).

Standard/Usage:	HTML 2	**Widely Supported:**	Yes

Sample:
```
<a href="/cgi-bin/imagemap/mymap">
<img ismap="ismap" src="images/main.gif" /></a>
```

longdesc="..."

Provides a long textual description of images, which is useful for users who have text-only browsers or who cannot view images for other reasons.

Standard/Usage:	HTML 4	**Widely Supported:**	No

Sample:
```
<img src="smiley.gif" alt=":-)"
  longdesc="This is a smiley face, placed here for decoration." />
```

loop="n|infinite"

Indicates the number of times a video file plays back.

Standard/Usage:	Internet Explorer 2	**Widely Supported:**	No

Sample:
```
<img dynsrc="bar.avi" loop="infinite" />
```

name="..."

Specifies a name by which bookmarks, scripts, and applets can reference the image. This attribute is deprecated; use the id attribute instead of or together with name.

Standard/Usage:	HTML 2; deprecated	**Widely Supported:**	No

Sample:
```
<img src="tweakie.jpg" name="img_1" id="img_1" />
```

src="url"

Specifies the relative or absolute location of a file that contains the graphic image you want to embed in a document.

Standard/Usage:	HTML 2; required	**Widely Supported:**	Yes

Sample:
```
<img src="images/left_arrow.gif" alt="&lt;-" />
```

style="..."

Specifies style sheet commands that apply to the inline image.

Standard/Usage:	HTML 4	**Widely Supported:**	No

Sample:
```
<img src="dots.gif" style="background: red" />
```

title="..."

Specifies text assigned to the element. You can use this attribute for context-sensitive help within the document. Browsers may use this to show tooltips over the image.

Standard/Usage:	HTML 4	**Widely Supported:**	No

Sample:
```
<img src="pics/jill.jpg" title="Image" />
```

usemap="url"

Specifies the location of the client-side image map data (see the map element). Because the map element gives the map data an anchor name, be sure to include the name with the URL of the document that contains the map data.

Standard/Usage: HTML 3.2 **Widely Supported:** Yes

Sample:
```
<img ismap="ismap" src="map1.gif" usemap="maps.html#map1" />
```

vrml="..."

Specifies the absolute or relative location of a VRML world to embed in a document.

Standard/Usage: Internet Explorer 2 **Widely Supported:** No

Sample:
```
<img vrml="vr/myroom.vrml" />
```

vspace="n"

Establishes a margin of white space (in pixels) above and below a graphic image. (See the hspace attribute for how to control the left and right margins of an image.) This attribute is deprecated in favor of style sheets.

Standard/Usage: HTML 3.2; deprecated **Widely Supported:** Yes

Sample:
```
<img src="pics/pinetree.jpg" hspace="20" vspace="15" />
```

width="n"

Specifies the horizontal dimension of the image (in pixels). If you don't use this attribute, the image appears in the default width. Use this attribute, along with the height attribute, to fit an image within a space. You can fit a large image into a smaller space, and you can spread a smaller image. Some Web designers use width and height to spread a single pixel image over a large space to produce the effect of a larger solid-color image.

Standard/Usage: HTML 3.2 **Widely Supported:** Yes

Sample:
```
<img src="images/smiley.jpg" width="50" height="50" />
```

Other Attributes

The img element also accepts the lang, dir, onclick, ondblclick, onmousedown, onmouseup, onmouseover, onmousemove, onmouseout, onkeypress, onkeydown, and onkeyup attributes.

input

Identifies several input methods for forms. This element must appear between the opening and closing form tags.

Standard/Usage: HTML 2 **Widely Supported:** Yes **Empty:** Yes

Sample:
```
<form action="/cgi-bin/order/" method="post">
  <input name="qty" type="text" size="5" />
  <input type="submit" value="order" />
</form>
```

align="left|center|right"

Lines up a graphical submit button (type="image"). The behavior of this element is identical to that of the align attribute of the img element. This attribute is deprecated in HTML 4 in favor of style sheets.

Standard/Usage: HTML 3.2; deprecated   **Widely Supported:**   Yes

Sample:

```
<input type="image" src="picture.gif" align="right" />
```

accept="..."

Specifies a comma-separated list of acceptable MIME types for submitted files.

Standard/Usage: HTML 4   **Widely Supported:**   No

Sample:

```
<input type="file" accept="image/gif, image/jpg" />Please submit an image.
```

accesskey="..."

Specifies a keyboard key sequence that users can use to navigate to the input field.

Standard/Usage: HTML 4   **Widely Supported:**   No

Sample:

```
<input type="checkbox" name="test" value="unproven" accesskey="t" />
```

alt="..."

Provides a textual description of the input element, which is useful for users who have text-only browsers. Some browsers may also display the alt text as a floating message when the user places the mouse pointer over the image.

Standard/Usage: HTML 2   **Widely Supported:**   Yes

Sample:

```
Age: <input type="text" name="age" alt="age" id="123" />
```

checked="checked"

Use with the type="radio" or type="checkbox" to set the default state of those input methods to True.

Standard/Usage: HTML 2   **Widely Supported:**   Yes

Sample:

```
One <input type="checkbox" checked="checked" name="foo" value="1" /><br />
Two <input type="checkbox" name="foo" value="2" /><br />
```

class="..."

Indicates which style class applies to the input element.

Standard/Usage: HTML 4   **Widely Supported:**   No

Sample:

```
<input class="casual" type="text" name="age" />
```

disabled="disabled"

Disables an instance of the input method so data cannot be accepted or submitted.

Standard/Usage: HTML 4   **Widely Supported:**   No

Sample:

```
<input type="password" name="pass" disabled="disabled" />
```

id="..."

Assigns a unique ID selector to an instance of the input element. When you then assign a style to that ID selector, it affects only that one instance of the input element.

Standard/Usage: HTML 4   **Widely Supported:**   No

Sample:

```
Age: <input type="text" name="age" id="123" />
```

ismap="ismap"

Indicates that the input element functions as a clickable image map. type must be equal to image.

Standard/Usage: HTML 2   **Widely Supported:**   Yes

Sample:

```
<input src="mapimage.gif" type="image" ismap="ismap" />
```

maxlength="n"

Indicates the number of characters you can enter into a text input field; only useful to input methods of type text or password. Contrary to the size attribute, maxlength does not affect the size of the input field shown on the screen.

Standard/Usage: HTML 2   **Widely Supported:**   Yes

Sample:

```
Phone: <input type="text" name="phone" maxlength="11" />
```

name="..."

Gives a name to the value you pass to the form processor. For example, if you collect a person's last name with an input method of type text, you assign a value to the name attribute similar to lastname. This establishes a *name-value pair* for the form processor.

Standard/Usage: HTML 2   **Widely Supported:**   Yes

Sample:

```
Enter your last name: <input type="text" name="lastname" size="25" />
```

readonly="readonly"

Indicates that changes to the input method data cannot occur.

Standard/Usage: HTML 4   **Widely Supported:**   No

Sample:

```
<input type="text" name="desc" value="1/4 inch flange assy" readonly="readonly" />
```

size="n"

Specifies the width of the input field, in characters for input fields of type text or password and in pixels for all other input methods.

Standard/Usage: HTML 2   **Widely Supported:**   Yes

Sample:

```
Your Age: <input type="text" name="age" size="5" />
```

src="url"

Implements a graphic image for a submit button. For this to work, indicate type="image".

Standard/Usage: HTML 3.2   **Widely Supported:**   Yes

Sample:

```
<input type="image" src="/images/push-button.gif" />
```

style="..."

Specifies style sheet commands that apply to the input element.

Standard/Usage:	HTML 4	Widely Supported:	No

Sample:

```
<input type="radio" name="food" value="1" style="background: red" />
```

tabindex="n"

Specifies where the input method appears in the tab order.

Standard/Usage:	HTML 4	Widely Supported:	No

Sample:

```
Information:
<input type="text" name="first name" tabindex="1" />
<input type="text" name="middle name" tabindex="2" />
<input type="text" name="last name" tabindex="3" />
```

title="..."

Specifies text assigned to the element. You can use this attribute for context-sensitive help within the document. Browsers may use this to show tooltips over the input method.

Standard/Usage:	HTML 4	Widely Supported:	No

Sample:

```
<input type="radio" name="cc" value="visa" title="visacard" />
```

type="button|checkbox|file|hidden|image|password|radio|reset|submit|text"

Indicates the kind of input method to use:

Value	Effect
button	Creates a generic button that can interact with scripts.
checkbox	Produces a small check box that the user can check or uncheck, depending on the settings.
file	Allows the user to submit a file with the form.
hidden	Creates a hidden field that the user cannot interact with. This field is typically used to transmit data to between the client and server.
image	Replaces the Submit button with an image. The behavior of this value is identical to that of the Submit button, except that the x,y coordinates of the mouse position over the image when selected are also sent to the form processor.
password	Gives the user a simple one-line text input field similar to the text type. However, when users enter data into the field, they do not see individual characters; rather, they see asterisks.
radio	Produces a small radio button that can be turned on and off (in groups of two or more). Use radio buttons when you want a user to select only one of several items. For multiple-value selections, see the checkbox type or the select element.
reset	Sets all the input methods to their empty or default settings.
submit	Produces a button that, when selected, submits all the name-value pairs to the form processor.
text	Produces a simple one-line text input field that is useful for obtaining simple data such as a person's name, a person's age, a dollar amount, and so on. To collect multiple lines of text, use the textarea element.

Standard/Usage: HTML 2   **Widely Supported:**   Yes
Sample:

```
<form method="post" action="/cgi-bin/thingie">
   Name:       <input type="text" name="name" /><br />
   Password:   <input type="password" name="pass" /><br />
   Ice Cream: Vanilla<input type="radio" value="1" checked="checked" name="ice_cream" />
              Chocolate<input type="radio" value="2" name="ice_cream" /><br />
   <input type="submit" value="Send Data..." />
</form>
```

usemap="url"

Indicates the relative or absolute location of a client-side image map to use with the form.

Standard/Usage: HTML 4   **Widely Supported:**   No
Sample:

```
<input src="mapimage.gif" usemap="maps.html#map1" />
```

value="..."

Sets the default value input method. Required when input is set to type="radio" or type="checkbox".

Standard/Usage: HTML 2   **Widely Supported:**   Yes
Sample:

```
<input type="hidden" name="id" value="123" />
```

Other Attributes

The input element also accepts the lang, dir, onfocus, onblur, onselect, onchange, onclick, ondblclick, onmousedown, onmouseup, onmouseover, onmousemove, onmouseout, onkeypress, onkeydown, and onkeyup attributes.

ins

Indicates text to be inserted in the document. May be either block-level or inline, as necessary.

Standard/Usage: HTML 4   **Widely Supported:**   No   **Empty:**   No
Sample:

```
<p>HTTP stands for Hypertext <ins>Transfer</ins> Protocol.</p>
```

cite="url"

Indicates the address of the reference (a definitive source, for example) for the insertion.

Standard/Usage: HTML 4   **Widely Supported:**   No
Sample:

```
<ins cite="http://www.w3.org/">HTML 2 was used for two years.</ins>
```

class="..."

Indicates which style class applies to the ins element.

Standard/Usage: HTML 4   **Widely Supported:**   No
Sample:

```
<ins class="joeadd">POP stands for Post Office Protocol.</ins>
```

datetime="..."

Indicates the date and time in precisely this format: YYYY-MM-DDThh:mm:ssTZD. For example, 2001-07-14T08:30:00-07:00 indicates July 14, 2001, at 8:30 a.m., in U.S. Mountain Time (7 hours from Greenwich time). This time could also be presented as 2001-07-14T08:30:00Z.

Standard/Usage:	HTML 4	**Widely Supported:**	No

Sample:
```
<ins datetime="2001-07-14T08:30:00Z">POP stands for Post Office Protocol.</ins>
```

id="..."

Assigns a unique ID selector to an instance of the ins element. When you then assign a style to that ID selector, it affects only that one instance of the ins element.

Standard/Usage:	HTML 4	**Widely Supported:**	No

Sample:
```
<ins id="123">WWW stands for World Wide Web.</ins>
```

style="..."

Specifies style sheet commands that apply to the inserted text.

Standard/Usage:	HTML 4	**Widely Supported:**	No

Sample:
```
<ins style="background: blue; color: white">ESP stands for extra-sensory perception.</ins>
```

title="..."

Specifies text assigned to the element. You can use this attribute for context-sensitive help within the document. Browsers may use this to show tooltips over the inserted text.

Standard/Usage:	HTML 4	**Widely Supported:**	No

Sample:
```
<ins title="Definition">More inserted text.</ins>
```

Other Attributes

The ins element also accepts the lang, dir, onclick, ondblclick, onmousedown, onmouseup, onmouseover, onmousemove, onmouseout, onkeypress, onkeydown, and onkeyup attributes.

isindex

Inserts an input field into the document so users can enter search queries. The queries then go to a CGI application indicated by the action attribute. This element is deprecated in HTML 4 in favor of the input element.

Standard/Usage:	HTML 2; deprecated	**Widely Supported:**	Yes	**Empty:**	Yes

Sample:
```
<isindex prompt="keyword search" action="/cgi-bin/search.cgi" />
```

prompt="..."

Changes the input prompt for keyword index searches. If you don't specify prompt, the browser displays a default prompt.

Standard/Usage:	HTML 3.2	**Widely Supported:**	Yes

Sample:
```
<isindex prompt="Search for something" />
```

Other Attributes

The isindex element also accepts the lang, dir, id, class, style, and title attributes.

k

kbd

Specifies text to be entered at the keyboard or keystrokes to be done by the user within a document.

| Standard/Usage: | HTML 2 | Widely Supported: | Yes | Empty: | No |

Sample:
```
Press <kbd>Ctrl+S</kbd> to save your document.
```

class="..."

Indicates which style class applies to the kbd element.

| Standard/Usage: | HTML 4 | Widely Supported: | No |

Sample:
```
Now press the <kbd class="casual">F4</kbd> key!
```

id="..."

Assigns a unique ID selector to an instance of the kbd element. When you then assign a style to that ID selector, it affects only that one instance of the kbd element.

| Standard/Usage: | HTML 4 | Widely Supported: | No |

Sample:
```
Press <kbd id="123">F1</kbd> for help.
```

style="..."

Specifies style sheet commands that apply to the text within the kbd tags.

| Standard/Usage: | HTML 4 | Widely Supported: | No |

Sample:
```
<kbd style="background: red">Type me</kbd>
```

title="..."

Specifies text assigned to the element. You can use this attribute for context-sensitive help within the document. Browsers may use this to show tooltips over the keyboard text.

| Standard/Usage: | HTML 4 | Widely Supported: | No |

Sample:
```
Now press the <kbd title="Keyboard stuff">F4</kbd> key.
```

Other Attributes

The kbd element also accepts the lang, dir, onclick, ondblclick, onmousedown, onmouseup, onmouseover, onmousemove, onmouseout, onkeypress, onkeydown, and onkeyup attributes.

l

label

Provides identifying text for a form widget.

Standard/Usage:	HTML 4	**Widely Supported:**	No	**Empty:**	No

Sample:

```
<label for="idname">First Name</label><input type="text" id="idname" />
```

accesskey="..."

Assigns a keystroke to the element.

Standard/Usage:	HTML 4	**Widely Supported:**	No

Sample:

```
<label for="idname" accesskey="h">...</label>
```

class="..."

Indicates which style class applies to the label element.

Standard/Usage:	HTML 4	**Widely Supported:**	No

Sample:

```
<label for="idname" class="short">First Name</label><input type="text" id="idname" />
```

disabled="disabled"

Denies access to the label input method.

Standard/Usage:	HTML 4	**Widely Supported:**	No

Sample:

```
<label for="idname" accesskey="h" disabled="disabled">...</label>
```

for="..."

Specifies the ID of the widget associated with the label.

Standard/Usage:	HTML 4	**Widely Supported:**	No

Sample:

```
<label for="idname">First Name</label><input type="text" id="idname" />
```

id="..."

Assigns a unique ID selector to an instance of the label element. When you then assign a style to that ID selector, it affects only that one instance of the label element.

Standard/Usage:	HTML 4	**Widely Supported:**	No

Sample:

```
<label for="idname" id="234">First Name</label><input type="text" id="idname" />
```

style="..."

Specifies style sheet commands that apply to the label element.

Standard/Usage:	HTML 4	**Widely Supported:**	No

Sample:

```
<label for="idname" style="background: red">First Name</label>
<input type="text" id="idname" />
```

tabindex="n"

Specifies where the label input method appears in the tab order. For example, `tabindex="3"` places the cursor at the label element after the user presses the Tab key three times.

Standard/Usage: HTML 4   **Widely Supported:** No

Sample:
```
Credit card number: <label for="ccard" tabindex="5">Credit Card</label>
<input type="text" name="ccard" />
```

title="..."

Specifies text assigned to the element. You can use this attribute for context-sensitive help within the document. Browsers may use this to show tooltips over the label.

Standard/Usage: HTML 4   **Widely Supported:** No

Sample:
```
<label for="ccard" title="credit card">Credit Card</label>
```

Other Attributes

The label element also accepts the `lang`, `dir`, `onfocus`, `onblur`, `onselect`, `onchange`, `onclick`, `ondblclick`, `onmousedown`, `onmouseup`, `onmouseover`, `onmousemove`, `onmouseout`, `onkeypress`, `onkeydown`, and `onkeyup` attributes.

layer

Defines a layer within a document, which you can then manipulate with JavaScript. Specify the layer's contents by placing markup between the layer tags or by using the src attribute.

Standard/Usage: Netscape Navigator 4   **Widely Supported:** No   **Empty:** No

Sample:
```
<layer src="top.html" height="100" width="100" z-index="4" name="top"
    visibility="show">…</layer>
```

above="..."

Specifies the name of a layer above which the current layer should appear.

Standard/Usage: Netscape Navigator 4   **Widely Supported:** No

Sample:
```
<layer src="grass.gif" z-index="1" name="grass" visibility="show">
    <layer src="dog.gif" above="grass" name="dog">…</layer>
</layer>
```

background="url"

Specifies the relative or absolute location of an image file that the browser tiles as the background of the layer.

Standard/Usage: Netscape Navigator 4   **Widely Supported:** No

Sample:
```
<layer z-index="5" name="info" background="goo.gif"><h1>Hi there</h1></layer>
```

below="..."

Specifies the name of a layer below which the current layer should appear.

Standard/Usage: Netscape Navigator 4   **Widely Supported:** No

Sample:
```
<layer background="road.jpg" name="Road" below="Car">…</layer>
```

bgcolor="#rrggbb" or "..."

Specifies the background color of the layer. Use either the hexadecimal RGB values or the color name.

Standard/Usage: Netscape Navigator 4   **Widely Supported:**   No

Sample:
```
<layer bgcolor="#ff0011">
<div align="center"><h1><blink>EAT AT JOE'S!</blink></h1></div></layer>
```

clip="x1,y1,x2,y2"

Indicates the dimensions of a clipping rectangle that specifies which areas of the layer are visible. Areas outside this rectangle become transparent.

You can give the *x* and *y* coordinates in pixels or as percentages to indicate relative portions of the layer. You can omit x1 and y1 if you want to clip from the top-left corner of the layer.

Standard/Usage: Netscape Navigator 4   **Widely Supported:**   No

Sample:
```
<layer src="hawk.jpg" clip="20%,20%">...</layer>
```

height="n"

Specifies the vertical dimension of the layer (in pixels or as a percentage of the browser window height).

Standard/Usage: Netscape Navigator 4   **Widely Supported:**   No

Sample:
```
<layer src="frame.gif" above="bg" name="frame" width="200" height="200">...</layer>
```

left="n"

Specifies the layer's horizontal position (in pixels) relative to the left edge of the parent layer. Use the top attribute for vertical positioning.

Standard/Usage: Netscape Navigator 4   **Widely Supported:**   No

Sample:
```
<layer left="100" top="150">This layer is at {100,150}.</layer>
```

name="..."

Gives the layer a name by which other layer definitions and JavaScript code can reference it.

Standard/Usage: Netscape Navigator 4   **Widely Supported:**   No

Sample:
```
<layer src="car.gif" name="carpic" above="road">...</layer>
```

src="url"

Specifies the relative or absolute location of the file containing the contents of the layer.

Standard/Usage: Netscape Navigator 4   **Widely Supported:**   No

Sample:
```
<layer src="ocean.jpg">...</layer>
```

top="n"

Specifies the layer's vertical position (in pixels) relative to the top edge of the parent layer. Use the left attribute for horizontal positioning.

Standard/Usage: Netscape Navigator 4   **Widely Supported:**   No

Sample:
```
<layer left="100" top="150">This layer is at {100,150}.</layer>
```

visibility="show|hide|inherit"

Indicates whether the layer is initially visible. A value of show indicates the layer is initially visible; hide indicates the layer is not initially visible; and inherit indicates the layer has the same initial visibility attributes as its parent layer.

Standard/Usage: Netscape Navigator 4 **Widely Supported:** No

Sample:
```
<layer src="grass.gif" z-index="1" name="grass" visibility="show">...</layer>
```

width="n"

Specifies the horizontal dimension of the layer (in pixels or as a percentage of the browser window width).

Standard/Usage: Netscape Navigator 4 **Widely Supported:** No

Sample:
```
<layer src="frame.gif" above="bg" name="frame" width="200" height="200">...</layer>
```

z-index="n"

Specifies where the layer appears in the stack of layers. Higher values indicate a position closer to the top of the stack.

Standard/Usage: Netscape Navigator 4 **Widely Supported:** No

Sample:
```
<layer z-index="0" name="bottom">
You may never see this text if are other layers are above it.</layer>
```

Other Attributes

The layer element also accepts the onfocus, onblur, onselect, onchange, onclick, ondblclick, onmousedown, onmouseup, onmouseover, onmousemove, onmouseout, onkeypress, onkeydown, and onkeyup attributes.

legend

Specifies a description for a fieldset. Use inside fieldset tags.

Standard/Usage: HTML 4 **Widely Supported:** No **Empty:** No

Sample:
```
<fieldset><legend valign="top" align="center">Grades for Cooking 101</legend>...</fieldset>
```

align="top|bottom|left|right"

Indicates whether the legend appears at the top or bottom, left or right of the fieldset. This attribute is deprecated in favor of style sheets.

Standard/Usage: HTML 4; deprecated **Widely Supported:** No

Sample:
```
<legend align="top">Seattle Staff Directory</legend>
```

accesskey="..."

Specifies a keyboard key sequence that users can use to navigate to the legend.

Standard/Usage: HTML 4 **Widely Supported:** No

Sample:
```
<legend accesskey="c">Criteria for Judging</legend>
```

class="..."

Indicates which style class applies to the legend element.

Standard/Usage: HTML 4 **Widely Supported:** No

Sample:
```
<legend class="chemical">Hydrogen vs. Oxygen</legend>
```

id="..."

Assigns a unique ID selector to an instance of the legend element. When you then assign a style to that ID selector, it affects only that one instance of the legend element.

Standard/Usage: HTML 4   **Widely Supported:**   No

Sample:
```
<legend id="123">Great Painters</legend>
```

style="..."

Specifies style sheet commands that apply to the contents of the legend tags.

Standard/Usage: HTML 4   **Widely Supported:**   No

Sample:
```
<legend style="background: red">…</legend>
```

title="..."

Specifies text assigned to the element. You can use this attribute for context-sensitive help within the document. Browsers may use this to show tooltips over the legend.

Standard/Usage: HTML 4   **Widely Supported:**   Yes

Sample:
```
<legend title="sleepy hollow">…</legend>
```

Other Attributes

The legend element also accepts the lang, dir, onclick, ondblclick, onmousedown, onmouseup, onmouseover, onmousemove, onmouseout, onkeypress, onkeydown, and onkeyup attributes.

li

Places items into ordered (see the ol element), menu (see the menu element), directory (see the dir element), and unordered (see the ul element) lists.

Standard/Usage: HTML 2   **Widely Supported:**   Yes   **Empty:**   No

Sample:
```
<p>My favorite foods are:
<ul>
   <li>Pepperoni pizza</li>
   <li>Lasagna</li>
   <li>Taco salad</li>
   <li>Bananas</li>
</ul></p>
```

class="..."

Indicates which style class applies to the li element.

Standard/Usage: HTML 4   **Widely Supported:**   No

Sample:
```
<li class="casual">Dogs</li>
```

compact="compact"

Specifies that the list item appears in a space-saving form. This attribute is deprecated in HTML 4.

Standard/Usage: HTML 2; deprecated   **Widely Supported:**   Yes

Sample:
```
<ul>
   <li>Cola</li>
   <li>Fruit drink</li>
   <li compact="compact">Orange juice</li>
   <li>Water</li>
</ul>
```

id="..."

Assigns a unique ID selector to an instance of the li element. When you then assign a style to that ID selector, it affects only that one instance of the li element.

Standard/Usage: HTML 4   **Widely Supported:**   No

Sample:
```
<li id="123">Bees</li>
```

style="..."

Specifies style sheet commands that apply to the list item.

Standard/Usage: HTML 4   **Widely Supported:**   No

Sample:
```
<li style="background: red">Fruit drink</li>
```

title="..."

Specifies text assigned to the element. You can use this attribute for context-sensitive help within the document. Browsers may use this to show tooltips over the list item.

Standard/Usage: HTML 4   **Widely Supported:**   No

Sample:
```
<li title="List Item">Thingie</li>
```

type="..."

Specifies the bullets for each unordered list item (see the ul element) or the numbering for each ordered list item (see the ol element). If you omit the type attribute, the browser chooses a default type.

Valid type values for unordered lists are disc, square, and circle.

Valid type values for ordered lists are 1 for Arabic numbers, a for lowercase letters, A for uppercase letters, i for lowercase Roman numerals, and I for uppercase Roman numerals.

The type attribute is deprecated in favor of style sheets.

Standard/Usage: HTML 3.2; deprecated   **Widely Supported:**   Yes

Sample:
```
<ul>
   <li type="square">Food</li>
   <ol>
      <li type="1">Spaghetti</li>
      <li type="1">Tossed salad</li>
   </ol>
</ul>
```

value="..."

Sets a number in an ordered list. Use this attribute to continue a list after interrupting it with something else in your document. You can also set a number in an ordered list with the `start` attribute of the `ol` element.

Because unordered lists do not increment, the `value` attribute is meaningless when used with them. This attribute is deprecated in favor of style sheets.

Standard/Usage: HTML 3.2; deprecated   **Widely Supported:**   Yes

Sample:
```
<ol type="1">
    <li value="5">Watch</li>
    <li>Compass</li>
</ol>
```

Other Attributes

The `li` element also accepts the `lang`, `dir`, `onclick`, `ondblclick`, `onmousedown`, `onmouseup`, `onmouseover`, `onmousemove`, `onmouseout`, `onkeypress`, `onkeydown`, and `onkeyup` attributes.

link

An empty element that establishes relationships between the current document and other documents. Use this element within the `head` section. For example, if you access the current document by choosing a hyperlink from the site's home page, you can establish a relationship between the current document and the site's home page (see the `rel` attribute). At this time, however, most browsers don't use most of these relationships. You can place several `link` elements within the `head` section of your document to define multiple relationships.

With newer implementations of HTML, you use the `link` element to establish information about Cascading Style Sheets (CSS). Some other relationships (link types) that the `link` element defines with either the `rel` or `rev` attribute include the following:

Value of `rel` or `rev`	References
alternate	A different version of the same document. When used with `lang`, `alternate` implies a translated document; when used with `media`, it implies a version for a different medium.
appendix	An appendix
bookmark	A bookmark, which links to a important entry point within a longer document
chapter	A chapter
contents	A table of contents
copyright	A copyright notice
glossary	A glossary of terms
help	A document offering help or more information
index	An index
next	The next document in a series (use with `rel`)
prev	The previous document in a series (use with `rev`)
section	A section
start	The first document in a series
stylesheet	An external style sheet
subsection	A subsection

Standard/Usage:	HTML 2	Widely Supported:	Yes	Empty:	Yes

Sample:

```
<head>
    <title>Prices</title>
    <link rel="top" href="http://www.lanw.com/" />
    <link rel="search" href="http://www.lanw.com/search.html" />
</head>
```

charset="..."

Specifies character encoding of the data designated by the link. Use the name of a character set defined in RFC2045. The default value for this attribute, appropriate for all Western languages, is ISO-8859-1.

Standard/Usage:	HTML 4	Widely Supported:	No

Sample:

```
<link rel="top" href="http://www.lanw.com/" charset="ISO-8859-1" />
```

href="url"

Indicates the relative or absolute location of the resource you're establishing a relationship to/from.

Standard/Usage:	HTML 2	Widely Supported:	Yes

Sample:

```
<link rel="prev" href="page1.html" />
```

hreflang="..."

Specifies the language used in the document linked to. Use standard codes for languages, such as DE for German, FR for French, IT for Italian, and HE for Hebrew. See ISO International Standard 639 at

```
www.oasis-open.org/cover/iso639a.html
```

for more information about language codes.

Standard/Usage:	HTML 4	Widely Supported:	No

Sample:

```
<link href="german.html" hreflang="DE" />
```

media="..."

Specifies the destination medium for style information. It may be a single type or a comma-separated list. Media types include the following:

Value	Description
all	Applies to all devices
braille	For Braille tactile feedback devices
print	For traditional printed material and for documents on screen viewed in print preview mode
projection	For projectors
screen	For online viewing (default setting)
speech	For a speech synthesizer

Standard/Usage:	HTML 4	Widely Supported:	No

Sample:

```
<link media="screen" rel="stylesheet" href="/global.css" />
```

rel="..."

Defines the relationship you're establishing between the current document and another resource. The values for this attribute are the link types provided in the element definition section.

Standard/Usage: HTML 2   **Widely Supported:**   Yes

Sample:
```
<head>
    <link rel="help" href="/help/index.html" />
    <link rel="stylesheet" href="sitehead.css" />
</head>
```

rev="..."

Establishes reverse relationships between the current document and other resources. The values for this attribute are the link types provided in the element definition section.

Standard/Usage: HTML 2   **Widely Supported:**   Yes

Sample:
```
<link rev="stylesheet" href="/global.css" />
```

target="..."

Specifies the name of a frame in which the referenced link appears.

Standard/Usage: HTML 4   **Widely Supported:**   No

Sample:
```
<link target="_blank" rel="home" href="http://www.lanw.com/" />
```

title="..."

Specifies text assigned to the element that can be used for context-sensitive help within the document. Browsers may use this to show tooltips.

Standard/Usage: HTML 4   **Widely Supported:**   Yes

Sample:
```
<link rel="top" href="/index.html" title="Home Page" />
```

type="..."

Specifies the MIME type of a style sheet to import with the link element.

Standard/Usage: HTML 4   **Widely Supported:**   No

Sample:
```
<link rel="stylesheet" type="text/css" href="/style/main.css" />
```

Other Attributes

The link element also accepts the lang, dir, onfocus, onblur, onchange, onselect, onclick, ondblclick, onmouse-down, onmouseup, onmouseover, onmousemove, onmouseout, onkeypress, onkeydown, and onkeyup attributes.

map   853

m

map

Specifies a container for client-side image map data. You use the area element inside the map tags.

Standard/Usage: HTML 3.2   **Widely Supported:** Yes   **Empty:** No

Sample:
```
<map name="mainmap" id="mainmap">
    <area nohref="nohref"    alt="home"   shape="rect"  coords="0,0,100,100" />
    <area href="yellow.html" alt="yellow" shape="rect"  coords="100,0,200,100" />
    <area href="blue.html"   alt="blue"   shape="rect"  coords="0,100,100,200" />
    <area href="red.html"    alt="red"    shape="rect"  coords="100,100,200,200" />
</map>
```

class="..."

Indicates which style class applies to the element.

Standard/Usage: HTML 4   **Widely Supported:** No

Sample:
```
<map class="casual" name="simba" id="simba">...</map>
```

id="..."

Indicates an identifier to associate with the map. You can also use this to apply styles to the object.

Standard/Usage: HTML 4   **Widely Supported:** No

Sample:
```
<map id="123" name="simba" id="simba">...</map>
```

name="..."

Establishes a name for the map information you can later reference using the usemap attribute of the img element. This attribute is deprecated; use the id attribute instead of or together with name.

Standard/Usage: HTML 3.2; deprecated   **Widely Supported:** Yes

Sample:
```
<map name="housemap" id="housemap">
    <img src="house.gif" usemap="#housemap" alt="map of house" />...</map>
```

style="..."

Specifies style sheet commands that apply to the contents of the map tags.

Standard/Usage: HTML 4   **Widely Supported:** No

Sample:
```
<map style="background: black">...</map>
```

title="..."

Specifies text assigned to the element. You can use this attribute for context-sensitive help within the document. Browsers may use this to show tooltips.

Standard/Usage: HTML 4   **Widely Supported:** No

Sample:
```
<map title="image map spec">...</map>
```

marquee

Displays a scrolling text message within a document. Only Internet Explorer recognizes this element. Use the more supported Java or JavaScript to achieve the same effect for a broader audience.

Standard/Usage: Internet Explorer 2   **Widely Supported:** No   **Empty:** No

Sample:

```
<marquee direction="left" behavior="scroll" scrolldelay="250" scrollamount="10">
    Big sale today on fuzzy wuzzy widgets!</marquee>
```

behavior="scroll|slide|alternate"

Indicates the type of scrolling. A value of scroll scrolls text from one side of the marquee, across, and off the opposite side; slide scrolls text from one side of the marquee, across, and stops when the text reaches the opposite side; and alternate bounces the marquee text from one side to the other.

Standard/Usage: Internet Explorer 2   **Widely Supported:** No

Sample:

```
<marquee direction="left" behavior="alternate">Go Bears! Win Win Win!</marquee>
```

bgcolor="#rrggbb" or "..."

Specifies the background color of the marquee. You use a hexadecimal RGB color value or a color name.

Standard/Usage: Internet Explorer 2   **Widely Supported:** No

Sample:

```
<marquee bgcolor="red" direction="left">Order opera tickets here!</marquee>
```

direction="left|right"

Indicates the direction in which the marquee text scrolls.

Standard/Usage: Internet Explorer 2   **Widely Supported:** No

Sample:

```
<marquee direction="left">Order opera tickets here!</marquee>
```

height="n"

Specifies the vertical dimension of the marquee (in pixels).

Standard/Usage: Internet Explorer 2   **Widely Supported:** No

Sample:

```
<marquee width="300" height="50">Go Bears!</marquee>
```

hspace="n"

Specifies the size of the margins (in pixels) to the left and right of the marquee.

Standard/Usage: Internet Explorer 2   **Widely Supported:** No

Sample:

```
<marquee direction="left" hspace="25">Check out our detailed product specs!</marquee>
```

id="..."

Assigns a unique ID selector to an instance of the marquee element. When you then assign a style to that ID selector, it affects only that one instance of the marquee element.

Standard/Usage: Internet Explorer 4   **Widely Supported:** No

Sample:

```
<marquee id="3d4">...</marquee>
```

loop="n|infinite"

Controls the appearance of the marquee text.

Standard/Usage: Internet Explorer 2 **Widely Supported:** No

Sample:

```
<marquee loop="5">December 12 is our big, all-day sale!</marquee>
```

scrollamount="n"

Indicates how far (in pixels) the marquee text shifts between redraws. Decrease this value for a smoother (but slower) scroll; increase it for a faster (but bumpier) scroll.

Standard/Usage: Internet Explorer 2 **Widely Supported:** No

Sample:

```
<marquee scrollamount="10" scrolldelay="40">Plant a tree for Arbor Day!</marquee>
```

scrolldelay="n"

Indicates how often (in milliseconds) the marquee text redraws. Increase this value to slow the scrolling action; decrease it to speed the scrolling action.

Standard/Usage: Internet Explorer 2 **Widely Supported:** No

Sample:

```
<marquee direction="right" scrolldelay="30">Eat at Joe's!</marquee>
```

style="..."

Specifies style sheet commands that apply to the text within the marquee tags.

Standard/Usage: Internet Explorer 4 **Widely Supported:** No

Sample:

```
<marquee style="background: red">...</marquee>
```

title="..."

Specifies text assigned to the element. You can use this attribute for context-sensitive help within the document. Browsers may use this to show tooltips over the marquee.

Standard/Usage: Internet Explorer 4 **Widely Supported:** No

Sample:

```
<marquee title="scrolling marquee">...</marquee>
```

truespeed="truespeed"

A stand-alone attribute that specifies that the scrolldelay values should be maintained. If this attribute is not used, scrolldelay values under 59 are rounded up to 60 milliseconds.

Standard/Usage: Internet Explorer 2 **Widely Supported:** No

Sample:

```
<marquee direction="right" scrolldelay="30" truespeed="truespeed">Eat at Joe's!</marquee>
```

vspace="n"

Specifies the size of the margins (in pixels) at the top and bottom of the marquee.

Standard/Usage: Internet Explorer 2 **Widely Supported:** No

Sample:

```
<marquee direction="left" vspace="25">Check out our detailed product specs!</marquee>
```

width="n"

Specifies the horizontal dimension (in pixels) of the marquee.

Standard/Usage:	Internet Explorer 2 **Widely Supported:** No
Sample:	

```
<marquee width="300">Go Bears!</marquee>
```

menu

Defines a menu list. Use the li element to indicate list items. However, use ul instead of this deprecated element.

Standard/Usage: HTML 2; deprecated   **Widely Supported:**   No   **Empty:**   No

Sample:

```
Now you can:<menu>
   <li>Eat the sandwich.</li>
   <li>Place the sandwich in the fridge.</li>
   <li>Feed the sandwich to the dog.</li>
</menu>
```

class="..."

Indicates which style class applies to the menu element.

Standard/Usage: HTML 4   **Widely Supported:**   No

Sample:

```
<menu class="casual">
   <li>Information</li>
   <li>Members</li>
   <li>Guests</li>
</menu>
```

compact="compact"

Specifies that the menu list appears in a space-saving form. This attribute is deprecated in HTML 4.

Standard/Usage: HTML 2; deprecated   **Widely Supported:**   Yes

Sample:

```
<h2>Drinks Available</h2>
<menu compact="compact">
   <li>Cola</li>
   <li>Fruit drink</li>
   <li>Orange juice</li>
   <li>Water</li>
</menu>
```

id="..."

Assigns a unique ID selector to an instance of the menu element. When you then assign a style to that ID selector, it affects only that one instance of the menu element.

Standard/Usage: HTML 4   **Widely Supported:**   No

Sample:

```
You'll need the following:<menu id="123">
   <li>Extra socks</li>
   <li>Snack crackers</li>
   <li>Towel</li>
</menu>
```

style="..."

Specifies style sheet commands that apply to the menu list.

Standard/Usage: HTML 4   **Widely Supported:**   Yes

Sample:

```
<menu style="background: black; color: white">…</menu>
```

title="..."

Specifies text assigned to the element. You can use this attribute for context-sensitive help within the document. Browsers may use this to show tooltips over the menu list

Standard/Usage: HTML 4   **Widely Supported:**   No

Sample:

```
<menu title="menu list">…</menu>
```

Other Attributes

The menu element also accepts the lang, dir, onclick, ondblclick, onmousedown, onmouseup, onmouseover, onmousemove, onmouseout, onkeypress, onkeydown, and onkeyup attributes.

meta

This empty element specifies information about the document to browsers, applications, and search engines. Place the meta element within the document head. For example, you can use the meta element to instruct the browser to load a new document after 10 seconds (client-pull), or you can specify keywords for search engines to associate with your document.

Standard/Usage: HTML 2   **Widely Supported:**   Yes   **Empty:**   Yes

Sample:

```
<head>
    <title>Igneous Rocks in North America</title>
    <meta http-equiv="keywords" content="geology, igneous, volcanos" />
</head>
```

content="..."

Assigns values to the HTTP header field. For example, when using the refresh HTTP header, assign a number along with a URL to the content attribute; the browser then loads the specified URL after the specified number of seconds.

Standard/Usage: HTML 2; required   **Widely Supported:**   Yes

Sample:

```
<meta http-equiv="refresh" content="2;url=nextpage.html" />
```

http-equiv="..."

Indicates the HTTP header value you want to define, such as refresh, expires, or content-language. Other header values are listed in RFC2068.

Standard/Usage: HTML 2   **Widely Supported:**   Yes

Sample:

```
<meta http-equiv="expires" content="Tue, 04 Aug 2001 22:39:22 GMT" />
```

name="..."

Specifies the name of the association you are defining, such as keywords or description.

Standard/Usage:	HTML 2	**Widely Supported:**	Yes

Sample:

```
<meta name="keywords" content="travel,automobile" />
<meta name="description" content="The Nash Metro moves fast and goes beep beep." />
```

scheme="..."

Specifies additional information about the association you're defining.

Standard/Usage:	HTML 4	**Widely Supported:**	No

Sample:

```
<meta name="number" scheme="priority" content="1" />
```

Other Attributes

The meta element also accepts the lang and dir attributes.

multicol

Formats text into newspaper-style columns.

Standard/Usage:	Netscape Navigator 4	**Widely Supported:**	No	**Empty:**	No

Sample:

```
<multicol cols="2" gutter="10">...</multicol>
```

cols="n"

Indicates the number of columns.

Standard/Usage:	Netscape Navigator 4	**Widely Supported:**	No

Sample:

```
<multicol cols="4">...</multicol>
```

gutter="n"

Indicates the width of the space (in pixels) between multiple columns.

Standard/Usage:	Netscape Navigator 4	**Widely Supported:**	No

Sample:

```
<multicol cols="3" gutter="15">...</multicol>
```

width="n"

Indicates the horizontal dimension (in pixels or as a percentage of the total width available) of each column.

Standard/Usage:	Netscape Navigator 4	**Widely Supported:**	No

Sample:

```
<multicol cols="2" width="30%">...</multicol>
```

n

nobr

Disables line-wrapping for a section of text. To force a word-break within a nobr clause, use the wbr empty element. The nobr element is a proprietary Internet Explorer element, which is also supported by Netscape but not the XHTML or HTML specification.

| **Standard/Usage:** | Internet Explorer 1, Netscape Navigator 1 | **Widely Supported:** | Yes | **Empty:** | No |

Sample:
```
<nobr>All this text will
remain on one single line in the
browser window, no matter how wide the
window is, until the closing
tag appears. That doesn't happen
until right now.</nobr>
```

class="..."

Indicates which style class applies to the element.

| **Standard/Usage:** | Internet Explorer 3, Netscape Navigator 4 | **Widely Supported:** | No |

Sample:
```
<nobr class="casual">...</nobr>
```

id="..."

Assigns a unique ID selector to an instance of the nobr element. When you then assign a style to that ID selector, it affects only that one instance of the nobr element.

| **Standard/Usage:** | Internet Explorer 3, Netscape Navigator 4 | **Widely Supported:** | No |

Sample:
```
You'll need the following:<nobr id="123">...</nobr>
```

style="..."

Specifies style sheet commands that apply to the nonbreaking text.

| **Standard/Usage:** | Internet Explorer 4, Netscape Navigator 3 | **Widely Supported:** | Yes |

Sample:
```
<nobr style="background: black">...</nobr>
```

noframes

Provides XHTML content for browsers that do not support frames or are configured not to present frames. In XHTML, the body element is required within the noframes section. It provides additional formatting and style sheet features.

| **Standard/Usage:** | HTML 4 (Frames) | **Widely Supported:** | Yes | **Empty:** | No |

Sample:
```
<frameset cols="*,70">…
    <noframes>
        <body>
            <p>Your browser doesn't support frames. Please follow the links below for
                the rest of the story.</p>
            <p><a href="prices.html">Prices</a> |
                <a href="about.html">About Us</a> |
                <a href="contact.html">Contact Us</a></p>
        </body>
    </noframes>
</frameset>
```

class="..."

Indicates which style class applies to the noframes element.

Standard/Usage: HTML 4   **Widely Supported:**   No

Sample:
```
<noframes class="short"><body>…</body></noframes>
```

id="..."

Assigns a unique ID selector to an instance of the noframes element. When you then assign a style to that ID selector, it affects only that one instance of the noframes element.

Standard/Usage: HTML 4   **Widely Supported:**   No

Sample:
```
<noframes id="234"><body>…</body></noframes>
```

style="..."

Specifies style sheet commands that apply to the noframes element.

Standard/Usage: HTML 4   **Widely Supported:**   No

Sample:
```
<noframes style="background: red"><body>…</body></noframes>
```

title="..."

Specifies text assigned to the element. You can use this attribute for context-sensitive help within the document. Browsers may use this to show tooltips.

Standard/Usage: HTML 4   **Widely Supported:**   No

Sample:
```
<noframes title="XHTML for nonframed browsers"><body>…</body></noframes>
```

Other Attributes

The noframes element also accepts the lang, dir, onclick, ondblclick, onmousedown, onmouseup, onmouseover, onmousemove, onmouseout, onkeypress, onkeydown, and onkeyup attributes

noscript

Provides XHTML content for browsers that do not support scripts. Use the noscript element inside a script definition.

| Standard/Usage: | HTML 4 | Widely Supported: | No | Empty: | No |

Sample:
```
<noscript>Because you can see this, you can tell that your browser
  will not run (or is set not to run) scripts.</noscript>
```

class="..."

Indicates which style class applies to the noscript element.

| Standard/Usage: | HTML 4 | Widely Supported: | No |

Sample:
```
<noscript class="short">...</noscript>
```

id="..."

Assigns a unique ID selector to an instance of the noscript element. When you then assign a style to that ID selector, it affects only that one instance of the noscript element.

| Standard/Usage: | HTML 4 | Widely Supported: | No |

Sample:
```
<noscript id="234">...</noscript>
```

style="..."

Specifies style sheet commands that apply to the noscript element.

| Standard/Usage: | HTML 4 | Widely Supported: | No |

Sample:
```
<noscript style="background: red">...</noscript>
```

title="..."

Specifies text assigned to the element. You can use this attribute for context-sensitive help within the document. Browsers may use this to show tooltips.

| Standard/Usage: | HTML 4 | Widely Supported: | No |

Sample:
```
<noscript title="XHTML for nonscript browsers">...</noscript>
```

Other Attributes

The noscript element also accepts the lang, dir, onclick, ondblclick, onmousedown, onmouseup, onmouseover, onmousemove, onmouseout, onkeypress, onkeydown, and onkeyup attributes

object

Embeds a software object into a document. The object can be an ActiveX object, a QuickTime movie, or any other object or data that a browser supports.

Use the param element to supply parameters to the embedded object. You can place messages and other elements between the object tags for browsers that do not support embedded objects.

Standard/Usage:	HTML 4	**Widely Supported:**	No	**Empty:**	No

Sample:

```
<object classid="/thingie.py">
    <param name="thing" value="1" />
    <param name="autostart" value="true" />
    Sorry. Your browser does not support embedded objects.
    If it supported these objects, you would not see this message.
</object>
```

align="left|center|right|texttop|middle|textmiddle|baseline|textbottom"

Indicates how the embedded object lines up relative to the edges of the browser windows and/or other elements within the browser window. This attribute is deprecated in favor of style sheets.

Value	Effect
left	Floats the embedded object between the edges of the window, on the left side
right	Floats the embedded object between the edges of the window, on the right side
center	Floats the embedded object between the edges of the window, evenly between left and right
texttop	Aligns the top of the embedded object with the top of the surrounding text
textmiddle	Aligns the middle of the embedded object with the middle of the surrounding text
textbottom	Aligns the bottom of the embedded object with the bottom of the surrounding text
baseline	Aligns the bottom of the embedded object with the baseline of the surrounding text
middle	Aligns the middle of the embedded object with the baseline of the surrounding text

Standard/Usage:	HTML 4; deprecated	**Widely Supported:**	No

Sample:

```
<object data="shocknew.dcr" type="application/director" width="288" height="200"
    align="right">...</object>
```

archive="url url url"

Specifies a *space-separated* list of URIs for archives containing resources relevant to the object, which may include the resources specified by the classid and data attributes. Preloading archives generally results in reduced load times for objects.

Standard/Usage:	HTML 4	**Widely Supported:**	No

Sample:

```
<object archive="bear.htm lion.htm">...</object>
```

border="n"

Indicates the width (in pixels) of a border around the embedded object. border="0" indicates no border. This attribute is deprecated in favor of style sheets.

Standard/Usage:	HTML 4; deprecated	**Widely Supported:**	No

Sample:

```
<object data="shocknew.dcr" type="application/director" width="288" height="200"
    border="10">...</object>
```

classid="url"

Specifies the location of an object resource, such as a Java applet. Use classid="java:appletname.class" for Java applets.

Standard/Usage:	HTML 4	**Widely Supported:**	No

Sample:

```
<object classid="java:appletname.class">...</object>
```

codebase="url"

Specifies the absolute or relative location of the base directory in which the browser will look for data and other implementation files.

Standard/Usage:	HTML 4	**Widely Supported:**	No

Sample:

```
<object codebase="/fgm/code/">...</object>
```

codetype="..."

Specifies the MIME type for the embedded object's code.

Standard/Usage:	HTML 4	**Widely Supported:**	No

Sample:

```
<object codetype="application/x-msword">...</object>
```

class="..."

Indicates which style class applies to the element.

Standard/Usage:	HTML 4	**Widely Supported:**	No

Sample:

```
<object class="casual" codetype="application/x-msword">...</object>
```

classid="url"

Specifies the URL of an object resource.

Standard/Usage:	HTML 4	**Widely Supported:**	No

Sample:

```
<object classid="http://www.lanw.com/bogus.class">...</object>
```

data="url"

Specifies the absolute or relative location of the embedded object's data.

Standard/Usage:	HTML 4	**Widely Supported:**	No

Sample:

```
<object data="/fgm/goo.avi">...</object>
```

declare="declare"

Defines the embedded object without actually loading it into the document.

Standard/Usage:	HTML 4	**Widely Supported:**	No

Sample:

```
<object classid="clsid:99B42120-6EC7-11CF-A6C7-00AA00A47DD3" declare="declare">...</object>
```

height="n"

Specifies the vertical dimension (in pixels) of the embedded object.

Standard/Usage:	HTML 4	Widely Supported:	No

Sample:

```
<object data="shocknew.dcr" type="application/director" width="288" height="200">…</object>
```

hspace="n"

Specifies the size of the margins (in pixels) to the left and right of the embedded object.

Standard/Usage:	HTML 4	Widely Supported:	No

Sample:

```
<object data="shocknew.dcr" width="288" height="200" hspace="10">…</object>
```

id="..."

Indicates an identifier to associate with the embedded object. You can also use this to apply styles to the object.

Standard/Usage:	HTML 4	Widely Supported:	No

Sample:

```
<object data="shocknew.dcr" width="288" height="200" id="swave2">…</object>
```

name="..."

Specifies the name of the embedded object.

Standard/Usage:	HTML 4	Widely Supported:	No

Sample:

```
<object data="shocknew.dcr" name="Very Cool Thingie">…</object>
```

standby="..."

Specifies a message that the browser displays while the object is loading.

Standard/Usage:	HTML 4	Widely Supported:	No

Sample:

```
<object standby="Please wait. Movie loading." width="100" height="250">…</object>
```

tabindex="n"

Indicates the place of the embedded object in the tabbing order.

Standard/Usage:	HTML 4	Widely Supported:	No

Sample:

```
<object classid="clsid:99b42120-6ec7-11cf-a6c7-00aa00a47dd3" tabindex="3">…</object>
```

title="..."

Specifies text assigned to the element. You can use this attribute for context-sensitive help within the document. Browsers may use this to show tooltips over the embedded object.

Standard/Usage:	HTML 4	Widely Supported:	No

Sample:

```
<object title="Earth Movie" width="100" height="250">…</object>
```

type="..."

Indicates the MIME type of the embedded object.

> **Standard/Usage:** HTML 4   **Widely Supported:** No
> **Sample:**

```
<object data="shock.dcr" type="application/x-director" width="288" height="200">...</object>
```

usemap="url"

Indicates the relative or absolute location of a client-side image map to use with the embedded object.

> **Standard/Usage:** HTML 4   **Widely Supported:** No
> **Sample:**

```
<object usemap="maps.html#map1">...</object>
```

vspace="n"

Specifies the size of the margin (in pixels) at the top and bottom of the embedded object.

> **Standard/Usage:** HTML 4   **Widely Supported:** No
> **Sample:**

```
<object data="shocknew.dcr" width="288" height="200" vspace="10">...</object>
```

width="n"

Indicates the horizontal dimension (in pixels) of the embedded object.

> **Standard/Usage:** HTML 4   **Widely Supported:** No
> **Sample:**

```
<object data="shock.dcr" type="application/director" width="288" height="200">...</object>
```

Other Attributes

The object element also accepts the lang, dir, onclick, ondblclick, onmousedown, onmouseup, onmouseover, onmousemove, onmouseout, onkeypress, onkeydown, and onkeyup attributes.

ol

Contains a numbered (ordered) list.

> **Standard/Usage:** HTML 2   **Widely Supported:** Yes   **Empty:** No
> **Sample:**

```
<ol>
   <li>Introduction</li>
   <li>Part One</li>
   <ol type="A">
      <li>Chapter 1</li>
      <li>Chapter 2</li>
   </ol>
</ol>
```

class="..."

Indicates which style class applies to the ol element.

> **Standard/Usage:** HTML 4   **Widely Supported:** No

Sample:

```
<ol class="car">
   <li>Check engine oil</li>
   <li>Check tire pressures</li>
   <li>Fill with gasoline</li>
</ol>
```

compact="compact"

Indicates that the ordered list appears in a compact format. This attribute may not affect the appearance of the list because most browsers do not present lists in more than one format. This attribute is deprecated in HTML 4.

Standard/Usage: HTML 2; deprecated   **Widely Supported:**   No

Sample:

```
<ol compact="compact">...</ol>
```

id="..."

Assigns a unique ID selector to an instance of the ol element. When you then assign a style to that ID selector, it affects only that one instance of the ol element.

Standard/Usage: HTML 4   **Widely Supported:**   No

Sample:

```
<ol id="123">...</ol>
```

start="..."

Specifies the value at which the ordered list should start. This attribute is deprecated in HTML 4.

Standard/Usage: HTML 2; deprecated   **Widely Supported:**   Yes

Sample:

```
<ol type="a" start="f">...</ol>
```

style="..."

Specifies style sheet commands that apply to the ordered list.

Standard/Usage: HTML 4   **Widely Supported:**   Yes

Sample:

```
<ol style="background: black; color: white">...</ol>
```

title="..."

Specifies text assigned to the element. You can use this attribute for context-sensitive help within the document. Browsers may use this to show tooltips over the ordered list.

Standard/Usage: HTML 4   **Widely Supported:**   No

Sample:

```
<ol title="ordered list">...</ol>
```

type="..."

Specifies the numbering style of the ordered list. Possible values are 1 for Arabic numbers, i for lowercase Roman numerals, I for uppercase Roman numerals, a for lowercase letters, and A for uppercase letters. This attribute is deprecated in HTML 4.

Standard/Usage: HTML 2; deprecated   **Widely Supported:**   Yes

Sample:
```
<ol type="a">
   <li>is for apple.</li>
   <li>is for bird.</li>
   <li>is for cat.</li>
   <li>is for dog.</li>
</ol>
```

Other Attributes

The ol element also accepts the lang, dir, onclick, ondblclick, onmousedown, onmouseup, onmouseover, onmouse-move, onmouseout, onkeypress, onkeydown, and onkeyup attributes.

optgroup

Specifies a description for a group of options. Use inside select tags, and use the option element within the opt-group element.

Standard/Usage:	HTML 4	**Widely Supported:**	No	**Empty:**	No

Sample:
```
<select name="dinner">
   <optgroup label="choices">
     <option>Vegan</option>
     <option>Vegetarian</option>
     <option>Traditional</option>
   </optgroup>
</select>
```

class="..."

Indicates which style class applies to the optgroup element.

Standard/Usage:	HTML 4	**Widely Supported:**	No

Sample:
```
<optgroup label="Fake or False" class="casual">
   <option>Fake</option>
   <option>False</option>
</optgroup>
```

disabled="disabled"

Denies access to the group of options.

Standard/Usage:	HTML 4	**Widely Supported:**	No

Sample:
```
<optgroup label="food" disabled="disabled">
   <option>Prime Rib</option>
   <option>Lobster</option>
</optgroup>
```

id="..."

Assigns a unique ID selector to an instance of the optgroup element. When you then assign a style to that ID selector, it affects only that one instance of the optgroup element.

Standard/Usage: HTML 4   **Widely Supported:** No

Sample:
```
<optgroup label="Fake or False" id="123">
  <option>Fake</option>
  <option>False</option>
</optgroup>
```

label="..."

Specifies alternative text assigned to the element. You can use this attribute for context-sensitive help within the document.

Standard/Usage: HTML 4; required   **Widely Supported:** Yes

Sample:
```
<optgroup label="Dinner selections">
  <option>Prime Rib</option>
  <option>Lobster</option>
</optgroup>
```

style="..."

Specifies style sheet commands that apply to the contents of the optgroup tags.

Standard/Usage: HTML 4   **Widely Supported:** No

Sample:
```
<optgroup label="dinner" style="background: red">…</optgroup>
```

title="..."

Specifies text assigned to the element. You can use this attribute for context-sensitive help within the document.

Standard/Usage: HTML 4   **Widely Supported:** No

Sample:
```
<optgroup label="party" title="Select a political party">…</optgroup>
```

Other Attributes

The optgroup element also accepts the lang, dir, onfocus, onblur, onchange, onselect, onclick, ondblclick, onmousedown, onmouseup, onmouseover, onmousemove, onmouseout, onkeypress, onkeydown, and onkeyup attributes.

option

Indicates items in a fill-out form selection list (see the select element).

Standard/Usage: HTML 2   **Widely Supported:** Yes   **Empty:** No

Sample:
```
Select an artist from the 1970s:<select name="artists">
  <option>Black Sabbath</option>
  <option selected="selected">Pink Floyd</option>
  <option>Boston</option>
</select>
```

class="..."

Indicate which style class applies to the element.

Standard/Usage: HTML 4 **Widely Supported:** No

Sample:

```
<option name="color" class="casual">…</option>
```

disabled="disabled"

Denies access to the input method.

Standard/Usage: HTML 4 **Widely Supported:** No

Sample:

```
<option value="Bogus" disabled="disabled">Nothing here.</option>
```

id="..."

Assigns a unique ID selector to an instance of the option element. When you then assign a style to that ID selector, it affects only that one instance of the option element.

Standard/Usage: HTML 4 **Widely Supported:** No

Sample:

```
<option id="123">Mastercard</option>
```

label="..."

Specifies shorter, alternative text assigned to the option element. You can use this attribute for context-sensitive help within the document. Browsers may use this to show tooltips over the group.

Standard/Usage: HTML 4 **Widely Supported:** Yes

Sample:

```
<option label="Trad">Traditional Dinner Menu</option>
```

selected="selected"

Marks a selection list item as preselected.

Standard/Usage: HTML 2 **Widely Supported:** Yes

Sample:

```
<option selected="selected" value="1">Ice Cream</option>
```

title="..."

Specifies text assigned to the element. You can use this attribute for context-sensitive help within the document. Browsers may use this to show tooltips over the selection list option.

Standard/Usage: HTML 4 **Widely Supported:** No

Sample:

```
<option title="Option">Thingie</option>
```

value="..."

Indicates which data is sent to the form processor if you choose the selection list item. If the value attribute is not present within the option element, the text between the option tags is sent instead.

Standard/Usage: HTML 2 **Widely Supported:** Yes

Sample:

```
<option value="2">Sandwiches</option>
```

Other Attributes

The option element also accepts the lang, dir, onfocus, onblur, onchange, onselect, onclick, ondblclick, onmousedown, onmouseup, onmouseover, onmousemove, onmouseout, onkeypress, onkeydown, and onkeyup attributes.

p

p

Indicates a paragraph in a document.

Standard/Usage:	HTML 2	**Widely Supported:**	Yes	**Empty:**	No

Sample:
```
<p>I'm a paragraph.</p>
<p>I'm another paragraph.</p>
```

align="left|center|right"

Aligns paragraph text flush left, flush right, or in the center of the document. This attribute is deprecated in HTML 4 in favor of style sheets.

Standard/Usage:	HTML 3.2; deprecated	**Widely Supported:**	Yes

Sample:
```
<p align="center">There will be fun and games for everyone!</p>
```

class="..."

Indicates which style class applies to the p element.

Standard/Usage:	HTML 4	**Widely Supported:**	No

Sample:
```
<p class="casual">Tom turned at the next street and stopped.</p>
```

id="..."

Assigns a unique ID selector to an instance of the p element. When you then assign a style to that ID selector, it affects only that one instance of the p element.

Standard/Usage:	HTML 4	**Widely Supported:**	No

Sample:
```
<p id="123">This paragraph is yellow on black!</p>
```

style="..."

Specifies style sheet commands that apply to the contents of the paragraph.

Standard/Usage:	HTML 4	**Widely Supported:**	No

Sample:
```
<p style="background: red; color: white">...</p>
```

title="..."

Specifies text assigned to the element. You can use this attribute for context-sensitive help within the document. Browsers may use this to show tooltips over the paragraph.

Standard/Usage:	HTML 4	**Widely Supported:**	No

Sample:
```
<p title="paragraph">...</p>
```

Other Attributes

The p element also accepts the `lang`, `dir`, `onclick`, `ondblclick`, `onmousedown`, `onmouseup`, `onmouseover`, `onmouse-move`, `onmouseout`, `onkeypress`, `onkeydown`, and `onkeyup` attributes.

param

Specifies parameters passed to an embedded object. Use the param element within the object or applet elements.

Standard/Usage:	HTML 3.2	Widely Supported:	No	Empty:	Yes

Sample:

```
<object classid="/thingie.py">
  <param name="thing" value="1" />
  Sorry. Your browser does not support embedded objects.
</object>
```

name="..."

Indicates the name of the parameter passed to the embedded object.

Standard/Usage:	HTML 3.2; required	Widely Supported:	No

Sample:

```
<param name="startyear" value="1920" />
```

type="..."

Specifies the MIME type of the data found at the specified URL. Use this attribute with the `valuetype="ref"` attribute.

Standard/Usage:	HTML 4	Widely Supported:	No

Sample:

```
<param name="data" value="/data/sim1.zip" valuetype="ref"
  type="application/x-zip-compressed" />
```

value="..."

Specifies the value associated with the parameter passed to the embedded object.

Standard/Usage:	HTML 3.2	Widely Supported:	No

Sample:

```
<param name="startyear" value="1920" />
```

valuetype="ref|object|data"

Indicates the kind of value passed to the embedded object. A value of ref indicates that the value of value is a URL passed to the embedded object; object indicates that the value attribute specifies the location of object data; and data indicates that the value attribute is set to a plain-text string. Use this for passing alphanumeric data to the embedded object.

Standard/Usage:	Internet Explorer 3, HTML 4	Widely Supported:	No

Sample:

```
<param name="length" value="9" valuetype="data" />
```

pre

Contains preformatted plain text. This is useful for including computer program output or source code within your document.

Standard/Usage:	HTML 2	**Widely Supported:**	Yes	**Empty:**	No

Sample:

```
Here's the source code:
<pre>
#include <stdio.h>
void main()
{
 printf("Hello World!\n");
}
</pre>
```

class="..."

Indicates which style class applies to the pre element.

Standard/Usage:	HTML 4	**Widely Supported:**	No

Sample:

```
<pre class="food">BBQ Info</pre>
```

id="..."

Assigns a unique ID selector to an instance of the pre element. When you then assign a style to that ID selector, it affects only that one instance of the pre element.

Standard/Usage:	HTML 4	**Widely Supported:**	No

Sample:

```
An example of an emoticon:<pre id="123"> :-) </pre>
```

style="..."

Specifies style sheet commands that apply to the contents of the pre tags.

Standard/Usage:	HTML 4	**Widely Supported:**	Yes

Sample:

```
<pre style="background: red">…</pre>
```

title="..."

Specifies text assigned to the element. You can use this attribute for context-sensitive help within the document. Browsers may use this to show tooltips over the preformatted text.

Standard/Usage:	HTML 4	**Widely Supported:**	No

Sample:

```
<pre title="preformatted text">…</pre>
```

width="n"

Specifies the horizontal dimension of the preformatted text (in pixels). This attribute is deprecated in favor of style sheets.

Standard/Usage:	HTML 4; deprecated	**Widely Supported:**	No

Sample:

```
<pre width="80">…</pre>
```

Other Attributes

The pre element also accepts the lang, dir, onclick, ondblclick, onmousedown, onmouseup, onmouseover, onmouse-move, onmouseout, onkeypress, onkeydown, and onkeyup attributes.

q

q

Quotes a direct source within a paragraph. Use blockquote to signify only a longer or block quotation.

| **Standard/Usage**: | HTML 4 | **Widely Supported**: | No | **Empty**: | No |

Sample:
```
Dr. Bob said <q>I really like the procedure.</q>
```

cite="url"

Specifies a reference URL for a quotation.

| **Standard/Usage**: | HTML 4 | **Widely Supported**: | No |

Sample:
```
<q cite="http://www.example.com/url.html">The book was good.</q>
```

class="..."

Indicates which style class applies to the q element.

| **Standard/Usage**: | HTML 4 | **Widely Supported**: | No |

Sample:
```
<q class="holiday">Twas the night before Christmas</q>
```

id="..."

Assigns a unique ID selector to an instance of the q element. When you then assign a style to that ID selector, it affects only that one instance of the q element.

| **Standard/Usage**: | HTML 4 | **Widely Supported**: | No |

Sample:
```
On July 12, John wrote a profound sentence in his diary:
<q id="123">I woke up this morning, and it was raining.</q>
```

style="..."

Specifies style sheet commands that apply to the contents of the q tags.

| **Standard/Usage**: | HTML 4 | **Widely Supported**: | No |

Sample:
```
<q style="background: red">…</q>
```

title="..."

Specifies text assigned to the element. You can use this attribute for context-sensitive help within the document. Browsers may use this to show tooltips over the quoted text.

| **Standard/Usage**: | HTML 4 | **Widely Supported**: | No |

Sample:
```
<q title="quotation">Quoted text goes here.</q>
```

Other Attributes

The q element also accepts the lang, dir, onclick, ondblclick, onmousedown, onmouseup, onmouseover, onmouse-move, onmouseout, onkeypress, onkeydown, and onkeyup attributes.

s

s

Deprecated. See strike.

samp

Indicates a sequence of literal characters.

Standard/Usage:	HTML 2	Widely Supported:	Yes	Empty:	No
Sample:					

An example of a palindrome is the word <samp>MOM</samp>.

class="..."

Indicates which style class applies to the samp element.

Standard/Usage:	HTML 4	Widely Supported:	No
Sample:			

The PC screen read: <samp class="casual">Command Not Found</samp>

id="..."

Assigns a unique ID selector to an instance of the samp element. When you then assign a style to that ID selector, it affects only that one instance of the samp element.

Standard/Usage:	HTML 4	Widely Supported:	No
Sample:			

Just for fun, think of how many words end with the letters <samp id="123">ing</samp>.

style="..."

Specifies style sheet commands that apply to the contents of the samp tags.

Standard/Usage:	HTML 4	Widely Supported:	Yes
Sample:			

<samp style="background: red">...</samp>

title="..."

Specifies text assigned to the element. You can use this attribute for context-sensitive help within the document. Browsers may use this to show tooltips.

Standard/Usage:	HTML 4	Widely Supported:	No
Sample:			

<samp title="Sample">...</samp>

Other Attributes

The samp element also accepts the lang, dir, onclick, ondblclick, onmousedown, onmouseup, onmouseover, onmousemove, onmouseout, onkeypress, onkeydown, and onkeyup attributes.

script

Contains browser script code. Examples include JavaScript and VBScript.

Standard/Usage:	HTML 3.2	**Widely Supported:**	Yes	**Empty:**	No

Sample:
```
<script type="text/javascript">…</script>
```

charset="..."

Specifies character encoding of the data designated by the script. Use the name of a character set defined in RFC2045. The default value for this attribute, appropriate for all Western languages, is ISO-8859-1.

Standard/Usage:	HTML 4	**Widely Supported:**	No

Sample:
```
<script type="text/javascript" charset="ISO-8859-1">…</script>
```

defer="defer"

Indicates to the browser that the script does not affect the initial document display, so the script can be processed after the page loads.

Standard/Usage:	HTML 4	**Widely Supported:**	No

Sample:
```
<script type="text/javascript" defer="defer">…</script>
```

language="..."

Indicates the type of script; deprecated in favor of type="…".

Standard/Usage:	HTML 4; deprecated	**Widely Supported:**	Yes

Sample:
```
<script language="JavaScript">…</script>
```

src="url"

Specifies the relative or absolute location of a script to include in the document.

Standard/Usage:	HTML 4	**Widely Supported:**	Yes

Sample:
```
<script type="text/javascript" src="http://www.example.com/sc/script.js">…</script>
```

type="..."

Indicates the MIME type of the script. This is a preferred alternative to the language element for declaring the type of scripting.

Standard/Usage:	HTML 3.2; required	**Widely Supported:**	Yes

Sample:
```
<script type="text/javascript">document.write ("<em>Great!</em>")</script>
```

XHTML Elements and Attributes

select

Specifies a selection list within a form. Use the option element to specify items in the selection list.

Standard/Usage: HTML 2   **Widely Supported:** Yes   **Empty:**   No

Sample:

```
What do you use our product for?<br />
<select multiple="multiple" name="use">
   <option value="1">Pest control</option>
   <option selected="selected" value="2">Automotive lubricant</option>
   <option value="3">Preparing pastries</option>
   <option value="4">Other</option>
</select>
```

accesskey="..."

Indicates a keystroke sequence associated with the selection list.

Standard/Usage: Internet Explorer 4   **Widely Supported:** No

Sample:

```
<select name="size" accesskey="s">...</select>
```

class="..."

Indicates which style class applies to the element.

Standard/Usage: HTML 4   **Widely Supported:** No

Sample:

```
<select name="color" class="casual">...</select>
```

disabled="disabled"

Denies access to the selection list.

Standard/Usage: HTML 4   **Widely Supported:** No

Sample:

```
<select name="color" disabled="disabled">...</select>
```

id="..."

Assigns a unique ID selector to an instance of the select element. When you then assign a style to that ID selector, it affects only that one instance of the select element.

Standard/Usage: HTML 3   **Widely Supported:** No

Sample:

```
<select id="123" name="salary">...</select>
```

multiple="multiple"

Indicates that a user can select more than one selection list item at the same time.

Standard/Usage: HTML 2   **Widely Supported:** Yes

Sample:

```
<select multiple="multiple">...</select>
```

name="..."

Gives a name to the value you are passing to the form processor. This establishes a *name–value pair* with which the form processor application can work.

Standard/Usage: HTML 2   **Widely Supported:** Yes

Sample:
```
What is your shoe size?
<select size="4" name="size">
   <option>5</option>
   <option>6</option>
   <option>7</option>
   <option>8</option>
   <option>9</option>
   <option>10</option>
</select>
```

size="n"

Specifies the number of visible items in the selection list. If there are more items in the selection list than are visible, a scroll bar provides access to the other items.

Standard/Usage: HTML 2   **Widely Supported:** Yes

Sample:
```
<select size="3">...</select>
```

style="..."

Specifies style sheet commands that apply to the contents of the select tags.

Standard/Usage: HTML 4   **Widely Supported:** Yes

Sample:
```
<select style="background: red" name="color">...</select>
```

tabindex="n"

Indicates where in the tabbing order the selection list is placed.

Standard/Usage: HTML 4   **Widely Supported:** No

Sample:
```
<select name="salary" tabindex="3">...</select>
```

title="..."

Specifies text assigned to the element. You can use this attribute for context-sensitive help within the document. Browsers may use this to show tooltips over the selection list.

Standard/Usage: HTML 4   **Widely Supported:** No

Sample:
```
<select title="select list" name="car">...</select>
```

Other Attributes

The select element also accepts the lang, dir, onfocus, onblur, onchange, onselect, onclick, ondblclick, onmousedown, onmouseup, onmouseover, onmousemove, onmouseout, onkeypress, onkeydown, and onkeyup attributes.

small

Specifies text that should appear in a small font.

Standard/Usage:	HTML 3.2	**Widely Supported:**	Yes	**Empty:**	No

Sample:
```
<p>Our lawyers said we need to include some fine print:</p>
<p><small>By reading this document, you're breaking the rules and will be assessed
   a $2000 fine.</small></p>
```

class="..."

Indicates which style class applies to the small element.

Standard/Usage:	HTML 4	**Widely Supported:**	No

Sample:
```
<small class="casual">Void where prohibited.</small>
```

id="..."

Assigns a unique ID selector to an instance of the small element. When you then assign a style to that ID selector, it affects only that one instance of the small element.

Standard/Usage:	HTML 4	**Widely Supported:**	No

Sample:
```
<p>Most insects are <small id="123">small</small>.</p>
```

style="..."

Specifies style sheet commands that apply to the contents of the small tags.

Standard/Usage:	HTML 4	**Widely Supported:**	Yes

Sample:
```
<small style="background: red">...</small>
```

title="..."

Specifies text assigned to the element. You can use this attribute for context-sensitive help within the document. Browsers may use this to show tooltips over the text inside the small tags.

Standard/Usage:	HTML 4	**Widely Supported:**	No

Sample:
```
<small title="Legalese">This will subject you to risk of criminal prosecution.</small>
```

Other Attributes

The small element also accepts the lang, dir, onclick, ondblclick, onmousedown, onmouseup, onmouseover, onmousemove, onmouseout, onkeypress, onkeydown, and onkeyup attributes.

spacer

A Netscape-specific element that specifies a blank space within the document. We recommend using style sheets or other formatting techniques unless you're developing documents exclusively for Netscape Navigator users.

Standard/Usage:	Netscape Navigator 3	**Widely Supported:**	No	**Empty:**	Yes

Sample:
```
<spacer type="horizontal" size="150" />
Doctors Prefer MediWidget 4 to 1
```

align="left|right|top|texttop|middle|abbsmib|baseline|bottom|absbottom"

Specifies the alignment of text around the spacer. Only used when `type="block"`.

Standard/Usage: Netscape Navigator 3 **Widely Supported:** No

Sample:
```
<spacer type="block" align="left" />
```

height="n"

Specifies the height of the spacer (in pixels). Only used when `type="block"`.

Standard/Usage: Netscape Navigator 3 **Widely Supported:** No

Sample:
```
<spacer type="block" height="50" />
<img src="rosebush.jpg" />
```

size="n"

Specifies the dimension of the spacer (in pixels).

Standard/Usage: Netscape Navigator 3 **Widely Supported:** No

Sample:
```
<spacer type="horizontal" size="50" />
<img src="rosebush.jpg" />
```

type="horizontal|vertical|block"

Indicates whether the spacer measures from left to right, from top to bottom, or a block (acts like a transparent image).

Standard/Usage: Netscape Navigator 3 **Widely Supported:** No

Sample:
```
<p>After you've done this, take a moment to review your work.
<spacer type="vertical" size="400" /></p>
<p>Now, isn't that better?</p>
```

span

Defines an inline section of a document affected by style sheet attributes. Use `div` to apply styles at the block element level.

Standard/Usage: HTML 4 **Widely Supported:** No **Empty:** No

Sample:
```
<span style="background: red">…</span>
```

class="..."

Indicates which style class applies to the span element.

Standard/Usage: HTML 4 **Widely Supported:** No

Sample:
```
<span class="casual">…</span>
```

id="..."

Assigns a unique ID selector to an instance of the span element. When you then assign a style to that ID selector, it affects only that one instance of the span element.

Standard/Usage:	HTML 4	Widely Supported:	No

Sample:
```
<span id="123">…</span>
```

style="..."

Specifies style sheet commands that apply to the contents of the span tags.

Standard/Usage:	HTML 4	Widely Supported:	No

Sample:
```
<span style="background: red">…</span>
```

title="..."

Specifies text assigned to the element. You can use this attribute for context-sensitive help within the document. Browsers may use this to show tooltips.

Standard/Usage:	HTML 4	Widely Supported:	No

Sample:
```
<span title="section" style="background: red">…</span>
```

Other Attributes

The span element also accepts the lang, dir, onclick, ondblclick, onmousedown, onmouseup, onmouseover, onmousemove, onmouseout, onkeypress, onkeydown, and onkeyup attributes.

strike

Indicates strikethrough text. This element is deprecated in HTML 4 in favor of style sheets.

Standard/Usage:	HTML 3.2; deprecated	Widely Supported:	Yes	Empty:	No

Sample:
```
My junior high biology teacher was <strike>sort of</strike> really smart.
```

class="..."

Indicates which style class applies to the strike element.

Standard/Usage:	HTML 4	Widely Supported:	No

Sample:
```
<strike class="casual">Truman</strike> lost.
```

id="..."

Assigns a unique ID selector to an instance of the strike element. When you then assign a style to that ID selector, it affects only that one instance of the strike element.

Standard/Usage:	HTML 4	Widely Supported:	No

Sample:
```
Don <strike id="123">ain't</strike> isn't coming tonight.
```

style="..."

Specifies style sheet commands that apply to the contents of the strike tags.

Standard/Usage: HTML 4   **Widely Supported:**   No

Sample:

```
<strike style="background: red">…</strike>
```

title="..."

Specifies text assigned to the element. You can use this attribute for context-sensitive help within the document. Browsers may use this to show tooltips over the text.

Standard/Usage: HTML 4   **Widely Supported:**   No

Sample:

```
<p>He was <strike title="omit">ambitious</strike>enthusiastic.</p>
```

Other Attributes

The strike element also accepts the lang, dir, onclick, ondblclick, onmousedown, onmouseup, onmouseover, onmousemove, onmouseout, onkeypress, onkeydown, and onkeyup attributes.

strong

Indicates strong emphasis. The browser will probably display the text in a boldface font.

Standard/Usage: HTML 2   **Widely Supported:**   Yes   **Empty:**   No

Sample:

```
If you see a poisonous spider in the room then <strong>get out of there!</strong>
```

class="..."

Indicates which style class applies to the strong element.

Standard/Usage: HTML 4   **Widely Supported:**   No

Sample:

```
Did you say my dog is <strong class="urgent">missing?!</strong>
```

id="..."

Assigns a unique ID selector to an instance of the strong element. When you then assign a style to that ID selector, it affects only that one instance of the strong element.

Standard/Usage: HTML 4   **Widely Supported:**   No

Sample:

```
Sure, you can win at gambling. But you'll probably <strong id="123">lose</strong>.
```

style="..."

Specifies style sheet commands that apply to the contents of the strong tags.

Standard/Usage: HTML 4   **Widely Supported:**   No

Sample:

```
<strong style="background: red">…</strong>
```

title="..."

Specifies text assigned to the element. You can use this attribute for context-sensitive help within the document. Browsers may use this to show tooltips over the emphasized text.

Standard/Usage: HTML 4   **Widely Supported:**   No

Sample:

```
I mean it was <strong title="emphasis">HOT!</strong>
```

Other Attributes

The strong element also accepts the lang, dir, onclick, ondblclick, onmousedown, onmouseup, onmouseover, onmousemove, onmouseout, onkeypress, onkeydown, and onkeyup attributes.

style

Contains style sheet definitions and appears in the document head (see the head element). Place style sheet data within comment markup (<!--...-->) to accommodate browsers that do not support the style element.

Standard/Usage: HTML 3.2   **Widely Supported:**   No   **Empty:**   No

Sample:

```
<html xmlns="http://www.w3.org/1999/xhtml">
    <head>
        <title>Edible Socks: Good or Bad?</title>
        <style type="text/css">
        <!--
            h1    { background: black; color: yellow }
            li dd { background: silver; color: black }
        -->
        </style>
    </head>
```

media="..."

Specifies the destination medium for style information. It may be a single type or a comma-separated list. Media types include the following:

Value	Media Type
all	Applies to all devices
aural	Speech synthesizer
braille	Braille tactile feedback devices
handheld	Handheld devices
print	Traditional printed material and documents on screen viewed in print preview mode
projection	Projectors
screen	Online viewing (default setting)
tty	Teletypes, terminals, or portable devices with limited display capabilities
tv	Television-type devices

Standard/Usage: HTML 4   **Widely Supported:**   No

Sample:

```
<style type="text/css" media="all">
   <!--
      h1    { background: black; color: white }
      li dd { background: silver; color: darkgreen }
   -->
</style>
```

title="..."

Specifies text assigned to the element. You can use this attribute for context-sensitive help within the document. Browsers may use this to show tooltips.

Standard/Usage:	HTML 4	Widely Supported:	No

Sample:

```
<style title="Stylesheet 1" type="text/css">
   <!--
      h1 { background: black; color: yellow }
      li dd { background: silver; color: black }
   -->
</style>
```

type="..."

Specifies the MIME type of the style sheet specification standard used.

Standard/Usage:	HTML 4; required	Widely Supported:	No

Sample:

```
<style type="text/css">
   <!--
      h1 { background: black; color: white }
      li dd { background: silver; color: darkgreen }
   -->
</style>
```

Other Attributes

The style element also accepts the lang and dir attributes.

sub

Indicates subscript text.

Standard/Usage:	HTML 3.2	Widely Supported:	Yes	Empty:	No

Sample:

```
<p>Chemists refer to water as H<sub>2</sub>O.</p>
```

class="..."

Indicates which style class applies to the sub element.

Standard/Usage:	HTML 4	Widely Supported:	No

Sample:

```
H<sub class="chemical">2</sub>O
```

id="..."

Assigns a unique ID selector to an instance of the sub element. When you then assign a style to that ID selector, it affects only that one instance of the sub element.

Standard/Usage:	HTML 4	**Widely Supported:**	No

Sample:

```
At the dentist I ask for lots of NO<sub id="123">2</sub>.
```

style="..."

Specifies style sheet commands that apply to the contents of the sub tags.

Standard/Usage:	HTML 4	**Widely Supported:**	No

Sample:

```
<sub style="background: red">…</sub>
```

title="..."

Specifies text assigned to the element. You can use this attribute for context-sensitive help within the document. Browsers may use this to show tooltips over the subscripted text.

Standard/Usage:	HTML 4	**Widely Supported:**	No

Sample:

```
Before he fell asleep, he uttered, "Groovy."<sub title="Footnote">2</sub>
```

Other Attributes

The sub element also accepts the lang, dir, onclick, ondblclick, onmousedown, onmouseup, onmouseover, onmousemove, onmouseout, onkeypress, onkeydown, and onkeyup attributes.

sup

Indicates superscript text.

Standard/Usage:	HTML 3.2	**Widely Supported:**	Yes	**Empty:**	No

Sample:

```
<p>Einstein's most famous equation is E=mc<sup>2</sup>.</p>
```

class="..."

Indicates which style class applies to the sup element.

Standard/Usage:	HTML 4	**Widely Supported:**	No

Sample:

```
z<sup class="exp">2</sup> = x<sup class="exp">2</sup> + y<sup class="exp">2</sup>
```

id="..."

Assigns a unique ID selector to an instance of the sup element. When you then assign a style to that ID selector, it affects only that one instance of the sup element.

Standard/Usage:	HTML 4	**Widely Supported:**	No

Sample:

```
Pythagorean theorem says z<sup id="123">2</sup> = 4 + 16.
```

table   885

style="..."

Specifies style sheet commands that apply to the contents of the sup tags.

Standard/Usage: HTML 4   **Widely Supported:** No

Sample:
```
<sup style="background: red">…</sup>
```

title="..."

Specifies text assigned to the element. You can use this attribute for context-sensitive help within the document. Browsers may use this to show tooltips over the superscripted text.

Standard/Usage: HTML 4   **Widely Supported:** No

Sample:
```
x<sup title="Exponent">2</sup>
```

Other Attributes

The sup element also accepts the lang, dir, onclick, ondblclick, onmousedown, onmouseup, onmouseover, onmousemove, onmouseout, onkeypress, onkeydown, and onkeyup attributes.

t

table

Specifies a container for a table within your document. Inside these tags you can place tr, td, th, caption, and other table elements.

Standard/Usage: HTML 3.2   **Widely Supported:** Yes   **Empty:** No

Sample:
```
<table border="0">
    <tr>
        <td><img src="pine.jpg" border="0" alt="pine" /></td>
        <td valign="middle">Pine trees naturally grow at higher elevations. They require
            less water and do not shed leaves in the fall.</td>
    </tr>
</table>
```

align="left|right|center"

Positions the table flush left, flush right, or in the center of the window. This attribute is deprecated in favor of style sheets.

Standard/Usage: HTML 3.2; deprecated   **Widely Supported:** Yes

Sample:
```
<table align="center">…</table>
```

background="url"

Specifies the relative or absolute location of an image file loaded as a background image for the entire table.

Standard/Usage: Internet Explorer 3, Netscape Navigator 4   **Widely Supported:** No

Sample:
```
<table background="paper.jpg">…</table>
```

bgcolor="#rrggbb" or "..."

Specifies the background color within all table cells in the table. You can substitute color names for the hexadecimal RGB values. This attribute is deprecated in favor of style sheets.

Standard/Usage: HTML 4; deprecated   **Widely Supported:**   No

Sample:
```
<table bgcolor="peach">...</table>
```

border="n"

Specifies the thickness (in pixels) of borders around each table cell. Use a value of 0 to produce a table with no visible borders.

Standard/Usage: HTML 3.2   **Widely Supported:**   Yes

Sample:
```
<table border="0">...</table>
```

bordercolor="#rrggbb" or "..."

Specifies the color of the borders of all the table cells in the table. You can substitute color names for the hexadecimal RGB values.

Standard/Usage: Internet Explorer 2, Netscape Navigator 4   **Widely Supported:**   No

Sample:
```
<table bordercolor="#3f9a11">...</table>
```

bordercolordark="#rrggbb" or "..."

Specifies the darker color used to draw 3-D borders around the table cells. You can substitute color names for the hexadecimal RGB values.

Standard/Usage: Internet Explorer 2   **Widely Supported:**   No

Sample:
```
<table bordercolordark="silver">...</table>
```

bordercolorlight="#rrggbb" or "..."

Specifies the lighter color used to draw 3-D borders around the table cells. You can substitute color names for the hexadecimal RGB values.

Standard/Usage: Internet Explorer 2   **Widely Supported:**   No

Sample:
```
<table bordercolorlight="white">...</table>
```

cellpadding="n"

Specifies the space (in pixels) between the edges of table cells and their contents.

Standard/Usage: HTML 3.2   **Widely Supported:**   Yes

Sample:
```
<table cellpadding="5">...</table>
```

cellspacing="n"

Specifies the space (in pixels) between the borders of table cells and the borders of adjacent cells.

Standard/Usage: HTML 3.2   **Widely Supported:**   Yes

Sample:
```
<table border="2" cellspacing="5">...</table>
```

table   887

class="..."

Indicates which style class applies to the table element.

Standard/Usage: HTML 4   **Widely Supported:** No

Sample:

```
<table class="table" border="2">…</table>
```

cols="n"

Specifies the number of columns in the table.

Standard/Usage: Internet Explorer 3, Netscape Navigator 4   **Widely Supported:** No

Sample:

```
<table border="2" cols="5">…</table>
```

frame="void|border|above|below|hsides|lhs|rhs|vsides|box"

Specifies the external borderlines *around* the table. For the frame attribute to work, set the border attribute to a nonzero value.

Value	Specifies
void	No borderlines
box or border	Borderlines around the entire table (the default)
above	A borderline along the top edge
below	A borderline along the bottom edge
hsides	Borderlines along the top and bottom edges
lhs	A borderline along the left edge
rhs	A borderline along the right edge
vsides	Borderlines along the left and right edges

Standard/Usage: HTML 4   **Widely Supported:** No

Sample:

```
<table border="2" rules="all" frame="vsides">…</table>
```

id="..."

Assigns a unique ID selector to an instance of the table element. When you then assign a style to that ID selector, it affects only that one instance of the table element.

Standard/Usage: HTML 4   **Widely Supported:** No

Sample:

```
<table id="123">…</table>
```

rules="none|rows|cols|all|groups"

Specifies where rule lines appear *inside* the table. For the rules attribute to work, set the border attribute to a nonzero value.

Value	Specifies
none	No rule lines
rows	Rule lines between rows
cols	Rule lines between columns
all	All possible rule lines
groups	Rule lines between the groups defined by the tfoot, thead, tbody, and colgroup elements

Standard/Usage:	HTML 4	Widely Supported:	No

Sample:

```
<table border="2" rules="all">…</table>
```

style="..."

Specifies style sheet commands that apply to the contents of cells in the table.

Standard/Usage:	HTML 4	Widely Supported:	No

Sample:

```
<table style="background: red">…</table>
```

summary="..."

Specifies descriptive text for the table. It's recommended that you use this attribute to summarize or describe the table for use by browsers that do not visually display tables (for example, Braille or text-only browsers).

Standard/Usage:	HTML 4	Widely Supported:	No

Sample:

```
<table summary="This table shows that 50% of sick days are taken on Mondays.">…</table>
```

title="..."

Specifies text assigned to the element. You can use this attribute for context-sensitive help within the document. Browsers may use this to show tooltips over the table.

Standard/Usage:	HTML 4	Widely Supported:	No

Sample:

```
<table title="table">…</table>
```

width="n"

Specifies the width of the table. You can set this value to an absolute number of pixels or to a percentage amount so the table is proportionally as wide as the available space.

Standard/Usage:	HTML 3.2	Widely Supported:	Yes

Sample:

```
<table align="center" width="60%">…</table>
```

Other Attributes

The table element also accepts the lang, dir, onclick, ondblclick, onmousedown, onmouseup, onmouseover, onmousemove, onmouseout, onkeypress, onkeydown, and onkeyup attributes.

tbody

Defines the table body within a table. This element must *follow* the tfoot element.

Standard/Usage:	HTML 4	Widely Supported:	No	Empty:	No

Sample:

```
<table>
    <thead>…</thead>
    <tfoot>…</tfoot>
    <tbody>…</tbody>
</table>
```

align="left|right|center|justify|char"

Specifies how text within the table footer will line up with the edges of the table cells, or if align="char", on a specific character (the decimal point by default).

Standard/Usage: HTML 4   **Widely Supported:**   Yes

Sample:
```
<tbody align="left">…</tbody>
```

char="..."

Specifies the character on which cell contents will align, if align="char". If you omit the char attribute, the default value is the decimal point in the specified language.

Standard/Usage: HTML 4   **Widely Supported:**   No

Sample:
```
<tbody align="left" char="a">…</tbody>
```

charoff="n"

Specifies the number of characters from the left at which the alignment character appears.

Standard/Usage: HTML 4   **Widely Supported:**   No

Sample:
```
<tbody align="char" char="," charoff="7">…</tbody>
```

class="..."

Indicates which style class applies to the tbody element.

Standard/Usage: HTML 4   **Widely Supported:**   No

Sample:
```
<tbody class="casual">…</tbody>
```

id="..."

Assigns a unique ID selector to an instance of the tbody element. When you then assign a style to that ID selector, it affects only that one instance of the tbody element.

Standard/Usage: HTML 4   **Widely Supported:**   No

Sample:
```
<tbody id="123"></tbody>
```

style="..."

Specifies style sheet commands that apply to the contents of the tbody tags.

Standard/Usage: HTML 4   **Widely Supported:**   No

Sample:
```
<tbody style="background: red">…</tbody>
```

title="..."

Specifies text assigned to the element. You can use this attribute for context-sensitive help within the document. Browsers may use this to show tooltips over the table body.

Standard/Usage: HTML 4   **Widely Supported:**   No

Sample:
```
<tbody title="Table Body">…</tbody>
```

valign="top|bottom|middle|baseline"

Specifies the vertical alignment of the contents of the table body.

Standard/Usage:	Internet Explorer 4	**Widely Supported:**	No

Sample:

```
<tbody valign="middle">...</tbody>
```

Other Attributes

The tbody element also accepts the `lang`, `dir`, `onclick`, `ondblclick`, `onmousedown`, `onmouseup`, `onmouseover`, `onmousemove`, `onmouseout`, `onkeypress`, `onkeydown`, and `onkeyup` attributes.

td

Contains a table cell. These elements go inside `tr` elements.

Standard/Usage:	HTML 3.2	**Widely Supported:**	Yes	**Empty:**	No

Sample:

```
<tr>
   <td>Bob Jones</td>
   <td>555-1212</td> <td>Democrat</td>
</tr>
```

abbr="..."

Specifies short replacement text associated with the element contents. When appropriate, browsers may use this text in place of the actual contents.

Standard/Usage:	HTML 4	**Widely Supported:**	No

Sample:

```
<td title="Year to Date Summary" abbr="ytd">Year to Date</td>
```

axis="..."

Specifies cell categories. The values can be a comma-separated list of category names.

Standard/Usage:	HTML 4	**Widely Supported:**	No

Sample:

```
<td axis="TV">Television</td>
```

align="left|right|center|justify|char"

Specifies how text within the table header will line up with the edges of the table cells, or if `align="char"`, on a specific character (the decimal point by default).

Standard/Usage:	HTML 4	**Widely Supported:**	Yes

Sample:

```
<tr>
   <td align="center">Television</td>
   <td><img src="tv.gif" alt="TV" border="0" /></td>
</tr>
```

background="url"

Specifies the relative or absolute location of an image file for the browser to load as a background graphic for the table cell.

Standard/Usage: Internet Explorer 4, Netscape Navigator 3 **Widely Supported:** No

Sample:
```
<td background="waves.gif">Oceanography</td>
```

bgcolor="#rrggbb" or "..."

Specifies the background color inside a table cell. You can substitute the hexadecimal RGB values for the appropriate color names. This attribute is deprecated in favor of style sheets.

Standard/Usage: HTML 4; deprecated **Widely Supported:** No

Sample:
```
<td bgcolor="pink">Course Number</td>
```

bordercolor="#rrggbb" or "..."

Indicates the color of the border of the table cell. You can specify the color with hexadecimal RGB values or by the color name.

Standard/Usage: Internet Explorer 2 **Widely Supported:** No

Sample:
```
<td bordercolor="blue">Time Taught</td>
```

bordercolordark="#rrggbb" or "..."

Indicates the darker color used to form 3-D borders around the table cell. You can specify the color with its hexadecimal RGB values or with its color name.

Standard/Usage: Internet Explorer 2 **Widely Supported:** No

Sample:
```
<td bordercolorlight="#ffffff" bordercolordark="#88aa2c">...</td>
```

bordercolorlight="#rrggbb" or "..."

Indicates the lighter color used to form 3-D borders around the table cell. You can specify the color with its hexadecimal RGB values or with its color name.

Standard/Usage: Internet Explorer 2 **Widely Supported:** No

Sample:
```
<td bordercolorlight="#ffffff" bordercolordark="#88aa2c">...</td>
```

char="..."

Specifies the character on which cell contents will align, if align="char". If you omit the char attribute, the default value is the decimal point in the specified language.

Standard/Usage: HTML 4 **Widely Supported:** No

Sample:
```
<td align="char" char=",">...</td>
```

charoff="n"

Specifies the number of characters from the left at which the alignment character appears.

    Standard/Usage: HTML 4   **Widely Supported:**   No

    Sample:

```
<td align="char" char="," charoff="7">…</td>
```

class="..."

Indicates which style class applies to the td element.

    Standard/Usage: HTML 4   **Widely Supported:**   No

    Sample:

```
<td class="casual">Jobs Produced</td>
```

colspan="n"

Specifies that a table cell occupies more columns than the default of 1. This is useful when you have a category name that applies to multiple columns of data.

    Standard/Usage: HTML 3.2   **Widely Supported:**   Yes

    Sample:

```
<tr>
   <td colspan="2">Students</td>
</tr>
<tr>
   <td>Bob Smith</td>
   <td>Jane Doe</td>
</tr>
```

id="..."

Assigns a unique ID selector to an instance of the td element. When you then assign a style to that ID selector, it affects only that one instance of the td element.

    Standard/Usage: HTML 4   **Widely Supported:**   No

    Sample:

```
<td id="123">…</td>
```

headers="..."

Specifies the ID names of table header cells associated with the current cell for use by browsers in presenting the table contents.

    Standard/Usage: HTML 4   **Widely Supported:**   No

    Sample:

```
<td title="Year to Date Summary" headers="th1,th4">Year to Date</td>
```

height="n"

Specifies the vertical dimension (in pixels) of the cell. This attribute is deprecated in favor of style sheets.

    Standard/Usage: HTML 3.2; deprecated   **Widely Supported:**   No

    Sample:

```
<td title="Year to Date Summary" height="200">Year to Date</td>
```

nowrap="nowrap"

Disables the default word-wrapping within a table cell, thus maximizing the amount of the cell's horizontal space. This attribute is deprecated in favor of style sheets.

Standard/Usage: HTML 3; deprecated   **Widely Supported:**   No

Sample:

```
<td nowrap="nowrap">The contents of this cell will not wrap at all</td>
```

rowspan="n"

Specifies that a table cell occupies more rows than the default of 1. This is useful when several rows of information are related to one category.

Standard/Usage: HTML 3.2   **Widely Supported:**   Yes

Sample:

```
<tr>
    <td valign="middle" align="right" rowspan="3">Pie Entries</td>
    <td>Banana Cream</td>
    <td>Mrs. Robinson</td></tr>
<tr>
    <td>Strawberry Cheesecake</td>
    <td>Mr. Barton</td></tr>
<tr>
    <td>German Chocolate</td>
    <td>Ms. Larson</td></tr>
```

scope="row|col|rowgroup|colgroup"

Specifies the row, row group, column, or column group to which the specific header information contained in the current cell applies. When appropriate, browsers may use this information to help present the table.

Standard/Usage: HTML 4   **Widely Supported:**   No

Sample:

```
<td title="Year to Date Summary" scope="rowgroup">Year to Date</td>
```

style="..."

Specifies style sheet commands that apply to the contents of the table cell.

Standard/Usage: HTML 4   **Widely Supported:**   No

Sample:

```
<td style="background: red">...</td>
```

title="..."

Specifies text assigned to the element. You can use this attribute for context-sensitive help within the document. Browsers may use this to show tooltips over the table header.

Standard/Usage: HTML 4   **Widely Supported:**   No

Sample:

```
<td title="table cell heading">...</td>
```

valign="top|middle|bottom|baseline"

Aligns the contents of a cell within the cell.

Standard/Usage:	HTML 3.2	**Widely Supported:**	Yes
Sample:			

```
<td valign="top"><img src="images/bud.gif" alt="bud.gif" border="0" /></td>
```

width="n"

Specifies the horizontal dimension of the cell in pixels or as a percentage of the table width. This attribute is deprecated in favor of style sheets.

Standard/Usage:	HTML 3.2; deprecated	**Widely Supported:**	Yes
Sample:			

```
<td width="200" align="left">African Species</td>
```

Other Attributes

The td element also accepts the lang, dir, onclick, ondblclick, onmousedown, onmouseup, onmouseover, onmousemove, onmouseout, onkeypress, onkeydown, and onkeyup attributes.

textarea

Defines a multiple-line text input field within a form. Place the textarea elements inside the form tags. To specify a default value in a textarea field, place the text between the textarea tags.

Standard/Usage:	HTML 2	**Widely Supported:**	Yes	**Empty:**	No
Sample:					

```
Enter any comments here:
<textarea name="comments" cols="40" rows="5">No Comments.</textarea>
```

accesskey="..."

Assigns a keystroke sequence to the textarea element.

Standard/Usage:	HTML 4	**Widely Supported:**	No
Sample:			

```
<textarea cols="40" rows="10" name="story" accesskey="s">…</textarea>
```

class="..."

Indicates which style class applies to the textarea element.

Standard/Usage:	HTML 4	**Widely Supported:**	No
Sample:			

```
<textarea cols="50" rows="3" class="casual">…</textarea>
```

cols="n"

Indicates the width (in character widths) of the text input field.

Standard/Usage:	HTML 2; required	**Widely Supported:**	Yes
Sample:			

```
<textarea name="desc" cols="50" rows="3">…</textarea>
```

disabled="disabled"

Denies access to the text-input field.

Standard/Usage:	HTML 4	Widely Supported:	No

Sample:

```
<textarea rows="10" cols="10" name="comments" disabled="disabled">…</textarea>
```

id="..."

Assigns a unique ID selector to an instance of the textarea element. When you then assign a style to that ID selector, it affects only that one instance of the textarea element.

Standard/Usage:	HTML 4	Widely Supported:	No

Sample:

```
<textarea rows="10" cols="10" id="123">…</textarea>
```

name="..."

Names the value you pass to the form processor. For example, if you collect personal feedback, assign the name attribute something like comments. This establishes a *name-value pair* with which the form processor can work.

Standard/Usage:	HTML 2	Widely Supported:	Yes

Sample:

```
<textarea cols="30" rows="10" name="comments">…</textarea>
```

readonly="readonly"

Specifies that the user cannot change the contents of the text input field.

Standard/Usage:	HTML 4	Widely Supported:	No

Sample:

```
<textarea rows="10" cols="10" name="notes" readonly="readonly">…</textarea>
```

rows="n"

Indicates the height (in lines of text) of the text input field.

Standard/Usage:	HTML 2; required	Widely Supported:	Yes

Sample:

```
<textarea name="desc" cols="50" rows="3">…</textarea>
```

style="..."

Specifies style sheet commands that apply to the textarea element.

Standard/Usage:	HTML 4	Widely Supported:	No

Sample:

```
<textarea rows="5" cols="40" style="background: red">…</textarea>
```

tabindex="n"

Indicates where textarea appears in the tabbing order.

Standard/Usage:	HTML 4	Widely Supported:	No

Sample:

```
<textarea rows="5" cols="40" name="story" tabindex="2">…</textarea>
```

title="..."

Specifies text assigned to the element. You can use this attribute for context-sensitive help within the document. Browsers may use this to show tooltips over the text entry input method.

Standard/Usage: HTML 4   **Widely Supported:** No

Sample:
```
<textarea cols="10" rows="2" name="tt" title="text entry box">...</textarea>
```

Other Attributes

The textarea element also accepts the lang, dir, onfocus, onblur, onchange, onselect, onclick, ondblclick, onmousedown, onmouseup, onmouseover, onmousemove, onmouseout, onkeypress, onkeydown, and onkeyup attributes.

tfoot

Defines a table footer within a table. It must *precede* the tbody element.

Standard/Usage: HTML 4   **Widely Supported:** No   **Empty:** No

Sample:
```
<table>
    <thead>...</thead>
    <tfoot>
        <tr><td>Totals</td><td>$100.25</td></tr>
    </tfoot>
    <tbody>...</tbody>
</table>
```

align="left|right|center|justify|char"

Specifies how text within the table footer will line up with the edges of the table cells, or if align="char", on a specific character.

Standard/Usage: HTML 4   **Widely Supported:** Yes

Sample:
```
<tfoot align="center">...</tfoot>
```

char="..."

Specifies the character on which cell contents will align, if align="char". If you omit the char attribute, the default value is the decimal point in the specified language.

Standard/Usage: HTML 4   **Widely Supported:** No

Sample:
```
<tfoot align="char" char=",">...</tfoot>
```

charoff="n"

Specifies the number of characters from the left at which the alignment character appears.

Standard/Usage: HTML 4   **Widely Supported:** No

Sample:
```
<tfoot align="char" char="," charoff="7">...</tfoot>
```

class="..."

Indicates which style class applies to the tfoot element.

Standard/Usage: HTML 4   **Widely Supported:**   No
Sample:
`<tfoot class="casual">...</tfoot>`

id="..."

Assigns a unique ID selector to an instance of the tfoot element. When you then assign a style to that ID selector, it affects only that one instance of the tfoot element.

Standard/Usage: HTML 4   **Widely Supported:**   No
Sample:
`<tfoot id="123">...</tfoot>`

style="..."

Specifies style sheet commands that apply to the contents of the tfoot tags.

Standard/Usage: HTML 4   **Widely Supported:**   No
Sample:
`<tfoot style="background: red">...</tfoot>`

title="..."

Specifies text assigned to the element. You can use this attribute for context-sensitive help within the document. Browsers may use this to show tooltips over the table footer.

Standard/Usage: HTML 4   **Widely Supported:**   No
Sample:
`<tfoot title="Table Footer">...</tfoot>`

valign="top|bottom|middle|baseline"

Aligns the contents of the table footer with the top, bottom, or middle of the footer container.

Standard/Usage: HTML 4   **Widely Supported:**   No
Sample:
`<tfoot align="center" valign="top">...</tfoot>`

Other Attributes

The tfoot element also accepts the lang, dir, onclick, ondblclick, onmousedown, onmouseup, onmouseover, onmousemove, onmouseout, onkeypress, onkeydown, and onkeyup attributes.

th

Contains table cell headings. The th element is identical to the td element except that text inside th is usually emphasized with boldface font, centered within the cell, and represents a table heading instead of table data.

Standard/Usage: HTML 3.2   **Widely Supported:**   Yes   **Empty:**   No

Sample:

```
<table>
   <tr>
      <th>Name</th>
      <th>Phone No.</th>
   </tr>
   <tr>
      <td>Jane Doe</td>
      <td>555-1212</td>
   </tr>
   <tr>
      <td>Bob Smith</td>
      <td>555-2121</td>
   </tr>
</table>
```

abbr="..."

Specifies short replacement text associated with the element contents. When appropriate, browsers may use this text in place of the actual contents.

Standard/Usage: HTML 4   **Widely Supported:**   No

Sample:

```
<th title="Year to Date Summary" abbr="ytd">Year to Date</th>
```

align="left|right|center|justify|char"

Specifies how text within the table header will line up with the edges of the table cells, or if `align="char"`, on a specific character (by default, the decimal point).

Standard/Usage: HTML 4   **Widely Supported:**   Yes

Sample:

```
<th align="right">Television</th>
<th align="left"><img src="tv.gif" alt="tv" border="0" /></th>
```

axis="..."

Specifies cell categories. The value can be a comma-separated list of category names.

Standard/Usage: HTML 4   **Widely Supported:**   No

Sample:

```
<th axis="TV">Television</th>
```

background="url"

Specifies the relative or absolute location of an image file for the browser to load as a background graphic for the table cell.

Standard/Usage: Internet Explorer 4, Netscape Navigator 3   **Widely Supported:** No

Sample:

```
<th background="waves.gif">Oceanography</th>
```

bgcolor="#rrggbb" or "..."

Specifies the background color inside a table cell. You can substitute the hexadecimal RGB values for the appropriate color names. This attribute is deprecated in favor of style sheets.

Standard/Usage: HTML 4; deprecated   **Widely Supported:** No

Sample:
```
<th bgcolor="pink">Course Number</th>
```

bordercolor="#rrggbb" or "..."

Indicates the color of the border of the table cell. You can specify the color with hexadecimal RGB values or by the color name.

Standard/Usage: Internet Explorer 2   **Widely Supported:** No

Sample:
```
<th bordercolor="blue">Time Taught</th>
```

bordercolordark="#rrggbb" or "..."

Indicates the darker color used to form 3-D borders around the table cell. You can specify the color with its hexadecimal RGB values or with its color name.

Standard/Usage: Internet Explorer 2   **Widely Supported:** No

Sample:
```
<th bordercolorlight="#ffffff" bordercolordark="#88aa2c">...</th>
```

bordercolorlight="#rrggbb" or "..."

Indicates the lighter color used to form 3-D borders around the table cell. You can specify the color with its hexadecimal RGB values or with its color name.

Standard/Usage: Internet Explorer 2   **Widely Supported:** No

Sample:
```
<th bordercolorlight="#ffffff" bordercolordark="#88aa2c">...</th>
```

char="..."

Specifies the character on which cell contents align, if `align="char"`. If you omit the char attribute, the default value is the decimal point in the specified language.

Standard/Usage: HTML 4   **Widely Supported:** No

Sample:
```
<th align="char" char=",">...</th>
```

charoff="n"

Specifies the number of characters from the left at which the alignment character appears.

Standard/Usage: HTML 4   **Widely Supported:** No

Sample:
```
<th align="char" char="," charoff="7">...</th>
```

class="..."

Indicates which style class applies to the th element.

Standard/Usage: HTML 4   **Widely Supported:** No

Sample:
```
<th class="casual">Jobs Produced</th>
```

colspan="n"

Specifies that a table header cell occupies more columns than the default of 1. Use this, for example, if a category name applies to more than one column of data.

Standard/Usage: HTML 3.2   **Widely Supported:**   Yes

Sample:
```
<tr>
   <th colspan="2">Students</th>
</tr>
<tr>
   <td>Bob Smith</td>
   <td>Jane Doe</td>
</tr>
```

height="n"

Specifies the vertical dimension (in pixels) of the cell. This attribute is deprecated in favor of style sheets.

Standard/Usage: HTML 3.2; deprecated   **Widely Supported:**   No

Sample:
```
<th title="Year to Date Summary" height="200">Year to Date</th>
```

id="..."

Assigns a unique ID selector to an instance of the th element. When you then assign a style to that ID selector, it affects only that one instance of the th element.

Standard/Usage: HTML 4   **Widely Supported:**   No

Sample:
```
<th id="123">...</th>
```

headers="..."

Specifies the ID names of table header cells associated with the current cell for use by browsers in presenting the table contents.

Standard/Usage: HTML 4   **Widely Supported:**   No

Sample:
```
<th title="Year to Date Summary" headers="th1,th4">Year to Date</th>
```

nowrap="nowrap"

Disables default word wrapping within a table cell, maximizing the cell's horizontal space. This attribute is deprecated in favor of style sheets.

Standard/Usage: HTML 4; deprecated   **Widely Supported:**   No

Sample:
```
<th nowrap="nowrap">The contents of this cell will not wrap at all</th>
```

rowspan="n"

Specifies that a table header cell occupies more rows than the default of 1. This is useful if several rows of informàtion relate to one category.

Standard/Usage: HTML 3.2   **Widely Supported:**   Yes

Sample:
```
<tr>
   <th valign="middle" align="right" rowspan="3">Pie Entries</th>
   <td>Banana Cream</td>
   <td>Mrs. Robinson</td></tr>
<tr>
   <td>Strawberry Cheesecake</td>
   <td>Mr. Barton</td></tr>
<tr>
   <td>German Chocolate</td>
   <td>Ms. Larson</td></tr>
```

scope="row|col|rowgroup|colgroup"

Specifies the row, row group, column, or column group to which the specific header information contained in the current cell applies. When appropriate, browsers may use this information to help present the table.

Standard/Usage:	HTML 4	**Widely Supported:**	No

Sample:
```
<th title="Year to Date Summary" scope="rowgroup">Year to Date</th>
```

style="..."

Specifies style sheet commands that apply to the contents of the table cell.

Standard/Usage:	HTML 4	**Widely Supported:**	No

Sample:
```
<th style="background: red">…</th>
```

title="..."

Specifies text assigned to the element. You can use this attribute for context-sensitive help within the document. Browsers may use this to show tooltips over the table header.

Standard/Usage:	HTML 4	**Widely Supported:**	No

Sample:
```
<th title="Table Cell Heading">…</th>
```

valign="top|middle|bottom|baseline"

Aligns the contents of a cell within the cell.

Standard/Usage:	HTML 3.2	**Widely Supported:**	Yes

Sample:
```
<th valign="top"><img src="images/bud.gif" alt="bud.gif" border="0" /></th>
```

width="n"

Specifies the horizontal dimension of the cell in pixels or as a percentage of the table width. This attribute is deprecated in favor of style sheets.

Standard/Usage:	HTML 3.2; deprecated	**Widely Supported:**	Yes

Sample:
```
<th width="200" align="left">African Species</th>
```

Other Attributes

The th element also accepts the lang, dir, onclick, ondblclick, onmousedown, onmouseup, onmouseover, onmousemove, onmouseout, onkeypress, onkeydown, and onkeyup attributes.

thead

Defines a table header section. At least one table row must go within thead.

| Standard/Usage: | HTML 4 | Widely Supported: | No | Empty: | No |

Sample:
```
<table rules="rows">
   <thead>
      <tr><td>Column 1</td><td>Column 2</td></tr>
   </thead>
</table>
```

align="left|right|center|justify|char"

Specifies how text within the table header will line up with the edges of the table cells, or if align="char", on a specific character (by default, the decimal point).

| Standard/Usage: | HTML 4 | Widely Supported: | Yes |

Sample:
```
<thead align="center">
   <tr>
      <th>Television</th>
      <th>Radio</th>
   </tr>
</thead>
```

char="..."

Specifies the character on which cell contents align, if align="char". If you omit the char attribute, the default value is the decimal point in the specified language.

| Standard/Usage: | HTML 4 | Widely Supported: | No |

Sample:
```
<thead align="char" char=",">...</thead>
```

charoff="n"

Specifies the number of characters from the left at which the alignment character appears.

| Standard/Usage: | HTML 4 | Widely Supported: | No |

Sample:
```
<thead align="char" char="," charoff="7">...</thead>
```

class="..."

Indicates which style class applies to the thead element.

| Standard/Usage: | HTML 4 | Widely Supported: | No |

Sample:
```
<thead class="casual">...</thead>
```

id="..."

Assigns a unique ID selector to an instance of the thead element. When you then assign a style to that ID selector, it affects only that one instance of the thead element.

Standard/Usage:	HTML 4	**Widely Supported:**	No
Sample:			

```
<thead id="123">...</thead>
```

style="..."

Specifies style sheet commands that apply to the contents of the thead tags.

Standard/Usage:	HTML 4	**Widely Supported:**	No
Sample:			

```
<thead style="background: red">...</thead>
```

title="..."

Specifies text assigned to the element. You can use this attribute for context-sensitive help within the document. Browsers may use this to show tooltips over the table head.

Standard/Usage:	HTML 4	**Widely Supported:**	No
Sample:			

```
<thead title="table heading">...</thead>
```

valign="top|middle|bottom|baseline"

Aligns the contents of the table header with respect to the top and bottom edges of the header container.

Standard/Usage:	HTML 4	**Widely Supported:**	No
Sample:			

```
<thead align="left" valign="top">...</thead>
```

Other Attributes

The thead element also accepts the lang, dir, onclick, ondblclick, onmousedown, onmouseup, onmouseover, onmousemove, onmouseout, onkeypress, onkeydown, and onkeyup attributes.

title

Gives the document an official title. The title element appears inside the document header inside the head tags and is required for valid XHTML.

Standard/Usage:	HTML 2; required	**Widely Supported:**	Yes	**Empty:**	No
Sample:					

```
<head><title>How To Build A Go-Cart</title>...</head>
```

This element accepts the lang and dir attributes.

tr

Contains a row of cells in a table. You must place the tr elements inside the table container, which can contain th and td elements.

Standard/Usage:	HTML 3.2	**Widely Supported:**	Yes	**Empty:**	No

Sample:
```
<table>
   <tr>
      <th colspan="3">Test Scores</th></tr>
   <tr>
      <td>Bob Smith</td>
      <td>78</td>
      <td>85</td></tr>
   <tr>
      <td>Jane Doe</td>
      <td>87</td>
      <td>75</td></tr>
</table>
```

align="left|right|center|justify|char"

Specifies how text within the table row will line up with the edges of the table cells, or if align="char", on a specific character (by default, the decimal point).

Standard/Usage:	HTML 4	Widely Supported:	Yes

Sample:
```
<tr align="center">
   <td>Television</td>
   <td>Internet</td>
</tr>
```

bgcolor="#rrggbb" or "..."

Specifies the background color of table cells in the row. You can substitute the color names for the hexadecimal RGB values. This attribute is deprecated in favor of style sheets.

Standard/Usage:	HTML 4; deprecated	Widely Supported:	No

Sample:
```
<tr bgcolor="yellow">
   <td><img src="bette.jpg" alt="bette" border="0" /></td>
   <td align="left" valign="middle">Bette Smith sitting at her desk.</td>
</tr>
```

bordercolor="#rrggbb" or "..."

Specifies the color of cell borders within the row. Currently, only Internet Explorer accepts this attribute. You can substitute color names for the hexadecimal RGB values.

Standard/Usage:	Internet Explorer 2	Widely Supported:	No

Sample:
```
<tr bordercolor="#3F2A55">
   <td align="right" valign="middle">Computers</td>
   <td><img src="computers.jpg" /></td>
</tr>
```

bordercolordark="#rrggbb" or "..."

Indicates the darker color for the 3-D borders around the table row. You can specify the color with its hexadecimal RGB values or with its color name.

Standard/Usage: Internet Explorer 2   **Widely Supported:** No

Sample:
```
<tr bordercolorlight="silver" bordercolordark="black">…</tr>
```

bordercolorlight="#rrggbb" or "..."

Indicates the lighter color for 3-D borders around the table row. You can specify the color with its hexadecimal RGB values or with its color name.

Standard/Usage: Internet Explorer 2   **Widely Supported:** No

Sample:
```
<tr bordercolorlight="silver" bordercolordark="black">…</tr>
```

char="..."

Specifies the character on which cell contents align, if align="char". If you omit the char attribute, the default value is the decimal point in the specified language.

Standard/Usage: HTML 4   **Widely Supported:** No

Sample:
```
<tr align="char" char=",">…</tr>
```

charoff="n"

Specifies the number of characters from the left at which the alignment character appears.

Standard/Usage: HTML 4   **Widely Supported:** No

Sample:
```
<tr align="char" char="," charoff="7">…</tr>
```

class="..."

Indicates which style class applies to the tr element.

Standard/Usage: HTML 4   **Widely Supported:** No

Sample:
```
<tr class="elementary">
  <td>Uranium</td>
  <td>Plutonium</td>
  <td>Radon</td>
</tr>
```

id="..."

Assigns a unique ID selector to an instance of the tr element. When you then assign a style to that ID selector, it affects only that one instance of the tr element.

Standard/Usage: HTML 4   **Widely Supported:** No

Sample:
```
<tr id="123">…</tr>
```

style="..."

Specifies style sheet commands that apply to all cells in the table row.

Standard/Usage:	HTML 4	Widely Supported:	No

Sample:

```
<tr style="background: red">…</tr>
```

title="..."

Specifies text assigned to the element. You can use this attribute for context-sensitive help within the document. Browsers may use this to show tooltips.

Standard/Usage:	HTML 4	Widely Supported:	No

Sample:

```
<tr title="table row">…</tr>
```

valign="top|middle|bottom|baseline"

Specifies the vertical alignment of the contents of all cells within the row.

Standard/Usage:	HTML 3.2	Widely Supported:	Yes

Sample:

```
<tr valign="top">
   <td align="center">Jane Smith</td>
   <td align="center">Bob Doe</td>
</tr>
```

Other Attributes

The tr element also accepts the lang, dir, onclick, ondblclick, onmousedown, onmouseup, onmouseover, onmousemove, onmouseout, onkeypress, onkeydown, and onkeyup attributes.

tt

Displays text in a monospace font.

Standard/Usage:	HTML 2	Widely Supported:	Yes	Empty:	No

Sample:

```
After I typed help, the words <tt>help: not found</tt> appeared on my screen.
```

class="..."

Indicates which style class applies to the tt element.

Standard/Usage:	HTML 4	Widely Supported:	No

Sample:

```
<p>I began to type. <tt class="casual">It was a dark and stormy night.</tt></p>
```

id="..."

Assigns a unique ID selector to an instance of the tt element. When you then assign a style to that ID selector, it affects only that one instance of the tt element.

Standard/Usage:	HTML 4	Widely Supported:	No

Sample:

```
<tt id="123">…</tt>
```

style="..."

Specifies style sheet commands that apply to the contents of the tt elements.

Standard/Usage: HTML 4   **Widely Supported:** No

Sample:
```
<tt style="background: red">...</tt>
```

title="..."

Specifies text assigned to the element. You can use this attribute for context-sensitive help within the document. Browsers may use this to show tooltips over the text within the tt elements.

Standard/Usage: HTML 4   **Widely Supported:** No

Sample:
```
<p>Now, type <tt title="user typing">mail</tt> and hit the <kbd>Enter</kbd> key.</p>
```

Other Attributes

The tt element also accepts the lang, dir, onclick, ondblclick, onmousedown, onmouseup, onmouseover, onmousemove, onmouseout, onkeypress, onkeydown, and onkeyup attributes.

u

u

Underlines text in a document. Use this element in moderation; underlined text can confuse users, because they're accustomed to seeing hyperlinks underlined. This element is deprecated in HTML 4 in favor of style sheets.

Standard/Usage: HTML 2; deprecated   **Widely Supported:** Yes   **Empty:** No

Sample:
```
After waterskiing, I was <u>really</u> tired.
```

class="..."

Indicates which style class applies to the u element.

Standard/Usage: HTML 4   **Widely Supported:** No

Sample:
```
Have you seen <u class="casual">Tomb Raider</u> yet?
```

id="..."

Assigns a unique ID selector to an instance of the u element. When you then assign a style to that ID selector, it affects only that one instance of the u element.

Standard/Usage: HTML 4   **Widely Supported:** No

Sample:
```
<u id="123">...</u>
```

style="..."

Specifies style sheet commands that apply to the contents of the u tags.

Standard/Usage: HTML 4   **Widely Supported:** No

Sample:
```
<u style="background: red">...</u>
```

title="..."

Specifies text assigned to the element. You can use this attribute for context-sensitive help within the document. Browsers may use this to show tooltips over the underlined text.

Standard/Usage:	HTML 4	**Widely Supported:**	No

Sample:
```
<p>Read the book <u title="BookTitle">Walden</u> and you'll be enlightened.</p>
```

Other Attributes

The u element also accepts the lang, dir, onclick, ondblclick, onmousedown, onmouseup, onmouseover, onmouse-move, onmouseout, onkeypress, onkeydown, and onkeyup attributes.

ul

Contains a bulleted (unordered) list. You then use the li (list item) element to add bulleted items to the list.

Standard/Usage:	HTML 2	**Widely Supported:**	Yes	**Empty:**	No

Sample:
```
Before you can begin, you need:
<ul>
    <li>Circular saw</li>
    <li>Drill with Phillips bit</li>
    <li>Wood screws</li>
</ul>
```

class="..."

Indicates which style class applies to the ul element. Use li elements within the ul tags.

Standard/Usage:	HTML 4	**Widely Supported:**	No

Sample:
```
<ul class="casual">...</ul>
```

compact="compact"

Indicates that the unordered list appears in a compact format. This attribute may not affect the appearance of the list because most browsers do not present lists in more than one format. This attribute is deprecated in HTML 4.

Standard/Usage:	HTML 2; deprecated	**Widely Supported:**	No

Sample:
```
<ul compact="compact">...</ul>
```

id="..."

Assigns a unique ID selector to an instance of the ul element. When you then assign a style to that ID selector, it affects only that one instance of the ul element.

Standard/Usage:	HTML 4	**Widely Supported:**	No

Sample:
```
<ul id="123">...</ul>
```

XHTML Elements and Attributes

style="..."

Specifies style sheet commands that apply to the contents of the unordered list.

Standard/Usage:	HTML 4	**Widely Supported:**	No

Sample:
```
<ul style="background: red">...</ul>
```

title="..."

Specifies text assigned to the element. You can use this attribute for context-sensitive help within the document. Browsers may use this to show tooltips over the unordered list.

Standard/Usage:	HTML 4	**Widely Supported:**	No

Sample:
```
<ul title="Food List">
   <li>Spaghetti</li>
   <li>Pizza</li>
   <li>Fettuccini Alfredo</li>
</ul>
```

type="square|circle|disc"

Specifies the bullet type for each unordered list item. If you omit the type attribute, the browser chooses a default type.

Standard/Usage:	HTML 2; deprecated	**Widely Supported:**	Yes

Sample:
```
<ul type="disc">
   <li>Spaghetti</li>
   <ul type="square">
      <li>Noodles</li>
      <li>Sauce</li>
      <li>Cheese</li>
   </ul>
</ul>
```

Other Attributes

The ul element also accepts the lang, dir, onclick, ondblclick, onmousedown, onmouseup, onmouseover, onmousemove, onmouseout, onkeypress, onkeydown, and onkeyup attributes.

V

var

Indicates a placeholder variable in document text. This is useful when describing commands for which the user must supply a parameter.

Standard/Usage:	HTML 2	**Widely Supported:**	Yes	**Empty:**	No

Sample:
```
To copy a file in DOS, type <samp>COPY <var>file1</var> <var>file2</var></samp>
   and press the Enter key.
```

class="..."

Indicates which style class applies to the var element.

Standard/Usage:	HTML 4	**Widely Supported:**	No

Sample:
```
<p>I, <var class="casual">your name</var>, solemnly swear to tell the truth.</p>
```

id="..."

Assigns a unique ID selector to an instance of the var element. When you then assign a style to that ID selector, it affects only that one instance of the var element.

Standard/Usage:	HTML 4	**Widely Supported:**	No

Sample:
```
<var id="123">…</var>
```

style="..."

Specifies style sheet commands that apply to the contents of the var tags.

Standard/Usage:	HTML 4	**Widely Supported:**	No

Sample:
```
<var style="background: red">…</var>
```

title="..."

Specifies text assigned to the element. You can use this attribute for context-sensitive help within the document. Browsers may use this to show tooltips over the text within the var tags.

Standard/Usage:	HTML 4	**Widely Supported:**	No

Sample:
```
Use an <code>h</code><var title="Heading level number">n</var> element.
```

Other Attributes

The var element also accepts the lang, dir, onclick, ondblclick, onmousedown, onmouseup, onmouseover, onmousemove, onmouseout, onkeypress, onkeydown, and onkeyup attributes.

W

wbr

Forces a word break. This is useful in combination with the nobr element to permit line-breaks where they could otherwise not occur. This element has no attributes.

Standard/Usage:	Netscape Navigator 1, Internet Explorer 1	**Widely Supported:**	No	**Empty:**	Yes

Sample:
```
<nobr>This line would go on
forever, except that I have
this neat tag called wbr
that does <wbr />this!</nobr>
```

Cascading Style Sheets
Reference

XHTML

Master's Reference
Part 2

This reference lists properties that you can use to set up style sheets or to introduce styles into a document. For a thorough introduction to style sheets and their capabilities, including an introduction to some of the specialized terminology used in this reference section, see Chapter 10.

This section includes a complete discussion of Cascading Style Sheets level 1 (traditionally noted as CSS1) as well as introductions to some of the Cascading Style Sheets level 2 (noted as CSS2) features, which are particularly useful to you as you're developing your XHTML documents. At the time of writing, most commonly available browsers support CSS1 completely, but only a few browsers support CSS2 features (and even then may not support all of them). So, as always, test your documents thoroughly on as many browsers and computers as possible before you use new features.

General Information

The CSS properties are organized into the following categories:

- Selectors, which summarize the combinations of selectors you can use

- Colors, which describe the many ways to specify colors in style sheets

- Universal properties and values, which apply in many or most cases through style sheets

- Font properties, which affect the style of the typeface

- Text properties, which control paragraph and line values

- Box padding, border, margin, and position properties, which place the box contents within its boundaries on a page

- Color and background properties, which specify background colors and images, not just for the whole page, but for each element

- Classification properties, which control the presentation of standard elements, such as display and lists

- Aural style sheet properties, which control the aural presentation of XHTML documents

- Printed style sheet properties, which add features specifically to control printed output of XHTML documents

- Auto-generated content properties, which add features that help automatically insert content or automatically number parts of XHTML documents

*We don't cover the CSS2 table properties in this Master's Reference because they're currently not widely supported and the XHTML table elements **are** still widely supported. If you're feeling brave and want to check out CSS2 tables for yourself, visit the CSS2 tables section at* www.w3.org/TR/REC-CSS2/tables.html. *If not, use the XHTML table elements discussed in Chapter 6 to develop your tables.*

In this reference, you'll generally find a description of the property, a list of the property's values, notes about the use of the property, and examples of the property used in statements. Note that in the "Values" sections, if the value is a keyword, it's in program font (`like this`) and you use it as written; if it's a category of value, such as "Length" or "Percentage," it just appears in the normal font and you use the appropriate values as discussed in the description.

At the time of writing, the newest released versions of Internet Explorer 5.5 and Netscape 6 supported CSS1 almost completely (but not always consistently) and support for the CSS2 features is buggy. Be sure to test extensively on a variety of browsers before relying on any of the properties listed in this reference. See Chapter 10 for additional information about tailoring your style sheets to specific browser capabilities.

Throughout this reference, you'll also see references to various element types. The common element types are defined as follows:

Inline element   Does not start and stop on its own line, but is included in the flow of another element. A standard inline element is em, for emphasis; you can also include images in the stream of text as an inline element.

Block element   Starts on its own line and ends with another line break.

List item   Is a subset of block elements, but is contained within a larger block element.

Comments

Comments in CSS begin with the characters /* and end with the characters */. Don't use the traditional XHTML comment markup <!-- --> within your CSS markup, and don't nest comments inside each other.

```
/* this is a comment in a css file */
```

Selectors

You use selectors to indicate to which XHTML elements a style statement applies. You can assemble selectors in several combinations, which will each have different meanings. Table MR2.1 shows selectors, examples, and descriptions. The first six selectors come from CSS1 and work for all CSS implementations; the remaining selectors come from CSS2 and work only in CSS2-compliant browsers. You can use these selectors individually or together.

Table MR2.1 Selectors

Selector Pattern	Example	Description
element	p {color: black}	Sets all p elements to black. (CSS1)
element element	p a {color: black}	Sets all a elements contained in p elements to black. Does not affect a elements contained in other elements (such as h1, for example). (CSS1)
element.classname	p.newclass {color: black}	Sets all p elements that have class="newclass" to black. (CSS1)
.classname	.newclass {color: black}	Sets all elements that have class="newclass" to black. (CSS1)
#idvalue	#uniqueid {color: black}	Sets the element with id="uniqueid" to black. (CSS1)
*	* {color: black}	Sets all elements to black. (CSS2)
element > element	p > a {color: black}	Sets any a element that is contained in a p element to black. (CSS2)
element + element	p + blockquote {color: black}	Sets any blockquote element that immediately follows a p element to black. (CSS2)
element[attribute]	a[href] {color: black}	Sets any a element that includes an href attribute to black. (CSS2)

Table MR2.1 continued Selectors

Selector Pattern	Example	Description
element[attribute ="value"]	a[href="http://www. example.com/"] {color: black}	Sets any a element that includes an href attribute with the value "http://www.example.com/ " to black (the value must be exact). (CSS2)
element[attribute~ ="value"]	a[href~="index"] {color: black}	Sets any a element that includes an href attribute with a value of a space-separated list of words contain-ing "index" to black. (CSS2)
element[attribute| ="value"]	a[lang|="en"] {color: black}	Sets any a element that includes a language attribute beginning with the value "en" in a hyphen-separated list of words to black (CSS2)

Pseudoclasses

Pseudoclasses, which are closely related to selectors, refer to elements that do not explicitly exist in XHTML documents but can be inferred from location. For example, CSS1 offers the pseudoclasses :first-letter and :first-line (although browsers have not yet done anything with these features). Table MR2.2 summarizes CSS1 and CSS2 pseudoclasses.

Table MR2.2 Pseudoclasses

Pseudoclass	Example	Description
:first-line	p:first-line {color: red} p {color: black}	Sets the first line of all p elements to red, with the remaining lines black. (CSS1)

Cascading Style Sheets Reference

Table MR2.2 continued Pseudoclasses

PSEUDOCLASS	EXAMPLE	DESCRIPTION
:first-letter	p:first-letter {color: red} p {color: black}	Sets the first letter of all p elements to red, with the remaining letters and lines black. (CSS1)
:first-child	h1:first-child {color: red}	Sets the first child element under a h1 element to red. (CSS2)
:hover	p:hover {color: red}	Sets all p elements to red when the mouse cursor hovers over them. (CSS2)
:lang	p:lang(en) {color: red}	Sets all p elements set to language "en" (English) to red. (CSS2)
:first	@page:first {page-break-before: left}	Specifies that the first printed page start on the left. (CSS2)
:left	@page:left {margin: 2in}	Specifies 2-inch margins on all left printed pages. (CSS2)
:right	@page:right {margin: 2in}	Specifies 2-inch margins on all right printed pages. (CSS2)
:before	p:before {content: "para: "}	Places "para: " before all paragraph elements. (CSS2)
:hover:after	p:after {content: "\""}	Places " after all paragraph elements (the \ escapes the " in the statement). (CSS2)
:focus	button:focus {color: red}	Sets button elements to red when they have the cursor focus. (CSS2)
:active	button:active {color: red}	Sets button elements to red when they are active. (CSS2)

See also the outline-color, outline-style, outline-width, and outline properties for use with the :focus pseudoclass in forms.

Inherit Values

The `inherit` value can apply for any property in a style sheet. It explicitly indicates that the value of that property must be inherited from the parent element's value. This value is new in CSS2. For example,

```
p {font-family: inherit}
```

means that every p element should inherit its `font-family` from its immediate parent.

Colors

You can set color values for many CSS properties. In all CSS properties that accommodate color specifications, you can use either color keywords or RGB values to specify border colors. If you name a color, the browser must be able to recognize the keyword. Because all browsers recognize the RGB colors, they're generally a safer choice.

Table MR2.3 lists the keyword, hexadecimal, integer, and percentage values for all colors that have generally recognized keywords (these colors are taken from the Windows VGA palette). You can actually include many more colors in style sheets.

Even though browsers recognize the RGB colors and you can use more than the ones listed here, they may not render some of the more obscure colors the way you expect. Therefore, always test your pages on as many browsers as you can.

Table MR2.3 Equivalent Color Specifications in Various Systems

Color Keyword	RGB Hex	RGB Integer	RGB Percentage
aqua	#00ffff	rgb(0,255,255)	rgb(0%,100%,100%)
black	#000000	rgb(0,0,0)	rgb(0%,0%,0%)
blue	#0000ff	rgb(0,0,255)	rgb(0%,0%,100%)
fuchsia	#ff00ff	rgb(255,0,255)	rgb(100%,0%,100%)
gray	#808080	rgb(128,128,128)	rgb(50%,50%,50%)
green	#008000	rgb(0,128,0)	rgb(0%,50%,0%)
lime	#00ff00	rgb(0,255,0)	rgb(0%,100%,0%)
maroon	#800000	rgb(128,0,0)	rgb(50%,0%,0%)
navy	#000080	rgb(0,0,128)	rgb(0%,0%,50%)

Table MR2.3 continued Equivalent Color Specifications in Various Systems

Color Keyword	RGB Hex	RGB Integer	RGB Percentage
olive	#808000	rgb(128,128,0)	rgb(50%,50%,0%)
purple	#800080	rgb(128,0,128)	rgb(50%,0%,50%)
red	#ff0000	rgb(255,0,0)	rgb(100%,0%,0%)
silver	#c0c0c0	rgb(192,192,192)	rgb(75%,75%,75%)
teal	#008080	rgb(0,128,128)	rgb(0%,50%,50%)
white	#ffffff	rgb(255,255,255)	rgb(100%,100%,100%)
yellow	#ffff00	rgb(255,255,0)	rgb(100%,100%,0%)

When specifying colors with RGB numbers, in any system, it's helpful (and good code form) to include a comment that indicates what color you expect. For example, reading this line,

```
p {border-color: #000080 #00008b blue #0000cd}
```

it's a little difficult to tell what the outcome should look like. But this code

```
p {border-color: #000080 #00008b blue #0000cd}
   /* TOP navy blue, R dark blue, BOT blue, L med. blue */
```

is much easier to picture.

For more information about choosing colors, visit Chapters 5 and 14. Or, for additional resources regarding browser-safe colors and values, visit Part 6 of this Master's Reference.

CSS2 Color Features

The following additional CSS2 color values let your XHTML documents use the user's operating system colors:

ActiveBorder	InfoBackground
ActiveCaption	InfoText
AppWorkspace	Menu
Background	MenuText
ButtonFace	Scrollbar

ButtonHighlight	ThreeDDarkShadow
ButtonText	ThreeDFace
CaptionText	ThreeDHighlight
GrayText	ThreeDLightshadow
Highlight	ThreeDShadow
HighlightText	Window
InactiveBorder	WindowFrame
InactiveCaption	WindowText

For example, the code

```
p {color: MenuText}
```

makes paragraph text the same color as the menu text on the user's computer.

Lengths

Many properties can be defined as a length. Length values set a property as a number plus a unit abbreviation as a measurement. Some standard units of measurement are described in Table MR2.4.

Table MR2.4 Standard Units of Measurement

ABBREVIATION	UNIT	EXAMPLE	NOTES
cm	Centimeters	2.5cm	
em	Ems	3em	1 em equals the font's point size.
in	Inches	1in	
mm	Millimeters	25mm	
pc	Picas	6pc	1 inch = 6 picas
px	Pixels	96px	
pt	Points	72pt	1 inch = 72 points
ex	X-heights	2ex	1 x-height usually equals the height of the letter x.

When you specify a length, relative units set up the property in relation to other font and size properties. Use relative units wherever you can, because they scale more easily from situation to situation (for example, in different browsers and displays, or in the transition from display to printer). Relative units include em (in CSS, 1 em is equal to the font's point size), ex (usually the height of the lowercase letters in a font that have no ascenders or descenders: *x* or *e*), and px (screen pixels). The em and ex settings usually generate a font size relative to the parent font.

Absolute lengths are useful when the properties of the browser are well known or when you want to set a particular value to conform to a specification. Absolute units include inches, millimeters, centimeters, points (1 point = 1/72 inch), and picas (1 pica = 12 points = 1/6 inch).

Percentages

You can set many properties as a percentage of something else—a percentage of the parent element's value for the property, or a percentage of another property of the current element. Specify this type of value simply by including a % symbol after the number, as in font-size: 90%.

Font Properties

The font properties control the display of text elements, such as headings and paragraphs. This is the most common type of formatting you'll use in style sheets. These properties—particularly the font-family property—are also the most problematic, because no standard exists for fonts. Therefore, what works on one system or one platform may not work on another. Fortunately, you can specify alternative font families, as well as a generic font family.

The six font properties cover the font family (typeface), weight, and effects such as small caps or italics. The first property, font, is a *shorthand* property, as explained next.

font

Use this property as a shortcut to incorporate any or all of the other font properties. If you use the font shorthand property, you can also set the line spacing, using the line-height property (listed later in the "Text Properties" section of this reference). You can include one, many, or all of the font properties in this one property.

If you do not set the font-style, font-variant, font-weight, or font-family in this statement, you're essentially accepting the document default values for these properties. Shorthand properties do not have default settings; refer to entries for the individual properties for their default values.

    If you set the font properties for an element, these settings are used by inline elements (such as em) that are nested within such an element and by all elements of that type unless a class definition overwrites the settings.

Values

The possible values for the font property are the set of all possible values listed in the individual property entries, which must be set in this order (though optional properties can be omitted altogether):

Property	Effect
font-style	Sets the font to an oblique or italic face (optional).
font-weight	Sets the font to lighter or bolder (optional).
font-variant	Sets the font to small-caps (optional).
font-size	Sets the size of the font (required).
line-height	Sets the line spacing for the font (optional).
font-family	Sets the font face or type used (required).

    See the entries for the individual properties for more details about these values. (Note that the sections for the individual properties are arranged alphabetically, whereas this table is arranged in the order in which the properties should occur.)

Notes

If you do not include a setting for a particular property (such as font-variant), the browser uses the parent value of that property.

Examples

```
h1 {font: bold 14pt/18pt Arial, Helvetica, sans-serif}
```

    This statement uses values for the font-style, font-size, line-height, and font-family (in that order). The font-style is bold. The font-size is 14 points, and the line-height is 18 points. For the font-family, three values are listed, telling the browser to use Arial, and if Arial is not available use Helvetica, and if Helvetica is not available use a generic sans-serif font.

```
h3 {font: 12pt/120% serif}
```

This statement sets the font-size, line-height, and font-family using a 12-point font, a line height of 120% (14.4 points), and a generic serif font family.

```
body {font: italic 100%/130% Helvetica}
```

This statement sets the base class for the document; all other elements will default to these values. It sets the font-style to italic, the font-size to normal (100% of the browser default), the line-height to 130%, and the font-family to Helvetica.

CSS2 Font Features

CSS2 adds values for caption, icon, menu, messagebox, smallcaption, and status-bar. Each of these should set the font characteristics to the same values used in the user's system. For example, if you want text in your XHTML document to look like the text displayed in your user's status bar, use a statement such as the following:

```
p {font: statusbar}
```

font-family

Use this property when you want to change just the font family for an XHTML element. This sets the font to a particular or generic font family. You can set a list of font families and include a generic family at the end of the list. The browser works through the list until it finds a matching font family on the user's system.

The font-family property defaults to the browser settings, which may be the browser preferences, the browser default style sheet, or the user's default style sheet. If the setting is the browser preferences or style sheet, your settings take precedence, but if it's the user's style sheet, your settings are overridden by the user's style sheet.

Inline elements (such as em) use this property, as do child elements and all elements of that type unless the settings are overwritten by a class definition.

A paragraph (p) or heading (h1, h2, and so on) element is the child of the body element, list items (li) are the children of a list element (ol and ul). Class definitions allow you to have more than one type or version of an element for formatting. For example, a warning note could have its own class of paragraph element, as discussed in Chapter 10.

Values

Family name   Use any specific font family name. For font names, check the list of fonts on your system.

Generic family   Use one of the following generic family names: `serif` for fonts such as Times or Palatino, `sans-serif` for fonts such as Helvetica, `cursive` for fonts such as Zapf Chancery, `fantasy` for fonts such as Western or Circus, or `monospace` for fonts such as System or Courier.

You can list several choices for the font family, specific or generic; it's best to at least conclude your list with one choice for a generic family. Separate the list members with a comma.

Notes

With this property, you have the option of listing a series of alternatives separated by commas. You should *end* each list with a generic family name; the browser can then substitute an available font of the correct generic type when none of your specific family types are available. The browser works through the list from left to right until it finds a match on the user's system.

If a font family name contains spaces, place that name in quotation marks.

Examples

```
h1 {font-family: "Comic Sans MS", Architecture, sans-serif}
```

In this statement, the font choices for heading 1 elements are Comic Sans MS, Architecture, and a generic sans-serif. If the user's system has Comic Sans MS, it will use that font. Notice that Comic Sans MS is enclosed in quotation marks, because it includes spaces. If Comic Sans MS is not available, the browser looks for Architecture. If neither font family is available, the browser uses a generic sans-serif font.

```
body {font-family: Arial, Helvetica, sans-serif}
```

This statement sets body, the base class for all text elements in your page, to Arial or Helvetica (in order of preference). If neither of these families is available, the browser uses a generic sans-serif font. Because this is a base class, all the elements in your page inherit this property. Apply the properties you want as defaults for the page to the body element.

font-size

Use this property when you want to control the size of text. This property lets you set the size using a variety of measurements. It's more flexible than the font element in the XHTML specification, which scales text only by reference to the default size.

Values

Absolute size   Defines the font-size using a table of computed font sizes. These values can be one of the following: xx-small, x-small, small, medium (the default), large, x-large, or xx-large. Different font families may have different table values; thus, a small in one family might not be exactly the same size as a small in another family.

Relative size   Defines the font-size by increasing it (larger) or decreasing it (smaller) relative to the parent container font size rather than to the base browser font size.

Length   Sets the font-size as a number plus a unit abbreviation as a measurement. See the "Lengths" section earlier in this reference.

Percentage   Sets the font-size as a percentage of the parent element's font-size.

Notes

You can assign a single value for this property. If you use a keyword, such as x-large or larger, the browser recognizes the keyword and acts accordingly. If you use a numeric value, make sure to follow it with the appropriate measurement indicator, such as pt to indicate a point size or % to indicate a percentage.

When you use the absolute size value, the browser adjusts the font size according to the user's preferences. For example, if the default font size for the browser is 10 points, this corresponds to the medium value. The adjustment from medium is a multiplier of 1.5 for each increment in the list. So, if medium is 10 points, small is 6.7 points, and large is 15 points. Relative size is the best choice for sizing fonts, because if the user changes the base font from 10 points to 14 points, your document scales with the change.

In terms of absolute size and relative size, the default is expressed as medium.

Length and percentage values do not use the absolute or relative tables of values. The font sizes are interpreted, so they may appear different in different situations.

For length values, the default is taken from the browser or user's settings. The em and ex values are interpreted as references to the parent font size. For example, 1.5em is equivalent to large, larger, and 150% for absolute, relative, and percentage font sizes.

If the size is expressed as a percentage, the default is 100%. Any value less than 100% is smaller than the parent, and any value more than 100% is larger than the parent. For example, if the parent font is 12 points, and this property is set to 110%, the font size for this element is 13.2 points. If the font size is set to 80% of the 12-point parent, the element appears as 9.6 points.

Examples

```
body {font-size: 14pt}
```

This statement sets the base class font-size to 14 points. This is useful for sites where you want the presentation of text to be large, such as a site for the visually impaired or for children.

```
p {font-size: 90%}
```

This statement uses a percentage value to make the font-size depend on the settings in the body element. So, if this statement and the preceding one appear in the same style sheet, the font in the paragraph (p) will be 12.6 points.

```
address {font-size: x-small}
```

This statement sets the font-size for the address element using an absolute value. If this statement appears in the same style sheet as the first example, the font-size for the address element will be 4 points.

font-style

Use this property to add emphasis with an oblique or italic version of the font. If the default setting inherited for a particular element is an italic style font, you can use the font-style property to set the current element to normal, sometimes called roman (or upright).

When you set the font-style for an element, inline elements (such as em) and included block elements use this style. Also, if you set the font-style for a body or list container, all the elements within it use the setting.

Values

Value	Effect
normal	Chooses the roman or upright style in a font family.
italic	Chooses the italic style in a font family. Fonts with *italic, cursive,* or *kursiv* in their names are usually listed as "italic" in the browser's database.
oblique	Chooses the oblique style in a font family. Fonts with *oblique, slanted,* or *incline* in their names are usually listed in the browser's database as "oblique" fonts. The browser may also generate an oblique font from a family that does not have an oblique or italic style.

Notes

The browser maintains a list of the fonts available on the system, with the font name, font family, and values of the font, such as oblique or italic.

Examples

```
body {font-style: oblique}
h1, h2, h3 {font-style: normal}
```

The first statement sets the base body (body) to an oblique version of the font. Because the heading levels 1, 2, and 3 (h1, h2, h3) inherit this from the body class, the second statement sets them to normal. If the base font is not oblique or italic, you do not need to set the font-style to normal.

```
body em {font-style: italic}
```

This statement sets up the emphasis element to be an italic font-style. This means that when you emphasize some inline text, it will be italicized automatically.

font-variant

Use this property to switch between normal and small-caps fonts. Similar to the font-style property, font-variant handles one piece of font information. If you assign this property to an element, all included blocks and inline elements use the setting.

Values

A value of small-caps sets the lowercase letters to display as uppercase letters in a smaller font size. If the element has inherited a small-caps setting from its parent, a value of normal sets the font-variant to the usual uppercase and lowercase; this is the default value.

Notes

In some cases, when a small-caps version of the font is not available to the browser, the browser creates small-caps by using scaled uppercase letters.

Examples

```
h1 {font-variant: small-caps}
```

This statement sets the level 1 headings to a small-cap version of the default font.

```
address {font-variant: small-caps}
```

This statement sets the contents of any address element to appear in small-caps, using the default body font.

```
body em {font-variant: small-caps}
```

This statement sets text in the inline element em to use the small-caps version of the default font.

font-weight

Use this property to set the weight of a font, creating darker or lighter versions of the normal font. You can set the font-weight property as a relative weight or as a specific numeric value that represents a degree of darkness (or heaviness) or lightness for the font.

Values

Use only one value from the following lists.

Relative weight Sets the font-weight relative to the weight inherited by the element. In this method, the value can be either bolder or lighter; these increase (bolder) or decrease (lighter) the font-weight by one setting from its current weight (but not beyond the limits of 100 and 900).

Absolute weight   Sets the `font-weight` as a degree of heaviness on a nine-point scale. The value can be one of the following: 100, 200, 300, 400 or `normal` (these two values are equivalent), 500, 600, 700 or `bold` (these two values are equivalent), 800, or 900. The default is `normal`.

Notes

When you set a `font-weight` value for an element, its child elements inherit the weight of the font. This weight becomes their default weight, and you can increase or decrease the weight based on the inherited weight. When you then set a child element's weight using a relative weight (for example, `bolder` or `lighter`), it's relative to the weight of the parent element's font. (However, the weight will never exceed 900 or go below 100; if you set `bolder` on an element that is already inheriting 900, it stays at 900.)

The numeric, gradient weight values give you greater control over the weight of the font. These values must be stated exactly; intermediate values such as 250 are not acceptable.

There are no guarantees that the font family will include the full range of weight values. The browser will map the values you assign to those available for the font it uses. Fonts that have a weight lighter than normal are usually listed in the browser's database as *thinner, light,* or *extra-light.*

Examples

```
p {font-weight: bold}
```

This statement makes the weight of the paragraph (p) font bold. Use this when your layout requires a heavier text presentation.

```
body {font-weight: 500}
```

This statement uses the numerical representation to set the base font weight to slightly heavier than normal. This will make the text for all the elements appear darker. All included and inline elements use this as their normal weight. If you then use the relative keywords, as in the next statement, the text is bolder or lighter (we specify bolder here) than the 500 weight set in body.

```
h1 {font-weight: bolder}
```

This statement makes the h1 elements darker than the base font, regardless of what setting the base font has for its weight. However, if your body element base font is 900, there's no value that is bolder; therefore, the browser cannot make the h1 text bolder.

```
body em {font-weight: 400}
```

This statement controls the weight of emphasized text in the document. If the body weight is 500, the emphasized text will be lighter. If you include emphasized text in a paragraph set to bold, as in the first statement in this section, the emphasized text would appear lighter.

Text Properties

Text properties control the layout or display of lines and words on a page and within a text element. These properties include the familiar values for spacing and aligning text within an area, as well as values for controlling text capitalization and effects (such as underlining and blinking). Combined with the font properties, the text properties give you almost complete control over the appearance of the text on your page. The font properties control the typeface; the text properties control the paragraph settings.

letter-spacing

Use this property to control the spacing between characters in words in a text element. The distance you set applies across the elements; you cannot insert larger or smaller spaces between characters. This property is useful if you want to add space between characters for an open-looking presentation.

This property defaults to the spacing set in the parent element, or in the browser if no style is set. Inline and included block elements use the value set with the letter-spacing property.

Values

Sets standard spacing length between characters with a number plus a unit abbreviation. (See the "Lengths" section earlier in this reference.) The value adds to the normal length inherited by the element from its parent, or reduces the normal length if you use a negative value.

To reset the distance between characters to whatever is common for the font and font size in use, use a value of normal. This is the default.

Notes

When you use a length unit, you can use a positive or negative number, or a decimal number (for example, 0.4em or 1.2em). If you use a negative value, be sure that you don't make your text illegible with spacing too small between characters.

Examples

```
h1 {letter-spacing: 2em}
```

This statement increases the character spacing in words found in the level 1 headings to twice the font size.

```
p {letter-spacing: -0.5em}
```

This statement decreases the character spacing for paragraphs in the document to half the font size.

line-height

Use this property to set the distance (leading or spacing) between lines of text within an element. Elements inherit the settings for this property; if you change the settings in the child element, you change the inherited results. For example, if you set unordered lists (ul) to 2 (for double-spaced) and then set list items (li) to 1.5, you've effectively triple-spaced list items (2 × 1.5). In other words, the inheritance is cumulative, rather than a setting for a child element replacing the parent's setting.

Values

To set the spacing value to default to the browser-specific setting, which is usually 1 to 1.2 times the font size, use the default value of normal. To change the spacing, use one of the following techniques:

Number   Sets the distance between the baselines of each line of text in the element to the font size multiplied by the specified number. For example, if the font size is 10 points and you set line-height to 2, the spacing will be 20 points.

Length   Sets the spacing using one of the standard relative or absolute measurements. See the "Lengths" section earlier in this reference.

Percentage   Sets the spacing to a percentage of the line's font size.

Notes

When you use a length unit, you can use a positive or negative number. If you use a negative number, you'll create overlapping text, which may make it illegible.

Using a percentage for the line-height property is a flexible way to set line spacing, because it adapts to the font and display of the browser. Child elements will inherit the result of this setting.

Examples

```
p {line-height: 1.2;   font-size: 10pt}
p {line-height: 1.2em; font-size: 10pt}
p {line-height: 120%;  font-size: 10pt}
```

These three statements produce the same result: The text will have 12 points between each line.

outline

Using this CSS2 shorthand property, you can outline individual elements, such as buttons, fields, or emphasized text. Outlines do not take space—they fit just outside the border (if any) and do not affect the layout of any elements. Additionally, they precisely enclose the text, even if the lines result in irregular shapes, rather than forming a rectangle.

The outline property is a shorthand property and sets any of outline-color, outline-style, and outline-width.

Values

The possible values for the outline property are the set of all possible values listed in the individual property entries:

Property	Effect
outline-color	Sets the color for all sides of the outline.
outline-style	Sets the pattern used for the outline.
outline-width	Sets the outline width.

See the border-color for outline-color values, border-style for outline-style values, and border-width for outline-width values. Possible values for outline-style are the same as for the border-style property, except that hidden is not permitted for outline-style.

The `outline-color` property accepts all colors, as well as the keyword `invert`, which is expected to perform a color inversion on the pixels on the screen. This is a common trick you can use to ensure that the focus border is visible, regardless of color background.

Notes

This property is a CSS2 property and, therefore, won't work in browsers that don't support CSS2.

See the "Notes" sections for the `border-width`, `border-style`, and `border-color` properties, under "Box Border Properties" later in this reference.

Example

```
input:focus {outline: 2px inset red}
```

This statement generates an outline around the `input` element that has the focus. The outline is a red, inset line that is 2 pixels wide.

text-align

Use this property to arrange the text horizontally within the element box. This is useful for centering headings or creating effects with justification. You can set the alignment on any block-level element, such as `p`, `h1`, `ul`, and so on. The browser sets the property default (either from the browser properties, browser style sheet, or user's style sheet). Inline and included block elements use the settings. For example, if you justify an unordered list (`ul`), the list items (which are included block elements) are justified.

Values

Value	Effect
`left`	Aligns text along the left margin, for a "ragged-right" layout.
`right`	Aligns text along the right margin, for a "ragged-left" layout.
`center`	Places the text a uniform distance from the left and right margins.

justify   Creates uniform line lengths. The browser will use word spacing to create lines of text that abut both the left and right margins of the element box.

Examples

```
h1, h2 {text-align: center}
```

This statement centers both level 1 and level 2 headings across the width of the page (however wide or narrow the display is).

```
p.emerg {text-align: right;
         background: url(exclaim.gif) no-repeat}
```

This statement aligns paragraphs of class `emerg` (that is, `<p class="emerg">...</p>`) with the right margin of the element box. `p.emerg` also has an icon that appears once in the top-left corner of the element box as a background.

text-decoration

Use this property to control the effects used on text elements. This property is particularly useful for drawing attention to text elements, such as notes and warnings.

The default is not to use any text decoration, and the property is not inherited, although some properties do continue throughout sections. For example, a p with underlining will be underlined throughout, even through sections with other formatting, such as boldface. The decoration uses the settings from the `color` property (listed in the "Background and Color Properties" section).

Values

Value	Effect
none	Leaves the text plain (unadorned). This is the default.
underline	Draws a single, thin line under the text.
overline	Draws a single, thin line above the text.
line-through	Draws a single, thin line through the text, similar to strikethrough text.
blink	Makes the text blink.

You can combine `underline`, `overline`, `line-through`, and `blink` in a single statement.

Notes

If you apply the `text-decoration` to an empty element (such as `br`) or an element that has no text, the property has no effect.

Be careful using underlined text in your Web pages. Users are accustomed to underlined text representing hyperlinks and may get confused if you use it for other reasons.

Examples

```
h1 {color: purple; text-decoration: underline}
```

This statement sets level 1 headings as purple underlined text.

```
p em {text-decoration: blink}
```

This statement sets the emphasis in paragraphs (p em) to blink. Because nothing else is set, the emphasis will use all the other paragraph (p) properties that you have set.

```
h1 em {text-decoration: overline}
```

This statement sets the emphasized text in level 1 headings to have a line above it. If this statement appears in the same style sheet as the first statement in this section, this emphasized text will have a line above and a line below.

text-indent

Use this property to create paragraphs with the first line indented. Traditionally, indented first lines compensate for a lack of space between paragraphs and act as a visual cue for the reader. You can set the indent as an absolute or relative measurement.

Elements use whatever setting the parent has, so if you set `text-indent` for body, all block elements, such as h1 and p, default to first-line indentation. The default value is 0, for no indentation.

Values

Length   Sets the size of the first-line indent to the specified measurement. Some measurements are relative, and some are absolute. See the "Lengths" section earlier in this reference.

Percentage Sets the first-line indent to a percentage of the line length.

Notes

For most browsers, you can use negative values to create a hanging-indent format.

An indent is not added to the first line of the second text stream if the text within the element is separated by an inline element that breaks the line (such as br).

Examples

```
body {text-indent: 1%}
```

This statement creates a base class body with a first-line indent of 1 percent of the line length. Because a percentage is used, the ratio of indent to line length stays the same whether the browser window or font is sized larger or smaller.

```
h1 {text-indent: 3em}
```

In this statement, the indentation for level 1 headings is also relative to the font size (em measurements are based on the font size). If this line appears in the same style sheet as the first statement, the indentation is the base 1% *plus* an additional 3 ems.

```
p.warn {text-indent: 2cm}
```

This statement specifies a 2-centimeter first-line indent. Because this is an absolute measurement, this setting can produce unexpected results on different machines.

text-shadow

Use this CSS2 property to control shadow effects on text elements. We recommend using this effect sparingly, because too much text shadow can make text difficult to read.

Values

To restore an element to no text shadow, use the default value none.

To set a text shadow, you *must* provide the horizontal and vertical shadow offsets, but the blur radius and color are optional. You can also specify separate groups of settings for multiple shadows under the same text.

Horizontal shadow offset Specifies the horizontal distance to the right that the shadow appears. Use negative numbers to move the shadow to the left from the text. Specify measurements in any units.

Vertical shadow offset   Specifies the vertical distance down that the shadow appears. Use negative numbers to move the shadow above the text. Specify measurements in any units.

Blur radius   Specifies the fuzziness of the shadow. Specify measurements in any units.

Color   Specifies the shadow color. See the "Colors" section earlier in this reference for more about colors.

Notes

This property is new in CSS2 and is supported only by CSS2-compliant browsers.

If you apply the text shadow to an empty element (such as `br`) or an element that has no text, the property has no effect.

Examples

```
h1 {text-shadow: 1px 1px}
```

This statement sets a shadow offset by 1 pixel horizontally and vertically for level 1 headings.

```
h1 {text-shadow: 2px 2px 1px blue}
```

This statement sets the level 1 headings to have a blue shadow offset by 2 pixels horizontally and vertically, with a 1-pixel blur radius for level 1 headings.

```
h1 {text-shadow: 2px 2px 1px blue, 1px 1px red}
```

This statement sets a blue shadow offset by two pixels horizontally and vertically, with a 1-pixel blur radius, and a red shadow offset by 1 pixel in both directions for level 1 headings.

text-transform

Use this property to set the capitalization standard for one or more elements. For example, if you want all uppercase letters for a warning or title case for all headings, you can set this property in one place and allow the browser to adjust the text. Child elements, including both block and inline elements, use the parent's setting for this property.

Values

Value	Effect
none	Does not change the case for any of the text. This is the default.
capitalize	Creates a title-cased element, capitalizing the first letter of each word in the element.
lowercase	Sets all the text to lowercase, eliminating any uppercase letters from the element text.
uppercase	Sets all the text to uppercase.

Examples

```
h1 {text-transform: capitalize}
```

This statement forces all the text in level 1 headings to use uppercase for the first letter of each word. This is a form of the title case.

```
p.headline {text-transform: uppercase}
```

In this statement, paragraphs with the class headline are rendered in uppercase (all capital letters). This is not the same as setting a small-caps font (font-variant: small-caps), because no adjustment is made to the size of the lowercase letters.

vertical-align

Use this property to set inline text elements within a parent element to have different vertical alignment from the parent. The vertical-align property is an important layout tool for document designers. You could, for example, define a class for superscript or subscript text and apply it where required. This property is typically used to set the alignment between inline graphics (such as keycaps or toolbar icons) and the surrounding text. The default value is for alignment along the baselines of the elements. These settings are not used by any other elements.

Values

Value	Effect
baseline	Aligns the bottom of lowercase letters in the two elements (the default setting).

`bottom`	Aligns the inline element with the lowest part of the parent element on the same line. Use with caution—may produce unexpected results.
`middle`	Centers the inline text and the parent element text, aligning the midpoints of the two elements. May be required when the two elements have different sizes or when the inline element is an image.
`sub`	Moves the inline element down below the baseline of the parent element.
`super`	Moves the inline element up from the baseline of the parent element.
`text-bottom`	Aligns the bottom of the inline element with the bottom of the parent font's descender. Preferred method for aligning inline elements with the bottom of a textual parent element.
`text-top`	Aligns the inline element with the top of the ascender in the parent element.
`top`	Aligns the inline element with the highest part of the parent element, similar to superscript. Works line by line—for example, if the line has no ascenders, `top` moves the inline text to the top of the x-height for the parent element.

The `vertical-align` property can also be set as a percentage, raising or lowering (with negative values) the baseline of the inline element the given percentage above or below the baseline of the parent element. Use this in combination with the `line-height` property of the element.

Notes

If you use subscript (`sub`) or superscript (`super`) alignment, decrease the font size in relation to the parent element.

If you want to include inline images that replace words or letters in your text (such as toolbar buttons or keycaps), use a percentage value with the `vertical-align` property. This allows you to obtain precision in the placement of inline elements, such as images, that do not have true baselines.

Examples

```
img.keycap {vertical-align: -20%}
```

This statement creates an image class (`img`) called `keycap`. Elements that you apply this class to will drop below the baseline of the parent text element; 20% of the image will be below the baseline of the parent element's text.

```
code.expo {vertical-align: super}
```

This statement creates a code class called `expo` for superscripting. You could, for example, use this for the exponents in equations.

```
.regmark {vertical-align: text-top}
```

In this statement, a generic class, called `regmark`, aligns the inline element to the top of the parent font.

word-spacing

Use this property to control the spacing between words in a text element. As with the `letter-spacing` property, the distance you set applies across the elements; you cannot insert larger and smaller spaces between words, as in typesetting. This property is useful if you want to add space between words for an open-looking presentation.

This property assumes the settings for its parent element or the browser, and inline or included block elements use any changes you make in the `word-spacing` property.

Values

Sets a standard spacing between words with a length value. (See the "Lengths" section earlier in this reference.) The value adds to the length inherited by the element from its parent, or reduces the length if you use a negative value. For example, if body sets the font size to `10pt` and the word spacing to `1em`, the child elements will use a 10-point word spacing (1 em = the point size). If you then add `0.4em` to the word spacing, the child element has a wider word spacing than the parent.

To reset the distance between words to whatever is usual for the font and font size in use, use a value of `normal` (which is the default).

Notes

When you use a length unit, you can use a positive or negative number, as well as a decimal number (such as 0.4em). If you use a negative value, be careful that you do not eliminate the spaces between words, making your text unreadable.

Examples

```
h1 {word-spacing: 1em}
p {word-spacing: 0.4em}
```

In both these statements, the space between words in the elements will increase; the spacing in heading level 1 elements increases by 1 em, and the spacing in paragraph elements increases by 0.4 (4/10 of the font size).

Box Padding Properties

In the element box, the padding provides the distance between the element contents and the border. You can use the padding shorthand property to set the padding on all sides of the element or use the individual properties to set the padding on each side separately.

With box properties, you can manipulate the layers around the element. These layers, from the element out, are padding, border, margin, and position. Each of these layers has its own set of properties, which are included in this reference in the order listed, beginning with box padding.

padding

Use this shorthand property to set the distance for all four padding directions (top, right, bottom, and left). This area uses the element's settings for background (such as color and image).

Padding is not inherited, so included and inline elements use the default of zero rather than the settings from the parent element.

Values

Length   Sets an absolute or relative distance between the element contents and the inside of the box border. See the "Lengths" section earlier in this reference.

Percentage   Sets the distance between the element contents and the inside of the box border as a percentage of the parent element.

Use a single value to make the padding on each side equidistant. If you use two values, the browser uses the first one for the top and bottom padding, and the second one for the left and right padding. If you provide three values, the browser assigns them to the top padding, the left and right padding, and the bottom padding. If you provide all four values, the browser assigns them, in order, to the top, right, bottom, and left padding. You can mix value types—specifying padding in percentage for some and absolute measurements for other values.

Notes

You cannot have negative padding values; however, you can use decimal numbers, such as 0.4 or 1.2.

Examples

```
h1 {font-size: 20pt; padding: 1em 0.5em; color: red;}
h2 {font-size: 15pt; font-weight: normal; padding: 1em 0.5em;
    color: blue;}
```

If you include these two statements in a style sheet, the headings at levels 1 and 2 will have 20 and 15 points, respectively, between the content and the top and bottom borders. Heading 1s will have a left and right padding of 10 points and be red; heading 2s will have a left and right padding of 7.5 points and be blue with a normal font weight.

padding-bottom

Use this property to add space between the bottom of the contents and the border below. Padding is not inherited, so included and inline elements use the default of zero rather than the settings from the parent element.

Values

Length   Sets an absolute or relative distance between the bottom of the contents and the border below. See the "Lengths" section earlier in this reference.

Percentage   Sets the bottom padding size to a percentage of the parent element.

Notes

You cannot have negative padding values; however, you can use decimal numbers, such as 0.4 or 1.2.

Examples

```
body {padding-bottom: 3em}
```

This statement sets the padding distance between the bottom of the page to 3 ems, which allows it to vary with the font size.

```
h1 {padding-bottom: 2pt}
```

This statement sets the distance for the bottom padding to 2 points for level 1 headings. It will add a distance of 2 points to the space between the text of the heading and the location of the border, regardless of the font size of the heading.

```
p.cap {padding-bottom: 0.5cm}
```

This statement sets up a paragraph class called cap (that is, `<p class="cap">...</p>`) in which the distance between the bottom of the element contents and the border location is an absolute value of 0.5 centimeters.

padding-left

Use this property to add space between the left edge of the contents and the border location. Padding is not inherited, so included and inline elements use the default of zero rather than the settings from the parent element.

Values

Length   Sets an absolute or relative distance between the left edge of the contents and the border. See the "Lengths" section earlier in this reference.

Percentage   Sets the left padding size to a percentage of the parent element.

Notes

You cannot have negative padding values; however, you can use decimal numbers, such as 0.4 or 1.2.

Example

```
address {padding-left: 10%}
```

This statement adds space to the left of the `address` elements. Unlike the left margin space, this padding space shows the element background. This space is a relative space; the amount of the space depends on the size of the element.

padding-right

Use this property to add space between the right edge of the contents and the border location. Padding is not inherited, so included and inline elements use the default of zero rather than the settings from the parent element.

Values

Length   Sets an absolute or relative distance between the right edge of the contents and the border. See the "Lengths" section earlier in this reference.

Percentage   Sets the right padding size to a percentage of the parent element.

Notes

You cannot have negative padding values; however, you can use decimal numbers, such as 0.4 or 1.2.

Examples

```
p {padding-left: 8px; padding-right: 8px}
p {padding: 0 8px}
```

These two statements produce the same result. The first one uses the individual properties to set the left and right padding to 8 pixels. The second one uses the shorthand `padding` property to set the top and bottom padding to zero and the left and right padding to 8 pixels.

padding-top

Use this property to add space between the top of the contents and the border location. Padding is not inherited, so included and inline elements use the default of zero rather than the settings from the parent element.

Values

Length   Sets an absolute or relative distance between the top of the contents and the border. See the "Lengths" section earlier in this reference.

Percentage   Sets the top padding size to a percentage of the parent element.

Notes

You cannot have negative padding values; however, you can use decimal numbers, such as 0.4 or 1.2.

Example

```
address {padding-top: 1cm}
```

This statement adds a centimeter above the element contents before placing the border. Using an absolute measurement such as this is less browser-sensitive than the relative values.

Box Border Properties

Every container has a border. Element borders reside between the padding and margin in the element container. By default, borders have no style set (are not visible), regardless of color or width.

The default for the border is a medium-width line with no pattern that inherits the color (foreground) setting for the parent element.

You can use the border shorthand property to set any of the border properties, or use the individual properties.

border

Use this shorthand property to set some or all of the border properties. You can set a single value for all four sides of the border.

See the sections on the border-color, border-style, and border-width properties for values and notes on each.

Values

The possible values for the border property are the set of all possible values listed in the individual property entries:

Property	Effect
border-color	Sets the color for all sides of the border.
border-style	Sets the pattern used to fill the border.
border-width	Sets the border width for the border.

Notes

Unlike other shorthand properties, you can use only one setting for each value you include (as opposed to separate settings for top, bottom, etc.). The property is applied evenly to all sides of the box border. To set borders differently on various sides, use the more specific shorthand properties such as border-bottom.

Examples

```
p.warn {border: 2em double red}
```

This statement generates a border around the paragraph class element warn (that is, <p class="warn">...</p>). The border is a red, double-line border that is 2 ems wide.

```
p.note {border: 2px ridge blue}
```

This statement generates borders around the paragraph elements of the class note. The border is a ridged, blue border that is 2 pixels wide.

border-bottom

Use this shorthand property to set some or all of the border properties for the bottom border of the element container.

See the sections on the border-color, border-style, and border-width properties for values and notes on each.

Values

The possible values for the `border-bottom` property are the set of all possible values listed in the individual property entries:

Property	Effect
`border-color`	Sets the color for the bottom border.
`border-style`	Sets the pattern used to fill the bottom border.
`border-width`	Sets the width for the bottom border.

Examples

```
p.sectend {color: blue; border-bottom: 0.5em dashed #ff0000}
```

This statement overrides the foreground color for the `sectend` class of paragraphs (that is, `<p class="sectend">...</p>`) and replaces it with an RGB value (`#ff0000`). See the entry for the `border-color` property for more information about specifying border colors. `sectend` paragraph text will appear blue and concludes with a dashed, red line that is 0.5 em thick. The `em` thickness associates the width of the border with the font size for the paragraph.

```
p.note {color: green; border-bottom: 5em groove}
```

This statement specifies that `note`-class paragraphs (that is, `<p class="note">...</p>`) will use the color green for foreground objects (such as text and the border) and have a grooved, 5 em terminating line.

border-bottom-width

Use this property to set the thickness of the bottom border for an element. The border width is, by default, a medium thickness, and is unaffected by any border settings for the parent element.

Values

Sets the bottom border width, using an absolute or a relative measurement. For valid absolute-value measurements, see the "Lengths" section earlier in this reference. Possible relative values are `thin`, `medium` (the default), and `thick`; the specific interpretation of these thicknesses is up to the browser.

Notes

See the "Notes" section for the border-width property.

Examples

```
p.under {border-style: solid; border-bottom-width: 0.5cm;
        border-color: gray}
```

This creates a class of paragraph called under (that is, <p class="under">...</p>) in which the bottom border is 0.5 centimeter. This is an absolute setting, unaffected by the browser, page size, or element properties such as font.

```
h1 {border-style: solid; border-bottom-width: thin;
    border-color: #f0f8ff}
```

This statement specifies the bottom border as a standard, thin line.

border-color

Use this property to create a border using different colors than the foreground color for the element. The border color uses the foreground color of the element as a default setting. This shorthand property sets the visible border to the selected color(s).

Values

The values for border-color can be predefined color names or RGB values. See the "Colors" section earlier in this reference.

Notes

If you specify a single color, all four borders will appear as that color. If you include two colors, the top and bottom borders use the first color, and the left and right borders use the second color. If you include three colors, the top border uses the first color, the left and right borders use the second color, and the bottom border uses the third color. To give each border a unique color, list four colors; the borders use them in the following order: top, right, bottom, left.

Examples

```
p.warn {border-color: #8b0000}
```

This statement specifies that the paragraphs of class warn (that is, <p class="warn">...</p>) are outlined with a dark red border.

```
p.dancing {border-color: #000080 #00008b blue #0000cd}
```

This statement sets the border on each side of the element to a different color. This creates a multihued line around paragraphs of class dancing. The top is navy blue, the right is dark blue, the bottom is blue, and the left is medium blue.

border-left

Use this shorthand property to set some or all of the border properties for the border on the left side of the element container.

See the sections on the border-color, border-style, and border-width properties for values and notes on each.

Values

The possible values for the border-left property are the set of all possible values listed in the individual property entries:

Property	Effect
border-color	Sets the color for the left border.
border-style	Sets the pattern used to fill the left border.
border-width	Sets the width for the left border.

Example

```
p.insert {border-left: thin solid red}
```

This statement places a thin, solid, red line next to the insert class paragraphs (that is, <p class="insert">…</p>). This is a useful way to create a class for all your elements that inserts "change bars" (a line that shows that changes have been made in the text) in the left border.

border-left-width

Use this property to set the thickness of the border on the left side of an element. The border width is, by default, a medium thickness, and is unaffected by any border settings for the parent element.

Values

Sets the left border width, using an absolute or a relative measurement. Possible relative values are thin, medium (the default), and thick; the specific interpretation of these thicknesses is up to the browser. For absolute values and other valid relative measurements, see the "Lengths" section earlier in this reference.

Notes

See the "Notes" section for the border-width property.

Example

```
p.insert {border-style: dashed;
          border-left-width: 5em;
          border-color: red}
```

This statement creates a paragraph class called insert (that is, `<p class="insert">` ...`</p>`) that uses a dashed, red line on the left border. The thickness of the line depends on the size of the paragraph font.

border-right

Use this shorthand property to set some or all of the border properties for the border to the right of the element contents.

See the sections on the border-color, border-style, and border-width properties for values and notes on each.

Values

The possible values for the border-right property are the set of all possible values listed in the individual property entries:

Property	Effect
border-color	Sets the color for the right border.
border-style	Sets the pattern used to fill the right border.
border-width	Sets the width for the right border.

Examples

```
p.news {padding-right: 15em;
           border-right: thick dotted navy}
```

This creates a thick, dotted line that appears to the right of paragraphs of the class news (that is, <p class="news">...</p>). The line is navy blue and is 15 ems from the element contents.

```
h3.strike {border-right: thick groove black}
```

This adds a thick, grooved, black line to the right of level 3 headings of the class strike (that is, <h3 class="strike">...</h3>). This is a useful way to create a class that inserts an indicator that the information is out-of-date and about to be removed.

border-right-width

Use this property to set the thickness of the border on the right side of an element. The border width is, by default, a medium thickness, and is unaffected by any border settings for the parent element.

Values

Sets the right border width, using an absolute or a relative measurement. Possible relative values are thin, medium (the default), and thick; the specific interpretation of these thicknesses is up to the browser. For absolute values and other valid relative measurements, see the "Lengths" section earlier in this reference.

Notes

See the "Notes" section for the border-width property.

Example

```
p.strike {border-style: dashed;
          border-right-width: 5px;
          border-color: blue}
```

This statement creates a paragraph class called strike (that is, <p class="strike">...</p>) that uses a dashed, blue, 5-pixel-wide line on the right border of the element.

border-style

Use this property to display a border and specify a border style. You can create different effects by combining line styles with color and width. This property uses none as the default, which doesn't display the border at all, regardless of the color or width settings.

Values

Value	Effect
none	Prevents the display of one or more borders. This is the default.
dashed	Sets the border as a series of dashes, alternating the element background and the border color.
dotted	Sets the border as a dotted line, with spaces where the element background shows through.
double	Sets the border as two solid lines in the border color or element foreground color.
groove	Sets the border as a 3-D rendering of a grooved line drawn in the border color.
hidden	Identical to none except in reference to table element border conflict resolution.
inset	Sets the border as a 3-D rendering, creating the illusion that the inside of the element is sunken into the page.
outset	Sets the border as a 3-D rendering, creating the illusion that the inside of the element is raised above the page.
ridge	Sets the border as a raised 3-D rendering, peaking in the middle of the line, drawn in the border color.
solid	Sets the border as a single, solid line in the border color or element foreground color.

Use up to four values from the preceding list to stylize the borders around an element. Because the initial setting for the border-style property is none, no borders are visible unless you set them up with a style plus a width.

Notes

Not all browsers are capable of displaying the more esoteric styles, such as `ridge`, `inset`, and `outset`. If the browser cannot interpret the style, it substitutes a solid line. Some browsers may simply render all borders as solid lines.

Examples

```
p.looknew {border-style: outset; border-width: 0.5cm;
           border-color: gray}
```

This statement creates the illusion that the `looknew` class paragraph elements (that is, `<p class="looknew">...</p>`) are set above the page in a raised box.

```
p.dancing {border-style: groove ridge inset outset;
           border-color: #f0f8ff #f0ffff blue #5f9ea0}
```

With these properties, each side of the paragraphs in the class `dancing` is a different shade of blue and a different style.

border-top

Use this shorthand property to set some or all of the border properties for the top border of the element container.

See the sections on the `border-color`, `border-style`, and `border-width` properties for values and notes on each.

Values

The possible values for the `border-top` property are the set of all possible values listed in the individual property entries:

Property	Effect
border-color	Sets the color for the top border.
border-style	Sets the pattern used to fill the top border.
border-width	Sets the width for the top border.

Example

```
h1 {margin-top: 0.5in; color: red; background: white;
    padding: 9em; border-top: thin solid blue}
```

This statement creates level 1 headings that have red text on a white background and a thin, solid, blue line positioned 9 ems above the text. There is another line 0.5 inch above the heading. The 9-em padding is a relative value that depends on the font size and is equivalent to 9 blank lines above the heading.

border-top-width

Use this property to set the thickness of the border along the top of an element. The border width is, by default, a medium thickness, and is unaffected by any border settings for the parent element.

Values

Sets the top border width, using an absolute or a relative measurement. Possible relative values are `thin`, `medium` (the default), and `thick`; the specific interpretation of these thicknesses is up to the browser. For absolute values and other valid relative measurements, see the "Lengths" section earlier in this reference.

Notes

See the "Notes" section for the `border-width` property.

Example

```
h1, h2, h3 {font-style: Futura, sans-serif;
            font-size: 15pt;
            border-style: solid;
            border-top-width: 1.5em}
```

This statement applies to the three levels of headings, giving each heading a solid line that is 1.5 ems. Because this is relative to the font, the line will be 22.5 points. The border color is not set, so the border uses the foreground color of the element.

border-width

Use this shorthand property to set the thickness of all the borders for an element. You can give the borders unique widths, or you can use a single width for all the borders.

Values

Sets the width of the border on all sides, using an absolute or a relative measurement. Possible relative values are thin, medium (the default), and thick; the specific interpretation of these thicknesses is up to the browser. For absolute values and other valid relative measurements, see the "Lengths" section earlier in this reference.

If you use one value, it applies evenly to the borders on the four sides of the element. If you use two values, the browser applies the first to the top and bottom borders of the element, and the second to the left and right borders. If you include three values, the browser uses the first for the top border, the second for the left and right borders, and the last for the bottom border. If you use four values, the browser applies them in the following order: top, right, bottom, left.

Notes

The thin setting will always be less than or equal to the medium setting, which will always be less than or equal to the thick setting. The border widths do not depend on the element font or other settings. The thick setting, for example, is rendered in the same size wherever it occurs in a document. You can use the relative length values to produce variable (font-dependent) widths.

With a length setting, you cannot have a border with a negative width. However, you can use a decimal number, for example, 0.4 or 1.2.

Examples

```
p.looknew {border-style: outset; border-width: 0.5cm;
          border-color: gray}
```

This statement sets all the borders for the paragraphs of class looknew (that is, <p class="looknew">...</p>) at 0.5 centimeter, outset, and gray.

```
p.dancing {border-style: groove ridge inset outset;
          border-width: thin thick medium 1cm;
          border-color: #f0f8ff #f0ffff blue #5f9ea0}
```

This statement sets each border in the paragraphs of class dancing at different widths. The top border is thin and grooved, the right border is thick and ridged, the bottom is medium and inset, and the left border is 1 centimeter and outset. Each border is also a different shade of blue.

CSS2 Border Properties

CSS2 also provides border properties that offer you even more control over border appearance. Choose from:

```
border-bottom-color

border-bottom-style

border-left-color

border-left-style

border-right-color

border-right-style

border-top-color

border-top-style
```

For example,

```
h1, h2, h3 {font-size: 15pt; font-style: Futura, sans-serif;
            border-left-style: solid; border-left-color: blue}
```

applies to the three levels of headings, giving each heading a solid blue line on the left. See the corresponding CSS1 properties for valid values and notes.

Box Margin Properties

Margins set the size of the box around an element. You measure margins from the border area to the edge of the box.

margin

This property is shorthand to set up all the margins for an element's box. This measurement gives the browser the distance between the element border and the edge of the box. This area is always transparent, so you can view the underlying page background.

Values

The value `auto` sets the margin to the browser's default.

Length Sets an absolute or relative distance between the border and the box edge. See the "Lengths" section earlier in this reference.

Percentage Sets the margin size as a percentage of the parent element's width.

Use one of the preceding values. For length and percentage, you can use one, two, three, or four numbers. If you use one number, the browser applies it to all four margins (top, right, bottom, and left). If you use two numbers, the first number sets the top and bottom margin, and the second number sets the left and right margin. If you use three numbers, you're setting the top margin with the first, the right and left margins with the second, and the bottom margin with the third. You can mix length and percentage values.

Notes

You can use negative values for margins, but not all browsers will handle the settings correctly, and some may ignore the setting and substitute the default of zero or use their own algorithm.

Examples

```
p.1 {margin: 5%}
```

This statement establishes paragraph margins, for paragraphs of class 1 (that is, `<p class="1">`...`</p>`), to 5% each of the total width of the box.

```
p {margin: 2em 3pt}
```

This statement sets all paragraph elements' top and bottom margins to 2 ems (relative to the size of the font) and the left and right margins to 3 points.

```
p.note {margin: 1em 3em 4em}
```

This statement sets the margins for paragraphs of class `note` (that is, `<p class="note">`...`</p>`). The top margin is 1 em (relative to the font size), the left and right margins are 3 ems, and the bottom margin is 4 ems. If the font size is 10 points, the top margin will be 10 points, the left and right margins will be 30 points, and the bottom margin will be 40 points.

margin-bottom

Use this property to set just the bottom margin of an element's box. The bottom margin is the distance between the bottom border and the bottom edge of the box. This generally defaults to zero and is not used by included block or inline elements.

Values

The value auto sets the bottom margin to the browser's default.

Length   Sets an absolute or relative distance between the border and the box's bottom edge. See the "Lengths" section earlier in this reference.

Percentage   Sets the bottom margin size as a percentage of the parent element's width.

Notes

You can use negative values for margins, but not all browsers will handle the settings correctly, and some may ignore the setting and substitute the default of zero or use their own algorithm.

Examples

```
p {margin-bottom: 4em}
```

This statement sets all paragraphs to have a bottom margin that is 4 ems. This is a relative measurement, so the actual distance depends on the font. For example, if the font size is 10 points, the bottom margin will be the equivalent of 4 blank lines, or 40 points. This establishes a distance of 4 ems between the border and the box bottom.

```
h1 {margin-top:5em; margin-bottom: 1em}
```

This statement positions level 1 headings with the equivalent of five lines above and one line below. This creates a separation between the preceding topic and the heading and strengthens the association between the heading and its topic contents below.

margin-left

Use this property to set just the left margin of an element's box. The left margin is the distance between the border and the left edge of the box. You can use this to create indented text or other element placements. The default for the left margin is zero, or no space. The settings in one element are not used by its included or inline elements.

Values

The value auto sets the left margin to the browser's default.

Length   Sets an absolute or relative distance between the border and the box's left edge. See the "Lengths" section earlier in this reference.

Percentage   Sets the left margin size as a percentage of the parent element's width.

Notes

You can use negative values for margins, but not all browsers will handle the settings correctly, and some may ignore the setting and substitute the default of zero or use their own algorithm.

Examples

```
body {margin-left: 3%}
```

This statement sets up a basic left margin for the page using the body element. The browser should display this margin as 3% of the width of the page. No element within the page will appear outside this margin. If the browser shows 600×480 pixels, the body's left margin uses 18 pixels.

```
p {margin-left: 1cm; margin-top: 0.5cm}
```

This statement sets a left margin for paragraphs at the absolute value of 1 centimeter. With this, you can add a left gutter to your page. It also sets the top margin to 0.5 centimeters.

```
p {margin-left: 4em}
```

This statement creates a variable gutter for the paragraphs on a page. The actual size of the 4-em margin depends on the font size used for the paragraphs.

margin-right

Use this property to set just the right margin of an element's box. The right margin is the distance between the border and the right edge of the box. You can use this to force the element away from the right edge of the page. This generally defaults to zero and is not used by included block or inline elements.

Values

The value auto sets the right margin to the browser's default.

Length   Sets an absolute or relative distance between the border and the box's right edge. See the "Lengths" section earlier in this reference.

Percentage   Sets the right margin size as a percentage of the parent element's width.

Notes

You can use negative values for margins, but not all browsers will handle the settings correctly, and some may ignore the setting and substitute the default of zero or use their own algorithm.

Examples

```
body {margin-right: 0.5in}
```

This statement creates a margin on your page that is a 0.5 inches wide. Nothing will appear in this margin area.

```
p {margin-right: 10%}
```

This statement establishes an outside gutter that is 10% of the paragraph width. The actual distance depends on the paragraph width.

```
h1 {margin-right: 15em}
```

This statement creates an outside gutter whose size depends on the heading font size. It inserts a distance equal to 1.5 times the heading font size. This means that if the level 1 heading uses a 15-point font, for example, the distance between the border and box edge would be less than it would be with a 20-point font. If you want all headings to wrap before the edge of the box, but at the same place in the page, use percentage or absolute measurements.

margin-top

Use this property to set just the top margin of an element's box. The top margin is the distance between the border and the top of the box. You can use this to insert space above an element, perhaps to visually reinforce its relationship with the elements around it. This generally defaults to zero and is not used by included block or inline elements.

Values

The value auto sets the top margin to the browser's default.

Length   Sets an absolute or relative distance between the border and the box's top edge. See the "Lengths" section earlier in this reference.

Percentage   Sets the top margin size as a percentage of the parent element's width.

Notes

You can use negative values for margins, but not all browsers will handle the settings correctly, and some may ignore the setting and substitute the default of zero or use their own algorithm.

Examples

```
h1 {margin-top:5em; margin-bottom: 1em}
```

This statement positions level 1 headings with the equivalent of five lines above and one line below. This creates a separation between the preceding topic and the heading and strengthens the association between the heading and its topic contents below.

```
body {margin-top: 1em}
```

This statement adds the equivalent of one line to the margin of any element inside the body of the document. The actual distance depends on the font size for the element.

```
p {margin-top: 5%}
```

This statement adds a variable distance (5% of the height) to paragraph elements.

```
h1 {margin-top: 1cm}
```

This statement adds an absolute distance of 1 centimeter to the space between the box edge and the border of level 1 headings. Whatever the environment, the browser tacks on a centimeter of transparent margin to the element's box.

Box Position Properties

The box position properties control the arrangement of elements in relation to each other and the page, rather than within themselves. The float and clear properties control which elements can sit next to each other. The width and height properties set dimensions for elements, giving you more control of the page layout.

clear

Use this property to allow or disallow other elements, usually inline images, to float beside the element specified. You can allow floating elements on either side, both sides, or neither side. The default is to allow floating elements on both sides of the element (the none setting). This property is not used by inline and included elements.

Values

Value	Effect
none	Allows floating elements on either side of this element. This is the default.
both	Does not allow floating elements on either side of this element.
left	Not on the left; moves the element below any floating elements on the left.
right	Not on the right; moves the element below any floating elements on the right.

Use one of these values to designate the position for floating elements in relation to a particular element.

Notes

This property indicates where floating elements are not allowed.

Examples

```
p.prodname {clear: none}
```

This statement creates a paragraph class called `prodname` (that is, `<p class="prodname">...</p>`) that allows floating elements to appear on either side of it.

```
p {clear: right}
```

In this statement, the paragraph element allows floating elements on its left side, but not the right.

```
h1, h2, h3 {clear: both}
```

This statement prevents elements from appearing next to the headings in the document. All floating elements, usually images, are pushed up or down and appear above or below the headings.

float

Use this property to set an element in a position outside the rules of placement for the normal flow of elements. For example, the `float` property can raise an element from an inline element to a block element. This is usually used to place an image. The default, which is not an inherited value, is to display the element where it appears in the flow of the document (`none`).

Values

Value	Effect
none	Displays the element where it appears in the flow of the parent element. This is the default.
left	Wraps other element contents to the right of the floating element.
right	Wraps other element contents to the left of the floating element.

Notes

A floating element cannot overlap the margin in the parent element used for positioning. For example, an illustration that is a left-floating element (pushes other contents to the right of itself) cannot overlap the left margin of its parent container.

Examples

```
p {clear: none}
img.keycap {float: none}
img.prodlogo {float: left}
```

These statements specify that if an image of class keycap (that is, <img class=
"keycap" />) is inserted in the course of a paragraph, it appears within the flow of the
text. If an image of class prodlogo is inserted, it appears against the left margin of the
parent element and the text wraps on its right.

height

Use this property to set the height of an element on a page. Browsers will enforce the
height, scaling the image to fit. This property will be familiar to anyone who has used
the height and width attributes of an image (img) element in XHTML or HTML.

Values

The value auto allows the browser to either set the height to the actual image height
or, if the width is set, preserve the aspect ratio of images. You can instead use absolute or
relative length measurements, as described in the "Lengths" section earlier in this reference. Use a percentage to set the image size as a percentage of the parent element's height.

Notes

Some browsers may not handle the height (or width) property if the element is not a
replaced element (one that uses a pointer in the XHTML source to indicate the file
with the actual content).

Generally, replaced elements have their own, intrinsic, measurements. If you want
to replace these dimensions with a height (and/or width) property setting, the browser
tries to resize the replaced element to fit. To maintain the aspect ratio, you need to set
one of the properties, height or width, to auto. To preserve the aspect ratio of images
positioned with height, include the width property in the statement and set the width
to auto. If you position an image with the width property, include the height property
in the statement and set the height to auto.

If you need to set the size of an image, it's usually best to set it in proportion to the
container element (using a relative setting); otherwise, leave these settings at auto,
which allows the browser to use the image's original size.

You cannot use a negative value for the height or width of an element.

Examples

```
img.keycap {float: none; width: auto; height: 1.2em;
            vertical-align: middle}
```

This statement creates an img class (that is, <img class="keycap" />) where the images appear in the text stream. These images have a controlled width, and a height that is 1.2 ems. For example, in a stream of text with a font size of 12 points, the image will be 14.4 points. The statement also adjusts the vertical position of the image in relation to the line.

```
img.prodlogo {float: left; width: 2cm; height: auto}
```

In this statement, images of class prodlogo, which have the text wrap on the right around them, have a controlled width of 2 centimeters. However, it's better to avoid absolute measurements and use relative values or the image's values (by setting width and height to auto).

width

Use this property to set the width of an element on a page. Browsers will enforce the width, scaling the image to fit. This property will be familiar to anyone who has used the height and width attributes of an image (img) element in XHTML or HTML.

Values

The value auto allows the browser to either set the width to the actual image height or, if the height is set, preserve the aspect ratio of images.

Length   Sets an absolute or relative width for images in a particular element or class. See the "Lengths" section earlier in this reference.

Percentage   Sets the image size as a percentage of the parent element's width.

Notes

See the "Notes" section for the height property.

Examples

```
img.keycap {float: none; width: auto; vertical-align: middle;
            height: 1.2em}
```

In this statement, images of class keycap (that is, <img class="keycap" />) will appear in the text stream aligned to the middle of the line of text where it appears. Its height is set to 1.2 ems and the width to auto, which allows the browser to position it properly (the height does not disturb the paragraph formatting around it, and the width is adjusted to fit).

```
img.prodlogo {float: left; height: auto; width: 2cm}
```

This statement creates an image class prodlogo that forces the text to wrap on the right of it, is 2 centimeters wide, and has whatever height is proportionate to the 2-centimeter width.

Background and Color Properties

Color affects the foreground elements, such as text and borders, and background properties affect the surface on which the document elements appear. You can set these globally and locally for individual elements. When you paint the background for an element, you're layering on top of the document's background. If you do not set a background for an element, it defaults to transparent, allowing the document background to show. The color property inherits from the document body.

You can control a wide variety of properties for backgrounds, including the position, repetition, and scrolling. You can use the background shorthand property to set all the background properties, or use the individual properties. The background is set relative to the element's box properties.

background

This is a shorthand property used to include the full collection of background values. The background property will be familiar to anyone who has changed the page color of a Web page or added a graphic as wallpaper. This property now extends to individual elements, allowing you to have a variety of backgrounds. It also allows more functionality in the background, including scrolling and repetitions.

Values

The possible values for background are the set of all possible values listed in the individual property entries:

Property	Effect
background-attachment	Sets up a background that scrolls with the element.

Property	Effect
background-color	Sets a background color for the page or elements on the page.
background-image	Sets an image behind the element.
background-position	Positions the background within the element's box.
background-repeat	Sets the number of times and direction that a background repeats.

See the sections for the individual properties for details about these values.

Notes

If you do not include a property (such as background-repeat), the browser uses the default.

The order of the properties in a statement is not important.

Examples

```
body {background: url(sunshine.gif) blue repeat-y}
```

This statement sets up a background for the page using the body element. If the browser cannot find the image, it uses a blue background. If needed, the background image repeats down the page (but not across the page).

```
h1 {background: white}
```

This statement changes the background for level 1 headings to white using a color keyword. If this statement appears in the same style sheet as the first statement, the sunshine background is overlaid with a white box where the level 1 headings appear.

```
p em {background: url(swirl.gif) yellow top left}
```

In this statement, any emphasis (em) within a paragraph (p) is changed to use as a background a swirl.gif file that starts at the top-left corner of the element's box. If the swirl.gif file cannot be found, the browser uses a yellow background.

background-attachment

Use this property to specify whether an image used for the background of an element will scroll with the element or remain at a fixed location on the page. If the image is larger than the element box, when users scroll down the screen, they either see different parts of the background image (a fixed attachment) or a single part of the image (a scrolling attachment) that moves with the display of the element down the page.

Inline and included block elements do not inherit this property.

Values

A value of scroll moves the image with the element on the page, so the same part is visible when users scroll down the screen. This is the default and it applies only to the element in the statement. A value of fixed keeps the image fixed in relation to the page so different parts are visible when users scroll down the screen.

Notes

Use this property in conjunction with the background-image property.

Example

```
p {background-image: url(logo.gif);
   background-attachment: fixed}
```

This statement uses the image logo.gif as the background for the paragraphs in the document. The image is fixed to the page, not the contents of the paragraph.

background-color

Use this property to set the background color for the page or elements on the page. If you set the background for the base class body, your other elements will appear to inherit that color unless you change their background colors from transparent.

Values

Sets the color for the background. This value can be one of the color names or RGB values. See the "Colors" section earlier in this reference. The keyword value transparent makes the page background the default for viewing.

Notes

This value sets the background color only. To set the background as an image, you need to use either the background property or the background-image property.

This property affects the box area owned by the element. This is set using the margin and padding properties, listed in the "Box Margin Properties" and "Box Padding Properties" sections.

When you set an element's background to transparent, or don't set it at all, the page's background color or image appears in its place.

Examples

```
h1 {background-color: blue}
```

In this statement, the background color for level 1 headings is set to blue using the color keyword.

```
p.note {background-color: #800000}
```

This statement creates a paragraph class called note (that is, <p class="note"> ...</p>) that has a background color of maroon using the RGB hexadecimal value for the color.

background-image

Use this property to define an image for the background. The browser will look for additional information about the image's position, repetition, and attachment (or association). If you accept the defaults for these properties, your background image will not repeat, will be attached to the page (not the element), and will have a starting position at the upper-left corner of the element's box.

Values

The default value, none, does not use an image for the background. A value of url(...) cues the browser that you're going to provide a filename. You must include the file with the page.

Notes

The images you use should be gif or jpg image files to ensure that all graphical browsers can read them.

You should also include a background-color property in case the image you have selected is not available.

Example

```
p {background-image: url(litelogo.jpg);
    background-repeat: no-repeat;
    background-attachment: fixed;}
```

This statement sets up the document paragraphs to have a background image (called litelogo.jpg) that does not repeat and is fixed to the document canvas rather than to the element.

background-position

Use this property to position the element background within its space, using the initial position as a mark. Every element has a box that describes the area it controls. The background-position property is useful when your image is not the same size as the element it provides a background for. With this property, you can indicate the position of the image relative to the element box.

Values

Length   Sets the starting point on the element's box edge, in an absolute or a relative measurement, and also gives the coordinates as measurements. See the "Lengths" section earlier in this reference.

Percentage   Indicates, as a percentage, where on the box edge the browser begins placing the image. You can repeat this value to give a vertical and horizontal starting point.

Vertical position   Sets the vertical starting position. Use the keyword top, center, or bottom. The browser determines the size of the element box and works from there.

Horizontal position   Sets the horizontal starting position. Use the keyword left, center, or right. The browser determines the width of the element box and works from there.

With the length and percentage settings, you can use two numbers to indicate the vertical and horizontal starting point. Unlike percentage, however, the length measurement does not apply to both the image and the element box in the same way. The length measurement indicates the coordinates inside the element box where the top-left corner of the image appears.

Notes

Using 0% 0% is synonymous with using `top left`. In the first case, the initial position of the image is determined this way; the upper-left corner of the image is considered to be 0% horizontal and 0% vertical, and the same is done with the element box. You could position an image using 50% 50%, and the browser would then begin at the middle of the element and the image. If the image is larger than the element box, you lose the edges that extend beyond the element box. Similarly, if your image is smaller than the element box, you will have an edge, inside your element box, with no image.

You can combine the percentage and length measurements. It's legal to set the property using 25% 2cm. This would start rendering the image at one-fourth the way into the image and at one-fourth the distance across the element box. The image would begin to appear 2 centimeters below the top of the element box.

The length measurements indicate the distance from the box border where the browser starts to render the image.

When you use a length unit, you can use a positive or negative number. You can, in some cases, use a decimal number. Whichever system of measurement you choose to use must be communicated with the short form for the system (for example, `cm` or `in`).

You can also use keywords to position the image within the element's box. Table MR2.5 gives you some corresponding values to work with.

Table MR2.5 Background Position Keywords

KEYWORD	PERCENTAGE	DESCRIPTION
`top left`, `left top`	0% 0%	The top-left corner of the image starts at the top-left corner of the element box.
`top`, `top center`, `center top`	50% 0%	The horizontal middle of the image appears in the horizontal middle of the element box. The top of the image begins at the top of the element box.
`right top`, `top right`	100% 0%	The top-right corner of the image starts at the top-right corner of the element box.
`left`, `left center`, `center left`	0% 50%	The vertical middle of the image appears in the vertical middle of the element box. The left side of the image is flush against the left side of the element box.

Table MR2.5 continued Background Position Keywords

KEYWORD	PERCENTAGE	DESCRIPTION
`center,center center`	50% 50%	The absolute middle of the image is positioned over the absolute middle of the element box.
`right,right center,center right`	100% 50%	The vertical middle of the image positions over the vertical middle of the element box. The right edge of the image is flush against the right side of the element box.
`bottom left,left bottom`	0% 100%	The bottom-left corner of the image is positioned at the bottom-left corner of the element box.
`bottom center,center bottom`	50% 100%	The horizontal centers of the image and element box appear together, and the bottom edges of each remain together.
`bottom right,right bottom`	100% 100%	The lower-right corner of the image positions in the lower-right corner of the element box.

Examples

```
body {background-image: url(litelogo.gif);
    background-position: 50% 50%}
```

This sets the class, **body**, to position a background image centered on the page.

```
h1 {background-image: url(exclaim.gif);
    background-position: top left}
```

In this statement, an image has been assigned to the background of heading level 1 elements that starts rendering at the upper-left corner of the element box.

background-repeat

Use this property to control whether an image repeats horizontally, vertically, both, or neither. Images normally repeat both horizontally and vertically, filling in the area within the element's margins. By default, backgrounds repeat both horizontally and vertically.

Values

Value	Effect
repeat	Sets horizontal and vertical repetitions of the image. This is the default.
repeat-x	Sets horizontal repetitions only.
repeat-y	Sets vertical repetitions only.
no-repeat	Prevents repeated copies of the image from displaying.

Notes

This property works in conjunction with the background-image and background-position properties. Combining these properties into a single statement enables you to create a pattern of background images that enhances the presentation of information.

Example

```
p {background-image: url(logo1.gif); background-color: blue;
    background-position: top left; background-repeat: repeat-y}
```

This statement adds a background to your document paragraphs. The first copy of the image, logo1.gif, appears in the top-left corner of the page and repeats down the page. If the image is not found, the browser uses a blue background.

color

Use this property to set the foreground, or element, color. If the element is text, you can set the color of the text with this property. Both inline (such as a) and included block elements (such as p) use this property.

Values

Sets the color using color names or RGB values. See the "Colors" section earlier in this reference.

Notes

You can set this property using one of the three RGB systems or by using a color keyword. Although most browsers should recognize the color keyword, individual browser/system configurations may display the same color differently.

Examples

```
body {color: black}
```

This statement uses the keyword black to set the default foreground color in the document to black.

```
p {color: #0000ff}
```

This statement changes the paragraph (p) foreground color to blue using the RGB hexadecimal value.

```
em {color: rgb(75%,0%,0%)}
```

In this statement, emphasis elements are set to maroon using the RGB percentage value.

Classification Properties

This group of properties controls the presentation of some standard elements, such as the display and lists. The properties can change the type of an element from an inline to a block, from a list item to an inline element, and so on. These properties also include controls for lists and list items, giving you more control over the presentation of the bulleted lists on your page.

display

Use this property to change the display values of an element. Every element has its own default value for display.

Values

Value	Effect
block	Sets the element with a line break before and after.
compact	Sets the display to compact, running the element into the margin of the next element if possible. This value is new in CSS2.
inline	Removes the line breaks from an element and forces it into the flow of another element.
list-item	Sets the element as an item in a list.
marker	Sets the display of an element to be a marker (for example, a bullet in a list). This value is new in CSS2.
none	Prevents the display of the element.
run-in	Sets the display to "run in," making the element an inline element at the beginning of the following block element. This value is new in CSS2.
table, inline-table, table-row-group, table-column, table-column-group, table-header-group, table-footer-group, table-row, table-cell, and table-caption	Make the element act like a table element.

Notes

You can use the display property values to create special elements such as run-in headings and running lists, as well as to force images into inline presentations.

Examples

```
h1 {display: inline}
```

This statement sets the browser not to force the level 1 headings onto a separate line. You could combine this with a line break (br) before the heading, to start a new line, but let the contents of the section start right after the heading. You may want to extend the right margin of the heading to add some space between the heading and the content.

```
li.intext {display: inline}
```

Use this if you want to reformat your lists of the class intext (that is, <li class= "intext">...</li>) as a integral part of a paragraph. For example, you could list:

```
block
```

```
inline
```

```
list-item
```

```
none
```

Or you could list them inline as block, inline, list-item, none.

list-style

Use this shorthand property to set all the list properties in a single statement. If you set this property for a list element (as opposed to the list-item elements), the list items use the settings you establish. You can override the list settings with individual list-item settings.

Values

The possible settings values for list-style are the set of all possible values listed in the individual property entries:

Property	Effect
list-style-image	Sets an image to use for a bullet.
list-style-position	Sets a traditional hanging bullet, which is not flush with the text of the list item, or an indented one that is flush with the text.
list-style-type	Sets the type of bullet used in the list.

See the entries for the individual properties for details about these values.

Notes

These values apply only to elements with a display characteristic of `list-item`.

If you use a URL to specify an image, you don't need to set the type, because the bullet position will be occupied by the image.

Examples

```
ol.outline {list-style: lower-roman inside}
```

This creates a list class called `outline` (that is, `<ol class="outline">...</ol>`) that numbers the list items.

```
li.comment {list-style: none}
```

If you use this statement in the same style sheet as the first statement, you can insert list items that have no numbering.

list-style-image

Use this property to replace the standard bullet characters with an image of your choice. If you set this property for a list element (as opposed to the list-item elements), the list items use the settings you establish. You can override the list settings with individual list-item settings.

Values

The keyword `none` (the default) suppresses the image bullets that the element may have inherited. A URL, in the format `url(...)`, identifies the URL of an image you want to use for a bullet.

Notes

If you use an image, be sure to resize it so it's a small image before using it as a bullet.

If the browser cannot find the image identified in the URL, it will default to `list-style-type` setting.

List items use the settings from the lists. You can insert list items with different settings, creating a series of effects (such as comments or highlights by using a different bullet or position).

Example

```
li.prodicon {list-style-image: url(logo.gif)}
```

This replaces the bullet character for list items of type prodicon (that is, <li class="prodicon">...</li>) with an image called logo.gif.

list-style-position

Use this property to set an indent or outdent for the bullet. This property allows the bullet to stand out from the list contents (outside) or lays it flush with the list items (inside). If you set this property for a list element (as opposed to the list-item elements), the list items use the settings you establish. You can override the list settings with individual list-item settings

Values

A value of inside indents the bullet character with the left margin of the list-item contents. A value of outside creates a hanging-indent (or "outdent") effect, with the bullet standing out from the left margin of the list-item contents.

Notes

List items use the settings from the lists. You can insert list items with different settings, creating a series of effects (such as comments or highlights by using a different bullet or position).

Examples

```
ul {list-style-position: outside; list-style-type: circle}
li.level2 {list-style-position: inside}
li.prodstart {list-style-image: url(logolit1.gif)}
```

If you combine these three statements in a style sheet, your basic list items in an unordered list will have a hollow circle that hangs outside the left margin of the list contents. You can add "second-level" list items (that is, <li class="level2">......</li>) that use the circle bullet but lay it flush to the list-item contents. This creates a visual effect where these list items appear to be secondary. The third statement creates the effect of list headings by replacing the circle with a logo, and these list items use the parent's list-style-position setting.

list-style-type

Use this property to indicate a style of bullet or numbering you want for your lists. You can create several list classes and list-item classes, and then combine them to give your information navigational structure. If you set this property for a list element (as opposed to the list-item elements), the list items use the settings you establish. You can override the list settings with individual list-item settings.

Values

Value	Effect
none	Suppresses the display of bullet characters.
circle	Places a hollow circle as the bullet.
disc	Places a filled circle as the bullet.
square	Places a filled square as the bullet.
decimal	Numbers the list items using Arabic numerals (1, 2, 3, …).
decimal-leading-zero	Numbers the list items using Arabic numerals with initial zeros (01, 02, 03, … , 10, 11, …).
lower-roman	Numbers the list items using lowercase Roman numerals (i, ii, iii, …).
upper-roman	Numbers the list items using uppercase Roman numerals (I, II, III, …).
lower-alpha	Letters the list items using lowercase letters (a, b, c, …).
upper-alpha	Letters the list items using uppercase letters (A, B, C, …).
armenian	Armenian numbering (CSS2).
cjk-ideographic	Ideographic numbering (CSS2).
georgian	Georgian numbering (an, ban, gan, …, he, tan, in, in-an, …) (CSS2).
hebrew	Hebrew numbering (CSS2).

Value	Effect
hiragana	a, i, u, e, o, ka, ki, ... (CSS2).
hiragana-iroha	i, ro, ha, ni, ho, he, to, ... (CSS2).
katakana	A, I, U, E, O, KA, KI, ... (CSS2).
katakana-iroha	I, RO, HA, NI, HO, HE, TO, ... (CSS2).

Notes

If you use numbering or lettering, and you insert list items with an alternate type, the numbering includes the unnumbered list items in its counts. For example:

```
a    full-featured
     WYSIWIG
     compliant
D    backward compatible
```

Examples

```
ol {list-style-type: lower-roman}
```

This statement sets up a numbering system for the ordered lists in the document. These lists will use i, ii, iii, and so on, as a "bullet" for each list item.

```
li.comment {list-style-type: none}
```

You can override the list settings with a list-item setting. If you apply the list-item class comment (that is, <li class="comment">...</li>) to an item in a numbered list, the browser includes it in the numbering, but does not display the number for the list item.

CSS2 Notes

CSS2 supports additional keywords for other numbering systems. Use the keywords hebrew, armenian, georgian, cjk-ideographic, hiragana, hiragana-iroha, katakana, katakana-iroha. For example, if you want to use a Hebrew numbering system, your code might look like this:

```
ol {list-style-type: hebrew}
```

white-space

Use this property to control the white space within an element. This setting controls the wrapping of text within the element.

Values

Value	Effect
normal	Keeps the default of wrapping lines at the browser page size. This is the default and produces results similar to what you see in Web pages already.
nowrap	Prevents the user from wrapping lines within an element.
pre	Assigns the formatting in the document source to the document display.

When you want to control the line wrap in paragraphs or headings, you can do it with this property. If you select normal, it overrides the settings of a parent element because browsers default to this setting. If your element is a preformatted entity (such as sample code), you may want to use the pre keyword to force the browser to display it exactly as it occurs in the source text. Use the nowrap keyword to prevent the browser from ending the line without an explicit instruction, such as br, in the source.

Notes

Some browsers may ignore this setting and retain their own defaults. Even though the default value for whitespace is listed as normal, some browsers will have a default setting for all XHTML elements as proposed in a specification.

Examples

```
pre {white-space: pre}
```

This statement indicates that the text in the element is preformatted. The spacing between characters, words, and lines is set in the source, as are the line breaks.

```
p {white-space: normal}
```

This statement sets the spacing in the paragraph elements (p) to normal, which is how text is currently displayed.

```
h1 {white-space: nowrap}
```

This statement prevents the browser from wrapping the level 1 headings. For these headings to break across more than one line, you explicitly add br elements at the break spots.

Positioning

Using positioning, one of the first CSS2 features to be supported by browsers, you can add properties to style rules to control the positioning of the element. For example, you can identify specific locations for elements, as well as specify locations that are relative to other elements. You can use other box properties to control the layout as well, in conjunction with the positioning features. Furthermore, these features, used with scripting features, allow you to create dynamic XHTML documents.

bottom

Use this property to specify how far a box's bottom content edge is offset above the bottom of the box's containing block.

Values

The value auto specifies automatic offset, based on related settings.

Length Specifies offset as a distance from the edge of the containing element. See the "Lengths" section earlier in this reference.

Percentage Specifies offset as a percentage of the containing element's size (vertical or horizontal, as appropriate).

Example

```
img.logo {position: fixed; bottom: 0px; right: 0px}
```

This sets the image with class logo to stay at the bottom right of the display at all times.

clear

Use this property to indicate which sides of an element's box(es) may not be adjacent to an earlier floating box.

Values

Value	Effect
left	Specifies that the element start below any left-floating elements above the current element.
right	Specifies that the element start below any right-floating elements above the current element.
both	Specifies that the element start below all floating boxes of earlier elements.
none	Specifies no constraints on element placement.

Example

```
img.picture {clear: all; float: left}
```

This sets the image with class `picture` to float to the left side with the text flowing around to the right. It also sets the `clear` property to ensure that no other floating elements appear on the same line.

clip

A clipping region defines which portion of an element's rendered content is visible. By default, the clipping region has the same size and shape as the element's box(es). However, the clipping region may be modified by the `clip` property.

Values

Specifies `rect` (for rectangle, which is the only valid shape in CSS2). Use code `rect` (`top, right, bottom, left`) with each value specifying the length offset from the respective sides of the box. Substitute an absolute or relative length or `auto` for each of top, right, bottom, and left. The keyword auto specifies that the clipping region has the same size and location as the element's box(es).

Example

```
p {clip: 15px 15px 15px 15px; overflow: hidden}
```

This example defines a clipping area 15 pixels in from the edges of the box and hides the extra content.

float

Use this property to specify that a box may shift to the left or right on the current line. The XHTML img element with clear and align attributes is similar to float.

Values

Value	Effect
left	Specifies a box that is floated to the left with other content flowing around the right.
right	Specifies a box that is floated to the right with other content flowing around the left.
none	Specifies that the box does not float.

Example

```
img.picture {float: left}
```

This sets the image with class picture to float to the left side with the text flowing around to the right.

left

Use this property to specify how far a box's left content edge is offset to the right of the left edge of the box's containing block.

Values

The value auto specifies automatic offset, based on related settings.

Length   Specifies offset as a distance from the edge of the containing element. See the "Lengths" section earlier in this reference.

Percentage   Specifies offset as a percentage of the containing element's size (vertical or horizontal, as appropriate).

Example

```
img.logo {position: fixed; top: 0px; left: 0px}
```

This sets the image with class logo to stay at the top left of the display at all times.

overflow

Use this property to specify what happens to the extra content when a box is too small for the content it includes. In this case, the box is often called "clipped."

Values

Value	Effect
auto	Specifies that a scrolling mechanism is to be provided when necessary, but not always.
hidden	Specifies that content is clipped and that users should be unable to access the hidden region.
scroll	Specifies that the content is clipped and that scrollbars (if applicable) should always be shown to allow access to the content.
visible	Specifies that content not be clipped to box boundaries.

Example

```
p {clip: 15px 15px 15px 15px; overflow: hidden}
```

This example defines a clipping area 15 pixels in from the edges of the box and hides the extra content.

position

Use this property to control the positioning of elements.

Values

Value	Effect
absolute	Specifies the element position and, optionally, size with respect to the containing element.
fixed	Specifies the element position and, optionally, size as with the absolute value, but with respect to a specific reference point (in the browser window or on a printed sheet, for example).

Value	Effect
relative	Specifies that the position be calculated relative to the position in the normal flow, with no effect on other elements. Relatively positioned elements can overlap.
static	Specifies that the element belongs to the normal document flow with no specific positioning requirements.

Example

```
img.logo {position: fixed; top: 0px; right: 0px}
```

This sets the image with the class `logo` (that is, `<img class="logo" />`) to stay at the top right of the display at all times.

right

Use this property to specify how far a box's right content edge is offset to the left of the right edge of the box's containing block.

Values

The value `auto` specifies automatic offset, based on related settings.

Length   Specifies offset as a distance from the edge of the containing element. See the "Lengths" section earlier in this reference.

Percentage   Specifies offset as a percentage of the containing element's size (vertical or horizontal, as appropriate).

Example

```
img.logo {position: fixed; top: 0px; right: 0px}
```

This sets the image with class `logo` to stay at the top right of the display at all times.

top

Use this property to specify the vertical offset for an element in relation to the containing block.

Values

The value auto specifies automatic offset, based on related settings.

Length   Specifies offset as a distance from the edge of the containing element. See the "Lengths" section earlier in this reference.

Percentage   Specifies offset as a percentage of the containing element's size (vertical or horizontal, as appropriate).

Example

```
img.logo {position: fixed; top: 0px; right: 0px}
```

This sets the image with class logo to stay at the top right of the display at all times.

visibility

Use the visibility property to specify whether the boxes generated by an element are rendered. Invisible boxes still affect layout (set the display property to none to suppress box generation altogether).

Values

Value	Effect
collapse	Specifies a collapsed (hidden) display for table rows and columns, or same as hidden for other elements.
hidden	Specifies that the box is invisible, but present for layout purposes.
visible	Specifies that the box is visible.

Examples

```
p.chosen {visibility: visible}
p.unchosen {visibility: hidden}
```

This example shows two paragraphs, each of which takes the same space, that can be either revealed or hidden (likely through scripts).

z-index

Using CSS2, you can *layer* box elements. Each box element has a position in three dimensions, including the normal horizontal and vertical positions and a vertical dimension, which is described on a *z*-axis. Each box belongs to one *stacking context* and has a number that indicates its position relative to other elements in the stack. The higher the number, the closer to the top (revealed) portion of the stack.

Use this property to specify the stack level of the box in the current stacking context. This property also implicitly specifies that new context is started.

Values

A numeric value specifies the stack level of the current element using an integer. The keyword `auto` specifies that the stack level is the same as the parent.

Examples

```
p.foreground {z-index: 10}
p.background {z-index: 3}
```

This sets the paragraphs with class `foreground` to have a `z-index` of 10, while the paragraphs with class `background` have a `z-index` of 3, so the background is behind the foreground.

Aural Style Sheets

Aural style sheets were introduced in CSS2; they specify how a document should be read aloud—for example, to a visually impaired person, in situations where reading is not possible, or as a supplement to the visual presentation.

With aural style sheets, you can specify where sound should come from, the characteristics of the sound, and other sounds to precede or follow the sound. These properties are important for accessibility reasons.

azimuth

You use the `azimuth` property to specify which direction the sound comes from on the horizontal plane—either from the left or right, from in front of or from behind, or from any point in between.

Values

Describes the sound source as an angle with 0 degrees directly in front of the listener, 90 degrees to the listener's right, 180 degrees behind the listener, and 270 degrees to the listener's left. All points in between are possible. Use a number to express the angle, or use one of the following keyword equivalents:

Value	Equivalent to
left-side	270 degrees
far-left	300 degrees (used with behind, specifies 240 degrees)
left	320 degrees (used with behind, specifies 220 degrees)
center-left	340 degrees (used with behind, specifies 200 degrees)
center	0 degrees (used with behind, specifies 180 degrees)
center-right	20 degrees (used with behind, specifies 160 degrees)
far-right	60 degrees (used with behind, specifies 120 degrees)
right-side	90 degrees
behind	180 degrees
leftwards	Moving the sound source counterclockwise by 20 degrees (subtracting 20 degrees)
rightwards	Moving the sound source clockwise by 20 degrees (adding 20 degrees)

Example

```
p.trick {azimuth: right-side; volume: 100}
```

This example sets the sound for all paragraphs with the trick attribute to come from the right at a volume of 100.

cue

You use this property to specify a sound to play before and after the specified element. The W3C suggests cues as "auditory icons." If you specify one value, it applies to both before and after; if you specify two values, one applies to before, and one applies to after.

Values

Specify the address of a sound file to play with the format url(...). The value none specifies no cueing.

Example

```
.example, .code {cue: url(codewarning.au);
                 pause-before: 20ms; pause-after: 50ms}
```

This example specifies that the codewarning.au sound should precede and follow anything in example or code classes. It also specifies that codewarning.au has a 50-millisecond pause before it plays and a 20-millisecond pause after it's played.

cue-after

Use this property to specify a sound to play after the specified element.

Values

Specify the address of a sound file to play with the format url(...). The value none specifies no cueing.

Example

```
.example, .code {cue-after: url(donenow.au);
                 pause-after: 5%}
```

This example specifies that the donenow.au sound follow anything in example or code classes and have a 5% pause after it's played.

cue-before

Use this property to specify a sound to play before the specified element.

Values

Specify the address of a sound file to play with the format url(...). The value none specifies no cueing.

Example

```
.example, .code {cue-before: url(codewarning.au);
                     pause-after: 5%}
```

This example specifies that the codewarning.au sound precede anything in example or code classes and have a 5% pause after it's played.

elevation

You use this property to specify the sound source in the vertical plane—points above or below the listener.

Values

Specifies the sound source as an angle between –90 degrees (directly below the listener) and +90 degrees (directly above the listener). Use a number to express the angle, or use one of the following keyword equivalents:

Value	Equivalent to
below	–90 degrees
level	0 degrees
above	+90 degrees
higher	Increasing elevation by 10 degrees
lower	Decreasing elevation by 10 degrees

Example

```
p.downhere {elevation: below; volume: 100}
```

This example sets the sound for all paragraphs with the class downhere to come from below.

pause

Use this property to specify the duration of a pause before or after an element is read. The pause occurs between element content and cues. If you specify one value, it applies before and after the element is read. If you specify two values, the first applies before and the second applies after an element is read.

Values

Time   Specifies the duration of the pause as a number of milliseconds.

Percentage   Specifies the duration of the pause as a percentage of the overall element length.

Examples

```
.example, .code {volume: 50; speak: spell-out; pause: 10 20}
```

This example specifies that anything in example or code classes should be spelled out at a volume of 50, preceded by a 10-millisecond pause and followed by a 20-millisecond pause.

```
.example, .code {volume: 50; speak: spell-out; pause: 10}
```

This example is the same as the first one, but the element will be preceded *and* followed by a 10-millisecond pause.

pause-after

Use this property to specify the length of a pause after an element is read. The pause occurs between element content and cues.

Values

Time   Specifies the duration of the pause as a number of milliseconds.

Percentage   Specifies the duration of the pause as a percentage of the overall element length.

Example

```
.example, .code {volume: 50; speak: spell-out;
                 pause-before: 10; pause-after: 5%}
```

This example specifies that anything in example or code classes be spelled out at a volume of 50, be preceded by a 10-millisecond pause, and be followed by a pause lasting 5% of the length of the element.

pause-before

Use this property to specify the length of a pause before an element is read.

Values

Time   Specifies the duration of the pause as a number of milliseconds.

Percentage   Specifies the duration of the pause as a percentage of the overall element length.

Example

```
.example, .code {volume: 50; speak: spell-out; pause-before: 10}
```

This example specifies that anything in example or code classes be spelled out and preceded by a 10-millisecond pause at a volume of 50.

pitch

Use this property to specify the pitch (frequency) of the voice.

Values

Specifies the pitch of the voice in hertz (Hz). Use a number for the value, or use x-low, low, medium, high, and x-high to specify relative pitches.

Example

```
.example, .code {pitch: medium}
```

This example specifies that anything in example or code classes be of medium pitch.

pitch-range

You use this property to specify variation in the pitch, which can range from a monotone to a highly inflected voice.

Values

Specifies a number in the range from 0 (monotone) to 100 (very energetic, highly inflected).

Example

```
.example, .code {volume: 50; pitch: medium; pitch-range: 10}
```

This example specifies that anything in example or code classes be inflected very little in a medium pitch at a volume of 50.

play-during

Use this property to specify a sound to play while the element's content is read.

Values

Value	Effect
url(...)	Specifies the address of a sound file.
mix	Specifies that any sound continuing from the parent element should continue to play in addition to the sound named in the url(...) value.
repeat	Specifies that the sound should repeat if necessary to fill the time that the element occupies. Otherwise, the sound plays once and then stops.
auto	Specifies that the sound of the parent element continues but no other sound plays. This is the default.
none	Specifies no cueing.

Example

```
.example, .code {volume: 50;
                 speak: spell-out;
                 cue-before: url(codewarning.au)
                 play-during: url(special.mid) repeat;
                 pause-after: 5%}
```

This example specifies that the special.mid sound should accompany anything in example or code classes.

richness

Use this property to specify the brightness or richness of the sound.

Values

Specifies a number in the range from 0 (a "smooth" voice that carries little) to 100 (a "rich" voice that carries well).

Example

```
.example, .code {volume: 50; richness: 90}
```

This example specifies that anything in example or code classes be very rich and played at a volume of 50.

speak

Use this property to specify whether text should be spoken, not spoken, or spelled-out.

Values

Value	Effect
none	Specifies that the element not be spoken.
normal	Specifies that the element should be spoken.
spell-out	Specifies that the element should be spelled one letter at a time.

Example

```
.example, .code {volume: 50; stress: 50;
                 richness: 90; speak: spell-out;}
```

This example specifies that anything in example or code classes be spelled out at a volume and stress of 50 and a richness of 90.

speak-numeral

Use this property to control how numbers are read.

Values

The value digits specifies that numbers be read as individual digits. The (default) value continuous specifies that numbers be read as a complete number.

Example

```
.example, .code {pitch: medium;
                 speak: spell-out;
                 speak-numeral: digits}
```

This example specifies that all numerals in example or code classes be spelled out and read digit by digit in a medium pitch.

speak-punctuation

Use this property to specify if or how punctuation should be spoken.

Values

The value code specifies that punctuation should be spoken explicitly. The (default) value none specifies that punctuation should be interpreted as pauses or inflection, but not spoken.

Example

```
.example, .code {volume: 50;
                 speak: spell-out;
                 speak-punctuation: code}
```

This example specifies that all punctuation in example or code classes be spelled out and spoken explicitly at a volume of 50.

speech-rate

Use this property to specify the rate of speech output for aural browsers.

Values

Specifies the rate in words per minute. Use a number to express the rate, or use one of the following keyword equivalents:

Value	Equivalent to
x-slow	80 words per minute
slow	120 words per minute
medium	180–200 words per minute (the default)
fast	300 words per minute
x-fast	500 words per minute
faster	Increasing rate by 40 words per minute
slower	Decreasing rate by 40 words per minute

Example

```
.example, .code {speech-rate: slow}
```

This example specifies that anything in example or code class be read slowly.

stress

This property is similar to pitch-range; however, it allows you to specify the amount of stress (inflection) of words and syllables.

Values

Specifies a number in the range from 0 (monotone) to 100 (highly inflected).

Example

```
.example, .code {volume: 50; pitch: medium; stress: 90}
```

This example specifies that anything in example or code classes be highly inflected at a volume of 50 and a medium pitch.

voice-family

Use this property to specify voice family names. You can specify multiple voice families, just as you can specify multiple font families.

Values

Specify either a generic voice, using the keywords male, female, or child, or a specific voice, assuming availability to the listener.

Example

```
h1 {voice-family: narrator, female}
```

This example specifies all level 1 headings be read in the narrator voice, or in a female voice if narrator is not available.

volume

Use this property to specify the relative volume of the text, where 1 is the minimum and 100 is the maximum. Users will likely be able to adjust or override volume settings.

Values

Value	Effect
nn	Sets a specific number between 1 and 100.
nn%	Sets a volume percentage.
x-soft	Identical to a value of 0.
soft	Identical to a value of 25.
medium	Identical to a value of 50.
loud	Identical to a value of 75.
x-loud	Identical to a value of 100.

Example

```
h1 {volume: 70}
```

This example sets a relatively high volume for level 1 headings.

Printed Media Style Sheets

Your users will view many of your documents online and scroll up or down to access page content. In some cases, however, your users might print your documents, rather than reading them online. You can use printed (or paged) media style sheets to set up documents to accommodate printing needs. These CSS2 properties let you set values for the page box, which you can think of as the area of your printout. For example, in hard copy, your page box might be the 8.5 × 11 piece of paper; the page box is the content, margins, and edges. Remember that these are only available to users using CSS2-compliant browsers.

@page

Use this special element to specify the dimensions, orientation, and margins of a page box. Use @page, which selects a page. For example,

```
@page {size: 8.5in 11in}
```

sets a standard North American paper size.

You can also use optional pseudoclasses, which are :first, :left, and/or :right to specify styles for the first, left, or right page of a document, respectively. For example,

```
@page :first {margin-top: 2em}
```

You can also use the names of specific pages, and any properties and declarations you want. For example,

```
@page squirrel {margin-bottom: 1in}
```

margin

Use this property to set up all the margins for a page. This shorthand measurement specifies the distance between the page box and the edge of the media.

Values

Length   Sets the border width using an absolute or a relative measurement. See the "Lengths" section earlier in this reference.

Percentage   Sets the margin size as a percentage of the page width.

Browser default   The value auto sets the margin to the browser's default on all four sides.

For length and percentage, you can use one, two, three, or four numbers. If you use one number, the browser applies it to all four margins (top, right, bottom, and left). If you use two numbers, the first number sets the top and bottom margins, and the second number sets the left and right margins. If you use three numbers, you're setting the top margin with the first, the right and left margins with the second, and the bottom margin with the third. You can mix length and percentage values.

Example

```
@page {margin: 1in}
```

This example sets a 1-inch margin around all sides of the pages.

margin-bottom

Use this property to set only the bottom margin of a page box. The bottom margin is the distance between the bottom border and the bottom edge of the box. This generally defaults to zero and is not used by included block or inline elements.

Values

Length   Sets an absolute or relative distance between the border and the box's bottom edge. See the "Lengths" section earlier in this reference.

Percentage   Sets the bottom margin size as a percentage of the parent element's width.

Browser default   The value auto sets the bottom margin to the browser's default.

Example

```
@page {margin: 1in; margin-bottom: 0.5in}
```

This example sets a 1-inch margin around all sides of the pages with a 0.5-inch margin at the bottom.

margin-left

Use this property to set only the left margin of a page box. The left margin is the distance between the border and the left edge of the box.

Values

Length Sets an absolute or relative distance between the border and the box's left edge. See the "Lengths" section earlier in this reference.

Percentage Sets the left margin size as a percentage of the parent element's width.

Browser default The value auto sets the left margin to the browser's default.

Example

```
@page {margin: 1in; margin-left: 0.5in}
```

This example sets a 1-inch margin around all sides of the pages with a 0.5-inch margin at the left.

margin-right

Use this property to set only the right margin of a page. The right margin is the distance between the border and the right edge of the page. You can use this to force the element away from the right edge of the page.

Values

Length Sets an absolute or relative distance between the border and the box's right edge. See the "Lengths" section earlier in this reference.

Percentage Sets the right margin size as a percentage of the parent element's width.

Browser default The value auto sets the right margin to the browser's default.

Example

```
@page:left {margin-left: 5cm; margin-right: 6cm}
```

This example sets the left margin at 5 cm and the right margin at 6 cm.

margin-top

Use this property to set only the top margin of a page box. The top margin is the distance between the page and the top of the physical page.

Values

Length Sets an absolute or relative distance between the border and the box's top edge. See the "Lengths" section earlier in this reference.

Percentage Sets the top margin size as a percentage of the parent element's width.

Browser default The value auto sets the top margin to the browser's default.

Example

```
@page:first {margin-top: 8cm}
```

Here, we set the top margin to 8 cm.

marks

You use this property to specify whether crop or cross marks should be printed outside the page box (if the output device can do so) to help with alignment of physical media for binding.

Values

The value crop specifies to print crop marks. The value cross specifies to print cross marks. The default value is none.

Example

```
@page {marks: crop}
```

This example specifies to print crop marks.

orphans

Use this property to specify the minimum number of lines of a paragraph that must be left at the bottom of a page. By using the orphans property, you can avoid a single line dangling at the bottom of a page.

Values

An integer that sets the minimum number of lines of a paragraph that must appear at the bottom of a page.

Example

```
p {orphans: 3}
```

This example requires at least three lines of a new paragraph to appear at the bottom of a page.

page

Using the page property, you can specify the specific page on which an element should appear.

Values

The value specifies the name or identification of a page.

Example

```
@page summary
h1 {page: summary}
```

This example specifies that the h1 element appear on the summary page.

page-break-after

Use this property to control page breaks after elements.

Values

Value	Effect
always	Specifies a page break after the element.
auto	Specifies default action for page breaks (this is the default value).
avoid	Specifies no page break after the element.
left	Specifies a page break after the element to make sure the element starts on a left-side page.
right	Specifies a page break after the element to make sure the element starts on a right-side page.

Example

```
table {page-break-after: auto}
```

This example specifies automatic page breaks after `table` elements.

page-break-before

Use this property to control page breaks before elements.

Values

Value	Effect
always	Specifies a page break before the element.
auto	Specifies default action for page breaks (this is the default value).
avoid	Specifies no page break before the element.
left	Specifies a page break before the element to make sure the element starts on a left-side page.
right	Specifies a page break before the element to make sure the element starts on a right-side page.

Example

```
h1 {page-break-before: right}
```

This example specifies a page break before `h1` elements and forces them to start on a right hand page.

page-break-inside

Use this property to control page breaks within elements.

Values

The (default) value `auto` specifies a default action for page breaks. The value `avoid` specifies no page break within the element.

Example

```
table {page-break-inside: avoid}
```

Using the `page-break-inside` property, we can avoid all page breaks within `table` elements.

size

Use this property to specify the size of the page box.

Values

Use a keyword value or a number. Numeric values specify the dimensions (horizontal and vertical) of the box, using an absolute or (in the case of pixels) a relative measurement. This type of sizing forces a particular measurement to be used for the element, ignoring any browser's settings. Specify the measurement after the number as follows: `in` for inches, `mm` for millimeters, `cm` for centimeters, `pt` for points, `px` for pixels, or `pc` for picas. If you provide one measurement, the box will be square. If you provide two, you specify the width and length of the box.

Possible keyword values are as follows:

Value	Effect
auto	Specifies that the page box be set to the size and orientation of the target sheet. This is the default.
landscape	Specifies that the long sides of the page box are horizontal.
portrait	Specifies that the long sides of the page box are vertical.

If you use `auto`, you can follow it with `landscape` or `portrait` to override the default orientation while maintain the `auto` setting for size.

Examples

```
@page {size: 8.5in 11in}
```

This example sets a standard North American paper size.

```
@page {size: auto landscape}
```

This example sets a horizontally oriented page of the default size for the output device.

widows

Use this property to set the minimum number of lines of a paragraph that must appear at the top of a page. Similar to the orphans property, widows will prevent a single line dangling at the top of a new page.

Values

An integer that sets the minimum number of lines of a paragraph that must appear at the top of a page.

Example

```
p {widows: 3}
```

This example requires at least three lines of a new paragraph to appear at the top of a page.

Auto-Generated Content

The properties in this section allow you to use CSS2 to automatically generate content for your pages. These properties are handy for generating content that you'd otherwise have to retype from document to document or line to line, such as boilerplate text, dates, or even counters.

content

With the content property, you can automatically include whatever text you want. You'll use this property with the :before and :after pseudoclasses.

Values

Value	Effect
text	Specifies text content.
url(...)	Specifies the URL from which the content should come.
open-quote	Specifies opening quotation marks based on the quote property.

Value	Effect
close-quote	Specifies closing quotation marks based on the quote property.
no-close-quote	Specifies not to display closing quotation marks, but to consider the quote closed.
no-open-quote	Specifies not to display opening quotation marks, but to consider a quote open.

Examples

```
q:before {content: open-quote}
q:after {content: close-quote}
```

This example places an opening quote before q elements and a closing quote after q elements.

counter

Use this property to set and display counters.

Values

This property takes two values: the name of the counter, and an optional style. counter(name, style) specifies to display the current count for *name*, with the count displayed in *style* format. All the styles shown as possible values for list-style-type are allowed here, including disc, circle, square, and none; see the section on list-style-type earlier in this reference.

Notes

If an element increments or resets a counter and also uses it (in the content property of its :before or :after pseudoclass), the counter is used *after* being incremented or reset.

Examples

```
ol {counter-reset: list}
li:before {content: counter(list) ". ";
          counter-increment: list}
```

This example resets the list counter and then displays the list counter before each item in the list.

```
ol {counter-reset: list}
li:before {content: counter(name, roman) ". ";
           counter-increment: list}
```

This example is the same as the previous, but sets the counter to display as Roman numerals.

counter-increment

The `counter-increment` property adjusts the value of one or more counters as a particular selector occurs in your document.

Values

This property takes a counter name or names as a value (the name of the counter[s] to increment) and an optional integer by which to increment. The default increment is 1. Zero and negative integers are allowed.

Example

```
h2:before {content: counter(chapter) "." counter(section) " ";
           counter-increment: section}
```

This example displays a heading format like *1.2* and increments the counter on the section (h2) part by 1.

counter-reset

Use this property to reset counters to zero or another value when a particular selector occurs in your document.

Values

This property takes the name(s) of a counter to reset, and an optional integer that the counter is reset to (default is to reset to zero).

Example

```
h1:before {counter-reset: section 1 headlevel 1}
```

This example resets the counter named `section` to 1 and also resets the counter named `headlevel` to 1.

quotes

Use this property to specify quotation marks for any number of embedded quotations.

Values

The value none specifies that open-quote and close-quote values of the content property produce no quotations marks.

To specify quotation marks for the open-quote and close-quote values of the content property, provide paired strings of quotation characters. The first pair represents the opening and closing characters for the first (or outer) level of quotation, the second pair defines the next included level of quotation, and so forth.

Examples

```
q:lang(en) {quotes: '"' '"' "'" "'"}
q:lang(fr) {quotes: "«" "»" "<" ">"}
```

This example sets double and single quotes for English-language quotations and double and single chevrons for French-language quotations.

Scripting Reference

XHTML

Master's Reference
Part 3

This reference covers scripting statement keywords, objects, methods and functions, event handlers, and properties. These are all the pieces that you need to build a script for your page. The information in this section is based on Netscape's JavaScript 1.3, which is compatible with the international standard ECMA-262 (ECMAScript) and to a large extent with Microsoft's JScript (which is itself ECMA-262-compatible).

We've included some examples here, but look in Chapter 11 to find the details of how to write scripts for your Web pages. Keep in mind that you should test your scripts in as many different browsers on different platforms as you can. Additionally, we have chosen not to include most scripting features that are in only a particular version of JavaScript or JScript. Although extra or additional features in XHTML cause no problems for browsers lacking support for those features, extra or additional script commands do not work and simply generate error messages in noncompliant browsers. For a complete JavaScript reference, see *Mastering JavaScript and JScript* by James Jaworski (also published by Sybex).

Throughout this reference, in our explanations of the examples, we've used the term *entry* (rather than parameter or operator) to refer to the various parts of the syntax.

This reference sorts entries by general purpose; the sections cover the constructs, operators, escape character, reserved words, objects, methods and functions, event handlers, and properties.

Category	Description
Constructs	Statement types that you can use to control the flow of a script
Operators	Algebraic, logical, and bitwise symbols for working with values in your statements
The escape character	Allows you to insert a special character into your text
Reserved words	Terms that JavaScript either currently uses or plans to use in the future
Objects	Containers in which properties reside and that are affected by methods and functions
Event handlers	Wait for the user or browser to do something and then tell the script to act, based on that event
Properties	Describe browser or scripting characteristics

Although we often use extra spaces, indents, and line breaks for readability in our printed code, do not insert any additional spaces or line returns in your JavaScript code. Make sure that each JavaScript statement is on a single line, and allow the text to wrap without a line return. JavaScript sees line returns as JavaScript characters and adds them to your code (which will make the code nonfunctional). It's fine to use line returns at the actual end of a line of code, before you start the next line, but not in the middle of a line of code.

Constructs

Constructs are the structures that you can use in JavaScript to control the flow of the script. If the course of the script depends on input or circumstance, you use a construct to direct the processing of the script. For example, to display the answer to a test question after a user has tried unsuccessfully to respond correctly, you can use a construct called an if statement.

This section contains an alphabetic list of JavaScript constructs. Each entry describes a single construct and provides its syntax and an example.

break

A break statement ends a repetitive series of while or for statements. Sometimes you want a condition that ignores everything else and jumps out of the loop to carry on with the rest of the script. You do this with a break statement. The syntax for the break statement is:

```
break;
```

Example

```
function alphacount (x) {
   var count = 0
   while (count < 1000) {
      if (990 == count)
         break;
      count += (getUserNumber())  }  }
```

This example is a function, alphacount, that adds user input until at least 990, but it could conceivably go as high as 1000. If the value is exactly 990, the break statement is triggered, and the while statement ends.

comment

You place comments within your scripts to help you recall what variables represent or which conditions that change over time may affect loops or other calls. A comment does not perform a function; it's simply a note to yourself or to future users of the script. The syntax of the comment statement is:

```
// comment text
```

Example

```
readMe = "" // set the readMe variable to null
bigNews = 1 // set the bigNews variable to 1
if (readMe < bigNews) {
    bigNews += song
    // Add song to bigNews, increments bigNews by a user.
    variable getStory(readMe)
    // This function retrieves the user's guess.
}
```

In this example, the variable declarations and the if statement are documented with comments.

continue

Like the break statement, continue breaks out of a for or a while loop. Instead of going to the next set of instructions past the loop, the continue statement sends the script back to the condition in the while statement or to the update expression in a for loop. The syntax of the continue statement is:

```
continue;
```

Example

```
while (cows != "home") {
    if (barnDoor = "open") {
        cows = "home"
        continue;  }
    callCows()
}
```

In this `while` loop, the condition checks the value of the variable `cows`. As long as the value is not equal to "home", the loop continues. Within the loop is an `if` statement that checks the state of the `barnDoor`; when the variable `barnDoor` is "open", the statement sets the value of `cows` to "home" and sends the script back up to the condition statement. Otherwise, the loop continues to run the function `callCows`.

for

The `for` statement repeats an action for a counted number of times. You give the script the starting conditions, ending conditions, and iteration information. A starting condition could be `month=1`, indicating the repetitions begin at January. The ending condition, in this case, could be `month=12`, indicating the repetitions continue through the months of the year. Inside this repetition, you include a series of statements that perform a function (such as displaying a result: "in January our sales were $1,500,000"). The increment would likely be `month++`, indicating that the value of `month` is increased by 1 as each repetition is completed. The syntax of the `for` statement is:

```
for ([initial expression]; [condition]; [update expression]) {
    statements; }
```

The `initial expression` entry is the statement or variable declaration, `condition` is the Boolean or comparison statement, and `update expression` is the scheme for incrementing tied in with a variable in the condition.

Example

```
horse = 100;
for (cows = 0; cows <= horse; cows++) {
    getCowCount(cows); }
```

This example simply repeats the function `getCowCount` until the number of cows is more than the number of horses. Each time the result of `getCowCount` is less than or equal to the number of horses (in the variable `horse`), the number of cows is incremented by 1. This loop could go on for a long time.

for in

The `for in` statement doesn't need counters to complete its repetitions. If, for example, you have a list of commands in objects that use the menu name (the `File` object contains all the menu items found under the File menu), you can iterate through the list, presenting them as part of a list of options. The benefit is that you can store the information in an object and update it once to use many times. When the list of menu items is complete, the script moves on to the next set of instructions. The syntax of the `for in` statement is:

```
for (variable in object) { statements; }
```
The `variable` entry represents a value, and `object` is an array of object properties.

Example

```
function house (rooms, location, floors, residents) {
    this.rooms = rooms;
    this.location = location;
    this.floors = floors;
    this.residents = residents;  }
while (newHome != "no") {
    description = "";
    var info;
    for (info in house) { description += house + "." + info +
        " = " + house[info] + "<br />" }
    description += "<hr />";
    return description;
    getNewHouse (newHome);  }
```

In this example, the function `house` fills the information about the object `house`. The object `house` contains the properties: rooms, location, floors, and residents. The statement inside the `for in` loop generates a series of statements that fill the object. For example, if the user provided the following information—10, London, 5, and 9—the variable description would end up being this series:

```
house.rooms = 10;
house.location = London;
house.floors = 5;
house.residents = 9;
```

function

This construct sets up a JavaScript function. The function makes some kind of calculation using information provided—words, numbers, or objects. With a function command, you can fill an object with the selected information. For example, if you collect information from a user in several boxes, you can put this together into a single variable that you then use to address the user throughout the session. It's best to define functions in the head section of the Web page, because functions must be declared before they can be used. The syntax of the `function` statement is:

```
function name ([parameter], [parameter], [parameter]) {
    statements; }
```

Example

```
// This function works out the grade for the test.
// The variables ans_right, ans_wrong, and ans_blank are used
// in other functions to determine the user's improvement over
// a series of tests.
function calc_pass_fail (ans_right, ans_wrong, ans_blank) {
    return ans_right / (ans_right + ans_wrong + ans_blank);   }
```

In this example, the function `calc_pass_fail` reads in the variables `ans_right`, `ans_wrong`, and `ans_blank` to produce the person's percentage grade for the most recent test. Subsequent JavaScripts control which page users see, depending on their grade.

if

The `if` statement works just like the spoken equivalent: *If this is true, do this.* Use this construct when you want the script to perform a task when the right conditions arise. For example, to include some information in a result page, use the `if` construct—if the user selects examples, include examples in the results page. The syntax of the `if` statement is:

```
if (condition) {
    statements; }
```

Example

```
if (tests == 0) {
    window.location.href = "test.html"; }
```

In this example, the `if` statement determines whether the user has taken any tests. If the user has not taken any tests (`tests = 0`), the user is taken to the test pages.

if else

Like the if statement, this construct allows you to apply decision-making to the script: *If this is true, do this; otherwise, do this.* Use this construct when you have two alternatives that depend on the conditions. For example, you want to display correct or incorrect notes next to the user's response in a test. If the user answers correctly, include a congratulations message; otherwise, show the correct answer. The syntax of the if else statement is:

```
if (condition) {
    statements; }
else {
    statements; }
```

Example

```
if (tests != 0) {
    if (tests == 1) {
        document.write("lesson 2"); }
    else {
        if (tests == 2) {
            document.write("lesson 3"); }
            else {
            if (tests == 3) {
                document.write("lesson 4"); }
        } } }
else {
    document.write("lesson 1"); }
```

In this example, the if statements check which test the user has completed and print the name of the next lesson. The first if statement simply tests whether the user has taken any tests; the test counter is incremented at the end of each test (not in this function or loop).

new

Use this construct to create a user-defined object. Creating an object is a process with two steps:

1. Define the object with a function.

2. Create an instance of the object with new.

The syntax of the new statement is:

```
objectName = new objectType (
    [parameter1], [parameter2], [parameterN] );
```

The objectName entry is the name of the new object; this is how you refer to it in later code. The objectType entry is the object type, a function that defines the object. The parameter1 … parameterN entries are the properties for the object.

Example

```
function house (rooms, location, floors, residents) {
    this.rooms = rooms;
    this.location = location;
    this.floors = floors;
    this.residents = residents;  }
newHouse = new house (8, Prairieville, 3, 4);
```

This example creates an object type called house and populates newHouse, which is of type house, with 8 rooms, a Prairieville location, 3 floors, and 4 residents.

return

The return statement works in conjunction with the function statement. To display a calculated value, you include a return statement to bring the value back to the script. The syntax of the return statement is:

```
return;
```

Example

```
function square (x) {
    return (x * x); }
```

This simple example uses the return statement with the expression that generates the value that should be returned (the square of the number x passed to the function).

switch

The switch statement is similar to the if else statement, in that it presents the script with a series of alternate routes that depend on conditions found. The switch statement is cleaner than nesting a series of `if else` statements. The syntax of the `switch` statement is:

```
switch (expression) {
   case1: statements;
      break;
   case2: statements;
      break;
   default: statements;
}
```

Example

```
switch (infoType) {
   case ("reference") : destination = "jref.html";
      break;
   case ("how-to") : destination = "instruct.html";
      break;
   case ("overview") : destination = "intro.html";
      break;
   default : destination = "toc.html";
}
```

This example takes the value in the variable `infoType` and compares it to a list of known values. If the value in `infoType` matches any of the stated cases (reference, how-to, or overview), the script stores a page name in the destination variable. If no match is found, the script sets the destination to the table of contents (`toc.html`).

this

The construct `this` refers to the object in focus. For example, when filling an object's array (list of properties), you would have a series of `this` statements, one for each property. The syntax of the `this` statement is:

```
this[.propertyName]
```

Example

```
function house (rooms, location, floors, residents) {
   this.rooms = rooms;
   this.location = location;
   this.floors = floors;
```

```
      this.residents = residents;   }
newHouse = new house (8, Prairieville, 3, 4);
```

This example creates an object type called house and populates newHouse, which is of type house, with 8 rooms, a Prairieville location, 3 floors, and 4 residents.

var

This is a keyword that indicates the statement is performing an assignment to a variable. You can use this to set the initial value of the variables (always a good idea!) outside the function (particularly if it has repetitions) or inside the function. The syntax of the var keyword is either one of the following lines:

```
var varName;
var varName = value;
```

The varName entry is the name of the variable, and value becomes the original contents of the variable.

Example

```
var cust_id = 0, reading = 0;
```

In this simple statement, customer ID (cust_id) and usage (reading) variables are set to zero. This is in preparation for a function in which a customer number is assigned and a variable that tracks session activities is launched.

while

The while statement is similar to the for statement; it creates a loop that repeats a set of statements as long as a condition is true. The syntax of the while statement is:

```
while (condition) { statements }
```

Example

```
copies = 0;
original = 0;
while (copies < 5) {
   copies++;
   while (original < 10) {
      original++; }
```

```
        original = 0;
        //reset original to 0 before re-entering first while loop
}
```

In this example, the two variables, `copies` and `original`, are set to zero before entering the `while` loop. The outside loop checks that the number of copies made is less than 5. If that condition is true, the number of copies is incremented by 1, and then a second `while` loop iterates through the pages in the original.

with

To use a series of statements from the same object, such as the `Math` object, place them inside a `with` statement. You then need not identify each function, method, or property as belonging to the `Math` object. Usually when you write a statement that uses a function from an object, you have to include the object in the statement. The `with` construct lets you group a series of statements and identifies the parent object for the functions, methods, and properties. The syntax of the `with` statement is:

```
with (object) { statements; }
```

Example

```
with (Math) {
    a = PI * r * r;
    x = r * cos(theta);
    y = r * sin(theta);
}
```

In this example, values are assigned to the properties `Math.a`, `Math.x`, and `Math.y`.

Operators

An operator is a symbol that represents an action; the most familiar operators are the mathematical symbols for addition, subtraction, multiplication, and division. JavaScript includes these basic actions and some more complex operations, each with a special symbol. As is the case with those familiar mathematical symbols, an order of operation defines the precedence (i.e., which operator is dealt with first) of each operator in an expression.

Table MR3.1 defines the operators and presents them in their order of operation. You can use parentheses to control the order or precedence in a statement. In the table, operators of equal precedence are grouped together, and the groups are divided by a single line. For example, ( ), [ ], and . (period) have the same precedence in the order of operation.

Some of these operators work on the bits in your values. To work on the bits, JavaScript converts your values to bits, performs the operation, and converts the value back to its original type. This can lead to some interesting results, particularly if you're unfamiliar with the bit values or if you miscalculate.

Because the category of "assignment" is so extensive, we've listed the assignment operators separately, in Table MR3.2.

Table MR3.1 JavaScript Operators

OPERATOR	DESCRIPTION	WHAT IT DOES
( )	Function call or statement organizer	Organizes functions and forces a different order on the equations: x+2*y is the same as x+(2*y) because multiplication takes precedence over addition.
[ ]	Subscript	Use when you have a pointer and an element. For example, if you have an associative list (a variable that contains a set of values), you can use this to identify individual members in the list. These lists are called arrays.
.	Members	Use when you're using the methods and properties for an object. For example, Math.abs() calls the absolute function from the Math object
!	NOT	The Boolean negation symbol. Use it when your expression is designed to include everything except the item marked with this NOT symbol. For example, if name !Bob, call calls everyone except people named Bob.
~	One's complement	The bitwise equivalent of the NOT operator. Using this changes a 0 (zero) to a 1 (one) and vice versa.

Table MR3.1 continued JavaScript Operators

OPERATOR	DESCRIPTION	WHAT IT DOES
++	Increment	Use in front of or behind a variable to add one to its value. For example, `right++` is the same as `right+1`.
--	Decrement	Use in front of or behind a variable to subtract one from its value. For example, `submits--` is the same as `submits-1`.
*	Multiply	Use to multiply two numeric values. These must be numbers.
/	Divide	Use to divide two numeric values. These must be numbers. If you use integers on both sides of the division expression, you won't get any decimal values. For example, if `in` and `out` are declared as integers, and `in` is 12 and `out` is 7, `in/out = 1`.
%	Modulo	Integer division does not use the remainder; it does not give you a decimal place in the result. If the division is not a clean division, you lose the remainder. Use this when you want the remainder from a division operation. For example, 7/2 as an integer division gives you a result of 3; 7%2 gives you 1.
+	Addition	Combines two values (numbers or words).
-	Subtraction	Takes one value (number or word) out of another.
<<	Bitwise left shift	Moves the contents of an object or element left. This works on the bits in the object, moving them left and filling in the right with zeros. For example, 7<<2 takes 111 (the binary representation of 7) and shifts it left 2 places (11100), which, when converted back to integer values, is 28.
>>	Bitwise right shift	Similar to the left shift in the preceding row, this moves the bits to the right; unlike the left shift, the bits shifted right drop out of the value. So, using the same example, 7>>2 becomes 1.

Table MR3.1 continued JavaScript Operators

Operator	Description	What It Does
>>>	Zero-fill right shift	This bitwise shift operator moves bits to the right and pads the left with zeros.
<	Less than	Compares two values. If the value on the right is larger than the value on the left, this operation returns True.
>	Greater than	Compares two values. If the value on the left is larger than the value on the right, this operation returns True.
<=	Less than or equal to	Compares two values. If the value on the right is equal to or larger than the value on the left, this operation returns True.
>=	Greater than or equal to	Compares two values. If the value on the left is equal to or larger than the value on the right, this operation returns True.
==	Equality	Compares two values. If they're equal, the operation returns True.
===	Strict equality	Compares two values. If they're equal and the same type, the operation returns True.
!=	Inequality	Compares two values. If they're not equal, the operation returns True.
!==	Strict inequality	Compares two values. If they're the same type and not equal, the operation returns True.
&	Bitwise AND	Checks the bits of two values and determines where they're both the same. If the value is a multibit value, the operation checks each position. If the two values do not have a matching number of bits, the smaller value is left-padded until the number of positions match. If they match, a 1 is returned. For example, 10&7 returns 2 because 1010 & 0111 only match in the second-to-last position, giving you 0010, which is 2.

Table MR3.1 continued JavaScript Operators

Operator	Description	What It Does
^	Bitwise EOR (exclusive OR)	Returns True if one or the other of the values is 1. When the values match, it returns a 0. So, using the previous example, 10^7 returns 1101 which is 13.
|	Bitwise OR (inclusive OR)	Returns true (1) if one value is 1. Unlike EOR, this operator returns True if both values are 1. So, the 10 | 7 expression returns 1111, which is 15.
&&	Logical AND	Unlike bitwise operators, logical operators compare expression results. Use the logical operators to link Boolean comparisons into a test for a branching statement. For example, if Bob is older than Ray, AND Ray is not working today, send the package to Ray. The package is sent to Ray only if the two conditions are met.
||	Logical OR	Results in True if either expression is true. So, using the same example as the previous cell, Ray would receive the package if either he was younger than Bob or was not working that day.
?:	If-else	This is the symbol for the if else construct, which is described in the "Constructs" section.
operator=	Assignment	Creates assignments. Table MR3.2 shows the range of possibilities.
,	Comma	Separates values in a sequence, such as assignments to an object that contains an array.

Table MR3.2 The Assignment Operators

OPERATOR	WHAT IT DOES
=	Puts the value on the right into the variable on the left; any contents of the variable on the left are replaced.
+=	Adds the value on the right to the variable on the left; the contents of the variable on the left are augmented.
-=	Subtracts the value on the right from the variable on the left; the contents of the variable on the left are decremented.
*=	Multiplies the variable on the left by the value on the right and places the result in the variable on the left.
/=	Divides the variable on the left by the value on the right and places the result in the variable on the left.
%=	Divides the variable on the left by the value on the right and places the difference in the variable on the left.
<<=	Performs a bitwise shift on the variable on the left equal to the value on the right; the result is placed in the variable on the left.
>>=	Performs a bitwise shift on the variable on the left equal to the value on the right; the result is placed in the variable on the left.
>>>=	Performs a bitwise shift on the variable on the left equal to the value on the right; the result is placed in the variable on the left.
&=	Performs a bitwise AND on the variable on the left and value on the right; the result is placed in the variable on the left.
^=	Performs a bitwise EOR on the variable on the left and the value on the right; the result is placed in the variable on the left.
|=	Performs a bitwise OR on the variable on the left and the value on the right; the result is placed in the variable on the left.

Escape Character

The backslash (\) is the escape character in JavaScript. An escape character tells the system that the next character in the sequence is either a special instruction or is a reserved character being used in quoted text. Table MR3.3 lists the escape sequences that JavaScript uses.

Table MR3.3 The JavaScript Escape Sequences

CHARACTER	FUNCTION
\b	Backspace
\n	New line
\t	Tab
\r	Carriage Return
\f	Form feed
\uhhhh	Unicode character (u + 4-digit hexadecimal number)
\\	Backslash (in text)
\'	Single quote (in text)
\"	Double quote (in text)
\ooo	Octal number
\xhh	Latin-1 character (x + 2-digit hexadecimal number)

Reserved Words

JavaScript has many reserved words—words that you cannot use for variables in your script. These words, listed in Table 3.4, are either in use—as functions, for example—or are reserved for future use.

Table MR3.4 JavaScript Reserved Words

abstract	final	protected
boolean	finally	public
break	float	return
byte	for	short
case	function	static
catch	goto	super
char	if	switch

Table MR3.4 JavaScript Reserved Words

class	implements	synchronized
comment	import	this
const	in	throw
continue	instanceof	throws
debugger	int	transient
default	interface	true
delete	label	try
do	long	typeof
double	native	var
else	new	void
enum	null	volatile
export	package	while
extends	private	with
false		

Also, operators (the following characters) may not be used in variable names:
- ! ~ % / * > < = & | + ?

Objects

An object is a simple way of referring to parts of a Web page. Using objects gives structure to your Web pages and JavaScript scripts. In general, you apply methods, functions, and properties to objects to achieve a result.

This section contains an alphabetic listing of the available JavaScript objects. Each entry describes the object, gives its format, and (in most cases) shows an example. Each entry also contains a list of the associated properties, methods, and event handlers.

anchor

The anchor object is text on a page that represents a destination for a link. The anchor object can also be a link object if it includes an href attribute. The browser creates an anchors array when it opens the page. This array contains information about each anchor object. You can access the anchors or their length from this array.

The anchor object has the following format:

```
<a name="anchorname" id="anchorname">anchorText</a>
```

To access the anchor object:

```
document.anchor.name
```

To access the anchors array:

```
document.anchors.length
document.anchors.[index]
```

The index entry is an integer representing an anchor in the document.

The anchor object had no properties or methods prior to the version 4 browsers in which the property name was introduced. The anchors array has the property length, which you can use to get the number of anchors on the page from the number of elements in the anchors array.

There are no event handlers for the anchor object, which is a property of document.

button

The button object represents an XHTML button element and creates a pushbutton on a form. The browser sets the appearance of the button, but you control the text prompt on the button and the action it performs. You create a button object by using the input element with a type attribute set to the value button. The button object has the following format:

```
<input type="button" name="buttonName" value="buttonText"
    [onclick="handlerText"] />
```

The buttonName entry is the name for the button, which is how you identify the button. Each button on the page needs a unique name. The buttonText entry is the label that appears on the button.

The name property corresponds to the value of the name attribute, and the value property corresponds to the value specified in the value attribute. The button uses the click, blur, and focus methods and the onblur, onclick, onfocus, onmousedown, and onmouseup event handlers. The button object is a property of the form object.

Example

```
<input type="button" name="goNow" value="Let's Go"
    onclick="buttonClick(this.form)" />
```

In this example, a Let's Go button appears on the form. When the user clicks the button, the event handler onclick runs the function buttonClick that processes the form.

```
var button1 = document.forms['form1'].elements['goNow'];
```

In this example, a variable named button1 has been created to represent the button named goNow in the form named form1.

checkbox

The checkbox object represents an XHTML checkbox element. A check box appears on a form to let users make selections (none, one, or more) from a list. You create a checkbox object by using the input element with a type attribute set to the value checkbox. The checkbox object has the following format:

```
<input type="checkbox" name="checkboxName"
    value="checkboxValue" [checked="checked"]
    [onclick="handlerText"] /> textToDisplay
```

The checkboxName entry is the name for the checkbox object; you identify the checkbox with this name if you reference it in your script. The checkboxValue entry is the return value when the checkbox is selected; the default is On. The checked entry specifies that the checkbox appear as checked when the browser first displays it. The textToDisplay entry is the label, the text next to the checkbox on the page.

You can set the checkbox checked property, changing the state (On or Off) of the checkbox. The checked property indicates whether the check box is currently checked. The defaultChecked property indicates if the check box is checked by default (checked= "checked"). The name property corresponds to the value of the name attribute, and the value property corresponds to the value specifed in the value attribute. The checkbox object uses the blur, click, and focus methods and the onblur, onclick, and onfocus event handlers; checkbox is a property of the form object.

Example

```
<h3>Pick the modules that you want to study:</h3>
<input type="checkbox" name="studymodul_newdocs"
```

```
        checked="checked" />Creating a new document<br />
<input type="checkbox" name="studymodul_trackdocs" />
    Tracking documents in the system<br />
<input type="checkbox" name="studymodul_routedocs" />
    Routing documents on the system<br />
...
```

In this example, you have a list of options; the first option appears with its check box selected.

```
var check1 = document.forms['modules'].
    elements['studymodul_newdocs'];
```

In this example, a variable named check1 has been created to represent the check-box named studymodul_newdocs in the form named modules.

date

The date object, which is built-in, lets you work with dates. It includes a large number of methods for getting date information, such as the calendar date or the time of day. Dates prior to 1970 are not allowed. The date object has the following format:

```
dateObjectName = new Date();
dateObjectName = new Date(
    "month day, year hours: minutes:seconds");
dateObjectName = new Date(year, month, day);
dateObjectName = new Date(
    year, month, day, hours, minutes,seconds, milliseconds);
```

The new keyword generates a new object using the date object. In the second statement, the properties month day, year hours: minutes: seconds are string values. In the third and fourth statements, they are integers.

The date method has the following format:

```
dateObjectName.methodName(parameters);
```

The date object has no properties and uses the following methods:

getDate	getUTCMilliseconds	setUTCDate
getDay	getUTCMinutes	setUTCFullYear
getFullYear	getUTCMonth	setUTCHours

getHours	getUTCSeconds	setUTCMilliseconds
getMilliseconds	getYear	setUTCMinutes
getMinutes	parse	setUTCMonth
getMonth	setDate	setUTCSeconds
getSeconds	setFullYear	setYear
getTime	setHours	toLocaleString
getTimeZoneOffset	setMilliseconds	toUTCString
getUTCDate	setMinutes	UTC
getUTCDay	setMonth	valueOf
getUTCFullYear	setSeconds	
getUTCHours	setTime	

The date object has no event handlers because built-in objects have no event handlers. The date object is the property of no other object.

Example

```
var logofftime= new Date();
logofftime = logofftime.getHours() + ":" +
    logofftime.getMinutes() + ":" + logofftime.getSeconds();
```

In this example, the script creates a new date variable called logofftime and then populates that variable with the current time.

document

The document object is the container for the information on the current page. This object controls the display of XHTML information for the user. The document object has the following format:

```
function setMeUp() {
    document.alinkColor="darkcyan";
    document.linkColor="yellow";
    document.vlinkColor="white";  }
...
<body onload="setMeUp()">...</body>
```

In this example, the settings for the link colors use the document properties alinkColor, linkColor, and vlinkColor. This is equivalent to the following body declaration:

```
<body alink="darkcyan" link="yellow" vlink="white">…</body>
```

The document object has the properties shown in Table MR3.5.

Table MR3.5 Properties of the document Object

Property	What It Is
alinkColor	Active link color
anchors	Array containing a list of the anchors on the document
bgColor	Background color
cookie	Cookie (information about the user/session)
fgColor	Foreground color for text and other foreground elements such as borders or lines
forms	Array containing a list of the forms in the document
lastModified	Date the document was last changed
linkColor	Basic link color
links	Link attributes
location	Location (URL) of the document
referrer	Location (URL) of the parent or calling document
title	Contents of the title element
vlinkColor	Color of past links activity

The document object also uses five methods—clear, close, open, write, and writeln—but uses no event handlers. Although the onload and onunload event handlers are included in the body element, they are window events. The document object is a property of the window object.

Example

```
function hello() {
    document.write("Hello, welcome to my site");  }
```

In this example, the message "Hello, welcome to my site" is written to the page when the `hello` function is called, using the `write` method of the `document` object.

elements

The `elements` object is an array of the `form` objects in the order in which they occur in the source code. This gives you an alternate access path to the individual `form` objects. You can also determine the number of `form` objects by using the `length` property. This is similar to the `anchors` array in that you can read from it, but not write to it. The `elements` object has the following format:

```
formName.elements[index]
formName.elements.length
```

The `formName` entry is either the name of the form or an element in the forms array. The `index` entry is an integer representing an object on a form.

The `elements` object uses the `length` property, which reflects the number of elements in a form. There are no methods and no event handlers for the `elements` object, which is a property of the `form` object.

Example

```
userInfo.username.value
userInfo.elements[0].value
```

Both statements return the same value if the element `username` is the first item in the elements array.

form

This object defines the form with which users interact. It includes checkboxes, text areas, radio buttons, and so on. You use the `form` object to post data to a server. It has the following format:

```
<form name="formName" id="formName" target="windowName"
    action="serverURL" method="get|post" enctype="encodingType"
    [onsubmit="handlerText"]>
</form>
```

The `windowName` entry is where form responses go. If you use this, the server responses are sent to a different window—another window, a frame, or a frame literal (such as _top). The `serverURL` is the location where the information from the form goes when it's posted. The `get|post` (`get` or `post`) commands specify how the information is sent to the server. With `get`, which is the default, the information is appended to the receiving URL. With `post`, the form sends the information in a data body that the server handles. The `encodingType` entry is the MIME encoding of the data sent. This defaults to `application/x-www-form-urlencoded`; you can also use `multipart/form-data`.

Here's the format for using the object's properties and methods:

```
formName.propertyName
formName.methodName(parameters)
forms[index].propertyName
forms[index].methodName(parameters)
```

The `formName` entry is the value of the `name` attribute and the `id` attribute of the form. The `propertyName` and `methodName` entries indicate one of the properties of form listed in Table MR3.6. The `index` entry is an integer representing the `form` object within the array at the position indicated by the integer. Statements one and three are equivalent, as are statements two and four—statements one and two use the `form` object and statements three and four refer to the `forms` array.

Table MR3.6 The Properties of the `form` Object

Property	What It Does/Is
action	Server URL
elements	List of the elements in the form
encoding	`enctype` attribute
length	Number of elements on the form (a property of the `forms` array)
method	How the information is processed (`get` or `post`)
name	Name of the form
target	Window where form responses go

The `form` object uses the `reset` and `submit` methods and the `onreset` and `onsubmit` event handlers, and is a property of the `document` object.

Example

```
<script type="text/javascript" language="javascript">
   <!--
      function welcome() {
         document.write("Thanks for joining us, " +
            membername + "!") }
   -->
</script>
…
<form name="members" id="members">
   <p>Please enter your name and e-mail address below.</p>
   <b>Name:</b>
   <input type="text" name="membername" size="40" /><br />
   <b>E-mail address:</b>
   <input type="text" name="email" size="40" />
   <input type="button" name="button1" value="Join now!"
      onclick="welcome()">
</form>
```

In this example, the user enters their name and e-mail address. When the user clicks the button, the welcome function is called and a message with their name is displayed on the page.

frame

The frame object is a window within a window and has its own URL. A page can contain a series of frames. There's also a frames array that lists all the frames in your code. The frame object has the following format:

```
<frameset rows="rowHeightList" cols="columnWidthList"
   [onload="handlerText"] [onunload="handlerText"]>
   [<frame src="locationOrURL" name="frameName"
      id="frameName" />]
   [<noframes>
      // XHTML elements and so on for browsers
      // that do not support frames
   </noframes>]
</frameset>
```

The `rowHeightList` entry is a comma-separated list of values that sets the row heights of the frame. The default unit of measure is pixels. The `columnWidthList` is a comma-separated list of values that sets the column widths of the frame. The default unit of measure is pixels.

The `locationOrURL` entry is the location of the document to be displayed in the frame. This URL cannot include an anchor name. The `location` object describes the URL components. The `frameName` entry is the target for links.

To use the object's properties, follow this format:
```
[windowReference.]frameName.propertyName
[windowReference.]frames[index].propertyName
window.propertyName
self.propertyName
parent.propertyName
```

The `windowReference` entry is a variable from the window object definition or one of the synonyms: top or parent. The `frameName` entry is the value of the name and of the `id` attribute in the `frame` element. The `index` entry is an integer representing a `frame` object in the array, and the `propertyName` entry is one of the properties listed in Table MR3.7.

Table MR3.7 The Properties of the `frame` Object

PROPERTY	WHAT IT IS
frames	Array, or list, of frames in the document
name	name attribute (as assigned in the `frame` element)
id	id attribute (as assigned in the `frame` element)
length	Integer that reflects the number of child frames within this frame
parent	Window or frame that contains this frame
self	Current frame
window	Current frame

To use the object's array, follow this format:
```
[frameReference.]frames[index]
[frameReference.]frames.length
[windowReference.]frames[index]
[windowReference.]frames.length
```

The frames array has a length property that reflects the number of child frames within a frame. The frame object uses the clearTimeout and setTimeout methods.

The frame object does not use event handlers. Although the onload and onunload event handlers appear within the frameset element, they are event handlers for the window object. The frame object is a property of the window object; the frames array is a property of both frame and window.

Example

This code sets up framed windows. The frameset comes after the head element and replaces the body element.

```
<!DOCTYPE html PUBLIC "-//W3C/DTD XHTML 1.0 Frameset//EN"
    "http://www.w3.org/TR/xhtml1/DTD/xhtml1-frameset.dtd">
<html xmlns="http://www.w3.org/1999/xhtml">
<head>
    <title>Central Zoo: Front Entrance</title>
</head>
<frameset cols="40%, 60%" onload="alert('We\'re in!')">
    <frame name="frame1" id="frame1" src="mainframe.html" />
    <frame name="frame2" id="frame2" src="littleframe.html" />
</frameset>
</html>
```

In this example, the page is set up to include two frames. When the frameset page loads, an alert box with the text "We're in!" will appear.

hidden

The hidden object represents an XHTML hidden element. The hidden object contains a text object that is suppressed (that is, not displayed) on a form. This object is used to pass information when the form is submitted. Although the user cannot change the value directly, the developer (you) can control the contents, changing it programmatically. You create a hidden object by using the input element with a type attribute with the value hidden. The hidden object has the following format:

```
<input type="hidden" name="hiddenName" [value="textValue"] />
```

The hiddenName entry is the name of the object, which allows you to access the object using the name property. The textValue entry is the initial value for the object.

The `hidden` object uses three properties—`name`, `type`, and `value`. These reflect the object name, type, and contents. The `hidden` object does not use any methods or event handlers; it's a property of the `form` object.

Example

```
<form name="form1" id="form1">
    <input type="hidden" name="hiddenPass" />
    <input type="text" name="password" value="" size="5" />
    <input type="button" name="test" value="Test"
        onclick="document.form1.hiddenPass.value=document.form1.
        password.value; alert(document.form1.hiddenPass.value)" />
</form>
```

This example reads in a password from a `text` object and stores it in the `hidden` object. As a test of the form, we've included a line that displays the `hidden` object in an alert, which is not something you would normally do.

history

The `history` object contains the list of URLs visited; this information is available in the history list of the browser. The `history` object has the following format:

```
history.length
history.methodName(parameters)
```

The `length` entry is an integer representing a position in the history list. The `method-Name` entry is one of the methods listed below.

The `history` object uses the `length` property. There are three methods for the `history` object: `back`, `forward`, and `go`; each of these navigates through the history list. The `history` object does not use event handlers; it's a property of the `document` object.

Example

```
if (score < 65) { history.go(-2); }
```

The `if` statement checks the score against a satisfactory performance measure of 65. If the student scores less than 65 on the test, the browser goes back to the beginning of the lesson, two pages earlier.

```
<input type="button" name="reviewButton" value="Look Again!"
    onclick="history.back()" />
```

The `reviewButton` button performs the same function as the browser's back button.

link

A link object includes the text and images that contain the information for a hypertext jump. A link object is also an anchor object if it has a name attribute. When the jump is complete, the starting page location is stored in the destination document's referrer property. The link object has the following format:

```
<a href="locationOrURL" [name="anchorName"] [id="anchorName"]
    [target="windowName"] [onclick="handlerText"]
    [onmouseover="handlerText"]>
    linkText</a>
```

The locationOrURL entry is the destination address. The anchorName entry is the current location within the jump-from page. The windowName is the window that the link is loaded into, if different from the current window. This can be an existing window, a frame, or a synonym such as _top or _self.

You can also define a link using the link method of the string object.

To use a link's properties, follow this format:

```
document.links[index].propertyName
```

The index entry is an integer representing the link object in the links array.

To use the links array, follow this format:

```
document.links[index]
document.links.length
```

You can read the links array, but you cannot write values to it.

Table MR3.8 lists the properties of the link object.

Table MR3.8 The Properties of the link Object

PROPERTY	WHAT IT IS
hash	Anchor name in the URL
host	hostname:port portion of the URL
hostname	Host and domain name, or IP address, of the network host
href	Entire URL
pathname	URL-pathname (directory structure/location) part of the URL
port	Communication port on the server

Table MR3.8 continued The Properties of the `link` Object

protocol	Type of URL (for example, `http` or `ftp`)
search	Page name (for example, `index.html`)
target	`target` attribute

The `links` array uses the `length` property. The `link` object does not use any methods. The `link` object uses the `onclick`, `onmouseover`, and `onmouseout` event handlers. The `link` object is a property of the `document` object.

Example

```
<script type="text/javascript" language="javascript">
   var there="http://www.example.com/";
</script>
...
<form name="form1" id="form1">
   <b>Choose a document, then click "Take me there!" below.</b>
   <br />
   <input type="radio" name="destination" value="Overview"
      onclick="there = 'http://www.example.com/intro.html'" />
   Overview of JavaScripting<br />
   <input type="radio" name="destination" value="howto"
      onclick="there = 'http://www.example.com/script.html'" />
   Learn to Make a Script<br />
   <input type="radio" name="destination" value="reference"
      onclick="there = 'http://www.example.com/jref.html'" />
   JavaScript Reference Information<br />
   <p><a href="" onclick="this.href = there"
      onmouseover="self.status = there; return true;">
      <b>Take me there!</b>
   </a></p>
</form>
```

In this example, a form gives users access to the set of chapters. They can select a chapter/destination or go to the default destination.

location

The `location` object contains information about the current URL. It contains a series of properties that describe each part of the URL. A URL has the following structure:

```
protocol://hostname:port pathname search hash
```

The `protocol` specifies the type of URL (for example, `http` or `ftp`). The `hostname` contains the host and domain name, or IP address, of the network host. The `port` specifies the communication port on the server (not all addresses use this). The `pathname` is the directory structure/location on the server. The `search` value is the query string and is preceded by a question mark. The `hash` value is preceded by the hash mark (#) and indicates a target anchor on the page.

Here are some common protocol types:

about	http
file	javascript
ftp	mailto
gopher	news

The `location` object has the following format:

```
[windowReference.]location.propertyName
```

The `location` object uses the same properties as the `link` object, as shown in Table MR3.5 earlier. However, unlike the `link` object, which represents a link in a document, the `location` object can be used to change the URL (as in the example below), either to a new page or to a different location on the same page. The `location` object uses the `reload` (reload current document) and `replace` (replace current document) methods, but does not use event handlers; it's a property of the `document` object.

Example

```
window.location.href=
    "http://www.pageresource.com/jscript/index.html";
```

In this example, the URL of the current page is set to the Page Resource JavaScript tutorials home page.

```
parent.frame3.location.href=
    "http://www.pageresource.com/jscript/index.html";
```

This example opens the Page Resource JavaScript tutorials home page in frame 3.

```
<script type="text/javascript" language="javascript">
    var takeLesson = "";
    document.write("Welcome to " + document.location +
        ". Not ever done!");
</script>
```

This example displays a message at the top of the page that welcomes users to the current location.

Math

This is a built-in object that includes a large set of methods and properties for mathematic constants and operations. An example of a constant is Π (pi), which is referenced as `Math.PI`. If you're using a series of expressions, you can use the `with` construct. In general, the `Math` object has the following format:

```
varName = Math.propertyName [expression];
varName = Math.method();
```

The actual format will vary with the property in use. Check the property entries for the exact syntax.

The `Math` object uses the following properties, each of which is described in the "Properties" section:

E	LOG10E
LN2	PI
LN10	SQRT1_2
LOG2E	SQRT2

The `Math` object uses the following methods, each of which is described in the "Methods and Functions" section:

abs	atan	cos	log	pow	sin
acos	atan2	exp	max	random	sqrt
asin	ceil	floor	min	round	tan

The Math object uses no event handlers because it's a built-in object. It's not a property of anything. See the entries for individual properties and methods for examples.

navigator

Use this object to determine a user's version of a browser. It has the following format:

```
navigator.propertyName
```

The navigator object uses the javaEnabled method to test whether Java is enabled in the browser, and it contains the properties shown in Table MR3.9. It does not use any event handlers. It's a property of the window object.

Table MR3.9 The Properties of the navigator Object

PROPERTY	WHAT IT IS
appCodeName	Internal code name of the browser
appName	External name of the browser
appVersion	Version number of the browser
platform	Operating sytem on which the browser is running
userAgent	User-agent header in HTTP requests

Example

```
var userBrowser = navigator.appName + " " +
    navigator.appVersion;
```

The values for the navigator properties appName and appVersion are in a variable called userBrowser. You can use this later to test the browser's suitability for the functionality available on your page.

password

The password object is a text field that conceals its value and displays asterisks in place of typed characters. A password object is part of a form and must be defined within a form element. You create a password object by using the input element with a type attribute with the value password. This object has the following format:

```
<input type="password" name="passwordName" [value="textValue"]
    size="integer" />
```

The passwordName entry is the name of the object. The textValue entry is a default value for the password, and size is the length of the password field.

To use the password properties and methods, follow this format:

```
passwordName.propertyName
passwordName.methodName(parameters)
formName.elements[index].propertyName
formName.elements[index].methodName(parameters)
```

The first and third statements are equivalents, as are the second and fourth statements. The passwordName entry is the value of the name attribute in the password object. The formName entry is the form container or an element in the forms array.

The propertyName is one of three properties: defaultValue is the value attribute, name is the name attribute, and value is the current contents of the password object's field. methodName is one of focus, blur, or select.

The password object does not use event handlers. It's a property of the form object.

Example

```
<input type="password" name="password" size="8"
    value="password.defaultValue" />
```

This is useful if the user has already visited the site and created a password or if you have assigned passwords to users.

radio

A radio button forces a single selection from a set of options. Similar to the checkbox, it's a part of a form; unlike the checkbox, only one radio button can be selected from the set. The radio object has the following format:

```
<input type="radio" name="radioName" value="buttonValue"
    [checked="checked"] [onclick="handlerText"] />textToDisplay
```

The radioName entry is the name of the object. This offers you one method for addressing the radio object in your script. The buttonValue entry is the value that is returned to the server when the button is selected. The default is On. You can access this value using the radio.value property. The checked attribute sets the button to selected, and textToDisplay is the label displayed next to the radio button.

The radio button uses the blur, click, and focus methods and the properties shown in Table MR3.10.

Table MR3.10 The Properties of the radio Object

PROPERTY	WHAT IT DOES/IS
checked="checked"	Lets you set the selection through your script (rather than user interaction); good for situations in which one choice automatically determines several others
defaultChecked	The settings for the checked attribute
length	The number of radio buttons in the object
name	The name attribute (radioName above)
value	The value attribute (buttonValue above)

The radio object uses the onblur, onclick, and onfocus event handlers, and it's a property of the form object.

Example

```
<script type="text/javascript" language="javascript">
var there="http://www.example.com/";
function checkThis() { confirm("Thanks for registering"); }
function welcome() {
    alert("Welcome! You can register through this page.
    For future reference, this page is ' + document.location); }
</script>
...
<body onload="welcome()">
// This loads a message that includes the page address through
// the document.location from the welcome function.
<form name="form1" id="form1" onsubmit="checkThis()">
// The form tag includes the onsubmit event handler and
```

```
// the form includes a submit button.
<b>Choose a document, then click "Take me there" below.</b>
<br />
<input type="radio" name="destination" value="Overview"
    onclick="there = 'http://www.example.com/intro.html'" />
Overview of JavaScripting<br />
// This is a typical radio button.
// These buttons all have the same name: destination.
// In this example, all the values reflect the destination/text
// display when the user makes a selection; the destination is
// stored in the variable *there*.
<input type="radio" name="destination" value="HowTo"
    onclick="there = 'http://www.example.com/script.html'" />
Learn to Make a Script<br />
<input type="radio" name="destination" value="Reference"
    onclick="there = 'http://www.example.com/jref.html'" />
JavaScript Reference Information<br />
<p><a href="" onclick="this.href = there"
        onmouseover="self.status = there; return true;">
    <b>Take me there!</b>
</a></p>
// This link includes the information to make the jump to
// a page, depending on the selection made above - using the
// variable *there* following this is another set of selections
// for a different mode. These radio buttons pick a lesson and
// use the submit button to run a function - in this case, the
// function just displays a message; ideally the function would
// process the information and display a message.
<p><input type="text" name="whoIs" value="user"
    size="15" /></p>
<p><input type="radio" name="lesson" value="Lesson 1"
    checked="checked" onclick="takeLesson = 'lesson1.htm'" />
    Lesson 1: Getting Started</p>
<p><input type="radio" name="lesson"  value="Lesson 2"
    onclick="takeLesson = 'lesson2.htm'" />
    Lesson 2: Concepts and Operations</p>
<p><input type="radio" name="lesson" value="Lesson 3"
    onclick="takeLesson = 'lesson3.htm'" />
    Lesson 3: Projects</p>
<p><input type="reset" value="Defaults" name="resetToBasic" />
```

```
    </p>
<p><input type="submit" value="Send it in!"
    name="submit_form1" /></p>
<hr />
</form>
...</body>
```

This example creates two groups of radio buttons that set up the destination for the link/jump for the user or the course selections. Users identify the kind of information they want (as in Getting Started, Concepts And Operations, Projects, and so on) and the lesson they want (selected from the list of radio buttons). The reset statement clears any changes the user may have made and resets the form to Getting Started. The submit statement sends the selections to be processed according to the instructions (not seen) for the form.

reset

This object is a reset button on a form. It clears the form fields of any user interaction/entries and resets their values to the default. You create a reset object by using the input element with a type attribute set to the value reset. The onclick event handler cannot be canceled. Once the reset object is clicked, the form is reset, and all user entries are lost. The reset object has the following format:

```
<input type="reset" name="resetName" value="buttonText"
    [onclick="handlerText"] />
```

The resetName entry is the name of the object. It allows you to access the object within your script. The buttonText entry is the label for the button.

To use the reset properties and methods, follow this format:

```
resetName.propertyName
resetName.methodName(parameters)
formName.elements[index].propertyName
formName.elements[index].methodName(parameters)
```

Statements one and three are equivalents, as are statements two and four.

The reset object has two properties—name and value (described earlier in Table MR.10). It uses the blur, click, and focus methods and the onblur, onclick, and onfocus event handlers. The reset object is a property of the form object.

Example

```
<input type="reset" name="clearForm" value="Start Over" />
```

This simple example should appear on all your forms. This statement places a reset button (this one says Start Over) that clears the current form when it's clicked.

For another example of a `reset` object, see the example in the `"radio"` section.

select

The `select` object presents the user with a drop-down list of pre-set choices. It contains an `options` array. The `select` object is created with an XHTML `select` element, and is part of a form. The `select` object has the following format:

```
<select name="selectName" [size="integer"] [multiple="multiple"]
   [onblur="handlerText"] [onchange="handerText"]
   [onfocus="handlerText"]>
   <option value="optionValue" [selected="selected"]>
   textToDisplay</option>
   [... <option>textToDisplay</option>]
</select>
```

The `selectName` entry is the name of the object; the `select` object contains the list. The `multiple` entry indicates that the object accepts multiple selections—such as checkboxes. If the list is not set to multiple, it's like a radio object and only one choice is available. The `option` entry is a selection element in the list, and `optionValue` is the value returned to the system when the option is selected. The `selected` entry indicates that the option is the default value for the list, and `textToDisplay` is the text shown in the list.

To select the object's properties and methods, follow this format:

```
selectName.propertyName
selectName.methodName(parameters)
formName.elements[index].propertyName
formName.elements[index].methodName(parameters)
```

To use an option's properties, follow this format:

```
selectName.options[index1].propertyName
formName.elements[index2].options[index1].propertyName
```

The index1 entry is an integer representing the sequence of options in the list (the first option in the sequence is 0), and index2 is an integer representing the element in the form.

To use the options array, follow this format:

```
selectName.options
selectName.options[index]
selectName.options.length
```

The selectName entry is the value of the name attribute in the select object. The index entry is an integer representing an option in the select object, and length is the number of options in the select object.

The elements in the options array are read-only. You can get the number of options from the list, but you cannot change the values in the list.

The select object uses the properties shown in Table MR3.11. The options array uses the properties listed in Table MR3.12.

Table MR3.11 The Properties of the select Object

PROPERTY	WHAT IT IS
length	Number of options
name	name attribute
options	Array of the option elements
selectedIndex	Position of the selected option in the list (or the first of multiple options)

Table MR3.12 The Properties of the options Array

PROPERTY	WHAT IT IS
defaultSelected	selected attribute indicating which option is the default selection for the list
index	Position of the option in the list (the list begins at zero)
length	Number of options
name	name attribute
selected="selected"	Lets you select an option from your script, rather than from user input

Table MR3.12 continued The Properties of the `options` Array

Property	What It Is
selectedIndex	Position of the selected option in the list
text	textToDisplay for the option list item
value	value attribute

The `select` object uses the `blur` and `focus` methods and the `onblur`, `onchange`, and `onfocus` event handlers. The `select` object is a property of `form`. The `options` array is a property of `select`.

Example

```
<select name="lesson_list">
    <option selected="selected">Introduction</option>
    <option>Installation</option>
    <option>Setting up an account</option>
    <option>Creating a document</option>
    <option>Filing a document</option>
    <option>Recovering a filed document</option>
    <option>Sending a document to the printer</option>
</select>
```

The form contains a list of chapters in a book, from which the user can select a single item.

string

A `string` object is a series of characters, such as a name, a phrase, or other information. It has the following format:

```
stringName.propertyName
stringName.methodName(parameters)
```

The `stringName` entry is the variable name (that owns the string). The `length` entry is the size of the string. This is a character count and includes spaces and special characters. The `methodName` entry is one of the methods listed below.

The `string` object has a single property, `length`, which is the number of characters in the string. The string `object` uses the following methods:

anchor	fromcharcode	small
big	indexof	split
blink	italics	strike
bold	lastindexof	sub
charAt	link	substr
charCodeAt	match	substring
concat	replace	sup
fixed	search	toLowerCase
fontcolor	slice	toUpperCase
fontsize		

Some of these methods will look familiar, as they deal with the format of the text in the `string` object.

Because it's a built-in object, the `string` object does not use event handlers. It's not a property of anything.

Example

```
var user_id = new string();
user_id = getUserText.value;
user_id.toUpperCase();
```

This simple example takes the contents of the text field `getUserText` and assigns it to a newly created string variable called `user_id`. The last statement shifts the contents of the variable to uppercase.

submit

This object is a button on a form that starts the processing of the form. The submission is controlled by the form's `action` property. You create a `submit` object by using the input element with a `type` attribute with the value `submit`. The `submit` object has the following format:

```
<input type="submit" name="submitName" value="buttonText"
    [onclick="handlerText"] />
```

To use the submit object's properties and methods, follow this format:
```
submitName.propertyName
submitName.methodName(parameters)
formName.elements[index].propertyName
formName.elements[index].methodName(parameters)
```

The `submit` object uses two properties—name and `value`. It uses the `blur`, `click`, and `focus` methods, and the `onblur`, `onclick`, and `onfocus` event handlers. The `submit` object is a property of the `form` object.

Example

For an example of a `submit` object, see the example in the `"radio"` section.

text

The `text` object is a field on the form used to collect information from the user. The user can type short string sequences, such as a word, a phrase, or numbers into the text object. You create a `text` object by using the `input` element with a `type` attribute with the value `text`. The `text` object has the following format:

```
<input type="text" name="textName" value="textValue"
    size="integer" [onblur="handlerText"]
    [onchange="handlerText"] [onfocus="handlerText"]
    [onselect="handlerText"] />
```

The `textName` entry is the variable name for the object. The `textValue` entry is the initial value for the `text` object, and `size` is the length of the box on the page.

To use the `text` object's properties and methods, follow this format:

```
textName.propertyName
textName.methodName(parameters)
formName.elements[index].propertyName
formName.elements[index].methodName(properties)
```

The `text` object has the three properties: `defaultValue` is the default value setting; `name` is the `name` attribute; and `value` is the current contents of the `text` object.

The text object uses three methods—focus, blur, and select—and it uses the onblur, onchange, onfocus, and onselect event handlers. The text object is a property of the form object.

Example

```
var userProfile="user";
<input type="text" name="usertype" value="user" size="15"
    onchange="userProfile=this.value" />
<input type="text" name="userGroup" value="" size="32"
    onchange="userProfile+=this.value" />
```

These statements create a user profile by getting the text entries the user makes in the text objects' fields. The first statement sets the default for the variable userProfile. The next two statements change this variable only if the user changes the contents of the fields.

textarea

Like the text object, the textarea object offers a way for users to enter textual data. The textarea object is a multiline field, whereas the text object is a single line. The textarea object must also be defined within a form element. If you want the text to wrap properly within the textarea object, verify the version of the browser. The Windows platform uses a slightly different new-line code (Unix uses \n, Windows uses \r\n, and Macintosh uses \n). If you use the appVersion property, you can set the new-line character correctly.

You can dynamically update the textarea object by setting the value property. The textarea object has the following format:

```
<textarea name="textareaName" rows="integer" cols="integer"
    [onblur="handlerText"] [onchange="handlerText"]
    [onfocus="handlerText"] [onselect="handlerText"]>
    textToDisplay</textarea>
```

The textareaName entry is the name of the object.

To use the properties and methods of the textarea object, follow this format:

```
textareaName.propertyName
textareaName.methodName(parameters)
formName.elements[index].propertyName
formName.elements[index].methodName(parameters)
```

The textarea object uses three properties—defaultValue, name, and value—and three methods: focus, blur, and select. It uses the onblur, onchange, onfocus, and onselect event handlers. The textarea object is a property of the form object.

Example

```
<p>Decribe the FOLD function and give three examples of what
    you can do with the FOLD function:</p>
<textarea name="foldEssay" rows="5" cols="65"
    onchange="question3Essay = this.value"></textarea>
```

This example gives the user a field in which to answer an essay question; the answer is stored in the variable question3Essay.

window

The window object is the topmost object for JavaScript's document, location, and history objects. The self and window properties are synonymous and refer to the current window. The keyword top refers to the uppermost window in the hierarchy, and parent refers to a window that contains one or more framesets. Because of its unique position, you do not have to address the properties of window in the same fashion as other objects: close() is the same as window.close() and self.close().

The window object uses event handlers, but the calls to these handlers are put in the body and frameset elements. It has the following format:

```
windowVar = window.open("URL", "windowName"[,"windowFeatures"]);
```

The windowVar entry is the name of a new window, and windowName is the target attribute of the form and a elements.

To use a window's properties and methods, follow this format:

```
window.propertyName
window.methodName(parameters)
self.propertyName
self.methodName(parameters)
top.propertyName
top.methodName(parameters)
parent.propertyName
parent.methodName(parameters)
windowVar.propertyName
windowVar.methodName(parameters)
propertyName methodName(parameters)
```

To define the `onload` or `onunload` event handlers, include the statement in the body *or* `frameset` elements.

```
<body ...
    [onload="handlerText"]
    [onunload="handlerText"]>
    ...
</body>

<frameset ...
    [onload="handlerText"]
    [onunload="handlerText"]>
    ...
</frameset>
```

The `window` object contains the properties shown in Table MR3.13.

Table MR3.13 The Properties of the `window` Object

PROPERTY	WHAT IT IS
defaultStatus	Default message for the window's status bar
frames	List (array) of the window's child frames
length	Number of frames in a parent window
name	name attribute
parent	Synonym for `windowName` where the window contains a frameset
self	Synonym for the current `windowName`
status	Priority or transient message for the status bar
top	Synonym for the topmost browser window
window	Synonym for the current `windowName`

The window object also uses these methods:

alert	moveBy	resizeTo
blur	moveTo	scroll
clearInterval	open	scrollBy

clearTimeout	print	scrollTo
close	prompt	setInterval
confirm	resizeBy	setTimeout
focus		

The window object uses two event handlers: onload and onunload. It's not a property of anything.

Example

```
<script type="text/javascript" language="javascript">
    function checkThis() {
        windowReply = window.open("reginfo.html", "answerWindow",
            "scrollbars = yes, width = 100, height = 200");
        document.form1.submit();
        confirm("Thanks for registering");
        self.close();
    }
</script>
```

This example opens a window with the registration information.

Methods and Functions

You use methods and functions to manipulate containers, which are objects. If you think of the browser as a stage, the actors and the sets are objects; the lines spoken and the actions taken (according to the script) are the methods and functions applied to the objects.

This section is an alphabetic listing of the available JavaScript methods and functions. Each entry describes a single method or function, includes syntax information and (where appropriate) examples, and identifies the object that the method or function belongs to or affects.

abs

The abs method belongs to the Math object and returns the absolute value (an unsigned number). It has the following syntax:

```
Math.abs(number)
```

The number entry is any numeric expression or a property of an object.

Example

```
var myNumber = -49
document.write(Math.abs(myNumber));
```

acos

The acos method belongs to the Math object and returns the arccosine of a number in radians. It has the following syntax:

```
Math.acos(number)
```

The number entry is any numeric expression or a property of an object.

Example

```
var myNumber = 45;
document.write(Math.acos(myNumber));
```

alert

The alert method belongs to the window object and displays a small dialog box with a message string and an OK button. The alert method is most commonly used for displaying error messages when a user's input to a form element is invalid. It has the following syntax:

```
window.alert("message")
```

The message is any string expression or a property of an object.

Example

```
window.alert("Welcome to my homepage.");
```

This example displays an alert box when the browser executes the code. You can also use an alert method with the onload event handler in the body element so the alert box will display as the page is initially being loaded.

```
<body onload="window.alert('Welcome! You can register through
    this page. For future reference, this page is ' +
    document.location)">...</body>
```

This loads a message that includes the page address through the document.location.

anchor

The anchor method belongs to the string object and generates an anchor for a hypertext target in a document. Use the anchor method with the write or writeln method. It has the following syntax:

```
text.anchor(nameAttribute)
```

The text and nameAttribute entries are any string or property of an object.

Example

```
var intro = "Welcome to the JavaScript Tutorial!";
tocWindow = window.open("","displayWindow");
tocWindow.document.write(intro.anchor("contents_anchor");
for (x = 0; x < 5; x++) {
   switch(x) {
      case[1]: if (c1 != "true") {
         tocWindow.document.write(
            c1 + c1.anchor("overviewtoC");   }
         break;
      case[2]: if (c2 != "true") {
         tocWindow.document.write(
            c2 + c2.anchor("ObjectstoC");   }
         break;
      case[3]: if (c3 != "true") {
         tocWindow.document.write(
            c3 + c3.anchor("structuretoC");   }
         break;   }   }
```

asin

The asin method belongs to the Math object and returns the arcsine of a number in radians. It has the following syntax:

```
Math.asin(number)
```

The number entry is any numeric expression or a property of an object.

Example

```
var myNumber = 190;
document.write(Math.asin(myNumber));
```

atan

The atan method belongs to the Math object and returns the arctangent of the number in radians. It has the following syntax:

```
Math.atan(number)
```

The number entry is any numeric expression or a property of an object.

Example

```
var myNumber = 155;
document.write(Math.atan(myNumber));
```

atan2

The atan2 method belongs to the Math object and computes the angle (in radians) between the x axis and the position represented by the x and y coordinates, which are passed as parameters. It has the following syntax:

```
Math.atan2(x,y)
```

The number entries (x,y) are the *x* and *y* coordinates of the point.

Example

```
var x = 45;
var y = 90;
document.write(Math.atan2(x,y));
```

back

The back method belongs to the history object and uses the history list to return to the previous document. You can use this method to give users an alternative to the browser's back button. It has the following syntax:

```
history.back()
```

Example

```
<p><input type="button" value="Take Me Back!"
    onclick="history.back()" />
  <input type="button" value="Let's Keep Going!"
    onclick="history.forward()" /></p>
```

This code puts two buttons beside each other on a line. The first button goes back to the last document; the second button is useful if the user has already moved back in the history list and is ready to go forward again.

big

The big method belongs to the string object and displays the associated string as a large font (as if the text were tagged with a big element). It has the following syntax:

```
stringName.big()
```

The stringName is any string expression or a property of an object.

Example

```
<script type="text/javascript" language="javascript">
  var welcome = "Welcome to our flashy new digs!";
  confirm(welcome);
  // This opens a small box with the text and an OK button.
  document.write(welcome.big());
  alert("That's All Folks!");
  self.close();
</script>
```

blink

The blink method belongs to the string object and displays the associated string blinking, as if the text were tagged with a blink element. It has the following syntax:

```
stringName.blink()
```

The stringName entry is any string expression or a property of an object.

Example

```
<script type="text/javascript" language="javascript">
```

```
    var welcome = "Welcome to our flashy new digs!";
    confirm(welcome);
    // This opens a small box with the text and an OK button.
    document.write(welcome.blink());
    alert("That's All Folks!");
    self.close();
</script>
```

blur

The blur method belongs to the password, select, text, textarea, and window objects and is the programmatic way to move the focus off a form object such as a text object. It has the following syntax:

```
password.blur()
selectName.blur()
textName.blur()
textareaName.blur()
window.blur()
```

The password entry is either the name of a password object or an element in the elements array. The selectName entry is either the name of a select object or an element in the elements array. The textName entry is either the name of a text object or an element in the elements array. The textareaName entry is either the name of a textarea object or an element in the elements array. The window entry is the name of the top-level browser window specified by the window object.

Example

```
<script type="text/javascript" language="javascript">
    var userPass = "";
    var userName = "";
    var formulate = new window();
    // set up the variables to be used later
    formulate.window.open();
    // open a window for the form
    document.formulate.userPass.focus();
    var timer = setTimeout(
        "document.formulate.userPass.blur()", 8000);
    // put the focus onto the password box
    // for 8 secs, then blur
```

```
        clearTimeout(timer);
        document.formulate.userName.focus();
        timer = setTimeout(
            "document.formulate.userName.blur()", 30000);
        // clear the timeout, put the focus on the username box for
        // 30 secs, then blur
        document.formulate.userAuth.click();
        // force a selection in the userAuth check box
        clearTimeout(timer);
        msgWindow.window.close();
        // clear the timeout variable and close the window
    </script>
    …
    <form name="formulate" id="formulate">
        <input type="password" name="userPass" size="5" />
            tell us your secret
        <input type="text" name="userName" value="Bob's your uncle"
            size="15" />
        <input type="checkbox" name="userAuth" value="Validate Me" />
            authorize us to check this stuff out!
    </form>
```

bold

The bold method belongs to the string object and displays the associated string as bold—as if the text were tagged with the b element. It has the following syntax:

```
stringName.bold()
```

The stringName is any string expression or a property of an object.

Example

```
<script type="text/javascript" language="javascript">
    var welcome = "Welcome to our flashy new digs!";
    confirm(welcome);
    // This opens a small box with the text and an OK button.
    document.write(welcome.bold());
    alert("That's All Folks!");
    self.close();
</script>
```

ceil

The `ceil` method belongs to the `Math` object and returns the nearest integer that is equal to or greater than the given number. It has the following syntax:

```
Math.ceil(number)
```

The `number` entry is any numeric expression or a property of an object.

Example

```
var myNumber = 4.7;
document.write(Math.ceil(myNumber));
```

This returns the integer nearest the number (greater or equal).

charAt

The `charAt` method belongs to the `string` object and returns the character found at the given `index` in the string. It has the following syntax:

```
stringName.charAt(index)
```

The `stringName` is any numeric expression or a property of an object.

Example

```
<script type="text/javascript" language="javascript">
   var welcome = "Welcome to our flashy new digs!";
   confirm(welcome);
   for (var place = 0; place < welcome.length; place++) {
      document.write(welcome.charAt(place) + "<br />");   }
   // This for loop displays each letter on its own line.
   alert("That's All Folks!");
   self.close();
</script>
```

charCodeAt

The `charCodeAt` method belongs to the `string` object and returns a number that represents the Unicode encoding of the character found at the given `index` in the string. The first character in a string is at the position numbered 0. It has the following syntax:

```
stringName.charCodeAt (index)
```

The stringName entry is any numeric expression or a property of an object.

Example

```
var myText = wobble;
document.write(myText.charCodeAt(5));
```

This example would display the Unicode encoding for the character at the fifth position in the string myText (the letter e), which is 0066.

clear

The clear method belongs to the document object and empties the contents of the document window. It has the following syntax:

```
document.clear()
```

Example

```
alert("That's All Folks!");
self.clear();
```

A box appears, with the message That's All Folks! and an OK button. The next line clears the document from the browser window.

clearInterval

The clearInterval method belongs to the frame and window objects and cancels an interval set with the setInterval method. It has the following syntax:

```
clearInterval (intervalID)
```

The intervalID entry is the name of the value returned by a previous call to set-Interval.

Example

```
<head>
<script type="text/javascript" language="javascript">
    function reminder() {
        window.alert("Don't forget to enter our contest!") }
    function setReminder() {
        var myReminder = window.setInterval("reminder()",8000); }
```

```
</script>
…</head>
<body onload="setReminder();">…
<script type="text/javascript" language="javascript">
    function noway() {
        clearInterval(myReminder); }
</script>
<form>
    <input type="button" value="pleasestop" name="stopmessage"
        onclick="return noway()" />
</form>
…</body>
```

In this example, as soon as the page loads, an alert box with the message "Don't forget to enter our contest!" will be displayed every eight seconds. The message will stop displaying when the "pleasestop" button is clicked, which calls the noway function.

clearTimeout

The clearTimeout method belongs to the frame and window objects and resets the variable for the setTimeout method. It has the following syntax:

```
clearTimeout(timeoutID)
```

The timeoutID entry is the name of the value returned by a previous call to setTimeout.

Example

```
<head>
<script type="text/javascript" language="javascript">
    var myTimer;
    function timesup() {
        myTimer = setTimeout("window.alert('It's time!')",3000);
    }
</script>
…</head>
<body onload="timesup()">…
<script type="text/javascript" language="javascript">
    function stopit() {
        clearTimeout(myTimer); }
</script>
```

```
<form>
   <input type="button" value="stop" name="stoptimer"
      onclick="return stopit()" />
</form>
...</body>
```

In this example, a timer is started when the pages loads. An alert message will be displayed unless the button labeled "stop" is clicked before three seconds have elapsed. Clicking the button calls the stopit function which clears the timer.

click

The click method belongs to the button, checkbox, radio, reset, and submit objects and simulates, programmatically, the user's click on a form object. The click method, however, does not invoke the onclick event handler. It has the following syntax:

```
password.click()
selectName.click()
textName.click()
textareaName.click()
```

The password entry is either the name of a password object or an element in the elements array. The selectName entry is either the name of a select object or an element in the elements array. The textName entry is either the name of a text object or an element in the elements array. The textareaName is either the name of a textarea object or an element in the elements array.

Example

```
<script type="text/javascript" language="javascript">
   likes.elements[0].click();
   //forces a selection in the icecream check box
</script>
...
<form name="likes" id="likes">
   <input type="checkbox" name="icecream" value="vanilla" />
   vanilla
</form>
```

In this example, the vanilla check box is checked through the use of the click method. However, you could get the same result by using checked="checked" within the input element.

close (document Object)

This close method belongs to the document object and closes the output stream to the specified document. It has the following syntax:

```
document.close()
```

Example

```
<script type="text/javascript" language="javascript">
    function openWin() {
        myWin= open("", "displayWindow",
            "width = 250, height = 300, status = no, toolbar = no,
            menubar = no");
        myWin.document.open();
        myWin.document.write("<html><head><title>My New Window");
        myWin.document.write("</title></head><body>");
        myWin.document.write("<p><font size='5'
            face='arial,helvetica'>");
        myWin.document.write("See how easy it is to create ");
        myWin.document.write("a new window using Javascript!");
        myWin.document.write("</font></p></body></html>");
        myWin.document.close();  }
</script>
...
<form name="popup" id="popup">
    <input type=button value="New Window" onClick="openWin()"
        name="button" />
</form>
```

In this example, a pop-up window is created when the button labelled "New Window" is clicked. The myWin.document.close statement closes input to this pop-up window, and returns the flow to the original document.

close (window Object)

This close method belongs to the window object and closes the active window. It has the following syntax:

```
windowReference.close()
```

A window can also close with the following syntax:

```
self.close()
close()
```

The windowReference is any valid means of identifying a window object.

Example

```
<script type="text/javascript" language="javascript">
    var welcome = "Welcome to our flashy new digs!";
    confirm(welcome);
    // This opens a small box with the text and an OK button.
    for (var place = 0; place < welcome.length; place++) {
        document.write(welcome.charAt(place) + "<br />");
    }
    // This for loop puts out each letter on its own line.
    alert("That's All Folks!");
    self.close();
</script>
```

A box appears, with the message That's All Folks! and an OK button. The next line clears the document from the browser window.

concat

The concat method belongs to the string object; it concatenates the strings supplied and returns the joined strings. It has the following syntax:

```
stringName.concat(value, ...)
```

The values are one or more strings to be added to the end of stringName. If a value is not a string, the concat method converts it to a string. The stringName is any numeric expression or a property of an object.

Example

```
<script  type="text/javascript" language="javascript">
    var myMsg = "Hello";
    var usrName = prompt("Please enter your name", " ");
    var myString;
    document.write(myMsg + " " + usrName + "<br>");
    myString = myMsg.concat(" ",usrName);
    document.write(myString);
</script>
```

In this example, the string myMsg ("Hello") is joined to the string usrName, which the user enters in response to the prompt. Each document.write statement displays the same output.

confirm

The confirm method belongs to the window object and displays a small dialog box with the message string and two buttons, OK and Cancel. It has the following syntax:

```
confirm("message")
```

The message entry is a string expression or a property of an object.

Example

```
<script type="text/javascript" language="javascript">
    function checkThis() {
        windowReply=window.open("reginfo.html", "answerWindow",
            "scrollbars = yes, width = 100, height = 200");
        document.form1.submit();
        confirm("Thanks for registering");
        self.close();
    }
</script>
...
<form name="form1" id="form1" onsubmit="checkThis()">
// The form element includes the onsubmit event handler
// and the form includes a submit button.
// Following this is a set of selections.
// These radio buttons pick a lesson and use the submit
// button to run a function - in this case, the function
// just displays a message; ideally the function would
// process the information and display a message.
    <p><input type="text" name="whoIs" value="user" size="15" />
        </p>
    <p><input type="radio" name="lesson" value="Lesson 1"
        checked="checked" onclick="takeLesson = 'lesson1.htm'" />
        Lesson 1: Getting Started</p>
    <p><input type="radio" name="lesson" value="Lesson 2"
        onclick="takeLesson = 'lesson2.htm'" />
        Lesson 2: Concepts and Operations</p>
```

```
<p><input type="radio" name="lesson" value="Lesson 3"
    onclick="takeLesson = 'lesson3.htm'" />
    Lesson 3: Projects</p>
<p><input type="reset" value="Defaults" name="resetToBasic" />
    <input type="submit" value="Send it in!"
        name="submit_form1" /></p>
<hr />
</form>
```

This example displays the confirmation message when the user clicks the Submit button.

cos

The cos method belongs to the Math object returns the cosine of the number. It has the following syntax:

```
Math.cos(number)
```

The number entry is any numeric expression or a property of an object.

Example

```
<script type="text/javascript" language="javascript">
    function tryMe(baseVal) {
        var baseVal = Math.random();
        showMe = window.open("");
        with (Math) {
            showMe.document.write(cos(baseVal) + "<br />");
            showMe.document.write(abs(cos(baseVal))+ "<br />");
            // return the cosine of the number
            showMe.alert("Close \'er up now, skip?");
            showMe.close();  }  }
</script>
```

escape

The escape function returns the ASCII encoded value for the given string. It has the following syntax:

```
escape("string")
```

The `string` entry is a nonalphanumeric string that represents a reserved or unprintable character from the ISO Latin-1 character set. For example, `escape(%26)` returns &.

eval

The `eval` function runs a JavaScript expression, statement, function, or sequence of statements. The expression can include variables and object properties. It has the following syntax:

```
eval("string")
```

The `string` entry is a JavaScript expression, statement, function, or sequence of statements.

exp

The `exp` method belongs to the `Math` object and returns the value equal to Euler's constant (e, the base of natural logarithms—approximately 2.718) raised to the power of the given number. It has the following syntax:

```
Math.exp(number)
```

The `number` entry is any numeric expression or a property of an object.

Example

```
<script type="text/javascript" language="javascript">
function tryMe(baseVal) {
    var baseVal = Math.random();
    showMe = window.open("");
    with (Math) {
        showMe.document.write(exp(baseVal) + "<br />");
        showMe.document.write(abs(exp(baseVal)) + "<br />");
        // return Euler's constant (e) to the power of the
        // number given
        showMe.alert("Close \'er up now, skip?");
        showMe.close();  }  }
</script>
```

fixed

The fixed method belongs to the string object and displays the associated string in a fixed width (monospaced) font, as if the text were tagged with a tt element. It has the following syntax:

```
stringName.fixed()
```

The stringName is any string expression or a property of an object.

Example

```html
<script type="text/javascript" language="javascript">
    var welcome = "Welcome to our flashy new digs!";
    confirm(welcome);
    // This opens a small box with the text and an OK button.
    document.write(welcome.fixed());
    alert("That's All Folks!");
    self.close();
</script>
```

floor

The floor method belongs to the Math object and returns the nearest integer that is equal to or less than the given number. It has the following syntax:

```
Math.floor(number)
```

The number entry is any numeric expression or a property of an object.

Example

```javascript
with (Math) {
    msgWindow.document.write(random());
    // generate a random number
    msgWindow.document.write(floor(random() * baseVal));
    // return the integer nearest the number (less or equal)
}
```

focus

The focus method belongs to the password, select, text, textarea, and window objects and allows you to programmatically move the focus to a form object or browser window. This simulates the user's moving the cursor to the object. It has the following syntax:

```
password.focus()
selectName.focus()
textName.focus()
textareaName.focus()
window.focus()
```

The password entry is either the name of a password object or an element in the elements array. The selectName entry is either the name of a select object or an element in the elements array. The textName is either the name of a text object or an element in the elements array. The textareaName is either the name of a textarea object or an element in the elements array. The window is the top-level browser window specified by the window object.

For an example of the focus method, see the "blur" section.

fontcolor

The fontcolor method belongs to the string object and displays the associated string in the given color as if the text were tagged with a font element with a color attribute. It has the following syntax:

```
stringName.fontcolor(colorKeyword)
```

The stringName entry is any string expression or a property of an object.

Example

```
<script type="text/javascript" language="javascript">
    var welcome = "Welcome to our flashy new digs!";
    confirm(welcome);
    // This opens a small box with the text and an OK button.
    document.write(welcome.fontcolor("crimson") + "<br />");
    document.write(welcome.fontsize(8) + "<br />");
    // Some more text attributes, these take arguments.
    alert("That's All Folks!");
    self.close();
</script>
```

fontsize

The fontsize method belongs to the string object and displays the associated string at the given size as if the text were tagged with a font element with a size attribute. It has the following syntax:

```
stringName.fontsize(size)
```

The stringName is any string expression or a property of an object.

Example

```
<script type="text/javascript" language="javascript">
    var welcome = "Welcome to our flashy new digs!";
    confirm(welcome);
    // This opens a small box with the text and an OK button.
    document.write(welcome.fontcolor("crimson") + "<br />");
    document.write(welcome.fontsize(8) + "<br />");
    // Some more text attributes, these take arguments.
    alert("That's All Folks!");
    self.close();
</script>
```

forward

The forward method belongs to the history object and uses the history list to recall a previously viewed document that the user has left via the Back button or the back method. You can use this method to give users an alternative to the browser's Forward button. You can also use history.go(1) method to perform this action. It has the following syntax:

```
history.forward()
```

Example

```
<p><input type="button" value="Take Me Back!"
    onclick="history.back()" />
  <input type="button" value="Let's Keep Going!"
    onclick="history.forward()" /></p>
```

This code puts two buttons beside each other on a line. The first button goes back to the last document. The second button is useful if the user has already moved back in the history list and is ready to go forward again.

getDate

The getDate method belongs to the date object and returns the day of the month (0–31) for the given date. It has the following syntax:

```
dateObjectName.getDate()
```

The datObjectName entry is any date object or a property of an object.

Example

```html
<script type="text/javascript" language="javascript">
   function callMe() {
      Xmas01 = new Date("December 25, 2001 23:15:00");
      weekday = Xmas01.getDate();
      confirm(weekday);
      var who = 1;
      var docMod = document.lastModified;
      switch (who) { // this switch has two streams
         case(1) :
            alert(docMod);
            chrono = new Date();
            alert(chrono.getDate());
            alert(chrono + " already?!");
            who++;
            break;
         case(2) :
            docMod = "";
            docMod.setDay(1);
            docMod.setMonth(6);
            docMod.setDate(30);
            docMod.setYear(2001);
            docMod.setTime(11, 59, 59);
            document.write(chrono.fontcolor("darkmagenta") +
               "<br />");
            who++;
            break;
      }
      alert("That's All Folks!");
      self.close();
   }
</script>
```

```
...
<form>
   <input type="button" value="click here" name="button1"
      onclick="callMe()" />
</form>
```

The getDate method returns local time; for Universal Coordinated Time (UTC time), use getUTCDate.

getDay

The getDay method belongs to the date object and returns the day of the week (0–6) for the given date. It has the following syntax:

```
dateObjectName.getDay()
```

The dateObjectName entry is any date object or a property of an object.

Example

```
<script type="text/javascript" language="javascript">
   function callMe() {
      Xmas01 = new Date("December 25, 2001 23:15:00");
      weekday = Xmas01.getDate();
      confirm(weekday);
      var who = 1;
      var docMod = document.lastModified;
      switch (who) { // this switch has two streams
         case(1) :
            alert(docMod);
            chrono = new Date();
            alert(chrono.getDay());
            alert(chrono + " already?!");
            who++;
            break;
         case(2) :
            docMod = "";
            docMod.setDay(1);
            docMod.setMonth(6);
            docMod.setDate(30);
            docMod.setYear(2001);
            docMod.setTime(11, 59, 59);
```

```
        document.write(chrono.fontcolor("darkmagenta") +
          "<br />");
        who++;
        break;
      }
      alert("That's All Folks!");
      self.close();
    }
  </script>
```

The getDay method returns local time; for Universal Coordinated Time (UTC time), use getUTCDay.

getFullYear

The getFullYear method belongs to the date object and returns all four digits of the year of the given date. It has the following syntax:

```
dateObjectName.getFullYear()
```

The dateObjectName entry is any date object or a property of an object.

Example

```
<script type="text/javascript" language="javascript">
  function callMe() {
    Xmas99 = new Date("December 25, 1999 23:15:00");
    weekday = Xmas99.getDate();
    confirm(weekday);
    var docMod = document.lastModified;
    alert(docMod);
    chrono = new Date();
    alert(chrono.getFullYear());
    alert(chrono + " already?!");
    alert("That's All Folks!");
    self.close();  }
</script>
```

The getFullYear method returns local time; for Universal Coordinated Time (UTC time), use getUTCFullYear.

getHours

The getHours method belongs to the date object and returns the hour (0–23) of the given date. It has the following syntax:

```
dateObjectName.getHours()
```

The datObjectName entry is any date object or a property of an object.

Example

```
<script type="text/javascript" language="javascript">
    function callMe() {
        Xmas01 = new Date("December 25, 2001 23:15:00");
        weekday = Xmas01.getDate();
        confirm(weekday);
        var docMod = document.lastModified;
        alert(docMod);
        chrono = new Date();
        alert(chrono.getHours());
        alert(chrono + " already?!");
        alert("That's All Folks!");
        self.close();   }
</script>
```

The getHours method returns local time; for Universal Coordinated Time (UTC time), use getUTCHours.

getMilliseconds

The getMilliseconds method belongs to the date object and returns the milliseconds (0–999) of the given date. It has the following syntax:

```
dateObjectName.getMilliseconds()
```

The datObjectName entry is any date object or a property of an object.

Example

```
<script type="text/javascript" language="javascript">
    function callMe() {
        var docMod = document.lastModified;
        alert(docMod);
```

```
        chrono = new Date();
        alert(chrono.getMilliseconds());
        alert(chrono + " already?!");
        alert("That's All Folks!")
        self.close();  }
</script>
```

The getMilliseconds method returns local time; for Universal Coordinated Time (UTC time), use getUTCMilliseconds.

getMinutes

The getMinutes method belongs to the date object and returns the minutes (0–59) for the given date. It has the following syntax:

```
dateObjectName.getMinutes()
```

The dateObjectName entry is any date object or a property of an object.

Example

```
<script type="text/javascript" language="javascript">
    function callMe() {
        Xmas01 = new Date("December 25, 2001 23:15:00");
        weekday = Xmas01.getDate();
        confirm(weekday);
        var docMod = document.lastModified;
        alert(docMod);
        chrono = new Date();
        alert(chrono.getMinutes());
        alert(chrono + " already?!");
        alert("That's All Folks!");
        self.close();  }
</script>
```

The getMinutes method returns local time; for Universal Coordinated Time (UTC time), use getUTCMinutes.

getMonth

The getMonth method belongs to the date object and returns the month (0–11) of the given date. It has the following syntax:

```
dateObjectName.getMonth()
```

The dateObjectName entry is any date object or a property of an object.

Example

```
<script type="text/javascript" language="javascript">
    function callMe() {
        Xmas01 = new Date("December 25, 2001 23:15:00");
        weekday = Xmas01.getDate();
        confirm(weekday);
        var docMod = document.lastModified;
        alert(docMod);
        chrono = new Date();
        alert(chrono.getMonth());
        alert(chrono + " already?!");
        alert("That's All Folks!");
        self.close();   }
</script>
```

The getMonth method returns local time; for Universal Coordinated Time (UTC time), use getUTCMonth.

getSeconds

The getSeconds method belongs to the date object and returns the seconds (0–59) of the given date. It has the following syntax:

```
dateObjectName.getSeconds()
```

The datObjectName entry is any date object or a property of an object.

Example

```
<script type="text/javascript" language="javascript">
    function callMe() {
        Xmas01 = new Date("December 25, 2001 23:15:00");
        weekday = Xmas01.getDate();
```

```
        confirm(weekday);
        var docMod = document.lastModified;
        alert(docMod);
        chrono = new Date();
        alert(chrono.getSeconds());
        alert(chrono + " already?!");
        alert("That's All Folks!");
        self.close();  }
</script>
```

The getSeconds method returns local time; for Universal Coordinated Time (UTC time), use getUTCSeconds.

getTime

The getTime method belongs to the date object and returns the time (number of milliseconds since January 1, 1970 00:00:00) for the given date. It has the following syntax:

```
dateObjectName.getTime()
```

The dateObjectName entry is any date object or a property of an object.

Example

```
<script type="text/javascript" language="javascript">
    function callMe() {
        Xmas01 = new Date("December 25, 2001 23:15:00");
        weekday = Xmas01.getTime();
        confirm(weekday);
        var docMod = document.lastModified;
        alert(docMod);
        chrono = new Date();
        alert(chrono.getHours());
        alert(chrono + " already?!");
        alert("That's All Folks!");
        self.close();  }
</script>
```

getTimezoneOffset

The getTimezoneOffset method belongs to the date object and returns the difference between local time and Universal Coordinated Time (UTC) or GMT in minutes. It has the following syntax:

```
dateObjectName.getTimezoneOffset()
```

The dateObjectName entry is any date object or a property of an object.

Example

```
<script type="text/javascript" language="javascript">
    function callMe() {
        Xmas01 = new Date("December 25, 2001 23:15:00");
        weekday = Xmas01.getDate();
        confirm(weekday);
        var docMod = document.lastModified;
        alert(docMod);
        chrono = new Date();
        alert(chrono.get.timezoneOffset());
        alert(chrono);
        alert("That's All Folks!");
        self.close();   }
</script>
```

getYear

The getYear method belongs to the date object and returns the last two digits of the year of the given date. It has the following syntax:

```
dateObjectName.getYear()
```

The dateObjectName entry is any date object or a property of an object.

Example

```
<script type="text/javascript" language="javascript">
    function callMe() {
        Xmas01 = new Date("December 25, 2001 23:15:00");
        weekday = Xmas01.getDate();
        confirm(weekday);
        var docMod = document.lastModified;
```

```
        alert(docMod);
        chrono = new Date();
        alert(chrono.getYear());
        alert(chrono + " already?!");
        alert("That's All Folks!");
        self.close();  ]
</script>
```

For Y2K (and beyond) compliance, use `getFullYear` instead.

go

The `go` method belongs to the `history` object and uses the history list to recall a previously viewed document. You can use this method to give users an alternative to the browser's Back and Forward buttons. You can also use the `back` and `forward` methods. The `go` method has the following syntax:

```
history.go(number)
```

The `number` entry is a positive or negative integer. A positive integer moves the user forward, and a negative integer moves the user back.

Example

```
<p><input type="button" value="Take Me Back!"
      onclick="history.back()" />
    <input type="button" value="Let's Keep Going!"
      onclick="history.forward()" /></p>
```

This code places two buttons beside each other on a line. The first button goes back to the last document. The second button is useful if the user has already moved back in the history list and is ready to go forward again.

Using the `go` method, these lines would appear like this:

```
<p><input type="button" value="Take Me Back!"
      onclick="history.go(-1)" />
    <input type="button" value="Let's Keep Going!"
      onclick="history.go(1)" /></p>
```

indexOf

The indexOf method belongs to the string object and returns the position of the first occurrence of the search value starting from the position given. It has the following syntax:

```
stringName.indexOf("searchValue"[, fromIndex])
```

The stringName entry is any string or object property. The searchValue is a string from within stringName. The fromIndex entry is the starting position for the search; the default is zero (first position).

Example

```
var champion = "We are the champions! We are the champions!";
champion.indexOf("are");
chamption.lastIndexOf("are);
```

This example returns the number 3 for the indexOf statement and 25 for the lastIndexOf statement.

isFinite

The isFinite function determines whether the number evaluated is finite. It has the following syntax:

```
isFinite(testValue)
```

This example returns true for finite numbers and false for infinite.

isNaN

The isNaN function determines whether the value given is a number. It has the following syntax:

```
isNaN(testValue)
```

Example

```
floatValue = parseFloat(toFloat);
if isNaN(floatValue) { not Float(); }
else { isFloat(); }
```

This example generates the value and then evaluates it.

italics

The `italics` method belongs to the `string` object and displays the associated string as italics or oblique as if the text were tagged with the i element. It has the following syntax:

```
stringName.italics()
```

The `stringName` entry is any string expression or a property of an object.

Example

```
<script type="text/javascript" language="javascript">
    var welcome = "Welcome to our flashy new digs!";
    confirm(welcome);
    // This opens a small box with the text and an OK button.
    document.write(welcome.italics() + "<br />");
    alert("That's All Folks!");
    self.close();
</script>
```

lastIndexOf

The `lastIndexOf` method belongs to the `string` object and returns the position of the last occurrence of the search value starting from the position given. It has the following syntax:

```
stringName.lastIndexOf("searchValue"[, fromIndex])
```

The `stringName` entry is any string or object property. The `searchValue` entry is a string from within `stringName`. The `fromIndex` entry is the starting position for the search; the default is zero (first position).

Example

```
var champion="We are the champions! We are the champions!";
champion.indexOf("are");
chamption.lastIndexOf("are);
```

This example returns the number 3 for the `indexOf` statement and 25 for the `lastIndexOf` statement.

link

The `link` method belongs to the anchor object and creates a jump to a URL. It has the following syntax:

```
linkText.link(hrefAttribute)
```

The `linkText` entry is a string or property that is used as the label for the link. The `hrefAttribute` entry is a valid URL for the destination.

Example

```
var c1="JavaScripting Overview";
var c2="JavaScript Objects";
var c3="JavaScript Constructs";
…
document.write(c1.link(
    "http://www.example.com/Courses/js_overview.html");
document.write(c2.link(
    "http://www.example.com/Courses/js_objects.html");
document.write(c3.link(
    "http://www.example.com/Courses/js_constructs.html");
```

You can use this example to build the table of contents for a dynamically selected course by including a selection form and a `switch` statement.

log

The `log` method belongs to the `Math` object and returns the natural logarithm (base e) of the given number. It has the following syntax:

```
Math.log(number)
```

The `number` entry is any numeric expression or a property of an object.

Example

```
with (Math) {
    msgWindow.document.write(random());
    // generate a random number
    msgWindow.document.write(log(baseVal));
    // return the natural logarithm (base of e) of the number
}
```

match

The match method belongs to the string object and is used to match a regular expression against a string. It has the following syntax:

```
stringName.match(regExp)
```

The stringName is any string expression or a property of an object. The regExp entry is a regular expression. A *regular expression* is an object that defines a group of characters. The match method searches a string for one or more matches of the regular expression and returns an array containing the results of the match.

max

The max method belongs to the Math object and returns the higher of two given numbers. It has the following syntax:

```
Math.max(number1, number2)
```

The number1 and number2 entries are any numeric expression or a property of an object.

Example

```
with (Math) {
    msgWindow.document.write(random());
    // generate a random number
    msgWindow.document.write(max(baseVal, (random() * 3)));
    // return the higher of the two values
}
```

min

The min method belongs to the Math object and returns the lower of two given numbers. It has the following syntax:

```
Math.min(number1, number2)
```

The number1 and number2 entries are any numeric expression or a property of an object.

Example

```
with (Math) {
    msgWindow.document.write(random());
    // generate a random number
    msgWindow.document.write(min(baseVal, (random()*3)));
    // return the lower of the two values
}
```

moveBy

The moveBy method belongs to the window object and moves the window to the position specified by px and py. It has the following syntax:

```
window.moveBy(px, py)
```

The px entry is the number of pixels to move the window to the right, and the py entry is the number of pixels to move the window down.

moveTo

The moveTo method belongs to the window object and moves the window to an absolute position. It has the following syntax:

```
window.moveTo(x,y)
```

The x entry is the *x*-coordinate of the new window position and the y entry is the *y*-coordinate of the new window position. The upper-left corner of the window is moved to the position specified by x and y.

open (document Object)

The open method for documents belongs to the document object and opens an output destination for the write and writeln statements. It has the following syntax:

```
document.open()
document.open(["mimeType"])
```

If the mime type is "text/html", you can use the first form of this statement—"text/html" is the default and does not have to be specified. If you want to use a different mime type, use the second form of this statement with one of the following:

```
text/plain

image/gif

image/jpeg

image/x-bitmap

plugIn
```

For an example of the open (document object) method, see the "close (document Object)" section.

open (window Object)

The open method for window objects belongs to the window object and allows you to set up and open an instance of the browser for displaying information. It has the following syntax:

```
windowVar=window.open("URL", "windowName" [,"windowsFeatures"])
```

The windowVar entry is the name of the new window, and URL is the location of the document to be loaded into the new window. The windowName entry is used in the target attribute of the form and a elements. The windowsFeatures entry is a comma-separated list that can contain one or more of the following:

```
toolbar[=yes|no] | [=1|0]
location[=yes|no] | [=1|0]
directories[=yes|no] | [=1|0]
status[=yes|no] | [=1|0]
menubar[=yes|no] | [=1|0]
scrollbars[=yes|no] | [=1|0]
resizable[=yes|no] | [=1|0]
width=pixels
height=pixels
```

Example

```
<script type="text/javascript" language="javascript">
  var userPass = "";
  var userName = "";
  var formulate =  new window();
  // set up the variables to be used later
  formulate.window.open('http://www.example.com'
     'titlebar = no,menubar = no,scrollbars = no');
  // open a window for the form
  document.formulate.userPass.focus();
  var timer = setTimeout(
     "document.formulate.userPass.blur()", 8000);
  // put the focus onto the the password box for 8 secs
  clearTimeout(timer);
  document.formulate.userName.focus();
  timer = setTimeout(
     "document.formulate.userName.blur()", 30000);
  // clear the timeout, put the focus on the username box
  // for 30 secs
  document.formulate.userAuth.click();
  // force a selection in the userAuth check box
  clearTimeout(timer);
  msgWindow.window.close();
  // clear the timeout variable and close the window
</script>
...
<form name="formulate" id="formulate">
  <input type="password" name="userPass" size="5" />
     tell us your secret
  <input type="text" name="userName" value="Bob's your uncle"
     size="15" />
  <input type="checkbox" name="userAuth" value="Validate Me" />
     authorize us to check this stuff out!
</form>
```

parse

The `parse` method belongs to the `date` object and returns the number of milliseconds between a given date string and January 1, 1970 00:00:00 local time. It has the following syntax:

```
Date.parse(dateString)
```

The `dateString` entry is a date or object property.

Example

```
checkValue = Date.parse("1, 1, 99");
if isNaN(checkValue) { notGood(); }
else { isGood(); }
```

This example generates the value and then evaluates it.

parseFloat

The `parseFloat` function determines whether a value is a number and returns a floating-point number for a string. It has the following syntax:

```
parseFloat(string)
```

The `string` entry is a string or object property.

Example

```
toFloat = "3.14";
floatValue = parseFloat(toFloat);
if isNaN(floatValue) { not Float(); }
else { isFloat(); }
```

This example generates the value and then evaluates it.

parseInt

The `parseInt` function determines whether a value is a number and returns an integer value of the given radix or base. It has the following syntax:

```
parseInt(string[, radix])
```

The `string` entry is a string or an object property, and the `radix` is an integer.

Example

```
document.write(parseInt("F", 16));
// the 16 indicates that the F is a hexidecimal number (base 16)
document.write(parseInt("1111", 2));
document.write(parseInt ("0xF"));
```

These examples return the same value, 15.

pow

The pow method belongs to the Math object and returns the first number raised to the power of the second number. It has the following syntax:

```
Math.pow(base, exponent)
```

The base and exponent entries are any numeric expression or a property of an object.

Example

```
with (Math) {
    msgWindow.document.write(random());
    // generate a random number
    msgWindow.document.write(pow(baseVal, random()));
    // raise the first number to the power of the second number
}
```

print

The print method belongs to the window object and prints the current document. It has the following syntax:

```
window.print()
```

The print method prints the document as if the user had clicked the browser's Print button.

prompt

The prompt method belongs to the window object and displays a dialog box with a message and an input field. Even though prompt is a window method, you do not have to include the windowReference in the statement. The prompt method has the following syntax:

```
prompt(message[, inputDefault])
```

The message entry is a text string or an object property, and inputDefault is a string, an integer, or an object property.

Example

```
<script  type="text/javascript" language="javascript">
    var myMsg = "Hello";
    var usrName = prompt("Please enter your name", " ");
    var myString = myMsg + " " + usrName;
    document.write(myString);
</script>
```

In this example, the string myMsg ("Hello") is joined to the string usrName, which the user enters in response to the prompt.

random

The random method belongs to the Math object and generates a random number between 0 and 1. It has the following syntax:

```
Math.random()
```

Example

```
<script type="text/javascript" language="javascript">
    function tryMe(baseVal) {
        var baseVal = Math.random();
        showMe = window.open("");
        with (Math) {
            var firstOne = (random());
            var secondOne = (abs(random()));
            showMe.document.write(firstOne + "<br />")
            showMe.document.write(secondOne + "<br />")  }  }
</script>
```

replace

The `replace` method belongs to the `string` object; it does a find and replace operation on `string`. It has the following syntax:

```
stringName.replace(regExp, replacementString)
```

The `stringName` is any string expression or a property of an object. The `regExp` entry is a regular expression, and `replacementString` is a string that specifies the replacement text for `regExp`. A *regular expression* is an object that defines a group of characters.

Example

```
<script type="text/javascript" language="javascript">
    function replace1 () {
        var myString;
        myString = "I feel cold."
        document.write(myString + "<br />");
        myString=myString.replace("cold"," hot");
        document.write(myString);   }
</script>
...
<body onload="replace1()">...</body>
```

In this example, the string `"cold"` is replaced by the string `"hot"`.

resizeBy

The `resizeBy` method belongs to the `window` object and resizes a window by a relative amount. It has the following syntax:

```
window.resizeBy(pw,ph)
```

The `pw` entry is the number of pixels increase in the width of the window, and the `ph` entry is the number of pixels increase in the height of the window.

Example

```
<script type="text/javascript" language="javascript">
    function openWin() {
        myWin = open("", "displayWindow", "width = 250,
            height = 300, status = no, toolbar = no,
            menubar = no");
        myWin.document.open();
```

```
    myWin.document.write("<html><head><title>My New Window");
    myWin.document.write("</title></head><body>");
    myWin.document.write("<p><font size='5'
       face='arial,helvetica'>");
    myWin.document.write("See how easy it is to create ");
    myWin.document.write("a new window using Javascript!");
    myWin.document.write("</font></p></body></html>");
    myWin.resizeBy(50,50);
    myWin.document.close();  }
</script>
...
<form name="popup" id="popup">
   <input type=button value="New Window" onClick="openWin()"
      name="button" />
</form>
```

In this example, the pop-up window increases by 50 pixels in width and 50 pixels in height as it displays.

resizeTo

The resizeTo method belongs to the window object and resizes a window to a specified size. It has the following syntax:

```
window.resizeTo(w,h)
```

The w entry is the new width of the window in pixels, and the h entry is the new height of the window in pixels.

Example

```
<script type="text/javascript" language="javascript">
   function openWin() {
      myWin= open("", "displayWindow", "width = 250,
         height = 300, status = no, toolbar = no,
         menubar = no");
      myWin.document.open();
      myWin.document.write("<html><head><title>My New Window");
      myWin.document.write("</title></head><body>");
      myWin.document.write("<p><font size='2'
         face='arial,helvetica'>");
      myWin.document.write("See how easy it is to create ");
      myWin.document.write("a new window using Javascript!");
```

```
        myWin.document.write("</font></p></body></html>");
        myWin.resizeTo(150,150);
        myWin.document.close();   }
</script>
...
<form name="popup" id="popup">
    <input type=button value="New Window" onClick="openWin()"
        name="button" />
</form>
```

In this example, the pop-up window resizes to 150 pixels in width and 150 pixels in height as it displays.

round

The round method belongs to the Math object and returns the value of the number given to the nearest integer. It has the following syntax:

```
Math.round(number)
```

The number entry is any numeric expression or a property of an object.

Example

```
<script type="text/javascript" language="javascript">
    function tryMe(baseVal) {
        var baseVal=Math.random();
        showMe = window.open("");
        with (Math) {
            var firstOne = (random());
            var secondOne = (abs(random()));
            showMe.document.write(firstOne + "<br />");
            showMe.document.write(secondOne + "<br />");
            // generate a random number
            showMe.document.write(round(baseVal * random()) +
                "<br />");
            showMe.document.write(abs(round(baseVal * random())) +
                "<br />");
            //rounds number to the nearest integer
            showMe.alert("Close \'er up now, skip?");
            showMe.close();   }   }
</script>
```

scrollBy

The scrollBy method belongs to the window object and scrolls a document by a relative amount. It has the following syntax:

```
window.scrollBy(px,py)
```

The px entry is the number of pixels the document is scrolled to the right, and the py entry is the number of pixels the document is scrolled down.

Example

```
<head>
<script type="text/javascript" language="javascript">
    function changeposition(x,y) {
        window.scrollBy(x,y);   }
</script>
...</head>
<body bgcolor="teal">
<table width="350" bgcolor="red">
    <tr><td> </td></tr>
</table>
<form name="scroll" id="scroll">
    <input type="button" value="Scroll Right"
        onClick="scroll(50,0)" />
</form>
...</body>
```

In this example, when the button labeled "Scroll Right" is clicked, the document scrolls 50 pixels to the right from its current position. For the scrollBy method to work in the browser window, though, the window must have scroll bars, i.e., must be sized by the user such that it requires scroll bars to display.

scrollTo

The scrollTo method belongs to the window object and scrolls a document to a specified position. It has the following syntax:

```
window.scrollTo(x,y)
```

The x entry is the *x*-coordinate of the new position, and the y entry is the *y*-coordinate of the new position. The document is scrolled within the window such that *x* and *y* are the coordinates of the upper-left corner of the window. This method has the same result as the `scroll` method but is preferred over that method because it has a more descriptive name.

Example

```
<head>
<script type="text/javascript" language="javascript">
    function changeposition(x,y) {
        window.scrollTo(x,y);   }
</script>
...</head>
<body bgcolor="teal">
<table width="350" bgcolor="red">
    <tr><td> </td></tr>
</table>
<form name="scroll" id="scroll">
    <input type="button" value="Change" onClick="scroll(50,0)" />
</form>
...</body>
```

In this example, when the button labeled "Change" is clicked, the document scrolls to the position (50,0), which is 50 pixels to the right of the upper left corner of the document (0,0). For the `scrollTo` method to work in the browser window, though, the window must have scroll bars, i.e., must be sized by the user such that it requires scroll bars to display.

search

The `search` method belongs to the `string` object and searches a string for the position of the first character of a specified substring. It has the following syntax:

```
stringName.search(regExp)
```

The `stringName` is any string expression or a property of an object. The `regExp` entry is a regular expression. A *regular expression* is an object that defines a group of characters. The `search` method returns the position of the start of the first substring that matches `regExp`.

Example

```
<script type="text/javascript" language="javascript">
    function search1() {
        var myString;
        myString = "I feel cold."
        var myExp = /cold/;
        myString.search(myExp);
        alert(myString.search(myExp));   }
</script>
...
<form>
    <input type="button" name="search" value="Search"
        onclick="search1()" />
</form>
```

In this example, when the button labeled "Search" is clicked, an alert box displays with the message "7". This is the position of the first character of our search string, cold.

select

Like the focus and blur methods, the select method performs an action programmatically. It belongs to the password, text, and textarea objects. The select method selects the input area of a given password, text, or text area form object. It has the following syntax:

```
passwordName.select()
textName.select()
textareaName.select()
```

The passwordName entry is the name attribute of the password object. The textName entry is the name attribute of the text object, and textareaName is the name attribute of the textarea object.

Example

```
<script type="text/javascript" language="javascript">
    var userPass = "";
    var userName = "";
    var formulate =  new window();
    // set up the variables to be used later
    formulate.window.open();
```

```
    // open a window for the form
    document.formulate.userPass.select();
    var timer = setTimeout(
        "document.formulate.userPass.blur()", 8000);
    // select the password box
    // for 8 secs, then blur
    clearTimeout(timer);
    document.formulate.userName.select();
    timer = setTimeout(
        "document.formulate.userName.blur()", 30000);
    // clear the timeout, select the username box
    // for 30 secs, then blur
    document.formulate.userAuth.click();
    // force a selection in the userAuth check box
    clearTimeout(timer);
    msgWindow.window.close();
    // clear the timeout variable and close the window
</script>
...
<form name="formulate" id="formulate">
    <input type="password" name="userPass" size="5" />
        tell us your secret
    <input type="text" name="userName" value="Bob's your uncle"
        size="15" />
    <input type="checkbox" name="userAuth" value="Validate Me" />
        authorize us to check this stuff out!
</form>
```

setDate

The setDate method belongs to the date object and sets the day of the month for a given date. It has the following syntax:

```
dateObjectName.setDate(dayValue)
```

The dateObjectName entry is any date object or a property of an object. The dayValue is an integer between 1 and 31 or a property of an object representing the month.

Example

```
<script type="text/javascript" language="javascript">
    function callMe() {
        Xmas01 = new Date("December 25, 2001 23:15:00");
        weekday = Xmas01.getDate();
        confirm(weekday);
        var docMod = "";
        docMod.setDay(1);
        docMod.setMonth(6);
        docMod.setDate(30);
        docMod.setYear(2001);
        docMod.setTime(11, 59, 59);
        alert(docMod);
        alert("That's All Folks!");
        self.close();  }
</script>
```

The `setDate` method uses local time; for Universal Coordinated Time (UTC time), use `setUTCDate`.

setFullYear

The `setFullYear` method belongs to the `date` object and sets the year for a given date. It has the following syntax:

```
dateObjectName.setFullYear(yearValue)
```

The `dateObjectName` entry is any `date` object or a property of an object. The `year-Value` entry is a four-digit integer or a property of an object representing the year.

Example

```
var docMod = "";docMod.setDay(1);
docMod.setMonth(12);
docMod.setDate(31);
docMod.setFullYear(2001);
docMod.setTime(23, 59, 59);
alert(docMod);
alert("That's All Folks!");
```

The setFullYear method uses local time; for Universal Coordinated Time (UTC time), use setUTCFullYear.

setHours

The setHours method belongs to the date object and sets the hour of the day for a given date. It has the following syntax:

```
dateObjectName.setHours(hoursValue)
```

The dateObjectName entry is any date object or a property of an object. The hoursValue entry is an integer between 0 and 23 or a property of an object representing the hour.

Example

```
<script type="text/javascript" language="javascript">
    function callMe() {
        Xmas01 = new Date("December 25, 2001 23:15:00");
        weekday = Xmas01.getDate();
        confirm(weekday);
        var docMod = "";
        docMod.setDay(1);
        docMod.setMonth(6);
        docMod.setDate(30);
        docMod.setYear(2001);
        docMod.setHours(11);
        docMod.setMinutes(59);
        docMod.setSeconds(59);
        alert(docMod);
        alert("That's All Folks!");
        self.close();   }
</script>
```

The setHours method uses local time; for Universal Coordinated Time (UTC time), use setUTCHours.

setInterval

The setInterval method belongs to the window object and periodically executes specified code at a fixed interval. It has the following syntax:

```
window.setInterval(code,interval)
window.setInterval(function,interval,values...)
```

The code entry specifies a string of JavaScript code. The interval entry is an integer that gives the interval in milliseconds between executions of the code. The function entry is a JavaScript function, and the values entries are parameters for this function.

The setInterval method is similar to the setTimeout method. The setInterval method periodically executes code at a given interval. The setTimeout method defers the code execution for a specified interval, but does not repeatedly execute the code.

For an example of the setInterval and clearInterval methods, see the "clearInterval" section.

setMilliseconds

The setMilliseconds method belongs to the date object and sets the milliseconds of the second of the minute for a given date. It has the following syntax:

```
dateObjectName.setMilliseconds(millisecondsValue)
```

The dateObjectName entry is any date object or a property of an object. The millisecondValue entry is an integer in the range 0–999 or a property of an object representing the milliseconds.

Example

```
function callMe() {
    var docMod = "";
    docMod.setDay(1);
    docMod.setMonth(6);
    docMod.setDate(30);
    docMod.setYear(2001);
    docMod.setHours(11);
    docMod.setMinutes(59);
    docMod.setSeconds(59);
    docMod.setMilliseconds(59);
    alert(docMod);
    alert("That's All Folks!");
    self.close();  }
```

The setMilliseconds method uses local time; for Universal Coordinated Time (UTC time), use setUTCMilliseconds.

setMinutes

The setMinutes method belongs to the date object and sets the minutes of the hour for a given date. It has the following syntax:

```
dateObjectName.setMinutes(minuteValue)
```

The dateObjectName entry is any date object or a property of an object. The minuteValue entry is an integer between 0 and 59 or a property of an object representing the minute.

Example

```
<script type="text/javascript" language="javascript">
    function callMe() {
        Xmas01 = new Date("December 25, 2001 23:15:00");
        weekday = Xmas01.getDate();
        confirm(weekday);
        var docMod = "";
        docMod.setDay(1);
        docMod.setMonth(6);
        docMod.setDate(30);
        docMod.setYear(2001);
        docMod.setHours(11);
        docMod.setMinutes(59);
        docMod.setSeconds(59);
        alert(docMod);
        alert("That's All Folks!");
        self.close();  }
</script>
```

The setMinutes method uses local time; for Universal Coordinated Time (UTC time), use setUTCMinutes.

setMonth

The setMonth method belongs to the date object and sets the month of the year for a given date. It has the following syntax:

```
dateObjectName.setMonth(monthValue)
```

The dateObjectName entry is any date object or a property of an object. The month-Value is an integer between 0 and 11 or a property of an object representing the month. It has the following syntax:

Example

```
<script type="text/javascript" language="javascript">
    function callMe() {
        Xmas01 = new Date("December 25, 2001 23:15:00");
        weekday = Xmas01.getDate();
        confirm(weekday);
        var docMod = "";
        docMod.setDay(1);
        docMod.setMonth(6);
        docMod.setDate(30);
        docMod.setYear(2001);
        docMod.setHours(11);
        docMod.setMinutes(59);
        docMod.setSeconds(59);
        alert(docMod);
        alert("That's All Folks!");
        self.close();  }
</script>
```

The setMonth method uses local time; for Universal Coordinated Time (UTC time), use setUTCMonth.

setSeconds

The setSeconds method belongs to the date object and sets the seconds of the minute for a given date. It has the following syntax:

```
dateObjectName.setSeconds(secondsValue)
```

The dateObjectName entry is any date object or a property of an object. The seconds-Value entry is an integer between 0 and 59 or a property of an object representing the seconds.

Example

```
<script type="text/javascript" language="javascript">
    function callMe() {
```

1106   MASTER'S REFERENCE · PART 3

Scripting Reference

```
            Xmas01 = new Date("December 25, 2001 23:15:00");
            weekday = Xmas01.getDate();
            confirm(weekday);
            var docMod = "";
            docMod.setDay(1);
            docMod.setMonth(6);
            docMod.setDate(30);
            docMod.setYear(2001);
            docMod.setHours(11);
            docMod.setMinutes(59);
            docMod.setSeconds(59);
            alert(docMod);
            alert("That's All Folks!");
            self.close();   }
    </script>
```

The setSeconds method uses local time; for Universal Coordinated Time (UTC time), use setUTCSeconds.

setTime

The setTime method belongs to the date object and sets the number of milliseconds since January 1, 1970 00:00:00. It has the following syntax:

```
dateObjectName.setTime(timeValue)
```

The dateObjectName entry is any date object or a property of an object. The timeValue entry is an integer or a property of an object representing the number of milliseconds since the epoch.

Example

```
<script type="text/javascript" language="javascript">
    function callMe() {
        Xmas01 = new Date("December 25, 2001 23:15:00");
        weekday = Xmas01.getDate();
        confirm(weekday);
        var docMod = "";
        docMod.setDay(1);
        docMod.setMonth(6);
        docMod.setDate(30);
```

```
            docMod.setYear(2001);
            docMod.setTime(11, 59, 59);
            alert(docMod);
            alert("That's All Folks!");
            self.close();  }
    </script>
```

setTimeout

The setTimeout method belongs to the frame and window objects and evaluates an expression after the set number of milliseconds have past. It has the following syntax:

```
    timeoutID = setTimeout(expression, msec)
```

The timeoutID entry is the identifier for the timeout variable; it's used later by the clearTimeout method. The expression entry is a string or a property of an object. The msec entry is a numeric value, a numeric string, or an object property representing the number of millisecond units for the timeout.

For an example of the setTimeout and the clearTimeout methods, see the "clearTimeout" section.

setYear

The setYear method belongs to the date object and sets the year for a given date. It has the following syntax:

```
    dateObjectName.setYear(yearValue)
```

The dateObjectName entry is any date object or a property of an object. The yearValue entry is a four-digit integer or a property of an object representing the year.

The setYear method is deprecated in JavaScript 1.2 in favor of the setFullYear method.

Example

```
    <script type="text/javascript" language="javascript">
        function callMe() {
            Xmas01 = new Date("December 25, 2001 23:15:00");
            weekday = Xmas01.getDate();
            confirm(weekday);
            var docMod = "";
            docMod.setDay(1);
            docMod.setMonth(6);
```

```
            docMod.setDate(30);
            docMod.setYear(2001);
            docMod.setTime(11, 59, 59);
            alert(docMod);
            alert("That's All Folks!");
            self.close();  }
    </script>
```

sin

The sin method belongs to the Math object and returns the sine of the given number. It has the following syntax:

```
Math.sin(number)
```

The number entry is any numeric expression or a property of an object.

Example

```
<script type="text/javascript" language="javascript">
    function tryMe(baseVal) {
        var baseVal = Math.random();
        showMe = window.open("");
        with (Math) {
            showMe.document.write(sin(random()) + "<br />");
            showMe.alert("Close \'er up now, skip?");
            showMe.close();  }  }
</script>
```

slice

The slice method belongs to the string object and extracts a slice, or substring, from a string. It has the following syntax:

```
stringName.slice(index1, index2)
```

The stringName entry is any string expression or a property of an object. The index1 entry is an integer representing the starting position of the substring within the string; this can be any integer from zero to stringName.length-1. The index2 entry is an integer representing the ending position of the substring within the string; this can be any integer larger than index1 from zero to stringName.length-1. If index1 or index2 are negative numbers, the position is measured from the end of the string. The slice method returns a substring containing all the characters from and including the character at index1, and up to but *not* including the character at index2.

Example

```
<script type="text/javascript" language="javascript">
    function slice1(){
        var myString;
        myString = "JavaScriptReference"
        myString = myString.slice(0,10);
        alert([myString]);  }
</script>
...
<form>
    <input type="button" name="slice" value="Slice"
        onclick="slice1()" />
</form>
```

In this example, when the button labeled "Slice" is clicked, an alert box displays with the message "JavaScript". This is the array myString, created by slicing the string myString from character 0 up to but not including character 10.

small

The small method belongs to the string object and displays the associated string using a smaller font, as if the text were tagged with a small element. It has the following syntax:

```
stringName.small()
```

The stringName entry is any string expression or a property of an object.

Example

```
<script type="text/javascript" language="javascript">
    var welcome = "Welcome to our flashy new digs!";
    confirm(welcome);
    // This opens a small box with the text and an OK button.
    document.write(welcome.small() + "<br />");
    alert("That's All Folks!");
```

```
        self.close();
    </script>
```

split

The `split` method belongs to the `string` object and breaks a string into substrings. It has the following syntax:

```
stringName.split(boundary)
```

The `stringName` entry is any string expression or a property of an object. The boundary entry is the character or characters that JavaScript uses to decide where to split the string. The substrings that are created by the `split` method are put into an array created by this method.

Example

```
<script type="text/javascript" language="javascript">
    function split1(){
        var myString;
        myString = "JavaScript Reference"
        myString = myString.split("");
        alert([myString]);   }
</script>
...
<form>
    <input type="button" name="split" value="Split"
        onclick="split1()" />
</form>...
```

In this example, when the button labeled "Split" is clicked, an alert box displays the `myString` array. Because we used the empty string (`""`) as our boundary entry, the `myString` array is a set of every letter in `myString` as a separate array element.

sqrt

The `sqrt` method belongs to the `Math` object and returns the square root of the given number. It has the following syntax:

```
Math.sqrt(number)
```

The `number` is any nonnegative numeric expression or a property of an object.

Example

```
<script type="text/javascript" language="javascript">
    function tryMe(baseVal) {
        var baseVal=Math.random();
        showMe = window.open("");
        with (Math) {
            showMe.document.write(sqrt(baseVal) + "<br />");
            showMe.document.write(abs(sqrt(baseVal)) + "<br />");
            // return the square root of the number
            showMe.alert("Close \'er up now, skip?");
            showMe.close();  }  }
</script>
```

strike

The strike method belongs to the string object and displays the associated string with strikethrough. It has the following syntax:

```
stringName.strike()
```

The stringName entry is any string expression or a property of an object.

Example

```
<script type="text/javascript" language="javascript">
    var welcome = "Welcome to our flashy new digs!";
    confirm(welcome);
    // This opens a small box with the text and an OK button.
    document.write(welcome.strike() + "<br />");
    alert("That's All Folks!");
    self.close();
</script>
```

sub

The sub method belongs to the string object and displays the associated string subscripted to the rest of the text. It has the following syntax:

```
stringName.sub()
```

The stringName entry is any string expression or a property of an object.

Example

```
<script type="text/javascript" language="javascript">
    var welcome = "Welcome to our flashy new digs!";
    confirm(welcome);
    // This opens a small box with the text and an OK button.
    document.write(welcome.sub() + "<br />");
    alert("That's All Folks!");
    self.close();
</script>
```

submit

The submit method belongs to the form object and submits a form. It has the following syntax:

```
formName.submit()
```

The formName entry is the name of a form or an element in the forms array.

Example

```
<head>
<script type="text/javascript" language="javascript">
    function checkThis() {
        document.form1.submit();
        confirm("Thanks for registering");
        self.close();
    }
</script>
...</head>
<body onload="window.alert('Welcome! You can register through
    this page. For future reference, this page is ' +
    document.location)">
<form name="form1" id="form1">
    <p><input type="text" name="whoIs" value="user" size="15" />
        </p>
    <p><input type="radio" name="lesson" value="Lesson 1"
        checked="checked" onclick="takeLesson='lesson1.htm'" />
        Lesson 1: Getting Started</p>
    <p><input type="radio" name="lesson" value="Lesson 2"
        onclick="takeLesson='lesson2.htm'" />
```

```
    Lesson 2: Concepts and Operations</p>
  <p><input type="radio" name="lesson" value="Lesson 3"
    onclick="takeLesson='lesson3.htm'" />
    Lesson 3: Projects</p>
  <p><input type="reset" value="Defaults"
    name="resetToBasic" />
    <input type="submit" value="Send it in!"
    name="submit_form1" onclick="checkThis()" /></p>
  <hr />
</form>
...</body>
```

substr

The `substr` method belongs to the `string` object and returns a portion of a given string. It has the following syntax:

```
stringName.substr(index1, length)
```

The `stringName` entry is the string or an object property. The `index1` entry is an integer representing the starting position of the substring within the string; this can be any integer from zero to `stringName.length-1`. The `length` entry is an integer representing the number of characters in the substring.

Example

```
var champion="We are the champions! We are the champions!";
document.write(champion.substr(11,9));
document.write(champion.substr(13,3));
```
This example returns `champions` and `amp`.

substring

The `substring` method belongs to the `string` object and returns a portion of a given string. It has the following syntax:

```
stringName.substring(index1, index2)
```

The `stringName` entry is the string or an object property. The `index1` entry is an integer representing the starting position of the substring within the string; this can be any integer from zero to `stringName.length-1`. The `index2` entry is an integer representing the ending position of the substring within the string; this can be any integer larger than `index1` from zero to `stringName.length-1`.

Example

```
var champion="We are the champions! We are the champions!";
document.write(champion.substring(11,19));
document.write(champion.substring(13,15));
```

This example returns `champions` and `amp`. In contrast to the `slice` method, the `substring` method includes the final character specified.

sup

The `sup` method belongs to the `string` object and displays the associated string as a superscript to the surrounding text. It has the following syntax:

```
stringName.sup()
```

The `stringName` entry is any string expression or a property of an object.

Example

```
<script type="text/javascript" language="javascript">
   var super = "Superscripted Term";
   confirm(super);
   // This opens a small box with the text and an OK button.
   document.write("Here is a " + super.sup() + "<br />");
   alert("That's All Folks!");
   self.close();
</script>
```

tan

The `tan` method belongs to the `Math` object and returns the tangent of the given number. It has the following syntax:

```
Math.tan(number)
```

The `number` entry is any numeric expression or a property of an object that represents the size of an angle in radians.

Example

```
<script type="text/javascript" language="javascript">
   function updateAnswers(objAcos, objCos, objSin, objAtan,
      objTan) {
//
// This function receives information from the form below.
// The form has a series of text input boxes that result in
// the variables listed in the function call above.
// The function generates the correct value for the trig
// function and then compares the correct answer to the
// student's answer.
// If the answer is correct, the answer appears in a text box.
// If the answer is incorrect, the text Try Again! appears.
//
      var wrong = "Try Again!";
      var trueAcos = Math.acos(0.5);
      if (objAcos == trueAcos) {
         document.TrigTest.user_acos.value = objAcos; }
      else document.TrigTest.user_acos.value = wrong;

      var trueCos = Math.cos(0.5);
      if (objCos == trueCos) {
         document.TrigTest.user_cos.value = objCos; }
      else document.TrigTest.user_cos.value = wrong;

      var trueSin = Math.sin(0.5);
      if (objSin == trueSin) {
         document.TrigTest.user_sin.value = objSin; }
      else document.TrigTest.user_sin.value = wrong;

      var trueAtan = Math.atan(0.5;)
      if (objAtan == trueAtan) {
         document.TrigTest.user_atan.value = objAtan; }
      else document.TrigTest.user_atan.value = wrong;

      var trueTan = Math.tan(0.5);
      if (objTan == trueTan) {
         document.TrigTest.user_tan.value = objTan; }
      else document.TrigTest.user_tan.value = wrong;
```

```
      }
   </script>
   …
   <form name="TrigTest" id="TrigTest">
      <p><center>Find the arc cosine (in radians) of .5.</center>
         </p>
      <input type="text" name="enterArcCosine" value="0" size="10"
         onblur="updateAnswers(this,
         document.TrigTest.enterCosine.value,
         document.TrigTest.enterSine.value,
         document.TrigTest.enterArcTangent.value,
         document.TrigTest.enterTangent.value)" />
      <p><center>Find the cosine (in radians) of .5.</center></p>
      <input type="text" name="enterCosine" value="0" size="10"
         onblur="updateAnswers(
         document.TrigTest.enterArcCosine.value,
         this, document.TrigTest.enterSine.value,
         document.TrigTest.enterArcTangent.value,
         document.TrigTest.enterTangent.value)" />
      <p><center>Find the sine (in radians) of .5.</center></p>
      <input type="text" name="enterSine" value="0" size="10"
         onblur="updateAnswers(
         document.TrigTest.enterArcCosine.value,
         document.TrigTest.enterCosine.value, this,
         document.TrigTest.enterArcTangent.value,
         document.TrigTest.enterTangent.value)" />
      <p><center>Find the arc tangent (in radians) of .5.</center>
         </p>
      <input type="text" name="enterArcTangent" value="0" size="10"
         onblur="updateAnswers(
         document.TrigTest.enterArcCosine.value,
         document.TrigTest.enterCosine.value,
         document.TrigTest.enterSine.value, this,
         document.TrigTest.enterTangent.value)" />
      <p><center>Find the tangent (in radians) of .5.</center></p>
      <input type="text" name="enterTangent" value="0" size="10"
         onblur="updateAnswers(
         document.TrigTest.enterArcCosine.value,
         document.TrigTest.enterCosine.value,
         document.TrigTest.enterSine.value,
         document.TrigTest.enterArcTan.value, this)" />
      <p>Results:</p>
```

```
<p>arcCosine:<input type="text" name="user_acos" value=""
    size="10" /></p>
<p>cosine:<input type="text" name="user_cos" value=""
    size="10" /></p>
<p>sine:<input type="text" name="user_sin" value=""
    size="10" /></p>
<p>arcTangent:<input type="text" name="user_atan" value=""
    size="10" /></p>
<p>tangent:<input type="text" name="user_tan" value=""
    size="10" /></p>
</form>
```

toLocaleString

The toLocaleString method belongs to the date object and converts a date to a string, using the local conventions. It's generally more reliable to use the getMonth, getDay, and other such date methods to get the information if you plan to manipulate it at all. The toLocaleString method has the following syntax:

```
dataObjectName.toLocaleString()
```

The dateObjectName entry is any date object or a property of an object.

Example

```
function (showDate) {
    var docMod = "";
    docMod.setDay(1);
    docMod.setMonth(6);
    docMod.setDate(30);
    docMod.setYear(2001);
    docMod.setTime(11, 59, 59);
    docMod.toLocaleString();
    document.write(docMod.fontcolor("darkmagenta") + "<br />");
    docMod.toUTCString();
    document.write(docMod.fontcolor("darkmagenta") + "<br />") }
```

This converts the contents of the date variable docMod first to local time and then to UTC time before printing out each value.

Older versions of browsers support toGMTString rather than toUTCString.

toLowerCase

The toLowerCase method belongs to the string object and converts the contents of a text string to all lowercase letters. It has the following syntax:

```
stringName.toLowerCase()
```

The stringName entry is any string expression or a property of an object.

Example

```
<script type="text/javascript" language="javascript">
function upAndDown() {
    confirm(document.WhoAreYou.nameInfo.value.toUpperCase());
    confirm(document.WhoAreYou.FavFoodGroup.value.toLowerCase());
}
</script>
...
<form name="WhoAreYou" id="WhoAreYou">
    <input type="text" name="nameInfo" value="" size="30"
        maxlength="30" />
    <input type="text" name="FavFoodGroup" size="15" />
    <input type="submit" name="getGoing" value="Yumm!"
        onclick="upAndDown()" />
</form>
```

toUpperCase

The toUpperCase method belongs to the string object and converts the contents of a text string to all uppercase letters. It has the following syntax:

```
stringName.toUpperCase()
```

The stringName is any string expression or a property of an object.

Example

```
<script type="text/javascript" language="javascript">
function upAndDown() {
    confirm(document.WhoAreYou.nameInfo.value.toUpperCase());
    confirm(document.WhoAreYou.FavFoodGroup.value.toLowerCase());
}
</script>
```

```
...
<form name="WhoAreYou" id="WhoAreYou">
   <input type="text" name="nameInfo" value="" size="30"
      maxlength="30" />
   <input type="text" name="FavFoodGroup" size="15" />
   <input type="submit" name="getGoing" value="Yumm!"
      onclick="upAndDown()" />
</form>
```

toUTCString

The toUTCString method belongs to the date object and converts a date to a string, using the international UTC conventions. The exact format varies according to the user's platform. It's generally more reliable to use the getMonth, getDay, and other such date methods to get the information if you plan to manipulate it at all. The toUTCString method has the following syntax:

```
dataObjectName.toUTCString()
```

The dateObjectName is any date object or a property of an object.

Example

```
function (showDate) {
   var docMod = "";
   docMod.setDay(1);
   docMod.setMonth(6);
   docMod.setDate(30);
   docMod.setYear(2001);
   docMod.setTime(11, 59, 59);
   docMod.toLocaleString();
   document.write(docMod.fontcolor("darkmagenta") + "<br />");
   docMod.toUTCString();
   document.write(docMod.fontcolor("darkmagenta"))+ "<br />"   }
```

This converts the contents of the date variable docMod first to local time and then to UTC time before displaying each value.

Older versions of browsers support toGMTString rather than toUTCString.

unescape

Like the unescape function, the unescape function converts an ASCII value. The unescape function takes the integer or hexadecimal value of the character and returns the ASCII character. Like the escape method, it's a built-in JavaScript method, and is not a method of any object. It has the following syntax:

```
unescape("string")
```

The string entry is either an integer ("%integer") or a hexadecimal value ("xx").

UTC

The UTC method belongs to the date object and returns the number of milliseconds between the contents of a date object and the epoch (January 1, 1970 00:00:00, Universal Coordinated Time [GMT]). It has the following syntax:

```
Date.UTC(year, month, day[, hrs][, min][, sec] )
```

The year entry is a two-digit or four-digit representation of a year (2000–2999). The month entry is a number between zero (January) and 11 (December) representing the month of the year. The day entry is a number between 1 and 31 representing the day of the month. The hrs entry is a two-digit number between 0 (midnight) and 23 (11 P.M.) representing the hour of the day. The min entry is a two-digit number between 0 and 59 representing the minute of the hour, and sec is a two-digit number between 0 and 59 representing the seconds.

Example

```
var myDate = new Date(Date.UTC(2001, 7, 1, 7, 30, 0));
```

In this example, you create a new date object using a UTC specification. The UTC string for our date (August 1, 2001 7:30 A.M.) is 1 Aug 2001 07:30:00 UTC (if our time zone is UTC zone 0, or London/Greenwich—otherwise, a time zone offset will convert the UTC time for our time zone). The value of our variable, myDate, will be the number of milliseconds from January 1, 1970 to our date and time.

valueOf

The valueOf method belongs to the date object and returns the time (number of milliseconds since January 1, 1970 00:00:00) for the given date. It has the following syntax:

```
dateObjectName.valueOf()
```

The dateObjectName entry is any date object or a property of an object. The value returned is the same as that returned by the getTime method of the date object.

Example

```
<script type="text/javascript" language="javascript">
    function callMe() {
        Xmas01 = new Date("December 25, 2001 23:15:00");
        weekday = Xmas01.valueOf();
        confirm(weekday);
        var docMod = document.lastModified;
        alert(docMod);
        chrono = new Date();
        alert(chrono.getHours());
        alert(chrono + " already?!");
        alert("That's All Folks!");
        self.close();  }
</script>
```

write

The write method belongs to the document object and sends expressions to the document as encoded HTML strings. It has the following syntax:

```
write(expression1 [, expression2] [..., expressionN])
```

The expression1 through expressionN entries are any JavaScript expression or a property of an object.

Example

```
<script type="text/javascript" language="javascript">
    var welcome = "Welcome to our flashy new digs!";
    confirm(welcome);
    // This opens a small box with the text and an OK button.
    document.write(welcome.small() + "<br />");
    document.write(welcome.big()+ "<br />");
    document.write(welcome.blink()+ "<br />");
    document.write(welcome.bold()+ "<br />");
    document.write("<br />")
    document.write(welcome.fixed()+ "<br />");
    // These write out the contents of welcome using
    // various text attributes.
</script>
```

writeln

Like the `write` method, the `writeln` method belongs to the `document` object and sends expressions to the document as encoded HTML strings. The `writeln` method generates a newline character (hard return) at the end of the written string. XHTML ignores the newline character except within elements such as `pre`. The `writeln` method has the following syntax:

```
writeln(expression1 [, expression2] […, expressionN])
```

The `expression1` through `expressionN` entries are any JavaScript expression or a property of an object.

Example

```
<script type="text/javascript" language="javascript">
    var welcome = "Welcome to our flashy new digs!";
    confirm(welcome);
    // This opens a small box with the text and an OK button.
    document.writeln(welcome.small());
    document.writeln(welcome.big());
    document.writeln(welcome.blink());
    document.writeln(welcome.bold());
    document.writeln(welcome.fixed() + "<br />");
    // These write out the contents of welcome using
    // various text attributes.
</script>
```

Event Handlers

When users interact with your Web page through JavaScript scripts, you need event handlers to recognize the event and communicate back to your script. Event handlers help manage the interaction between your users and your JavaScript objects by providing the information in the user response to the JavaScript for later use.

This section is an alphabetic listing of the available JavaScript event handlers. Each entry describes a single event handler, includes examples, and identifies the objects for which the event handler works. The syntax for these event handlers can be seen in the corresponding object listings.

onblur

A blur occurs when the focus moves from one object to another on the page. The object that was in focus loses focus and is blurred. The onblur event handler works for the select, text, and textarea objects.

Example

```
onblur="document.login.submit()";
```

When the user leaves the field, the system submits the information for logging into the next page.

onchange

A change occurs when the user alters the contents of an object and then moves the focus from the object. The object is changed. Use the onchange event handler to validate the information submitted by users. The onchange event handler works for the select, text, and textarea objects.

Example

```
onchange="testName(this.value)";
```

This example sends the contents of the field to the testName function when the user changes information and leaves the field.

onclick

A click occurs when the user clicks an object on the page with the mouse. This event could lead to a selection or a change or could launch a piece of JavaScript code.

The onclick event handler works for the document, button, checkbox, radio, link, reset, and submit objects. It has been updated to *not* act if the event handler returns false when it's employed by a checkbox, radio, submit, or reset object.

Example

```
onclick="compute(this.form)";
```

When the user clicks the object, the script runs the compute function and sends the form contents.

ondblclick

A double-click occurs when the user clicks twice very quickly on an object on the page.

This event handler was introduced in JavaScript 1.2, so it will not work with versions of Netscape Navigator 3 or earlier or with Internet Explorer 3 or earlier. The ondblclick event handler is not implemented in the Macintosh versions of the Netscape Navigator browser. It works for the document, area (in an image map), and link objects.

Example

```
<a href="seeMyFamily.html" ondblclick="this.href =
'theFastTour'">
```

This example loads a different page if the user double-clicks a link.

ondragdrop

A drag-and-drop occurs when the user drops an object, such as a file, onto the browser window.

Note that this event was introduced in JavaScript 1.2, so it will not work with versions of Netscape Navigator 3 or earlier or with Internet Explorer 3 or earlier. The ondragdrop event handler works for the window object.

Example

```
ondragdrop="send(newInfo)";
```

This passes the dropped object to a function called send. This could be preformatted data that the user can mail to you by dropping the file onto the Web page.

onfocus

The focus on a page is selected when the user either tabs or clicks a field or an object on the page. Selecting within a field does not create a focus event; rather, it generates a select event. The onfocus event handler works for the select, text, and textarea objects.

Example

```
onfocus="msgWindow.document.write('Tell me what you want!')";
```

When the user clicks in the field object, the script writes out the phrase "Tell me what you want!"

onkeydown

A key down occurs as the user presses a keyboard key. This event precedes the keyPress event.

This event was introduced in JavaScript 1.2, so it will not work with versions of Netscape Navigator 3 or earlier or with Internet Explorer 3 or earlier. The onkeydown event handler works for the document, image, link, and textarea objects.

Example

```
onkeydown="msgWindow.document.write('Tell me what you want!')";
```

When the user presses the key, the script writes out the phrase "Tell me what you want!"

onkeypress

A key press occurs when the user presses or holds a keyboard key. You can use this in combination with fromCharCode and charCodeAt methods to determine which key was pressed. This is useful for operations where you prompt the user to type **Y** for yes and any other key for no.

The onkeypress event handler works for the document, image, link, and textarea objects. This event was introduced in JavaScript 1.2, so it will not work with versions of Netscape Navigator 3 or earlier or with Internet Explorer 3 or earlier.

Example

```
onkeypress="msgWindow.document.write('Tell me what you want!')";
```

When the user presses the key, the script writes out the phrase "Tell me what you want!"

onkeyup

A key up occurs when the user releases the keyboard key. You can use this to clear the results of the onkeypress or onkeydown event handlers.

The onkeyup event handler works for the document, image, link, and textarea objects. This event was introduced in JavaScript 1.2, so it will not work with versions of Netscape Navigator 3 or earlier or with Internet Explorer 3 or earlier.

Example

```
onkeyup="msgWindow.document.write('Tell me what you want!')";
```

When the user releases the key, the script writes out the phrase "Tell me what you want!"

onload

A load event occurs when the browser receives all the page information, including framesets, and displays it. Locate the onload event handler inside the body or frameset elements. The onload event handler works for the window object.

Example

```
<body onload="window.alert('Current as of ' +
    document.lastModified + '!')">
```

This example opens an alert window after the page is loaded and displays a message that includes the lastModified property. This gives the user the document's modification date.

onmousedown

A mouse button down occurs when the user presses one of the mouse buttons. You can use the event properties to determine which button was pressed.

The onmousedown event handler works for the button, document, and link objects. This event was introduced in JavaScript 1.2, so it will not work with versions of Netscape Navigator 3 or earlier or with Internet Explorer 3 or earlier.

Example

```
onmousedown="msgWindow.document.write
    ('Tell me what you want!')";
```

When the user moves the mouse button down, the script writes out the phrase "Tell me what you want!"

onmousemove

A mouse movement occurs when the user moves the mouse over any point on the page. This is not an event handler that works for any particular object, but can be invoked if an object requests the event. This event was introduced in JavaScript 1.2, so it will not work with versions of Netscape Navigator 3 or earlier or with Internet Explorer 3 or earlier.

Example

```
onmousemove="msgWindow.document.write
   ('Tell me what you want!')";
```

When the user moves the mouse, the script writes out the phrase "Tell me what you want!"

onmouseout

An onmouseout event occurs when the user moves the mouse point off an object on the page. This event handler defines what should happen when the user removes the mouse from an object such as a link.

This event was introduced in JavaScript 1.2, so it will not work with versions of Netscape Navigator 3 or earlier or with Internet Explorer 3 or earlier. The onmouseout event handler works for the area, layer, and link objects.

Example

```
<a href="myFamily.html" onmouseout="alert
   ('Hey, we've got great pics down this way, come back!')">
Meet My Family</a>
```

When the user's mouse passes off the Meet My Family link, an alert box appears with the message "Hey, we've got great pics down this way, come back!"

onmouseover

An onmouseOver event occurs when the user passes the mouse pointer over an object on the page. You must return True within the event handler if you want to set the status or defaultStatus properties.

The onmouseover event handler works for the area, layer, and link objects. The area object is a type of link object which defines an area of an image as an image map. The layer object is part of the document object's layers array property, and is referenced by id or index value.

Example

```
onmouseover="window.status="Come on in!"; return true";
```

When the user's mouse pointer passes over the object, the message "Come on in!" appears in the status line. You can also change the image in place, highlighting image links on the page.

```
<a href="intropage.html"
   onmouseover="document.pic1.src='images/jumpwild.jpg'"
   onmouseout="document.pic1.src='images/jump.jpg'"
   onclick="return true"></a>
```

In this example, the page displays the image jump.jpg, which is linked to the XHTML page intropage. When the user passes the mouse pointer over the image but does not click, the image changes to jumpwild.jpg. When the user clicks the image to jump, the return value of True is set by the onclick event handler before the jump is made.

onmouseup

A mouse button up event occurs when the user releases the mouse button. This event was introduced in JavaScript 1.2, so it will not work with versions of Netscape Navigator 3 or earlier or with Internet Explorer 3 or earlier. The onmouseup event handler works for the button, document, and link objects.

Example

```
<a href="myFamily.html" onmouseup="alert
   ('Hey, we've got great pics down this way, come back!')">
Meet My Family</a>
```

When the user's mouse button moves back up while over the Meet My Family link, an alert box appears with the message "Hey, we've got great pics down this way, come back!"

onmove

A move occurs when the user or a browser-driven script moves a window or a frame.

This event was introduced in JavaScript 1.2, so it will not work with versions of Netscape Navigator 3 or earlier or with Internet Explorer 3 or earlier. The onmove event handler works for the window and frame objects.

Example

```
onmove="window.status='Come on in!'";
```

When the window moves, the message "Come on in!" appears in the status line.

onselect

A select event occurs when the user highlights text inside a text or textarea field (the onselect event handler works for the text and textarea objects).

Example

```
onselect="document.bgColor=blue";
```

The background color of the document changes to blue when the user selects text from the field.

onresize

A resize occurs when the user or a browser-driven script changes the size of the window or frame.

This event was introduced in JavaScript 1.2, so it will not work with versions of Netscape Navigator 3 or earlier or with Internet Explorer 3 or earlier. The onresize event handler works for the window and frame objects.

Example

```
onresize="window.status='Stop that!'";
```

When the window is resized, the message "Stop that!" appears in the status line.

onreset

Use the onreset event handler to act when the form is reset; it works for the form object.

Example

```
<body>
<form name="form1" id="form1"
    onreset="alert('Please try again!')" … >
    <input type="text" name="newInTown" value="" size="100"
        maxlength="25" />
    <input type="Reset" name="Reset" value="Reset" />
</form>
```

This example prints a "Please try again!" alert box when the user resets the form.

onsubmit

When the document is one or more forms, use the onsubmit event handler to validate the contents of the form. This event handler works for the form object.

Example

```
<script type="text/javascript" language="javascript">
    function hotelGuys (checksOut) {
        if (checksOut == "false") {
            alert("Please fill in all fields.");  }
        else {
            document.forms[0].submit();
            alert("We came here Jasper");  }  }
</script>
…
<form name="form1" id="form1"
    onsubmit="hotelGuys(checksOut = 'true')">
    <input type="text" name="newInTown" value="" size="100"
        maxlength="25" />
    <input type="submit" name="register" value="" />
</form>
```

This example uses an if/else statement either to request more information from the user or to submit the form. Normally, you wouldn't set the state in the call. You would call another function that would test the entries, and that function would then call hotelGuys.

onunload

Like the load event, the unload event occurs when the browser leaves a page. One good use for the onunload event handler is to clear any function variables you may have set into motion with the onload or other event handlers. The onunload event handler works for the window object.

Example

```
<body onload="CountOn(4)" onunload="ClearCount()">...</body>
```

A counter starts when the page begins loading. You can use this to display a splash screen for a limited time. When the user leaves the page, the counter is reset to zero by the ClearCount function.

Properties

Properties affect objects. Unlike methods and functions, which do something within an object, properties assign attributes, such as appearance or size.

This section is an alphabetic listing of the JavaScript properties. Each entry describes a single property, includes syntax information and (typically) examples, and identifies which object the property affects.

action

The action property is part of the form object and contains the URL to which the form is submitted. You can set this property at any time. It has the following syntax:

```
formName.action=formActionText
```

The formName entry is either the form or an element from the forms array.

Example

```
document.lesson3.action=http://www.example.com/L3results.htm
```

This example loads the URL http://www.example.com/L3results.htm into the action property for the form lesson3.

alinkColor

The alinkColor property is part of the document object and sets the color for an active link. Once the layout of the XHTML code is complete, this becomes a read-only property of the document object, so you cannot change the alinkColor property. The color is expressed in RGB hexadecimal (three sets of double hex digits) or as one of the color keywords. Place the code that sets this property before the body element, and do not use the alink attribute in the body element. The alinkColor property has the following syntax:

```
document.alinkColor="colorLiteral"
document.alinkColor="colorRGB"
```

Example

```
document.alinkColor="green"
document.alinkColor="008000"
```

The two statements are equivalent. The first statement sets the alinkColor using the keyword green, which is 008000 in hex.

anchors

The anchors property is part of the anchor object and is the array of objects listing the named anchors in the source. The array lists the anchors in the order in which they appear in the document. The anchors property has the following syntax:

```
document.anchors[index]
document.anchors.length
```

The index entry is an integer that represents the anchor's position in the list; length returns the number of items in the array.

Example

```
var visitor = document.anchors.length;
document.write("There are " + visitor +
    " links to other pages… can you visit them all?");
```

The script stores the number of anchors in the variable visitor and uses that in a statement written out for the user.

appCodeName

The appCodeName property is a read-only part of the navigator object. It has the following syntax:

```
navigator.appCodeName
```

Example

```
var whoAreYou = navigator.appCodeName;
if(whoAreYou = "Mozilla") {
    document.write("Good job, carry on!");  }
```

This example gets the code name of the browser and, if it's Mozilla, writes a note to the user.

appName

The appName property is a read-only part of the navigator object. It has the following syntax:

```
navigator.appName
```

Example

```
var whoAreYou = navigator.appName;
document.write("Hey! Good thing you're using " +
    whoAreYou + "!");
```

This example puts the application name into the variable whoAreYou and includes it in a statement displayed for the user.

appVersion

The appVersion property is a read-only part of the navigator object. It has the following syntax:

```
navigator.appVersion
```

The version is in the following format:

```
releaseNumber (platform; country)
```

Example

```
document.write("You're checking us out with " +
    navigator.appVersion + ".");
```

This statement displays a result similar to this:

```
You're checking us out with 2.0 (Win95, I).
```

bgColor

The bgColor property is part of the document object and reflects the bgcolor attribute of the body element, but can be changed at any time. The default for bgColor is in the user's browser preferences. The bgColor property has the following syntax:

```
document.bgColor="colorLiteral"
document.bgColor="colorRGB"
```

Example

```
document.bgColor="darkblue"
document.bgColor="00008B"
```

These statements are equivalent. Both set the background color to dark blue—one through the keyword, and the other through the hex value for the color.

checked

The checked property is a Boolean value representing the state of a radio or checkbox object. True or 1 is checked; false or 0 is cleared. The checked property has the following syntax:

```
checkboxName.checked
radioName[index].checked
```

The checkboxName entry is the name attribute of a checkbox object. The radioName entry is the name attribute of a radio object. The index entry represents the radio button with the radio object.

Example

```
<input type="radio" name="courseOption1" value="courseOption"
    checked="checked" onclick="techComm.checked = '1'" />
```

This example sets the checkbox for the techComm value of courseOption1 to checked when the user selects the courseOption1 radio button.

cookie

A cookie is information stored by the browser. The cookie property is part of a document object that you can read using the substring, charAt, indexOf, and lastIndexOf methods. You can also write information to a cookie. The cookie property has the following syntax:

```
document.cookie
```

Example

```
document.cookie="expires in " + counter + " days";
```

This example assigns the string that reads "expires in *n* days"; *n* is the number of days remaining and is set with counter.

defaultChecked

The defaultChecked property is part of the checkbox and radio objects. It indicates the default state (checked or not checked) of a checkbox or a radio button. You can read or set the property at any time. The defaultChecked property has the following syntax:

```
checkboxName.defaultChecked
radioName.[index].defaultChecked
```

Example

```
document.chartForm.dataFocus[i].defaultChecked = true;
```

The statement sets the radio button at position i in the array to the default for the dataFocus group of buttons.

defaultSelected

This property is similar to the defaultChecked property; it indicates whether the option in a select object is the default selection. Only multiple select objects can

1136   **MASTER'S REFERENCE · PART 3**

Scripting Reference

have more than a single item selected. The defaultSelected property is part of the options array and has the following syntax:

```
selectName.options[index].defaultSelected
```

The selectName entry refers to the select object either by the name attribute or as an element within an array. The index entry is an integer representing an option in a select object.

Example

```
<script type="text/javascript" language="javascript">
function backAgain () {
   alert(document.javajive.lessonList.length);
   for (var a = 0; a < document.javajive.lessonList.length;
      a++) {
      if (document.javajive.lessonList.options[a].
         defaultSelected == true) {
         document.javajive.lessonList.options[a].selected=true;
      } } }
</script>
...
<form name="javajive" id="javajive" onsubmit="backAgain ()">
   <select name="lessonList">
      <option selected="selected">Introduction</option>
      <option>Installation</option>
      <option>Setting up an account</option>
      <option>Creating a document</option>
      <option>Filing a document</option>
      <option>Recovering a filed document</option>
      <option>Sending a document to the printer</option>
   </select>
   <input type="submit" name="getchathere" value="Submit" />
</form>
```

In this example, the form contains a list of chapters in a book, from which the user can select a single item. The backAgain function cycles through the list of options to find which ones should be selected by default and resets the default.

defaultStatus

This property is part of the window object and contains the default message displayed in the status bar. You can set the defaultStatus property at any time. If you plan to use the status bar for an onmouseOver event handler statement, you must return True. The defaultStatus property has the following syntax:

```
windowReference.defaultStatus
```

The windowReference entry is one of the available window identifiers (such as self).

Example

```
window.defaultStatus="Finish the modules in less than a week!";
```

The default contents for the status bar display are set to a phrase that complements the purpose of the site.

defaultValue

This property is part of the hidden, password, text, and textarea objects. It contains the default information for a password, text, or text area object. If the object is a password, the initial value is null, regardless of the defaultValue. For a text object, the defaultValue reflects the value attribute. For textarea objects, it's the contents of the object found between the textarea tags.

If you set defaultValue through a script, it overrides the initial value. The immediate display value of the object is not changed when you change the defaultValue through your script; if you later run a function that resets the defaults, your change appears.

The defaultValue property has the following syntax:
```
passwordName.defaultValue
textName.defaultValue
textareaName.defaultValue
```

Example

```
document.javajive.lessonLeader.defaultValue="E. E. Cummings";
...
<input type="reset" name="resetScoreCard"
   value="Reset the Scores" />
```

A line in your script changes the default value of the `lessonLeader text` object, and later in the script, the default values are reset. When this second line is executed, the contents of the `lessonLeader` text object is updated with "E. E. Cummings".

E

This read-only `Math` property is approximately 2.718, which is Euler's constant, the base of natural logarithms. It's part of the `Math` object and has the following syntax:

```
Math.E
```

Example

```
document.write("The base of natural logarithms is Euler's
    constant, which is: " + Math.E);
```

This statement displays the phrase followed by the value stored in the E property.

elements

The `elements` property is an array of the items in a form such as `checkbox`, `radio`, and `text` objects. These items are listed in the array in the order in which they occur. It has the following syntax:

```
document.form.elements[indexentry]
document.form.elements.length
document.forms[indexentry].elements[indexentry]
```

`form` is a form object, `elements` is the array of items contained in the form, and `forms` is the array of all forms on the page. The `indexentry` is an integer representing the position of an element within an array, or the name of an array element.

Example

```
var button1 = document.forms['form1'].elements['goNow'];
```

In this example, a variable named `button1` has been created to represent the button named goNow in the form named form1. If form1 is the first form on the page, and goNow is the third element in the form, the code could also be written as:

```
var button1 = document.forms[0].elements[2];
```

encoding

The encoding property is part of the form object and contains the MIME-encoding format information for the form. You can set the encoding property at any time; the initial value is the enctype attribute of the form element. The various encoding types may require specific values; check the specifications for the encoding type. The encoding property has the following syntax:

    formName.encoding

Example

    function formEncode() { return document.javajive.encoding; }

The formEncode function gets the MIME-encoding information from the form.

fgColor

This property is part of the document object and specifies the foreground color of the text. You can express the color using one of the color keywords or the hexadecimal RGB value. This property uses the browser preference settings as its initial value. You can change this value by either setting the color attribute of the font element or by using the fontcolor method. The fgColor property has the following syntax:

    document.fgColor

Example

    document.fgColor="darkred";
    document.fgColor="8B0000";

These two statements are equivalent. The first uses the color keyword, and the second uses the hexadecimal RGB value for the same color.

forms

The forms property is an array that lists the objects in a form, in the order in which they occur in the code.

frames

The frames property is an array that lists the child frames within a frame.

hash

The hash property is part of the URL, and it identifies an anchor on the destination page. It's part of the link and location objects and has the following syntax:

```
location.hash
```

(See the examples for the anchor object and the href property.)

host

The host property is part of the URL and it identifies the hostname:port for the page. This property is a concatenation of the hostname and port properties. You can set the host property; it's better to set the href property, however, if you want to change a location. The host property is part of the link and location objects and has the following syntax:

```
links[index].host
location.host
```

(See the examples for the link and location objects.)

hostname

The hostname property is part of the URL and identifies the host server by its DNS or IP address. If the port property is null, the hostname and host properties are the same. The hostname property is part of the link and location objects and has the following syntax:

```
links[index].hostname
location.hostname
```

(See the examples for the link and location objects.)

href

The href property is part of the link and location objects and contains the full URL. The protocol, host, port, pathname, search, and hash properties are substrings within the href property, which has the following syntax:

```
links[index].href location.href
```

Example

```
<script type="text/javascript" language="javascript">
var question1="false";
var question2="false";
var question3="false";
var question4="false";
var question5="false";
var question6="false";
var question7="false";
function roundTheClock() {
    for (var x = 0; x < 6; x++) {
        switch(x) {
            case(1): if (question1 != "true") {
              win1 = new window.open (answer1.location.href); }
              break;
            case(2): if (question2 != "true") {
              win2 = new window.open (answer2.location.href); }
              break;
            case(3): if (question3 != "true") {
              win3 = new window.open (answer3.location.href); }
              break;
            case(4): if (question4 != "true") {
              win4 = new window.open (answer4.location.href); }
              break;
            case(5): if (question5 != "true") {
              win5 = new window.open (answer5.location.href); }
              break;
            case(6): if (question6 != "true") {
              win6 = new window.open (answer6.location.href); }
              break;
            case(7): if (question7 != "true") {
              win7 = new window.open (answer7.location.href); }
              break;  }  }  }
</script>
```

In this example, the loop opens a series of windows with the answers to questions that the user answered incorrectly.

index

The index property is part of the options array. It's an integer value that gives the position of an object within the options array of a select object. The index property has the following syntax:

```
selectName.options[indexValue].index
```

The selectName entry is the name of the select object or element in the elements array. The indexValue entry is an integer representing the option in a select object.

Example

```
for (var x = 0; x < document.jivejingle.courseSelect.length;
    x++) {
document.write(
    document.jivejingle.courseSelect.options[x].index);   }
```

This example displays the contents of the list of courseSelect.

Infinity

The Infinity property (primitive value) represents a positive infinite value.

lastModified

The lastModified property is part of the document object. It's a read-only date string indicating when the document was last changed or updated and has the following syntax:

```
document.lastModified
```

Example

```
<script type="text/javascript" language="javascript">
document.write(
    "Welcome, this course description is current as of " +
    document.lastModified);
</script>
```

This script keeps the date current without manual intervention.

length

The `length` property works with objects and arrays; you can use it to get the number of elements within the object or array. It has the following syntax:

Statement	Returns the Number Of
`formName.length`	Elements on a form
`frameReference.length`	Frames within a frame
`history.length`	Entries in the `history` object
`radioName.length`	Buttons within a `radio` object
`select.Name.length`	Objects in a `select` list object
`stringName.length`	Character spaces in a `string`
`windowReference.length`	Frames in a parent window
`anchors.length`	Entries in the stated array
`elements.length`	Entries in the stated array
`forms.length`	Entries in the stated array
`frameReference.frames.length`	Entries in the stated array
`windowReference.frames.length`	Entries in the stated array
`links.length`	Entries in the stated array
`selectName.options.length`	Entries in the stated array

The `length` property is found in the following objects and arrays:

Objects	Arrays
frame	anchors
history	elements
radio	forms
select	frames
string	links
window	options

Example

```
var visitor = document.anchors.length document.write(
    "There are " + visitor +
    " links to other pages… can you visit them all?");
```

In this example, the script stores the number of anchors in the variable `visitor` and uses that in a statement displayed to the user.

linkColor

The `linkColor` property is part of the `document` object. It contains the setting for the inactive and unused links in a document. This property reflects the setting in the body element of a document. After the layout, this is a read-only property. To set this property in a script, place the code before the body element, and do not use the `link` attribute in the body element. The `linkColor` property has the following syntax:

```
document.linkColor
```

Example

```
document.write("The " + document.linkColor +
    " jumps are places you've never been!");
```

This statement displays the link color for the user.

links

The `links` property is an array of document links listed in source order.

LN2

The LN2 property is part of the built-in `Math` object. It's a read-only constant that represents the natural logarithm of two (approximately 0.693) and has the following syntax:

```
Math.LN2
```

Example

```
document.write("Bob says your chances of winning are: " +
    longShot + " in " + longShot / Math.LN2 + ".");
```

This example computes a value and displays the results in a statement for the user.

LN10

The LN10 property is part of the built-in Math object. It's a read-only constant that represents the natural logarithm of 10 (approximately 2.302) and has the following syntax:

```
Math.LN10
```

Example

```
document.write("Bob says your chances of winning are: " +
    longShot + " in " + longShot * Math.LN10 + ".");
```

This example computes a value and displays the results in a statement for the user.

location

The location property is part of the document object. It contains the complete URL of the document. Unlike the location object, you cannot change the document's location property. The location property has the following syntax:

```
document.location
```

Example

```
<script type="text/javascript" language="javascript">
    var there="http://www.example.com/";
    var takeLesson="";
    function weAre() {
        self.status = 'Welcome, this is ' + document.location +
        '. Our site is NEVER done!';   }
    function checkThis() { alert("Thanks for registering"); }
</script>
...<body onload="window.alert('Welcome!'); weAre()">...</body>
```

This displays a notice to the user, including the document's location, in the status line of the window.

LOG2E

The LOG2E property is part of the built-in Math object. It's a read-only constant that represents the base 2 logarithm of E (approximately 1.442). It has the following syntax:

```
Math.LOG2E
```

Example

```
document.write("Bob says your chances of winning are: " +
    longShot + " in " + longShot * Math.LOG2E + ".");
```

This example computes a value and displays the results in a statement for the user.

LOG10E

The LOG10E property is part of the built-in Math object. It's a read-only constant that represents the base 10 logarithm of E (approximately 0.434). It has the following syntax:

```
Math.LOG10E
```

Example

```
document.write("Bob says your chances of winning are: " +
    longShot + " in " + longShot / Math.LOG10E + ".");
```

This example computes a value and displays the results in a statement for the user.

method

The method property is part of the form object. It indicates how a form is sent to the server when it's submitted. This reflects the contents of the method attribute of the form element. This property contains either get or post. You can set this property at any time. The method property has the following syntax:

```
formName.method
```

Example

```
if (document.javajive.method == "get") {
    document.write("The server will get your answers now."); }
else {
    document.write(
        "Your answers will be posted to the server now."); }
```

This example displays different text depending on the method.

name

This property is used to identify the objects and elements contained by a number of objects and arrays. For window objects, this is a read-only property; you can set the name of other objects.

In a window object, the name reflects the windowName attribute. In other objects, it reflects the name attribute. The name property is the same for all radio buttons in a radio object.

The name property differs from the label used for the button, reset, and submit objects. The name property is not displayed; it's an internal, programmatic reference.

If a frame object contains several elements or objects with the same name, the browser creates an array using the name and listing the objects as they occur in the frame source.

The name property has the following syntax for window objects:

```
windowReference.name
window.Reference.frames.name
```

The name property has the following syntax for other objects:

```
objectName.name
frameReference.name
frameReference.frames.name
radioName[index].name
selectName.options.name
```

For a select object, objectName.name and selectName.options.name produce the same result. For a frame object, objectName.name, frameReference.name, and frameReference.frames.name produce the same result.

Example

```
newWindow = window.open("http://www.webwonders.net/test1.htm");
function whatYouBuilt () {
   for (var counter = 0, counter < document.elements.length,
      counter++) {
      msgWindow.document.write(
         document.sample.elements[counter].name + "<br />");
   }  }
```

In this example, the function loops through the loaded document and displays a list of the elements.

The name property is found in the options array and in the following objects:

button	hidden	reset text
checkbox	password	select textarea
frame	radio	submit window

NaN

The NaN property determines whether the value given is a number. Use the isNaN method to check the (Boolean) value of NaN.

options

The options property is an array that contains a list of the options in a select object.

parent

The parent property is one of the synonyms available for referencing a window that contains the current frame. This is a read-only property for the window and frame objects. You can use this property when referencing one frame from another within a window or parent frame. It has the following syntax:

```
parent.propertyName
parent.methodName
top.frameName
top.frames[index]
```

The propertyName entry is the defaultStatus, status, length, name, or parent property. This could also be the length, name, or parent property when the reference is from a parent to a frame. The methodName entry is any method associated with the window object. (See the window object entry for more information about the available methods.) The frameName and frames[index] entries reference individual frames by either their name value or their position in an array of frames.

Example

```
<input type="button" name="doItButton" value="Make it so!"
    onclick="parent.frames[1].document.bgColor=colorChoice" />
```

This example is part of the `frame` object example. In this statement, the background color of the sibling (index value 1, or the second element in the frames array) of the current frame is set to the user's color choice.

pathname

The `pathname` property is part of the `link` and `location` objects. It's the part of the URL that indicates the directory location for the page on the server. You can set the `pathname` at any time, but if you need to change the document pathname, it's safer to use the `href` property. The `pathname` property has the following syntax:

```
location.pathname
```

(See the examples for the `location` object.)

PI

The `PI` property is part of the built-in `Math` object. It's a read-only constant that represents the ratio of circle circumference to diameter (approximately 3.14). The PI property has the following syntax:

```
Math.PI
```

Example

```
document.write("Bob says your chances of winning are: " +
    longShot + " in " + longShot * Math.PI + ".");
```

This example computes a value and displays the results in a statement for the user.

port

The `port` property is part of the `link` and `location` objects. It's the `port` element in the URL and identifies the port, if any, used on the server. If this property is null, the `host` and `hostname` properties are the same. The `port` property has the following syntax:

```
location.port
```

(See the example for the `location` object.)

protocol

The protocol property is part of the link and location objects. It's part of the URL and uses the following protocols:

Protocol	Description
file	Accesses a local filesystem
ftp	Uses the FTP protocol (File Transfer Protocol)
gopher	Uses the gopher protocol
http	Uses the HTTP protocol (Hypertext Transfer Protocol)
mailto	Uses the SMTP protocol (Simple Mail Transfer Protocol)
news	Uses the NNTP protocol (Network News Transfer Protocol)
snews	Uses the secure NNTP protocol
https	Uses the secure HTTP protocol
telnet	Uses the telnet protocol
tn3270	Uses the 3270 telnet protocol

The port property has the following syntax:

```
location.protocol
```

(See the examples for the link and location objects.)

referrer

The referrer property is part of the document object. It's a read-only property of the document object that contains the originating document URL when a user jumps from an originating document to a destination document. The referrer property has the following syntax:

```
document.referrer
```

Example

```
document.write("welcome, I see you joined us from " +
    document.referrer + ". How's the weather back there?");
```

This statement displays a message for the user that includes the location URL of the original document.

search

The search property is found in the link and location objects. It's part of the URL; although you can change this property at any time, it's best to use the href property to change location attributes. The search property has the following syntax:

```
location.search
```

Example

```
newWindow = window.open
    ("http://www.example.com/Look/scripts?qt=property=elements");
with (document) {
  write("The href property is " +
      newWindow.location.href + "<br />");
  write("The protocol property is " +
      newWindow.location.protocol + "<br />");
  write("The host property is " +
      newWindow.location.host + "<br />");
  write("The host name is " +
      newWindow.location.hostName + "<br />");
  write("The port property is " +
      newWindow.location.port + "<br />");
  write("The pathname property is" +
      newWindow.location.pathname + "<br />");
  write("The search property is " +
      newWindow.location.search + "<br />");
  write("The hash property is " +
      newWindow.location.hash + "<br />");
  close();  }
```

which displays the following:

```
The href property is http://www.example.com/Look/scripts?qt=
property=elements
The protocol property is http:
The host property is www.example.com
The host name is www.example.com
The port property is
```

```
The pathname property is /Look/scripts
The search property is ?qt=property=elements
The hash property is
```

selected

The selected property is part of the options array. It contains a Boolean value that indicates whether the option in a select object is currently selected. For selected options, this property is True. You can set this property programmatically. It has the following syntax:

```
selectName.options[index].selected
```

Example

```
for (x = document.saleForm.buyTheseThings.length; x > 0; x--) {
    if (document.saleForm.buyTheseThings.options[x].selected =
        "true") {
        document.saleForm.buyTheseThings.options[x].selected =
        "false"; }
    else {
        document.saleForm.buyTheseThings.options[x].selected =
        "true"; }   }
```

In this example, the for loop traverses the list of options altering the selections. The result is an inversion of the user's selections.

selectedIndex

The selectedIndex property is part of the select object and the options array. It contains information about the order in which a select object was defined. You can set the selectedIndex property at any time, and the displayed information is updated. The selectedIndex property works well with select objects that are not multiple select objects. It has the following syntax:

```
selectName.selectedIndex
selectName.options.selectedIndex
```

Example

```
function whatSelection () {
    return document.saleForm.giveAwayOptions.selectedIndex; }
```

This simple function brings back the selection from the list of options.

self

The self property is part of the window object. This property is a synonym for the current window or frame object. Use this read-only property to help keep your code clear. It has the following syntax:

```
self.propertyName
self.methodName
```

Example

```
self.javatest.whichIsFunction.index[x];
document.javatest.whichIsFunction.index[x];
```

These two statements are equivalent.

SQRT1_2

The SQRT1_2 property is part of the built-in Math object. It's a read-only constant that represents the inverse of the square root of 2 (approximately 0.707). It has the following syntax:

```
Math.SQRT1_2
```

Example

```
document.write("Bob says your chances of winning are: " +
    longShot + " in " + longShot / Math.SQRT1_2 + ".");
```

This example computes a value and displays the results in a statement for the user.

SQRT2

The SQRT2 property is part of the built-in Math object. It's a read-only constant that represents the square root of 2 (approximately 1.414). It has the following syntax:

```
Math.SQRT2
```

Example

```
document.write("Bob says your chances of winning are: " +
    longShot + " in " + longShot * Math.SQRT2 + ".");
```

This example computes a value and displays the results in a statement for the user.

status

The `status` property is part of the `window` object. It contains a priority or transient message that is displayed in the status bar of the window. It has the following syntax:

```
windowReference.status
```

Example

```
self.status = "Welcome to our little home away from home!";
```

This example puts the message onto the window's status line.

target

The `target` property is part of the `form`, `link`, and `location` objects. For the `link` and `location` objects, the `target` property contains the window name for a jump. It works slightly differently for the `form` object: it contains the destination for form submissions. Although you can set the `target` property at any time, it cannot assume the value of an expression or a variable (meaning you can't build those fancy statements such as `document.write`). The `target` property has the following syntax:

```
formName.target
linkName.target
```

Example

```
self.status("When you submit your request, the information
    will appear in " + self.buyTheseThings.target + ".");
```

This statement displays a message in the window status bar telling users where their selections will appear. This is useful if you want to confirm the request before displaying the information.

text

The `text` property is part of the `options` array. It's the displayed value in an options list. If you change the `text` property for an option list, the display character, initially set in the `option` element, does not change, but the internal information does change. The `text` property has the following syntax:

```
selectName.options[index].text
```

Example

```
for (x = 0; x < self.javajive.pickMe.length; x++) {
    if (self.javajive.pickMe.option[x].select == true) {
        document.write(self.javajive.pickMe.option[x].text); } }
```

This example tests to see whether the option has been selected; if it has, it displays the option text. If you change the text property programmatically, the resulting list is different from the list of options the user sees and selects from.

title

The title property is part of the document object. It reflects the value of the title element, and you cannot change this value. The title property has the following syntax:

```
document.title
```

Example

```
self.status(self.title);
```

top

The top property is part of the window object. It's a read-only synonym for the topmost window and has the following syntax:

```
top.propertyName
top.methodName
top.frameName
top.frames[index]
```

The propertyName entry is defaultStatus, status, or length. The methodName entry is any window method. The frameName and frames[index] entries are frame references for frames within the window.

Example

```
top.close();
```

This closes the topmost window.

```
for (x = 0, x < top.length, x++) {
    top.frame[x].close(); }
```

This closes all the frames on a page.

undefined

The undefined property (primitive value) is the value of a variable that has not been assigned a specific value.

userAgent

The userAgent property is part of the navigator object. It's part of the Hypertext Transfer Protocol (HTTP) information. Servers use this property to identify the client browser. The userAgent property has the following syntax:

```
navigator.userAgent
```

Example

```
document.write("You're using " + navigator.userAgent + ".");
```

This displays the browser information, as in:

```
You're using Mozilla/4.0 (compatible; MSIE 5.5; Windows 98).
```

value

The value property differs for the various objects. In all cases, it reflects the value attribute of the object.

For hidden, password, text, and textarea objects or for an item in the options array, you can programmatically change the property. If you change it for the text and textarea objects, the display updates immediately. If you change it for the password object, security could give you some pause. If you evaluate your changes, you'll get the current value back; if a user changes it, security will not pass the changes. For the options array, the value attribute is not displayed but is an internal representation.

For the button, reset, and submit objects, the value property is a read-only reflection of the text on the face of the button.

For checkbox and radio objects, the value property is returned to the server when the check box or radio button is selected. It's not the value of the selection; it's simply On or Off.

The value property has the following syntax:

```
objectName.value
radioName[index].value
selectName.options.[index].value
```

(For examples of the `value` property, see the appropriate object entry.)
The `value` property is part of the `options` array and of the following objects:

button	password	submit
checkbox	radio	text
hidden	reset	textarea

vLinkColor

The `vLinkColor` is a part of the `document` object. It contains the color settings for the links on the page that have been visited. To set this value programmatically, place your script before the `body` element; once the layout has been done, this becomes a read-only property. If you do set the property in a script, do not use the `vlink` attribute of the `body` element. To set the color, use either the color keyword or a hexadecimal RGB number (three double digits). The `vLinkColor` has the following syntax:

```
document.vLinkColor="colorLiteral"
document.vLinkColor="colorRGB"
```

Example

```
document.vlinkColor="red"
document.vlinkColor="ff0000"
```

The two statements are equivalent. The first statement sets the `vlinkColor` using the keyword `red`, which is `ff0000` in hex.

window

The `window` property is part of the `frame` and `window` objects. It's a synonym for the current window. Although you can use the `window` property to refer to the current frame, it's better to use the `self` property in that situation. This property is read-only and has the following syntax:

```
window.propertyName
window.methodName(parameters)
```

Example

```
window.status="Welcome to our humble home away from home!";
```

This example displays the message in the status bar.

Working with the W3C Validator

XHTML

Master's Reference
Part 4

One of the easiest ways to validate an XHTML document is to use the W3C's free online validator. It supports validation of both public and local documents and can be accessed from any Web browser. We highly recommend that you validate your XHTML documents using this tool, which can be found at `http://validator.w3.org/`.

Validator Interface

The interface for the validator is not elegant; however, it's very usable (see Figure MR4.1). Validating a document using this tool is simple. You have two choices: You can either upload a local file, or you can point the validator to a public document on the Web. With either approach, you have a few options you can select to tailor your validation experience.

Figure MR4.1 *The simple interface of the W3C validator*

Document Type pull-down menu You can either select the value Specified Inline, which tells the validator that the document uses a DOCTYPE declaration to define the appropriate DTD, or you can select the version of XHTML or HTML you wish to use. You have eight options:

XHTML 1.0 Strict

XHTML 1.0 Transitional

XHTML 1.0 Frameset

HTML 4.01 Strict

HTML 4.01 Transitional

HTML 4.01 Frameset

HTML 3.2

HTML 2.0

Show Source Input checkbox   Presents the user with a listing of the source document, including line numbers.

Show An Outline Of This Document checkbox   Presents the user with a visual outline of the document based on heading markup.

Show Parse Tree checkbox   Presents the user with a parsed tree of the document, using indentation for layout.

Exclude Attributes From The Parse Tree checkbox   Tells the validator to exclude attributes from the parse tree. This function only works if you select to show the parse tree.

URL

If the file you want to validate is on the Web, all you have to do is enter the full URL into the Address field (shown in Figure MR4.1). To do this:

1. Visit `http://validator.w3.org/`.

2. Enter the URL of the document into the Address field.

3. Click the Validate this document button.

That's how easy this process is!

Upload Files

If the file you want to validate is on your local drive, you need to upload the file to the validator. To do this:

1. Visit `http://validator.w3.org/`.

2. Select the Upload Files hyperlink in the upper right of the window or under the Validate This Page button.

3. Select the Browse button.

4. Select the document to be validated from your hard drive.

5. Click the Validate This Page button.

Now, you need to know how to decrypt the sometime cryptic error messages displayed by the validator.

Translating Error Messages

If you make a mistake that violates any of XML's well-formedness rules, or the DTD's validity rules, the validator will present error messages. We used Listing 9.1 from Chapter 9 and ran it through the validator. The results are shown in Figure MR4.2.

Figure MR4.2 Screen shot of typical error messages

At first glance, the error messages seem a bit overwhelming. However, after you run a few documents through the validator, you'll get used to the cryptic messages—we promise. Until then, we've translated a few of the common error messages for you, in Table MR4.1.

Table MR4.1 Common W3C Validator Error Messages

ERROR	TRANSLATION
Missing a required sub-element of "head"	You forgot to include a required child of the head element, such as the title element.
End tag for "p" omitted; end tags are required in XML for non-empty elements; empty elements require an end tag or the start tag must end with "/>"	You forgot to close the p element.
Required attribute "alt" not specified	You forgot to add the alt attribute to the img element, and it's required.
Element "p" not allowed here; possible cause is an inline element containing a block-level element	You accidentally nested a p element where it isn't allowed. Although the error message states "inline element containing a block-level element," the actual mistake made for this document cites the misuse of a block-level element.
End tag for "img" omitted; end tags are required in XML for non-empty elements; empty elements require an end tag or the start tag must end with "/>"	You forgot to terminate the empty element—for example, <img />.

Adding the Icon

If your XHTML document validates, and you receive the following message, you can add the XHTML icon to your Web page:

```
Congratulations, this document validates as XHTML 1.0
    Transitional!
```

The XHTML icon (shown in Figure MR4.3) shows users that your page strictly conforms to the XHTML specification.

Figure MR4.3 *The XHTML icon shown when your document is validated against a DTD (in this case, the XHTML 1.0 Transitional DTD)*

To add the icon to your page, add the following XHTML markup to your Web page:

```
<p>
  <a href="http://validator.w3.org/check/referer">
    <img src="http://www.w3.org/Icons/valid-xhtml10"
    alt="Valid XHTML 1.0!" height="31" width="88" />
  </a>
</p>
```

All in all, understanding the validator is not that difficult. We hope you found this Master's Reference helpful. Happy validating!

XHTML Special Characters

XHTML

Master's Reference
Part 5

XHTML documents, like all documents based on XML, include only plain-text characters. This raises a very interesting issue: how should you go about including special characters, such as a tilde (~), the copyright symbol (©), or even some of the special characters that normally delimit XHTML markup (such as <, >, and so forth), in XHTML documents?

The good news is that it's easy to add special characters to XHTML documents, as long as you do so properly. The bad news (if you want to call it that) is that inserting special characters usually involves a bit of extra work. In fact, because of the notation that XHTML requires to reference such special characters, the ratio of keystrokes in a source XHTML document to the characters that they produce when that document is rendered in a browser is usually four to one or higher. In plain English, this means you often need to type four or more characters in an XHTML source document to produce a single special character when that document is displayed.

XHTML Entities

In the specialized language associated with XHTML (and other markup languages, including XML and XHTML), the strings that produce special characters when interpreted and rendered by a Web browser are called *entities*. Entities come in two forms:

Character entities   Such an entity refers to a character by some name. For example, the character entity for a quotation mark is ", and the character entity for the left angle bracket, < (also known as the less than symbol), is <.

Numeric entities   Such an entity refers to a character using a numeric code (for those with mathematical tendencies, these are normally integers in the range of 0 to 65,535). The numeric entity that represents the quotation mark is ", and the numeric entity that represents the left angle bracket is <.

These entities are often necessary to alert browsers that you want to use a character as plain text, not as markup, computer data, or programming instructions. For example, the left angle bracket (<) denotes the beginning of a markup element, so if you just type <, browsers and the like will assume that what follows is markup. If you have text that must be surrounded by angle brackets when viewed by users (like `<this>`), you signal it by typing `&lt;this&gt;`.

Entities always begin with an ampersand (&) and end with a semicolon (;). Character entities use names between those two bracketing characters; numeric entities follow the opening ampersand with a pound sign (#) before the numeric code and also end with a semicolon.

XHTML and Character Sets

By default, XHTML uses the same character set that's used by default with HTML—namely the standard ISO-8859-1 character set, also known as ISO-Latin-1. This name breaks down as follows:

- *ISO* stands for the International Organization for Standardization.

- *8859* uniquely identifies the standard by number.

- *Latin* indicates that this standard is based on the Roman alphabet so familiar to speakers of Western languages.

- The final number 1 indicates that this is the first version for this character set definition.

Table MR5.1 documents all of the known variants of the ISO-8859 character sets and indicates which particular alphabets they support.

Table MR5.1 ISO 8859 Character Sets

CHARSET	SCRIPT	LANGUAGES
ISO-8859-1	Latin-1	ASCII plus most Western European languages, including Albanian, Afrikaans, Basque, Catalan, Danish, Dutch, English, Faroese, Finnish, Flemish, Galician, German, Icelandic, Irish, Italian, Norwegian, Portuguese, Scottish, Spanish, and Swedish. Omits certain Dutch, French, and German characters.
ISO-8859-2	Latin-2	ASCII plus most Central European languages, including Czech, English, German, Hungarian, Polish, Romanian, Croatian, Slovak, Slovene, and Serbian.
ISO-8859-3	Latin-3	ASCII plus characters required for English, Esperanto, German, Maltese, and Galician.
ISO-8859-4	Latin-4	ASCII plus most Baltic languages, including Latvian, Lithuanian, German, Greenlandic, and Lappish; now superseded by ISO-Latin-6.
ISO-8859-5		ASCII plus Cyrillic characters for Slavic languages, including Byelorussian, Bulgarian, Macedonian, Russian, Serbian, and Ukrainian.
ISO-8859-6		ASCII plus Arabic characters.
ISO-8859-7		ASCII plus Greek characters.
ISO-8859-8		ASCII plus Hebrew.

Table MR5.1 continued ISO 8859 Character Sets

CHARSET	SCRIPT	LANGUAGES
ISO-8859-9	Latin-5	Latin-1 except that some Turkish symbols replace Icelandic ones.
ISO-8859-10	Latin-6	ASCII plus most Nordic languages, including Latvian, Lithuanian, Inuit, non-Skolt Sami, and Icelandic.
ISO-8859-11		ASCII plus Thai.
ISO-8859-12	Latin-7	ASCII plus Celtic.
ISO-8859-13	Latin-8	ASCII plus the Baltic Rim characters.
ISO-8859-14	Latin-9	ASCII plus Sami (Finnish).
ISO-8859-15	Latin-10	Variation on Latin-1 that includes euro currency sign, plus extra accented Finnish and French characters.

Please note that the foundation for all these character sets is the ASCII characters familiar to computer users everywhere. ASCII stands for American Standard Code for Information Interchange, and for the purposes of this discussion, should be considered to consist of uppercase Roman alphabetic characters (A–Z), lowercase Roman alphabetic characters (a–z), numbers (0–9), and common punctuation marks. The ASCII character set uses 8-bit codes—that is, numeric values between 0 and 255. The ISO-8859 character sets use only 7-bit, or lower order ASCII characters—those numbered from 0 to 127. Thus, higher-order ASCII characters—those numbered from 128 to 255—are not supported in the ISO-8859 character sets.

If you're familiar with numeric ASCII codes for higher-order ASCII characters, you'll have to do some research to identify either character or numeric entities that work with XHTML to represent those characters. Also be forewarned that the numeric codes you have to use to represent those characters will not be the same as the ASCII codes you're probably used to!

Because XHTML follows XML syntax rules, and XML requires that there be an entity declaration for every entity used in an XML document, all characters that XHTML supports are defined as part of the XHTML Document Type Declarations (DTDs). These declarations are divided into three different sets, and may be downloaded as such from the following W3C Web pages. (All these files end with a .ent extension, but they are plain-text files and may be viewed inside any text editor or word processor. Please note that we got strange results from Notepad, but good ones from other plain-text editors and MS Word.)

Latin-1	www.w3.org/TR/xhtml1/DTD/xhtml-lat1.ent
Special characters	www.w3.org/TR/xhtml1/DTD/xhtml-special.ent
Symbols	www.w3.org/TR/xhtml1/DTD/xhtml-symbol.ent

Readers who download and examine these files will notice several key items of information relevant to using character and numeric entities with XHTML:

- Character codes included also reference the ISO-8879 and ISO-10646 standards.

- Numeric codes go well beyond the range of 0–255 associated with ISO-8859 codes—in fact, that's where ISO-8879 and ISO-10646 come into play.

- ISO-10646 is nearly synonymous with the Unicode character set, which treats ISO-8859 and ISO-8879 as subsets of itself, and uses up to 16 bits for numeric character codes. (This is why we said that numeric entities typically fall in the range of 0–65,535 at the outset of this reference; 65,535 is equal to $2^{16}-1$, or the biggest integer that a 16-bit number can represent.)

In fact, the Unicode character set encompasses an incredibly broad range of character and numeric entities, along with nearly every written alphabet known to man. As such, it provides the broadest possible definition for characters that might appear in an XML or XHTML document. Just remember that if you want to use any characters outside those defined in ISO-Latin-1 in any XHTML documents you create, you must be sure to include the appropriate entity definitions in a DTD or schema that you invoke as part of your XHTML document. As long as you follow this guideline, you can take full advantage of what Unicode has to offer. For more information about Unicode, and a complete listing of Unicode characters, please visit that organization's Web site at www.unicode.org.

XHTML Color Codes

XHTML

Master's Reference
Part 6

U sing either Cascading Style Sheets (CSS) or deprecated XHTML elements, you can define display colors for almost any element on your Web page. Although users can define browser preferences to override your color selections, you can define the default colors in case they don't use preferences.

There are two ways you can define colors:

Hexadecimal value   A "hex" number defines the red, green, and blue (RGB) components of a color. A hexadecimal number is signaled by a pound sign (#) followed by six digits. The first two digits are for the red component, the next two digits define the amount of green in the color, and the last two digits are for the blue component. The hex code ff indicates the maximum of a component. If you want red, green, or blue to be "turned off" or not represented, you use a 00 combination. For example, #0000ff means no red or green at all and the maximum possible amount of blue.

Color name   You can also use one of the standard 16 color names that are predefined—for example, red. These are listed in Table MR6.1 along with their corresponding hexadecimal values.

Table MR6.1 Standard Colors

STANDARD COLOR NAME	HEXADECIMAL VALUE
aqua	#00ffff
black	#000000
blue	#0000ff
fuchsia	#ff00ff
gray	#808080
green	#008000
lime	#00ff00
maroon	#800000
navy	#000080
olive	#808000
purple	#800080
red	#ff0000
silver	#c0c0c0

XHTML Color Codes

Table MR6.1 continued Standard Colors

STANDARD COLOR NAME	HEXADECIMAL VALUE
teal	#008080
yellow	#ffff00
white	#ffffff

Many designers misspell gray *and use an* e *instead of the* a*. If you use* **grey***, the browser will display the color green because that is the closest spelling. So be careful when using* **gray***.*

Luckily, as designers, we're not limited to just those sixteen colors. Many browsers support hundreds of color names, and you can always use hexadecimal values. Keep in mind that some users have machines that can only display 256 colors. In this case, the browser either uses an existing color that is close to the defined color or "dithers" the color using available colors.

It's difficult to talk about color if you can't see the colors in action. The following Web sites contain a variety of useful color information, from color charts to interesting articles, and even some great interactive color pickers and decimal/hexadecimal converters:

Clear Ink's Pallete Man

www.paletteman.com

HyperSolutions' RGB color chart

www.hypersolutions.org/rgb.html

Microsoft's "The Safety Pallete," by Robert Hess

http://msdn.microsoft.com/workshop/design/color/safety.asp

Tucow's HTML color chart

http://look.html.tucows.com/designer/colorhexchart.html

VisiBone's Webmaster's Color Library

www.visibone.com/colorlab/

Webmonkey's color chart

`http://hotwired.lycos.com/webmonkey/reference/color_codes/`

ZDNet "Colors in HTML and CSS"

`www.zdnet.com/devhead/resources/tag_library/misc/colors.html`

The XHTML Specification

XHTML

Master's Reference
Part 7

The XHTML Specification

This section provides you with a complete copy of the W3C's XHTML 1.0 Recommendation, so you can refer to it at any time without having to get online. This specification can be found at `http://www.w3.org/TR/xhtml1` and is copyrighted by the W3C. You can access the full copyright statement of the W3C at

`http://www.w3.org/Consortium/Legal/ipr-notice-20000612`

Within the body of the specification, bracketed items, such as [HTML], are citations to works listed in the References section at the end. Some parenthetical material represents hotlinks on the W3C site that aren't expanded or explained in the Recommendation itself.

XHTML™ 1.0: The Extensible HyperText Markup Language

A Reformulation of HTML 4 in XML 1.0

W3C Recommendation 26 January 2000

This version:	`http://www.w3.org/TR/2000/REC-xhtml1-20000126`
	(Postscript version, PDF version, ZIP archive, or Gzip'd TAR archive)
Latest version:	`http://www.w3.org/TR/xhtml1`
Previous version:	`http://www.w3.org/TR/1999/PR-xhtml1-19991210`
Authors:	See acknowledgements.

Abstract

This specification defines XHTML 1.0, a reformulation of HTML 4 as an XML 1.0 application, and three DTDs corresponding to the ones defined by HTML 4. The semantics of the elements and their attributes are defined in the W3C Recommendation for HTML 4. These semantics provide the foundation for future extensibility of XHTML. Compatibility with existing HTML user agents is possible by following a small set of guidelines.

Status of This Document

This section describes the status of this document at the time of its publication. Other documents may supersede this document. The latest status of this document series is maintained at the W3C.

This document has been reviewed by W3C Members and other interested parties and has been endorsed by the Director as a W3C Recommendation. It is a stable document and may be used as reference material or cited as a normative reference from another document. W3C's role in making the Recommendation is to draw attention to the specification and to promote its widespread deployment. This enhances the functionality and interoperability of the Web.

This document has been produced as part of the W3C HTML Activity. The goals of the HTML Working Group (members only) are discussed in the HTML Working Group charter (members only).

A list of current W3C Recommendations and other technical documents can be found at `http://www.w3.org/TR`.

Public discussion on HTML features takes place on the mailing list `www-html@w3.org` (archive).

Please report errors in this document to `www-html-editor@w3.org`.

The list of known errors in this specification is available at `http://www.w3.org/2000/01/REC-xhtml1-20000126-errata`.

Contents

1. What Is XHTML?

XHTML is a family of current and future document types and modules that reproduce, subset, and extend HTML 4 [HTML]. XHTML family document types are XML
based, and ultimately are designed to work in conjunction with XML-based user
agents. The details of this family and its evolution are discussed in more detail in the
section on Future Directions.

XHTML 1.0 (this specification) is the first document type in the XHTML family. It
is a reformulation of the three HTML 4 document types as applications of XML 1.0
[XML]. It is intended to be used as a language for content that is both XML-conforming

and, if some simple guidelines are followed, operates in HTML 4 conforming user agents. Developers who migrate their content to XHTML 1.0 will realize the following benefits:

- XHTML documents are XML conforming. As such, they are readily viewed, edited, and validated with standard XML tools.

- XHTML documents can be written to to operate as well or better than they did before in existing HTML 4-conforming user agents as well as in new, XHTML 1.0 conforming user agents.

- XHTML documents can utilize applications (e.g. scripts and applets) that rely upon either the HTML Document Object Model or the XML Document Object Model [DOM].

- As the XHTML family evolves, documents conforming to XHTML 1.0 will be more likely to interoperate within and among various XHTML environments.

The XHTML family is the next step in the evolution of the Internet. By migrating to XHTML today, content developers can enter the XML world with all of its attendant benefits, while still remaining confident in their content's backward and future compatibility.

1.1 What Is HTML 4?

HTML 4 [HTML] is an SGML (Standard Generalized Markup Language) application conforming to International Standard ISO 8879, and is widely regarded as the standard publishing language of the World Wide Web.

SGML is a language for describing markup languages, particularly those used in electronic document exchange, document management, and document publishing. HTML is an example of a language defined in SGML.

SGML has been around since the middle 1980's and has remained quite stable. Much of this stability stems from the fact that the language is both feature-rich and flexible. This flexibility, however, comes at a price, and that price is a level of complexity that has inhibited its adoption in a diversity of environments, including the World Wide Web.

HTML, as originally conceived, was to be a language for the exchange of scientific and other technical documents, suitable for use by non-document specialists. HTML addressed the problem of SGML complexity by specifying a small set of structural and semantic tags suitable for authoring relatively simple documents. In addition to simplifying the document structure, HTML added support for hypertext. Multimedia capabilities were added later.

In a remarkably short space of time, HTML became wildly popular and rapidly outgrew its original purpose. Since HTML's inception, there has been rapid invention of new elements for use within HTML (as a standard) and for adapting HTML to vertical, highly specialized, markets. This plethora of new elements has led to compatibility problems for documents across different platforms.

As the heterogeneity of both software and platforms rapidly proliferate, it is clear that the suitability of 'classic' HTML 4 for use on these platforms is somewhat limited.

1.2 What Is XML?

XML™ is the shorthand for Extensible Markup Language, and is an acronym of Extensible Markup Language [XML].

XML was conceived as a means of regaining the power and flexibility of SGML without most of its complexity. Although a restricted form of SGML, XML nonetheless preserves most of SGML's power and richness, and yet still retains all of SGML's commonly used features.

While retaining these beneficial features, XML removes many of the more complex features of SGML that make the authoring and design of suitable software both difficult and costly.

1.3 Why the Need for XHTML?

The benefits of migrating to XHTML 1.0 are described above. Some of the benefits of migrating to XHTML in general are:

- Document developers and user agent designers are constantly discovering new ways to express their ideas through new markup. In XML, it is relatively easy to introduce new elements or additional element attributes. The XHTML family is designed to accommodate these extensions through XHTML modules and techniques for developing new XHTML-conforming modules (described in the forthcoming XHTML Modularization specification). These modules will permit the combination of existing and new feature sets when developing content and when designing new user agents.

- Alternate ways of accessing the Internet are constantly being introduced. Some estimates indicate that by the year 2002, 75% of Internet document viewing will be carried out on these alternate platforms. The XHTML family is designed with general user agent interoperability in mind. Through a new user agent and document profiling mechanism, servers, proxies, and user agents will be able to perform best effort content transformation. Ultimately, it will be possible to develop XHTML-conforming content that is usable by any XHTML-conforming user agent.

2. Definitions

2.1 Terminology

The following terms are used in this specification. These terms extend the definitions in [RFC2119] in ways based upon similar definitions in ISO/IEC 9945-1:1990 [POSIX.1]:

Implementation-defined   A value or behavior is implementation-defined when it is left to the implementation to define [and document] the corresponding requirements for correct document construction.

May   With respect to implementations, the word "may" is to be interpreted as an optional feature that is not required in this specification but can be provided. With respect to Document Conformance, the word "may" means that the optional feature must not be used. The term "optional" has the same definition as "may".

Must   In this specification, the word "must" is to be interpreted as a mandatory requirement on the implementation or on Strictly Conforming XHTML Documents, depending upon the context. The term "shall" has the same definition as "must".

Reserved   A value or behavior is unspecified, but it is not allowed to be used by Conforming Documents nor to be supported by a Conforming User Agents.

Should   With respect to implementations, the word "should" is to be interpreted as an implementation recommendation, but not a requirement. With respect to documents, the word "should" is to be interpreted as recommended programming practice for documents and a requirement for Strictly Conforming XHTML Documents.

Supported   Certain facilities in this specification are optional. If a facility is supported, it behaves as specified by this specification.

Unspecified   When a value or behavior is unspecified, the specification defines no portability requirements for a facility on an implementation even when faced with a document that uses the facility. A document that requires specific behavior in such an instance, rather than tolerating any behavior when using that facility, is not a Strictly Conforming XHTML Document.

2.2 General Terms

Attribute   An attribute is a parameter to an element declared in the DTD. An attribute's type and value range, including a possible default value, are defined in the DTD.

DTD   A DTD, or document type definition, is a collection of XML declarations that, as a collection, defines the legal structure, elements, and attributes that are available for use in a document that complies to the DTD.

Document   A document is a stream of data that, after being combined with any other streams it references, is structured such that it holds information contained within elements that are organized as defined in the associated DTD. See Document Conformance for more information.

Element   An element is a document structuring unit declared in the DTD. The element's content model is defined in the DTD, and additional semantics may be defined in the prose description of the element.

Facilities   Functionality includes elements, attributes, and the semantics associated with those elements and attributes. An implementation supporting that functionality is said to provide the necessary facilities.

Implementation   An implementation is a system that provides collection of facilities and services that supports this specification. See User Agent Conformance for more information.

Parsing   Parsing is the act whereby a document is scanned, and the information contained within the document is filtered into the context of the elements in which the information is structured.

Rendering   Rendering is the act whereby the information in a document is presented. This presentation is done in the form most appropriate to the environment (e.g. aurally, visually, in print).

User Agent   A user agent is an implementation that retrieves and processes XHTML documents. See User Agent Conformance for more information.

Validation   Validation is a process whereby documents are verified against the associated DTD, ensuring that the structure, use of elements, and use of attributes are consistent with the definitions in the DTD.

Well-formed   A document is well-formed when it is structured according to the rules defined in Section 2.1 of the XML 1.0 Recommendation [XML]. Basically, this definition states that elements, delimited by their start and end tags, are nested properly within one another.

3. Normative Definition of XHTML 1.0

3.1 Document Conformance

This version of XHTML provides a definition of strictly conforming XHTML documents, which are restricted to tags and attributes from the XHTML namespace. See Section 3.1.2 for information on using XHTML with other namespaces, for instance, to include metadata expressed in RDF within XHTML documents.

3.1.1 Strictly Conforming Documents

A Strictly Conforming XHTML Document is a document that requires only the facilities described as mandatory in this specification. Such a document must meet all of the following criteria:

1. It must validate against one of the three DTDs found in Appendix A.

2. The root element of the document must be <html>.

3. The root element of the document must designate the XHTML namespace using the xmlns attribute [XMLNAMES]. The namespace for XHTML is defined to be http://www.w3.org/1999/xhtml.

4. There must be a DOCTYPE declaration in the document prior to the root element. The public identifier included in the DOCTYPE declaration must reference one of the three DTDs found in Appendix A using the respective Formal

Public Identifier. The system identifier may be changed to reflect local system conventions.

```
<!DOCTYPE html
     PUBLIC "-//W3C//DTD XHTML 1.0 Strict//EN"
     "DTD/xhtml1-strict.dtd">
<!DOCTYPE html
     PUBLIC "-//W3C//DTD XHTML 1.0 Transitional//EN"
     "DTD/xhtml1-transitional.dtd">
<!DOCTYPE html
     PUBLIC "-//W3C//DTD XHTML 1.0 Frameset//EN"
     "DTD/xhtml1-frameset.dtd">
```

Here is an example of a minimal XHTML document.

```
<?xml version="1.0" encoding="UTF-8"?>
<!DOCTYPE html
     PUBLIC "-//W3C//DTD XHTML 1.0 Strict//EN"
     "DTD/xhtml1-strict.dtd">
<html xmlns="http://www.w3.org/1999/xhtml"
     xml:lang="en" lang="en">
  <head>
    <title>Virtual Library</title>
  </head>
  <body>
    <p>Moved to <a href="http://vlib.org/">vlib.org</a>.</p>
  </body>
</html>
```

Note that in this example, the XML declaration is included. An XML declaration like the one above is not required in all XML documents. XHTML document authors are strongly encouraged to use XML declarations in all their documents. Such a declaration is required when the character encoding of the document is other than the default UTF-8 or UTF-16.

3.1.2 Using XHTML with other namespaces

The XHTML namespace may be used with other XML namespaces as per [XML-NAMES], although such documents are not strictly conforming XHTML 1.0 documents as defined above. Future work by W3C will address ways to specify conformance for documents involving multiple namespaces.

The following example shows the way in which XHTML 1.0 could be used in conjunction with the MathML Recommendation:

```
<html xmlns="http://www.w3.org/1999/xhtml"
      xml:lang="en" lang="en">
  <head>
    <title>A Math Example</title>
  </head>
  <body>
    <p>The following is MathML markup:</p>
    <math xmlns="http://www.w3.org/1998/Math/MathML">
      <apply> <log/>
        <logbase>
          <cn> 3 </cn>
        </logbase>
        <ci> x </ci>
      </apply>
    </math>
  </body>
</html>
```

The following example shows the way in which XHTML 1.0 markup could be incorporated into another XML namespace:

```
<?xml version="1.0" encoding="UTF-8"?>
<!-- initially, the default namespace is "books" -->
<book xmlns='urn:loc.gov:books'
      xmlns:isbn='urn:ISBN:0-395-36341-6'
      xml:lang="en" lang="en">
  <title>Cheaper by the Dozen</title>
  <isbn:number>1568491379</isbn:number>
  <notes>
    <!-- make HTML the default namespace
         for a hypertext commentary -->
    <p xmlns='http://www.w3.org/1999/xhtml'>
        This is also available
        <a href="http://www.w3.org/">online</a>.
    </p>
  </notes>
</book>
```

3.2 User Agent Conformance

A conforming user agent must meet all of the following criteria:

1. In order to be consistent with the XML 1.0 Recommendation [XML], the user agent must parse and evaluate an XHTML document for well-formedness. If the user agent claims to be a validating user agent, it must also validate documents against their referenced DTDs according to [XML].

2. When the user agent claims to support facilities defined within this specification or required by this specification through normative reference, it must do so in ways consistent with the facilities' definition.

3. When a user agent processes an XHTML document as generic XML, it shall only recognize attributes of type ID (e.g. the id attribute on most XHTML elements) as fragment identifiers.

4. If a user agent encounters an element it does not recognize, it must render the element's content.

5. If a user agent encounters an attribute it does not recognize, it must ignore the entire attribute specification (i.e., the attribute and its value).

6. If a user agent encounters an attribute value it doesn't recognize, it must use the default attribute value.

7. If it encounters an entity reference (other than one of the predefined entities) for which the User Agent has processed no declaration (which could happen if the declaration is in the external subset which the User Agent hasn't read), the entity reference should be rendered as the characters (starting with the ampersand and ending with the semi-colon) that make up the entity reference.

8. When rendering content, User Agents that encounter characters or character entity references that are recognized but not renderable should display the document in such a way that it is obvious to the user that normal rendering has not taken place.

9. The following characters are defined in [XML] as whitespace characters:

    - Space ( )
    - Tab (	)
    - Carriage return ()
    - Line feed (
)

The XML processor normalizes different system's line end codes into one single line-feed character, that is passed up to the application. The XHTML user agent in addition, must treat the following characters as whitespace:

- Form feed ()

- Zero-width space ()

In elements where the 'xml:space' attribute is set to 'preserve', the user agent must leave all whitespace characters intact (with the exception of leading and trailing whitespace characters, which should be removed). Otherwise, white-space is handled according to the following rules:

- All whitespace surrounding block elements should be removed.

- Comments are removed entirely and do not affect whitespace handling. One whitespace character on either side of a comment is treated as two white space characters.

- Leading and trailing whitespace inside a block element must be removed.

- Line feed characters within a block element must be converted into a space (except when the 'xml:space' attribute is set to 'preserve').

- A sequence of white space characters must be reduced to a single space character (except when the 'xml:space' attribute is set to 'preserve').

- With regard to rendition, the User Agent should render the content in a manner appropriate to the language in which the content is written. In languages whose primary script is Latinate, the ASCII space character is typically used to encode both grammatical word boundaries and typographic whitespace; in languages whose script is related to Nagari (e.g., Sanskrit, Thai, etc.), grammatical boundaries may be encoded using the ZW 'space' character, but will not typically be represented by typographic whitespace in rendered output; languages using Arabiform scripts may encode typographic whitespace using a space character, but may also use the ZW space character to delimit 'internal' grammatical boundaries (what look like words in Arabic to an English eye frequently encode several words, e.g. 'kitAbuhum' = 'kitAbu-hum' = 'book them' == their book); and languages in the Chinese script tradition typically neither encode such delimiters nor use typographic whitespace in this way.

Whitespace in attribute values is processed according to [XML].

4. Differences with HTML 4

Due to the fact that XHTML is an XML application, certain practices that were perfectly legal in SGML-based HTML 4 [HTML] must be changed.

4.1 Documents must be well-formed

Well-formedness is a new concept introduced by [XML]. Essentially this means that all elements must either have closing tags or be written in a special form (as described below), and that all the elements must nest.

Although overlapping is illegal in SGML, it was widely tolerated in existing browsers.

CORRECT: nested elements.

```
<p>here is an emphasized <em>paragraph</em>.</p>
```

INCORRECT: overlapping elements

```
<p>here is an emphasized <em>paragraph.</p></em>
```

4.2 Element and Attribute Names Must Be in Lower Case

XHTML documents must use lower case for all HTML element and attribute names. This difference is necessary because XML is case-sensitive e.g. <li> and <LI> are different tags.

4.3 For Non-Empty Elements, End Tags Are Required

In SGML-based HTML 4 certain elements were permitted to omit the end tag; with the elements that followed implying closure. This omission is not permitted in XML-based XHTML. All elements other than those declared in the DTD as EMPTY must have an end tag.

CORRECT: terminated elements

```
<p>here is a paragraph.</p><p>here is another
paragraph.</p>
```

INCORRECT: unterminated elements

```
<p>here is a paragraph.<p>here is another paragraph.
```

4.4 Attribute Values Must Always Be Quoted

All attribute values must be quoted, even those which appear to be numeric.

CORRECT: quoted attribute values

```
<table rows="3">
```

INCORRECT: unquoted attribute values

```
<table rows=3>
```

4.5 Attribute Minimization

XML does not support attribute minimization. Attribute-value pairs must be written in full. Attribute names such as compact and checked cannot occur in elements without their value being specified.

CORRECT: unminimized attributes

```
<dl compact="compact">
```

INCORRECT: minimized attributes

```
<dl compact>
```

4.6 Empty Elements

Empty elements must either have an end tag or the start tag must end with />. For instance, <br/> or <hr></hr>. See HTML Compatibility Guidelines for information on ways to ensure this is backward compatible with HTML 4 user agents.

CORRECT: terminated empty tags

```
<br/><hr/>
```

INCORRECT: unterminated empty tags
```
<br><hr>
```

4.7 Whitespace Handling in Attribute Values

In attribute values, user agents will strip leading and trailing whitespace from attribute values and map sequences of one or more whitespace characters (including line breaks) to a single inter-word space (an ASCII space character for western scripts). See Section 3.3.3 of [XML].

4.8 Script and Style Elements

In XHTML, the script and style elements are declared as having #PCDATA content. As a result, < and & will be treated as the start of markup, and entities such as < and & will be recognized as entity references by the XML processor to < and & respectively. Wrapping the content of the script or style element within a CDATA marked section avoids the expansion of these entities.

```
<script>
 <![CDATA[
 ... unescaped script content ...
]]>
 </script>
```

CDATA sections are recognized by the XML processor and appear as nodes in the Document Object Model, see Section 1.3 of the DOM Level 1 Recommendation [DOM].

An alternative is to use external script and style documents.

4.9 SGML Exclusions

SGML gives the writer of a DTD the ability to exclude specific elements from being contained within an element. Such prohibitions (called "exclusions") are not possible in XML.

For example, the HTML 4 Strict DTD forbids the nesting of an 'a' element within another 'a' element to any descendant depth. It is not possible to spell out such prohibitions in XML. Even though these prohibitions cannot be defined in the DTD, certain elements should not be nested. A summary of such elements and the elements that should not be nested in them is found in the normative Appendix B.

4.10 The Elements with 'id' and 'name' Attributes

HTML 4 defined the name attribute for the elements a, applet, form, frame, iframe, img, and map. HTML 4 also introduced the id attribute. Both of these attributes are designed to be used as fragment identifiers.

In XML, fragment identifiers are of type ID, and there can only be a single attribute of type ID per element. Therefore, in XHTML 1.0 the id attribute is defined to be of type ID. In order to ensure that XHTML 1.0 documents are well-structured XML documents, XHTML 1.0 documents MUST use the id attribute when defining fragment identifiers, even on elements that historically have also had a name attribute. See the HTML Compatibility Guidelines for information on ensuring such anchors are backwards compatible when serving XHTML documents as media type text/html.

Note that in XHTML 1.0, the name attribute of these elements is formally deprecated, and will be removed in a subsequent version of XHTML.

5. Compatibility Issues

Although there is no requirement for XHTML 1.0 documents to be compatible with existing user agents, in practice this is easy to accomplish. Guidelines for creating compatible documents can be found in Appendix C.

5.1 Internet Media Type

As of the publication of this recommendation, the general recommended MIME labeling for XML-based applications has yet to be resolved.

However, XHTML Documents which follow the guidelines set forth in Appendix C, "HTML Compatibility Guidelines" may be labeled with the Internet Media Type "text/html", as they are compatible with most HTML browsers. This document makes no recommendation about MIME labeling of other XHTML documents.

6. Future Directions

XHTML 1.0 provides the basis for a family of document types that will extend and subset XHTML, in order to support a wide range of new devices and applications, by defining modules and specifying a mechanism for combining these modules. This mechanism will enable the extension and sub-setting of XHTML 1.0 in a uniform way through the definition of new modules.

6.1 Modularizing HTML

As the use of XHTML moves from the traditional desktop user agents to other platforms, it is clear that not all of the XHTML elements will be required on all platforms. For example a hand held device or a cell-phone may only support a subset of XHTML elements.

The process of modularization breaks XHTML up into a series of smaller element sets. These elements can then be recombined to meet the needs of different communities.

These modules will be defined in a later W3C document.

6.2 Subsets and Extensibility

Modularization brings with it several advantages:

- It provides a formal mechanism for sub-setting XHTML.

- It provides a formal mechanism for extending XHTML.

- It simplifies the transformation between document types.

- It promotes the reuse of modules in new document types.

6.3 Document Profiles

A document profile specifies the syntax and semantics of a set of documents. Conformance to a document profile provides a basis for interoperability guarantees. The document profile specifies the facilities required to process documents of that type, e.g. which image formats can be used, levels of scripting, style sheet support, and so on.

For product designers this enables various groups to define their own standard profile.

For authors this will obviate the need to write several different versions of documents for different clients.

For special groups such as chemists, medical doctors, or mathematicians this allows a special profile to be built using standard HTML elements plus a group of elements geared to the specialist's needs.

Appendix A. DTDs

This appendix is normative.

These DTDs and entity sets form a normative part of this specification. The complete set of DTD files together with an XML declaration and SGML Open Catalog is included in the zip file for this specification.

A.1 Document Type Definitions

These DTDs approximate the HTML 4 DTDs. It is likely that when the DTDs are modularized, a method of DTD construction will be employed that corresponds more closely to HTML 4.

- XHTML-1.0-Strict
- XHTML-1.0-Transitional
- XHTML-1.0-Frameset

A.2 Entity Sets

The XHTML entity sets are the same as for HTML 4, but have been modified to be valid XML 1.0 entity declarations. Note the entity for the Euro currency sign (€ or € or €) is defined as part of the special characters.

- Latin-1 characters
- Special characters
- Symbols

Appendix B. Element Prohibitions

This appendix is normative.

The following elements have prohibitions on which elements they can contain (see Section 4.9). This prohibition applies to all depths of nesting, i.e. it contains all the descendant elements.

a   cannot contain other a elements.

pre   cannot contain the img, object, big, small, sub, or sup elements.

button   cannot contain the input, select, textarea, label, button, form, fieldset, iframe or isindex elements.

label   cannot contain other label elements.

form   cannot contain other form elements.

Appendix C. HTML Compatibility Guidelines

This appendix is informative.

This appendix summarizes design guidelines for authors who wish their XHTML documents to render on existing HTML user agents.

C.1 Processing Instructions

Be aware that processing instructions are rendered on some user agents. However, also note that when the XML declaration is not included in a document, the document can only use the default character encodings UTF-8 or UTF-16.

C.2 Empty Elements

Include a space before the trailing / and > of empty elements, e.g.
, <hr /> and <img src="karen.jpg" alt="Karen" />. Also, use the minimized tag syntax for empty elements, e.g.
, as the alternative syntax
</br> allowed by XML gives uncertain results in many existing user agents.

C.3 Element Minimization and Empty Element Content

Given an empty instance of an element whose content model is not EMPTY (for example, an empty title or paragraph) do not use the minimized form (e.g. use <p> </p> and not <p />).

C.4 Embedded Style Sheets and Scripts

Use external style sheets if your style sheet uses < or & or]]> or --. Use external scripts if your script uses < or & or]]> or --. Note that XML parsers are permitted to silently remove the contents of comments. Therefore, the historical practice of "hiding" scripts and style sheets within comments to make the documents backward compatible is likely to not work as expected in XML-based implementations.

C.5 Line Breaks within Attribute Values

Avoid line breaks and multiple whitespace characters within attribute values. These are handled inconsistently by user agents.

C.6 Isindex

Don't include more than one isindex element in the document head. The isindex element is deprecated in favor of the input element.

C.7 The *lang* and *xml:lang* Attributes

Use both the lang and xml:lang attributes when specifying the language of an element. The value of the xml:lang attribute takes precedence.

C.8 Fragment Identifiers

In XML, URIs [RFC2396] that end with fragment identifiers of the form "#foo" do not refer to elements with an attribute name="foo"; rather, they refer to elements with an attribute defined to be of type ID, e.g., the id attribute in HTML 4. Many existing HTML clients don't support the use of ID-type attributes in this way, so identical values may be supplied for both of these attributes to ensure maximum forward and backward compatibility (e.g., <a id="foo" name="foo">...</a>).

Further, since the set of legal values for attributes of type ID is much smaller than for those of type CDATA, the type of the name attribute has been changed to NMTOKEN. This attribute is constrained such that it can only have the same values as type ID, or as the Name production in XML 1.0 Section 2.5, production 5. Unfortunately, this constraint cannot be expressed in the XHTML 1.0 DTDs. Because of this change, care must be taken when converting existing HTML documents. The values of these attributes must be unique within the document, valid, and any references to these fragment identifiers (both internal and external) must be updated should the values be changed during conversion.

Finally, note that XHTML 1.0 has deprecated the `name` attribute of the `a`, `applet`, `form`, `frame`, `iframe`, `img`, and `map` elements, and it will be removed from XHTML in subsequent versions.

C.9 Character Encoding

To specify a character encoding in the document, use both the encoding attribute specification on the xml declaration (e.g. `<?xml version="1.0" encoding="EUC-JP"?>`) and a meta http-equiv statement (e.g. `<meta http-equiv="Content-type" content='text/html; charset="EUC-JP"' />`). The value of the encoding attribute of the xml processing instruction takes precedence.

C.10 Boolean Attributes

Some HTML user agents are unable to interpret boolean attributes when these appear in their full (non-minimized) form, as required by XML 1.0. Note this problem doesn't affect user agents compliant with HTML 4. The following attributes are involved: `compact`, `nowrap`, `ismap`, `declare`, `noshade`, `checked`, `disabled`, `readonly`, `multiple`, `selected`, `noresize`, `defer`.

C.11 Document Object Model and XHTML

The Document Object Model level 1 Recommendation [DOM] defines document object model interfaces for XML and HTML 4. The HTML 4 document object model specifies that HTML element and attribute names are returned in upper-case. The XML document object model specifies that element and attribute names are returned in the case they are specified. In XHTML 1.0, elements and attributes are specified in lower-case. This apparent difference can be addressed in two ways:

1. Applications that access XHTML documents served as Internet media type `text/html` via the DOM can use the HTML DOM, and can rely upon element and attribute names being returned in upper-case from those interfaces.

2. Applications that access XHTML documents served as Internet media types `text/xml` or `application/xml` can also use the XML DOM. Elements and attributes will be returned in lower-case. Also, some XHTML elements may or

may not appear in the object tree because they are optional in the content model (e.g. the tbody element within table). This occurs because in HTML 4 some elements were permitted to be minimized such that their start and end tags are both omitted (an SGML feature). This is not possible in XML. Rather than require document authors to insert extraneous elements, XHTML has made the elements optional. Applications need to adapt to this accordingly.

C.12 Using Ampersands in Attribute Values

When an attribute value contains an ampersand, it must be expressed as a character entity reference (e.g. "&"). For example, when the href attribute of the a element refers to a CGI script that takes parameters, it must be expressed as

```
http://my.site.dom/cgi-bin/myscript.pl?class=guest&amp;name=user
```

rather than as

```
http://my.site.dom/cgi-bin/myscript.pl?class=guest&name=user
```

C.13 Cascading Style Sheets (CSS) and XHTML

The Cascading Style Sheets level 2 Recommendation [CSS2] defines style properties which are applied to the parse tree of the HTML or XML document. Differences in parsing will produce different visual or aural results, depending on the selectors used. The following hints will reduce this effect for documents which are served without modification as both media types:

1. CSS style sheets for XHTML should use lower case element and attribute names.

2. In tables, the tbody element will be inferred by the parser of an HTML user agent, but not by the parser of an XML user agent. Therefore you should always explicitly add a tbody element if it is referred to in a CSS selector.

3. Within the XHTML name space, user agents are expected to recognize the "id" attribute as an attribute of type ID. Therefore, style sheets should be able to continue using the shorthand "#" selector syntax even if the user agent does not read the DTD.

4. Within the XHTML name space, user agents are expected to recognize the "class" attribute. Therefore, style sheets should be able to continue using the shorthand "." selector syntax.

5. CSS defines different conformance rules for HTML and XML documents; be aware that the HTML rules apply to XHTML documents delivered as HTML and the XML rules apply to XHTML documents delivered as XML.

Appendix D. Acknowledgements

This appendix is informative.

This specification was written with the participation of the members of the W3C HTML working group:

Steven Pemberton, CWI (HTML Working Group Chair)

Murray Altheim, Sun Microsystems

Daniel Austin, AskJeeves (CNET: The Computer Network through July 1999)

Frank Boumphrey, HTML Writers Guild

John Burger, Mitre

Andrew W. Donoho, IBM

Sam Dooley, IBM

Klaus Hofrichter, GMD

Philipp Hoschka, W3C

Masayasu Ishikawa, W3C

Warner ten Kate, Philips Electronics

Peter King, Phone.com

Paula Klante, JetForm

Shin'ichi Matsui, Panasonic (W3C visiting engineer through September 1999)

Shane McCarron, Applied Testing and Technology (The Open Group through August 1999)

Ann Navarro, HTML Writers Guild

Dave Raggett, W3C/HP (W3C lead for HTML)

Patrick Schmitz, Microsoft

Sebastian Schnitzenbaumer, Stack Overflow

Peter Stark, Phone.com

Chris Wilson, Microsoft

Ted Wugofski, Gateway 2000

Dan Zigmond, WebTV Networks

Appendix E. References
This appendix is informative.

[**CSS2**] "Cascading Style Sheets, level 2 (CSS2) Specification", B. Bos, H. W. Lie, C. Lilley, I. Jacobs, 12 May 1998. Latest version available at: `http://www.w3.org/TR/REC-CSS2`

[**DOM**] "Document Object Model (DOM) Level 1 Specification", Lauren Wood et al., 1 October 1998. Latest version available at: `http://www.w3.org/TR/REC-DOM-Level-1`

[**HTML**] "HTML 4.01 Specification", D. Raggett, A. Le Hors, I. Jacobs, 24 December 1999. Latest version available at: `http://www.w3.org/TR/html401`

[**POSIX.1**] "ISO/IEC 9945-1:1990 Information Technology - Portable Operating System Interface (POSIX) - Part 1: System Application Program Interface (API) [C Language]", Institute of Electrical and Electronics Engineers, Inc, 1990.

[**RFC2046**] "RFC2046: Multipurpose Internet Mail Extensions (MIME) Part Two: Media Types", N. Freed and N. Borenstein, November 1996. Available at `http://www.ietf.org/rfc/rfc2046.txt`. Note that this RFC obsoletes RFC1521, RFC1522, and RFC1590.

[**RFC2119**] "RFC2119: Key words for use in RFCs to Indicate Requirement Levels", S. Bradner, March 1997. Available at: `http://www.ietf.org/rfc/rfc2119.txt`

The XHTML Specification

[**RFC2376**]   "RFC2376: XML Media Types", E. Whitehead, M. Murata, July 1998. Available at: http://www.ietf.org/rfc/rfc2376.txt

[**RFC2396**]   "RFC2396: Uniform Resource Identifiers (URI): Generic Syntax", T. Berners-Lee, R. Fielding, L. Masinter, August 1998. This document updates RFC1738 and RFC1808. Available at: http://www.ietf.org/rfc/rfc2396.txt

[**XML**]   "Extensible Markup Language (XML) 1.0 Specification", T. Bray, J. Paoli, C. M. Sperberg-McQueen, 10 February 1998. Latest version available at: http://www.w3.org/TR/REC-xml

[**XMLNAMES**]   "Namespaces in XML", T. Bray, D. Hollander, A. Layman, 14 January 1999. XML namespaces provide a simple method for qualifying names used in XML documents by associating them with namespaces identified by URI. Latest version available at: http://www.w3.org/TR/REC-xml-names

Index

E

G